SOVEREIGNTY AND TERRITORIAL TEMPTATION

This powerful study stands on its head the most venerated tradition in international law and discusses the challenges of scarcity, sovereignty, and territorial temptation. Newly emergent resources, accessible through global climate change, discovery, or technological advancement, highlight time-tested problems of sovereignty and challenge liberal internationalism's promise of beneficial or shared solutions. From the High Arctic to the hyperarid reaches of the Atacama Desert, from the South China Sea to the history of the Law of the Sea, from doctrinal and scholarly treatments to institutional forms of global governance, the historically recurring problem of territorial temptation in the ageless age of scarcity calls into question the future of the global commons, and illuminates the tendency among states to share resources, but only when necessary.

Christopher R. Rossi is an adjunct faculty member in Public International Law at the University of Iowa College of Law.

Sovereignty and Territorial Temptation

THE GROTIAN TENDENCY

CHRISTOPHER R. ROSSI

University of Iowa College of Law

CAMBRIDGE
UNIVERSITY PRESS

CAMBRIDGE
UNIVERSITY PRESS

University Printing House, Cambridge CB2 8BS, United Kingdom

One Liberty Plaza, 20th Floor, New York, NY 10006, USA

477 Williamstown Road, Port Melbourne, VIC 3207, Australia

314-321, 3rd Floor, Plot 3, Splendor Forum, Jasola District Centre, New Delhi-110025, India

79 Anson Road, #06-04/06, Singapore 079906

Cambridge University Press is part of the University of Cambridge.

It furthers the University's mission by disseminating knowledge in the pursuit of education, learning and research at the highest international levels of excellence.

www.cambridge.org
Information on this title: www.cambridge.org/9781316634974
DOI: 10.1017/9781316871935

First published 2017
First paperback edition 2018

A catalogue record for this publication is available from the British Library

Library of Congress Cataloging in Publication data
Names: Rossi, Christopher R., author.
Title: Sovereignty and territorial temptation: the Grotian tendency / Christopher R. Rossi, University of Iowa College of Law.
Description: Cambridge, United Kingdom; New York, NY, USA: Cambridge University Press, 2017.
Identifiers: LCCN 2016052789 | ISBN 9781107183537 (hardback)
Subjects: LCSH: Territory, National. | Grotius, Hugo, 1583-1645–Influence.
Classification: LCC KZ3675 .R67 2017 | DDC 341.4/2–dc23
LC record available at https://lccn.loc.gov/2016052789

ISBN 978-1-107-18353-7 Hardback
ISBN 978-1-316-63497-4 Paperback

Contents

Acknowledgments

I am grateful to Ed Gordon, Giuseppe Nesi, Joe Phillips, Rut Diamint, and Lawson Brigham who provided much appreciated feedback. I thank John Reitz, Edward Carmody Professor of International and Comparative Law, and Iowa Law College students Yifeng Bao, Wuyan Wang, and especially Antonio I. Martinez for institutional and research support. John Bergstrom, Iowa Law College librarian, located difficult-to-find material, as did Alexandra McCallen, Department Librarian at the Naval History and Heritage Command, Washington Navy Yard, Washington, D.C. I owe special thanks to Arthur E. Bonfield, Allan D. Vestal Chair and Associate Dean Emeritus at the Iowa Law College. Arthur was instrumental in constructing one of the world's great law libraries at the University of Iowa College of Law. To the uninformed, that statement may appear to be an exaggeration, but it is not. Arthur also pinpointed numerous primary documents and readings from the early modern age. He provided me access to his astonishing private collection of sixteenth- and seventeenth-century works on the age of exploration and the birth of Westphalian sovereignty. I cannot thank Arthur enough for his friendship, kindness, and assistance. Ciarán Burke illuminated pathways and provided penetrating comments about the Svalbard Treaty. My former student Drew Cumings-Peterson provided valuable feedback on an early draft chapter, and Claudio Hidalgo-Wohlleben walked me through the drawn-out history of the Atacama Desert dispute. My editor at Cambridge University Press, John Berger, provided exceptional guidance, and I am grateful to him along with the support staff, including Hrishikesh Perumethu, Kanimozhi Ramamurthy, Sarah Starkey, Steve Aylett, and Sam Shaw. Mostly, I am indebted to Nick Onuf for the same reasons so many scholars of international law and international relations hold him in almost reverential esteem. His exceptionally nuanced understanding of international law and international relations, his targeted critiques, his generous commitment of time and effort, his lifelong support as mentor and friend, and his inspiring ability to unlock problems or restate them as if they were ever so simple and clear to begin with, combine to make him out to be what is well-known: a colleague's colleague. He was all of these things to me before he started all of the conversation about that term, constructivism.

Publishers and journals have allowed me to reprint or reformulate material, including Routledge Taylor & Francis Group for "The Club Within the Club: The Challenge of a Soft Law Framework in a Global Arctic Context," 5(1) *The Polar Journal* 8–34 (2015); Brill Nijhoff, for "The Northern Sea Route and the Seaward Extension of *Uti Possidetis (Juris),*" 83 *Nordic Journal of International Law* 476–508 (2014); the University of Iowa for "Russian Arctic Straits and the Temptation of *Uti Possidetis,*" 24(1) *Transnational Law & Contemporary Problems* 19–68 (2014); The University of Toronto for "A Particular Kind of *Dominium*: The Grotian 'Tendency' and the Global Commons in a Time of High Arctic Change," 11(1) *Journal of International Law and International Relations* 1–60 (2015); The University of Houston for "Jura Novit Curia? Condominium in the Gulf of Fonseca and the 'Local Illusion' of a Pluri-State Bay," 37(3) *Houston Journal of International Law* 793–840 (2015); and Washington University for "'A Unique International Problem': The Svalbard Treaty, Equal Enjoyment, and Terra Nullius: Lessons of Territorial Temptation from History," 15(1) *Washington University Global Studies Law Review* 93–136 (2016); The University of Miami for "A Case Ill Suited for Judgment: Constructing 'A Sovereign Access to the Sea' in the Atacama Desert," 48(2) *Inter-American Law Review* 28–86 (2016). Above all, I thank my children, Nicholas "Christian" and Sigrid Sophia, and my wife, Monica, for their patience, love, and support.

Table of Cases

1

Tradition, Tendency, Temptation

Hugo Grotius (1583–1645) overlooked the North Sea from Holland's shore in the early seventeenth century and observed an "immense, infinite" waterway,[1] so vast it could not be possessed,[2] so unbounded, except by the heavens,[3] it could only admit to uses such as navigation, fishing, and trade.[4] He claimed in *Mare Liberum* (The Free Sea, 1609), his small pamphlet quickly destined to become a classic, that the seas represented a shared resource, like air, which allowed for a "common use" to benefit mankind.[5] According to Grotius, Providence bestowed on humanity a particular kind of *dominium* (ownership) over the seas, which, unlike land, granted individuals a freedom of use but enjoined proprietary claims.[6] One could not give away what one never owned, he reasoned;[7] one could not discover what already belonged to someone else,[8] and one could not appropriate what was common to all.[9] According to Grotius, the seas represented a *res communis*, a common good.[10]

By the time Grotius died, *Mare Liberum* had cycled through thirteen editions,[11] securing its place among the classics of international law. Curiously, far less secure were its main claims that the seas could not be owned and were to be used in common. These assertions generated intense discussion and

---

[1] HUGO GROTIUS, MARE LIBERUM 1609–2009, at 81 (Robert Feenstra, ed., with a general introduction by Jeroen Vervliet, 2009) (1609) [hereinafter GROTIUS, MARE LIBERUM].
[2] *See id.* at 63.
[3] *See id.* at 81.
[4] *See id.* at 63 (navigation and fishing), and 25 (trade).
[5] *Id.* at 63 (emphasis added).
[6] *See id.* at 9.
[7] *See id.* at 15.
[8] *See id.*
[9] *See id.* at 63 ("the sea is an element common to all … no one could possibly take possession of it").
[10] *See* Jeroen Vervliet, *General Introduction, in* GROTIUS, MARE LIBERUM, *supra* note 1, at xv.
[11] *See* CHRISTIAN GELLINEK, HUGO GROTIUS at 147 (1983).

criticism during his time and ours: many claim Grotius' view of freedom of the seas has prevailed,[12] yet "few works of such brevity have caused arguments of such global extent and striking longevity."[13]

What did Grotius mean when he labeled the seas a *res communis*, the use of which was reserved for humanity's benefit? Consider the following points: almost four hundred years after publication, on August 2, 2007, Russian explorer and parliamentarian, Artur Chilingarov, piloting the mini-submarine, *Mir-I*, planted a rustproof titanium Russian tricolor flag on the seabed, fourteen thousand feet below the ice-covered North Pole. Russia's Arctic and Antarctic Institute hailed it as a "massive scientific achievement," likening it to placing a flag on the moon.[14] Canada's Foreign Minister called it a stunt: "This isn't the fifteenth century," he chafed; "you can't go around the world and just plant flags and say 'We're claiming this territory'."[15]

The well-publicized gesture generated pithy headlines about a coming "Race to the Pole" and a new "Cold War in the Arctic."[16] But the headlines eclipsed the expedition's far more significant mission, which foretells of Russia's greatest Arctic ambition.[17] The mission was to take core seabed

---

[12] *See, e.g.*, Jon Miller, *Hugo Grotius, in* STANFORD ENCYCLOPEDIA OF PHILOSOPHY, http://plato
.stanford.edu/entries/grotius/ (conceding that history may have favored Grotius and his view
that the seas are open to all); ANTHONY D'AMATO & JOHN LAWRENCE HARGROVE, ENVIRONMENT
AND THE LAW OF THE SEA: A REPORT OF THE WORKING GROUP ON OCEAN ENVIRONMENT OF
THE AMERICAN SOC'Y OF INTERNATIONAL LAW 15 (1974) (noting "[h]istorically it was of course
the Grotian position [freedom of the seas] that prevailed"); and Alison Reppy, *The Grotian
Doctrine of the Freedom of the Seas Reappraised*, 19 FORDHAM L. REV. 243, 264 (1950) (declaring
Grotius the victor in doctrinal battle of freedom of the seas versus closed seas).

[13] David Armitage, *Introduction, in* THE FREE SEA: HUGO GROTIUS at xi (translated by Richard
Hakluyt with William Welwod's Critique and Grotius' Reply, edited, and with an intro-
duction, by David Armitage, 2004). The book was placed on the list of forbidden works in
1610. *Id.* at xviii [footnote omitted], as was much of the author's *oeuvre*. *See* IDEX LIBRORUM
PROHIBITORUM SANCTISSIMI DOMINI NOSTRI, GREGORII XVI. PONTIFICUS MAXIMI. JUSSU
EDITUS. EDITIO NOVISSIMA IN QUA LIBRI OMNES AB APOSTOLICA SEDE USQUE AD ANNUM
MDCCCLII PROSCRIPTI, SUIS LOCIS RECENSENTU 188–189 (1853).

[14] *Russia Plants Flag under N Pole*, BBC News (Aug. 2, 2007), http://news.bbc.co.uk/2/hi/europe/
6927395.stm.

[15] *Id.*

[16] Jamie Doward, Robin McKie, & Tom Parfitt, *Russia Leads Race for North Pole Oil*, THE
GUARDIAN (July 28, 2007), www.theguardian.com/world/2007/jul/29/russia.oil; Doug Struck,
Russia's Deep-Sea Flag-Planting at North Pole Strikes a Chill in Canada, WASH. POST (Aug. 7,
2007), www.washingtonpost.com/wp-dyn/content/article/2007/08/06/AR2007080601369.html;
Owen Matthews, *The Coldest War: Russia and U.S. Face Off over Arctic Resources*, THE MAIL
ONLINE (May 19, 2009), www.dailymail.co.uk/news/article-1184291/The-coldest-war-Russia-U-
S-face-Arctic-resources.html;

[17] *See generally* Pavel K. Baev, *Sovereignty Is the Key to Russia's Arctic Policy*, 37 STRATEGIC
ANALYSIS 489 (2013).

samples of the Arctic Basin's massive underwater Lomonosov Ridge; the ambition is to prove to the United Nations Commission on the Limits of the Continental Shelf (CLCS) that the geological structure of the seabed of the Ridge is exclusively an extension of Russia's continental shelf, which would extend Russia's sovereignty over its abundant mineral resources.[18]

According to the United Nations Convention on the Law of the Sea (UNCLOS),[19] which Russia ratified,[20] each coastal state may claim a 200 nautical mile continental shelf as measured from its baseline.[21] Each state may file continental shelf extension claims with the CLCS beyond the 200 nautical mile swath granted by UNCLOS up to 350 nautical miles, but the state must pass a *test of appurtenance*[22] and show scientifically that its continental margin extends beyond 200 nautical miles and is part of the submerged prolongation of its mainland.[23] The CLCS rejected Russia's "sloppily prepared" 2001 submission due to lack of evidence[24] and recommended that Russia fortify and refile its claim.[25] Russia has already applied for extensions of its territories in the Barents, Bering, and Okhotsk Seas and recently signaled it will refile its Lomonosov claim, along with a claim over the Mendeleev Ridge off the South Siberian Sea.[26]

[18] *Infra*, note 19, pt. XI, §§ 1–3.

[19] United Nations Convention on the Law of the Sea, *opened for signature* Dec. 10, 1982, 1833 U.N.T.S. 397 (entered into force Nov. 16, 1994) [hereinafter UNCLOS], *available at* www.un.org/depts/los/convention_agreements/convention_overview_convention.htm.

[20] UN Treaty Collection, Multilateral Treaties Deposited with the Secretary-General, Status of Treaties, United Nations Convention on the Law of the Sea, *available at* http://treaties.un.org/doc/Publication/MTDSG/Volume%20II/Chapter%20XXI/XXI-6.en.pdf

[21] UNCLOS, *supra* note 19, pt. VI, art. 76, ¶ 1.

[22] *Id.* pt. VI, art. 76, ¶¶ 1–7. *See* Elizabeth Riddell-Dixon, *Canada and Arctic Politics: The Continental Shelf Extension*, 39 OCEAN DEV. & INT'L L. 343, 345 (2008).

[23] UNCLOS, *supra* note 19, Annex II, art. 4. The provision holds: "Where a coastal State intends to establish, in accordance with Article 76, the outer limits of its continental shelf beyond 200 nautical miles, it shall submit particulars of such limits to the Commission along with supporting scientific and technical data as soon as possible but in any case within ten years of the entry into force of this Convention for that State. The coastal State shall at the same time give the names of any Commission members who have provided it with scientific and technical advice." Under a separate provision, refilings are admissible beyond the ten year period. *Id.* annex II, art. 8 ("In the case of disagreement by the coastal State with the recommendations of the Commission, the coastal State shall, within a reasonable time, make a revised or new submission to the Commission").

[24] Baev, *supra* note 17. The Russian Federation was in fact the first country to submit a claim. For a summary of submissions, *see* CONTINENTAL SHELF: THE LAST MARITIME ZONE 30–33 (Tina Schoolmeester & Elaine Baker, eds., 2009) [hereinafter Schoolmeester & Baker].

[25] The Secretary-General, Oceans and the Law of the Sea: Report of the Secretary General, Addendum, ¶ 41, delivered to the General Assembly, U.N. Doc. A/57/57/Add.1 (Oct. 8, 2002).

[26] *Russia to Apply for Extension of Arctic Shelf Boundaries in 2014*, ARCTIC INFO (Aug. 26, 2013), www.arctic-info.com/News/Page/russia-to-apply-for-extension-of-arctic-shelf-boundaries-in-2014-

If successful, Russia will be allowed legally to extend its control over about 1.2 million square kilometers of underwater terrain that formerly had been considered part of the deep seabed, which is the seafloor beyond the scope of national jurisdiction – an area meant to be administered for the benefit of all countries in trust, as part of a Grotian-inspired Common Heritage of Mankind.[27]

From a global Arctic perspective, Russia's filings portend gloom for the shrinking global commons – as they would enclose almost half of the territory beneath the Arctic Ocean for its own resource exploitation.[28] From a management perspective, capturing efficient economies of scale makes sense; from a stewardship perspective, extending decision-making and police powers to the adjacent coastal state have bases in law; from parochial political and national security perspectives, the attractions of extending sovereign control over the world's diminishing unsecured geospatial regimes are enticing.

Russia's claims are unexceptional. All circumpolar states are seeking continental shelf extensions into the Arctic cryosphere.[29] Denmark has identified five potential claim areas off the Faroe Islands and its territory, Greenland;[30] Norway presented three separate claims,[31] which extend its continental shelf by the equivalent of seven soccer fields for each of its almost five million people;[32] Canada's Arctic Ocean extension claim covers three-quarters of a million square kilometers; when added to its claims in the Atlantic and Pacific Oceans, Canada's total claim approaches 1.75 million square kilometers, which equals the combined size of its three prairie provinces, Alberta, Saskatchewan, and Manitoba.[33] The United States, although not party to UNCLOS, has amassed scientific evidence to support a continental shelf extension claim, which "could extend more than six hundred nautical miles from the north coast of

---

[27] UNCLOS, *supra* note 19, pt. I, arts. 1.1 (pertaining to the "The Area," which is defined as "the seabed and ocean floor and subsoil thereof, beyond the limits of national jurisdiction) and 136 (referring to the Area and its resources as the "common heritage of mankind").

[28] Roderick Kefferpütz, *On Thin Ice? (Mis)interpreting Russian Policy in the High North*, at 3, CEPS Policy Brief, No. 205 (Feb. 2010).

[29] UNCLOS and the Commission on the Limits of the Continental Shelf (CLCS), Munk School of Global Affairs, http://gordonfoundation.ca/sites/default/files/images/UNCLOS%20 and%20the%20Commission%20on%20the%20Limits%20of%20the%20Continental%20Shelf .pdf

[30] *See* the Continental Shelf Project of the Kingdom of Denmark, Ministry of Science, Innovation and Higher Education, http://a76.dk/lng_uk/main.html.

[31] Summary of the recommendations of the Commission on the Limits of the Continental Shelf in regard to the submission made by Norway in respect of the areas in the Arctic Ocean, the Barents Sea, and the Norwegian Sea on November 27, 2006 (Mar. 27, 2009) www.un.org/ Depts/los/clcs_new/submissions_files/nor06/nor_rec_summ.pdf.

[32] *UN Backs Norway's Claim to Arctic Seabed Extension*, AFP (Apr. 15, 2009), www.google.com/ hostednews/afp/article/ALeqM5gQORJjsuFpxulrmjBRhjCNlQyhjg?hl=en.

[33] Riddell-Dixon, *supra* note 22, at 347.

Alaska."[34] The legal basis underpinning this claim remains oblique. But one might wonder legitimately what portion of the global commons will be left of the Arctic once circumpolar states complete their Arctic extensions.[35]

Expansive as these claims are, set against the geomorphology of the world's smallest ocean,[36] they are surpassed by continental shelf extension claims elsewhere. Australia submitted ten claims for continental shelf extension in its surrounding oceans and seas,[37] resulting in its May 25, 2012 proclamation of exclusive rights to oil, gas, mineral, and biological resources over eleven million square kilometers of continental shelf;[38] New Zealand, Sri Lanka, the United Kingdom, France, Portugal, and South Africa filed claims exceeding the scope of Russia's claims;[39] the total area of seabed under review by the CLCS in 2009, involving (at that time) fifty-one submissions, covered an area almost as large as the North American continent; since that time, twenty-six additional claims have been filed.[40]

Some Arctic claims overlap[41] and will doubtless generate delicate diplomatic negotiations.[42] But focusing on extant and emerging bilateral boundary

---

[34] National Strategy for the Arctic Region, May 2013, 1–11, www.whitehouse.gov/sites/default/files/doc/nat_arctic_strategy.pdf, with a cover letter from President Barak Obama dated May 10, 2013.

[35] Continental shelf extension claims do not affect the legal status of the superjacent water column. Reports of a melting polar ice cap, an increasingly long and warmer polar summer, and prospects for an ice-free Arctic summer within 30–100 years, suggest a northern movement in migratory fish patterns toward warmer Arctic waters, attracting a variety of international fishing fleets and the prospect of overfishing. A race for the fish and to control overfishing are two likely issues of coming concern. *See generally* Myron H. Nordquist, John Norton Moore, & Ronán Long, Challenges of the Changing Arctic: Continental Shelf, Navigation, and Fisheries (2016); *see also* Allison Winter, *U.S. Bans Commercial Fishing in Warming Arctic*, N.Y. Times (Aug. 21, 2009), www.nytimes.com/gwire/2009/08/21/21greenwire-us-bans-commercial-fishing-in-warming-arctic-33236.html.

[36] Vladimir Golitsyn, *Climate Change, Marine Science and Delineation of the Continental Shelf, in* 235 Beiträge zum ausländischen öffentlichen Recht und Völkerrecht 245, 248 (Susanne Wasum-Rainer, Ingo Winkelmann, & Katrin Tiroch, eds., 2011), *available at* http://link.springer.com/content/pdf/10.1007%2F978-3-642-24203-8.pdf.

[37] Continental Shelf Submission of Australia, Executive Summary Aus-Doc-ES, *available at* www.un.org/depts/los/clcs_new/submissions_files/aus04/Documents/aus_doc_es_web_delivery.pdf

[38] Proclamation on the continental shelf, Senator the Hon. Bob Carr, Australian Minister for Foreign Affairs, May 25, 2012, http://foreignminister.gov.au/releases/2012/bc_mr_120525.html.

[39] Schoolmeester & Baker, *supra* note 24, at 17.

[40] *Id.* at 16. For claim filings, *see* www.un.org/depts/los/clcs_new/commission_submissions.htm.

[41] *See generally Overlapping Sovereignty Claims in the Arctic*, International Institute for Strategic Studies, Mar. 7, 2012, www.openbriefing.org/regionaldesks/polarregions/arcticsovereigntymap/. *See also* UNCLOS, *supra* note 19, art. 83 (providing that delimitation of the continental shelf between States with opposite or adjacent coasts shall be effected by agreement on the basis of international law).

[42] Michael Becker, *Russia and the Arctic: Opportunities for engagement Within the Existing Legal Framework*, 25 Am. U. Int'l L. Rev. 225, 227 (noting ample opportunities for constructive engagement).

disputes miss a larger point about the changing circumstances and improving technological abilities to exploit resources formerly considered too remote, inaccessible, or unworthy of attention.

A rapidly receding polar ice cap[43] and new information about the value of potentially accessible resources[44] have altered circumpolar state calculations dramatically vis-à-vis the interests of the rest of the world. This alteration exposes a strong state tendency to territorialize resources formerly considered beyond the control of any state's national jurisdiction. In a variation of this theme, for the first time in history, states actively contemplate commercial trans-arctic voyages across the Northwest Passage, the amorphous waterway straddling the North American landmass and connecting the Atlantic and Pacific Oceans. The thought is mind-boggling. For over four centuries, explorers and nations competed to unlock the icebound secrets of this Arctic labyrinth in a frustrating, deadly search for an ever-shifting navigable route through the nineteen thousand islands of the Canadian Archipelagic island chain. After Portugal (da Gama) cracked the navigational sea code, enabling expedited passage to India around Africa (1498), and Spain (Magellan) rounded Cape Horn into the Pacific Ocean (1520), Elizabethan through Victorian sea interests made conquest of the Northwest Passage a national objective. Joseph Conrad wrote in *Heart of Darkness* that the "tidal currents of the Thames" launched "the great knights-errant of the sea" down its stream, pursuing dreams of men, sowing seeds of commonwealths, and spreading germs of empire in search of fame, gold, and the elusive route.[45] Counted among these wandering sea knights were Francis Drake, John Cabot, William Bligh, Henry Hudson, William Baffin, James Cook, George Vancouver, James Clark Ross, and, most psychologically enervating for the British, Sir John Franklin, whose 1845 expedition aboard the *Erebus* and *Terror* vanished.[46] The

---

[43] The National Snow and Ice Data Center records a 10.6 percent per decade decline in monthly August Arctic Sea Ice Extent measurements from 1979 to 2013. *Arctic Sea Ice News & Analysis*, National Snow & Ice Data Center (Sept. 4, 2013), http://nsidc.org/arcticseaicenews/.

[44] *See generally Circum-Arctic Resource Appraisal: Estimates of Undiscovered Oil and Gas North of the Arctic Circle*. United States Geological Survey Fact Sheet (2008), https://pubs.usgs.gov/fs/2008/3049/fs2008-3049.pdf.

[45] JOSEPH CONRAD, HEART OF DARKNESS 8–9 (2003) [1899].

[46] *Id.* at 9 ("never returned"). *See generally* GLYN WILLIAMS, VOYAGES OF DELUSION: THE NORTHWEST PASSAGE IN THE AGE OF REASON (2002); GLYN WILLIAMS, ARCTIC LABYRINTH: THE QUEST FOR THE NORTHWEST PASSAGE (2011). Traces of Franklin's expedition were located in 1859 on remote King William Island along with evidence that Franklin's men may have endured for months, possibly succumbing to temptations of cannibalism or sickness due to botulism, conveyed by shoddily made and improperly sealed canned meats and vegetables. For a reconstructed

chimera of a passageway connecting the Mississippi-Missouri River System to the Pacific Ocean occupied the American mind and motivated US President Thomas Jefferson's commissioning of the 1804 Corps of Discovery expedition, captained by Meriwether Lewis and William Clark. But it was not until 1906, with Norway's supreme discoverer Roald Amundsen at the helm of the tiny *Gjøa*, that a mariner proved it could be traversed. The voyage took him three years to complete. As improbable as it seems, slightly more than one century after Amundsen's feat, recreational sailing vessels, including row boats, ply these waters;[47] some vessels, including private yachts, have completed passage during a single season of the Canadian Arctic's lengthening summer.[48]

Likewise, global climate change is "creating conditions of siege for the oceans and coasts of the world,"[49] altering the fourteen million square kilometers of the "world's next resource frontier" – the Arctic Ocean.[50] This alteration is particularly pronounced along Arctic coastlines, where significant portions are now "ice-free for a substantial period of time each year,"[51] including substantial portions of the coastal seascape of the Northeast Passage, which connects Asia and Europe via waterways atop Russia. Scarcely any such traffic ever before had ventured this far north. The first non-Russian navigation of the Northern Sea Route, a treacherous Siberian stretch of the waterway, took place in the summer of 2009; but as recently as 2013, 450 vessels queued up for commercial voyage of the entire passage.[52] Canada and Russia straddle an ideological divide, but in mirror image fashion, they have long made similar sovereign claims over these waterways adjacent to their respective continental landmasses.[53] Both countries regard the passages as internal waters and have fortified their claims with

---

account of the ordeal, *see generally* SCOTT COOKMAN, ICE BLINK: THE TRAGIC FATE OF SIR JOHN FRANKLIN'S LOST POLAR EXPEDITION (2000).

[47] Scott Yorko, *Rowing the Northwest Passage – Because They Can*, OUTSIDE (July 10, 2013), www .outsideonline.com/1917256/rowing-northwest-passage%E2%80%94because-they-can.

[48] Elaine Lembo, *Northwest Passage Routes Made Passable: With the Retreat of Arctic Ice, Boat Traffic in the Northwest Passage is Rising*, CRUISING WORLD (Feb. 14, 2013), www.cruisingworld .com/northwest-passage-routes-made-passable.

[49] *See* Randall S. Abate & Dr. Sarah Ellen Krejci, *Climate Change Impacts on Ocean and Coastal Law: Scientific Realities and Legal Responses*, *in* CLIMATE CHANGE IMPACTS ON OCEAN AND COASTAL LAW: U.S. AND INTERNATIONAL PERSPECTIVES 2 (Randall S. Abate, ed., 2015).

[50] Kamrul Hossain, *Governance of Arctic Ocean Marine Resources*, *in* CLIMATE CHANGE IMPACTS ON OCEAN AND COASTAL LAW: U.S. AND INTERNATIONAL PERSPECTIVES 273–275 (Randall S. Abate, ed., 2015).

[51] *Id.* at 273–274.

[52] Ben Anderson, *Yong Sheng: Why Arctic Voyage of Chinese Cargo Ship Is Business as Usual*, ALASKA DISPATCH (Sept. 1, 2013), www.alaskadispatch.com/article/20130901/yong-sheng-why-arctic- voyage-chinese-cargo-ship-business-usual.

[53] Robert Dufresne, *Controversial Canadian Claims over Arctic Waters and Maritime Zone*, at 2, Law and Government Division, Parliamentary Information and Research Service,

domestic environmental and administrative legislation.[54] UNCLOS lends some support to their coast state regulatory claims by acknowledging that costal states may exercise special environmental police powers over ice-covered areas.[55] But global warming has made the legal status of these waterways, and the extent to which they constitute internal waters or international straits, much more of a topical concern to other maritime powers.[56]

Global warming also has prompted interest in other Arctic realms, ranging from environmental concerns such as ocean acidification and loss of marine and aboriginal habitat, to sovereignty issues. These sovereignty issues involve extended continental shelf claims of circumpolar powers, ownership of resources in and under the waters adjacent to the High Arctic archipelago of Svalbard, and establishing the proper governance regime for Arctic waters. This latter interest increasingly involves inputs from non-circumpolar states and nongovernmental actors, and envisions a new stewardship arrangement more expressive of the establishment of a global Arctic.

In the aggregate, these claims signify that a dramatic territorialization of this geospatial resource is underway. This book argues that it has long been underway – reflecting a tendency present at the creation of the Grotian Tradition and embraced personally or at least politically by the master himself. Recognizing this coastal state interest in extending *dominium* over the seas gives rise to

PRB 07-47E, Library of Parliament (Jan. 10, 2008), *available at* www.parl.gc.ca/Content/LOP/researchpublications/prb0747-e.pdf; Central Executive Committee of the U.S.S.R., Decree of April 15, 1926, *reprinted in* Leonid Timtchenko, *The Russian Arctic Sectoral Concept: Past and Present*, 50 ARCTIC 30 (1997), http://pubs.aina.ucalgary.ca/arctic/Arctic50-1-29.pdf. *See also* WILLIAM E. BUTLER, NORTHEAST ARCTIC PASSAGE 72 (1978).

[54] Arctic Waters Pollution Prevention Act, R.S.C. ch 2 (1970), amended by S.C. ch 41 (1977–1978) (Can.) (imposing safety and environmental regulations on all shipping within 100 nautical miles of Canada's Arctic coast); Russian Federation Federal Law N132-Ф3 On Amendments to Specific Legislative Acts of the Russian Federation related to Governmental Regulation of Merchant Shipping in the Water Area of the Northern Sea Route, adopted by the State Duma, July 3, 2012, approved by The Council of Federation July 18, 2012, *available at* www.arctic-lio.com/docs/nsr/legislation/federal_law_nsr.pdf (establishing, *inter alia*, navigation rules and administrative requirements for pilotage of vessels in the waters of the Northern Sea Route).

[55] UNCLOS, *supra* note 19, art. 234 (granting coastal states the right to adopt and enforce nondiscriminatory regulations for the prevention, reduction, and control of marine pollution where particularly severe climatic conditions and ice covering for most of the year create obstructions or exceptional hazards to navigation and where pollution could cause major harm or irreversible disturbance of the ecological balance).

[56] Michael Byers, *How the Arctic Ocean Could Transform World Trade*, AL JAZEERA (Aug. 27, 2013), www.aljazeera.com/indepth/opinion/2013/08/201382273357893832.html (noting US objections to Russian and Canadian sovereignty claims). *See also* Scott G. Borgerson, *Arctic Meltdown: the Economic and Security Implications of Global Warming*, FOREIGN AFF. 63 (March-April 2008); and James Kraska, *International Security and International Law in the Northwest Passage*, 42 VAND. J. TRANSNAT'L L. 1109–1132 (2009).

fundamental questions about the global commons and sovereignty, not simply in the Arctic region but also elsewhere in international relations, making Grotius' problematic introduction of common use relevant and worthy of reconsideration.

THE SUSTAINING POWER OF THE GROTIAN TRADITION

This book investigates the significance of common use as a legal and political construct. It sets the concept of the global commons against the historical backdrop of the law of the sea, which, famously, has been informed by the Dutchman, or the Hollander as he preferred to be called, and his seventeenth-century classic, *Mare Liberum*. A key interest here is the future of common use in relation to the global commons, given its historical treatment in pelagic space. This historical treatment itself is informed by a misreading of *Mare Liberum* and the context in which Grotius presented it. It is based on a misreading of the intentions of states as applied to the freedom of navigation in the high seas, a freedom driven historically by commercial and security interests. It is also based on a misunderstanding of the so-called Grotian Tradition in international relations, which affirms a luminous and rational complementarity between passions and interests,[57] where the totality of international relations conforms to the rule of law,[58] where a sense of epochal or profound change monumentally transformed the previous world disorder into our emerging new world order.[59]

The sustaining power of the Grotian Tradition in international law and relations credits the important contribution of Cornelis Van Vollenhoven[60] and, later, Hersch Lauterpacht, and many subsequent scholars who advanced the twentieth-century belief in the moral necessity of international law, its binding force, and its value as a normative approach. John T. Parry recounted the contributions of some of these scholars, including Hans Kelsen, Louis Henken, and Thomas Franck, along with more recent presentations by Mary Ellen O'Connell and Michael Scharf.[61] "In 'semiotic' terms," according to Scharf,

---

[57] See A. Claire Cutler, *The 'Grotian tradition' in International Relations*, 17 Rev. of Int'l Stud. 41, 41 (1991).

[58] Hersch Lauterpacht, *The Grotian Tradition in International Law*, 23 Brit. Y.B. Int'l L. 1 (1946).

[59] See Antony Anghie, *The Grotius Lecture: ASIL 2010: International Law in a Time of Change: Should International Law Lead or Follow?* 26 Am.U. Int'l L. Rev. 1318 (2011) (linking the genius of Grotius to the phenomenon of profound change).

[60] See, e.g., Cornelis Van Vollenhoven, De drie treden van het volkenrecht (1918; English translation, 1919); Randall Lesaffer, *The Grotian Tradition Revisited: Change and Continuity in the History of International Law*, 73 Brit. Y.B. Int'l L. 103, 108 (2003) (crediting Van Vollenhoven's publication of The Three States in the Evolution of the Law of Nations).

[61] John T. Parry, *What is the Grotian Tradition in International Law?* 35 U. Pa. Int'l L. Rev. 299, 300–301 (2014).

"the 'Grotian Tradition' has come to symbolize the advent of the modern international legal regime, characterized by a community of states operating under binding rules."[62] The English school of international relations, headed by Hedley Bull, Martin Wight, and Barry Buzan, championed its place among leading theoretical traditions, envisioning it as the offsetting fulcrum between the international relations traditions of realism and idealism, and international law's traditions of positivism and naturalism. In this position, the Grotian Tradition portrays international society as an ordered system of territorial states, neither in perpetual conflict nor peace, but governed by the idea of sovereignty. Sovereignty, despite its many detractors and potential challenges, remains the stable centerpiece of the Grotian Tradition.[63] Occupying this "middle position,"[64] the Grotian Tradition shaped the foundation for modern liberal internationalism,[65] which essentially combines multidimensional projects of republicanism, commercial liberalism, and regulatory institutionalism to promote peace, freedom, human rights, and liberal democracy.[66] Few introductory textbooks on international relations or international law fail to discuss its pragmatism, principles, and significance.

According to Benedict Kingsbury, this popular placement between the Machiavellian and Kantian Traditions became a kind of trilectic Tradition within international relations theory.[67] Its viability, as noted by C. G. Roelofsen, made it a convenient twentieth-century starting-place for reflections in international relations despite its reflexive invocation as a shibboleth.[68] Randall Lesaffer labeled the twentieth century as "Grotian,"[69] although he and others recognized that Emmerich de Vattel's (1714–1767) more systematic and succinct treatment of the law of nations would expand Grotius' teachings and dominate international legal thinking into the twentieth century.[70] Vattel's

---

[62] Michael P. Scharf, CUSTOMARY INTERNATIONAL LAW IN TIMES OF FUNDAMENTAL CHANGE RECOGNIZING GROTIAN MOMENTS 4 (2013); Parry, *supra* note 61, at 301.

[63] *See generally* F. H. HINSLEY, SOVEREIGNTY (1986); ALAN JAMES, SOVEREIGN STATEHOOD: THE BASIS OF INTERNATIONAL SOCIETY (1988); ROBERT H. JACKSON, QUASI-STATES: SOVEREIGNTY, INTERNATIONAL RELATIONS, AND THE THIRD WORLD (1990).

[64] MARK WESTON JANIS, AMERICA AND THE LAW OF NATIONS, 1776–1939, at 52 (2010); *see also* MARTIN WIGHT, INTERNATIONAL THEORY: THE THREE TRADITIONS 15 (1991) (arguing Grotius occupied "a broad middle road" between Machiavellian and Kantian thought); Parry, *supra* note 61, at 318.

[65] *See* Parry, *supra* note 61, at 306–311.

[66] *See* MARTIN GRIFFITHS, RETHINKING INTERNATIONAL RELATIONS THEORY 19–32 (2011).

[67] *See* Benedict Kingsbury, *A Grotian Tradition of Theory and Practice?: Grotius, Law, and Moral Skepticism in the Thought of Hedley Bull*, 17 Q.L.R. 8 (1997).

[68] C. G. Roelofsen, *Grotius and the 'Grotian Heritage' in International Law and International Relations; the Quatercentenary and Its Aftermath (circa 1980–1990)*, 11 GROTIANA 11 (1990).

[69] Lesaffer, *supra* note 60, at 108–109.

[70] *See* Randall Lesaffer, *A Schoolmaster Abolishing Homework? Vattel on Peacemaking and Peace Treaties, in* VATTEL'S INTERNATIONAL LAW IN A XXIST CENTURY PERSPECTIVE / LE

most vocal twentieth-century critic, Van Vollenhoven, complained Vattel's rational emphasis on a voluntary law, which made each state the sovereign judge of its international duties, "gave a Judas-kiss to Grotius' system;" that Vattel's "pathetic" support of external sovereignty concealed the thinking of a man who "could not hold a candle to Grotius."[71] Despite Vattel's "most disheartening" rise to prominence, even Van Vollenhoven admitted that Grotius' conception of the state coincided with organizational platforms of early twentieth century, including the League of Nations, making Grotius and his tradition quite modern.[72]

LIFE EXPRESSIONS OF TRADITION

Usage of the term "Tradition" imputes an attempt to capture the entirety of a meaning; it implies a "handing on of formed ways of acting;"[73] of transmitting customs and behaviors along a metaphoric arc involving the turning of history's wheel. Tradition serves as the backstop for Thomas Kuhn's *The Structure of Scientific Revolutions* (1962), the most cited work in the canon of modern social science, which details the importance of paradigms in the transmission of scientific advancement and folly.[74] The sociologist Edward Shils reduced the meaning of tradition to the *traditum*: "anything which is transmitted or

DROIT INTERNATIONAL DE VATTEL VU DU XXIe SIÈCLE 352, 358–359 (Vincent Chetail & Peter Haggenmacher, eds., 2011); Lucius Caflisch, *Vattel and the Peaceful Settlement of International Disputes, in id.* at 266 (noting citations to and judicial quotations of Vattel *Droit des gens* as compared to Grotius, Pufendorf, and Bynkershoek in Edwin Dickinson's empirical survey of American case law between 1789–1820). *See also* Nicholas Greenwood Onuf, *Civitas Maxima: Wolff, Vattel and the Fate of Republicanism*, 88 AM. J. INT'L L. 280, 299 (1994) (noting Vattel's supreme authority in the eighteenth century, especially in the newly independent United States). For evidence of Vattel's supreme doctrinal sway from 1770–1914, as measured in part by translations and editions of his work, *see* C. VAN VOLLENHOVEN, THE THREE STAGES IN THE EVOLUTION OF THE LAW OF NATIONS (1919).

[71] VAN VOLLENHOVEN, *supra* note 70, at 29 ("Judas-kiss"), 31 ("pathetic"), and 32 ("could not hold a candle to Grotius").

[72] *See id.* at 32 ("most disheartening"); *see also* C. Van Vollenhoven, *Grotius and the Study of Law*, 19 AM. J. INT'L L. 1, 3 (1925) (comparing Grotius' conception of the state favorably to the 1915 American League to Enforce Peace, the 1919 League of Nations Covenant, and the 1924 Geneva Protocol).

[73] NICHOLAS GREENWOOD ONUF, THE REPUBLICAN LEGACY IN INTERNATIONAL THOUGHT 8 (1998) (quoting J. G. A. POCOCK, THE MACHIAVELLIAN MOMENT).

[74] *See generally* THOMAS S. KUHN, THE STRUCTURE OF SCIENTIFIC REVOLUTIONS (1962). On its position as the most cited publication in the social sciences, *see* Elliott Green, *What are the most-cited publications in the social sciences (according to Google Scholar)?* LSE, http://blogs.lse.ac.uk/impactofsocialsciences/2016/05/12/what-are-the-most-cited-publications-in-the-social-sciences-according-to-google-scholar/?utm_content=bufferobc47&utm_medium=social&utm_source=facebook.com&utm_campaign=buffer.

handed down from the past to the present."[75] Tradition's "implied continuity
with the past" – continuity imbued with a sense of invariance – is an essential
component of its meaning and transmission, points recognized even among
historians who notionally debunk the idea of tradition.[76] This transmission of
custom, the passing down of beliefs, practices, and ideas, denotes common
definitional usages of the term – usages that impute a coherence that may be
self-evident,[77] or unwarranted, especially if aspects of tradition do not conform
to broader, perhaps invented, understandings.[78]

The handing down of tradition from one generation to the next creates a
dynamic. This dynamic calls into question the notion of invariance, which
begins to reframe the understanding of knowledge in terms of the "life expressions" of those who bear witness to history.[79] Historian Mark Salber Phillips
pointed to an under-examined historiographical bias: while historians regard
the passage of time as a secret weapon – calendrical distance promotes disin-
terestedness; it removes historians from the clutter of the present and enables
them to study clearly and accurately the past – they fail "to think historically
about the historical discipline itself."[80] There is a "plasticity" to historical
distance that admits to "richly variable designs."[81] R. G. Collingwood noted
these designs require the dialectical study of the "outside" [objective] and
"inside" [hermeneutic] of events, where historians must "re-enact the past" in
"[their] own minds."[82] This reenactment assigns to historians the task of knowledge interlocutor. They cannot rely exclusively on testimony even when it
exists, because "that kind of mediation would give at most not knowledge but
belief."[83] E. H. Carr labeled the disinterested mediation of the past a "prepos-
terous fallacy." The investigation of "hard core" historical facts unavoidably

---

75   EDWARD SHILS, TRADITION 12 (1981).
76   Eric Hobsbawm, *Introduction: Inventing Traditions, in* THE INVENTION OF TRADITION 1
     (Eric Hobsbawm & Terence Ranger, eds., 1983) ("implied continuity with the past"). *See
     also* Mark Salber Phillips, *What Is Tradition When It Is Not 'Invented'? A Historiographical
     Introduction, in* QUESTIONS OF TRADITION 1, 2 (Mark Salber Phillips & Gordon Schochet,
     eds., 2004) (discussing the complex problem of culturally transmitting traditions and the pop-
     ularity of Hobsbawm and Ranger's oxymoronic idea of "invented traditions"); and *id.* at 7 (on
     Hobsbawm and invariance).
77   SHILS, *supra* note 75, at 13 ("Those who accept a tradition need not call it a tradition; its
     acceptability might be self-evident to them).
78   *See* ONUF, *supra* note 73, at 8 (borrowing from his discussion of republicanism).
79   Wilhelm Dilthey, *The Understanding of Other Persons and Their Life-Expressions, in* THEORIES
     OF HISTORY 213 (Patrick Gardiner, ed., 1959).
80   MARK SALBER PHILLIPS, ON HISTORICAL DISTANCE 5 (2013).
81   *Id.* at 9.
82   R. G. COLLINGWOOD, THE IDEA OF HISTORY 282 (1946).
83   *Id.* at 282.

involves a culling of events. Historical facts are never "pure;" "the historian is necessarily selective,"[84] and facts "are always refracted through the mind of the recorder."[85] Study the historian before studying the facts, wrote Carr, for "the main work of the historian is not to record, but to evaluate; for if he does not evaluate, how can he know what is worth recording?"[86]

Traditions embed refractions, as well, prompting discussions about how they are recorded and evaluated. Hans-Georg Gadamer claimed the art of understanding history and tradition necessarily required the "conscious assimilation of one's own fore-meanings and prejudices."[87] His intentional assimilation of prejudice into process reflected the irredeemably human quality of hermeneutics. Reinhart Koselleck's approach to *Begriffsgeschichte* (conceptual history) emphasized that "measurable time" (the chronological auxiliary dealing with questions of dating) "cannot be transformed unmediated into a historical concept of time." Historical time "is bound up with social and political actions, with concretely acting and suffering human beings and their institutions and organizations."[88]

In his book, *The Republican Legacy in International Thought* (1998), Nicholas Onuf reflected on the meaning of a tradition and how historians, in contemplation of the legacy of the Republican Tradition in international relations, conflated terms and were inclined to refer to republicanism as an ideology, or something akin to a paradigm.[89] Useful as these terms were, Onuf underscored that these usages only captured *aspects* of the idea; attempting to call republicanism a tradition, however, captured some sense of it as a whole way of life.[90] Unlike some unself-conscious invocations of the term, however, Onuf paused to reflect on the meaning of tradition.[91] Like Shils and the intellectual historian J. G. A. Pocock, Onuf was influenced by the prospect "that tradition contains the seeds of its own undoing;" that the *process* of "carrying on with tradition goes hand in hand with its conceptualization;"[92] and

---

[84] E. H. Carr, What is History? 10 (1964).
[85] *Id.* at 24.
[86] *Id.* at 26 ("study the historian before" the facts) and 22.
[87] Hans-Georg Gadamer, Truth and Method 238 (1975).
[88] Reinhart Koselleck, Futures Past: On the Semantics of Historical Time 1–2 (Translated and with an Introduction by Keith Tribe, 2004).
[89] Onuf, *supra* note 73, at 8.
[90] *Id.* at 8. The preservation of the whole in terms of the transmission of tradition has a separate and involved history among nineteenth-century clergymen – John Henry Newman, John Keble, and Edward Pusey – who formed the Tractarian movement to preserve catholic heritage against doctrinal manipulation, laxity and political adulteration. Its influences can be felt in social science discussions. *See* Stephen Prickett, Modernity and the Reinvention of Tradition: Backing into the Future 169–188 (2009).
[91] *See* Onuf, *supra* note 73, at 8ff.
[92] *Id.* at 9 and 8 (agreeing with Pocock).

that a part of a tradition can get "lifted out," "reflected upon," and "altered" so much that "it no longer fits where it did."[93] Shils wrote that the identity of transmitted things "does not remain identical through its career of trans-missions over generations;" that the *traditum's* constellations of images and understandings "are received and modified;" that a "chain of transmitted variants of a tradition is also called a tradition."[94] Phillips sensed these variants from his reworking of Benadetto Croce's maxim: Every telling of history is adequate to its own time and inadequate to the next.[95] Aspects of tradition get "left behind;" but when tradition is accepted, it comes to represent the "past in the present," but it is nevertheless "as much part of the present as any very recent innovation."[96] Thus, cut and pasted aspects appear; reassembled and truncated traditions emerge; new foundation myths arise.[97] Where rapid social transformation destroys previously established social patterns, traditions may even be invented.[98] Referencing the Platonic Tradition, the Kantian Tradition, the Grotian Tradition, or the Republican Tradition (Onuf avoided that latter construction by titling his work, *The Republican Legacy*, instead) indeed warrants consideration of multiple meanings within each generational pathway giving expression to the *traditum* or, perhaps better put, the evolving *tradita*.

RECONSTRUCTING THE GROTIAN TRADITION: SOVEREIGNTY

Reconstructing traditions can be undertaken to shore up perspectives that get left behind or tear up interpretations that are unduly selective. For instance, in *The Twenty Years' Crisis, 1919–1939* (1939) Carr invoked the Realist Tradition to diminish the prestige of the Idealist Tradition because Idealism selectively distorted the increasingly turbulent events of the interwar period. Carr later wrote: "The facts seemed to smile on us less propitiously than in the years before 1914,"[99] making necessary for Carr his devastating critique of Idealism as an anachronism. Jonathan Haslam's *No Virtue Like Necessity* (2002) attempted to support the value of the Realist Tradition by emphasizing the overlooked context in which realist concepts emerged.[100] He claimed "[i]t is

---

[93] *Id.* at 9.
[94] Shils, *supra* note 75, at 13.
[95] Phillips, *supra* note 80, at 232.
[96] Shils, *supra* note 75, at 12 and 13.
[97] *See* Onuf, *supra* note 73, at 9.
[98] *See* Hobsbawm, *supra* note 76, at 4.
[99] Carr, *supra* note 84, at 23.
[100] *See* Jonathan Haslam, No Virtue Like Necessity: Realist Thought in International Relations since Machiavelli 1 (2002).

time those who teach the history of political thought interested themselves in international relations and vice versa."[101] Georg Cavallar argued in *The Rights of Strangers* (2002) that postcolonial and Eurocentric interpretations of positivism disconnected a universal, Kantian Tradition of hospitality and cosmopolitanism dating to the scholastic age.[102]

And what to make of the constellation of images attaching to the Grotian Tradition? What should be shored up; what should be torn up? International relations specialists tend to employ the Grotian Tradition as a means of conveying the broader significance of its foundation myth – the epochal birth of liberal internationalism and the state-centric world. Edward Keene's reconstruction of Hedley Bull's *The Anarchical Society* (1977) focused on the latter's selective but enormously influential view of Grotius. In *Beyond the Anarchical Society* (2002), Keene admirably recast the rationalist penumbra surrounding Grotius and his association with the idea of sovereign equality. Together with other scholars such as Peter Borschberg and Martina Van Ittersum, aspects of competing *tradita* emerge: Grotius the mercantilist; Grotius the convoluted Just War theorist; Grotius the divisible sovereignty supporter; Grotius the hired gun for an agency of empire, the Dutch East India Company. Terms have been conflated and lifted out of their context; some terms have been left behind in the historically unfolding conceptualization process of the Grotian Tradition.

The concept of state sovereignty, which is routinely connected to the Peace of Westphalia in 1648,[103] and further described as the *fount* of the Grotian Tradition,[104] provides a good example of a term that has been lifted out of the Grotian conceptual framework, where it may no longer fit where it once did. In the Grotian Tradition, it occupies its own temporal and conceptual space as international law's birth certificate – sometimes referred to as international

---

[101] *Id.* at 6.

[102] *See generally* GEORG CAVALLAR, THE RIGHTS OF STRANGERS: THEORIES OF INTERNATIONAL HOSPITALITY, THE GLOBAL COMMUNITY, AND POLITICAL JUSTICE SINCE VITORIA (2002).

[103] *See* JONATHAN HAVERCROFT, CAPTIVES OF SOVEREIGNTY 51 (2011); KEN MACMILLAN, SOVEREIGNTY AND POSSESSION IN THE ENGLISH NEW WORLD: THE LEGAL FOUNDATIONS OF EMPIRE, 1576–1640 at 18 (2006); BENNO TESCHKE, THE MYTH OF 1648: CLASS, GEOPOLITICS, AND THE MAKING OF MODERN INTERNATIONAL RELATIONS 2–3 (2003). The Peace of Westphalia pertains to two treaties signed in the towns of Münster and Osnabrück in the region of Westphalia. The peace conference was divided between the two cities because papal representatives refused to negotiate in the presence of Protestants. *See* DEREK CROXTON & ANUSCHKA TISCHER, THE PEACE OF WESTPHALIA: A HISTORICAL DICTIONARY 211(2001).

[104] *See, e.g.,* Ove Bring, *The Westphalian Peace Tradition in International Law: from Jus ad Bellum to Jus contra Bellum, in* 75 INTERNATIONAL LAW ACROSS THE SPECTRUM OF CONFLICT: ESSAYS IN HONOUR OF PROFESSOR L. C. GREEN ON THE OCCASION OF HIS EIGHTIETH BIRTHDAY 57, 58–62 (Michael N. Schmitt, ed., 2000) (discussing 'The Peace of Westphalia and the Grotian Legacy').

law's Grotian Moment, or as an analytic assumption for neoliberalism.[105] State sovereignty's sudden appearance on the international stage made it seem as if it was a phenomenon.[106] Its identification with modernity became so commonplace thereafter, and its normative implications "went largely unchallenged" until criticisms of modernity's accomplishments cast "unaccustomed scrutiny" on its meaning and future.[107] Emphasis on its invariance negated consideration of its diachronic trajectory or its social construction.[108] Subsequent scholarly treatments of sovereignty's ontological status critically implicated the narrowness of this lifting out. The widely proclaimed erosion of sovereignty in the globalized present,[109] the construction of vernacular law schemes (a common law of the people) beyond the state,[110] the nuances of soft law, and the mutable and contingent treatment of sovereignty as symbolic form[111] indicate the concept is still traveling, perhaps, some scholars say, ever-changing.[112]

Certainly the concept of state sovereignty traveled across time, pre- and postdating by centuries the epochal arrival of 1648.[113] Benno Teschke identified modern forms of sovereignty before Westphalia and premodern forms after it.[114] Jens Bartelson argued the "history of sovereignty ought to be studied not in isolation or within a narrow temporal frame of inferential and rhetorical connections," but in terms of its multiple relations within the larger discursive whole.[115] Hent Kalmo construed this discursive whole as emanating from the "thick web" of medieval jurisprudence where, as early as the eleventh century, a proto-plenipotentiary space between the double sword of imperial

---

[105] Stephen D. Krasner, *Compromising Westphalia*, 20 INT'L SEC. 115, 121 (1995/96).
[106] *See* STEPHEN TOULMIN, COSMOPOLIS: THE HIDDEN AGENDA OF MODERNITY 76 (1990), noting the crucial timeliness of Grotius' publication of *De Jure Belli ac Pacis* (1625)
[107] Nicholas Greenwood Onuf, *Sovereignty: Outline of a Conceptual History*, 16 ALTERNATIVES 425, 425 (1991).
[108] *See, e.g.,* STATE SOVEREIGNTY AS SOCIAL CONSTRUCT (Thomas J. Biersteker & Cynthia Weber, eds., 1996).
[109] *See, e.g.,* BEYOND WESTPHALIA? *State Sovereignty and International Intervention* (Gene M. Lyons & Michael Mastanduno, eds., 1995)
[110] *See, e.g.,* BURNS H. WESTON & DAVID BOLLIER, GREEN GOVERNANCE: ECOLOGICAL SURVIVAL, HUMAN RIGHTS, AND THE LAW OF THE COMMONS (2013).
[111] *See generally* JENS BARTELSON, SOVEREIGNTY AS SYMBOLIC FORM (2014).
[112] *See, e.g.,* Thomas J. Biersteker & Cynthia Weber, *The Social Construction of State Sovereignty, in* STATE SOVEREIGNTY AS SOCIAL CONSTRUCT, *supra* note 108, at 3 (arguing against the modern state system as some timeless principle).
[113] *See generally* STEPHEN D. KRASNER, SOVEREIGNTY: ORGANIZED HYPOCRISY (1999); Stephen D. Krasner, *'Westphalia and All That', in* IDEAS AND FOREIGN POLICY: BELIEFS, INSTITUTIONS AND POLITICAL CHANGE 235–64 (Judith Goldstein & Robert O. Keohane, eds., 1993).
[114] TESCHKE, *supra* note 103, at 26 (citing Stephen D. Krasner).
[115] JENS BARTELSON, A GENEALOGY OF SOVEREIGNTY 2 (1995).

and papal power began to appear.[116] This space achieved a special status and over time attached to the *person* of the rule-maker. Feudal status-conferring terms included *sovereign, seigneur, suzerain, sire, sir, sieur, monsieur, monseigneur*.[117] Quentin Skinner traced sovereignty's genealogy from the princely concern toward the end of the sixteenth century of maintaining this personal status, which over time required a container to preserve the welfare of the body politic (*corpus politicum*).[118] "[T]he awe-inspiring formality and dignity" of the personal ruler transposed into a corporate office (which survived the individual inspiring it), solidifying an important antecedent of the sovereign state – the concept of *majestas* (majesty of office).[119] *Majestas* was central to Jean Bodin's (1530–1596) concept of absolute sovereignty, but its roots resided in the Roman law of *patria potestas* – the father of the household.[120] The end result, according to Bartelson, was the relocation of authority in the form of the depersonalized abstract state "conceptualized independently of rulers as well as ruled."[121]

But this relocation did not coalesce in a moment, it developed through a process. Bartelson noted that the concept of sovereignty, taken as a snapshot in 1648, "did not ... contain any recognizably modern notion of territorially bounded sovereignty;" the connection between sovereignty and territory arose in the aftermath of the Peace of Westphalia.[122] To forge this connection, the concept of the state first had to develop *into* the post-Westphalian world.

In 1648, the state remained an etymological hybrid, "combining roots from *estate* ([meaning] land, property, rights) and *status* (authority, standing, rights);" it was a territorially grounded object of property rights pertaining to monarchs.[123] Early modern rulers endured practicalities of limited authority. They were poorly equipped, feebly financed, spatially tethered to their immediate surroundings, and in need of assistance from advisory assemblies.[124] Derek Croxton argued sovereignty emerged as a historical fact over

---

[116] *See* Hent Kalmo, *Sovereignty: A Painful State*, 63 Hist. *Today* (2013), www.historytoday.com/hent-kalmo/sovereignty-painful-state.

[117] Kurt Burch, "Property" and the Making of the International System 143 (1988).

[118] Quentin Skinner, *The Sovereign State: A Genealogy, in* Sovereignty in Fragments: The Past, Present and Future of a Contested Concept 26, 27–28 (Hent Kalmo & Quentin Skinner, eds., 2010).

[119] Onuf, *supra* note 107, at 435.

[120] Jean Bethke Elshtain, Sovereignty: God, State, Self 54 (2008); Onuf, *supra* note 107, at 437–438.

[121] Bartelson, *supra* note 111, at 19 (referencing Skinner).

[122] *Id.* at 28.

[123] Burch, *supra* note 117, at 143–144.

[124] *Id.* at 144.

the course of three hundred years before Westphalia, and transmuted from the rule over people to the rule over territory only after the post-Westphalian principalities internalized notions of autonomy – a process that was hardly momentary: indeed, the Holy Roman Empire, which state sovereignty superseded, lasted another 158 years following the Peace of Westphalia.[125] Almost immediately after the Holy Roman Empire's formal expiration, the emerging state system would again draw from Roman law's deep wellspring of property analogies to help fill the spatial vacuum created by retreating Metropolitan powers in the New World after 1810 – hence the modern birth of *uti possidetis*.

What made sovereignty harden into the state system's "protective shell" was the eventual reconciliation of a paradox whereby sovereignty could be internally construed as divisible, allowing for the fulfilment of multiple enterprises within the state, and yet indivisible externally, whereby external sovereignty denied changes in the relations of states.[126] The process of "unbundling" territoriality became the basis for a new international order once spatial demarcations between public and private realms and internal and external realms consolidated, the latter taking the form of reciprocal sovereignty.[127] Multiple internal and divisible constructions could render the holder of sovereignty a *dominus* or usufruct (an intermediary/agent constituted to serve the public interest).[128] These constructions could take the form of a monarch, or the people (popular sovereignty), or a constitution. External sovereignty imposed a condition of anarchy – not equated with chaos – which immunized the particular holder of internal sovereignty from external interference and fixed state relations foremost around a principle analogized from private property law: no-trespassing (nonintervention).[129]

This norm of autonomy – the core of Westphalian sovereignty – inconsistently reflected actual practice.[130] But more than the practical inconsistencies, Friedrich Kratochwil claimed conceptual confusion regarding sovereignty's relocation arose from the conflation of sovereignty with will, owing to the enduring spatial representations of authority presented by Hobbes and

[125] See Derek Croxton, *The Peace of Westphalia of 1648 and the Origins of Sovereignty*, 21 INT'L HIST. REV. 569, 573 (1999). Napoleon dissolved the empire in 1806.

[126] Onuf, *supra* note 107, at 432.

[127] John Gerard Ruggie, *Territoriality and Beyond: Problematizing Modernity in International Relations*, 47 INT'L ORG. 139, 151 and 162 (1993).

[128] See Daniel Lee, *Popular Liberty, Princely Government, and the Roman Law in Hugo Grotius's De Jure Belli ac Pacis*, 72 J. HIST. IDEAS 371, 391 (July 2011).

[129] Daniel Philpott, *Ideas and the Evolution of Sovereignty, in* STATE SOVEREIGNTY: CHANGE AND PERSISTENCE IN INTERNATIONAL RELATIONS 15, 20 (Sohail H. Hashmi, ed., 1997).

[130] Stephen Krasner noted history shows states pursue a logic of consequences guided by power and interest, as opposed to a logic of appropriateness supported by institutionalized norms,

Bodin.[131] Sovereignty's conceptual derailment arose when it "became no longer simply attributable to a real person."[132] Over time, the *jus publicum europaeum* conceived of a state as a *persona moralis* and other states as *personae morales*, "each one free and independent of its inner constitution."[133] Left behind in modernity's treatment of sovereignty was an aspect common to the writings of Grotius, Samuel Pufendorf (1632–1694), and John Selden (1585–1654), which construed sovereignty as analogous to the exclusionary character of private property in Roman law,[134] where its civil exercise was not "easily defeasible by moral considerations;"[135] where "right use" was moderated by "background conditions" such as the *sic utere tuo ut alienum non laedas* (and also the doctrine of usufruct, which frowned on waste), but which allowed not simply a right of ownership, but a broader right of rule, even "to do the wrong thing."[136] Sovereignty in this sense evolved from the waning of princely fealty to hierarchies of European Christendom, but it also reflected nuanced understandings of political authority stemming from Roman law, especially the embedded idea of *dominium*, where restrictions on sovereign privilege of use were few.[137] If *imperium* imparted a power to rule, *dominium* allowed a right to own or possess.[138] This concept became well developed and differentiated within the context of ownership and control over land use within the king's territorial jurisdiction, and, until the rise of popular sovereignty, over the people as well.[139] Joseph Chan noted this ownership perspective of political authority was prominent in Europe in the sixteenth century and after, and was frequently invoked to define royal rights.[140] Others also have made the connection between sovereignty and the genealogical backdrop of Roman property law.[141] Nicholas Onuf and Peter Onuf contended "Roman civil law fostered an analogy between property and territory as a basis for jurisdiction – for deciding which persons

---

notwithstanding what they may claim. To Krasner, the normal state of affairs long has revolved around organized hypocrisy. KRASNER, ORGANIZED HYPOCRISY, *supra* note 113, at 8–9.

[131] Friedrich Kratochwil, *Sovereignty as Dominium: Is There a Right of Humanitarian Intervention?*, in BEYOND WESTPHALIA? STATE SOVEREIGNTY AND INTERNATIONAL INTERVENTION, *supra* note 109, 21, at 22–23.

[132] *Id.* at 23.

[133] REINHART KOSELLECK, CRITIQUE AND CRISIS: ENLIGHTENMENT AND THE PATHOGENESIS OF MODERN SOCIETY 43 (1988).

[134] *Id.* at 22.

[135] *Id.* at 26

[136] *Id.* at 26.

[137] *Id.* at 25.

[138] *See* MACMILLAN, *supra* note 103, at 6.

[139] JOSEPH CHAN, CONFUCIAN PERFECTIONISM: A POLITICAL PHILOSOPHY FOR MODERN TIMES 214 (2014).

[140] *Id.* at 213.

[141] *See* ELSHTAIN, *supra* note 120, at 24, 41 and 54–55 (2008); Ben Holland, *Sovereignty as Dominium? Reconstructing the Constructivist Roman Law Thesis*, 54 INT'L STUD. Q. 449 (2010);

are subject to given rules in what circumstances."[142] As a property right, Kurt Busch argued sovereignty was the highest expression of ownership (*dominium*), combining perfect title with possession.[143] Jean Bethke Elshtain connected the development of the modern state to the medieval incorporation of Roman law, where the state was conceived along the lines of private property, immune from public control, and where sovereignty was conceived along the lines of the rule of a *paterfamilias* over the Roman *domus* (a form of *dominium*), which is capable of legally representing the (Roman) people as a unified subject.[144] Like others, she recognized "[i]t took time for this redolent little seed to germinate meaningfully."[145] Situating sovereignty's institutional roots in the private law of Rome and its treatment of *proprietas* presents new angles to consider common use doctrine, certainly as it relates to the historical development of *dominium*, and, as we shall discuss, in relation to *uti possidetis* (as you possess, so you may possess), itself a hallmark feature of Roman property law. Grotius was deeply concerned with *dominium*; that he incorporated discussion of *dominium* into questions involving proprietary claims relating to the seas makes him a shining example in favor of shared access for the common good. But his subjective expression of a natural right of *dominium*, left behind in progressive and modern expressions of his eponymous Tradition, underscores fissures in the relationship between sovereignty and territory, which pose problems for international relations specialists who seek to move beyond the Westphalian world. *Dominium*, with its lingering connection to *patria potestas*, was an idea connected to the evolving Grotian Tradition, and the Grotian Tradition never completely detached from it. Although overlooked or lifted out of modern discussions, his disturbing normative construction of sovereignty as a form of *dominium* reverberates worldwide in the disparate settings of the High Arctic, the hyperarid Atacama Desert in South America, in the South China Sea, and, doubtless, in the coming discussions on the fate of the global commons.

HISTORICAL ANACHRONISM AND THE GROTIAN TRADITION

When we witness a modern notion improperly applied to the past, we witness the anachronism of historical research.[146] Quentin Skinner thought some

---

BURCH, *supra* note 117, at 143–148 (1998); NICHOLAS ONUF & PETER ONUF, NATIONS, MARKETS, AND WAR: MODERN HISTORY AND THE AMERICAN CIVIL WAR 56–58 (2006).

[142] ONUF & ONUF, *supra* note 141, at 47 (2006).

[143] *See* BURCH, *supra* note 117, at 145.

[144] ELSHTAIN, *supra* note 120, at 41.

[145] *Id.*

[146] *See* Peter Cryle, *Anachronistic Readings of Eighteenth-Century Libertinage in Nineteenth- and Twentieth-Century France, in* SEX, KNOWLEDGE, AND RECEPTIONS OF THE PAST 66, 66 (Kate Fischer & Rebecca Langlands, eds., 2015).

anachronism unavoidable; it arises in the form of conceptual parochialisms that inhere in looking at the past from modernity's window.[147] But conceptual historians are mindful of the value-laden political implications of anachronistic imagery, which can be used as tools or as weapons in relation to social change.[148] When current historiographies become "contaminated by unconscious application of paradigms [that] disguise[] an essential inapplicability to the past," we create a mythology wrought by historical anachronism.[149]

Complaints now arise that the Grotian Tradition embodies endemic and anachronistic mythologies, calling into question its applicability to the past and future. Peter Haggenmacher, for instance, questioned the novelty of the Grotian Tradition, placing Grotius in a continuum of scholarly discourse relating to just war theory that dates to Gratian's *Decretum*.[150] Others have been more critical, forwarding a new foundation myth based on the Grotian Tradition's "peculiarly narrow and twisted perspective on order in modern world politics,"[151] suggesting the tradition has been "invented,"[152] not "meaningfully definable,"[153] and not what it appears to be.[154] David Armitage has pointed out that multiple Grotian narratives, along with narratives about early modernity, comprise "foundation myths retailed by later communities of historians and diplomats, international lawyers and proto-political scientists, seeking historical validation for their ideological projects and infant professions."[155]

One intriguing and influential *aspect* lifted out of the Grotian Tradition has been its identification with the still-popular crystallization of the Grotian Moment, an "irresistible catchphrase"[156] coined by Richard Falk in 1980.[157]

---

[147] Quentin Skinner, *Meaning and Understanding in the History of Ideas*, in 8 HISTORY AND THEORY 3, 22–27 (1969) (discussing parochialism).

[148] *See* Sami Syrjämäki, *Sins of a Historian: Perspectives on the Problem of Anachronism* 18 (dissertation, University of Tampere, 2011).

[149] Skinner, *supra* note 147, at 7.

[150] *See, e.g.*, PETER HAGGENMACHER, GROTIUS ET LA DOCTRINE DE LA GUERRE JUSTE (1983).

[151] EDWARD KEENE, BEYOND THE ANARCHICAL SOCIETY: GROTIUS, COLONIALISM AND ORDER IN WORLD POLITICS 38 (2002).

[152] RENÉE JEFFERY, HUGO GROTIUS IN INTERNATIONAL THOUGHT 17–26 (2006); Parry, *supra* note 61, at 305.

[153] Parry, *supra* note 61, at 302.

[154] Anghie, *supra* note 59, at 1321 (contrasting Grotius as a heroic figure with ambitious and self-interested aspects of his character). *See also* MARTINE VAN ITTERSUM, PROFIT AND PRINCIPLE: HUGO GROTIUS, NATURAL RIGHTS THEORIES AND THE RISE OF DUTCH POWER IN THE EAST INDIES 1595–1615 (2006); Peter Borschberg, Hugo Grotius, *The Portuguese, and Free Trade in the East Indies* (NUS Press, 2011); and Christopher R. Rossi, *A Particular Kind of Dominium: The Grotian Tendency and the Global Commons in a Time of High Arctic Change*, 11 J. INT'L L. & INT'L REL. 1 (2015).

[155] DAVID ARMITAGE, FOUNDATIONS OF MODERN INTERNATIONAL THOUGHT 9–10 (2013).

[156] Parry, *supra* note 61, at 316 ff (discussing Richard Falk's "irresistible catchphrase" – the Grotian Moment).

[157] Richard Falk, *Some Thoughts on the Decline of International Law and Future Prospects*, 9 HOFSTRA L.R. 399, 408 (1980) (describing the Grotian Moment as a time when a "new kind of

Falk argued that creation of the Westphalian state system in 1648 ushered in with unusual rapidity and acceptance a transformative system of rules in an epochal turn of history's wheel. Falk's elegant and timely portrayal of Grotius' emergence from the shadow land of Europe's Thirty Years' War informs a variety of scholarly and political perspectives today, including former United Nations Secretary-General Boutros Boutros-Ghali's perspective in relation to the international community's establishment of the International Tribunal for the Former Yugoslavia.[158] Many of these Grotian Moments succumb to a new temptation: forecasting the erosion of territorial sovereignty and the passing of the Westphalian order. One might wonder how many Grotian Moments have we witnessed since Falk coined the term? – the United Nations Security Council's awakening from rhetorical torpor when it authorized "all necessary means" to compel Iraq to quit Kuwait,[159] the fall of communism, US President George H. W. Bush's pronouncement of a New World Order,[160] Francis Fukuyama's culminating *End of History* thesis,[161] the democracy movement in China before the Tiananmen Square massacre, the 1992 Maastrict Treaty creating the European Union, the response to 9/11, the introduction of the Responsibility to Protect doctrine and the attempted reformulation of international humanitarian law, the Arab Spring, responses to Abu Bakr al-Baghdadi's June 29, 2014 declaration of the Islamic State in Iraq and Greater Syria (ISIS), efforts to combat global climate change – all of these examples suggest Grotian possibilities for profound change, perhaps Grotian Moments.

Phillips cautioned that the general coinage of any phrase acquiring quick popularity results often in loose use of the idea.[162] Perhaps this point is correct

order is trying to emerge ... synthesizing the old that is dying with the new that is emerging in a way that goes beyond evolutionary statism ...".). For elaboration, *see generally* INTERNATIONAL LAW: A CONTEMPORARY PERSPECTIVE, ch. 1 (Richard Falk, Friedrich Kratochwil & Saul H. Mendlovitz eds., 1985) (presenting interpretations of the Grotian Moment by Lauterpacht and Falk).

158 Boutrous Boutrous-Ghali, *The Role of International Law in the Twenty-First Century: A Grotian Moment*, 18 FORDHAM INT'L L.J. 1609, 1612 (1995); *See generally* Scharf, *supra* note 62; Melena Sterio, *A Grotian Moment: Changes in the Legal Theory of Statehood*, 39 DENV. J. INT'L L. & POL'Y 209 (2010–2011); Ibrahim J. Gassama, *International Law at a Grotian Moment: The Invasion of Iraq in Context*, 18 EMORY INT'L L. REV. 1 (2004). *See also* Christopher Weeramantry, *The Grotius Lecture Series: Opening Tribute to Hugo Grotius*, 14 AM. U. INT'L L. REV. 1516, 1518 (1999) (claiming "we are living at a 'Grotian moment' in world history").

159 UN SC Res 678, Nov. 29, 1990, Security Council Resolutions – 1990, http://daccess-dds-ny.un.org/doc/RESOLUTION/GEN/NR0/575/28/IMG/NR057528.pdf?OpenElement.

160 George Bush, Address before a Joint Session of the Congress on the State of the Union, Jan. 29, 1991, reprinted in THE AMERICAN PRESIDENCY PROJECT, www.presidency.ucsb.edu/ws/?pid=19253.

161 *See generally* FRANCIS FUKUYAMA, THE END OF HISTORY AND THE LAST MAN (1992).

162 *See* PHILLIPS, *supra* note 76, at 4 (discussing coinage of the phrase "invented tradition").

about of the Grotian Moment. Its invocation seems to distort or misrepresent a genuine want among enthusiastic proponents of the Grotian Tradition by constructing, accelerating, and punctuating the normative preference for liberal internationalism. Timur Kuran cautioned against misperceived norm construction, generically labeling such an idea a "preference falsification" – a misrepresentation of a genuine want that may not genuinely exist.[163] Do some Grotian Moments reflect preference falsifications that mask tensions within liberal internationalism's Grotian Tradition?

The conflation of the Grotian Tradition with the Grotian Moment imputes to the former an unwarranted coherence and to the latter an overstated significance. Michael Scharf, in his monograph on *Customary International Law in Times of Fundamental Change* (2013), subtitled his work: "*Recognizing Grotian Moments.*" Although only the Grotian Tradition is referenced in his index, he acknowledged the concept of the Grotian Moment "denotes a radical development in which new rules and doctrines … emerge with unusual rapidity and acceptance,"[164] and he proceeds to analyze it through a series of case studies, some mentioned earlier.[165] He noted the Grotian Moment's reworking in the context of "international constitutional moments," for instance, the drafting of the United Nations Charter, the establishment of the Nuremberg Principles on individual responsibility for war crimes, crimes against peace, and crimes against humanity.[166] But he also noted the sudden paradigm-shifting Grotian Moment "is not entirely accurate;"[167] that the ontology of the state system coexisted with empire one hundred years before the Peace of Westphalia.[168] One of Keene's main points was that the Grotian Tradition never truly existed outside of Europe; in the European colonial world, it poorly reflected the values and structures later associated with it. It seems the dramaturgy of the Grotian Moment, punctuating global liberalism's arrival on stage, was lifted out of the Grotian Tradition inchoate or as overworked, as some productions of the Grotian Moment may be. Indeed, scholars have noted the anachronistic portrayal of the Peace of Westphalia as *the* original Grotian Moment. The inaccurate and retrospective identification of Grotius with the birth of state

[163] *See generally* PRIVATE TRUTHS, PUBLIC LIES: THE SOCIAL CONSEQUENCES OF PREFERENCE FALSIFICATION (1995).

[164] Scharf, *supra* note 62, at 1.

[165] His case studies include: The development of the Nuremberg Principles; the Truman Proclamation on the Continental Shelf; Outer Space law; the Yugoslav Tribunal's Tadic Decision; NATO's air attack against Serbia in defense of Albanian Kosovars; and responses to 9/11. *See id.*

[166] *Id.* at 5–6.

[167] *Id.* at 24.

[168] *Id.* at 24–25.

sovereignty more properly and historically belongs to Vattel, when he clarified con-
structs of internal and external sovereignty and the norm of nonintervention in the
internal affairs of other states.[169] This clarification would make the Grotian Moment
wholly anachronistic – a misnomer better expressed as a Vattellian Moment
and more properly located in the latter stages of the eighteenth century (with a
nineteenth-century assist from Henry Wheaton[170]), not in the seventeenth century.

TRADITION AND HISTORICISM

Tradition is a term of great historical depth.[171] Uncovering the deep meaning
of the Grotian Tradition involves an appreciation of the "road to wisdom"[172]
that history provides. History imparts knowledge within a specific context; and
the belief that history imparts contextual knowledge reflects a mode of thinking referred to as historicism.

There is debate about historicism and the degree to which it frames or
determines reality. Benedetto Croce wrote of a *storicismo assoluto* and understood historicism as an absolute and scientific determinant of succeeding
events; in *History as the Story of Liberty* (1941) he famously defined historicism
as "the affirmation that life and reality are history and history alone;"[173] that
"historicism is the true humanism" and "the truth of humanism."[174] His greatest critic was Karl Popper, who labeled historicism a "poor method"[175] because
it negated volitional and associational (cultural) aspects of human interaction
and agency, presenting not truth but the "myth of destiny" traceable to Plato's
seducing, authoritarian, proto-illiberal spell over western methodology.[176] But

---

[169] *See* EMER DE VATTEL & JOSEPH CHITTY, THE LAW OF NATIONS, OR PRINCIPLES OF THE LAW
OF NATURE, APPLIED TO THE CONDUCT OF NATIONS AND SOVEREIGNS: A WORK TENDING TO
DISPLAY 11 (1829) [1758] ("distinguishing carefully the internal law from the external law, that
is, the necessary from the voluntary law of nations"). *See also* Sovereignty: Conversation with
Stephen D. Krasner [conversation with Harry Kreisler], Mar. 31, 2003, http://globetrotter
.berkeley.edu/people3/Krasner/krasner-con3.html; Stéphane Beaulac, *Emer de Vattel and the
Externalization of Sovereignty*, 5 J. HIST. INT'L L. 237 (2003).

[170] ONUF & ONUF, *supra* note 141, at 50, 60, and 63 (associating Wheaton with Vattel's establishment of the conceptual autonomy of the law of nations; crediting Wheaton in a line of
descent separating legal relations among states from legal relations within states; acknowledging Wheaton as an exemplary figure in this discussion, but noting his error and imaginative
and anachronistic reconstructions).

[171] PHILLIPS, *supra* note 76, at 4.

[172] MORRIS R. COHEN, THE MEANING OF HUMAN HISTORY 16 (1947) ("the main road to human
wisdom").

[173] BENEDETTO CROCE, HISTORY AS THE STORY OF LIBERTY 65 (Sylvia Sprigge trans., 1947).

[174] *Id.* at 315.

[175] KARL R. POPPER, THE POVERTY OF HISTORICISM vi (1964).

[176] KARL R. POPPER, THE OPEN SOCIETY AND ITS ENEMIES, VOLUME 1: THE SPELL OF PLATO
(1966) (referencing chapter 1, "Historicism and the Myth of Destiny").

there is plenty of room for middle ground even among intramural discussions of historicists. Robert Pois contrasted Croce's view of historicism with Friedrich Meinecke's understanding,[177] which at its core defined historicism as "compensation, through individual reflection, for a generalizing view of historical-human forces;" and as a search for "general lawfulness and types of human life ... simultaneously blend[ed] with its sense for the individual."[178] Pois noted "[b]oth Croce and Meinecke eschewed transcendentalism" in history,[179] and indeed "almost all the proponents of historicism repudiate any search for 'laws'" that aim at historical prediction;[180] and historicists generally understand that the ordering of historical facts involves a human vetting process. Historicism is broad enough to involve the consideration of the changing social and political conditions that intersect with legal norms. These conditions are not fixed over time, and legal norms are not fixed either. Consequently, emphasizing a historical approach to the study of the global commons imparts an appreciation of the "changing structures of legal consciousness"[181] and the evolving *tradita* of the Grotian legacy. Historicism values the importance and meaning of history not because it results in a formal brand of determinism but because it reflects an important wake charted by human activity.

Taking a page from Popper, who debunked the historical narrative based on the undue influences of Plato and his blameworthy followers Hegel and Marx,[182] international law's history may be occluded by Grotius' heralded reputation, a reputation that compounds this misreading of the history of the law of the sea and overshadows consideration of Grotius' complexity, which uncharitably might be expressed as his hidden agenda. Grotius' Free Sea thesis is not what many international legal scholars think it to be. In fact, Grotius' misunderstood contribution to international law actually validates the disturbing *tendency* – herein modestly referred to (with a small "t") as the *Grotian tendency* – of states to territorialize emergent claims over unsecured global resources when interests and abilities align. The Grotian tendency is an *aspect* of the Grotian Tradition. It is traceable to restrictions on use – on

---

[177] *See generally* Robert A. Pois, *Two Poles within Historicism: Croce and Meinecke*, 31 J. Hist. of Ideas 253 (1970).

[178] *Id.* at 253 (quoting Meinecke's Die Entstehund des Historismus (1936)).

[179] *Id.*

[180] Dwight E. Lee & Robert N. Beck, *The Meaning of "Historicism,"* 59 Am. Hist. Rev. 568, 577 (1954).

[181] Jack M. Balkin & Sanford Levinson, *Legal Historicism and Legal Academics: The Roses of Law Professors in the Wake of Bush v. Gore*, 90 Geo. L.J. 173, 181 (2001)

[182] *See generally* Karl Popper, The Open Society and Its Enemies, Volume II, The High Tide of Prophecy: Hegel, Marx and the aftermath (1966).

the alienability of use – found in the concept of *dominium* within the civil
law of Rome and its development of *proprietas*. It is not an ironclad rule;
it is not presented to trump the sudden crystallization of Grotian Moment
mentality. It is a historically present inclination that helps to inform a broader
perspective on the Grotian Tradition and those scholars who prefer to write
with grander capital Ts in mind. In my view, it is a salient, persistent feature
of Grotius' impressive imprint on modern international relations; it appears
when possibilities arise to territorialize resources either within the common
realm or newly emergent; and it is as relevant as wishful identifications with
the Grotian Moment.

In this book, I lift out the Grotian tendency from the Grotian Tradition,
involve it in the rapidly changing circumstances of the Arctic and other
pelagic and proximate spaces as a platform for discussing resources, globalization and post-sovereignty prospects (in forms such as soft law, vernacular
law, adaptations of common pool resource theory), the often disparaged possibility of condominium arrangements in international law, and extant and
prospective discussions about common space and about the Grotian Tradition
itself. Grotius had a complex agenda, which, contrary to his revered historical
treatment as the progenitor of a liberal Grotian Tradition in international law,
supports the long-standing and ongoing tendency of states to lay sovereign
claim to emerging resources once interests and abilities align. Grotius should
be given full credit for his tradition in international law, which involves proto-
territorializing tendencies more complex and parochial than his praiseworthy proto-liberal life suggests and is more textured, especially with regard to
dominium, than the historiography of the Grotian Tradition records.

THE PATH OF THIS BOOK

I begin Chapter 2 with a discussion of Hugo Grotius, the most celebrated
authority in international law. In his famous work, *Mare Liberum*, he articulated the doctrine of freedom of the seas. In support of the claim that states
could not enclose or appropriate the seas for private use, Grotius forwarded
the idea that the seas were a common good, the use of which must be shared
by all of humanity. I reconsider Grotius' common use argument and note
problems with his original formulation in the context of his own time and
in light of dramatic current attempts by certain states to capitalize on changing climate conditions and ambiguities in the international law of the sea to
extend their control over new resources. Drawing from the history of international law, the current and future significance of common use doctrine begins
to reflect the grander lesson of the Grotian Tradition involving the embedded

Grotian tendency of states to appropriate rather than share scarce extant or emerging resources.

Once considered impassable due to icebound conditions of the High Arctic, Chapter 3 considers the prospect of a coming clash over the legal status of the Northern Sea Route, the major stretch of waterway atop Russia, straddling Eurasia from Providence Bay to Murmansk. Through analogous application of the Roman law principle of *uti possidetis*, a presumptive proprietary judge-made principle adapted to international law – with serious criticism – I argue that Russia's claim of sovereign control over the route finds legal support but is pragmatically and strategically weak. Existing *lacunae* in the governing international law of the sea, nevertheless, make consideration of the principle valuable, particularly components of the principle that emphasize factual circumstances, called *effectivités*, which support Russia's claim. The creeping pelagic significance of this principle, historically tethered to terrestrial border delimitations and more recently to factual patterns involving gross human rights abuse, underscores a central and recurring component of the Grotian tendency.

How well states work together to forward common interests in the shrinking global commons is explored in Chapter 4, which introduces the unique international problem of the High Arctic archipelago, Svalbard. The 1920 Svalbard Treaty conferred its full and absolute sovereignty on Norway but paradoxically limited that sovereignty by conferring on states party to the treaty equal enjoyment and liberty of access provisions on Svalbard *and in its territorial waters*. This curious example of divisible sovereignty, perhaps better expressed as shared sovereignty, generates interesting but challenging prospects. Whether these provisions now extend to geographic areas adjacent to Svalbard's territorial sea – specifically to Svalbard's oil-rich continental shelf and abundant fishing stock of the superjacent waters of its Exclusive Economic Zone (EEZ) – is a matter of considerable debate. Norway repudiates the dynamic legal extension of the Svalbard Treaty to these geographic areas, which postdate the treaty; other Arctic stakeholders disagree. In this chapter I concentrate on the problematic meaning of full and absolute yet qualified sovereignty within the context of the Svalbard Treaty. Focusing on the factual and historical *effectivités* pertaining to the archipelago's four hundred year human history is of essential but limited use given competing historical narratives. Instead, I concentrate on the historical and legal development of the concept of *terra nullius*, a term more elusive than commonly thought, and the ways in which states historically made use of that concept to forward territorializing interests over Svalbard's newly emergent resources, even when pronouncing or professing interest in shared or condominium-like resource management arrangements. In an age of rapid ice melt in the cryosphere, emergent technology and increasing access to previously unavailable or uncontemplated resources present questions regarding Svalbard and sovereignty. Svalbard's extended geographical area challenges global governance regimes and presents a cautionary tale about territorial temptation in the High Arctic's diminishing global commons.

Challenges to Arctic governance presented by rapid ice melt are assessed in Chapter 5 in light of structural problems facing the region's preeminent soft law regime structure, the Arctic Council. I argue the territorializing temptations of the subregional Arctic 5 states that ring the Arctic Ocean, which among themselves may overlap and conflict, nevertheless align to keep the Arctic Council focus on functional objectives, notwithstanding attempts at internal reform, calls for a new Arctic treaty, or emerging assessments of a global understanding of Arctic issues, as represented by the newly founded Arctic Circle Assembly. The jurisdictional designs for the Arctic Ocean, as preferenced by the Arctic 5, counter proposals to revise the soft law and functional orientation of the current Arctic regime and evidence a corollary to the Grotian tendency: when states are not able to appropriate resources, they work together to alienate their interests vis-à-vis the rest of the world.

In Chapters 6 and 7, I move away from the High Arctic in pursuit of the concept and problem of condominium or shared sovereignty arrangements. Two historical examples involving pelagic interests in the Pacific Ocean present interesting case studies. Both examples involve Latin American countries, the Grotian tendency, and add the element of third-party dispute settlement. The first case involves the International Court of Justice's (ICJ's) 1992 Chamber ruling, which affirmed a joint ownership agreement over a body of water known as the Gulf of Fonseca. The three states adjoining the Pacific Ocean shores of the Gulf of Fonseca – El Salvador, Honduras, and Nicaragua – were declared joint sovereigns over the water. The decision affirmed a ruling of the 1917 Central American Court of Justice and gave renewed prominence to the concept of condominium arrangements in international law. This chapter critically analyzes the bases for both Courts' decisions in light of the factual and historical circumstances that the Chamber uncovered and applied to what it declared to be a *sui generis* circumstance. Drawing from references to *uti possidetis*, and mindful of the belligerent pre and postcolonial histories of the states assigned this shared sovereignty, the Chamber constructed a condominium arrangement. But this solution's uneasy reception among the three states continues to this date and has complicated the administration of justice by courts and tribunals in ways not fully apparent. The condominium concept as applied to the Gulf of Fonseca calls into question the proper role of decision-makers in the pacific settlement of disputes.

Studying problems in the High Arctic takes an ironic turn with an examination of the second case study, which involves, except for Antarctica's Dry Valleys, the most arid spot in the world – the Atacama Desert. There, similar questions of condominium and control over emergent resources inform a case currently before the ICJ. In 2015, the ICJ ruled that Bolivia's claim against Chile could proceed to the merit stage, setting up a discussion of perhaps the most intractable border dispute in South American history – Bolivia's attempt to reclaim from Chile a sovereign access to the Pacific Ocean. This chapter investigates the international law and deeply commingled regional history pertaining to the Atacama Desert region, the resource-rich region where Bolivia seeks to secure its long-lost access to the sea. Investigating the *effectivités*, the postcolonial international legal principle of *uti possidetis*, territorial temptations arising from resource discoveries, and the duty to negotiate based on a *pactum de contrahendo*, a *pactum de negotiando*, or unilateral declarations, this chapter concludes this case is less suited for adjudicative settlement than resolution by the principal three parties involved in the region – Bolivia, Chile, and Peru – primarily because the parties have, over the course of this protracted dispute, constructed intersubjective modalities for a shared sovereignty arrangement facilitated by subregional economic growth relations. It is here that I want to suggest an avenue for meaningful cooperation among states in shared sovereignty relationships. It is not a solution amenable to third-party dispute settlement, particularly when a cohabitation solution is imposed rather than universally accepted, as was the case in the Gulf of Fonseca. But the tortured and commingled history of these Andean countries reveals that a regional reconstruction of sovereignty in the northern Atacama region presents the better prospect for resolution than is possible through the limited outcomes presented by formal third-party dispute settlement. This is a lesson that potentially could lead to strengthened governance regimes in the High Arctic and prospects for common use elsewhere.

But the problem of *elsewhere* arises in the final chapter, first with a consideration of China's bold and rapidly unfolding claim of *dominium* over the South China Sea. The normatively disquieting implications of the Grotian tendency in that realm may serve as a precursor to discussions on the not-too-distant horizon, either in the geo-spatial regime of Antarctica, the ozone-depleted atmosphere, the coming colonization of outer space, or the all-too-real but intangible world of cyberspace. The management of these coming worlds most certainly occupies attention today, and this discussion ends with a consideration of how best to apply the time-tested lessons of the Grotian tendency, embedded and occluded as they tend to be, in the powerful significance and promise of the Grotian Tradition.

2

The Grotian Tendency in His Time and Ours

In *Mare Liberum*, Grotius argued the common seas were part of Nature's plan.[1] Drawing from Roman law and the Greek poet, Hesiod (c. 750 BCE), he recognized three possible legal descriptions of the seas: they could belong to nobody (*res nullius*), in which case they could be appropriated by individuals through effective occupation; they could belong to everybody, in which case they would form a common possession (*res communis*); or they could belong to the public (*res publicae*), in which case they could be subject to administrative regulation.[2]

According to what he labeled "primary law,"[3] which was the immutable law of nature (as distinguished from a secondary and mutable law of nations[4]), the seas were a gift from God "not to this or that individual, but to the human race."[5] In this original sense, ownership imparted a universal meaning,[6] which prevented individual appropriations or enclosures of this common area. He noted immutable qualities of Nature's gift – claiming common use was a common right "since the beginning of the world," over which no other right could be asserted.[7] He believed Nature created a hybrid brokerage account for the

---

[1] HUGO GROTIUS, MARE LIBERUM [THE FREE SEA] 1609–2009, translated by Robert Feenstra (Leiden: Brill Academic Publishers, 2009) at 65 [hereinafter MARE LIBERUM] ("[i]t is, then, quite impossible for the sea to be made the private property of any individual: for nature does not merely permit, but rather commands, that the sea shall be held in common").

[2] *Id.* at 49.

[3] *Id.* at 51.

[4] For a fuller discussion of Grotius' primary and secondary views of law, the scholastic influences on development of these views, and Iberian assailants of these views, *see generally* Mónica Brito Vieira, *Mare Liberum vs. Mare Clausum: Grotius, Freitas, and Selden's Debate on Dominion over the Seas*, 64 J. HIST. IDEAS 361 (2003).

[5] MARE LIBERUM, *supra* note 1, at 53.

[6] *Id.*

[7] *Id.* at 115.

seas, as "there was nothing to prevent a number of persons from being joint owners, in this fashion, of one and the same thing."[8]

Grotius' particular view of *dominium* grew out of two proprietary claims relating to the seas: some things are consumed through use and "therefore admit of no further use," and other things, through use, "are rendered less fit for additional service."[9] To claim ownership, a thing (*res*) had to be consumed or converted and thereby altered from its original condition. A quantitative or qualitative diversion of use had to take place in order for the *res* to become private property.[10] But the seas produce no such diversion. Nature intended them to be free and open because a claim of ownership would serve no purpose; at most, they only could be occupied temporarily. He argued they would always retain their original character following use, undisturbed by consumption[11] and incapable of conversion.

Grotius also construed ownership as an alienable right – as a personal right – which allowed a person "to exclude others from using and benefiting from a thing."[12] But *dominium*, in this sense, could be established only "through the industry and labor of each man,"[13] who also must refrain from unjustly laying hands on the property of others.[14] He claimed wild beasts, fish, and birds were not items assigned for common use, even though nobody owned them, because they could be subjected to private ownership – "provided that someone does take possession of them."[15] This *proviso* became a pillar of his argument: "For the essential characteristic of private property is the fact that

[8]   *Id.* at 53.

[9]   *Id.* at 55.

[10] *Id.* at 63. This notion would profoundly affect John Locke's ideas on private property; *see generally* JOHN LOCKE, THE SECOND TREATISE ON CIVIL GOVERNMENT 22–25 (1986); *see also id.* at 19 (indigenous peoples' proprietary rights as a tenancy-in-common in the original state of nature; *see generally* Karl Olivecrona, *Appropriation in the State of Nature: Locke on the Origin of Property*, 35 J. HIST. IDEAS 211 (1974).

[11] Scottish Professor of Civil Law, William Welwood (1578–1622), objected sharply to Grotius' claim regarding the inexhaustibility of the living resources of the seas in his 1613 rejoinder to *Mare Liberum*: "If the uses of the seas may be in any respect forbidden and stayed it should be chiefly for the fishing, as by which the fishes may be said to be exhaust and wasted, which daily experience these twenty years past and more hath declared to be overttrue. For whereas aforetime the white fishes daily abounded [a reference probably to cod] even into all the shores on the eastern coast of Scotland, … the shoals of fishes are broken and so far scattered away from our shores and coasts that no fish can now be found worth of any pains and travails, to the impoverishing of all … our home fishers and to the great damage of all the nation." WILLIAM WELWOOD, OF THE COMMUNITY AND PROPRIETY OF THE SEAS (1613), *reprinted in* David Armitage, *Introduction, in* THE FREE SEA: HUGO GROTIUS 73–74 [spelling his name Welwod].

[12] Martin J. Schermaier, *Res Communis Omnium: The History of an Idea from Greek Philosophy to Grotian Jurisprudence*, 30 GROTIANA 20, 22 (2009).

[13] MARE LIBERUM, *supra* note 1, at 9.

[14] *Id.*

[15] *Id.* at 65.

it belongs to a given individual in such a way as to be *incapable* of belonging to someone else as well."[16] Thus, *dominium* could be achieved only through physical seizure (*apprehensio*) leading to private use through the construction or definition of boundaries.[17] Unlike lakes or "mere rivers," which "wash against the land on all sides,"[18] the seas retain a fluid character that wash away bids to occupy or enclose them,[19] making them "forever exempt from … ownership by the unanimous agreement of mankind,"[20] – and forever free.

THE SIGNIFICANCE

Grotius' argument was important for his time and ours. The argument that a thing cannot be appropriated and must be available for use by everybody, as long as its use does not impede someone else's future enjoyment, adumbrated development of the now well-established four high seas' freedoms;[21] it stands behind the development of a *res communis omnium* or *res communis humanitatus*, conventionally expressed by the Common Heritage of Mankind principle[22] as applied to the moon,[23] the deep

[16] *Id.* ("[f]or there are some things which are consumed by use, either in the sense that they are converted … and therefore admit of no further use, or … in the sense that they are rendered less fit …" at 55).

[17] *See id.* at 57. *See also* Armitage, *supra* note 11, at xiii (distinguishing possession (*possession*), use (*usus*) and ownership (*dominium*)).

[18] MARE LIBERUM, *supra* note 1, at 81.

[19] *Id.* (citing Cicero and Ovid for the proposition that most running water is classified "among the things that are common to all" at 61); but *see* WILLIAM WELWOOD, AN ABRIDGMENT OF ALL SEA-LAWES (1613) (arguing that although the sea is "liquid, fluid, and unstable in the particles thereof, yet in the whole body it is not so, because it keeps the prescribed bounds strictly enough concerning the chief places and limits thereof" at 67); *see also id.* (claiming, despite its constantly changing appearance, that "the sea most constantly keeps the set place prescribed by the Creator [and so lends itself to] conquest" at 72). *See also* Alison Reppy, *The Grotian Doctrine of the Freedom of the Seas Reappraised*, 19 FORDHAM L. REV. 243, 270 (1950).

[20] MARE LIBERUM, *supra* note 1, at 65.

[21] *See* Convention on the High Seas, art. 2, Apr. 29, 1958, 450 U.N.T.S.82, 82 (comprising, *inter alia*, both for coastal and non-coastal States: (1) Freedom of navigation; (2) Freedom of fishing; (3) Freedom to lay submarine cables and pipelines; and (4) Freedom to fly over the high seas.

[22] *See* KEMAL BASLAR, THE CONCEPT OF THE COMMON HERITAGE OF MANKIND IN INTERNATIONAL LAW 40–43 (1998). *See generally* Christopher Joyner, *Legal Implications of the Concept of the Common Heritage of Mankind*, 35 INT'L & COMP. L.Q. 190 (1986); Charlotte Ku, *The Concept of Res Communis in International Law*, 12 HIST. EUR. IDEAS 459 (1990); Mathias Risse, *Common Ownership of the Earth as a Non-Parochial Standpoint: A Contingent Derivation of Human Rights*, 7 EUR. J. PHIL. 277 (2008). *See also* Schermaier, *supra* note 12; and Scott J. Shackelford, *The Tragedy of the Common Heritage of Mankind*, 28 STAN. ENVTL L.J. 109 (2009).

[23] Agreement Governing the Activities of States on the Moon and Other Celestial Bodies, opened for signature Dec. 18, 1979, G.A. Res 34/68, U.N. GAOR, 34th Sess., Agenda Items 48, 49, at 1, U.N. Doc. A/Res/34/68 (1979), reprinted in 18 ILM 1434–1441 (1979).

seabed,[24] and outer space;[25] it informs debates on international resource management,[26] and arises in legal discussions on intergenerational equity,[27] cultural heritage,[28] climate change,[29] biodiversity,[30] the geo-synchronous orbit,[31] cyberspace,[32] North-South relations,[33] Antarctica,[34] sequencing the human genome,[35] and the High Arctic, where recent

[24] *Third United Nations Conference on the Law of the Sea: Final Act,* Dec. 10 1982, U.N. Doc. A/CONF. 62/121.

[25] Treaty on Principles Governing the Activities of States in the Exploration and Use of Outer Space, Including the Moon and other Celestial Bodies, Jan. 27, 1967, 18 U.S.T. 2416, 610 U.N.T.S. 205 (entered into force October 10, 1967).

[26] *See, e.g.,* Burns H. Weston & David Bollier, Green Governance: Ecological Survival, Human Rights and the Law of the Commons (2013).

[27] *See, e.g.,* Edith Brown Weiss, *Planetary Trust: Conservation and Intergenerational Equity,* 11 Ecology L.Q. 551 (1984); James C. Wood, *Intergenerational Equity and Climate Change,* 8 Geo. Int'l Envtl L. Rev. 293, 325 (1995–1996).

[28] *See, e.g.,* John E. Noyes, *The Common Heritage of Mankind: Past, Present, and Future,* 40 Denv. J. Int'l L. & Pol'y 447 (2011); and Anastasia Strati, The Protection of the Underwater Cultural Heritage: An Emerging Objective of the Contemporary Law of the Sea (1995).

[29] *See, e.g.,* Mathias Risse, *Who Should Shoulder the Burden? Global Climate Change and Common Ownership of the Earth,* HKS Working Paper No. RWP08-075 (Jan. 15, 2009); and Kristen H. Engel & Scott R. Saleska, *Subglobal Regulation of the Global Commons: The Case of Climate Change,* Ecol. L.Q. 183 (2005).

[30] *See, e.g.,* Kathryn Milun, The Political Uncommons: The Cross-Cultural Logic of the Global Commons (2011); and Jonathan Curci, The Protection of Biodiversity and Traditional Knowledge in International Law of Intellectual Property (2010).

[31] *See generally,* UN World Comm'n on Environ. & Dev., Report, "Our Common Future," A/42/427, II (2) (1982), www.un-documents.net/ocf-10.htm (referring to the geostationary orbit as the 'geosynchronous orbit). *See also* Marvin S. Soroos, *The Commons in the Sky: The Radio Spectrum and Geosynchronous Orbit as Issues in Global Policy,* 36 Int'l Org. 665 (1982); and Shane Chaddha, *A Tragedy of the Space Commons?* (2010), *available at* http://papers.ssrn.com/sol3/papers.cfm?abstract_id=1586643 (arguing that the space environment is a finite resource system that is susceptible to self-interested use and exploitation).

[32] *See, e.g.,* Maj. Gen. Mark Barrett, Dick Bedford, Elizabeth Skinner & Eva Vergles, *Assured Access to the Global Commons,* Supreme Allied Command Transformation, North Atlantic Treaty Organization (April 2011), www.act.nato.int/multimedia/video?task=alphabetic&id=43&sl=alphabetic&layout=simple&start=55&Itemid=179&option=com_videoflow&limitstart=55&view=videoflow&fontstyle=f-smaller.

[33] *See, e.g.,* Jennifer Frakes, *Common Heritage of Mankind Principle and Deep Seabed, Outer Space, and Antarctica: Will Developed and Developing Nations Reach a Compromise,* 21 Wis. Int'l L.J. 409 (2003); Bradley Larschan & Bonnie C. Brennan, *Common Heritage of Mankind Principle in International Law,* 21 Columb. J. Transnt'l L. 305 (1983).

[34] *See, e.g.,* Marvin S. Soroos, The Endangered Atmosphere: Preserving a Global Commons 2 (1997); Magnus Wijkman, *Managing the Global Commons,* 36 Int'l Org. 511 (1982); M. C. W Pinto, *The International Community and Antarctica,* 33 U. Miami L. Rev. 479 (1978–1979).

[35] *See, e.g.,* Jasper A. Bovenberg, Property Rights in Blood, Genes & Data: Naturally Yours? (2006).

claims of *dominium* are advancing as quickly as the polar ice cap is receding.[36] Importantly, Grotius' common use characterization has affected profoundly the development in international law of the global commons – those geo-spatial areas beyond the national jurisdiction of any state, where exploration and exploitation of resources are subject to principles of non-appropriation, common management, peaceful purpose, and preservation for future generations.[37] Sometimes called the "transnational commons,"[38] and with distinct connections to common pool resource theory,[39] this area of law presents regulatory challenges in a world conditioned by scarcity. A deeper consideration of Grotius and his times provides helpful context for interpreting the status and prospects of common use in geo-spatial areas where proprietary claims never before have been contemplated.[40]

[36] Terry Macalister, *Climate Change Could Lead to Arctic Conflict, Warns Senior NATO Commander*, THE GUARDIAN (Oct. 11, 2010), www.theguardian.com/environment/2010/oct/11/nato-conflict-arctic-resources; Nataliya Vasilyeva, *Russia, Canada Make Competing Claims to Artic Resources*, WINNIPEG FREE PRESS (Sept. 16, 2010), www.winnipegfreepress.com/breakingnews/russia-canada-in-rivalry-over-arctic-resources-expect-favourable-un-ruling–103033134.html; Tony Halpin, *President Medvedev Threatens Russian Arctic Annexation*, TIMES ONLINE (Sept. 18, 2008), www.timesonline.co.uk/tol/news/world/europe/article4773567.ece.

[37] *See* Frakes, *supra* note 33, at 411–414 (2003); B. Larschan & C. B. Brennan, *The Common Heritage of Mankind Principle in International Law*, 21 COLUM. J TRANSNT'L L. 305, 336 (1983); J. Van Dyke and C. Yuen, *Common Heritage v. Freedom of the Seas: Which Governs the Seabed?*, 19 SAN DIEGO L. REV. 493 (1982); F. FRANCIONI AND T. SCOVAZZI, eds., INTERNATIONAL LAW FOR ANTARCTICA (1996); C. Christol, *The Common Heritage of Mankind Provision in the 1979 Agreement Governing the Activities of States on the Moon and Other Celestial Bodies*, 14 INT'L LAWYER 429 (1980); BIN CHENG, STUDIES IN INTERNATIONAL SPACE LAW 155–157 (1997); and P. P. C. Hannapel, THE LAW AND POLICY OF AIR SPACE AND OUTER SPACE: A COMPARATIVE APPROACH (2003).

[38] *See* Scott J. Shackelford, *Was Selden Right? The Expansion of Closed Seas and its Consequences*, 47 STAN. J. INT'L L. 47 n. 7 and accompanying text (2011) (preferring usage of the term "transnational commons" instead of "global commons" because the former term is broad enough to incorporate outer space and cyberspace).

[39] *See* ELINOR OSTROM, GOVERNING THE COMMONS: THE EVOLUTION OF INSTITUTIONS FOR COLLECTIVE ACTION (1990) (discussing self-management prospects for natural or human made resources – goods – generally deemed too large to exclude beneficiaries from use). It appears Ostrom's ideas have found a place in American legal circles, but mostly in those related to general property theory, environmental and natural resource law, and intellectual property. *See* Carol M. Rose, OSTROM AND THE LAWYERS: THE IMPACT OF GOVERNING THE COMMONS ON THE AMERICAN LEGAL ACADEMY 10 (2010), Arizona Legal Studies Discussion Paper, *available at* http://papers.ssrn.com/sol3/papers.cfm?abstract_id=1701358.

[40] *See* Karl Zemanek, *Was Hugo Grotius Really in Favour of the Freedom of the Seas?*, 1 J. HIST. INT'L L. 46, 59 (1999) (noting "[v]ery few of the scholars who refer to the Grotian idea in their teaching present it in its true context)."

THE CONTEXT

Grotius' articulation of a common use doctrine was astonishing given the internecine violence that beset Europe throughout his life.[41] He died at the cusp of an age that ushered in, with the Treaty of Westphalia in 1648, a new ordering construct for international relations and the law of nations: territorial sovereignty. Writing in the shadow land[42] of this new age of state-centric *imperium* (the power to rule), one cannot help but wonder if he truly intended to introduce a major exception to territorial rule through the articulation of an ownership-free international commons.

SPANISH-LUSO COMPETITION

Grotius' common use argument was contentious, and he knew it, certainly because few people believed it at that time: Luso-Spanish competition for conquest and settlement of the Azores, Madeira, Canary, and Cape Verde Islands earlier in that century prompted Alexander VI to issue four papal bulls that ultimately produced the 1494 Treaty of Tordesillas,[43] which divided the non-Christian world on a north-south line 370 leagues west of the Cape Verde Islands;[44] newly discovered territory west of that line was to belong to the Castilian crown; territory discovered east of that demarcation became the right of Portugal. Commercial monopolies also were granted to the respective crowns in these spheres, and other nations could not trade without proper license (*cartaz*).[45] In effect, Iberian colonizers attempted to divide the western

---

[41] In 1568, hostilities broke out between the Low Countries and the reigning King of Spain, Philip II. By 1579, the Dutch Provinces had created a collective self defense pact through the Union of Utrecht. Under Prince William of Orange, a general assembly was created – the States-General – which, in 1581, declared independence as the Dutch Republic. The republic was a federation of seven provinces with Holland serving as the richest and most powerful.

[42] *See* Richard Falk, *The Grotian Quest, in* INTERNATIONAL LAW: A CONTEMPORARY PERSPECTIVE 36–37(Richard Falk et al., eds., 1985).

[43] The principal Alexandrine bulls, the so-called *bulls of donation* (granting overseas territorial control to Iberian powers), were *Inter caetera* (May 3, 1493, relating to Spanish grants; May 4, 1493, relating to Portuguese grants), and *Eximiae devotionis* (May 3, 1493) followed by *Dudum siquidem* (Sept. 26, 1493). *See* H. Vander Linden, *Alexander VI and the Demarcation of the Maritime and Colonial Domains of Spain and Portugal, 1493–1494*, 22 AM. HIST. REV. 3, 8 (1916). For accounts of competition between Spain and Portugal in the 'African Atlantic,' *see generally* Felipe Fernández-Armesto, *Spanish Atlantic Voyages and Conquests before Columbus, in* MARITIME HISTORY: THE AGE OF DISCOVERY 136 ff (John B. Hattendorf, ed.,1996) [hereinafter HATTENDORF, MARITIME HISTORY].

[44] *See* Elizabeth Mancke, *Oceanic Space and the Creation of a Global International System, 1450–1800, in* MARITIME HISTORY AS WORLD HISTORY 149–150 (Daniel Finamore, ed., 2004).

[45] Bo Johnson Theutenberg, *Mare Clausum et Mare Liberum*, 37 ARCTIC 481, 490 (1984).

hemisphere in half.[46] Northern European powers balked at this claim of sovereignty *ad absurdum*, but "it would take most of three centuries to sort out the radically new international order that oceanic expansion created."[47]

THE TREATY OF TORDESILLAS; LETTERS OF MARQUE AND REPRISAL; DIVIDED SOVEREIGNTY

The importance of the Treaty of Tordesillas related to the sheer size of the appropriation and its distance so far from shore.[48] It was the largest but not the first attempt to close the seas. Sovereigns of this period, even those who objected to the Treaty of Tordesillas, commonly claimed areas they "saw as a continuation of the already-known land masses. If the king had sovereignty over the lands enclosing the sea areas, why shouldn't he also claim the sea between?"[49] Moreover, a self-help enforcement system took hold in fifteenth-century Europe; French, German, and English sovereigns joined the Iberians in commissioning "Letters of Marque and Reprisal," which empowered privateers to cruise against an enemy's merchant fleet or neutral ships dealing in enemy trade, and seize and return cargo to the sovereign's admiralty courts. If condemned as lawful prize, the spoils would then be sold to indemnify the treasury and reward the auxiliaries for their private, yet warlike, captures at sea.[50]

This loose and abused system of enforcement and spoils-recovery vexed maritime relations for centuries.[51] Privateer to one sovereign meant buccaneer to another. But the issuance of such letters hardened into a

---

[46] A. N. Ryan notes that confusion regarding Columbus' discovery of the New World and its relationship to India prompted negotiators to decline to nominate a complementary meridian in the eastern hemisphere. A. N. Ryan, *The New World and Asia 1492–1606, in* MARITIME HISTORY AS WORLD HISTORY, *supra* note 44, at 259. The Treaty of Zaragoza (Apr. 22, 1529) established a demarcation line between Spain and Portugal in the eastern sphere.

[47] Elizabeth Mancke, *Early Modern Expansion and the Politicization of Oceanic Space*, 89 THE GEOGRAPHICAL REV. 225, 229 (1999).

[48] Mancke, *supra* note 44, at 151.

[49] Theutenberg, *supra* note 45, at 482.

[50] *See* FRANCIS H. UPTON, THE LAW OF NATIONS AFFECTING COMMERCE DURING WAR: WITH A REVIEW OF THE JURISDICTION, PRACTICE AND PROCEEDINGS OF PRIZE COURTS 100–101 (1863). *See also* Robert Fruin, *An Unpublished Work of Hugo Grotius's*, 13 BIBLIOTHECA VISSERIANA 26–27 (1925), who notes that the Dutch Admiralty regulation of Aug. 13, 1597 required privateers to remunerate 20 percent of the booty to the state, 10 percent to the admiral-general (navy), and the remainder to the ship owner, captain, and crew. In the case of the *Santa Catarina, infra*, the captain and crew received no more than 4 percent, which the captain protested.

[51] *See* JERALD A. COMBS, THE JAY TREATY: POLITICAL BATTLEGROUND OF THE FOUNDING FATHERS 140 (1970).

relatively uniform practice until privateering was abolished in the 1856 Paris Declaration.[52] This practice modified Bodin's original idea of absolute and indivisible sovereignty,[53] opened the door to the concept of divided sovereignty through use of auxiliaries, which would characterize "extra-European" practices employed by Dutch and British imperial systems in the East,[54] and informed Grotius' opinion on just war theory, as expressed on the final pages of *Mare Liberum*. There, Grotius noted: "He who prevents … or who in any way hinders another in the use of something which is his by common right" creates an injustice,[55] and, absent judicial administration ("where a judgment cannot be given"[56]), the aggrieved can make recourse to just war. Here, Grotius stands almost alone among writers of the early modern age, taking a step backward from positions crafted by important scholastic luminaries such as Aquinas (1225–1274), Vitoria (1492–1546), and the particularly influential Gentili (1552–1608).[57] He justified belligerent actions of private individuals to punish transgressors of the natural order to make right violations of the *jus mercandi* (the freedom to trade) and the *jus navigandi* (the freedom to navigate) – where no judge can be found.[58] This vigilantism, encased in a pamphlet rhetorically devoted to making the seas free, depended necessarily on private policing, which even today complicates the idea of a global commons. Index-linked to prevailing norms of dominant power, Grotius presented an enigmatic ethic of war.[59]

---

[52] Paris Declaration Respecting Maritime Law (Apr. 16, 1856). The granting of Letters of Marque and Reprisal find textual expression in the U.S. Constitution as an enumerated power of Congress. *See* U.S. Const., art. I, § 8, cl. 11.

[53] *See* JEAN BODIN, LES SIX LIVRES DE LA RÉPUBLIC, at I.VIII and I.IX (1576).

[54] EDWARD KEENE, BEYOND THE ANARCHICAL SOCIETY: GROTIUS, COLONIALISM AND ORDER IN WORLD POLITICS 3 and 93 (2002).

[55] MARE LIBERUM, *supra* note 1, at 153.

[56] *Id.*

[57] Zemanek, *supra* note 40, at 50 n 7. *See also* MARTINE JULIA VAN ITTERSUM, PROFIT AND PRINCIPLE: HUGO GROTIUS, NATURAL RIGHTS THEORIES AND THE RISE OF DUTCH POWER IN THE EAST INDIES (1595–1615), at 487 (2006). Carl Schmitt noted Grotius' views on trade were repetitive of Gentili's ideas. *See* CARL SCHMITT, THE NOMOS OF THE EARTH IN THE INTERNATIONAL LAW OF THE JUS PUBLICUM EUROPAEUM 179 (2006).

[58] *See* MARE LIBERUM, *supra* note 1, at 153–155. Peter Borschberg discusses Grotius' usages of these concepts as extensions of the broader notions of the jus communicationis (the right of free and unimpeded communication), which Grotius adapted from Francisco de Vitoria. *See* PETER BORSCHBERG, HUGO GROTIUS, THE PORTUGUESE AND FREE TRADE IN THE EAST INDIES, 83, 84, and 89 (2010) [hereinafter BORSCHBERG, HUGO GROTIUS]; *see also* Kenneth R. Simmonds, *Grotius and the Law of the Sea – a Reassessment*, *in* GROTIUS ET L'ORDRE JURIDIQUE INTERNATIONAL, 43, 45 (Alfred Dufour, Peter Haggenmacher, & and Jiří Toman, eds., 1985).

[59] *See* Karma Nabulsi, *An Ideology of War, Not Peace: Jus in Bello and the Grotian Tradition of War*, 4 J. POL. IDEOLOGIES 17–18 (1999).

THALASSOCRACY AND MARE CLAUSUM

Assertions of *dominium* over the seas predated Grotius' world by centuries. Thucydides and Herodotus, the greatest Greek historians, wrote of thalassocracy, or the hegemonic control of the sea.[60] They wrote of the Minoan sea-borne empire (c. 1600–1400 BCE) as well as the Athenian rule over the Aegean (c. 500–400 BCE).[61] The Romans, though reputed landlubbers, effectively asserted their *mare nostrum* (our sea) over the entire Mediterranean around 67 BCE to protect grain shipments.[62] Rome's thalassocracy extended into the Atlantic and as far as North Sea shores of Western Europe.[63] The Hanseatic League of merchants forced its will on trading communities of the Baltic region from Bergen, Norway to Novgorod, Russia from around 1300–1600.[64] And an assortment of Republican city-states, importantly Monaco, Genoa, Pisa, and Florence, displayed pretentions of controlling the Tyrrhenian Sea;[65] the Genoese made additional and effective claims over the Ligurian Sea; and thirteenth-century Venice would rise to become the thalassocracy of the Mediterranean world,[66] effectively controlling all passage on the Adriatic.[67] In 1563, the prominent Spanish jurist, Fernando Vázquez y Menchaca (1512–1569) attacked claims of *dominion* in the Mediterranean, and Queen Elizabeth of England (1533–1603), while overlooking her county's exclusionary practices, lectured the Spanish Ambassador that the ocean was as "common to all as the use of sea and air,"[68] but these arguments were not in the main.[69] Norwegian kings forbade foreign merchants from trading in Norwegian ports from the mid-thirteenth century (a practice the English would adopt with passage of the Navigation Acts in 1651) and prohibited foreigners from trading in areas north

[60] CLARK G. REYNOLDS, HISTORY AND THE SEA: ESSAYS ON MARITIME STRATEGIES 20 (1989).
[61] *See* John B. Hattendorf, *The Sea as an Arena for Conflict, in* Hattendorf, *supra* note 43, at 130 (noting the development of a Minoan sea network in the Aegean and Eastern Mediterranean).
[62] *See* J. H. THIEL, STUDIES ON THE HISTORY OF ROMAN SEA-POWER IN REPUBLICAN TIMES 21–22 (1946).
[63] *See* Richard W. Unger, *Power and Domination: Europe and the Sea in the Middle Ages and the Renaissance, in* MARITIME HISTORY AS WORLD HISTORY, *supra* note 44, at 140.
[64] *See generally* Mike Burkhardt, *The German Hanse and Bergen: New Perspectives on an Old Subject,* 58 SCAN. ECON. HIST. REV. 60 (2010).
[65] J. E. S. Fawcett, *How Free Are the Seas?,* 49 INT'L AFF. 14 (1973).
[66] Reynolds, *supra* note 60, at 40.
[67] *See* Theutenberg, *supra* note 45, at 488.
[68] Edward Gordon, *Grotius and the Freedom of the Seas In the Seventeenth Century,* 16 WILLAMETTE J. INT'L L. & DISP. RES. 252, 253 (2008), citing Vázquez y Menchaca's *Controversiarum illiustrium usuque frequentium libri tres* and 254, noting that Queen Elizabeth demanded that foreign vessels entering English waters strike their topsails and take in their flags in recognition of Britain's sovereign jurisdiction.
[69] In the main or not, Grotius cited Vázquez seventy-four times in *De Jure Praeda Commentarius. See* Vieira, *supra* note 4, at 361.

of Bergen,[70] effectively claiming the Northern Sea (*Mare Septentrionalis*) as a *mare clausum* (closed sea).[71] England, Scotland, Holland, Norway, and Denmark squabbled for centuries over fishing licenses in their waters;[72] if a private person could prevent others from fishing in a creek or nook of the sea through prescriptive use, argued Welwood, "by what reason should a private man ... be thus privileged and preferred to a prince[?]"[73] Indeed, England's kings, James I and Charles I (who reigned during 1603–1625 and1625–1649), became chief proponents of *mare clausum*. Like the similarly apportioned squadrons of the French fleet, led by ships titled governors of the sea (*praefectus maris*), England divided its fleet into three squadrons, each with a different charge, but all with the same aim of "keeping the narrow sea."[74] The northern seas between Norway, the Faroes, Iceland, and Greenland became the scene of prolonged disputes at the beginning of the seventeenth century.[75] The Danes would make a historic claim to the Skagerrak Strait leading to the Baltic,[76] and, indeed, over the entire North Sea to Iceland.[77] Sweden and Poland also laid claim to the Baltic,[78] and Sweden additionally regarded the Gulf of Bothnia as a *mare clausum*, given that Finland had been part of the Swedish kingdom until 1809.[79] And history records claims over the North Sea, the Black Sea, the Persian Gulf, the Red Sea,[80] and the eastern Mediterranean.[81] By Grotius' time, this list of European enclosure-claims had extended to Asian waters,[82] but most certainly "there was hardly any part of the European seas free from

[70] *See* Theutenberg, *supra* note 45, at 482.

[71] *Id.* at 483.

[72] *See* Welwood, *supra* note 11, at 71 (noting specifically the "covenant twixt Scottish men and Hollanders concerning ... fishing).

[73] *Id.* at 73 (noting that the alienation of use itself fostered a diversion of use (*diverticulum*)).

[74] *See* T. W. Fulton, The Sovereignty of the Sea: An Historical Account of the Claims of England to the Dominion of the British Seas, and of the Evolution of the Territorial Waters 30 (1911). 'Keeping the narrow sea' is a poetic refrain from the old English poem *The Libelle of Englyshe Polycye* in reference to exercising control over the strategic English Channel.

[75] *See* Fawcett, *supra* note 65, at 49. *See also* Anna Agnarsdóttir, *The Danish Empire: The Special Case of Iceland, in* Europe and its Empires 59 (Mary N. Harris et al., 2008); *see also* H. S. K. Kent, *Historical Origins of the Three-Mile Limit*, 48 Am. J. Int'l L. 537 (1954).

[76] *See* Theutenberg, *supra* note 45, at 485–487.

[77] *See* Peter Borschberg, *Hugo Grotius' Theory of Trans-Oceanic Trade Regulation: Revisiting Mare Liberum (1609)*, 29 Itinerario 31, 41 n. 71 (2005).

[78] *See* Susan J. Buck, The Global Commons: An Introduction 76 (1998).

[79] *See* Theutenberg, *supra* note 45, at 489.

[80] Mancke, *supra* note 44, at 150–151 [footnote omitted].

[81] *See* Hugh Bicheno, Crescent and Cross: The Battle of Lepanto 1571, at 210 (2003) (discussing the papal formation of the Holy League).

[82] Most importantly, the Portuguese claim to exclude the Dutch from the Malaccan Strait, sometimes called the Strait of Singapore, which separates Sumatra from Malacca.

proprietary claim."[83] The history of *mare clausum* casts a long shadow over Grotius' claim that the common use doctrine was based on the "unanimous agreement" that the seas were exempt from ownership.

Mare Liberum details some of this history in the latter part of its formidable fifth chapter. It reads like an impressive testament to Grotius' command of geography and ancient seafaring. But he missed an important point. He proffered his review to counter "absurd" Portuguese claims that they were the first navigators of the "sea leading to the Indians"; "that no one had sailed over the aforesaid tracts of the Ocean before they themselves did so;"[84] that they had come to occupy (*occupare*) the seas and establish good title through navigation, prior use, and prescriptive right. Grotius retorted that the seas had always been navigated and there had never been a first voyager;[85] he reiterated his notion of private property and his conclusion that the seas are a *res communis* ("since it is as incapable of being seized as the air"[86]), holding that navigating the seas leaves no wake, no consequence, no diversion of use: "[A] ship sailing over the sea no more leaves behind itself a right than it leaves a permanent track."[87] But Grotius' history lesson, undertaken to refute title by navigation *qua* occupation, contained a brief narrative relating to *dominium* and *imperium*. He noted Rome's thalassocracy secured its reign and riches not through a prescriptive right of navigation or by claims of discovery (first voyage), but through the simple yet effective means of stationing "companies of archers" on their ships to fend off pirates[88] and, doubtless, all other challengers.

In *Mare Liberum*, Grotius sought a rational, natural law justification for common use, deriving it from the *jus naturale*. But he scantily involved himself with the historical and customary practice that dramatically inclined toward the opposite conclusion. His insignificant treatment of customary practice in *Mare Liberum* has been linked to a complaint that he cited to history only if the material suited his thesis.[89] His most famous critic, John Selden (1584–1654), devoted several chapters of *Mare Clausum* (1635) to prove that the customs of many kingdoms and commonwealths allowed for *dominion*

---

[83] Michael Bertram Crowe, *An Eccentric Seventeenth-Century Witness to the Natural Law: John Selden (1584–1654)*, in GROTIUS, PUFENDORF AND MODERN NATURAL LAW 107, 110 (Knud Haakonssen, ed., 1998).

[84] MARE LIBERUM, *supra* note 1, at 85.

[85] *Id.* (arguing "there is no part of the sea upon which someone has not been the first to enter" at 85); he also rejected the more modest Portuguese claim that "[they] were the first to restore to use a navigable area which had lain neglected for perhaps many centuries." *Id.* at 89.

[86] *Id.* at 85.

[87] *Id.*

[88] *Id.* at 89.

[89] *See* Zemanek, *supra* note 40, at 53–54.

over the sea.[90] Regarding Grotius' assertion that nature commanded the seas
to be common, Welwood laconically responded: "And for what reason?"[91]

A BRASH RESPONSE

Perhaps to preempt criticism of his common use thesis, Grotius brashly
labeled as "completely irrational" any other modern usage of the term ownership that deviated from his own construction.[92] Spanish and Portuguese
assertions of prescriptive rights over their sea realms were "no less *wildly
erroneous* than the opinions of those who are wont to embrace a very similar
delusion in regard to the Genoese and the Venetians."[93] Elsewhere, however,
he distinguished "vast maritime tracts" such as oceans from seas such as the
Mediterranean and other mere gulfs,[94] which, he conceded, could be owned
(citing specifically Venetian and Genoese powers as examples), because
they were "the possessors of the shores boarding on the sea."[95] This curious
distinction indicates that *Mare Liberum* specifically targeted Spanish and
Portuguese maritime policies of exclusion, and did not treat as a serious
controversy Venetian and Genoese exercise of *dominium* over the Adriatic
and Ligurian Seas,[96] or many of the other seaward extensions of sovereign
control.

THE POLITICAL CONTEXT

Grotius published his *quarto* volume anonymously, opting to "skulk" behind
it in anticipation of doctrinal ripostes,[97] of which the arguments of Vázquez y
Menchaca, Welwood, Freitas (c.1570–1633), Pereira (1575–1655), and the most
noted Selden remain of great historical importance.[98] Political considerations

---

90 *See generally* JOHN SELDEN, OF THE DOMINION; OR, OWNERSHIP OF THE SEA (translated by
    Marchamont Nedham, 1972); Vieira, *supra* note 4, at 373; and Crowe, *supra* note 83, at 110–111
    (Selden wrote the response in 1617, but publication was withheld for fear of complicating
    relations with Scandinavian powers, until published by order of Charles I in 1635).

91 Welwood, *supra* note 11, at 72. For a listing of British jurists advocating a *mare clausum* before
    the time of James I, *see* Simmonds, *supra* note 58, at 45 (citing works of John Dee (1577),
    Edmund Plowden (1578), Welwood, and Thomas Craig (1603)).

92 MARE LIBERUM, *supra* note 1, at 55.

93 *Id.* at 113.

94 *Id.* at 123 (referencing, presumably, the Gulf of Genoa in the northernmost waters of the
    Ligurian Sea).

95 *Id.*

96 BORSCHBERG, HUGO GROTIUS, *supra* note 58, at 164–165.

97 ARMITAGE, *supra* note 11, at xi. *See also* Borschberg, *supra* note 77, at 32.

98 *See* Welwood, *supra* note 19; JOHN SELDEN, MARE CLAUSUM (1635); SERAFIM DE FREITAS, DE
    IUSTO IMPERIO LUSITANORUM ASIATICO (1625). Alexandrowicz noted strong points of connection

also prompted a broader need for discretion: the Dutch Republic's burgeoning economic power had seriously damaged Hanseatic and English interests, but Spain and Portugal (a united monarchy during 1580–1640) still possessed the economic and administrative power to curtail Dutch maritime expansion.[99] Spanish embargoes against Dutch trade in the massive Mediterranean market,[100] in force since 1598, had punishing effect.[101] Warring to the point of financial ruin brought the countries into delicate truce negotiations between 1606 and 1609. Grotius' political mentor, Johan van Oldenbarnevelt (1547–1619), the Land's Advocate of Holland,[102] represented the Dutch Republic at the negotiating table,[103] and he doubtless sought to avoid any untimely association of his relationship to Grotius with the official Dutch position on navigation. "As Oldenbarnevelt foresaw, Spanish dissatisfaction with *Mare Liberum* would jeopardize a positive outcome of the negotiations on a peace or truce."[104] From the Iberian perspective, Spanish king Philip III (1598–1621) and his Great Favorite the duke of Lerma (1553–1625) faced an "awesome dilemma:"[105] They could not allow the Dutch Republic's hegemonic rise in Asia to continue, but they did not have the economic or military tools to stop it.[106] The duke of Lerma entered into negotiations and offered Oldenbarnevelt independence for the Dutch Republic from the Spanish crown in exchange for an evacuation of settlements in Asia and the Americas and a cessation of all commercial activities in Asia.[107] The offer presented Oldenbarnevelt with his own dilemma: acceptance of the Iberian offer would lift an embargo against Dutch access to the neighboring and desperately desired Mediterranean market but surrender imperial pretensions to the East and West Indies. An uneasy truce – the Armistice of Antwerp, or, the so-called Twelve Years' Truce – was

---

between Freitas' critique and Selden's critique of Grotius. *See* C. H. Alexandrowicz, *Freitas versus Grotius*, 35 Brit. Y.B. Int'l L. 1959, 162 (1960). Edward Gordon notes that some Spanish scholars regard Juan de Solorzano Pereira's *De Indiarum iure* as the most systematic juridical formulation of a prescriptive right argument favoring Iberian claims; he notes Pereira's treatise receives scantily any attention in the English speaking world. *See* Gordon, *supra* note 68, at 262.

[99] *See* Jonathan I. Israel, Dutch Primacy in World Trade, 1585–1740, at 80 (1989).

[100] *See id.*

[101] *Id.* at 82.

[102] Oldenbarnevelt was also recognized as the *de facto* political leader of the United Provinces: Van Ittersum, Profit and Principle, *supra* note 57, at xxiv.

[103] *See* Geoffrey Parker, Global Crisis: War, Climate Change & Catastrophe in the Seventeenth Century 218 (2013).

[104] Henk Nellen, *The History of Grotius and His Printers, Explained on the Basis of Five Portraits*, 39 Int'l J. Legal Info. 210, 212 (2011).

[105] Israel, *supra* note 99, at 81.

[106] *Id.*

[107] *Id.*

indeed negotiated and it did forestall war between the Spanish Crown and the Low Countries until 1621, but it "brought neither absolute recognition of Dutch independence nor Dutch concessions regarding Indian commerce."[108] It did, however, buy much needed time for the Dutch to develop their Asian colonial campaign. Jonathan I. Israel called the truce "a key political watershed" with "immense implications for the whole of the world economy" due to the lifting of Spanish embargoes, which allowed Dutch access to trade in the Mediterranean.[109]

At Oldenbarnevelt's insistence, Grotius postponed publication until after the truce had been signed in April 1609,[110] but he published the work with the famous House of Elzevier and his authorship quickly became an open secret.[111]

A LUMINOUS LEGACY, A TROUBLESOME TENDENCY

History's treatment of Grotius' common use argument, couched in terms of the freedom of navigation, has been kind, until recently.[112] And with good reason. He was a prodigy, brilliantly versed in letters and languages,[113] with

---

[108] *See* Zemanek, *supra* note 40, at 51 n 9.

[109] ISRAEL, *supra* note 99, at 80–81.

[110] *See* Martine Julia Van Ittersum, *Preparing Mare Liberum for the Press: Hugo Grotius' Rewriting of Chapter 12 of De Jure Praedae Commentarius in November-December 1608*, 26 GROTIANA 246, at 248, 256 (2007). Van Ittersum notes the Twelve Years' Truce delayed war between Spain's Philip III and the Low Countries until 1621, yet failed to take hold in the East Indies, where the Dutch solidified interests versus Iberian powers using *Mare Liberum* as a perfect justification for war-by-proxy fought thousands of miles from Europe. *Id.* at 273.

[111] *See* Armitage, *supra* note 11, at xi. Though published in Latin in 1609, the Dutch translation issued in 1614 was the first to reveal the author's name. *See also* Jeroen Vervliet, *General Introduction, in* GROTIUS, MARE LIBERUM, at xv [hereinafter Vervliet].

[112] *See generally* BORSCHBERG, HUGO GROTIUS, *supra* note 58; Eric Wilson, *Erasing the Corporate Sovereign, Inter-Textuality and an Alternative Explanation for the Publication of Hugo Grotius' Mare Liberum (1609)*, 30 ITINERARIO 78 (2006); Van Ittersum, PROFIT AND PRINCIPLE, *supra* note 57; Georg Cavallar, *Vitoria, Grotius, Pufendorf, Wolff and Vattel: Accomplices of European Colonialism and Exploitation or True Cosmopolitans*, 10 J. HIST. INT'L L. 181 (2008); and KEENE, *supra* note 54.

[113] CHRISTIAN GELLINEK, HUGO GROTIUS, 147–150 (1983) (Grotius mastered Latin and Greek by age eight and published numerous highly regarded poems and plays, almost all of which remained in print throughout his life). Nellen referred to him as a master propagandist: "Whether he wrote in Latin, Dutch or French made no difference. His style was always clear, succinct and eloquent." Henk J. M. Nellen, *Hugo Grotius's Political and Scholarly Activities in the Light of His Correspondence, in* PROPERTY, PIRACY AND PUNISHMENT: HUGO GROTIUS ON WAR AND BOOTY IN DE IURE PRAEDAE – CONCEPTS AND CONTEXTS 16, at 21 (Hans W. Blom, ed., 2009). Gordon notes he wrote some sixty books in Latin, two biblical dramas, translated into Latin from Dutch a paper on navigation, and wrote works on astronomy. Gordon, *supra* note 68, at 259.

a thirst for knowledge that ran in his family;[114] he was born a patrician and matriculated at the University of Leiden at age eleven; he was awarded a doctorate in laws from the University of Orléans at fifteen;[115] and he was admitted to the bar in Holland the following year, immediately launching into a spectacular legal career.[116] At Oldenbarnevelt's suggestion, he accompanied Dutch diplomats to the French Court, where Henri IV proclaimed him the miracle of Holland,[117] and awarded him a gold medallion for his political poem, *Pontifex Romanus.*[118] At age eighteen, he was commissioned to write the history of the Dutch Revolt against Spain.[119] Already, he had edited the *Martianus Capella Encyclopedia*, which was published in 1599.[120] The dedication page features Jacques de Gheyn's engraving of him with the medallion in hand.[121] It was an artful reminder of his juvenilia,[122] which he was bent on making known to all,[123] even as a juvenile.

HIS DAZZLING EFFECT ON INTERNATIONAL LAW AND RELATIONS

Grotius' literary genius and textured legal thinking extended beyond his precocious youth and contributed in additional ways to his luminous legacy

---

[114] Martine J. Van Ittersum, *Knowledge Production in the Dutch Republic: The Household Academy of Hugo Grotius*, 72 J. Hist. Ideas 523, 523 (2011).

[115] Van Ittersum notes Grotius purchased the doctorate in law from Orléans, which was "a perfectly normal thing to do for a seventeenth-century gentleman on the *grand tour*." Van Ittersum, Profit and Principle, *supra* note 57, at xxiv–xxv.

[116] Gellinek, *supra* note 113, at 2. (Grotius was appointed attorney general and first public comptroller at the Courts of Holland, Westfriesland, and Zeeland in 1607 – the highest legal office a Dutch lawyer could hold). In 1613, he became pensionary (legal advisor) of Rotterdam, later deputed to the States of Holland; he then served as a representative of his home province in the States General. *See* Van Ittersum, *Preparing Mare liberum for the Press*, *supra* note 110, at 250.

[117] Gellinek, *supra* note 113, at 2.

[118] *Id.* at 28.

[119] *See* Van Ittersum, Profit and Principle, *supra* note 57, at xxv.

[120] Martianus Capella, Martiani Capellae de nuptii Philologiae et Mercurii (H. Grotius ed., 1599). The work goes by various names, including: *Liber de nuptiis Mercurii e Philologiae* (referring to the first two books); other books are titled: *De arte grammatical*, and *De arte dialectica*. It has been referred to as *De septem disciplinis*. Martianus may have called it *Disciplinae*; it has also been referred to as *Satyricon*. *See* I. Martianus Capella and the Seven Liberal Arts 20–21 n. 2 (William Harris Stahl et al., eds., 1971).

[121] *See* Nellen, *supra* note 104, at 211–212.

[122] *See* Eric Wilson, *The VOC, Corporate Sovereignty and the Republican Sub-Text of De iure praedae*, 26 Grotiana 310, 313 (2007) (listing *De republica emendanda* (c. 1600), *Annales et historiae de rebus Belgicis* (1601–1612), *Commentarius in theses XI* (1603–1608), Mare liberum (1609), and *De antiquitate Republicae Bataviae* (c.1610) as examples of juvenile works by Grotius, discursive of his Republicanism).

[123] Nellen, *Grotius and His Printers*, *supra* note 104, at 211. *See also* Henk J. M. Nellen, Hugo de Groot: Een leven in strijd om de vrede (official Dutch State biography) (2007).

as a polymath. In the legal field, he revolutionized juridical technique by introducing subjects in treatise form, stylistically and systematically advancing discourse away from the cloistered, lecture-orientation of his scholastic predecessors.[124] His use of authority was "dazzling" and eclectic,[125] although not always accurate or discriminating.[126] He innovated in conceptual ways: he made important contributions to subjective natural rights theory,[127] the early modern Republican Tradition,[128] and the doctrine of divided sovereignty;[129] he famously employed (but is erroneously credited with inventing[130]) the *etiamsi daremus*, the impious hypothesis[131] that allowed thinkers to theorize *as if* God did not exist. This was a useful rhetorical technique in an age of the Thirty Years' War (1618–1648), where impiety provoked maximum punishment.[132] His bold, secular orientation was stated in *Mare Liberum's* preface: "What we here

[124] CHRISTOPHER R. ROSSI, BROKEN CHAIN OF BEING: JAMES BROWN SCOTT AND THE ORIGINS OF MODERN INTERNATIONAL LAW 47–48 (1998); *see also* Laurens Winkel, *Problems of Legal Systematization from De iure praedae to De iure belli ac pacis. De iure praedae Chapter II and the Prologomena of De iure belli ac pacis*, 26 GROTIANA 61 (2007).

[125] *See* Hersch Lauterpacht, *The Grotian Tradition in International Law*, 23 BRIT. Y.B. INT'L L. 3 (1946); *see also* Patrick Riley, *The Legal Philosophy of Hugo Grotius*, in THE PHILOSOPHERS' PHILOSOPHY OF LAW FROM THE SEVENTEENTH CENTURY TO OUR DAYS 11, 11 (Enrico Pattaro, ed., 2009).

[126] *See* NICHOLAS GREENWOOD ONUF, THE REPUBLICAN LEGACY IN INTERNATIONAL THOUGHT 130 (1998) (citing Tadashi Tanaka, *State and Governing Power*, and Masaharu Yanagihara, *Dominium* and *Imperium*, in A NORMATIVE APPROACH TO WAR: PEACE, WAR, AND JUSTICE IN HUGO GROTIUS (Yasuaki Onuma ed. 1993)); Henk J. M. Nellen, *Hugo Grotius's Political and Scholarly Activities in the Light of his Correspondence*, 26 GROTIANA 16, 20 (2007) (noting Grotius collected citations that had to fit as material in his line of reasoning, without much attention to original context).

[127] *See generally* Benjamin Straumann, *Is Modern Liberty Ancient? Roman Remedies and Natural Rights in Hugo Grotius's Early Works on Natural Law*, 27 LAW AND HIST. REV. 55 (2009).

[128] *See generally* ONUF, *supra* note 126. See also RICHARD TUCK, PHILOSOPHY AND GOVERNMENT 1572–1651, at 154–169 (1993).

[129] *See generally* Keene, *supra* note 54 (referring to the concept as 'divisible sovereignty').

[130] *See generally* William P. George, *Grotius, Theology, and International Law: Overcoming Textbook Bias*, 14 J. LAW AND RELIGION 605 (1999).

[131] Michael Bertram Crowe, *The 'Impious Hypothesis': A Paradox in Hugo Grotius?*, in GROTIUS, PUFENDORF AND MODERN NATURAL LAW 3 (Knud Haakonssen ed., 1998).

[132] *See* PROLOGOMENA, HUGO GROTIUS, DE JURE BELLI AC PACIS LIBRI TRES 11, at 13 (Translated by F. Kelsey, 1925) [Prologomena] ("What we have been saying would have a degree of validity even if ... there is no God, or that the affairs of men are of no concern to Him"). *See also* JAMES ST. LEGER, THE "ETIAMSI DAREMUS" OF HUGO GROTIUS: A STUDY IN THE ORIGINS OF INTERNATIONAL LAW (1962). As Haakonssen has noted, however, the *etiamsi daremus* passage marking Grotius as a great secularizer did little more than rephrase a technique borrowed from the mid-fourteenth-century scholastic tradition and what his contemporary Spanish neo-Thomist had written. *See* Knud Haakonssen, *Hugo Grotius and the History of Political Thought*, 13 POL. THEORY 239, 248–249 (1985). On the importance of fictions, *see* Hans Vaihinger, THE PHILOSOPHY OF 'AS IF'; A SYSTEM OF THE THEORETICAL, PRACTICAL AND RELIGIOUS FICTIONS OF MANKIND (1924).

submit ... does not depend upon an interpretation of Holy Writ."[133] He was among the first to conceive of the seas in terms of geo-spatial uses; by doing so he, in all but name, introduced regime analysis to the study of world politics[134] almost four hundred years before the subject gained currency in international relations circles.

Often, international relations scholars reflexively address him as the putative father of international law,[135] a sobriquet that spawned a debate on international law's paternity.[136] Important Dutch scholars, such as Van Vollenhoven, Willem J. M. van Eysinga, and Christian Meurer, viewed him with a "beaming sense of enthusiasm."[137] Others regard him with a Kuhnian sense of significance,[138] as a transformative developer of a new paradigm of constitutive rules and doctrines – crystallizing unusually quickly into a so-called Grotian Moment.[139] In influential Anglophone circles, he became not so much the father of international law as the *paterfamilias* of a so-called Grotian Tradition in international relations,[140] which, prosaically, sought to "endow international

---

[133] MARE LIBERUM, *supra* note 1, at 19. Edward Gordon notes Grotius' most influential erudition lay in his familiarity with the history and tenets of Christianity and his ability to remove barriers of inessential dogma. Gordon, *supra* note 68, at 259–260. For Grotius' treatment of biblical authority, which cautioned against "rival traditions of biblical exegesis" to show the Bible should not be referenced in international law, *see* Mark Somos, *Secularization in De Iure Praedae: From Bible Criticism to International Law, in* Blom, *supra* note 113, at 147.

[134] Stephen D. Krasner, *Structural Causes and Regime Consequences: Regimes as Intervening Variables, in* INTERNATIONAL REGIMES 1 (Stephen D. Krasner, ed., 1983); Oran R. Young, *Regime Dynamics: The Rise and Fall of International Regimes, in id.* at 93; Stephan Haggard & Beth A Simmons, *Theories of International Regimes*, 41 INT'L ORG. 491 (1987); Friedrich Kratochwil & John Gerard Ruggie, *International Organization: A State of the Art on the Art of the State*, 40 INT'L ORG. 753 (1986).

[135] *See* ROSSI, BROKEN CHAIN OF BEING, *supra* note 124, at 2–5.

[136] *Id. See also* John D. Haskell, *Hugo Grotius in the Contemporary Memory of International Law: Secularism, Liberalism, and the Politics of Restatement and Denial*, 25 EMORY INT'L L. REV. 269, 270 (2011) (noting cyclical and fetishistic attraction to Grotius in fields of international law and politics).

[137] BORSCHBERG, HUGO GROTIUS, *supra* note 58, at 103–105.

[138] *See* THOMAS S KUHN, THE STRUCTURE OF SCIENTIFIC REVOLUTIONS (4th edn., 2012) (discussing the importance of paradigms, how they inform, mislead, and change).

[139] *See* Richard Falk, *The Grotian Moment, in* INTERNATIONAL LAW: A CONTEMPORARY PERSPECTIVE 7 (Richard Falk, Friedrich V. Kratochwil & Saul H. Mendlovitz, eds., 1985); Boutrous Boutros-Ghali, *The Role of International Law in the Twenty-First Century: A Grotian Moment*, 18 FORDHAM INT'L L. J. 1609, 1613 (1995); Michael P. Scharf, *Seizing the "Grotian Moment": Accelerated Formation of Customary International Law in Times of Fundamental Change*, 43 CORNELL INT'L L. J. 439, 441 (2010); Milena Sterio, *A Grotian Moment: Changes in the Legal Theory of Statehood*, 39 DEV. J. INT'L L. & POL'Y 209, 211–215 (2011).

[140] *See generally* Lauterpacht, *supra* note 125. *See also* Benedict Kingsbury, *A Grotian Tradition of Theory and Practice?: Grotius, Law, and Moral Skepticism in The Thought of Hedley Bull*, 17 Q.L.R. 3 (1997); MARTIN WIGHT, GABRIELE WIGHT, & BRIAN PORTER, eds., INTERNATIONAL

law with unprecedented dignity and authority;"[141] or, more concretely, strove
to find a place for law in a dangerous time.[142]

Hersch Lauterpacht coined the term Grotian Tradition in an eponymous
essay marking the tercentenary of Grotius' death, but he quixotically paused
to wonder if Grotius was really a Grotian.[143] The phrase seems glib in an article Lauterpacht considered his most important contribution to the field.[144]
Readers are left to discern which of the eleven features of his own tradition
Grotius failed to embrace.[145] Lauterpacht's equivocation is awkward but in one
sense justified; he unwittingly alit on a problem he did not explore fully: the
Grotian tradition, at least in relation to the global commons thesis, harbored
a hidden pelagic agenda.

HIS HIDDEN AGENDA

This agenda casts doubt on Grotius' suggestively munificent notion of common use, undercuts the importance of *Mare Liberum's* writings on freedom of
navigation, reveals Grotius to be as much a propagandist for Dutch colonial

THEORY: THE THREE TRADITIONS (1991); A. Claire Cutler, *The 'Grotian Tradition' in
International Relations*, 17 REV. OF INT'L STUD. 41 (1991); and John T. Parry, *What is the
Grotian Tradition in International Law?* 35 U. PENN. J. INT'L L. 299 (2013).

[141] Lauterpacht, *supra* note 125, at 51. *See also* Hedley Bull, *The Grotian Conception of
International Society*, in DIPLOMATIC INVESTIGATIONS: ESSAYS IN THE THEORY OF WORLD
POLITICS 51 (Herbert Butterfield & Martin Wight, eds., 1966); Martin Wight, *Western Values
in International Relations*, in *id.*, 89; and GEORG SCHWARZENBERGER, POWER POLITICS: AN
INTRODUCTION TO THE STUDY OF INTERNATIONAL RELATIONS AND POST-WAR PLANNING (1941).
Renée Jeffery notes the influence of Lauterpacht's "Grotian Tradition," which emphasized
principles of "generosity, gratitude, pity [and] charity." *See* Renée Jeffery, *Hersch Lauterpacht,
the Realist Challenge and the 'Grotian Tradition' in 20th Century International Relations*, 12
EUR. J. INT'L REL. 223, 238 (2006).

[142] *See* MARTTI KOSKENNIEMI, THE GENTLE CIVILIZER OF NATIONS: THE RISE AND FALL OF
INTERNATIONAL LAW 1870–1960, at 355 (2001). *See also* Martti Koskenniemi, *Lauterpacht: The
Victorian Tradition in International Law*, 8 EUR. J. INT'L L. 215 (1997).

[143] *Lauterpacht, supra* note 125, at 5.

[144] *See* Editor's note, *The Grotian Tradition in International Law*, in INTERNATIONAL LAW,
BEING THE COLLECTED PAPERS OF HERSCH LAUTERPACHT, VOL 2, at 307 (Elihu Lauterpacht
ed., 1975).

[145] According to Lauterpacht, "[t]he fact seems to be that on most subjects which he discusses in
his treatise [i.e., MARE LIBERUM] it is impossible to say what is Grotius's view of the legal position." Lauterpacht, *supra* note 125, at 5. Lauterpacht's eleven main features of the Grotian tradition include: (1) The Subjection of the Totality of International Relations to the Rule of Law;
(2) The Acceptance of the Law of Nature as an Independent Source of International Law;
(3) The Affirmation of the Social Nature of Man as the Basis of the Law of Nature; (4) The
Recognition of the Essential Identity of Sates and Individuals; (5) The Rejection of 'Reason
of State'; (6) The Distinction between Just and Unjust Wars; (7) The Doctrine of Qualified
Neutrality; (8) The Binding Force of Promises; (9) The Fundamental Rights and Freedoms of
the Individual; (10) The Idea of Peace; and (11) The tradition of idealism and progress. *Id.*

administration in the Malay Archipelago specifically and Asia generally as a humanist-advocate for peace, freedom, and the rule of law, and – ultimately – colors negatively ongoing prospects for state cooperation in the global commons.

His treatment of the seas calls into question the value of common use and reveals a state-centric *tendency* – as opposed to a tradition[146] – that reframes our understanding of the tragedy of the commons. Unlike the formulation of its ecological expositor, biologist Garrett Hardin,[147] who postulated a "remorseless" overworking of a common space by rational actors focused on individual gain,[148] the Grotian tendency views the tragedy in terms of having one state's individual interests cut off by another more capable state's ability to appropriate effectively that resource; the Grotian tendency has little to do with overuse, common use, or the concern that "freedom in a commons brings ruin to all;"[149] it has more to do with laying parochial claim to resources previously considered unattainable. Maritime history, viewed as world history, details the prevalence of this tendency to assert sovereign claims over resources once the means to the extract them become available and interests become dominant. And with all due respect to Professor Hardin, maritime nations, before and after Grotius, never "responded automatically to the shibboleth of the 'freedom of the seas'."[150]

WHAT *MARE LIBERUM* IS ABOUT

Perhaps, Grotius too did not respond in any way. He may have intentionally mistitled his great work, or at least he buried its true orientation in the subtitle,[151] given his admitted desire to skulk behind the implications of its message. *Mare Liberum* – as its subtitle suggests – reads at times more like a political tract advancing monopoly claims involving unimpeded Dutch access to Asian trade than a legal treatise about the freedom of the seas. It bears little, if any,

---

[146] The term *tradition* is sometimes unselfconsciously employed, but generally it has been described as "the handing on of formed ways of acting, a formed way of living;" by "communicative and self-conscious creatures;" as "a cluster of institutionalized continuities." *See* Onuf, *supra* note 126, at 8.

[147] Garrett Hardin, *The Tragedy of the Commons*, 162 SCIENCE 1243 (1968).

[148] *Id.* at 1244.

[149] *Id.*

[150] Hardin's actual quote was: "… the oceans of the world continue to suffer from the survival of the philosophy of the commons. Maritime nations still respond automatically to the shibboleth of the 'freedom of the seas.'" *Id.* at 1245)

[151] The full title is: *Mare Liberum sive De iure quod Batavis competit ad Indicana commercio [-] Dissertatio* (The Free Sea or a Dissertation on The Right Which the Dutch Have to Carry on Indian Trade).

modern resemblance to the idea of free trade; rather, Grotius revealed himself as a major theorist of mercantilism.[152] He was, of course, writing well before economist David Ricardo (1772–1823) advanced economics' "beautiful proof" of comparative advantage in 1817,[153] which today provides much of the theoretical basis for trade. He also was writing during a time in which maritime powers could paradoxically equate free trade and open seas with an *exclusive* right of unimpeded access. Thus, free trade as a proto-economic idea was distinct from a right to trade, and Grotius' arguments advancing that right deserve an evaluation on their merits, apart from the complicating political practices of the time. But such an evaluation is complicated given Grotius' commingled ideological and political interests.

Exclusivity was precisely the complaint Grotius had launched against the Portuguese noblemen (*Fidalgos*) and their attempt to establish their colonial empire (the *Estado da Índia*). No prescriptive right or passage of time "avails to make a private property of the right to trade," wrote Grotius, because it is a "right which is incapable of assuming the character of private property."[154] Curiously, he amended that thought by adding that the lawful establishment of any such claim would require "coercion," "the absence of resistance," and no exceptions in terms of application[155] – criteria pursued with alacrity by the interests Grotius was hired to support. The result created something of a strange parallel, to borrow Victor Lieberman's phrase:[156] "Dutch practice towards Asian seaborne trade and towards European competitors proved not a whit more liberal than Portuguese custom, which in many respects was even copied by the [Dutch]."[157] Peter Borschberg noted the Dutch, through its corporate agent, the United Dutch East India Company (VOC: Verenigde Oostindische Compagnie),[158] "excluded all real and potential competitors, and bound princes in Asia to abide by their contracts with the Dutch – no matter how dubious the conditions might have been under which these contracts were conceded."[159] The VOC's military assault on the Asian trade diaspora included demands for privileges from the Mughal Empire, attempts to

---

[152] *See* Van Ittersum, Profit and Principle, *supra* note 57, at 487.

[153] Paul A Samuelson, Economics 670 (9th edn., 1973).

[154] Mare Liberum, *supra* note 1, at 137.

[155] *Id.* at 139.

[156] From his heralded two-volume book, *Strange Parallels: Southeast Asia in Global Context, c. 800–1830*, vol 1 & 2 (2003 & 2009).

[157] C. G. Roelofsen, *Grotius and International Law, in* Grotius Reader: a reader for students of international law and legal history 3, 12 (L. E. van Holk & C. G. Roelofsen, eds., 1983).

[158] *Id.*

[159] Borschberg, Hugo Grotius, *supra* note 58, at 101 (referencing specifically the Dutch East India Company, *infra*) [footnote omitted].

exclude Gujarati traders from Southeast Asian ports, establishing genuine monopoly control over nutmeg and clove production of the Maluku, Banda, and Ambon islands, and restricting both intra-Asian and Asia-European trade through licenses (*cartazes*) in imitation of Portuguese practice.[160] Although *Mare Liberum's* full title linked freedom of the seas to a right to trade, much of Grotius' emphasis was on freedom of navigation, which actually "forms a sub-set to the overarching arguments on the freedom of access."[161] This insight from Borschberg, "stands in sharp contrast to past interpretations, insofar as these have placed the 'freedom of the seas' – and not the broader issues surrounding 'free trade' – at the forefront of scholarly attention."[162] In this light, *Mare Liberum* was an illiberal tract reinterpreted by the bedazzled keepers of his name, moment, and tradition, as a grand liberal tract in support of modernity's twin pursuits of openness and common use of the seas. These pursuits support liberalism's ideas of navigation and commerce. But the Grotian tendency, apart from the man himself, saw them as avenues for allowing an emerging pelagic power to gain unimpeded access to newly accessible resources and to maintain a hegemonic command of the commons.

THE CONTEXT REVISITED: ANOTHER VIEW
OF SEVENTEENTH-CENTURY HOLLAND

There is another view of the seas from Grotius' time. It helps to explain a skeptical view of Grotius' common use argument. By the earliest years of the seventeenth century, the view from Holland's shore was decidedly global; and Dutch economic interests were forging into new territory and drafting on the achievements of others: Renaissance discoverers a century before had carried Europeans across great distances and had turned oceans into highways.[163] In little more than a generation, Renaissance exploration outlined a world map not drastically different than our own atlases,[164] and provided "the sensationally rapid opening of the aperture through which Europeans looked at their world."[165] Norse, Celtic, Polynesian, Arab, Indian, and Chinese mariners

---

[160] Philip D. Curtin, Cross-Cultural Trade in World History 153–154 (1984).

[161] Borschberg, Hugo Grotius, *supra* note 58, at 102.

[162] *Id.*

[163] Olaf U. Janzen, *A World-Embracing Sea: The Oceans as Highways, 1604–1815, in* Maritime History as World History *supra* note 44, at 102.

[164] J. R. Hale, Renaissance Exploration 7 (1968) (noting, with the exception of Australia and the Antarctic and the northern coasts of America and Asia, the "outlines of the world map were not drastically dissimilar to those in our own atlases").

[165] *Id.* Felipe Fernandez-Armesto referred to it as the "breakthrough" generation of the 1490s. Felipe Fernandez-Armesto, *The Indian Ocean in World History, in* Vasco da Gama and the

most certainly accomplished astonishing and earlier open sea voyages of their own;[166] but indisputably the Renaissance explorers set the stage for worldwide exchanges of biota and culture[167] and created global connections that mark our modern and worldwide economic system.

We may leave to Renaissance historians and geographers the detailed task of determining how and why Europeans were able to "swagger across the globe,"[168] unraveling so quickly the seemingly insurmountable secrets of open-sea navigation to create a new spatial order based on a *jus publicum europaeum*.[169] A cursory review is helpful for understanding the Grotian tendency of capable states to appropriate resources for themselves, and points toward certain causes or historical tenets: a Christian worldview that conscripted Nature as a thing to be enjoyed, not endured (will);[170] shipwright advancements in outrigging and large-ship design to better withstand punishing gales of high-seas transit (technology);[171] the development of insurance

LINKING OF EUROPE AND ASIA 11, 14 (Anthony Disney & Emily Booth, eds., 2000). J. R. Hale called it "possibly the climactic generation in world history." Hale, *supra* note 164, at 7. Diaz rounded the Cape of Good Hope (1488); Columbus discovered the West Indies (1492); da Gama charted a sea route to Calicut, India (1498); Cabral opened up Brazil for exploration (1500); Balboa sighted the Pacific Ocean (1513), confirming the continental discovery of the Americas; and Magellan's crew (minus Magellan, who had been killed in The Philippines) circumnavigated the globe (1519–1522). *See generally* A GENERAL COLLECTION OF VOYAGES AND DISCOVERIES MADE BY THE PORTUGUESE AND THE SPANIARDS, DURING THE FIFTEENTH AND SIXTEENTH CENTURIES, CONTAINING THE INTERESTING AND ENTERTAINING VOYAGES OF THE CELEBRATED, GONZALEZ AND VAZ [AND OTHERS] (1789).

166 John L. Allen, *From Cabot to Cartier: The Early Exploration of Eastern North America, 1497–1543*, 82 ANNALS OF THE ASSOC. AM. GEOGRAPHERS 500 (1992); *see also* K. M. PANIKKAR, ASIA AND WESTERN DOMINANCE: A SURVEY OF THE VASCO DA GAMA EPOCH OF ASIAN HISTORY 1498–1945, at 29–31 (1953) (recounting specifically accomplishments of Arab, Chinese and Hindu mariners); C. E. M. Pearce & F. M. Pearce, *Transoceanic Trade and Migration: Following Currents from the West Pacific Warm Pool into the Indian Ocean: The Cinnamon Route and the Colonization of Madagascar*, OCEANIC MIGRATION 67 (2010); and Lionel Casson, *Seaborne Exploration in the Ancient World*, in *Maritime History as World History*, *supra* note 44, at 35–46.

167 Fernandez-Armesto, *Maritime History and World History*, in MARITIME HISTORY AS WORLD HISTORY, *supra* note 44, at 30.

168 Hale, *supra* note 164, at 22. *See also* Philip T. Hoffman, WHY DID EUROPE CONQUER THE WORLD? (2015).

169 Schmitt, *supra* note 57, at 140.

170 *See* Hale, *supra* note 164, at 26; *see also* Philipp Pattber, *Conquest, Domination and Control: Europe's Mastery of Nature in Historic Perspective*, 14 J. POL. ECOL. 1 (2007). William Welwood, in his 1613 critique of Grotius' MARE LIBERUM, citing *Genesis* I:28 ("Subdue the earth, and rule over the fish"), noted God's command "could not be but by a subduing of the waters also." *See, Of the Community and Propriety of the Seas, in* THE FREE SEAS: HUGO GROTIUS, *supra* note 11, at 66.

171 *See* Ian Friel, *Guns, Gales and God: Elizabeth I's 'Merchant Navy'*, 60 HIST. TODAY 45 (2010); *see also* Unger, *supra* note 63, at 143–144, on the evolution of the Celtic cog vessel

and finance capital to offset risks of piracy and shipwreck (means);[172] the "twin impulses of cupidity and curiosity,"[173] sparked by insatiable appetite for exotic imports (demand); and Europe's "peculiar" geographic station, which conferred wind advantages on Atlantic mariners unattainable elsewhere (discovery/fortuna).[174] Atlantic trade winds drew ships south to the latitudes of the roaring forties, which "girdle" the earth and lead to the West Australia current, making back-and-forth circumnavigation of the world possible.[175] It took centuries of sailing before Vasco da Gama "cracked this Atlantic wind code,"[176] the discovery of which revolutionized world history by providing Europeans with the transmission belt to pursue global ambition[177] – and global war.[178]

and full-rigged square and triangular sail design. Technological improvements in navigation began to replace dead reckoning more routinely by the end of the fifteenth century, including widespread use of the compass and the magnetized needle, the gimbal (a suspension device to stabilize the compass in rough sea), and advancements in chart use and cartography. *See generally* Richard W. Unger, *Theoretical and Practical Origins of Methods of Navigation, in* HATTENDORF, MARITIME HISTORY, *supra* note 43, at 21–33; *see also* John H Pryor, GEOGRAPHY, TECHNOLOGY, AND WAR: STUDIES IN THE MARITIME HISTORY OF THE MEDITERRANEAN, 649–1571, at 53 (1988).

[172] FERNAND BRAUDEL, CIVILIZATION & CAPITALISM 15TH-18TH CENTURY (THE WHEELS OF COMMERCE), vol 2, 365–369 (Siân Reynolds, translator, 1983) [hereinafter 2 Braudel].

[173] Allen, *supra* note 166, at 500; *see also* PHILLIP LAWSON, THE EAST INDIA COMPANY: A HISTORY 2 and 3 (1993).

[174] *See generally* Fernandez-Armesto, *supra* note 167. *See also* C. R. BOXER, THE PORTUGUESE SEABORNE EMPIRE: 1415–1825, 2 (1969): "the peoples of the Iberian peninsula – and particularly the Portuguese – were peculiarly fitted to inaugurate the series of maritime and geographical discoveries which changed the course of world history."

[175] Fernandez-Armesto, *supra* note 167, at 30. Hendrik Brouwer, a master of the Dutch United East India Company, later a governor-general, discovered a westerly route that would carry ships even more swiftly across the Indian Ocean to the Indonesian Archipelago; this route avoided the east coast of Africa and Madagascar, which da Gama and former trading companies had hugged. Faster, cooler, and less addled by pirates, the "Brouwer route" became the mandatory route of the Dutch East India Company in 1616. *See* ELS M. JACOBS, IN PURSUIT OF PEPPER AND TEA: THE STORY OF THE DUTCH EAST INDIA COMPANY 58(1991).

[176] De Gama had the crucial help of a Gujarati Muslim pilot, whose services he enlisted on the way to India from Malindi on the southeastern coast of Africa. *See* Charles Verlinden, *The Big Leap under Dom João II: From the Atlantic to the Indian Ocean, in* HATTENDORF, MARITIME HISTORY, *supra* note 43, at 79–80.

[177] Fernandez-Armesto, *supra* note 167, at 30.

[178] Boxer, *supra* note 174 argues that the Dutch-Iberian struggle from 1600 to 1663 was "waged in four continents and on seven seas" and was "indubitably world-wide … this seventeenth-century contest deserves to be called the First World War rather than the holocaust of 1914–18 which is commonly awarded that doubtful honour." *See also* Mancke, *supra* note 44, at 149, who notes the "new" development of European politicization and militarization of the world's oceans between 1450 and 1800.

THE ROARING FORTIES

It was the discovery of the roaring forties – this resource of untapped trade wind – that allowed European merchants direct access to eastern emporia, circumventing centuries of chokepoints along the silk routes from Asia.[179] Control of these routes built empires, none greater from their western trunk points than the Venetian Republic, which, after protracted conflict, defeated its Genoese competitor,[180] monopolized control over trade terminuses across the Levant and Black Sea, and brokered European access to silk routes until ceding control to the Ottomans, first at Constantinople in 1453,[181] and twenty-two years later at Caffa in the Black Sea.[182] The Ottomans, in turn, exacted their own tolls and choke holds,[183] but allowed the uneasy relationship with western merchants to continue because they "could not afford not to."[184]

In search of means to outflank Islamic control of ports on the Mediterranean, as well as on the Red Sea, the Persian Gulf, and the Black Sea,[185] Spanish, Portuguese, English, and later Dutch mariners set sail northwest, northeast and south in search of any other strategic passage to access directly Asian sources of trade.[186]

Between the late fifteenth and early sixteenth centuries, a European world-economy developed along these maritime highways,[187] and if this economy

[179] *See* Richard W. Unger, *Politics, Religion and the Economy of Renaissance Europe, in* Hattendorf, Maritime History, *supra* note 43, at 5, discussing the perils of overland trade from Asia following the breakdown of Mongolian authority over Central Asian routes to the Black Sea.

[180] David S. Kelly, *Genoa and Venice: An Early Commercial Rivalry, in* Great Power Rivalries 125 (William R. Thompson, ed., 1999) 125 (discussing the periods of Venetian-Genoese warfare beginning in 1205 and ending in 1381 with the Venetian victory at Chioggia); *see also* Fernand Braudel, Civilization & Capitalism 15th-18th Century (The Perspective of the World), vol 3, 125–126 (Siân Reynolds, translator, 1984) [3 Braudel].

[181] *See generally* Steven Runciman, The Fall of Constantinople 1453 (1990).

[182] 3 Braudel, *supra* note 180, at 137.

[183] John E. Dotson, *Foundations of Venetian Naval Strategy from Pietro II Orseolo to the Battle of Zonchio 1000–1500*, 32 Viator 113, 123 (2001).

[184] 3 Braudel, *supra* note 180, at 137 (noting also the relationship between the Turkish empire and the West "was a classic example of 'complementary enemies': everything separated them, but vital interests forced them to coexist").

[185] *See* Mancke, *supra* note 47, at 228.

[186] *Id. See also* Panikkar, *supra* note 166, at 13, arguing that a major strand of the Vasco da Gama "epoch" following his arrival at the port of Calicut, India, in 1498 was the European desire to "crusade against Islam and a strategic outflanking of Muslim power" that was motivated originally by desire for the monopoly of the spice trade. *See also* Lawson, *supra* note 173, at 7–8, discussing the English merchant community's predicament vis-à-vis Portuguese and Spanish closures of trade routes.

[187] Immanuel Wallerstein, The Modern World-System: Capitalist Agriculture and the Origins of the European World-Economy in the Sixteenth Century, with a New Prologue, vol. 1, 13 (2011).

had not yet congealed around the determinants of capitalism,[188] the profit motive everywhere was understood.[189] Fourteenth-century Venetian merchants already had created the blueprint for a trading-post empire (*fondachi*) in the Adriatic, which made Venice "a sort of universal warehouse of the world;"[190] mid-fifteenth-century European quaysides offered a potpourri of goods imported from Benin to Borneo;[191] and by the early years of the seventeenth century, at the cusp of the age introducing the state system, another age was in the making: the rapidly advancing archipelagic age of Dutch colonial rule. By mid-century, roughly, Dutch corporate interests controlled twenty-three trading posts to Asia, ranging from the Cape of Good Hope to Japan.[192]

DUTCH COMMERCIAL INTERESTS AND TECHNOLOGICAL ADVANTAGE

Grotius' early seventeenth-century view of the sea reflected clearly the rapidly expanding commercial interests of the Dutch. By this time, the Dutch had established a worldwide trading presence, "one of the wonders of commercial history,"[193] which would make them the greatest commercial power in seventeenth-century Europe.[194] Holland's comparative advantage took hold on many fronts, including, importantly, shipbuilding, with the introduction of the flat-bottomed *fluitschip* in the waning years of the sixteenth century. These vessels spectacularly reduced shipping costs and crew size and produced

---

[188] Mercantilism reigned supreme as the predominant economic practice at this time. Market impediments in the pepper trade led the Dutch to conclude in 1599 that free competition increased prices to the point of rendering trade unremunerative. By 1602, the Dutch government oversaw the consolidation of various trading companies, leading to the creation of the Dutch United East India Company. *See* ALAN K. SMITH, CREATING A WORLD ECONOMY: MERCHANT CAPITAL, COLONIALISM, AND WORLD TRADE, 1400–1825, at 105 (1991). Elizabethan England depended heavily on imports of pepper from the Dutch but had little to trade in exchange for the commodity, causing exports of "specie" in violation of controlling mercantile economic thought. When Holland increased the price of pepper in 1599 from 3s to 8s per pound in England, British merchants, under Queen Elizabeth's Charter of the English East India Company, decided to outflank the Dutch monopoly and enter the Eastern trade themselves. *See* Panikkar, *supra* note 166, at 49–50. This decision cast two emerging seaborne empires on a collision course, which would prompt two Anglo-Dutch colonial conferences in 1613 and 1615, and which would account for the viciousness of three Anglo-Dutch wars over the course of one generation (1650–1680). *See* Reynolds, *supra* note 60, at 44.

[189] Hale, *supra* note 164, at 11.

[190] 3 Braudel, *supra* note 180, at 125.

[191] Hale, *supra* note 164, at 11.

[192] VICTOR LIEBERMAN, STRANGE PARALLELS, VOL. 2: MAINLAND MIRRORS: EUROPE, JAPAN, CHINA, SOUTH ASIA, AND THE ISLANDS (2009) 863 [hereinafter Lieberman, STRANGE PARALLELS].

[193] D. W. DAVIES, A PRIMER OF DUTCH SEVENTEENTH CENTURY OVERSEAS TRADE 2 (1961).

[194] *Id.* at 1.

efficiencies not profitably exceeded until the introduction of iron hulls in the nineteenth century.[195] Until well into the seventeenth century, most ships that engaged in oceanic shipping were Dutch.[196] By one calculation, the Dutch owned more tonnage than the rest of Atlantic Europe combined, and the size of the Dutch merchant fleet probably exceeded the combined fleets of England, France, Spain, Portugal, and Germany.[197] It would grow to equal "roughly half of the world's total stock of seagoing ships,"[198] making it, according to Fernand Braudel, the real instrument of Dutch greatness.[199]

A catalog of places where this fleet carried Dutchmen highlights "the strength, complexity, and wealth of their commercial structure,"[200] as well as the burgeoning need for a legal protection of claim. They hunted whales off Spitsbergen, traded Norwegian timber for falcons and fish in Iceland and the Shetlands, fished herring off England to peddle to the Catholic South of Europe, stowed grain from Baltic trade and exchanged it for Italian marble, traded slaves in Curaçao, smuggled Brazilian sugar to Amsterdam (which had twenty-five sugar refineries), trafficked Venezuelan salt, harvested West Indies tobacco, dealt coffee from Surat, Mocha, and Ceylon, paid tribute to Arabian and Persian brokers to access the silk trade, established entrepôts in India, Ceylon, and Burma to secure cloths, cotton, lacquers, elephants' tusks, and precious stones in intra-Asian exchange for Japanese gold, silver, and vast supplies of copper.[201] And, they would monopolize the lucrative trade in Asian spice – pepper, cinnamon, clove, mace, nutmeg, ginger, and turmeric. "There was scarcely a region where they did not trade,"[202] and like Venice before, Amsterdam became Europe's new commodity clearinghouse, only much larger and more complex.[203] And of all the world's riches, none would become more consistently important to the Dutch than spice.[204]

---

[195] Jan de Vries, The Economy of Europe in an Age of Crisis, 1600–1750, at 117 (1976). *See also* 3 Braudel, *supra* note 180, at 190–193.

[196] Janzen, *supra* note 163, at 103.

[197] de Vries, *supra* note 195, at 118.

[198] Israel, Dutch Primacy, *supra* note 99, at 12.

[199] 3 Braudel, *supra* note 180, at 190.

[200] Davies, A Primer of Dutch Seventeenth Century Overseas Trade, *supra* note 193, at 1.

[201] *Id.* at 1–2. *See also* Kristof Glamann, Dutch-Asiatic Trade 1620–1740 (1958). For a discussion of the Dutch creation of a profitable intra-Asian trade network, *see* Femme S. Gaastra, *War, Competition and Collaboration: Relations between the English and Dutch East India Company in the Seventeenth and Eighteenth Centuries, in* The Worlds of the East India Company 51 (H. V. Bowen, Margarette Lincoln & Nigel Rigby, eds., 2002); and Lieberman, Strange Parallels, *supra* note 192, at 841ff.

[202] Davies, A Primer of Dutch Seventeenth Century Overseas Trade 1, *supra* note193, at 2.

[203] 3 Braudel, *supra* note 180 at 35, 125.

[204] Israel, Dutch Primacy, *supra* note 99, at 67.

GROTIUS' CORPORATE AGENDA

This was the commercial world that Grotius saw in the seventeenth century. And this was also the corporate world he was hired to protect. In 1603, the Dutch United East India Company (VOC),[205] the first-ever trading company formed with permanent share capital – fast to become the most powerful and richest company in the world (indeed, the first great global corporation)[206] – hired the twenty-one-year-old to legitimize and defend its expanding interests in Asia.[207] By this time, Grotius was "renown[ed] throughout Europe for his prodigious erudition,"[208] and his recruitment was akin to a "celebrity endorsement" – "as valuable to the [VOC] in this respect as by the persuasiveness of whatever legal arguments he could muster in support of its actions."[209]

The VOC had a curious, hybrid identity. It was created by the States-General of the United Provinces to consolidate six smaller Dutch commercial enterprises in Asia after Oldenbarnevelt became convinced those chaotic rivalries bid up the purchase price of spice in Asia and bid down the sale price in Dutch ports.[210] It was chartered as a private commercial corporation and granted an initial twenty-one-year monopoly to trade east of the Cape of Good Hope or through the Straits of Magellan. Its funding came from investors, not taxpayers, but its directors swore an oath of allegiance to the States-General, though they often were beholden to neither. It had the capacity to enter into contracts and treaties alike; it could declare war or sue for peace; it was a trading company with a large fleet of merchant ships, but it also maintained giant warships, a huge private army, and fortifications spanning the Indian Ocean to the Malay Archipelago and Japan. There had never been anything like it, ever. It operated as a state within a state, formed within the unique politico-commercial and federated structure of the United Provinces.[211] And in obvious ways, it appears more like a twenty-first-century creation than a totem of the seventeenth-century reformation.[212]

---

[205] The Dutch East India Company was founded in 1602 following the consolidation of six smaller Dutch trading companies that had been trading in Asia since 1594. *See* Gaastra, *supra* note 201, at 50.

[206] STEPHEN R. BROWN, MERCHANT KINGS: WHEN COMPANIES RULED THE WORLD, 1600–1900, at 16 (2009).

[207] There is some dispute as to who exactly commissioned the work from Grotius, but Borschberg notes: "It is now an academic commonplace to treat … *De iure praedae* … as a commissioned response to the seizure of the Portuguese-flagged carrack." *See* Peter Borschberg, *Grotius, Maritime Intra-Asian Trade and Portuguese Estado da Índia: Problems, Perspectives and Insights from De iure praedae, in* Blom, *supra* note 113, at 32.

[208] Gordon, *supra* note 68, at 255.

[209] *Id.*

[210] ISRAEL, DUTCH PRIMACY, *supra* note 99, at 68–69.

[211] *Id.* at 71.

[212] *See* Pratap Chatterjee, HALLIBURTON'S ARMY: HOW A WELL-CONNECTED TEXAS OIL COMPANY REVOLUTIONIZED THE WAY AMERICA MAKES WAR (2009); P. W. Singer, *Outsourcing War*, 82

AN AGENCY OF EMPIRE

Historian Philip D. Curtin called the VOC "a syndicate for piracy,"[213] but it could as easily double as an agency of empire in an increasingly belligerent relationship between the Dutch and Portuguese for control of the East Indies seas.[214] In the three short years since its incorporation, the VOC managed to transform "into a full-scale strategic offensive." In 1605 alone, it conquered Amboina, Tidor, and Ternate (the legendary Spice Islands) from the Portuguese, and solidified its colonial presence with fortifications and fixed garrisons.[215] The VOC and its private army would oust the Portuguese from Jakarta (1619), and from their bastion at Malacca (1641); it would advance toward India and control the coastal tracts of Ceylon (1654) and Cochin on the Indian peninsula (1660); it would oust the Portuguese from the Indian Ocean and the Pacific and it would put an end to the *Estado da Índia*, save for establishments in Goa, Macao, and Timor.[216] And all along the way, it would subdue and enter into trade agreements with the great sultanates of Indonesia and Malaya.[217]

THE TAKING OF THE *SANTA CATARINA*

Most immediately, the VOC sought Grotius' aid to defend its capture of the Portuguese carrack, *Santa Catarina*, off the coast of Singapore in 1603.[218] The proceeds, distributed following a ruling by a Dutch admiralty court,[219] instantaneously replenished a substantial portion of the paid-in capital for the company's central governing board of directors – the Gentlemen XVII – and their one thousand eight hundred shareholders.[220]

FOREIGN AFF. at 119 (2005); Larry W. Isaac & Daniel M. Harrison, *Corporate Warriors: The State and Changing Forms of Private Armed Force in America* 24 CURRENT PERSPECTIVES IN SOCIAL THEORY 153–188 (2006). *See also* Michael N Schmitt, *Humanitarian Law and Direct Participation in Hostilities by Private Contractors or Civilian Employees*, 5 CHI. J. INT'L L. 511 (2005).

[213] Curtin, *supra* note 160, at 153.

[214] Vieira, *supra* note 4, at 361.

[215] ISRAEL, DUTCH PRIMACY, *supra* note 99, at 73.

[216] Panikkar, *supra* note 166, at 47–59.

[217] LIEBERMAN, STRANGE PARALLELS, *supra* note 192, at 845–857 (noting VOC influence on the five major coastal realms of Ache, Hohor, Banten, Makasar, and Maluku, and on the interior Javanese empire of Mataram).

[218] *See* Fruin, *supra* note 50, at 13 (contending the seizure was "the most direct cause of writing *De Jure Praedae Commentarius*).

[219] Fruin notes that the proceedings of the condemnation hearing were lost in a fire at the Ministry of the Navy, save for some minutes. *Id.* at 23–24.

[220] C. R. BOXER, FIDALGOS IN THE FAR EAST 1550–1770, at 50–51 (1968). *See also* Martine Julia Van Ittersum, *Hugo Grotius in Context: Van Heemskerck's Capture of the Santa Catarina and its Justification in De Jure Praedae Commentarius (1604–1606)*, 31 ASIAN J. SOC. SCI. 511, 511 (2003).

The cargo yielded three and a half million Dutch guilders upon sale in Amsterdam,[221] and attracted "an incredible multitude" of gawkers and bidders from across Europe.[222] Booty included Ming porcelain, unrefined gold, Chinese silks, a royal chair set with gems, lacquer, curiosities, and gifts deemed worthy of offer to the kings of England and France.[223] But criticisms abounded from the public and, importantly, from angry shareholders. The seizure set a dubious standard as "one of the best-known acts of freebooting" committed during the Dutch dominance over Asian trade[224] – a period noted for "its injustice, perfidy, cruelty,"[225] and "mafia-like enforcers."[226]

But from the Dutch perspective, it was a justifiable reprisal for injuries suffered due to a Portuguese attack against a small Dutch fleet commanded by Jacob van Neck. In September 1601, following an unsuccessful attack against the Portuguese fortress at Tidore in the Moluccas that previous June, van Neck's fleet, blown off course, reconnoitered the port of Macao, where ships from a Portuguese garrison, through perfidious use of a white flag,[227] intercepted seventeen of his crew, converted them to Catholicism, and then executed them as pirates in response to the Tidore attack.[228] Letters detailing the event were seized from a Portuguese frigate during another act of Dutch privateering and fell into the hands of Jacob van Heemskerck, a commander of yet another Dutch fleet operating in Asian waters. He "flew into a passion" upon reading of the fate of van Neck's men, and he made it his object to retaliate. Acting on a tip from agents of the prince of Johor, who had his own grievance against the Portuguese, van Heemskerck and his seamen caught up with the *Catarina* at the mouth of the Johor River in the straits of Singapore, laid siege "all day long," killed seventy Portuguese, and ultimately released the remainder of the seven hundred and fifty aboard before taking the prize back to a Dutch harbor for condemnation proceedings.[229]

---

[221] BOXER, FIDALGOS IN THE FAR EAST, *supra* note 220, at 50–51.

[222] Fruin, *supra* note 50, at 22–23.

[223] *Id.* at 18, 29–30.

[224] Borschberg, *supra* note 77, at 31. For discussions of Dutch dominance over Asian markets, dated between 1602 and 1684, *see* Gaastra, *supra* note 201, at 50–55. *See also* LIEBERMAN, STRANGE PARALLELS, *supra* note 192, at 857–868.

[225] Gaastra, *supra* note 201, at 52. *See generally* BROWN, MERCHANT KINGS, *supra* note 206.

[226] LIEBERMAN, STRANGE PARALLELS, *supra* note 192, at 865.

[227] VAN ITTERSUM, PROFIT AND PRINCIPLE, *supra* note 57, at 9 n8.

[228] *See* Boxer, *supra* note 220, at 49. Twenty Dutchmen were actually captured at Macao, but two were released because of their young age, as was the ship's Factor [legal counselor/agent].

[229] Fruin, *supra* note, 50 at 15–17.

TROUBLE WITH FRISIANS AND MENNONITES;
COMMON USE AND NO COMPETITION

A rearguard action sparked among discontented Dutch investors, principally Frisians and Mennonites. The Frisians had advanced the company seven hundred thousand guilders but soon found out they had no voice in corporate decisions.[230] Controlling interests in the VOC vested in the hands of its board, the Gentlemen XVII, eight of whom came from the Holland Chamber (Amsterdam) and four from the Zeeland Chamber.[231] These principal directors controlled the decisions not to pay out dividends,[232] never to seek capital through additional stock offerings,[233] when to take out short-term loans, where to reinvest, and which voyages to undertake next. Their insular use of authority gave early modern expression to concerns about securities regulation, closely held corporations, fiduciary duty, and unjust enrichment. "Heated conflicts" broke out over investment policy, the lack of transparency of the Gentlemen XVII, and military expenditures of the corporation.[234] The prospect of the corporation's break up into its constituent parts presented "a real danger."[235] Pamphleteers charged that the VOC was a government proxy, using shareholder capital to finance political objectives of the Dutch state rather than to maximize the financial interests of shareholders.[236] Their claims had a basis in fact: after only four years of operating, all six million guilders of start-up capital had been spent financing the corporation's military activities in Asia.[237]

---

[230] *See* ISRAEL, DUTCH PRIMACY, *supra* note 99, at 72.

[231] *Id.* at 69. In addition to the twelve seats allocated to Holland and Zeeland, two seats each went to the North Quarter and South Holland chambers (departments). The last seat on the board went to a member nominated in rotation by Zeeland, the North Quarter, and South Holland: id at 69–70. The Holland and Zeeland chambers raised the lion's share of capital, about 5 million guilders of the 6.5 million initially deposited (with the Holland chamber accounting for 3.7 million guilders and the Zeeland chamber contributing 1.3 million guilders). Other chambers formed in Rotterdam, Delft, Hoorn and Enkhuizen.

[232] The VOC did begin issuing dividends following the first few years of its existence. Jacobs, IN PURSUIT OF PEPPER AND TEA, *supra* note 175, at 17. It paid out more than 230 million guilders during its two centuries of existence. *Id.* at 16. The company averaged about a 20 percent annual return for Dutch investors between 1605 and 1620. *See* Douglas A Irwin, *Mercantilism as Strategic Trade Policy: The Anglo-Dutch Rivalry for the East India Trade*, 99 J. POL. ECON. 1296, 1320 (1991).

[233] VOC directors, when in need of additional capital, would issue advances against future earnings or take out short-term loans. It was a practice that would continue over the course of the VOC's existence. *See* JACOBS, IN PURSUIT OF PEPPER AND TEA, *supra* note 175, at 15.

[234] *Id.* at 17.

[235] VAN ITTERSUM, PROFIT AND PRINCIPLE, *supra* note 57, at 151.

[236] ISRAEL, DUTCH PRIMACY, *supra* note 99, at 72.

[237] *See* VAN ITTERSUM, PROFIT AND PRINCIPLE, *supra* note 57, at 153.

Grotius entered into this fray unperturbed by shareholder concerns. Scholarly assessments of *Mare Liberum* and *De Jure Praedae Commentarius* (Commentary on the Law of Prize; 1604–1606), the grander, unpublished tract from which *Mare Liberum* was reworked, praised their literary qualities: they were a "triumph of juristic art" in which Grotius "abounds with patriotic fervor and zeal for his countrymen" in a struggle for liberty against oppression; where Grotius appears as a citizen of a republic fighting to secure its independence.[238] But these characterizations, reflecting the gilded rays of the Grotian Tradition advocates, block out complex implications brought up by Frisian concerns, and avoid ethical implications of pacifist Mennonite and other Anabaptist shareholders.

The Mennonites were appalled by the seizure of the *Catarina*, which to them smacked of an act of piracy or unjust war. Their position gained a measure of notoriety and public sympathy when some Mennonites deeded their VOC shares to the poor in protest.[239] Perhaps their numbers were not great enough to affect VOC policy, but one among them, Pieter Lijntgens, was influential in Amsterdam commercial circles and held the most VOC shares; his threat to dump them[240] created problems for management. Although "quietly prosperous and self-contained," the Mennonite protest was bold. The Mennonites had a complicated status in the United Provinces. They were often "mocked by Calvinists and 'libertines' alike" for their sobriety and dress. Their active persecution ended in 1581, but they endured without full citizenship until 1672.[241]

Grotius knew of the Mennonites' poor treatment; later, in a famous address to the Amsterdam city council in April 1617, he chastised his own political party for conniving against "Mennonite conventicles out of expediency rather than principle."[242] He would add to his reputation as a defender of religious toleration with his publication of *De Veritate Religionis Christianae* (1627), which solidified his key place in culture discussions advancing Dutch tolerance doctrine in the 1620s.[243] But his biblically

---

[238] Edward Dumbauld, Life and Legal Writings of Hugo Grotius 29–30 (1969) at 29–30.

[239] Gellinek, *supra* note 11, at 98.

[240] *See* Van Ittersum, Profit and Principle, *supra* note 57, at 153. *See also* Fruin, *supra* note 50, at 33 (noting Lijntgens headed one of the great commercial houses in Amsterdam and had invested more than one ton gold in the company).

[241] C. R. Boxer, The Dutch Seaborne Empire, 1600–1800, at 129 (1965).

[242] Jonathan I. Israel, *Toleration in Seventeenth-Century Dutch and English Thought*, in Conflicts of Empires: Spain, the Low Countries and the Struggle for World Supremacy 1585–1713, at 253 (Jonathan I. Israel, ed., 1997).

[243] *Id.* at 252. Indeed, Grotius was well known in his century for this contribution on Christian truth, not for *De Jure Belli ac Pacis*, as many now retrospectively tend to believe. *See* Antonio

suffused, yet mild, writings on Christianity, lauded as intellectually crisp and free of denominational diatribe, "stressed the vital importance of freedom of conscience" but are, nevertheless, "remarkably reticent on freedom of practice and expression."[244] This observation would seem to characterize part of his decision to represent VOC interests in face of Mennonite complaints, which, combined with the Frisians' concerns, led to some pointed invectives in defense of the corporate objective. In *De Jure Praedae*, he alluded to both factions, but most discernibly the Mennonites. He complained about their "blameworthy"[245] convictions; their "artless innocence;"[246] their spread of "malicious falsehoods" and "insufficient devotion to the commonwealth;"[247] their "superstitious self-restraint"[248] and "anxious and overnice avoidance of things;"[249] and their "betray[al of] their own possessions to the enemy because some conscientious scruple prevented them from fighting."[250] In the complex mix of sacred and profane interests, Edward Dumbauld concluded, "[t]he growing wealth which was put into circulation as the result of Dutch maritime prowess doubtless proved more convincing to the thrifty populace than the conscientious scruple of the Mennonites against the use of armed force."[251]

But the Frisians and Mennonites were not finished. They responded in an astonishing resourceful fashion and in a way that would make Grotius' mentor, Oldenbarnevelt, "extremely alarmed."[252] After first discussing a plan to form a Frisian East India Company, an initiative Holland and Zeeland ably blocked,[253] they joined forces with other discontented merchants[254] and turned to the one man Oldenbarnevelt knew the Dutch Republic "could not afford

---

Cassese, *The Martens Clause: Half a Loaf or Simply Pie in the Sky?*, 11 Eur. J. Int'l L. 187, 200 (2000) (referencing the great Dutch historian Johan Huizinga's essay, "Grotius' Plaats in de Geschiedenis van den Manschelijken Geest").

[244] Israel, *supra* note 242, at 253.

[245] 1 Hugo Grotius, De Iure Praedae Commentarius 2 (translated by Gwladys L. Williams and Walter H. Zeydel, 1950).

[246] *Id.* at 1.

[247] *Id.*

[248] *Id.*

[249] *Id.* at 2.

[250] *Id.* at 3.

[251] Dumbauld, *supra* note 238, at 26. But cf. Van Ittersum, Profit and Principle, *supra* note 57, at 153, who notes that, despite his Mennonite pacifism and Anabaptist scruples, Pieter Lijntgens, nevertheless, served as an agent to purchase guns and ammunition for Zeeland voyages to the East Indies.

[252] Israel, Dutch Primacy, *supra* note 99, at 72.

[253] *Id.*

[254] Van Ittersum notes two disaffected shareholders in particular, the Flemish *émigrée* merchants Balthasar de Moucheron and Isaac le Maire; both resigned their VOC directorships and

to antagonize:"[255] Henri IV, king of France. Seen as the protector and greatest ally of the United Provinces, and implicitly aware of the advantages to France of a Franco-Dutch East India Company[256] – in view of Dutch, Portuguese, and English attempts to create the same[257] – Henri's "avid interest" in the proposal made for Oldenbarnevelt a huge political problem.[258] "But such was the determination to keep all Dutch investment in the East India trade within the confines of the VOC that it was decided to risk an outright rejection of the king's request."[259] Oldenbarnevelt told the king no such deal would be allowed to take place.[260] A particular kind of *dominium* over the seas began to develop on the home front as it would in Asia – Grotius' doctrine of freedom of the seas and its emphasis on common use were written against the backdrop of a state-sponsored and enforced no-compete clause – the signature piece of *mare clausum*; the remnant of a kind of *majestas* owed to the *patria potestas*.

SELF-DEFENSE AND *MARE LIBERUM*

In view of the shareholder row and the concern that Oldenbarnevelt might concede the VOC's Asian agenda at the armistice table,[261] the Gentlemen XVII petitioned Grotius for help. Grotius legitimized the seizure of the *Santa Catarina* in the famous twelfth chapter of his tract, *De Jure Praedae Commentarius*. He reworked this chapter and published it separately as *Mare Liberum*.[262]

"became involved in attempts to create a French East India Company." *See* Van Ittersum, Profit and Principle, *supra* note 57, at 151.

[255] Israel, Dutch Primacy, *supra* note 99, at 72.

[256] Fruin, *supra* note 50, at 34 (noting French mariners' lack of seafaring knowledge of Indo-Asian waters at this time).

[257] In 1600, under the auspices of the Lord Mayor of London, London merchants and their British political allies decided to establish their own trading company in the East, in view of Dutch intentions to do the same. By Royal Charter, Queen Elizabeth established the company in the same year; it became known as the British East India Company, which functioned well into the nineteenth century. *See generally* Lawson, *supra* note 173.

[258] *See* Israel, Dutch Primacy, *supra* note 99, at 72. *See also* Van Ittersum, Profit and Principle, *supra* note 57, at 153 (noting: "Oldenbarnevelt wrote one letter after another to the French monarch in order to warn him against the nefarious schemes of 'Anabaptists and libertines,' and even suggested that the projected establishment of a French East India Company was part of a Spanish conspiracy...);" and Fruin, *supra* note 50, at 34 (concluding Lijntgen's plan "threatened to become a dangerous rival of the Dutch Company"); and at 35 (noting Oldenbarnevelt "combatted the scheme" with all means of statecraft at his service).

[259] Israel, Dutch Primacy, *supra* note 99, at 72.

[260] *Id.*

[261] *See* Roelofsen, *supra* note 157, at 9–10.

[262] *See* Vervliet, *supra* note 111, at xiv (not until 1864, when Grotius' heirs put his papers up for auction at The Hague, did it become apparent that *Mare Liberum* was but one chapter of a

Grotius crafted a defense, which not only strategically couched the conflict in terms of the secondary concern for freedom of navigation, but also forwarded a natural rights argument that justified the private recourse to war as a means of self defense and for the protection of rights "common to all."[263] He argued the taking of spoils – absent the presence of a third party adjudicator – was proper recompense for injuries suffered to an ally of the Dutch, the sultan of Johor, although there is ample evidence the sultan never staked a claim to the *Catarina* and could not have assigned a good cause of action to the VOC even according to Grotius' theory.[264] His development of a divided sovereignty doctrine allowed a sovereign to assign a public right of war, in terms of self-defense (alternatively described as a right to punish[265]), to a private, corporate entity on the basis of a subjective natural right of *dominium*.[266] These traits of indirect rule are at odds with the Grotian Tradition's construct of indivisible sovereignty. They indicate counterrevolutionary and imperial tendencies rather than the proto-liberal and republican virtues that led Lauterpacht to conclude Grotius endowed international law with unprecedented dignity.

"The crucial element in Grotius' legal thought on divisible sovereignty, then, is that the law of nations was not exclusively a law for nations, but also included rights and duties for individuals and private companies."[267] From this example of the taking of the *Catarina*, one might come to understand why Lauterpacht detailed eleven main features[268] of the Grotian Tradition; so many of them are relevant to this case at hand, but few of them are relevant to the praiseworthy and liberal legacies intended by Sir Hersch's gilded portrait of Grotius. To justify an

---

much larger manuscript written in defense of Dutch colonial interests. Historian Robert Fruin made the connection, Leiden University purchased the manuscript, and the long dormant larger work was finally published in 1868 as *De Jure Praedae Commentarius*. The full title of the tract, *De Jure Praedae Commentarius, ex auctoris codice descripsit et vulgavit*, was the title given to the work by its first editor, H. G. Hamaker; Grotius, however, usually referred to the work as *De rebus Indicis* – "On the Affairs of the Indies." *See id.* at xiv. *See also* Armitage, *supra* note 11, at xiii; and Van Ittersum, *Preparing Mare liberum for the Press*, *supra* note 110, at 26–28. Much has been written about the importance of the *Commentarius*, but not enough has been written about the fact that Grotius never published the work).

[263] MARE LIBERUM, *supra* note 1, at 64 and 151.

[264] Van Ittersum, HUGO GROTIUS IN CONTEXT, *supra* note 220, at 514, 535 (Van Ittersum also notes that following the carrack's capture, it was Van Heemskerck who rewarded the sultan, not the other way around, at 541).

[265] BORSCHBERG, HUGO GROTIUS, *supra* note 58, at 86.

[266] *See* Martti Koskenniemi, *Empire and International Law: The Real Spanish Contribution*, 61 U. TORONTO L.J. 32 (2011).

[267] Oliver Jütersonke & Rolf Schwarz, *Slicing up the Cake: Divisible Sovereignty in the Pre and Post-Westphalian Order*, EISA (Sept. 12, 2007) at 4, www.eisa-net.org/be-bruga/eisa/files/events/turin/Schwarz-divsov_and_westphalian_order.pdf.

[268] *See supra* note 145.

act of privateering in which "a private individual could punish transgressors of the natural law and act as judge and executioner in his own cause"[269] could not have any other consequence than problematizing Grotius' notion of common use while undercutting the declaration of the "progressive triumph of Grotius' thesis of *mare liberum* and its concomitant prohibition on claims of territorial sovereignty."[270]

REQUIEM FOR *MARE LIBERUM*

Grotius' involvement in law of the sea matters was not the product of his deliberate design to craft an argument about the global commons. Rather, he backed into the subject while advancing the parochial interest of a state-sponsored corporation in pursuit of *raison d'état*. C. G. Roelofsen argues the epoch-making qualities ascribed to *Mare Liberum* are "the result of an accident."[271] Indeed, classifying the seas as a common use and vindicating a corporation's violent act of privateering by highlighting Portuguese interferences with the natural right to trade and travel, only to justify an appropriation of that same space by the superceding power, seem disturbingly precedential if not indicative of the Grotian tendency of capable states to commandeer resources in increasingly diminishing areas described as the global commons.

There is irony here. Grotius' expedient legal argument on behalf of the VOC caught up with him at the Anglo-Dutch colonial conferences of 1613–1615. Sent to England to defend the Dutch maritime monopoly policy of excluding competitors from trade in the Spice Islands and elsewhere, "the Dutch were somewhat embarrassed by having Grotius, their foremost champion of the freedom of the seas, constantly quoted against them."[272] Embarrassed perhaps, but the significance of Grotius' earlier view presumably indicated there was more to it than political expediency. Nevertheless, according to historian, C. R. Boxer, the Dutch, in the final analysis, "relied less on their rather dubious legal arguments than on their practical preference for:

> The good old rule, the simple plan,
> That they should take who have the power,
> And they should keep who can.[273]

---

[269] Van Ittersum, Profit and Principle, *supra* note, 57 at 29.

[270] Bernard H. Oxman, *The Territorial Temptation: A Siren Song at Sea*, 100 Am. J. Int'l L. 830, 830 (2006).

[271] *See* Roelofsen, *supra* note, 157 at 5 and 6.

[272] Boxer, The Dutch Seaborne Empire, *supra* note 241, at 102.

[273] *Id.* (paraphrasing a stanza from William Wordsworth's poem, *Rob Roy's Grave* (1807)).

Recent scholarly readings of *Mare Liberum* pick up on Roelofsen's "uncomfortable thought."[274] Although received in the canon of international legal literature as a masterwork of independent scholarship and the basis for the principle of freedom of navigation, and, indeed, proto-liberal thinking relating to natural rights theory, these scholars have highlighted the complexities of *Mare Liberum*'s legacy: Peter Borschberg viewed it as fundamentally political, not legal, in nature, expressing minimal familiarity with accepted maritime or commercial practice;[275] it was crafted to influence the Amsterdam Admiralty Court's verdict on the capture and to persuade the Dutch Estates General to assist the VOC;[276] Martine Van Ittersum labels Grotius an "unyielding VOC apologist,"[277] who readily collated Company-supplied "transcripts, attestations, letters, maps and books"[278] and the personal account of the VOC's admiral who took the *Catarina* as prize[279] into a legal doctrine justifying a private right to war. More astonishing is the fact that Grotius accomplished this aim by configuring his legal argument in terms of common use, just war, and, above all else, freedom of the seas – concepts "more honored in the breach than the observance."[280] Van Ittersum also highlights Grotius' skills of "forensic oratory," turning *Mare Liberum* into a villainous encomium of Iberian intentions to conquer the Low Countries, akin to Spanish subjugation of the indigenous peoples of the Americas.[281] More thought should be directed toward the self-determination implications of Grotius' *Mare Liberum*. His embedded concept of divided sovereignty, which contributed to corporate and colonial rule over indigenous populations, elevated the doctrine of *pacta sunt servanda* (the good faith performance of obligations) to a position of supreme primacy (which, incidentally, Lauterpacht lauded[282]). But he treated corporate contracts of adhesion in Asia no differently than the Spanish administered the *Requerimiento*[283] in the

---

[274] Roelofsen, *supra* note 157, at 5.

[275] *See* Borschberg, *supra* note 77, at 32.

[276] *See* VAN ITTERSUM, PROFIT AND PRINCIPLE, *supra* note 57, at 488.

[277] *Id.*

[278] *See* Van Ittersum, *Hugo Grotius in Context, supra* note 220, at 512–513 (citing fifteen notarized attestations put together by the VOC and sent to Grotius in 1604).

[279] *Id.* at 511.

[280] With apologies to the Bard, who was actually referring to a custom that is more honorably ignored than observed, not one that is more often ignored. *See* William Shakespeare, *Hamlet*, Reprint (1963) at act 1, scene iv. *See also* Philip B Corbett, *Mangled Shakespeare*, N.Y. TIMES (Jan. 17, 2012), http://afterdeadline.blogs.nytimes.com/2012/01/17/mangled-shakespeare/?_php=true&_type=blogs&_r=0.

[281] *See generally* VAN ITTERSUM, PROFIT AND PRINCIPLE, *supra* note 57, Ch. 2 (discussing the so-called Spanish Black Legend regarding the conquistadores' treatment of aborigines in the New World).

[282] *See* Lauterpacht, *The Grotian Tradition in International Law, supra* note 125.

[283] Sixteenth-century Spanish colonial policy, chiefly through the writings of scholastic friar, Francisco de Vitoria, held that aborigines "discovered" in the New World were endowed with

colonization of the Americas, and these coerced agreements had a retrograde significance and relationship to the right of self-determination.

Others have noted Grotius' rhetorical tactic of quoting and often misquoting Iberian doctrinal authorities for the sake of discrediting the Iberian positions in their own tongues. Karl Zemanek criticized Grotius' apologists for presenting his work as a successful application of the *jus naturale*, ostensibly hewn from references to classical, biblical, patristic, and theological authority as "a sudden inspiration of *recta ratio* (right reason) in the *opinio juris* of states," rather than as "the success of an economic doctrine which determined the new foreign policy."[284] Grotius' Free Sea thesis was meant to substantiate the claim that no nation had exclusive rights to the common seas – to navigation and trade through discovery, occupation, prescription or donation by the pope – but to prove it, he had to force a dichotomy between the Scylla of lawful privateering (which he admitted was opposed by "a considerable number" of his own people)[285] and the Charybdis of piracy. And as Michael Kempe pointed out: "By naming each other 'pirates,' the Portuguese as well as the Dutch would both have agreed to label the native resistance against their conquest as 'piracy' too."[286]

THE GROTIAN TENDENCY ON DISPLAY

It is ironic that this concept of the global commons, which arises across such a wide spectrum of international law topics, is under assiduous attack in the seaborne realm that gave rise to its early modern expression. Since the end of World War II, the world has witnessed a series of creeping appropriations of pelagic space formerly considered to be part of a global commons, or at least beyond the scope of national jurisdiction. These enclosures are every bit as significant and expansive as the fifteenth-century attempt to divide the world – except, they have been much more effective.

A sublime indeterminacy thesis accompanies Grotius' idea of the global commons: on one level, the term serves as a stable rubric for international cooperation and mutual benefit, but only as long as capable states remain

---

rational capacity and free will. Consequently the pope's exercise of universal temporal authority over the inhabitants, through his agent, the Spanish crown, hinged on the legal "requirement" that aborigines consent to and acknowledge the universal temporal authority of the pope, who had granted dominium to the Spanish crown. Failure to consent to the *Requerimiento* provided the Spanish conquerors with a right to determine and resort to extreme measures. *See* Rossi, Broken Chain of Being, *supra* note 124, at 121–125.

[284] *See* Zemanek, *supra* note 40, at 60.

[285] Hugo Grotius, De Iure Praedae Commentarius 1 (translated by G. L. Williams 1950).

[286] Michael Kempe, *Beyond the Law. The Image of Piracy in the Legal Writings of Hugo Grotius*, 26 Grotiana 379, 385 (2007).

uninterested in or incapable of exercising effective control over a resource. On another level, because states tend to lay claim to geo-spatial areas they are determined to control, the significance of the global commons dilutes and become a rhetorical or political trope more than a term of legal art and significance. Nowhere has the receding importance of the global commons or the lingering significance of the Grotian tendency been more pronounced than in the modern history of the seas. And as D. P. O'Connell noted, it is easy to understand why: proximity to the sea assigns to coastal states primordial rights over its resources.[287]

Perhaps a territorial temptation is at work here. Scholars claim that "the law of the land and the law of the sea have developed in very different ways,"[288] that the regimes for establishing sovereignty rights to land and sea are "fundamentally different,"[289] with title to land established primarily through physical appropriation by powerful states and title to the seas remaining *res communis* due to sheer practical difficulties in establishing *dominium*.[290] Thus, the history of the international law of the land has led to the progressive triumph of the territorial temptation, and the history of the international law of the sea has led to the progressive triumph/myth of Grotius' thesis of *mare liberum*.[291] The more interesting historical point for consideration is the way in which the territorial temptation supports the pelagic adaptation of that most terrestrial and presumptive form of *dominium*: *uti possidetis juris* (as you possess, so you may possess).[292]

THE TWENTIETH-CENTURY TERRITORIALIZATION
OF THE GLOBAL COMMONS

Prompted by the discovery of offshore oil and gas deposits, Harry S. Truman, President the United States – on behalf of the world's then and current naval superpower – issued two proclamations –the so-called 1945 Truman Proclamations:[293] The first proclamation asserted jurisdiction over the subsoil and seabed of the

---

[287] 1 D. P. O'CONNELL, THE INTERNATIONAL LAW OF THE SEA 476 (I. A. Shearer, ed., 1982) (writing in relation to a coastal state's inherent and primordial rights over the continental shelf).

[288] Oxman, *supra* note 270, at 830.

[289] Lea Brilmayer & Natalie Klein, *Land and Sea: Two Sovereignty Regimes in Search of a Common Denominator*, 33 N.Y.U. INT'L L. & POL. 703, 703–704 (2001).

[290] *Id.*

[291] Oxman, *supra* note 270, at 830.

[292] *See generally* Giuseppe Nesi, *Uti possidetis iuris e delimitazioni maritime*, 74 RIVISTA DI DIRITTO INTERNAZIONALE 534 (1991).

[293] Proclamation No. 2667, Sept. 28, 1945, Policy of the United States with Respect to the Natural Resources of the Subsoil and Sea Bed of the Continental Shelf, 13 DEP'T ST. BULL., 485 (1945).

continental shelf while preserving the high-seas character of the historically defined right of freedom of navigation; the second claimed a right of the United States to regulate coastal fisheries, which presaged a coming coastal state interest over the superjacent water column of the continental shelf to control and harvest the living resources of the sea. The proclamations amounted to stunning encroachments into the seas, as related to coastal states' creeping jurisdiction over the seabed, subsoil, and, later, the superjacent water column of the continental shelf. The proclamations signified a major step toward the end of the classical law of the sea[294] and presaged a coming "land grab" over the mineral and living resources of the sea.

The US justification for these proclamations "sprang from the two-fold claim that the continental shelf was naturally appurtenant to the landmass of the coastal state and that the most effective measures of utilization and conservation were necessarily contingent on cooperation and protection from the shore."[295] Both justifications suited well the interests of coastal states and provided them with an easy invitation from the leading thalassocracy to extend control over resources of the sea. Merely thirteen years after introduction, the Truman Proclamations and their appropriative design became the cornerstone of continental shelf law,[296] which was one of four weighty conventions and an optional protocol on dispute settlement[297] produced at the First United Nations Conference on the Law of the Sea (1958).[298] This conference, held in Geneva, marked the successful launch of the twentieth-century movement to codify the law of the sea,[299] and to enclose major portions of it, too. The

---

[294] L. D. M. Nelson, *The Patrimonial Sea*, 22 INT'L & COMP. L.Q. 668, 669 (1973).

[295] CHRISTOPHER R. ROSSI, EQUITY AND INTERNATIONAL LAW: A LEGAL REALIST APPROACH TO INTERNATIONAL DECISIONMAKING 205 (1993) at 205.

[296] *See generally* Convention on the Continental Shelf, April 29,1958, 499 U.N.T.S. 311.

[297] Three other conventions were produced at the First United Nations Conference on the Law of the Sea. *See* Convention on the Territorial Sea and Contiguous Zone, April 29, 1958, 516 U.N.T.S. 205; Convention on the High Seas, April 29, 1958, 450 U.N.T.S. 11; Convention on Fishing and Conservation of the Living Resources of the High Seas, April 29, 1958, 559 U.N.T.S. 285; Optional Protocol of Signature Concerning the Compulsory Settlement of Dispute, April 29, 1958, 450 U.N.T.S. 169.

[298] *See* UNCLOSOR, 1958, 1st-21st Plen Mtgs, UN Doc A/CONF.13/38 (Sales No# 58 V. 4, Vol. II). A second conference was convened in 1960 to address the breadth of the territorial sea, which had been left unresolved by the first conference, but it also failed to resolve the issue. *See* UNGAOR, 15th Sess., UN Doc A/CONF.19/C.1/L.9 (1960). A third conference resolved the issue of the breadth of the territorial sea and numerous other issues but gave rise to new considerations, particularly the EEZ zone, *infra*, which now presents major considerations relating to attempts to claim sovereign rights over the seas. *See* UNCLOSOR, 11th Sess, UN Doc A/CONF.62/121 (1982).

[299] It should be noted that the League of Nations attempted with the 1930 Hague Law of the Sea Conference to begin the codification process, but the successful conclusion of the four Geneva Conventions mark, for many, the starting point for discussions.

appropriative design was succinctly stated by a member of the International Law Commission: the Continental Shelf Convention "had been drafted in light of the eventual exploitation of the natural resources of the seabed."[300] While establishing "sovereign rights" over the continental shelf, but not sovereignty itself, the convention did not interfere with modern applications of the *jus mercandi* and the *jus navagandi*.

Since that time, the appropriative designs of capable states over the living and mineral resources of the sea have been on display.[301] Although essentially somnambulant for three hundred and fifty years,[302] the doctrine of the territorial sea, reawakened in this same postwar period as the Truman Proclamations, resulted in coastal state extensions of sovereign rights from three to twelve nautical miles,[303] along with the creation of the contiguous zone,[304] which extended coastal state police powers an additional twelve nautical miles seaward.[305] The Geneva Conventions forwarded an *ab initio* doctrine,[306] which based acquisition to pelagic space on geographic proximity rather than on the military muscle via the terrestrial concept of effective or physical occupation.[307] Acceptance of this doctrine was done "without hesitation" to prevent a "rush and grab for sea-bed resources being undertaken by a few [powerful] states on the basis of the Grotian dogma of 'freedom of the sea'."[308] And a sense of attitudinal change developed. The ICJ validated the *ab initio* doctrine,[309]

---

[300] "Chapter IV: Revised Draft Articles on the Continental Shelf and Related Subjects" (UN Doc A/CN.4/60) in 1 Y.B. OF THE INT'L L. LAW COMM'N 1953, 73, 77 (1959) (UNDOC.A/CN.4/ SER.A/1953) (comment of Mr Zourek).

[301] See Fisheries Case (United Kingdom v. Norway) 1951 I.C.J. 116; Fisheries Jurisdiction Case (United Kingdom v Iceland) 1974 I.C.J. 3; Fisheries Jurisdiction Case (Federal Republic of Germany v Iceland) 1974 I.C.J. 175.

[302] The generally accepted view is that the three-mile territorial sea developed from the "cannon-shot" rule, most famously articulated but not conceived of by Dutch publicist Cornelius van Bynkershoek (1673–1743) in 1709. That delimitation hardened as a compromise between Danish-Norwegian and later Swedish four-mile claims to a neutral belt and Mediterranean countries' claim, along with Holland's, to a three-mile zone, later enforced by the cannon-shot rule, to guard neutral states from quarrels of warring powers. See generally Kent, *The Historical Origins of the Three-Mile Limit, supra* note 75.

[303] See UNCLOS, arts. 2–8.

[304] See id. art 33.

[305] Id. art 33 (2). For a discussion of the historical development of the contiguous zone, see Shigeru Oda, *The Concept of the Contiguous Zone*, 11 INT'L & COMP. L.Q. 131 (1962).

[306] Convention on the Continental Shelf, art. 2, April 29, 1958, 499 U.N.T.S. 314; UNCLOS, pt VI, art 77.

[307] Brilmayer & Klein, *supra* note 289, at 710 (noting that the *ab initio* doctrine conferred the title from the outset and did not require any actions by the coastal state to perfect it).

[308] *Case Concerning the Continental Shelf (Tunis v Libyan Arab Jamahiriya)*, (Feb. 24, 1982), I.C.J. 123 (separate opinion of Judge de Arechaga)

[309] *North Sea Continental Shelf Cases (Federal Republic of Germany v Denmark, Federal Republic of Germany v the Netherlands)*, 1969 I.C.J. 30, at 39. See also Wolfgang Friedmann, *The North*

and some scholars argued the legal regime based on geographical proximity rather than prior occupation expanded the rule of law and promoted a sense of attitudinal change by forestalling the interests of Western colonial powers that "were poised at that very moment to claim and exploit vast ocean areas," noting that "by the time that developing nations obtained comparable technological capability it would have been much too late."[310]

In retrospect, the *ab initio* doctrine did not appear to be too far removed from the concept of effective occupation. In direct response to the Truman Proclamations, Latin American countries forwarded claims of a Patrimonial Sea or Epicontinental Sea, which asserted prescriptive or sovereign rights over a 200 nautical mile economic zone measured from the baseline of the territorial sea.[311] Over time, major maritime powers came to embrace a reformulated version of these concepts, which contributed directly to "the most fundamental change"[312] of UNCLOS – the establishment of the EEZ.[313] The EEZ established sovereign rights for the purpose of exploring and exploiting, conserving and managing the natural resources, both living and nonliving, as well as the seabed and its subsoil out to 200 nautical miles from shore.[314] It "extended the same sort of protection to interests of coastal states in the living resources of the waters over the continental shelf ... as the continental shelf regime previously had extended only to coastal state interests in the resources on or beneath the ocean floor."[315] Embracing about one-third of the marine environment and encasing all of the "important seas and gulfs of the world,"[316] it was an enclosure every bit as significant as the Treaty of Tordesillas.[317]

Sea Continental Shelf Cases – A Critique, 64 Am. J. Int'l L. 229, 232 (1970) (noting the ICJ's brief, almost casual, recognition of coastal state authority over the continental shelf independent of the 1958 Conventions). *See also* Aegean Sea Continental Shelf (Greece v. Turkey), 1978 I.C.J. 3, at 36.

[310] Brilmayer & Klein, *supra* note 289, at 713.

[311] Chile, Peru, Costa Rica, and El Salvador laid claim to Patrimonial Seas by decree in 1947 and 1948; Argentina's decree of an Epicontinental Sea, which asserted sovereign rights, was claimed in 1946. The movement congealed around the Declaration of Santiago of August 18, 1952. *See* Nelson, *supra* note 294, at 669–670. Other Latin American states joined in endorsement of the 200-mile territorial sea with the *Montevideo Declaration on the Law of the Sea*, May 8, 1970, UN Doc. A/AC 138/34.

[312] Zouhair A. Kronfol, *The Exclusive Economic Zone: A Critique of Contemporary Law of the Sea*, 9 J. Marine L. & Commerce 461, 463 (1977).

[313] UNCLOS, pt VII, arts 86–90.

[314] *Id.* arts 56–57.

[315] Brilmayer & Klein, *supra* note 289, at 723.

[316] Oxman, *supra* note 270, at 839.

[317] The establishment of the EEZ is substantively distinct from sovereign claims to the territorial sea. As Oxman has noted, "what really separates the EEZ from the territorial sea is that the former embraces freedom of navigation, overflight, and communications, and is not

But UNCLOS was crafted as a package deal:[318] The agreement reached to delimit the territorial sea, to establish the EEZ, and to afford maritime powers protections for military and national security interests, such as unimpeded transit through straits,[319] was offered in exchange for economic concessions to developing and landlocked countries. These developing countries, numerically powerful in the United Nations following postwar decolonization, and aligned through a host of organizations promoting a rebalancing of the extant international economic order,[320] also expected the new law of the sea to manage the remaining global commons of the high seas and deep seabed according to the principle of distributive justice, with the principle of the Common Heritage of Mankind[321] as the guiding light.

It was not to be. In an obvious display of power politics, reminiscent of Grotius' parochial defense of seventeenth-century VOC interests, the United States and other powers reversed their long-standing negotiating positions, refused to sign the treaty, accepted the vast majority of the non-seabed provisions of the Convention as existing customary law, and on the basis of customary, not conventional, law, proclaimed a 200 nautical mile EEZ.[322] The United States (and the former Soviet Union) also made explicitly clear that any extension of the territorial sea would not be accommodated without acceptance of

in principle subject to comprehensive coastal state jurisdiction, while the latter is subject to comprehensive coastal state jurisdiction and, outside of straits, includes only a very limited, and suspendable, right of innocent passage that is subject to both important qualifications and unilateral coastal state regulation." Oxman, *supra* note 270, at 839. Innocent passage refers to the right of all states to navigate through the territorial sea so long as passage is continuous, expeditious, and not prejudicial to the peace. *See* UNCLOS, pt II, arts 17–19.

[318] James Kraska, *International Law and the Future of Indian Ocean Security, in* Deep Currents and Rising Tides: The Indian Ocean and International Security 213, 224 (John Garofano & Andrea J. Dew, eds., 2013).

[319] John R. Stevenson, Speech by US representative to the Second Session of UNCLOS III (July 11, 1974) 71 Dep't. St. Bull. 232, 233. *See also* M. Nordquist & C. Park, eds., Reports of the United States Delegation to the Third United Nations Conference on the Law of the Sea (1983).

[320] *See* Rossi, *Equity and International Law, supra* note 295, at 195–204 (noting the rise of the Group of 77, the New International Economic Order, the UNCTAD movement, and the debate on permanent sovereignty over natural resources).

[321] *See* UNCLOS, pt XI, arts 136–137 (establishing an International Seabed Authority to regulate the exploration and exploitation of the resources of the "Area" – denoting the seabed, ocean floor, and subsoil thereof beyond the limits of national jurisdiction – in accordance with the Common Heritage of Mankind principle). *See generally* Hugo Caminos & Michael R. Molitor, *Progressive Development of International Law and the Package Deal*, 79 Am. J. Int'l L. 871 (1985). *See also* Declaration of Principles Governing the Sea-Bed and the Ocean Floor, and the Subsoil Thereof, beyond the limits of National Jurisdiction, GA Res 2749, UNGAOR, 25th Sess, (1970) at ¶ 1.

[322] Ronald Reagan, Statement on United States Oceans Policy (Mar. 10, 1983), www.reagan.utexas.edu/archives/speeches/1983/31083c.htm.

thalassocratic interests relating to military transit through international straits, a demand that gave birth to the doctrine of transit passage.[323]

THE TWENTY-FIRST-CENTURY CONTINUATION

Long before the EEZ became established law, Wolfgang Friedmann, Georges Scelle, Robert Jennings, Cecil Hurst, Hersch Lauterpacht, and other twentieth-century international legal scholars began writing of the radical post-war reformulation of the classical law of the sea, noting the expanding, almost inexorable movement toward closed seas.[324] Hurst interpreted the movement as sovereignty by another name;[325] Bernard H. Oxman noted more recently this "territorial temptation thrust seaward with a speed and geographic scope that would be the envy of the most ambitious conquerors in human history,"[326] giving rise to the prospect that the classical law of the sea had not ever radically transformed. Several other resource scrambles are underway at the beginning of the twenty-first century, one in the High Arctic,[327] the other spanning the globe, but including the High Arctic, and stretching into the outer

---

[323] UNCLOS, pt III, arts 37–44. *See* John Norton Moore, *Regime of Straits and the Third United Nations Conference on the Law of the Sea*, 74 Am. J. Int'l L. 71, 100 (1980), (noting that both the United States and the Soviet Union "repeatedly made clear that they could not accept a law of the sea treaty that did not provide for freedom of navigation through straits).

[324] *See* Wolfgang Friedmann, *Selden Redivivus: Towards a Partition of the Seas?* 65 Am. J. Int'l L. 757, 763 (1971); Hubert Thierry, *The Thought of Georges Scelle*, 1 Eur. J. Int'l L. 193, 207–208 (1990); R. Y. Jennings, *A Changing International Law of the Sea*, 3 Cambridge L.J. 32, 34 (1972); Cecil Hurst, *The Continental Shelf*, 34 Transactions of the Grotius Soc'y 153 (1948); Hersch Lauterpacht, *Sovereignty Over Submarine Areas*, 27 Brit. Y.B. Int'l L. 376 (1950). *See also* Nelson, *supra* note 294, at 669ff.

[325] Hurst, *supra* note 324, at 161 (interpreting the distinction between the Truman Proclamation's exercise of exclusive control and sovereignty as "so small as to be little more than a question of name," at 161).

[326] Oxman, *supra* note 270, at 832.

[327] The "High Arctic" region is a term used to distinguish the colder climates of the Arctic, which are closer to the North Pole, than the relatively warmer environs of the lower or subarctic regions. Definitions of the Arctic region differ, but not materially for purposes of this paper. The Arctic Research and Policy Act (ARPA), 15 USC Title I of PL 1984, Section 112 § 4111 defines the Arctic as "all United States and foreign territory north of the Arctic Circle and all United States territory north and west of the boundary formed by the Porcupine, Yukon, and Kuskokwim Rivers [in Alaska]; all contiguous seas, including the Arctic Ocean and the Beaufort, Bering, and Chukchi Seas; and the Aleutian chain." A helpful map of this area can be found at Allison Gaylord, "Arctic Boundary as defined by the Arctic Research and Policy Act (ARPA)" *USARC – United States Arctic Research Comm'n* (May 27, 2009), www.arctic .gov/publications/maps/ARPA_Polar_150dpi.jpg. For the definition and map of the Arctic used by a working group of the Arctic Council, the eight member group formed in 1996 for purposes of promoting cooperation in the region, adopted by the Arctic Monitoring and Assessment Programme (AMAP), *see Geographical Coverage*, AMPAP, www.amap.no/about/ geographical-coverage.

reaches of the continental shelf. Together, they amount to "one of the biggest territorial grabs in history"[328] and continue the encroachment on remaining unsecured space.

THE HIGH ARCTIC

Arctic sea ice typically covers fourteen to sixteen million square kilometers in late winter. Satellite data accumulated since 1972 suggests that Arctic ice has decreased by an average rate of 3 percent per decade, with more dramatic reductions apparent beginning in September 2002, leading to average current estimates that Arctic sea ice is decreasing at a rate of 7.7 percent per decade; sea ice measurements average almost an 11 percent per decade decline in monthly August Arctic measurements from 1979 to 2013.[329] Prompted by this dramatic Artic ice melt, and scientific estimates that the Arctic Circle holds approximately 13 percent of the world's recoverable oil and 30 percent of the world's undiscovered gas deposits, as well as vast quantities of mineral resources,[330] states adjacent to the Arctic are laying claim to previously inaccessible resources. Since 2001, seventy-seven continental shelf extension claims, some of them included in the current Arctic enclosure bid, have been presented to the CLCS,[331] which was established by UNCLOS to receive information and make recommendations to coastal states on the establishment of the outer limits of their continental shelves.[332] None of these claims, proffered by rich and poor countries alike, are motivated by a protection of or interest in the global commons machinery set up by UNCLOS' International Seabed Authority machinery.[333] This machinery had to be modified extensively by the

---

[328] Shackelford, *supra* note 38, at 2.

[329] *Environment: Trends*, National Snow and Ice Data Center, http://nsidc.org/cryosphere/ seaice/environment/trends.html. Sea ice extent for August 2013 averaged 6.09 million square km (2.35 million square miles), or 1.03 million square km (398,000 square miles) below the 1981–2010 average for August. *Arctic Sea ice news & Analysis*, National Snow and Ice Data Center, (Sept. 4, 2013), http://nsidc.org/arcticseaicenews/.

[330] National Strategy for the Arctic Region, May 2013, at 5 www.whitehouse.gov/sites/default/files/ doc/nat_arctic_strategy.pdf, with a cover letter from President Barak Obama dated May 10, 2013 (citing US Geological Survey fact sheet, 2008).

[331] Submissions, through the Secretary-General of the United Nations, to the Commission on the Limits of the Continental Shelf, pursuant to Article 76, ¶ 8, of the United Nations Convention on the Law of the Sea of December 10, 1982, *United Nations – Oceans & Law of the Sea*, www .un.org/depts/los/clcs_new/commission_submissions.htm. The Canadian Foreign Ministry estimates that eighty-five countries have an extended continental shelf claim. *See Canada's Extended Continental Shelf*, FOREIGN AFFAIRS, TRADE AND DEVELOPMENT CANADA (Dec. 9, 2013), www.international.gc.ca/arctic-arctique/continental/index.aspx?lang=eng.

[332] *See* UNCLOS, pt VI, art 76 (8).

[333] *See id.*, pt XI, arts 156–158.

1994 New York Amendments to prevent the outright rejection by the developed world of the once proud Common Heritage of Mankind concept.[334] Moreover, "the 1994 Agreement changed the nature of the [International Seabed Authority] into a market-based concept fully compatible with private economic activity."[335] Never embraced completely, the Common Heritage principle now may be undergoing a *de facto* deconstruction, given the expanding interest of coastal states, much like its perceived undoing in the management of the geosynchronous orbit and international space commons.[336] Every incremental seaward extension of the continental shelf amounts to a *de facto* reduction of deep seabed, which was to be regulated by UNCLOS itself.[337] The result, according to Scott Shackelford, is that the "world's largest 'commons' is being, at least in part nationalized"[338] along the lines suggested almost four hundred years ago by John Selden, and objected to by Grotius, except when it served his interests.

THE NORTHERN SEA ROUTE AND THE NORTHWEST PASSAGE

Receding Arctic ice also makes possible increased commercial shipping on two trans-Arctic sea routes: the Northern Sea Route, part of the Northeast Passage, which traverses the top of Russia connecting Europe and Asia, and the Northwest Passage, which connects the Atlantic and Pacific Oceans through the ice pack of Canada's northern archipelago.

Already, Canada claims the Northwest Passage as part of its inland waters, which is tantamount to a nonnegotiable claim of full sovereignty over the area;[339] the United States and the European Union dispute this claim and

---

[334] Jasper A. Bovenberg, *Mining the Common Heritage for Our DNA: Lessons Learned from Grotius and Pardo*, 8 Duke L. & Tech. Rev. at 29 (2006), http://scholarship.law.duke.edu/cgi/viewcontent.cgi?article=1154&context=dltr. Importantly, the United States still refuses to ratify the treaty, notwithstanding six main revisions. *See UN: Agreement Relating to the implementation of Part XI of UNCLOS – Content Summary*, 33 ILM 1309 (1994).

[335] Shackelford, *supra* note 38, at 26–27.

[336] For a discussion on the problems and prospects of proprietary interests in enclosing portions of outer space, including the geostationary and low earth orbits, *see* Shane Chaddha, "Hardin Goes to Outer Space – 'Space Enclosure'" (Feb. 8, 2011), *available at* http://ssrn.com/abstract=1757903; and Ole Varmer, *The Third World's Search for Equitable Access to the Geostationary Satellite Orbit*, 6 ILSA J. Int'l L. at 175) (1987). For discussion of the enduring significance of Common Heritage concept, *see* Graham Nicholson, *The Common Heritage of Mankind and Mining: An Analysis of the Law as to the High Seas, Outer Space, the Antarctic and World Heritage*, N.Z. J. Envtl L. 177, 197 (2002).

[337] Shackelford, *supra* note 38, at 25 and 30ff.

[338] *Id.* at 4.

[339] *Canada's Northern Strategy: Our North, Our Heritage, Our Future*, Ministry of Indian Affairs and Northern Development and Federal Interlocutor for Métis and Non-Status

assert the passage is an international strait between two high seas.[340] The legal distinction fundamentally affects the right to regulate shipping, marine pollution, and military surface and submerged transit.[341] It also affects air traffic, including foreign military aircraft. International law allows expeditious and nonhostile military air traffic over international straits. The United States rhetorically asserts this right *vis-à-vis* its close ally, Canada, leading to mischievous Canadian speculation about the US policy were Russia to assert the same right of North American passage for its airborne arsenal of bombers.[342]

To accommodate increasing traffic in the Northeast Passage, Russia has budgeted $1.2 billion to develop ice-resistant tankers and is expanding its considerable fleet of icebreakers, some of which are nuclear powered.[343] Like the Dutch and Venetians before, Russia has invested in an extended series

INDIANS (2009), www.northernstrategy.gc.ca/cns/cns-eng.asp (noting establishment of an Army Training Centre in Resolute Bay on the shore of the Northwest Passage and the "managed disagreements" between the United States and Canada regarding the maritime boundary in the Beaufort Sea and the legal status of the various waterways known as the Northwest Passage). *See also* Rob Huebert, *Climate Change and Canadian Sovereignty in the Northwest Passage*, in CALGARY PAPERS IN MILITARY AND STRATEGIC STUDIES (Occasional Paper Number 4) 383, 385 (John Ferris & P. Whitney Lackenbauer, eds., 2011). Most important, the Canadian claim that the Northwest Passage constitutes internal waters renders inapplicable the conventional right of "innocent passage." *See* Donat Pharand, *The Arctic Waters and the Northwest Passage: A Final Revisit*, 38 OCEAN DEV. & INT'L L. 3, 4 (2007).

[340] United States, National Security Presidential Directive and Homeland Security Presidential Directive, NSPD-66/HSPD-25 (Jan. 9, 2009), www.fas.org/irp/offdocs/nspd/nspd-66.htm (declaring the Northwest Passage and the Northern Sea Routes as straits used for international navigation, to which the regime of transit passage applies through both). *See also* Huebert, *supra* note 339, at 388 (noting "the United States and the European Union position is that, contrary to Canadian claims, the Northwest Passage is an international strait").

[341] The establishment of a Northwest Passage route would save 9,000km (4,860 nautical miles) in travel distance over traditional routes between Europe and Asia via the Panama Canal; larger vessels unable to transit the Panama Canal would save 17,000 km (9,180 nautical miles) as opposed to rounding Cape Horn; use of a Northern Sea Route rather than transiting the Suez Canal could cut the transit distance between Germany and Japan from around 11,400 to 7,200 nautical miles. *See* Clive Schofield, *Cold Rush: Exploring Arctic Myths and Misconceptions*, CURRENT INTELLIGENCE – THE ARCTIC (Mar. 27, 2013), www.currentintelligence.net/analysis/2013/3/27/cold-rush-exploring-arctic-myths-and-misconceptions.html.

[342] *See, e.g.*, Michael Byers, *The Northwest Passage Dispute Invites Russian Mischief*, NATIONAL POST (April 28, 2015), http://news.nationalpost.com/full-comment/michael-byers-the-northwest-passage-dispute-invites-russian-mischief. The observation is specious, however. It is doubtful Russia would attempt to assert the international character of the Northwest Passage as it would amount to a declaration against its own interests vis-à-vis the Northeast Passage. The important point to note is that Russia and Canada appear to be the best of enemies in relation to Arctic strait issues: They embrace the same territorializing interests over the respective passages.

[343] *Russia's Atomflot Inks Deal to Build World's Largest Nuclear Icebreaker*, BELLONA (Aug. 24, 2012), www.bellona.org/articles/articles_2012/biggest_icebreaker.

of (Arctic) trading posts,[344] and has been investing in its shore-based Siberian infrastructure since Stalin's 1932 announcement of the grand strategy to make the Soviet Arctic a symbol of national pride.[345] And like maritime nations of the seventeenth century, Russia's Northern Sea Route Administration has issued licenses, akin to Iberian *cartazes*, to numerous countries that seek transit across these northern waters, maintaining, like the European monarchs of the late-scholastic and early modern age, and over the objections of competing thalassocratic interests,[346] that the route traverses a *mare clausum* because the Northern Sea Route forms part of Russia's internal waters.[347]

We now turn our attention to the rise of territorial temptation with regard to this key strategic route followed by a discussion of the governing regime structure of the Arctic. The Ilulissat Declaration of May 2008,[348] issued by five countries rimming the Arctic Ocean (Canada, Denmark (via Greenland), Russia, Norway, and the United States), promised cooperation rather than competition in the area of the High Arctic. The creation of an Arctic Council in 1996 underscores this commitment as well.[349] But the coastal state signatories (the Arctic 5) made the claim that by virtue of their proximity to the Arctic Ocean, they were in the unique position to address unfolding possibilities and challenges, even more than Finland, Sweden, and Iceland, the other members of the eight-country Arctic Council not fronting the Arctic Ocean.[350] With the most capable, and in this case proximate, states suggesting that no new comprehensive regime would be needed to manage the Arctic, it remains to be seen whether the

---

[344] *See Arctic Ports*, NORTHERN SEA ROUTE INFORMATION OFFICE, www.arctic-lio.com/arcticports (the Russians are currently building the seventeenth Northern Sea Route port-city at Sabetta).

[345] *See* CHARLES EMMERSON, THE FUTURE HISTORY OF THE ARCTIC 36–42, (2010) (noting Stalin's Arctic initiative to establish *Glavsevmorput* in 1932, the Soviet agency charged with the development of the Arctic as a commercial and military asset).

[346] The United States and European Community object to Russia's claim of sovereignty over the Northern Sea Route.

[347] *See* Ronald O'Rourke, *Changes in the Arctic: Background and Issues for Congress*, Congressional Research Service 51 (Apr. 28, 2014), www.fas.org/sgp/crs/misc/R41153.pdf; and, Amendments to Certain legislative Acts of the Russian Federation Concerning State Regulation of Merchant Shipping in the Area of the Northern Sea Route, President of Russia (July 28, 2001), http://eng. kremlin.ru/news/4232 (defining the Northern Sea Route as encompassing Russia's internal waters).

[348] *The Ilulissat Declaration*, Arctic Ocean Conference (Greenland, May 27–29, 2008), www .oceanlaw.org/downloads/arctic/Ilulissat_Declaration.pdf.

[349] The 1996 Ottawa Declaration formally established the Arctic Council "to provide a means for promoting cooperation, coordination and interaction among the Arctic States, with the involvement of the Arctic Indigenous communities and other Arctic inhabitants on common Arctic issues; in particular, issues of sustainable development and environmental protection in the Arctic." *History of the Arctic Council*, THE ARCTIC COUNCIL (Apr. 7, 2011), www.arctic-council.org/index.php/en/about-us/arctic-council.

[350] *See* Margaret Blunden, *Geopolitics and the Northern Sea Route*, 88 INT'L AFF. 115, 121 (2012).

guiding principle will take the form of *mare liberum's* common use resurgent or *uti possidetis juris* recrudescent. Those who support the former idea, as is indicated by the movement to establish a democratic Arctic Circle Assembly,[351] have good reason to expect the latter in view of the Grotian tendency.

What also remains to be seen is whether these developments act as a bellwether for the deconstruction of the common use idea in other regions of a real or imagined transnational commons.[352] These areas include the problem of Antarctica,[353] where a moratorium holds in abeyance sovereign claims for the duration of the Antarctic Treaty;[354] in the East China and South China Seas, where competing claims of sovereignty clash with the ascending military and economic might of China and its emerging thalassocratic intentions;[355] and outer space, the last bastion of the Common Heritage idea, where once far-flung discussions of human colonization and resource extraction now take the form of earthly appropriations planning at the dawn of the age of outer space development.[356] Some of these regions are beyond the scope of this

---

[351] *See* Address of Ólafur Grímsson, President of Iceland, National Press Club, Apr. 15, 2013, http://press.org/news-multimedia/videos/npc-luncheon-%C3%B3lafur-gr%C3%ADmsson.

[352] *See* Shackelford, *supra* note 38, at 30. *See also* Nicholson, *supra* note 336 at 198 (concluding a need for more effective and universal enforcement of the common heritage principle to forestall "dissentient state action, confrontation and disunity" in areas including the moon and other celestial bodies, outer space, and world heritage areas).

[353] *See generally*, ERIC WILLIAM HUNTER CHRISTIE, THE ANTARCTIC PROBLEM: AN HISTORICAL AND POLITICAL STUDY (1951) (discussing specifically the historical territorial disputes among Great Britain, Argentina, and Chile).

[354] 1959 Antarctic Treaty, December 1, 1959, 402 UNTS 71, art IV(2), (entered into force June 23, 1961) (safeguarding the interests of states asserting, supporting, or denying a claim of territorial sovereignty while the treaty is in force). *See generally* Francesco Francioni, *Resource Sharing in Antarctica: For Whose Benefit?* EUR. J. INT'L L. 258 (1990).

[355] Currently seven Asian countries (China, Taiwan, The Philippines, Vietnam, Malaysia, Indonesia, Brunei) have made various and conflicting claims over the continental shelf of the South China Sea and its huge oil and gas reserves. *See South China Sea*, US ENERGY INFORMATION ADMINISTRATION (Feb. 7, 2013), www.eia.gov/countries/regions-topics.cfm?fips=SCS (estimating approximately 11 billion barrels of oil and 190 trillion cubic feet of natural gas in proved and probable reserves). *See also* Zrasul, *Politics Aside, The South China Sea Controversy Raises the Old Issue of How Far Does Your Continental Shelf Extend*, POLITICOANALYST (June 1, 2012), http://politicoanalyst.com/2012/06/01/politics-aside-the-south-china-sea-controversy-raises-the-old-issue-of-how-far-does-your-continental-shelf-extend/. A "war of diplomatic notes" has erupted over continental shelf extension claims. *See* Guifang (Julia) Xue, *Deep Danger: Intensified Competition in the South China Sea and Implications for China*, 17 OCEAN & COAST. L.J. 307, 311 (2012).

[356] EDYTHE WEEKS, OUTER SPACE DEVELOPMENT, INTERNATIONAL RELATIONS AND SPACE LAW: A METHOD FOR ELUCIDATING SEEDS xiii–xiv, and 6 (2012) (noting plans in the $58.4 billion 2010 NASA Authorization Act to privatize spacecraft development; create commercial space habitats, stations, and settlements; to initiate commercial space mining; and to engage in commercial spaceport construction in light of the 1967 Outer Space Treaty, which deems Outer Space "the province of mankind").

inquiry. But control over the Northeast and Northwest Passages, the Svalbard case, the regime structure of the Arctic and two unusual non-Arctic analogues involving Pacific waters – the Gulf of Fonseca and the arid corridor stretching to the Pacific across the Atacama Desert – each present a variation on the theme of common use and directly impact the problem of territorializing interests and the commons.

3

The Temptation of *Uti Possidetis*

On August 8, 2013, the *Yong Sheng*, a nineteen thousand ton cargo vessel laden with heavy equipment and steel operated by the Chinese-owned state-trading company, Cosco Group, set sail from the northeastern Chinese port of Dalian, en route to Rotterdam, The Netherlands.[1] The journey, between the world's largest exporting nation and Europe, the largest importer of Chinese goods, marked the maiden voyage of a Chinese merchant ship through the Northern Sea Route, a 5,400 kilometer (3,380 mile) passageway from the Bering to Kara Straits, a historically icebound and treacherous stretch of the fabled Northeast Passage, which straddles Eurasia from Providence Bay to Murmansk.[2] The route bypasses the traditional shipping lane around India and through the Suez Canal and Mediterranean Sea, and could potentially change global shipping patterns forever. It can shorten distance traveled by as much as 5,700 nautical miles,[3] or up to 60 percent over established southern routes,[4] reduce transit

---

[1] Tom Mitchell & Richard Milne, *Chinese Cargo Ship Sets Sail for Arctic Short-cut*, Fin. Times (Aug. 11, 2013), www.ft.com/intl/cms/s/2/05daa11e-0274-11e3-88od-00144feab7de.html# axzz2cnjuZR1n.

[2] *Id.*

[3] Distances vary depending on loading and discharge ports and detours encountered along the ice-riddled way. Norwegian shipping magnate, Felix Tschudi, in partnership with the Danish operator, Nordic Bulk Carriers, completed a voyage in September 2010 from Kirkenes, Norway, to Lianyungang, China, shortening the trip by 5,700 nautical miles over southern canal routes. See Felix H. Tschudi, *Time Equals Money: Developing a Profitable Shipping System Using the Northern Sea Route*, 70 Proceedings, Summer 2013, at 17–18, *available at* www.uscg.mil/proceedings/archive/2013/Vol70_No2_Sum2013.pdf. The *Young Sheng* arrived in Rotterdam on September 10, 2013, shaving approximately 2,800 nautical miles and nine transit days off the distance and time normally associated with the conventional routes through the Strait of Malacca and the Suez Canal. COSCO *Voyage Yong Sheng Arrives in Rotterdam, The Netherlands*, Xinhuanet News (Sept. 11, 2013), http://news.xinhuanet.com/english/photo/2013-09/11/c_132711222.htm.

[4] Nathan D. Mulherin, The Northern Sea Route: Its Development and Evolving State of Operations in the 1990s, US Army Corps of Engineers Cold Regions Research & Engineering

time by two to three weeks,[5] save five hundred metric tons of fuel[6] (equivalent to about six hundred thousand dollars per trip),[7] and avoid pirate-infested waters.[8] The voyage showcases clearly what geographers and discoverers have understood for more than a century: the Northeast Passage is the shortest maritime link between Europe and the Asia-Pacific region – were it only navigable.

Once considered completely impassable due to the icebound condition of the High Arctic, now with receding Arctic sea ice,[9] and projections of nearly ice-free polar seasons by century's end,[10] development of this geo-spatial region is a probability, with important consequences for an assortment of issues beyond sea transport.[11] But, rapid ice depletion presents questions about

---

Laboratory Report 96-3, 1 (Apr. 1996), *available at* http://acwc.sdp.sirsi.net/client/search/asset/ 1001334. *Cf.* David W. Titley & Courtney St. John, *Arctic Security Considerations and the U.S. Navy's Roadmap for the Arctic*, 63 NAVAL WAR C. REV. 35, 39 (Spring 2010).

[5] See Stan Jones, *Northern Sea Route Beckons LNG Shippers*, ALASKA NAT. GAS TRANSP. PROJECTS OFF. FED. COORDINATOR (Oct. 9, 2013), www.arcticgas.gov/northern-sea-route-beckons-lng-shippers (finding that by using the Northern Sea Route versus the Suez Canal, between sixteen and twenty-and-a-half days in transit are saved).

[6] See Tschudi, *supra* note 3, at 18.

[7] See Jennifer Cayias, *The Arctic Silk Road: As the U.S. Pivots East, Russia Pivots North*, STRATRISKS (Apr. 22, 2013), http://stratrisks.com/geostrat/12047 (referencing fuel savings projected by the Director General of Sovcomflot, Russia's state-owned oil and liquid natural gas shipping fleet). Other estimates project savings on the order of $3.5 million per transit. See Frédéric Lasserre & Sébastien Pelletier, *Polar Super Seaways? Maritime Transport in the Arctic: An Analysis of Shipowners' Intentions*, 19 J. TRANSP. GEOGRAPHY 1465, 1466 (2011), *available at* www.sciencedirect .com/science/article/pii/S0966692311001414.

[8] For a discussion of the prevalence of piracy, see Ved P. Nanda, *Maritime Piracy: How Can International Law and Policy Address This Growing Global Menace?* 39 DENV. J. INT'L L. & POL'Y 177 (2011).

[9] See Jason Samenow, *Snow and Arctic Sea Ice Extent Plummet Suddenly as Globe Bakes*, WASH. POST (July 18, 2013), www.washingtonpost.com/blogs/capital-weather-gang/wp/2013/07/18/snow-and-arctic-ice-extent-plummet-suddenly-as-globe-bakes/. In scientific terms, "ice-free" conditions do not necessitate complete lack of ice. For scientific definitions of varieties of sea ice, see *All About Sea Ice: Characteristics*, NAT'L SNOW & ICE DATA CENTER, http://nsidc.org/cryosphere/ seaice/characteristics/index.html.

[10] CTR. FOR ICE, CLIMATE AND ECOSYSTEMS, NORWEGIAN POLAR INST., MELTING SNOW AND ICE: A CALL FOR ACTION 36 (2009), *available at* www.regjeringen.no/upload/UD/Vedlegg/klima/melting_ ice_report.pdf. The US Navy's "Arctic Roadmap" projects ice-free conditions for portions of the summer beginning as early as 2030. See Titley & St. John, *supra* note 4, at 36. The term "ice free" does not mean water "free of ice": it means "the ice that once survived the seasonal melt cycle (the multiyear ice) will disappear leaving only first-year ice or annual sea ice[,]" which would be much thinner ice and easier to break up for marine transit. Lawson W. Brigham, *Arctic Marine Transportation*, in Y.B. SCI. & TECH. 9 (2012).

[11] RODERICK KEFFERPÜTZ, CTR. FOR EUROPEAN POLICY STUDIES, ON THIN ICE? (MIS)INTERPRET- ING RUSSIAN POLICY IN THE HIGH NORTH 1, 4–5 (2010), *available at* http://aei.pitt.edu/14550/ (noting the potential for oil, gas, and base and precious mineral resource exploitation); Robin McKie, *Russia Blocks Greenpeace Ship from Entering Arctic Waters*, THE GUARDIAN (Aug. 21, 2013), www.theguardian.com/environment/2013/aug/21/russia-blocks-greenpeace-ship-arctic

the legal status of increasingly accessible High Arctic resources, including the Northern Sea Route itself.

Current transits are miniscule in number compared to sea freight traffic elsewhere,[12] but an uptick in barge volume indicates heightened interest in using the Northeast Passage as an artery for world trade. The Soviets opened the route for international navigation in 1967, but vessels steered completely clear due to safety and profitability concerns.[13] The first non-Russian navigation of the route occurred in the summer of 1997.[14] In the summer of 2009, two German ships delivered oil-service equipment from South Korea to Rotterdam.[15] Four ships navigated the passage in 2010, thirty-four in 2011, forty-six in 2012; Russian authorities granted four hundred and fifty permits in 2013, and received over six hundred applications to sail all or part of the route in 2014.[16] Seventy-one vessels completed the whole or part of the route between the Bering Strait and the Barents Sea during the 2013 navigation season; twenty-three vessels sailed the entire route in 2014.[17] The captain of Russia's fleet of nuclear-powered icebreakers estimates that by 2021, fifteen million tons of cargo will traverse the full route and twenty-five million tons of Russian oil and liquefied natural gas will traffic the route as exports to Asia and Europe.[18] This latter point indicates that most of the volume of trade for possibly

(discussing global warming and Arctic environmental consequences); MARK BURNETT ET AL., WORLD WILDLIFE FUND, ILLEGAL FISHING IN ARCTIC WATERS: CATCH OF TODAY – GONE TOMORROW? 1 (2008), *available at* www.wwf.se/source.php/1173651/Illegal%20fishing%20in%20 Arctic%20waters.pdf (reporting on illegal, unregulated, and unreported fishing in Arctic waters as a significant threat).

12 *Arctic Shipping Holds Great Promise for Asia*, UPI (Aug. 21, 2013), www.upi.com/Business_ News/Energy-Resources/2013/08/21/Arctic-shipping-holds-great-promise-for-Asia/ 1842137108030/ (noting in 2011 almost eighteen thousand vessels transporting 929 million tons of cargo passed through the Suez Canal).

13 Alexander S. Skaridov, *Northern Sea Route: Legal Issues and Current Transportation Practice, in* CHANGES IN THE ARCTIC ENVIRONMENT AND THE LAW OF THE SEA 283, 294 (Myron H. Nordquist et al., eds., 2010) [hereinafter CHANGES IN THE ARCTIC ENVIRONMENT].

14 See Andrew C. Revkin, *Commercial Arctic Passage Nearing Goal*, N.Y. TIMES (Sept. 4, 2009), http://dotearth.blogs.nytimes.com/2009/09/04/commercial-arctic-passage-nearing-goal/ (noting the transit in summer of 1997 of the *Uikku*, under a Finnish flag, and Russian reports of a Latvian-flag tanker also completing a full transit in 1997).

15 See Andrew E. Kramer & Andrew C. Revkin, *Arctic Shortcut Beckons Shippers as Ice Thaws*, N.Y. TIMES (Sept. 10, 2009), www.nytimes.com/2009/09/11/science/earth/11passage.html?_r=0.

16 See Ben Anderson, *Yong Sheng: Why Arctic Voyage of Chinese Cargo Ship is Business as Usual*, ALASKA DISPATCH NEWS (Sept. 1, 2013), www.alaskadispatch.com/article/20130901/yong-sheng-why-arctic-voyage-chinese-cargo-ship-business-usual; see also Hector Martin, *Northern Sea Route: From Short-Cut to Long-Shot*, THE ARCTIC JOURNAL (Jan. 9, 2016), http://arcticjournal .com/business/1229/short-cut-long-shot (noting over six hundred applications).

17 See Trude Pettersen, *Fifty Percent Increase on Northern Sea Route*, BARENTS OBSERVER (Dec. 3, 2013), http://barentsobserver.com/en/arctic/2013/12/fifty-percent-increase-northern-sea-route-03-12; and Martin, *supra* note 16 (noting "immense" interest but a slight dip in transits).

18 *See generally* Mitchell & Milne, *supra* note 1.

decades to come will be limited to and directed from *entrepôts* in Russia accessed through the Barents Sea in the west, or the Bering Sea in the east. Geographers and oceanographers repeatedly tamp down enthusiastic political assessments of trans-arctic passage,[19] noting the region remains an exceedingly dangerous place for human activity.[20] They caution one should not soon expect the opening of an Arctic version of the Panama or Suez Canal.[21] But potential gains from a rapidly changing environment and costs associated with a lack of contingency planning contribute to a sense of urgency among US policy-makers.[22]

In May 2010, the Obama Administration released its National Security Strategy document, which specifically referenced the Arctic region. The United States proclaimed itself "an Arctic Nation with broad and fundamental interests in the Arctic region, where we seek to meet our national security needs, protect the environment, responsibly manage resources, account for indigenous communities, support scientific research, and strengthen international cooperation on a wide range of issues."[23]

[19] *See* Gleb Bryanski, *Russia's Putin Says Arctic Trade Route to Rival Suez*, REUTERS CAN. (Sept. 22, 2011), *available at* http://ca.reuters.com/article/topNews/idCATRE78L5TC20110922 (quoting Russian Prime Minister Vladimir Putin's 2011 prediction that the Northern Sea route would soon "rival traditional trade lanes").

[20] See Thor Edward Jakobsson, *Climate Change and the Northern Sea Route: An Icelandic Perspective, in* INTERNATIONAL ENERGY POLICY, THE ARCTIC AND THE LAW OF THE SEA 285, at 292–301 (Myron H. Nordquist et al., eds., 2005) (referring specifically to the Arctic coastal region from the Vilkitsky Strait to the Bering Strait as "one of the most challenging ship operating environments on the planet").

[21] Lawson W. Brigham, *Think Again: The Arctic*, FOREIGN POL'Y (Aug. 6, 2010), www.foreignpolicy .com/2010/08/06/think-again-the-arctic/; see also comments by Lawson Brigham, *Edited Transcription of Question and Answer Session Panels III & IV, in* CHANGES IN THE ARCTIC ENVIRONMENT, *supra* note 13, at 307–308 (questioning the economics of Arctic coastal routes); and Skaridov, *supra* note 13, at 283, 299–300 (questioning the profitability of the Northern Sea Route as a European-Asian transit route).

[22] *See, e.g.,* H.R. REP. NO. 111–491 (2010) (accompanying H.R. 5136 the National Defense Authorization Act for Fiscal Year 2011), *available at* www.gpo.gov/fdsys/pkg/CRPT-111hrpt491/ html/CRPT-111hrpt491.htm; The White House, National Security Presidential Directive and Homeland Security Presidential Directive NSPD-66/HSPD-25 (2009), *available at* http://fas .org/irp/offdocs/nspd/nspd-66.htm (establishing US policy with respect to the Arctic region) [hereinafter National Security Presidential Directive 66]; DEP'T OF DEF., REPORT TO CONGRESS ON ARCTIC OPERATIONS AND THE NORTHWEST PASSAGE (2011), *available at* www.defense.gov/ pubs/pdfs/tab_a_arctic_report_public.pdf; *see also* Ariel Cohen, *Russia in the Arctic: Challenges to U.S. Energy and Geopolitics in the High North, in* RUSSIA IN THE ARCTIC 1, 2 (Stephen Blank, ed., 2011) (noting the USA "largely ignored" the region until the "11th hour of the Bush administration," and noting also the Obama Administration has been "slow to move on the issue"); *see also* Scott Borgerson, *The Coming Arctic Boom*, 92 FOREIGN AFF., 76, 86 (July–Aug. 2013) (noting the United States still seems asleep while the rest of the world has woken to the Arctic's growing importance).

[23] THE WHITE HOUSE, NATIONAL SECURITY STRATEGY 50 (2010), *available at* www.whitehouse.gov/ sites/default/files/rss_viewer/national_security_strategy.pdf.

The document reiterated national security interests identified in National Security Presidential Directive 66, released on January 12, 2009 by President George W. Bush.[24] On May 10, 2013, the Obama Administration supplemented emerging Arctic policy by releasing its National Strategy for the Arctic Region.[25] This document specifically sets forth strategic priorities to respond to challenges emerging "from significant increases in Arctic activity due to the diminishment of sea ice."[26] One of the priorities is enabling US "vessels and aircraft to operate, consistent with international law, through, under, and over the airspace and waters of the Arctic."[27] Safe commercial operations and national defense are specific US Arctic interests.[28] Underscoring US interest in the area is the February 14, 2014 State Department announcement creating an Arctic Ambassador position to deal with the "very rare convergence of almost every national priority in the most rapidly-changing region on the face of the earth."[29]

The inclusion of Arctic issues in the US National Security Strategy blueprint indicates that the United States intends to make this mostly landless mass its next frontier.[30] It is not alone. On February 20, 2013, Russian President Vladimir Putin announced Russia's Arctic development strategy for the period up to 2020,[31] an encompassing two-part action plan foreshadowed by Soviet General Secretary Mikhail Gorbachev's important 1987 Murmansk Initiative speech. There, Gorbachev pledged to open the Northern Sea Route to foreign

[24] National Security Presidential Directive 66, *supra* note 22 (proclaiming the United States "an Arctic nation, with varied and compelling interests in that region").

[25] THE WHITE HOUSE, NATIONAL STRATEGY FOR THE ARCTIC REGION 1–11 (2013), *available at* www.whitehouse.gov/sites/default/files/docs/nat_arctic_strategy.pdf (with a cover letter from President Barack Obama dated May 10, 2013).

[26] *Id.* at 2.

[27] *Id.*

[28] Press Release, White House Office of the Press Sec'y, National Security Presidential Directive/ NSPD–66: Arctic Region Policy (Jan. 9, 2009), *available at* www.marad.dot.gov/documents/ Arctic_Policy_White_House.pdf.

[29] Press Statement, Sec'y of State, US Dept. of State, Secretary Kerry Announces Department Will Establish a Special Representative for the Arctic Region (Feb. 14, 2014), *available at* www.state .gov/secretary/remarks/2014/02/221678.htm.

[30] *See generally* HEATHER A. CONLEY ET AL., THE NEW POLICY FRONTIER: U.S. INTERESTS AND ACTORS IN THE ARCTIC (2013). But cf. Brigham, *supra* note 21 (discounting prospects the Arctic region will turn into a geopolitical flashpoint).

[31] *Putin Approved the Arctic Development Strategy to 2020*, ARCTIC INFO (Feb. 20, 2013), www.arctic-info.com/News/Page/putin-approved-the-arctic-development-strategy-to-2020. The English translation of the document is: "The Strategy for the Development of the Arctic Zone of the Russian Federation and National Security up to 2020." *See* Lassi Heininen et al., *New Russian Arctic Doctrine: From Idealism to Realism?* VALDAI (July 15, 2013), http://valdaiclub .com/russia_ and_the_world/60220.html.

commercial traffic.[32] Now, Putin has made that pledge Russia's national ambition. Putin's strategy extends Russia's complicated psychological history with its northern expanse. This history is marked by Russia's long-held desire to conquer its Arctic interior. Russia intends to civilize its economic geography, rebrand Siberia as the engine of Russia's prosperous future rather than the gulag-region of its notorious past, and shed its ambivalent, sometimes suspicious, attitude toward the High North by dominating this harsh natural world through science and technology.[33]

Despite fits and starts, Russia's presence in the Arctic is now commanding. While US lawmakers debate adding an icebreaker to their aging fleet of four (commissioned to patrol both polar seas),[34] Russia launched in June 2016 the world's most advanced nuclear-powered icebreaker,[35] with more of them planned,[36] to complement its Arctic fleet of seven atomic vessels[37] and

---

[32] Heather Exner-Pirot, *How Gorbachev Shaped Future Arctic Policy 25 Years Ago*, ALASKA DISPATCH (Oct. 1, 2012), www.alaskadispatch.com/article/how-gorbachev-shaped-future-arctic-policy-25-years-ago. *See also* Ronald Purver, *Arctic Security: The Murmansk Initiative and Its Impact*, 11 CURRENT RESEARCH ON PEACE & VIOLENCE 147–158 (1988). Part one of the strategy calls for a formulation of internal boarders by 2015, followed by a second stage, which will create sustainable means for resource extraction, socioeconomic development and environmental and security improvements. *See Russia Pushing Ahead with Arctic Development in New Strategy Document*, BELLONA (Mar. 5, 2013), www.bellona.org/articles/articles_2013/Russia_arctic_push.

[33] *See* CHARLES EMMERSON, THE FUTURE HISTORY OF THE ARCTIC 35–42 (2010) (discussing the Czar's imperial economic and managerial policy of maintaining Moscow's periphery as a pool of historical stagnation and Stalin's 1932 establishment of *Glavsevmorput*, a bureaucratic consolidation of Arctic agencies with a mandate to develop the region economically).

[34] The Coast Guard maintains three multi-mission icebreaking vessels: the *Polar Star*, *Polar Sea*, and *Healy*. Ronald O'Rourke, *Coast Guard Polar Icebreaker Modernization: Background and Issues for Congress* 2–6 (Congressional Research Service, RL34391, 2015), www.fas.org/sgp/crs/weapons/RL34391.pdf. The first two were commissioned in the early 1970s and designed for thirty years of service. *Id.* at 3. The *Polar Star* has been placed in caretaker status in 2006 but has undergone extensive repairs and became operational again in 2012; the *Healy* was commissioned in 2000. *Id.* at 4–5. The National Science Foundation operates a fourth icebreaker, a single-mission ship built in 1992 to support scientific research in Antarctica, the *Nathaniel B. Palmer*. *Id.* at 6.

[35] *See* Camila Domonoske, *Russia Launches World's Biggest, Most Powerful Icebreaker*, NPR (June 16, 2016), www.npr.org/sections/thetwo-way/2016/06/16/482288188/russia-launches-worlds-biggest-most-powerful-icebreaker.

[36] *Russia as a World Leader in Nuclear-Powered Icebreaker Fleet Construction*, SPUTNIK (Sept. 9, 2012), http://sputniknews.com/voiceofrussia/2012_09_09/Russia-as-a-world-leader-in-nuclear-powered-icebreaker-fleet-construction/.

[37] Jared Allen, *The Northern Sea Route as a Viable Development–Russia's Fleet of Atomic Icebreakers*, ARCTICECON (Oct. 1, 2012), http://arcticecon.wordpress.com/2012/10/01/the-northern- sea-route-as-a-viable-development-russias-fleet-of-atomic-icebreakers/.

twenty smaller diesel-powered ships.[38] In 2012, the State of Alaska undertook a one million dollar feasibility study to create an Arctic deep water port along its 927–mile Arctic coastline;[39] that same year, Russia began constructing a $2.25 billion port at Sabetta on the Yamal Peninsula[40] – its seventeenth deep water port along its 10,874–mile Arctic coastline.[41] With not a single search-and-rescue aircraft based in the Arctic,[42] the Canadian Coast Guard once took six days to rescue a stranded cruise ship and oil tanker; the Commandant of the US Coast Guard estimated it would have taken the United States six weeks to mount a similar rescue mission.[43] Indeed, "[t]he United States has no Arctic deep water port, no military aviation facility in the region, and no comprehensive network for monitoring Arctic shipping."[44] Russia, however, is building ten search-and-rescue stations in the Arctic and fortifying each with aircraft, icebreakers, on-board helicopters, and military-support capability.[45]

Bureaucratic inefficiency has been identified as the Achilles' heel of US policy implementation in the Arctic,[46] a claim also, certainly historically, associated with Russian administrative acumen.[47] While serious logistical concerns

---

[38] Paul Gobel, *Window on Eurasia: "How Many Icebreakers Does Russia Need?,"* JOHNSON'S RUSSIA LIST (Aug. 14, 2013), http://russialist.org/how-many-icebreakers-does-russia-need/. Estimates suggest five to six nuclear ships and up to ten nonnuclear icebreakers would be needed to keep open and safe the Northern Sea Route corridor. *Id.*

[39] Paula Lowther, *Arctic Deep Water Port,* ALASKA BUS. MONTHLY (Jan. 4, 2012), *available at* www .akbizmag.com/Alaska-Business-Monthly/January-2012/Arctic-Deep-Water-Port/.

[40] The port at Sabetta includes construction of a twenty-five-billion-ruble liquid natural gas plant and has been acclaimed by officials as the "beginning of the future development of the entire Arctic region." *Construction of Sabetta Port on the Yamal Peninsula,* ARCTIC INFO (July 23, 2012), www.arctic-info.com/News/Page/construction-of-sabetta-port-on-the-yamal-peninsula.

[41] *See* Michael Byers, *Canada's Arctic Nightmare Just Came True: The Northwest Passage is Commercial,* GLOBE & MAIL (Sept. 20, 2013), www.theglobeandmail.com/globe-debate/canadas-arctic-nightmare-just-came-true-the-northwest-passage-is-commercial/article14432440/.

[42] *See* Michael Byers, *The (Russian) Arctic is Open for Business,* GLOBE & MAIL (Aug. 12, 2013), www .theglobeandmail.com/commentary/the-russian-arctic-is-open-for-business/article13696054/.

[43] *See* Ronald O'Rourke, *Changes in the Arctic: Background and Issues for Congress* 45 (Congressional Research Service., R41153, 2014), www.fas.org/sgp/crs/misc/R41153.pdf (footnote omitted). *See also* Lowther, *supra* note 39 (noting the port at Kodiak Island, 940 air miles from Point Barrow, Alaska, is the most northern base for the US Coast Guard, greatly reducing its ability to respond to Arctic emergencies).

[44] Borgerson, *supra* note 22, at 87.

[45] *See* Byers, *supra* note 42.

[46] CONLEY ET AL., *supra* note 30, at 5.

[47] Soviet management of the Northern Sea Route began in 1932 with the Glavsevmorput administration which operated until 1954, when administrative responsibilities were turned over to the Ministry of Maritime Fleet (MINMORFLOT), followed by another administrative reshuffling in 1970. Skaridov, *supra* note 13, at 292. Following dissolution of the USSR, the Russian Ministry of Transportation took charge. *Id.* Thereafter, icebreaker administration was privatized. *Id.* Following the promulgation of the Merchant Maritime Code in 1999, the Ministry of Transportation again took charge of navigation safety and hydrographic survey. *Id.* Later,

persist,[48] Russia recently consolidated its Northern Sea Route Administration under an eponymous title, located the agency in Moscow to quiet bickering among competing cities on its northern tier,[49] and identified regional stream-lining as the first prong of its two-part Arctic development strategy.[50] Like sixteenth-century European advocates of *mare clausum*, Russia recently began collecting tolls, issuing licenses, regulating traffic, providing escort service, and policing the route's sea-lanes.[51]

Russia is the only country with millions of citizens living above the Arctic Circle.[52] It generates 20 percent of its Gross Domestic Product in the Arctic, has $355 billion in energy projects underway or planned with the Chinese alone,[53] a "tricky" but formidable Arctic economic relationship with Europe,[54]

Atomflot took control of management and operational safety of Russia's nuclear powered icebreaker fleet. *Id.*

[48] *See* Revkin, *supra* note 14 (referencing retired US Coast Guard polar Captain Lawson Brigham's observation that Russian bureaucracy more than sea ice may be impeding international use of the Northern Sea Route). *See also* Pavel Baev, *Op-Ed.*, *Putin's Blurred Arctic Vision*, Moscow Times (Aug. 15, 2013), www.themoscowtimes.com/opinion/article/putins-blurred-arctic-vision/484579 .html (assessing Russia's Arctic policy as "a muddle of inflated goals and eroding capabilities").

[49] Atle Staalesen, *Opening the Northern Sea Route Administration*, Barents Observer (Mar. 21, 2013), http://barentsobserver.com/en/arctic/2013/03/opening-northern-sea-route-administration-21-03.

[50] *See Putin Approved the Arctic Development Strategy to 2020, supra* note 31.

[51] *See*, e.g., Steven Lee Myers, *Russia Seizes Greenpeace Ship and Crew for Investigation*, N.Y. Times (Sept. 20, 2013), www.nytimes.com/2013/09/21/world/europe/russia-seizes-greenpeace-ship-for-investigation.html?_r=0 (reporting on Russia's Federal Security Service seizure of a Greenpeace International ship in the Pechora Sea near the island of Novaya Zemlya and the gateway to the Northern Sea Route).

[52] *Population*, The Arctic, http://arctic.ru/geography-population/population (undated) (citing about half of the Arctic's population of four million lives in Russia). For a demographic breakdown of polar populations by country, *see* Hugo Ahlenius, UNEP/GRID-Arendal, Population Distribution in the Circumpolar Arctic, by Country (Including Indigenous Population) (2008), *available at* www.grida.no/graphicslib/detail/population-distribution-in-the-circumpolar-arctic-by-country-including-indigenous-population_1282.

[53] Michael Byers, *China Could Be the Future of Arctic Oil*, Aljazeera (Aug. 22, 2013), www .aljazeera.com/indepth/opinion/2013/08/201382113589162420.html (noting $25 billion in Chinese investments in Siberian-to-China pipeline and offshore Arctic oil fields). A "break-through" of understanding signed between Russia's state oil company, OAO Rosneft, and China National Petroleum Corp. in October 2013 allows for a massive oil and gas joint venture in the Arctic, adding three hundred thousand barrels per day increase of crude exports from Russia to China in a deal valued at $270 billion. *See* Wayne Ma & Lukas Alpert, *Russia Lets Down Guard on China: Deal by Oil Giants to Jointly Explore Siberia Reserves Follows Spate of Chinese Inroads Around Globe*, Wall St. J. (Oct. 19, 2013), http://online.wsj.com/news/articles/SB1000142405270 2304410204579143001850172282.

[54] Christophe-Alexandre Paillard, *Russia and Europe's Mutual Energy Dependence*, 63 Colum. J. Int'l Aff. 65 (Spring/Summer 2010); *see also* Leon Aron, *The Political Economy of Russian Oil and Gas*, Am. Enterprise Inst. (May 29, 2013), www.aei.org/outlook/foreign-and-defense-policy/regional/europe/the-political-economy-of-russian-oil-and-gas/ (noting Russia's leading role as a

and a "firm and persistent" declaratory policy toward the region, which is enhanced by strengthened border controls[55] and newly deployed army brigades and navy vessels.[56]

A swirl of international activity now surrounds the High Arctic. Already multiple disputes have arisen regarding competing claims of sovereignty over mineral resources on the floor of the Arctic Ocean.[57] Three Arctic coastal states – Canada, Russia, and Norway – are preparing territorial claims over vast portions of the Arctic Basin, including claims for extended continental shelves, which are to be submitted to the CLCS in accordance with Article 76 of UNCLOS; Denmark submitted a claim in late 2014, which includes the North Pole and 895,000 square kilometers of the Arctic.[58] The fifth Arctic coastal state, the United States, is not a party to UNCLOS, but, nevertheless, has been gathering scientific data since 2001,[59] which could serve as the basis for its own claim to an extended continental shelf.[60] All of these claims, if perfected, will substantially close off the continental margins of the Artic Basin and dramatically decrease access to mineral resources sometimes regarded as part of the global commons, to the extent the global commons is an object of attention at all.[61]

European energy provider and Europe's increasing concerns about Russian energy price-fixing); and *Statoil Writes Off $336 mln Shtokman Gas Investment*, REUTERS (Aug. 7, 2012), *available at* www.reuters.com/article/2012/08/07/statoil-shtokman-idUSL6E8J76LB20120807 (detailing the breakdown of Norwegian/French/Russian joint venture to develop the huge offshore Shtokman gas project in the Barents Sea).

55 *See* Lawson W. Brigham, *Russia Opens Its Maritime Arctic*, U.S. NAVAL INST.: PROCE., May 2011, at 50, 54 (noting enhancement efforts of Russia's Federal Security Service); *see also* Margaret Blunden, *Geopolitics and the Northern Sea Route*, 88 INT'L AFF. 115, 116 (2012).

56 *See Russia Dispatches Naval Force to Reopen Arctic Base*, YAHOO NEWS (Sept. 6, 2014), http:// news.yahoo.com/russia-dispatches-naval-force-reopen-arctic-112019010.html (discussing Russia's reopening of mothballed Cold War naval base on the New Siberian islands); *Putin Vows to Beef Up Russia's Arctic Military Presence*, CBS NEWS (Dec. 10, 2013, 11:33 A.M.), www .cbsnews.com/news/putin-vows-to-beef-up-russias-arctic-military-presence/ (specifically noting enhancement of Soviet-era military bases to protect Arctic shipping routes); David Greene, *Russia Pushes to Claim Arctic as Its Own Pt. 2*, NAT'L PUB. RADIO SPECIAL SERIES (Aug. 16, 2011), www.npr.org/2011/08/16/139577789/russia-pushes-to-claim-arctic-as-its-own (noting Russia's two new army brigade deployments to the region).

57 *See*, e.g., Mel Weber, *Defining the Outer Limits of the Continental Shelf Across the Arctic Basin: The Russian Submission, States' Rights, Boundary Delimitation and Arctic Regional Cooperation*, 24 INT'L J. MARINE & COASTAL L. 653 (2009).

58 For background information on the convention, *see generally* THE UNITED NATIONS LAW OF THE SEA TREATY INFORMATION CENTER, www.unlawoftheseatreaty.org/. On Denmark's submission, *see* Richard Milne, *Denmark's Claim to North Pole Fans Geopolitical Rivalry*, FIN. TIMES (Dec. 18, 2015), www.ft.com/intl/cms/s/0/49a5a1ca-85e3-11e4-b11b-00144feabdc0.html#axzz3wmSe5p8c.

59 *See* Weber, *supra* note 57, at 669–670, 677–679.

60 National Strategy for the Arctic Region, *supra* note 25, at 9 (noting that a US claim could extend more than six hundred nautical miles from the north coast of Alaska).

61 *See generally* Scott J. Shackelford, *Was Selden Right?: The Expansion of Closed Seas and Its Consequences*, 47 STAN. J. INT'L L. 1 (2011).

Changes to the Arctic cryosphere, attributed to global warming, have also generated renewed focus on unresolved territorial disputes among Arctic powers: the United States and Canada dispute their boundary in the Beaufort Sea;[62] the United States and Russia have yet to perfect an agreement delimiting a shared border in the Bering Sea;[63] Canada and Denmark contest territorial control over Hans Island, a barren rock-scape between Greenland and Canada's Ellesmere Island;[64] and Canada claims the Northwest Passage as part of its internal waters, making it subject to its complete sovereign control.[65]

This latter claim created what is possibly the greatest fissure in United States-Canadian relations since the *Caroline Incident* of 1837,[66] a relationship commonly regarded as among the closest bilateral relationships in the world.[67] The United States, and less explicitly the European Union,[68] counter that this passageway, consisting of varying routes through the nineteen thousand–island Canadian Arctic Archipelago, constitutes an international strait between two high seas, affording any country the right to pass freely in accordance with

---

[62] *See, e.g.,* James S. Baker & Michael Byers, *Crossed Lines: The Curious Case of the Beaufort Sea Maritime Boundary Dispute*, 43 OCEAN DEV. & INT'L L. 70 (2012).

[63] The US Senate provided its advice and consent to the agreement in 1991, but the Russian *Duma* has refused to take action. Alex G. Oude Elferink, *Arctic Maritime Delimitations: The Preponderance of Similarities with Other Regions, in* THE LAW OF THE SEA AND POLAR MARITIME DELIMITATION AND JURISDICTION 179, 183 n. 15 (Alex G. Oude Elfernick & Donald R. Rothwell, eds., 2001).

[64] Michael Byers, *Hans Island: Creative Thinking on Sovereignty, Who Owns the Arctic?*, ARCTIC SOVEREIGNTY & INT'L REL. (Mar. 7, 2014), http://byers.typepad.com/arctic/hans-island/.

[65] *See generally* Donat Pharand, *Canada's Sovereignty over the Northwest Passage*, 10 MICH. J. INT'L L. 653 (1989).

[66] *See generally* Kenneth R. Stevens, BORDER DIPLOMACY: THE CAROLINE AND MCLEOD AFFAIRS IN ANGLO-AMERICAN-CANADIAN RELATIONS, 1837–1842 (1989) (involving a violent cross-border skirmish between American and British subjects, and its aftermath, which resulted in the doctrine of anticipatory self defense). *See also* R. Y. Jennings, *The Caroline and McLeod Cases*, 32 AM. J. INT'L L. 82 (1938) (discussing the incident and seizure of a British subject associated with the incident subsequently found on American territory).

[67] *See, e.g., U.S. Relations with Canada*, U.S. DEP'T OF STATE (Sept. 10, 2014), www.state.gov/r/pa/ei/bgn/2089.htm (describing the bilateral relationship as "one of the closest and most extensive in the world"). *See also Canada-U.S. Relations*, GOV'T OF CANADA, www.can-am.gc.ca/relations/index.aspx?lang=eng (describing the bilateral relationship as "unique," "deep," and "powerful").

[68] Michael Byers, *Toward a Canada-Russia Axis in the Arctic*, GLOBAL BRIEF (Feb. 6, 2012), http://globalbrief.ca/blog/2012/02/06/toward-a-canada-russia-axis-in-the-arctic/ (noting the focus of the European objection centered on the "unusual length of several of the baselines rather than on "the adoption of the lines as such, or the internal waters claim specifically"). The European Community, through the British High Commission in Ottawa, also contested Canada's claim of historic title. *See* Michael Byers & Suzanne Lalonde, *Who Controls the Northwest Passage?* 42 VAND. J. TRANSNAT'L L. 1133, 1162 (citing British High Comm'n Note No. 90/86 of July 1986) (footnote omitted).

the doctrine of transit passage.[69] The right of submarines to pass through international straits without surfacing, and the right of overflight – rights that do not extend to regimes governing internal or territorial waters – are critical.[70]

International law distinguishes between internal waters and other pelagic regimes.[71] Foreign vessels have no right to access the former without permission.[72] With respect to Canada, the United States has gone out of its way twice to assert the international character of the waterway. In 1969, it sent the ice-strengthened supertanker, *USS Manhattan*, and in 1985 the Coast Guard Cutter (USCGC), *Polar Sea*, through the Northwest Passage without seeking Canada's permission.[73] These actions caused an uproar in Canada and resulted in numerous consequences that complicated US policy interests,[74]

---

[69] Byers, *supra* note 68. *See* O'Rourke, *supra* note 43, at 17 (noting the interests of the US Navy and Coast Guard for expanded surface ship operations to defend the US and EU claim that the Northern Sea Route (and the Northwest Passage) constitute international straits, which allow right of innocent passage).

[70] *See* UNCLOS, *supra* note 58, art. 39, ¶ 2 (requiring "ships and aircraft, while exercising the right of transit passage, shall … refrain from any activities other than those incident to their normal modes of continuous and expeditious transit unless rendered necessary by *force majeure* or by distress"). A normal mode of transit for a submarine includes submerged transit.

[71] *See id.*, art. 8, ¶ 1 (defining internal waters as "waters on the landward side of the baseline of the territorial sea").

[72] Louise de La Fayette, *Access to Ports in International Law*, 11 INT'L J. MARINE & COASTAL L. 1, 1 (1996) (noting ports situated in a state's internal waters form part of its sovereign territory).

[73] *See* Elizabeth B. Elliot-Meisel, *The Northwest Passage in Canadian-American Relations, 1946–1998*, AM. REV. CANADIAN STUD. 407, 412–415 (1999) (noting the United States specifically did not ask Canada for permission and avoided any gesture that "could be interpreted as recognition of Canadian sovereignty"). *The Manhattan* diverted its intended route after encountering ice trouble in the M'Clure Strait, forcing it to double back and pass through Canadian territorial waters. *See* Byers & Lalonde, *supra* note 68, at 1149–1150.

[74] The incidents galvanized Canadian public and political opinion and resulted in numerous and significant responses. Canada redefined the breadth of its territorial sea from three nautical miles to twelve, affecting entrances to the Northwest Passage at the Barrow Strait in the Pacific and the Prince of Wales Strait in the Atlantic. *See generally* Elliot-Meisel, *supra* note 73. Canada pushed through the controversial Canadian Arctic Water Pollution Prevention Act, which articulated a 100-mile environmental protection zone, which affected shipping regulation. *Id.* It also broadened its understanding of the doctrine of "innocent passage" to include environmental issues. *Id.* In 1973 and 1975, Canada reasserted its claim over all archipelagic waters as historic internal waters and took a leading role – along with the Soviets – in conversations leading up to the adoption of Article 234 of the 1982 UNCLOS, which grants coastal states upgraded administrative and environmental regulatory authority in ice-covered areas. *Id.* Following the *Polar Sea* transit in 1985, Canada also implemented the practice of drawing straight baselines; commissioned construction of an addition to its icebreaker fleet; dramatically committed to enlarging its military presence with a "three ocean navy," with specific intentions of acquiring ten to twelve nuclear-powered attack submarines at the feared expense of its NATO financial commitments; and enhanced sonar and aerial surveillance measures. *Id. See also* Donald R. Rothwell, *The Canadian-U.S. Northwest Passage Dispute: A Reassessment*, 26 CORNELL INT'L L.J. 331, 339–345 (1993) (discussing Canadian responses to the incidents).

some with lingering effect.[75] But these events have underscored the US assertion that the Northwest Passage is an international strait between high seas that has an international navigation use, an essential criterion identified by the ICJ in the 1949 *Corfu Channel Case.*[76]

As the closest of allies, Canada and the United States politely agreed to disagree on the legal status of the Northwest Passage.[77] In the joint 1988 Agreement on Arctic Cooperation, the United States pledged, without conceding its position, that all future "navigation by US icebreakers within waters claimed by Canada to be internal will be undertaken with the consent of the Government of Canada."[78] Interestingly, the United States' persistent objection to Canada's claim probably does not concern Canada at all, and perhaps never did. Rather, recognition of Canada's claim would compromise US seaborne interests elsewhere, most proximately with Russia, its far less accommodating neighbor.[79] Like Canada, and again over the objections of the United

---

[75] *See generally* Byers, *supra* note 68. For an example of the negative lingering effect of Canadian Arctic policy on an American scholar's perspective, *see* James Kraska, *International Security and International Law in the Northwest Passage*, 42 Vand. J. Transnat'l L. 1109 (2009) (referring to Canada's Arctic policy as "audacious," "hypersensitive," projecting a "Northern mythos," operating under a "unilateralist spell," with Canadian scholars projecting "slightly tortured theories").

[76] Corfu Channel Case (U.K. v. Alb.), Judgment, 1949 I.C.J. 4, 28 (holding that the right of innocent passage in straits used for international navigation in time of peace is a customary norm of general international law).

[77] Telegram from US State Department to Canada (May 17, 1985), reprinted in J. Ashley Roach & Robert W. Smith, Excessive Maritime Claims 209 (1994).

[78] Agreement Between the Government of Canada and the Government of the United States of America on Arctic Cooperation, U.S.-Can., Jan. 11, 1988, 1852 U.N.T.S. 60, reprinted in Roach & Smith, *supra* note 77, at 212–213.

[79] *See generally* Suzanne Lalonde & Frédéric Lasserre, *The Position of the United States on the Northwest Passage: Is the Fear of Creating a Precedent Warranted?*, 44 Ocean Dev. & Int'l L. 28, 54–58 (2013), surveying cases involving US protests of straits declared internal to coastal states; the authors surveyed thirty-four potential straits worldwide and concluded seven, possibly eight, straits involving, *inter alia*, the Mediterranean Sea, Sea of Japan, Black Sea, South China Sea, and Indian Ocean might be affected by US recognition of Canadian sovereignty over the Northwest Passage. *See also* Byers & Lalonde, *supra* note 68, at 1187 (noting the US Navy concern that recognizing Canada's claim could "create a precedent for coastal state control over other contested waterways") (footnote omitted). In a most thorough review of the military and strategic value of the Northern Sea Route and US (and Russian) interest in preserving a right of submerged transit through straits, R. Douglas Brubaker and Willy Østreng concluded that the military interests in the Northern Sea Route are "low" but that the supreme consideration for the US military is preserving the freedom of navigation globally and in regions "far removed from" the Northern Sea Route itself, listing specifically the Gibraltar Straits, the Indonesian Straits, the Indian Ocean, the GIUK gap, the Barents Sea, the deep Arctic MIZ, and polynias of the Central Arctic Basin. *See generally* R. Douglas Brubaker & Willy Østreng, *The Northern Sea Route Regime: Exquisite Superpower Subterfuge?* 30 Ocean Dev. & Int'l L. 299 (1999) (assessing overbroad security and commercial claims by the United States and Russia).

States[80] (with some muted support from the European Union[81]), Russia lays claim to the Northern Sea Route, part of the Northeast Passage,[82] as part of its internal waters.[83] This latter claim, in light of increasingly viewed commercial prospects of trans-arctic commerce, is the subject of this chapter.

The freeing up of Arctic ice during the lengthening Arctic summer and promising commercial prospects regarding High Arctic's resources[84] prompt questions about the legal status of the Northern Sea Route. These questions have burdened US-Soviet/Russian relations for decades and remain a divisive political issue in bilateral Arctic relations.[85] Russia regards the Northern Sea Route as internal waters, making these "enclosed" waters subject only to Russian sovereign decisions.[86] Russia's Northern Sea Route claim extends into its EEZ, but has been criticized as vague and lacking in legal authority.[87] Nonetheless, Russian authorities claim that the integral nature of the Northern Sea Route as a national transport route is unaffected by portions of the route that may pass outside of its internal waters, territorial sea, and EEZ.[88]

[80]   *See* MICHAEL BYERS, INTERNATIONAL LAW AND THE ARCTIC 129–130 (2013).

[81]   *See* Blunden, *supra* note 55, at 120–124 (discussing heightened European Union interest in the Northern Sea Route, and specifically Germany's emerging Arctic trade interests and view of the region as the "common heritage of mankind").

[82]   The Northern Sea Route is the name Russians have used for the passage that others have called the Northeast Passage. The Russian term "holds different connotations" than an "adventurous shortcut" and "evokes visions of a grand national transport corridor, created by the efforts of the Russian people, and mainly used for bringing natural resources out, and for bringing deliveries in to the many settlements in the Russian Arctic." Claes Lykke Ragner, *The Northern Sea Route*, 2008 BARENTS NORDEN ASSOC. Y.B. 114, 114 (Torsten Hallberg, ed., 2008) (English translation from Swedish), *available at* www.fni.no/doc&pdf/clr-norden-nsr-en.pdf.

[83]   *See* ANA G. LÓPEZ MARTIN, INTERNATIONAL STRAITS: CONCEPT, CLASSIFICATION AND RULES OF PASSAGE 70 (2010).

[84]   *See* Donald Rothwell, *The Arctic in International Affairs*, *supra* note 65, 241–243 (noting the long neglected Arctic region has the potential to take "center stage").

[85]   Brubaker & Østreng, *supra* note 79, at 301.

[86]   Willy Østreng, *Ocean Futures 2010, The Northern Sea Route and Jurisdictional Controversy*, ARCTIS, www.arctis-search.com/Northern+Sea+Route+and+Jurisdictional+Controversy.

[87]   R. Douglas Brubaker canvassed five alternative jurisdictional views of the Northern Sea Route, noting Russia's composite view, which others note for its "creative ambiguity." R. DOUGLAS BRUBAKER, THE RUSSIAN ARCTIC STRAITS 29–30 (Gerald J. Mangone, ed., 2005). *See also* Ragner, *supra* note 82, at 119 (noting that Russia's formal jurisdiction over the Northern Sea Route is based on Article 234 of UNCLOS, which gives coastal states unilateral rights to enforce nondiscriminatory environmental regulations in their EEZs where ice coverage and particularly severe climate conditions cause exceptional hazards to navigation and ecological balance, and on claims of "internal waters" pertaining to straits). While noting the importance of Article 234 to Russian and Canadian claims of special police powers in ice-covered regions, Byers and Lalonde question whether the provision applies in international straits, because "the negotiators did not expressly deal with the issue." Byers & Lalonde, *supra* note 68, at 1182 (footnote omitted).

[88]   Katarzyna Zysk, *Russia's Arctic Strategy: Ambitions and Constraints*, 57 JOINT FORCE Q. 103, 107 (2010), *available at* www.intelros.ru/pdf/JFQ/57/16.pdf.

Russia's resolve is to assert sovereignty over key chokepoints of the Northern Sea Route through which most, if not all, commercial traffic currently must transit. Russia claims historic title to these waters, which include the Vilkitsky and Shokalsky Straits, the Dmitry Laptev and Sannikov Straits,[89] and the Proliv Long Strait.[90] These straits are crucial shortcuts that may determine the commercial viability of the entire Northeast Passage.[91] The Vilkitsky and Shokalsky Straits are located in the Severnaya Zemlya archipelago and connect the Kara and Laptev Seas; the Dimitry Laptev and Sannikov Straits are in the Novosbirsky island chain and connect the Laptev and East Siberian Seas;[92] the Proliv Long Strait joins the East Siberian and the Chukchi Seas off Wrangel Island.[93]

The United States regards the Northern Sea Route as one, long international strait, making the waterway open and free to all countries in accordance with the established law of the sea.[94] It is the only country that explicitly challenges the Russian claim.[95] The United States' competing claim, as one of history's few thalassocracies, portends trouble.[96] Both countries justify their opposing views on grounds of national security.[97] "It is only a matter of time," predicts one respected Canadian international legal scholar, before other countries join in the fray to oppose Russian claims of sovereignty.[98]

[89] *See* Byers, *supra* note 68.

[90] López Martín, *supra* note 83, at 85 n. 273.

[91] *See* Alexandr̆ Golts, *The Arctic: A Clash of Interests or Clash of Ambitions, in* Russia in the Arctic, *supra* note 22, at 50 (noting a leading Russian marine official's downplaying of the commercial viability of the route, specifically in light of shallow sections of the Sannikov and Vilkitsky straits).

[92] *See* Mulherin, *supra* note 4, at 32.

[93] López Martín, *supra* note 83, at 85.

[94] *See* Bureau of Oceans & Int'l Envtl. & Sci. Aff., U.S. Dep't of State, Pub. No. 112, Limits in the Seas: United States Responses to Excessive National Maritime Claims 71–73 (1992), *available at* www.state.gov/documents/organization/58381.pdf [hereinafter Limits in the Seas]. *See also* UNCLOS, *supra* note 58, arts. 35(c), 36, 38(1) & 41(b).

[95] Østreng, *supra* note 86.

[96] Brubaker & Østreng, *supra* note 79, at 301.

[97] *Id.*

[98] Byers, *supra* note 68. *See generally* Lincoln E. Flake, *Russia's Policy on the Northern Sea Route in an Era of Climate Change*, 158 RUSI J. 44 (2013) (noting that issues of freedom of navigation in the Arctic may pose more challenges to stability than competing claims for mineral resources). Margaret Blunden has specifically taken up consideration of Chinese Arctic policy regarding the Northeast Passage, which to date has been relatively low profile. *See* Blunden, *supra* note 55, at 125–129. It is worth noting China has constructed the world's largest nonnuclear icebreaker, *Snow Dragon*, which regularly undertakes Arctic voyages. *Id.* at 126. *See also* Pavel Baev, *Putin's Blurred Arctic Vision*, Moscow Times (Aug. 15, 2013), www .themoscowtimes.com/opinion/article/putins-blurred-arctic-vision/484579.html (noting China's "persistent interest in Arctic affairs" and "superficial respect to Russia's obsession with sovereignty" in the northern seas).

IDIOSYNCRASY, AMBIGUITY, AND AMBIVALENCE
IN THE ARCTIC CRYOSPHERE

The Northern Sea Route is the Russian name for a part of the Northeast Passage,[99] but it is not a fixed route.[100] "Unlike most other sea routes, there is no single, set channel for ships to follow."[101] Like its equally fabled counterpart, the Northwest Passage, which straddles the North American landmass connecting the Atlantic and Pacific Oceans, the Northern Sea Route is "a series of shipping routes"[102] through the icy waters atop Eurasia. The Arctic's notoriously harsh and changing weather diverts and often closes traffic routes yearly, seasonally, and often more frequently than that, with dangerous consequences for vessels trapped in nature's vice.[103] The Northern Sea Route's treacherous unfixed sea-lane character is its hallmark feature.[104] This fluidity, paradoxically matched by months of icebound rigidity, adds confusion to discussions about its geographical, environmental, and legal dimensions.[105]

---

[99] Irina Nossova, *Russia's International Legal Claims in Its Adjacent Seas: The Realm of Sea as Extension of Sovereignty* 26 (dissertation, University of Tartu, Estonia, 2013), *available at* http://dspace.utlib.ee/dspace/bitstream/handle/10062/31198/nossova_irina.pdf?sequence=1.

[100] A. L. Kolodkin & M. E. Volosov, *The Legal Regime of the Soviet Arctic: Major Issues*, 14 MARINE POL'Y 158, 164 (1990).

[101] Brubaker & Østreng, *supra* note 79, at 299.

[102] Y. Ivanov & A. Ushakov, *The Northern Sea Route Now Open*, 12 INT'L CHALLENGES 15 (1992).

[103] *See, e.g.,* Mulherin, *supra* note 4, at 14 (discussing fervent rescue efforts in 1983, when approximately fifty ships became trapped during an early October cold spell in locations around the East Siberian and Chukchi Seas). Search and rescue coordination covering an area of about 13 million square miles in the Arctic is the subject of an international agreement prepared through the aegis of the eight-member Arctic Council. *See* Press Release, "U.S. Dep't of State, Secretary Clinton Signs the Arctic Search and Rescue Agreement with Other Arctic Nations" (May 12, 2011), *available at* www.state.gov/r/pa/prs/ps/2011/05/163285.htm (discussing the Agreement on Cooperation on Aeronautical Maritime Search and Rescue (SAR) in the Arctic). Most recently, the *Nordvik*, a 138 meter, 6,403 d.w.t. tanker loaded with diesel fuel, and purportedly classified as capable of encountering light ice conditions, reportedly struck an ice floe north of the Taimyr Peninsula and was taking on water. The head of Russia's Seafarer's Union was quoted as saying "vessels like that should not be sailing on the [Northern Sea Route], simply because they are not capable of withstanding the ice conditions." Trude Pettersen, *Tanker Accident on Northern Sea Route*, BARENTS OBSERVER (Sept. 9, 2013), http://barentsobserver.com/en/nature/2013/09/tanker-accident-northern-sea-route-09-09.

[104] *See* W. Østreng, *The Northern Sea Route: A New Era in Soviet Policy?* 22 OCEAN DEV. & INT'L L. 259, 260 (1991).

[105] Leonid Tymchenko, *The Northern Sea Route: Russian Management and Jurisdiction Over Navigation in Arctic Seas, in* THE LAW OF THE SEA AND POLAR MARITIME DELIMITATION AND JURISDICTION, *supra* note 63, at 269, 269–270. *See also* S. M. OLENICOFF, TERRITORIAL WATERS IN THE ARCTIC: THE SOVIET POSITION 2 (1972) (discussing the unique and unusual nature of the Arctic Ocean and the difficulty resolving "questions of exactly where 'Arctic waters' end and 'Arctic territories' begin."). *See also* Kurt M. Shusterich, *International Jurisdictional Issues in the Arctic Ocean*, 14 OCEAN DEV. & INT'L L. 235, 241 (1984) (discussing difficulties distinguishing between landfast and drifting ice in boundary delimitations).

THE ARCTIC OCEAN GEOMORPHOLOGY AND THE
NORTHERN SEA ROUTE

The geomorphology of the Arctic Ocean presents fundamental problems of analysis. The Arctic Ocean is the world's smallest and shallowest ocean.[106] It is closely confined by continents, except in the vicinity of Canada's Queen Elizabeth Islands, and is surrounded by local seas.[107] Soviet scholars argued that the Arctic Ocean bore characteristics of a lake rather than a high seas regime.[108] Numerous chokepoints impede transit through its shallow straits. Some straits, notably existing in the Laptev Sea, are only eight meters deep; minimum depth in the Sannikov section of the East Siberian Sea is thirteen meters;[109] and portions of the Vilkitsky Strait, "which constitutes the most convenient shipping route between the Kara and the Laptev Sea,"[110] are seventeen meters deep.[111] Shallow seas limit a ship's size, weight, and cargo-capacity due to Archimedes' principle of water displacement.[112] Apart from the legal questions, the shallow channels of the Northern Sea Route may defeat the draft requirements of massive commercial vessels.[113] An ice-free route does not guarantee a competitive route. Shallow straits also create dangerous ice conditions.[114] Although straighter than the Northwest Passage, the Northern Sea Route generally retains its longitudinal direction,[115] but frequently presents

[106] See JOINT RESEARCH CTR., EUROPEAN COMM'N, SOIL ATLAS OF THE NORTHERN CIRCUMPOLAR REGION 15 (2009), available at http://eusoils.jrc.ec.europa.eu/library/Maps/Circumpolar/Index.html.

[107] VICTOR PRESCOTT & CLIVE SCHOFIELD, THE MARITIME POLITICAL BOUNDARIES OF THE WORLD 519 (2nd edn., 2005).

[108] See W. Lakhtine, Rights Over the Arctic, 24 AM. J. INT'L L. 703, 713 (1930) (noting the inadequacy of the high seas regime to the Arctic and the notion that portions conform to the idea of a "national sea"). See also Donald R. Rothwell, THE POLAR REGIONS AND THE DEVELOPMENT OF INTERNATIONAL LAW 288–289 (1996).

[109] Brubaker & Østreng, supra note 79, at 301.

[110] Eric Franckx, New Developments in the North-East Passage, 6 INT'L J. ESTUARINE & COASTAL L. 33, 36 (1991). A US Army Corps of Engineers 1996 Cold Regions Research & Engineering Laboratory Report noted the southernmost Vilkitsky Strait is the "most often-used" passage through or around the Severnay Zemly archipelago. Due to southwesterly ice drift in the western Laptev Sea, compounded by eastwardly ice floe from the Kara Sea, the Vilkitsky Strait and Taymyr Peninsula present serious navigation challenges "at all times of the year." Mulherin, supra note 4, at 27, 31.

[111] Golts, supra note 91, at 50.

[112] See generally David Biello, Fact or Fiction?: Archimedes Coined the Term "Eureka!" in the Bath, SCIENTIFIC AMERICAN (Dec. 8, 2006), www.scientificamerican.com/article.cfm?id=fact-or-fiction-archimede (discussing Archimedean principle of water displacement).

[113] It is estimated that Northern Sea Route vessel size is restricted to around fifty thousand d.w.t., a much smaller, thus less cost effective, substitute for the container vessels navigating the Suez Canal. See Ragner, supra note 82, at 117. Seafaring authorities note an additional restriction: cargo vessels cannot be wider than ice-breaking vessels. See id.

[114] Brubaker & Østreng, supra note 79, at 310.

[115] Kolodkin & Volosov, supra note 100, at 164.

latitudinal obstructions due to ice jams, compounded by rotational patterns of wind and current called Arctic Oscillation.[116] These factors make navigation treacherous, forcing mariners to make circuitous detours.

DEFINITIONS AND DIMENSIONS: NOMENCLATURE

Nomenclature presents a problem as well. The Northern Sea Route is often called the Northeast Passage, but these terms are not interchangeable. The Northern Sea Route is part of the much longer Northeast Passage, but a universal definition remains elusive. Leonid Tymchenko noted a variety of scholarly, geographical, and political definitions,[117] which complicate the international legal discussion of the Northern Sea Route.[118] For instance, distinguished American scholar of Soviet law, William Butler, broadly viewed the route as connecting Leningrad (Saint Petersburg) and Vladivostok.[119] This definition essentially equated the two as one and the same, a representation found often in western publications.[120] Elsewhere, Butler carefully distinguished the geographical area of the Northeast Passage and the lesser-included stretch of waterway that developed as a Siberian "domestic transport concept," which became known as the Northern Sea Route.[121] A geographer at the famed Fridtjof Nansen Institute argued the route escaped linear definition and instead should be "thought of as the whole *sea area* north of Russia."[122] The Soviet Encyclopedic Dictionary (1989) defined it as the 5,600 kilometer (3,024 nautical miles) stretch from the Kara Gates Strait to Providenya Bay (Providence Bay);[123] other scholars claimed the Northern Sea Route was bounded by the western approaches to the Novaya Zemlya's straits and the meridian going north of Zhelaniia Cape to the 66° latitude north and the 168°

---

[116] Byers & Lalonde, *supra* note 68, at 1138.

[117] *See* Tymchenko, *supra* note 105, at 269–271.

[118] *See id.* at 269 (noting particularly the "rather complicated and unclear" legal regime of the Northeast Passage's Northern Sea Route).

[119] BUTLER, NORTHEAST ARCTIC PASSAGE 42 (1978). The distance from Saint Petersburg to Vladivostok via the Northern Sea Route is 14,280 kilometers (7,710 nautical miles); via the Suez Canal, 23,200 kilometers (12,527 nautical miles); and round the Cape of Good Hope, 29,400 kilometers (15,875 nautical miles). *See Northern Sea Route: History of Development*, WAY TO SIBERIA, www.ikz.ru/siberianway/engl/sevmorput.html.

[120] For examples of synonymous treatments of the Northern Sea Route and the Northeast Passage, *see* Shih-Ming Kao, Nathaniel S. Pearre, & Jeremy Firestone, *Adoption of the Arctic Search and Rescue Agreement: A Shift of the Arctic Regime Toward a Hard Law Basis?* 36 MARINE POL'Y 832, 835 (2012).

[121] WILLIAM V. DUNLAP, TRANSIT PASSAGE IN THE RUSSIAN ARCTIC STRAITS 2–3 (1996) (quoting a later distinction by Butler).

[122] Ragner, *supra* note 82, at 114 (emphasis in original).

[123] *See* Tymchenko, *supra* note 105, at 269–270.

55' 37" – a distance of 2,200–2,900 nautical miles, with the variance attributed to prevailing ice conditions.[124]

In Russia, the route bears close association with truncated portions of the Northeast Passage, which facilitated cabotage transport and "played an important economic role for the Soviet Union around World War II."[125] In this historical sense, it took on a functional definition by serving as a "means of transporting goods into, and mineral resources out of, Siberia."[126] In 1984, the Supreme Soviet of the USSR decreed the Northern Sea Route extended from Novaya Zemlya in the west to the Bering Strait in the east,[127] demarcating the route as consisting of four individual seas (the Kara, Laptev, East Siberian, and Chukchi), linked by fifty-eight straits running through three archipelagos (the Novaya Zemlya, Severnaya Zemlya, and East Siberian Islands).[128] With this decree, the Soviet Council of Ministers for the first time approved drawing straight baselines along these respective archipelagos, linking these islands with the adjacent mainland, and enclosing the waters as internal to the Soviet Union.[129] In 1990, the Supreme Soviet decreed the Northern Sea Route to be

---

[124] *See id.* at 270 (citing Y. Ivanov and A. Ushakov).

[125] *Shipping: Northeast Passage,* ARCTIC PORTAL: SHIPPING PORTLET, http://portlets.arcticportal.org/northeast-passage.

[126] Franckx, *supra* note 110, at 35.

[127] Tymchenko, *supra* note 105, at 271 (quoting On Measures for Securing the Implementation of the Edict of the Presidium of the USSR, Article 1(2)). The edict provided the essential transportational line situated within the USSR that is located within its inland seas, territorial sea (territorial waters), or EEZ adjacent to the USSR Northern Coast, and includes seaways by the western entrances to the Novaia Zemlia Straits and the meridian running north through Mys Zhelaniia, and in the east (in the Bering Strait) by the parallel 66° N and the meridian 168° 58' 37" W. *Id.*

[128] Brubaker & Østreng, *supra* note 79, at 299.

[129] Rothwell, *supra* note 108, at 186. Maritime zones are measured from baselines. Rules on baselines are found in articles 3–13 of the Convention on the Territorial Sea and the Contiguous Zone, Apr. 29, 1958, 516 U.N.T.S. 205; and in the UNCLOS, *supra* note 58, arts. 5–11, 13, 14. Normally, baselines follow the low-water line along coasts; straight baselines are employed, however, where the coastline is deeply indented or fringed with islands. *See* J. Ashley Roach & Robert W. Smith, *Straight Baselines: The Need for a Universally Applied Norm,* 31 OCEAN DEV. & INT'L L. 47, 47 (2000); Convention on the Territorial Sea and the Contiguous Zone, art. 7(6) and UNCLOS art. 10(6) (exempting "historic bays" from rules describing closing lines). In the *Norwegian Fisheries Case,* the ICJ validated the use of straight baselines for geographic configurations involving "deeply indented" coasts or where a coast is "bordered by an archipelago." Fisheries Case (U.K. v. Nor.), Judgment, 1951 I.C.J. 116, 128–129. Donat Pharand, the Canadian international legal scholar, concluded in his 1978 study on Canadian jurisdiction over Arctic waters that to ensure full control over Arctic waters, Canada needed to assert its straight baselines around the northern archipelago off Canada's coast to bolster claims enclosing waters as "internal" – a recommendation adopted by a Canadian Order-in-Council on Sept. 10, 1985. See Suzanne Lalonde & Ronald St. J. Macdonald, *Donat Pharand: The Arctic Scholar,* 44 CAN. Y.B. INT'L L. 3, 34–35 (2007).

the middle part of the Northeast Passage.[130] Most recently, on July 28, 2012, President Putin signed into law amendments adopted by the State Duma and approved by the Russian Federation Council that consolidated Russian Arctic policy and defined the Northern Sea Route. Accordingly:

> The water area of the Northern Sea Route shall be considered as the water area adjacent to the Northern coast of the Russian Federation, comprising the internal sea waters, the territorial sea, the adjacent zone and the exclusive economic zone of the Russian Federation and confined in the East with the Line of Maritime Demarcation with the United States of America and Cape Dezhnev parallel in Bering Strait, with the meridian of Cape Mys Zhelania to the Novaya Zemlya Archipelago in the West, with the eastern coastline of the Novaya Zemlya Archipelago and the western borders of Matochkin Strait, Kara Strait and Yugorski Shar.[131]

A DIFFERENCE OF OPINION

The legal status of the Northern Sea Route has been disputed by United States and Soviet/Russian officials for more than fifty years. The Soviets "began considering the waters around its Siberian archipelagos as Soviet internal waters as early as the 1940s."[132] In 1965, they advanced a formal international legal claim declaring the waters internal to the country.[133] The declaration was meant to counter the presence of the *USCGC Northwind* and *USS Burton Island* in Arctic waters. These vessels had been dispatched in the summers of 1964 and 1965 "ostensibly" to conduct oceanographic surveys of the Arctic north.[134] Given the prevailing Cold War, others viewed their presence as an open assertion of "the high seas status of these waters."[135] The *Northwind* penetrated the Laptev Sea and the *Burton Island* entered the East Siberian Sea. A stiff *aide-mémoire* from the Soviet Ministry of Foreign Affairs to the

---

[130] *See* ALEXANDER ANTONOVICH KOVALEV, CONTEMPORARY ISSUES OF THE LAW OF THE SEA: MODERN RUSSIAN APPROACHES 189 (W. E. Butler ed., trans., 2003).

[131] Federal Law of the Russian Federation on Amendments to Specific Legislative Acts of the Russian Federation Related to Governmental Regulation of Merchant Shipping in the Water Area of the Northern Sea Route, 2012, N 132-Ф3, cl. 5.1, *available at* www.arctic-lio.com/docs/nsr/legislation/federal_law_nsr.pdf (English translation); *see also Legislation*, N. SEA ROUTE INFO. OFF., www.arctic-lio.com/nsr_legislation (posting current Russian legislation on the Northern Sea Route).

[132] Lalonde & Lasserre, *supra* note 79, at 38–39 (footnote omitted).

[133] *Id.* at 38.

[134] *Id.* (maintaining there was little doubt the US oceanographic research claim was a pretext for challenging Soviet assertions of sovereignty over the waters around its Siberian archipelagos).

[135] Erik Franckx, *Non-Soviet Shipping in the Northeast Passage, and the Legal Status of Proliv Vil'kitskogo*, 24 POLAR REC. 269, 270 (1988).

American Ambassador in Moscow informed that "the Dmitry, Laptev, and Sannikov Straits, which unite the Laptev and Eastern-Siberian Seas ... belong historically to the Soviet Union;" that the route "has been used and is used only by ships belonging to the Soviet Union;" and that, "not one of these stated straits, as is known, serves for international navigation."[136]

The United States responded by acknowledging the Soviet Union's efforts to develop the "Northern Seaway Route" but rejected the assertion that those efforts "ha[d] the effect of changing the status of the waters of the route under international law."[137] The two countries argued at cross-purpose: The United States asserted a freedom of navigation through these international straits while the Soviets claimed their historic entitlement turned them into internal waters.[138] Interestingly, the United States "sidestep[ped] the awkward fact that the waterways were not used for international shipping."[139] After failing to satisfy this criterion of the *Corfu Channel Case*, the United States tautologically asserted, "the waterways are international straits because they are international straits."[140] The US view of straits has long been based on geographical factors, not functional use; consequently, the classification of a strait does not depend on satisfying a minimum threshold of seafaring traffic.[141] The Soviets facilitated confusion by conflating the distinct legal terms "territorial sea" and "internal waters" and asserting rather than substantiating its claim of "historic right."[142]

Challenges arose again in 1967 when the United States commissioned two Coast Guard icebreakers, *Edisto* and *East Wind*, to circumnavigate the Arctic Ocean.[143] They entered the Severo-Karsky bloc of the Kara Sea, but encountered severe ice conditions that blocked the passage north of the Severnaya Zemlya archipelago.[144] The ships changed course and headed in a southern

[136] LIMITS IN THE SEA, *supra* note 94, at 71 (providing excerpts of *aide-mémoire* from the Soviet Ministry of Foreign Affairs to the American Embassy in Moscow on July 12, 1964).

[137] *Id.* at 71–72 (providing excerpts from reply *aide-memoire* from the United States to USSR on June 22, 1965).

[138] R. Douglas Brubaker, *Straits in the Russian Arctic*, 32 OCEAN DEV. & INT'L L. 263, 266 (2001).

[139] Byers, *supra* note 80, at 145.

[140] *Id.*

[141] *See* James Kraska, *The Law of the Sea Convention and the Northwest Passage*, 22 INT'L J. MARINE & COASTAL L. 257, 274 (2007). *See also* MICHAEL BYERS, WHO OWNS THE ARCTIC? UNDERSTANDING SOVEREIGNTY DISPUTES IN THE NORTH 55 (2009) (quoting US Naval authorities Richard Grunawalt and J. C. Kraska); *see also* Byers & Lalonde, *supra* note 68, at 1173 (citing US Naval authorities' view that international straits require potential and not actual use).

[142] *See* Brubaker & Østreng, *supra* note 79, at 311; *see also* López Martin, *supra* note 83, at 85 n. 273 (disputing Russian historic claims to the Vilkitsy, Dimitry Laptev, and Proliv Long Straits).

[143] *See generally* Donat Pharand, *Soviet Union Warns United Sates Against Use of Northeast Passage*, 62 AM. J. INT'L L. 927 (1968) (summarizing the incident and discussing whether the icebreakers also could have been classified as warships).

[144] *See* Franckx, *supra* note 135, 270–271 (noting *Edisto* and *Eastwind's* encounter with "some of the most difficult ice conditions in recent history," slowing transit to about one mile per day). *See also*

direction toward the Vilkitsky Strait, the sixty nautical mile long and thirty nautical mile wide passage[145] situated off the northernmost promontory of the Eurasian landmass (the Taimyr Peninsula).[146] Respected authorities regard this conduit connecting the Kara and Laptev Seas as the crucial chokepoint along the Northern Sea Route.[147] Its legal status alone – were it a waterway internal to Russia's sovereign decisions and not an aquatic highway of international transit – could affect practical calculations pertaining to the economic viability of the entire route, if the Russians restricted access to it.[148] The US Embassy informed the Soviets of the change in course, but the Soviets refused permission to transit.[149] The Soviets twice warned the United States, bluntly threatening to detain or "otherwise interfere" if the vessels attempted to pass through the strait.[150] The Soviets again specifically referred to the Vilkitsky Strait as "territorial waters," which not only negated its claim of historic right but seemingly supported a right of innocent passage afforded by an exception to the 1958 Geneva Convention on the Territorial Sea and Contiguous Zone (1958 Geneva Convention).[151] The United States issued a strong protest but terminated the circumnavigation,[152] ending the brinkmanship but not the legal dispute.[153] It has never again dispatched icebreakers to access disputed Arctic

Department Statement of Aug. 31, 1967, *Soviet Union Bars Completion of U.S. Scientific Voyage*, 57 DEP'T ST. BULL. 362 (1967) (citing impossibility of transit due to heavy ice conditions).

[145] *See* Mulherin, *supra* note 4, at 32–34.

[146] *See generally Taimyr (Taymyr) Peninsula*, ENCYCLOPEDIA BRITANNICA, www.britannica.com/EBchecked/topic/584942/Taymyr-Peninsula.

[147] Byers, *supra* note 80, at 145; Franckx, *supra* note 110, at 36.

[148] *See* Rothwell, *supra* note 108, at 288 ("While it may be true that much of the Arctic Ocean is open to high seas navigation, the reality is that because access to the high seas portions of the Arctic is so difficult, only vessels from the Arctic states frequent the area on any regular basis."). *See also id.* at 288 n. 142 ("[N]o non-Soviet/Russian vessel has in recent times passed through the Northeast Passage without using the Vilkitsky Strait, as access north of Severnaya Zemlya is extremely difficult, even in high summer").

[149] *See* Roach & Smith, *supra* note 77, at 315 (citing American Embassy in Moscow Note No. 340 to the Soviet Ministry of Foreign Affairs, Aug. 25, 1976). The Soviets invoked internal regulations requiring thirty days advance notice. *See id.* at 316 (referencing Soviet *aide-mémoire* of Aug. 25, 1967).

[150] *Id.* at 316. The Soviet *aide-mémoire* from Aug. 24, 1967 and oral démarche from Aug. 28, 1967 were referenced in the US Note and were delivered to the Soviet Ministry of Foreign Affairs in Moscow on Aug. 30, 1967. *Id.*

[151] *See* Brubaker, *supra* note 138, at 265–266 (2001) (noting art. 5(2) of the 1958 Convention, a grandfather clause, which preserves the right of innocent passage for areas enclosed by straight baselines that were formerly considered as part of the territorial sea or high seas). *See also* Dunlap, *supra* note 121, at 40 (quoting USSR Ministry of Maritime Fleet radio message informing the icebreakers that the "Vilkitsky Straits are within USSR territorial waters").

[152] Dunlap, *supra* note 121, at 72–73.

[153] Michael Byers cites a US State Department official as claiming the Soviets threatened to "go all the way" if the *Northwind* entered the strait. Byers, *supra* note 80, at 145.

straits, but periodically asserts its right to do so.[154] The emerging prospect of an increasingly ice-free passageway now stirs somnambulant passions.[155]

INTERNATIONAL STRAITS: AN AMBIGUOUS TENSION INVOLVING COASTAL STATES AND MARITIME POWERS

Scholars debate these Cold War events in light of intervening legal developments and receding Arctic ice, focusing on three interrelated issues: (1) Does the Northern Sea Route actually constitute a strait within the meaning of UNCLOS? (2) Does the right of transit passage, a neologism introduced by UNCLOS, apply to straits never before used for international navigation? and (3) Must newly accessible or increasingly used straits sustain or attract a minimum volume of international traffic in order to guarantee a right of unimpeded passage?

GEOGRAPHIC VERSUS FUNCTIONAL PERSPECTIVES

In their leading study on the law of the sea, R. R. Churchill and A. V. Lowe concluded that "doubts arise" as to designating the Northern Sea Route, and indeed the Northeast Passage, an international strait given the functional inability of but a handful of ships to access and traverse its waters.[156] Erik Bruël also recognized that international straits needed to demonstrate a functional use.[157] Suzanne Lalonde and Michael Byers surveyed the question and concluded that the general view supported a "certain level of actual use."[158] *Dicta* from the *Corfu Channel Case* are subject to interpretation: the English text holds "the decisive criterion is rather its geographical situation as connecting two parts of the high seas and the fact of its being used for international navigation."[159] This wording, framed with the usage of a single "criterion" rather than "criteria," imparts greater importance to the geographical character of the strait, as opposed to actual volume of ship traffic – which, incidentally,

---

[154] *See* Lalonde & Lasserre, *supra* note 79, at 38–39.
[155] *See* Terry Macalister, *Climate Change Could Lead to Arctic Conflict, Warns Senior NATO Commander*, THE GUARDIAN (Oct. 11, 2010), www.theguardian.com/environment/2010/oct/11/nato-conflict-arctic-resources (quoting NATO Supreme Allied Commander for Europe, Admiral James G. Stavridis, warning that the "broad implications … of climate change" could turn the Arctic into a zone of conflict).
[156] R. R. CHURCHILL & A. V. LOWE, THE LAW OF THE SEA 106 (3rd edn., 1999).
[157] 1 ERIK BRUËL, INTERNATIONAL STRAITS 42–43 (1947) (noting factors such as the number of ships passing through, tonnage, aggregate value of cargo, ship size, and number of different flags).
[158] Byers & Lalonde, *supra* note 68, at 1173.
[159] Corfu Channel (U.K. v. Alb.), Judgment, 1949 ICJ. 4, 28.

involved 2,884 transits by seven foreign-flagged countries.[160] But, as Donat Pharand has argued, the equally authoritative French text gives equal weight to the two criteria.[161]

Interestingly, before 1940, only three ships actually had traversed the Northern Sea Route – the *Vega*, piloted by the Finnish-Swedish explorer, Adolf Erik Nordenskjöld, in 1878–1879; the *Maud*, captained by the Norwegian, Roald Amundsen, in 1918–1919; and the Third Reich's *Komet* in 1940.[162] The first two ships predated modern development of the cabotage system,[163] and the third required a Soviet icebreaker escort, leading Pharand to conclude "it is doubtful if any foreign ship has ever crossed the Vilkitsky Strait without being escorted by a Soviet icebreaker pilot or receiving special permission from the Soviet Union."[164] In 1965, the Soviets promulgated internal regulations requiring compulsory pilotage for vessels navigating the Vilkitsky and Shokalsky Straits. Similar regulations followed in 1972 for passage through the Dimitry Laptev and Sannikov Straits.[165] Compulsory pilotage requires ships to take on board or follow pilots knowledgeable of local waters, a safety practice that continues to date.[166] Although pilotage has a long and secure history in maritime relations, particularly within internal waters and ports, the coastal state seaward extension of its police, environmental, and safety interests have raised "certain tensions,"[167] particularly as applied to international straits.[168] In 1991 and 1993, Russia extended domestic escort rules to warships, requiring icebreaker assisted pilotage and a host of other regulatory controls for all surface vessels transiting Russian Arctic straits.[169] These regulations affected only

[160] Brubaker, *supra* note 138, at 267.

[161] *See* Lalonde & St. J. Macdonald, *supra* note 129, at 80 (referencing Pharand's work).

[162] A. Donat Pharand, *Innocent Passage in the Arctic*, 6 CAN. Y.B. INT'L L. 3, 40 (1968).

[163] *See* PIER HORENSMA, THE SOVIET ARCTIC 68 (1991) (noting around this time the Northern Sea Route was "not much beyond the pioneering stage").

[164] Pharand, *supra* note 162, at 40.

[165] Brubaker, *supra* note 151, at 266.

[166] *See* Donald R. Rothwell, *Compulsory Pilotage and the Law of the Sea: Lessons Learned from the Torres Strait* 2 (Austl. Nat'l Univ. Coll. of Law, Research Paper No. 12-06, 2012), *available at* http://papers.ssrn.com/sol3/papers.cfm?abstract_id=2020781. *See also* Revkin, *supra* note 14 (quoting report by the chief executive officer of the Beluga Group on Russian pilotage service employed to transit the "most demanding" Vilkitsky Strait).

[167] Rothwell, *supra* note 166, at 2.

[168] *See generally* EDWIN EGEDE, INTERNATIONAL STRAITS, COMPULSORY PILOTAGE AND THE PROTECTION OF THE MARINE ENVIRONMENT 10 (2010), *available at* http://works.bepress.com/cgi/viewcontent.cgi?article=1011&context=edwin_egede.

[169] Brubaker & Østreng, *supra* note 79, at 319. The authors note Russia's icebreaker-assisted pilotage requirement for warships would include submarines, giving rise to a problematic application for submerged transit through the straits. *See id.* Surreptitious, submerged passage is the *sine qua non* (the essential condition) of transit passage, one of the few points of agreement shared by submariners from China, the United States, Russia, France, Great Britain, and

the scant Russian traffic that plied these waters; before 1991, the route was essentially closed to foreigners.

UNCLOS AND A MULTIPLICATION OF CATEGORIES

The governing legal order regarding straits has been described as "confused,"[170] even before concerns about global climate change. Unlike the historical development of the law of the sea, which has led to seaward extensions of coastal state sovereignty, straits have bucked this trend because navigational interests of maritime powers remain strong.[171] The extension of the territorial sea to twelve nautical miles also has presented challenges and more confusion regarding international straits. Before UNCLOS, the customary practice of states generally resulted in territorial sea claims of three to six nautical miles. Such claims enclosed hardly more than ten international straits in territorial waters. But UNCLOS' introduction of a twelve nautical mile territorial sea regime increased the number of international straits from ten to more than one hundred that now overlap with coastal state territorial waters.[172]

UNCLOS also introduced a variety of categories of straits, which has further complicated discussion.[173] The 1958 Geneva Convention made no distinction between straits used for international navigation, but dealt with two types of regimes: those uniting two parts of the high seas, and those connecting the high seas with the territorial sea of a coastal state.[174] UNCLOS causes a multiplication of categories to arise: straits including internal waters prior

other countries with such fleets. *Id.* at 314. It is doubtful that tensions between transit passage and assisted pilotage can be reconciled, unless submarines surface to transit straits – a practice that no submarine power, including Russia, would countenance except as an act of comity. The key political component to Russia's claim of historic title to these straits clearly relates to denying invocation of transit passage by foreign submarine fleets, presumably and most probably, the US submarine fleet. The United States could not seek legal support from a claim of prescriptive right, because the requisite element of notoriety is "virtually nonexistent concerning submarine passage." *Id.* at 316.

[170] Brubaker, *supra* note 138, at 263, 265; *see also* López Martin, *supra* note 83, at 65 (noting that the 1982 Convention added confusion and imprecision to the concept of straits by breaking up the unified treatment of the concept in the 1958 Geneva Convention and constructing a diversified range of legal regimes depending on the category of strait involved).

[171] López Martin, *supra* note 83, at 202 (arguing the order of primacy regulating international straits favors freedom of navigation over coastal state sovereignty due to the globalization of capitalism and US maritime supremacy).

[172] *See id.* at 18–19.

[173] *Id.*

[174] 1958 Geneva Convention, *supra* note 129, art. 16(4) ("There shall be no suspension of the innocent passage of foreign ships through straits which are used for international navigation between one part of the high seas and another part of the high seas or the territorial sea of a foreign state").

to the establishment of straight baselines (Article 35(a)); straits regulated by long-standing and non-long-standing international conventions (Article 35(c); Article 311(2)); straits involving EEZs (Article 36), and archipelagic waters (part IV); two types of straits involving innocent passage (formed by an island separating EEZs and high seas; straits involving high seas and economic zones and territorial seas of another state (Article 45(1) (b)); and straits involving the right of transit passage between one part of the high seas or EEZ and another part of the high seas or EEZ (Article 37).[175]

William Dunlap studied forty-three straits in Russian Arctic waters to determine if conditions requiring transit passage applied.[176] He concluded that all straits examined met the conditions favoring application of UNCLOS Part III (which deals with straits used for international navigation)[177] – *assuming* the straits were used for international navigation. He labeled this assumption "an open question," and predicted, absent a new treaty, the question likely will remain unresolved "long after foreign ships are regularly plying the Northern Sea Route."[178] Thus, despite UNCLOS' attention to the complicated geography of international straits, it failed to resolve doctrinal uncertainty about the functional use criterion. And while scholars and diplomats continue to debate the issue, Dunlap may have partly answered his own open question. Vessels increasingly queue to transit the Northeast Passage. They likely do so, as Dunlap noted, for one basic reason: the Northern Sea Route appears to have been "effectively nationalised" years ago.[179] There is no alternative to the essential support services only Russia can provide; without this support, commercial vessels would not risk the voyage. This observation buttresses Russia's *de facto* control over key portions of the Northern Sea Route and gives rise to the prospect of *uti possidetis juris'* creeping pelagic significance.

ENTER UTI POSSIDETIS JURIS: *A SHORT MODERN HISTORY*

Uti possidetis juris is an important building block of the state system. It emphasizes order, stability, finality, and respect for territorial borders.[180] Arising

[175] López Martin, *supra* note 83, at 66.
[176] See Dunlap, *supra* note 121, at 53.
[177] *Id.* at 54 (emphasis omitted).
[178] *Id.* at 54–55.
[179] *Id.*
[180] See GIUSEPPE NESI, L'UTI POSSIDETIS IURIS NEL DIRITTO INTERNAZIONALE 3 (1996); Tomáš Bartoš, *Uti Possidetis. Quo Vadis?* 18 AUST. Y.B. INT'L L. 37, 39 (1997); Daniel Bardonnet, *Frontières Terrestres et Frontiers Maritimes*, 35 ANNUAIRE FRANÇAIS DE DROIT INT'L 1, 59–60 (1989); *see* Temple of Preah Vihear (Cambodia v. Thai.), Judgment, 1962 I.C.J. 6, 34 (emphasizing a "primary" objective of achieving frontier stability on the basis of certainty and finality).

against the backdrops of decolonization and emerging statehood, it expresses international law's rudimentary concern for minimizing violence and "obviating territorial disputes."[181] Its application is considered necessary for maintaining "a modicum of international order"[182] and is fundamental to the concept of territorial integrity – the "great principle of peace, indispensable to international stability"[183] – and that "most glittering and controversial notion in the history ... of international law – sovereignty."[184] The ICJ recognized its place "among the most important legal principles."[185]

However, its application is contentious. By legalizing the territorial possessions of the *de facto* occupier at a critical date, usually the date of independence,[186] *uti possidetis juris* opens itself to criticism because of its agnostic regard for human populations and peoples' right of self-determination.[187] Its "rote application" favoring the status quo[188] fuels complaints that it facilitates inequality and economic dependency.[189] Steven Ratner noted its simplicity

---

[181] Malcolm N. Shaw, *The Heritage of States: The Principle of Uti Possidetis Juris Today*, 67 BRIT. Y.B. INT'L L. 75, 76 (1996); *see also* Marcelo G. Kohen, *L'Uti Possidetis Iuris et Les Espaces Maritimes*, *in* LIEBER AMICORUM JEAN-PIERRE COT: LE PROCÈS INT'L 154, 159–167 (2009) (discussing historical modern origins in Latin America and Africa).

[182] INT'L COMM. ON INTERVENTION AND STATE SOVEREIGNTY [ICISS], THE RESPONSIBILITY TO PROTECT: RESEARCH, BIBLIOGRAPHY, BACKGROUND 9 (Dec. 2001), *available at* www.bits.de/NRANEU/docs/ICISS1201supplement.pdf.

[183] Alain Pellet, *The Opinions of the Badinter Arbitration Committee: A Second Breath for the Self-Determination of Peoples*, 3 EUR. J. INT'L L. 178, 180 (1992).

[184] *See* Nico Schrijver, *The Changing Nature of State Sovereignty*, 70 BRIT. Y.B. INT'L L. 65, 69–70 (2000) (quoting Steinberger's reference in the Encyclopedia of Public International Law).

[185] Frontier Dispute (Burk. Faso/Mali), Judgment, 1986 I.C.J. 554, 567.

[186] *See id.* at 568 (discussing *uti possidetis*' immediate application, capturing "the photograph of the territor[y]" at the critical date of independence; and "freez[ing] the territorial title"); *see also* Land, Island and Maritime Frontier Dispute (El Sal./Hond.: Nicar. Intervening), Judgment, 1992 I.C.J. 351, 401 (acknowledging that the critical date of independence is not always determinative).

[187] *See* JOSHUA CASTELLINO & STEVE ALLEN, TITLE TO TERRITORY IN INTERNATIONAL LAW: A TEMPORAL ANALYSIS 10 (2003) (negating claims of aspirants, leading to a fundamental clash between territorial integrity and self-determination); *see also* W. Michael Reisman, *Protecting Indigenous Rights in International Adjudication*, 89 AM. J. INT'L L. 350, 352 (1995) (noting *uti possidetis* "bestowed an aura of historical legality to the expropriation of lands of indigenous peoples"). *See also* Frontier Dispute, 1986 I.C.J. at 567 (holding in *obiter dictum* that "at first sight [*uti possidetis*] conflicts outright with ... self-determination"). In Opinion No. 2, the Badinter Arbitration Commission held: "whatever the circumstances, the right to self-determination must not involve changes to existing frontiers at the time of independence (*uti possidetis juris*) except where the states concerned agree otherwise." Opinion No. 2, 92 I.L.R. 167, 168.

[188] Steven R. Ratner, *Drawing a Better Line: Uti Possidetis and the Borders of New States*, 90 AM. J. INT'L L. 590, 601 (1996); *see also* Shaw, *supra* note 181, at 78 (discussing the "perception of artificiality" surrounding *uti possidetis* because it does not conform with indicia between groups).

[189] *See generally* PAUL R. HENSEL, MICHAEL E. ALLISON & AHMED KHANANI, THE COLONIAL LEGACY AND BORDER STABILITY: UTI POSSIDETIS AND TERRITORIAL CLAIMS IN THE AMERICAS, *available at* www.paulhensel.org/Research/i005.pdf.

and clarity, but observed that it has both positive and negative aspects when dealing with the complex and emotional subject of reallocating territory.[190] Joshua Castellino and Steve Allen also acknowledged its duality, labeling it a "cornerstone for the maintenance of the system of sovereign states,"[191] but also a "problematic bedrock of the treatment of territory within modern international law."[192]

Yet it keeps its place among the most important legal principles delimiting boundaries and governing title to territory.[193] *Uti possidetis juris* holds that "states emerging from decolonization shall presumptively inherit the colonial administrative borders that they held at the time of independence."[194] This presumption freezes territorial title at the moment of independence, "no matter how arbitrary those boundaries may have been drawn."[195]

It began as a regional principle in Latin America in the early nineteenth century, when former Spanish colonies applied it to frontier disputes with each other and Brazil to protect against the revanchism of the Metropolitan power.[196] In the case of Spanish withdrawal from the New World, the principle relied on Spanish colonial legal documents to establish boundary contours (*uti possidetis juris*) rather than on the principle of effective possession (*uti possidetis de facto*). The principle mandated that newly established national borders coincide exactly with former colonial borders to avoid stimulating territorial claims based on *terra nullius* (land belonging to no one).[197] A territorial transition allowing for *terra nullius* would tempt further land disputes and produce the precise outcome *uti possidetis'* application sought to avoid.[198] Thus, in the decolonization of the Americas, conveyance of territory was not meant to be held in abeyance and *uti possidetis juris* was to serve as the guarantor of the seamless, gap-free, nonviolent transition to sovereignty. As

[190] Ratner, *supra* note 188, at 617.

[191] Castellino & Allen, *supra* note 187, at 7–8.

[192] *Id.* at 229.

[193] Frontier Dispute (Burk. Faso/Mali), Judgment, 1986 I.C.J. 554, 567.

[194] Ratner, *supra* note 188, at 590.

[195] Jan Klabbers & Rene Lefeber, *Africa: Lost between Self-Determination and Uti Possidetis, in* PEOPLES AND MINORITIES IN INTERNATIONAL LAW 37, 37 and 54 (Catherine Brölmann, René Lefeber & Marjoleine Zieck, eds., 1993) [hereinafter PEOPLES AND MINORITIES].

[196] *See* Frontier Dispute (Burk. Faso/Mali), 1986 I.C.J. at 566 (citing its employment "to scotch any designs which non-American colonizing powers might have" on former metropolitan regions); Territorial and Maritime Dispute between Nicaragua and Honduras in the Caribbean Sea, Judgment, 2007 I.C.J. 659, 706.

[197] Enver Hasani, *Uti Possidetis Juris: From Rome to Kosovo,* 27 FLETCHER F. OF WORLD AFF. 85, 86 (2003).

[198] *See* Gino J. Naldi, *The Case Concerning the Frontier Dispute (Burkina Faso/Republic of Mali): Uti Possidetis in an African Perspective,* 36 INT'L & COMP. L.Q. 893, 897 (1987); *see also* Beagle Channel Arbitration (Arg. v. Chile), 17 ILM 634, 644–645 (1978) (noting a main aspect of the principle was to negate the status of *res nullius* in Spanish America).

the ICJ Chamber laconically reaffirmed in the *El Salvador/Honduras* case: "a key aspect of the principle ... is the denial of the possibility of *terra nullius*."[199] In a modern permutation of the *terra nullius* temptation, the melting Arctic has spurred warnings of a coming land grab for its previously ice-entombed resources, which historically may have belonged to no one because they simply were unavailable to (and uncontemplated by) everyone. Rapid Arctic ice melt makes *uti possidetis juris* again a worthy subject of consideration.

In the case of Brazil, which was the successor to Portuguese colonial holdings, border demarcation depended on actual possession (*uti possidetis de facto*),[200] which gave rise to alternative usages of the term: *Uti possidetis juris* and *uti possidetis de facto*. Steven Ratner noted that the *"juris"* addition became somewhat of a fixture alongside *uti possidetis*, signifying the primary importance of the legal instruments.[201] But the tribunal in the 1933 *Honduras Borders* arbitration (Guat./Hond.) equivocated on the dispositive interpretation of *uti possidetis*,[202] and it appears the Chamber in *El Salvador/Honduras* did so too.[203] Castellino and Allen concluded the modern interpretation "seems to favor the Brazilian approach of *de facto* possession over any other system,"[204] – a conclusion supported by William Dunlap's observation regarding Russia and the Northern Sea Route – although established authorities such as John Basset Moore and Humphrey Waldock did not place much stock in the distinction,[205] and, in the case of Waldock, the concept.[206]

---

[199] Land, Island, and Maritime Frontier Dispute (El Sal./Hond.: Nicar. Intervening), Judgment, 1992 I.C.J. 351, 387 (referencing as well the Arbitral Award of the Swiss Federal Council of Mar. 24, 1922 in the boundary dispute case between Colombia and Venezuela, 1 R.I.A.A. 228 (1922)).

[200] Nesi, *supra* note 180, at 7; Ratner, *supra* note 188, at 595 (noting Brazil "claimed, through possession alone, large stretches of land beyond the borders set in treaties by Spain and Portugal") (footnote omitted).

[201] Ratner, *supra* note 188, at 594–595.

[202] Honduras Borders (Guat./Hond.), 2 R.I.A.A. 1309, 1323 (1933) (finding that an examination of the views of eminent jurists "fails to disclose such a consensus of opinion (as to the "historic utilization of the phrase '*uti possidetis*'") as would establish a definite criterion for [its] interpretation").

[203] The Chamber acknowledged "that when the principle of the *uti possidetis juris* is involved, the *jus* referred to is not international law but the constitutional or administrative law of the pre-independence sovereign." *Land, Island and Maritime Frontier Dispute*, 1992 I.C.J. at 558–559. The Chamber recognized, however, the possible failings of colonial law to give a "clear and definite answer," in which case it would be perfectly appropriate to examine the demarcation line as effectively administered ("colonial *effectivité*") or to examine the postcolonial conduct of the new State. *Id.*

[204] Castellino & Allen, *supra* note 187, at 11.

[205] *See* Ratner, *supra* note 188, at 594–595 (and accompanying footnotes, quoting Moore and Waldock).

[206] C. H. M. Waldock, *Disputed Sovereignty in the Falkland Islands Dependencies*, 25 Brit. Y.B. Int'l L. 311, 325 (1948) (criticizing *uti possidetis* as "indefinite and ambiguous").

Uti possidetis had a more tumultuous reception in Africa, where it appeared along with decolonization after World War II. Its application there has been pilloried for imposing coerced boundaries that disrupted local populations across the continent.[207] But its simplicity and clarity won the favor of African elites. Further, it was reflected in the Charter of the Organization of African Unity (OAU),[208] and directly incorporated into the 1964 OAU Cairo Declaration,[209] which heavily influenced the ICJ Chamber decision in the *Frontier Dispute (Burk. Faso/Mali)* case.[210] It surfaced again in Southeast Asia beginning in the 1950s,[211] although arguably less contentiously, due to the region's fuller restoration of precolonial forms of state organization,[212] and it arose beyond the colonial context when the Badinter Arbitration Commission, set up by the European Commission in 1991, applied *uti possidetis* following ethnic cleansing in the former Yugoslavia, holding that the internal boundaries between Croatia and Serbia and between Bosnia-Herzeginia and Serbia had been transformed into international boundaries.[213]

The ICJ took the principle out of its regional context and validated it in the *Frontier Dispute (Burk. Faso/ Mali)* case as a general principle – "not a special rule which pertains solely to one specific system of international law"[214] – "which is logically connected with the phenomenon of obtaining independence, wherever it occurs."[215] Here, the ICJ attached increasing significance to the principle: "Its obvious purpose is to prevent the independence and stability of new states being endangered by fratricidal struggles provoked

[207] *See* SAADIA TOUVAL, THE BOUNDARY POLITICS OF INDEPENDENT AFRICA 3–17 (1972) (noting that while all boundaries are artificial, African boundaries did not crystallize naturally, were largely imposed by outside powers, were drawn in disregard of local circumstances and the wishes of local populations, and that an "element of coercion was almost universally involved").

[208] Charter of the Organization of the African Unity art. III (3), Sept. 13, 1963, 479 U.N.T.S. 39. Art. 3(3) of the OAU Charter affirms the principle of respect for the sovereignty and territorial integrity of every State. *Id.*

[209] Resolution on the Intangibility of Frontiers, OAU Doc. AGH/Res. 16(I) (1964), reprinted in DOCUMENTS OF THE ORGANIZATION OF AFRICAN UNITY 49 (Gino J. Naldi ed., 1992).

[210] *See* Frontier Dispute (Burk. Faso/Mali), Judgment, 1986 I.C.J. 554, 565–566; *see also* Reisman, *supra* note 187, at 360–361.

[211] *See generally* Temple of Preah Vihear (Cambodia v. Thai.), Judgment, 1962 ICJ. 6; Rann of Kutch Arbitration (India/Pak.), *reprinted in* 7 ILM 633 (1968); *accord* Ratner, *supra* note 188, at 590.

[212] Hasani, *supra* note 197, at 89.

[213] Conference on Yugoslavia, Arbitration Comm'n Opinion No. 3 (Jan. 11, 1992), 31 ILM 1499 (1992) [hereinafter the Badinter Commission]. *See also* Castellino & Allen, *supra* note 187, 179–190.

[214] *Frontier Dispute* (Burk. Faso/Mali), 1986 I.C.J. at 565. *See also* Territorial Dispute (Libya/Chad), Judgment, 1994 I.C.J. 6, 89 (separate opinion of Judge Ajibola) (affirming it as a "principle of general application"); *see also* Badinter Commission, *supra* note 216 (recognizing *uti possidetis* as a "general principle").

[215] *Frontier Dispute* (Burk. Faso/Mali), 1986 I.C.J. at 565.

by the changing of frontiers following the withdrawal of the administering power."[216]

Connecting *uti possidetis* to gross violations of human rights has tended to crowd out a more nuanced adaptation of the principle. For example, in *El Salvador/Honduras*, the ICJ Chamber described it as an "essentially retrospective principle, investing as international boundaries administrative limits intended originally for quite other purposes."[217] Its retrospective utility was evident in *Nicaragua/Honduras*, which the Chamber specifically applied to offshore holdings and maritime space.[218] This extension of its applicability to pelagic space gave rise to some consideration by the ICJ about circumstances in which, in principle, *uti possidetis* might apply to maritime delimitation and historic claims over bays and territorial seas.[219]

Even so, applying this fundamentally terrestrial and decolonial tool of boundary delimitation to pelagic space may seem problematic,[220] notwithstanding the jurisprudential slide toward its seaward application. With regard to the status of the Northern Sea Route, there has been no evident withdrawal of an administering power, and, if the United States is correct, there has never been an administering power. What significance can a terrestrial default rule requiring respect for prior boundaries have on a non-colonial pelagic space historically addled by featureless distinctions between frozen land and sea? Indeed, not all aspects of the principle may apply, but the argument here is to note its analogous significance rather than its seamless adaptation to the Arctic. Its lifelong association with terrestrial boundary formation and now its dramatic – some would say retrospective – role in fratricidal and ethnic-cleansing exigencies spark criticism of its application as a cure for disputes far removed from its origins. However, debates about its unwieldy modern application tend to overlook the inescapable and time-tested possessory elements which have always affected *uti possidetis'* practical presumption of

---

[216] *Id.*

[217] Land, Island, and Maritime Frontier Dispute (El Sal./Hond.: Nicar. Intervening), Judgment, 1992 ICJ. 351, 388.

[218] Territorial and Maritime Dispute between Nicaragua and Honduras in the Caribbean Sea, Judgment, 2007 I.C.J. 659, 707. *See also Land, Island and Maritime Frontier,* 1992 I.C.J. at 558–559 (discussing that *uti possidetis* was the starting point for the Chamber's treatment of sovereignty over disputed islands).

[219] *Territorial and Maritime Dispute,* 2007 I.C.J. at 728 (emphasizing as well consideration of "circumstances"). The Court ultimately rejected applying the principle because "no persuasive case had been made by Honduras." Yoshifumi Tanaka, *Case Concerning the Territorial and Maritime Dispute between Nicaragua and Honduras in the Caribbean Sea (8 October 2007),* 23 INT'L J. MARINE & COASTAL L. 327, 333 (2008).

[220] Kohen, *supra* note 181, at 156 (L'émergence de nouveaux espaces maritimes a posé le problème de l'applicabilité de l'uti possidetis à ce qu'on appellee les "frontiers maritimes").

ownership. These elements are summed up by *uti possidetis'* emphasis on *effectivités*, or factual circumstances. A brief review of *uti possidetis'* origins, as opposed to its more modern treatment, contributes to an appreciation of what Thomas Franck regarded as its historical "redefinition,"[221] or what Giuseppe Nesi called its "evolution;"[222] both views reflect *uti possidetis'* connection to *effectivité*. A review of this historical ontology helps explain its relevance to the Northern Sea Route.

UTI POSSIDETIS: *ORIGINS AND DEVELOPMENT OF THE* EFFECTIVITÉS

Uti possidetis originated in Roman law at a time when the Republic's proto-civil and proto-equitable practices were hardening into legal systems known as the *ius civile* and *ius honorarium*.[223] During this period, Roman magistrates, called *praetors*, began issuing specific orders, called interdicts, to resolve disputes involving the acquisition, retention, or recovery of property.[224] As a starting point, *praetors* presumed that possession itself constituted *prima facie* evidence of ownership. Therefore, they issued provisional orders allowing possessors to continue in possession against all who could not claim better title.[225] This *praetorian*-inspired practice hardened over time into the doctrine of *uti possidetis*, which in its full exposition provides: "As you possess, so may you possess (*uti possidetis, ita possideatis*)."[226]

Uti possidetis originally pertained to interdicts involving the retention of immovable property, such as land. If retention questions involved movable or personal property, *praetors* issued a different interdict, called the *utribi* interdict.[227] Regardless of type, these possessory interdicts gave rise to procedural considerations: complainants allegedly dislodged of property automatically carried the burden of proving the property was taken, possessed, or

---

[221] T. M. Franck, *Postmodern Tribalism and the Right to Secession, in* PEOPLES AND MINORITIES, *supra* note 195, at 3, 20.

[222] Giuseppe Nesi, *Uti Possidetis Doctrine, in* MAX PLANCK ENCYCLOPEDIA OF PUBLIC INTERNATIONAL LAW. 7 (2011).

[223] Historians date this period between the end of the Monarchy, in the late sixth-century BCE and the beginning of the Empire, alternatively dated in 31 or 27 BCE. *See* George Mousourakis, THE HISTORICAL AND INSTITUTIONAL CONTEXT OF ROMAN LAW 1 (2003).

[224] *See* THE COMMENTARIES OF GAIUS 325 (J. T. Abdy & Bryan Walker trans., 1870). *See also*, LORD MACKENZIE, STUDIES IN ROMAN LAW WITH COMPARATIVE VIEWS OF THE LAWS OF FRANCE, ENGLAND, AND SCOTLAND 310, 361–363 (4th edn., John Kirkpatrick, ed., 1880).

[225] *See* THE COMMENTARIES OF GAIUS, *supra* note 224, at 327; *see also* Mackenzie, *supra* note 224, at 181.

[226] Ratner, *supra* note 188, at 553.

[227] *See* THE COMMENTARIES OF GAIUS, *supra* note 224, at 327–328.

encumbered wrongfully. If an aggrieved party convinced the *praetors* that the property had been obtained violently (*vi*), clandestinely (*clam*), or without permission (*aut praecario*) – factual questions that essentially "temporalized" the taking by identifying a critical time of wrongful possession – the *praetors* then shifted the burden of proof to the possessor, who then had to prove possession indeed was rightful.[228] In its original form, *uti possidetis* was a judicial tool applied presumptively to "confirm [lawful] possession of property by open, peaceful occupation."[229] The presumption could be overcome or fortified by consideration of factual circumstances relating to *vi, clam,* and *praecario* – the three original, or proto-*effectivités*. Grotius' common use doctrine abstractly adapted this possessory element to the seas, arguing in *a contrario* fashion that the seas belonged to everyone precisely because they could not be possessed or have their use altered or converted.

During its nascent stages in Roman law, *praetors* relied on certain maxims of justice to help determine rightful possession: Rome's civil law increasingly refused to reward occupiers who fell into possession through ill-gotten means or who sought to reclaim possession with unclean hands.[230] Roman law placed proactive duties on victims to assume the burden of proof and to seek timely remedies: it punished those who slumbered on their rights to assert a claim, deliberately delayed the presentation of facts, or silently expected a remedy based on self-inflicted inaction or acquiescence.[231] These Roman law maxims seep into modern scholarly opinions about the Northern Sea Route, given the quiescence or acquiescence of the vast majority of states to Russian claims of sovereignty. These maxims are implicitly recognized by the United States as well, which steadfastly, persistently, and notoriously objects to Russia's claim.

---

[228] *See* Ratner, *supra* note 188, at 592–593; Mackenzie, *supra* note 224, at 363–364. *See also* John Bassett Moore, *Memorandum on Uti Possidetis: Costa Rica – Panama Arbitration* (1911), reprinted in 3 THE COLLECTED PAPERS OF JOHN BASSETT MOORE 328, 328 (1944). There is some translation variance: Gaius held: "*eum potiorum esse Praetor iubet qui eo tempore quo interdictum redditur nec vi nec clam nec precario ab adversario possidet*" ("[T]he Praetor orders that he is to be preferred who at the time of the grant of the interdict is in possession, provided it be without violence, clandestinity, or sufferance on the part of his opponent"); THE COMMENTARIES OF GAIUS, *supra* note 224, at 327.

[229] *See* Reisman, *supra* note 187, at 352 n. 8 (citation omitted).

[230] The proscription against legally validating ill-gotten gains found expression in the Roman law maxim, *ex injuria jus non oritur*. For a discussion of the origins of the "clean hands" doctrine, *see* David Daube, *Turpitude in Digest 12.5.5*, *in* STUDIES IN ROMAN LAW IN MEMORY OF A. ARTHUR SCHILLER 33, 36 (Roger S. Bagnall & William V. Harris, eds., 1986) (discussing its exposition in Justinian's *Digest*).

[231] *See* Ashraf Ray Ibrahim, *The Doctrine of Laches in International Law*, 83 VA. L. REV. 647, 647 (1997) (noting the Roman law maxim, *vigilantibus non dormientibus aequitas subvenit* – "equity aids the vigilant, not those who sleep on their rights").

Uti possidetis' influences profoundly affected private law, which concerns the interests of individuals. For example, its influence is now seen most obviously in the distinction between possession and ownership, as reflected in the common law doctrine of adverse possession.[232] But this *praetorian*-inspired (judge-made) private law presumption, involving first immovable and then movable property, made a dramatic, non-ontological pivot into modern international law where its Roman law ergonomics felt familiar to its Castilian-Luso-New World handlers. This principle quickened into a pragmatic, political default setting applied to territory to forestall the emerging threat to decolonizing regional order – *terra nullius*.[233] If not completely ready-made for the task, key attributes of *uti possidetis* made it an attractive and adaptable gap-filler for unanticipated exigencies of decolonization – and later, state disintegration in the post-Yugoslavia context.[234] The *praetorian* presumption equating possession with proof of ownership became *uti possidetis'* most immediately adaptable element.[235]

Uti possidetis' after the fact (retrospective) application was one part palliative – to quiet disputes and stabilize claims secured by deed or occupation to regional territorial frontiers – and another part prophylactic – to forestall future conflict fostered by decolonization.[236] By acknowledging the political situation on the ground, *uti possidetis* facilitated the infant industry of post-colonial succession and late-modern state-creation.[237] However, its juridical mission creep has been noted, and not simply in terms of its uprooting from private to public international law. Thomas Franck discussed its development within international law: it appeared first as a rule emerging from colonial empires renouncing external territorial claims of other emerging states; then, it became associated with new states in general; then, it was connected to "entities" (in the Eastern European context in the early 1990s) succeeding from non-colonial states; and lately, it has been applied to buttress preexisting boundaries as against internal, not exclusively external, claims.[238]

The utility of the principle is well understood, but its broadening adaptation has generated concern: Roslyn Higgins cautioned against careless usages, or else it will come to mean all things to all people;[239] Tomáš Bartoš lamented

---

[232] *See* Bartoš, *supra* note 180, at 40.
[233] Malcolm N. Shaw, *Peoples, Territorialism and Boundaries*, 8 Eur. J. Int'l L. 478, 492–499 (1997).
[234] *See id.*
[235] *See id.*
[236] *Id.* (discussing the principle's two roles).
[237] *See id.*
[238] T. M. Franck, *supra* note 221, at 20.
[239] R. Higgins, *Postmodern Tribalism and the Right to Secession. Comments, in* Peoples and Minorities, *supra* note 195, at 29, 34.

its open-texturedness,[240] as did Jan Klabbers and René Lefeber, who cited specifically its unwitting employment as both a principle and a rule.[241]

International courts and tribunals have dealt with its open-textured potential by connecting the principle to discernible expressions of sovereign authority, *à titre de souverain*.[242] These expressions focus in part on the actions and intentions of the occupier. To occupy territory *à titre de souverain* requires that a state exercises "functions of state authority [over the territory] on behalf of those authorities."[243] These two elements, namely "the intention and will to act as sovereign, and some actual exercise or display of such authority," were noted by the Permanent Court of International Justice (PCIJ) as key ingredients of sovereign authority.[244] In discussions of *uti possidetis*, the factual acts that demonstrate the exercise of state authority became known as *effectivités*. They "play an essential role in showing how [a] title is interpreted in practice."[245] The *effectivités* provide important concrete considerations that merit close attention in the debate regarding the status of the Northern Sea Route.

Where definitive legal title or historic title is lacking, due to historical confusion or disputes regarding frontier delimitation, pre- and postcolonial *effectivités* become relevant means of ascertaining sovereignty.[246] In contrast, where good title exists, no appeal to *effectivités* can upend the legal status quo.[247] Here, the *effectivités*, in line with the general rule of treaty interpretation, become complimentary or supplementary hermeneutic tools to validate, or confirm, sovereignty, not to create it.[248] In the *Frontier Dispute Case (Burk.*

[240] Bartoš, *supra* note 180, at 39.

[241] Klabbers & Lefeber, *supra* note 195, at 61 (arguing *uti possidetis* is better thought of as a principle rather than as a rule).

[242] Malcolm Shaw, *The International Court of Justice and the Law of Territory, in* THE DEVELOPMENT OF INTERNATIONAL LAW BY THE INTERNATIONAL COURT OF JUSTICE 151, at 151, 168 (Christian J. Tams & James Sloan, eds., 2013). *See also* Eritrea v. Yemen, 22 R.I.A.A. 268, ¶ 241 (Perm. Ct. Arb. 1998) (where the tribunal determined that claims regarding *à titre de souverain* required evidence of consolidation of title).

[243] Kasikili/Sedudu Island (Bots./Namib.), Judgment, 1999 I.C.J. 1045, 1105.

[244] Legal Status of Eastern Greenland (Den. v. Nor.), 1933 P.C.I.J. (serv. A/B) No. 53, at 45–46 (Apr. 5).

[245] Frontier Dispute (Burk. Faso/Mali), Judgment, 1986 I.C.J. 554, 587; cf. Maritime Delimitation and Territorial Questions between Qatar and Bahrain, Judgment, 2001 I.C.J. 248, 255 (separate opinion of Judge Al-Khasawneh).

[246] Honduras Borders (Guat./Hond.), 2 R.I.A.A. 1307, 1325 (Perm. Ct. Arb. 1933) (noting difficulties encountered in drawing a *uti possidetis* line due to a lack of trustworthy information during colonial times involving great areas where there had been no semblance of administrative authority).

[247] *Frontier Dispute* (Burk. Faso/Mali), 1986 I.C.J. at 586–587.

[248] *Id.* at 587. *See also* Vienna Convention on the Law of Treaties, arts. 31–32, May 23, 1969, 1155 U.N.T.S. 331 (detailing the general rule of treaty interpretation and supplementary means of interpretation).

Faso/Mali), the ICJ Chamber determined "the *effectivités* can … play an essential role in showing how … title is interpreted in practice," and defined the test for *colonial effectivités* as "the conduct of the administrative authorities as proof of the effective exercise of territorial jurisdiction in the region during the colonial period."[249] In *El Salvador/Honduras*, the Chamber characterized the colonial record as "confused and contradictory," a circumstance prompting consideration of effective possession as a postcolonial *effectivité*.[250] But in *Eritrea v. Yemen*, the factual evidence in support of *effectivités* was deemed "voluminous in quantity but … sparse in useful content."[251]

Malcolm Shaw's reading of international jurisprudence led him to a situationally specific conclusion, similar to the relevant-circumstances requirement that accompanies application of equitable principles in maritime boundary delimitation jurisprudence:

> [A]lthough it must be effective, control does not necessarily have to amount to possession and settlement of all of the territory claimed. Precisely what acts of sovereignty are necessary to found title will depend in each instance upon all the relevant circumstances of the case, including the nature of the territory involved, the amount of opposition (if any) that such acts on the part of the claimant state have aroused, and international reaction.[252]

THE PROBLEM OF EFFECTIVE POSSESSION AND THE ARCTIC

For more than a century, jurisdictional claims over the Arctic cryosphere were easy to dismiss given the barren, uninhabitable, and inaccessible nature of the region. Generally, the international law pertaining to territorial acquisition, and specifically the doctrine of effective occupation, proved less than a neat fit for Arctic claims,[253] given the remoteness of the region. The 1931 *Clipperton Island Arbitration* between Mexico and France presupposed the "actual and not the nominal" taking of possession as a "necessary condition of occupation," involving "steps to exercise exclusive authority."[254] Through

---

[249] *Frontier Dispute* (Burk. Faso/Mali), 1986 I.C.J. at 586–587. *See also Frontier Dispute (Benin/ Niger)*, Judgment, 2005 I.C.J. 90, 120–121 (illustrating how the Chamber first considered "regulative or administrative act[s]").

[250] Malcolm D. Evans, *Case Concerning the Land, Island and Maritime Frontier Dispute (El Salvador/Honduras: Nicaragua Intervening), Judgment of 11 September 1992*, 42 INT'L & COMP. L.Q. 929, 934 (1993).

[251] Eritrea v. Yemen, 22 R.I.A.A. 268, ¶ 241 (Perm. Ct. Arb. 1998) (five-person panel).

[252] Shaw, *supra* note 242, at 168.

[253] *See* Lakhtine, *supra* note 108, at 705.

[254] Arbitral Award on the Subject of the Difference Relative to the Sovereignty over Clipperton Island (Fr./Mex.), reprinted in 26 AM. J. INT'L L. 390, 393 (1932).

immemorial usage, the establishment of title required an *animus occupandi*, or an actual intent to possess, as a precedent condition. Grotius implied as much with his emphasis on a diversion or conversion of use as an indicator of possessory interest. "[A]n intentional display of power and authority" by "the exercise of jurisdiction and state functions, on a continuous and peaceful basis" were criteria deemed relevant by the tribunal in the first *Eritrea v. Yemen Arbitration Award*.[255] The famous 1928 *Island of Palmas Arbitration* whittled away at the association between the act of discovery and *terra nullius*, noting that additional administrative or occupational acts were needed to establish title.[256] The arbitration's rationale also cut against the grain of broad but never-accepted sector proposals, which sought to carve up the Arctic into Gargantuan pie-like geo-spatial slices[257] and make continental propinquity to the pole – as opposed to actual possession – the controlling legal consideration for title to Arctic territory. Scholars have noted the problem of adapting the concept of *terra nullius* to the essentially landless realm of the Arctic, prompting thoughtful ruminations on the legal status of ice regions.[258] A crowning achievement of Canadian and Russian diplomacy was UNCLOS Article 234, which grants coastal states unilateral rights to promulgate and enforce non-discriminatory environmental regulations in their EEZs where severe climate conditions and ice coverage create exceptional hazards. These powers do not approach sovereign control but provide considerable regulatory allowance to

---

[255] Eritrea v. Yemen, 22 R.I.A.A. 268, ¶ 239 (Perm. Ct. Arb. 1998).

[256] Island of Palmas Arbitration (U.S.A./Neth.), 2 R.I.A.A. 829, 839 (1928) (sole arbitrator Huber).

[257] A Canadian Senator (Poirier) first proposed jurisdictional delimitations of the Arctic according to sector theory in 1907, which proposed employing a meridian line drawn from termini of land or maritime boundaries straight to the North Pole, carving up the region into pie slices; it officially abandoned the idea in 2006. *See* Byers, *supra* note 80 at 66, 117. The Soviet Union applied sector theory by decree of the Central Presidium on Apr. 15, 1926, as a means of avoiding the doctrine of "effective possession," but subsequently fell short of endorsing the principle as applied to the water and ice areas of the Arctic. *Id.* Interestingly, William Butler claims no state seems to have contested the Soviet's claims over lands and islands lying within the geographic coordinates of the 1926 decree, acknowledging the decree's general acceptance over these land claims. *See* Butler, *supra* note 119, at 71–77. For an involved discussion of sector theory, *see generally* Horensma, *supra* note 163; *see generally* SERGE M. OLENICOFF, TERRITORIAL WATERS IN THE ARCTIC: THE SOVIET POSITION (1972), *available at* www.rand.org/content/dam/rand/pubs/reports/2009/R907.pdf.

[258] *See generally* Christopher Joyner, *Ice-Covered Regions in International Law*, 31 NAT. RESOURCES J. 213 (1991) (discussing possible application of baselines to subglacial continental landmass or ice shelves); *see also* Rothwell, *supra* note 108, at 5; Willy Østreng, *The Northern Sea Route and Jurisdictional Controversy*, ARCTIS, www.arctis-search.com/Northern+Sea+Route+and+Jurisdictional+Controversy (posing the question: "Should sea ice be regarded as 'Arctic ocean water' (which in fact is what it is), or as 'Arctic ocean territory' (which is what it is from any functional practical point of view")). For a general discussion of differences between territorial and maritime boundaries, *see* Bardonnet, *supra* note 180, at 1–6.

these two countries, which together form 75 percent of the Arctic Ocean's coastline.[259] But scholars have noted that the interplay between UNCLOS Part III, which governs straits used for international navigation, and Article 234 is not clear, underscoring the long-standing call for a new international treaty, because no such regime governs the Arctic.[260] The legal status of the Northern Sea Route is emerging quickly as an issue, giving credence, once again, to international law's old but formidable nemesis, the doctrine of *non liquet*.[261]

ANALOGOUS RECOURSE TO UTI POSSIDETIS
TO AVOID NON LIQUET

If it is assumed that law, like nature, abhors gaps, how does international law provide a framework for dealing with the status of this passageway in a rapidly emerging area of international significance? How might established legal principles help close the gap regarding the legal status of this waterway and resolve questions pertaining to its legal use?

The problem of gaps in the law is a familiar problem, particularly in the field of third-party dispute settlement, where the judicial temptation to innovate extra-legal solutions to disputes is discouraged mightily.[262] Generally in international law, one important way to approach the problem of gaps has been to borrow concepts from municipal law and apply them by analogy to international legal problems – that is, to draw from municipal law's wellspring of relevant legal stopgap measures and apply them on the international level to prevent gaps from forming or spreading. This idea was laid out by Hersch Lauterpacht in his doctoral

---

[259] Ariel Cohen, *Russia in the Arctic: Challenges to U.S. Energy and Geopolitics in the High North*, in RUSSIA IN THE ARCTIC *supra* note 22, at 1, 13–14 (Stephen Blank, ed., 2011).

[260] See T. E. M. McKitterick, *Validity of Territorial and Other Claims in Polar Regions*, 21 J. COMP. LEGIS. & INT'L L. 89, 97 (1939); *see also* Joyner, *supra* note 256, at 217; Matin Rajabov, Note and Comment, *Melting Ice and Heated Conflicts: A Multilateral Treaty as a Preferable Settlement for the Arctic Territorial Dispute*, 15 S.W. J. INT'L L. 420 (2008–2009). It should be noted the Arctic has been subject to many and productive bilateral or regional legal initiatives. *See* Rothwell, *supra* note 108, at 160 (referencing, for example, the 1911 Fur Seal Convention, the 1920 Spitsbergen (Svalbard) Treaty, the 1973 Polar Bear Agreement, and the 1991 Arctic Environmental Protection Strategy).

[261] *Non liquet*, for purposes here, draws from Lucien Siorat's usages in LE PROBLÈME DES LACUNES EN DROIT INTERNATIONAL: CONTRIBUTION À L'ÉTUDES DES SOURCES DU DROIT ET DE LA FONCTION JUDICIAIRE (1958), in which decision-makers fail to render a decision due to the obscurity, logical or social insufficiency, silence, or absence of law. The doctrine finds principal explication in the field of judicial settlement of disputes, where its application is prohibited as a general principle of international law. *See* Hersch Lauterpacht, THE FUNCTION OF LAW IN THE INTERNATIONAL COMMUNITY 67 (1966).

[262] *See generally* Gerald Fitzmaurice, *Judicial Innovation – Its Uses and Its Perils – As Exemplified in Some of the Works of the International Court of Justice During Lord McNair's Period of Office*, in CAMBRIDGE ESSAYS IN INTERNATIONAL LAW: ESSAYS IN HONOUR OF LORD McNAIR 24–47 (1965).

dissertation, *Private Law Sources and Analogies of International Law* (1925), and came to fruition in *The Function of Law in the International Community* (1933), "his most important doctrinal work."[263] Georg Schwarzenberger noted the "natural tendency" to borrow from private law – in particular Roman law – to lift the fog surrounding operative rules to territory.[264] This tendency has particular but relatively unrecognized application in the High Arctic today.

There is ample political evidence to suggest that circumpolar states – the fortuitous five: Russia, Canada, the United States, Norway, and Denmark (via its territory, Greenland) – have cooperated, notwithstanding notable differences, and will continue to cooperate, to carve up the Arctic Ocean among themselves, thus avoiding the development of legal gaps pertaining to control over resources. The stakes are doubtless substantial, and continental proximity to the pole may provide its own reward in terms of territorializing or enclosing the mineral resources of this pelagic space. These countries, along with Finland, Iceland, and Sweden comprise the select Arctic Council,[265] and may render moot discussions of legal status by turning this ocean space into a *de facto* and quite possibly *de jure mare clausum*,[266] a gap-filling enclosure that would certainly lay bare pieties regarding the future role of the Common Heritage of Mankind principle in international law.

But this deal is not yet done, and even if members of the Arctic Council were to hold sway over the future distribution of mineral and possibly living resources of the Arctic Ocean, questions would persist over the legal control of the Northern Sea Route, and particularly, those stretches along the route that historically served Russia's cabotage system. In the backwaters and eddies of the circumpolar mind-set, this cabotage system may expose enough of a territorial temptation to help explain how a much underexplored and often maligned municipal law concept may have analogous relevance in the High Arctic. The questions have been asked before, with specific reference to a maritime setting: To what extent can a traditional principle of territorial

[263] Martti Koskenniemi, *Lauterpacht: The Victorian Tradition in International Law*, 8 Eur. J. Int'l L. 215, 223 (1997).

[264] Georg Schwarzenberger, *Title to Territory: Response to a Challenge*, 51 Am. J. Int'l L. 308, 309 (1957).

[265] Declaration on the Establishment of the Arctic Council [Ottawa Declaration], Sept. 19, 1996, *available at* www.arctic-council.org/index.php/en/document-archive/category/4-founding-documents.

[266] *See* Anton Vasiliev, Russian Ambassador-at-Large to the Arctic Council, *The Arctic, Our Home and Future*, Arctic Info, www.arctic-info.com/ExpertOpinion/Page/the-arctic–our-home-and-future (citing Danish claims that up to 97 percent of proven reserves are located within EEZs of Arctic States, making the race to recover resources moot because "there's nothing to divide, everything has been already divided").

sovereignty be applied in areas remote from metropolitan power where there is no immediate intent to colonize as distinct from acquire?[267] To what extent can a domestic law principle, historically applicable only to things and *terra firma*, apply in the vastly landless High Arctic? Admittedly, the answers seem incongruous, but no more incongruous than applying the doctrine of freedom of the seas to areas of the High Arctic that historically could not be navigated, and still cannot be navigated by surface transit.[268] The recourse to municipal law analogies highlights a clarifying element missing from the legal discourse; for this reason it is worthwhile to consider elements of the Roman law concept of *uti possidetis* applied by analogy and *in extenso* to questions regarding the legal status of the Northern Sea Route.

UTI POSSIDETIS *AND THE NORTHERN SEA ROUTE*

The fundamental historical condition involving application of *uti possidetis* does not arise in the context of the Northern Sea Route. Most obviously, its legal status does not involve decolonization or legal title deriving from a colonial power and transferring to a new state. But the Badinter Commission's application of *uti possidetis* did not involve the fundamental historical condition of decolonization either.[269] Additionally, while the Arctic region is home to over forty ethnic peoples, including Saami, Nenets, Khanty, Evenk, and Chukchi who inhabit Russia's High Arctic,[270] the sovereignty questions addressed here involve no intra-colonial or administratively apportioned boundaries to bisect human geography and complicate claims of indigenous peoples.[271] But *uti possidetis* is meant to apply to frontiers in flux, and in this general sense, with the rapidly receding icecap serving as the stand-in for the

---

[267] Rothwell, *supra* note 108, at 4.

[268] Emmerson, *supra* note 33, at 87 (raising an evocative point). *See also* Donald R. Rothwell & Stuart Kaye, *Law of the Sea and the Polar Regions: Reconsidering the Traditional Norms*, 18 Marine Pol'y 41, 54 (1994) (noting the impossibility of vessels enjoying "normal" high seas freedoms due to the region's enclosure by landmasses and ice coverage).

[269] *See* Suzanne Lalonde, Determining Boundaries in a Conflicted World: The Role of Uti Possidetis 192 (2012).

[270] *See Arctic Indigenous Peoples*, Arctic Centre, www.arcticcentre.org/EN/SCIENCE-COMMUNICATIONS/Arctic-region/Arctic-Indigenous-Peoples. For detailed demographic information regarding indigenous peoples of the Arctic, *see generally* Laurence C. Smith, *Agents of Change in the New North*, 52 Eurasian Geography & Econ. 30 (2011).

[271] It must be noted, however, that development activities in the Arctic associated with climate change already have acutely impacted the interests of indigenous communities, prompting suggestions for multipronged involvement of indigenous communities in designing climate-change solutions. *See generally* Patricia Cochran et al., *Indigenous Frameworks for Observing and Responding to Climate Change in Alaska*, 117 Climate Change 1 (2013), *available at* www.lter.uaf.edu/pdf/1733_Cochran_Huntington_2013.pdf.

retreating Metropolitan power, the Russian Arctic coastal perimeter presents prospects for its analogous *de facto* application.[272]

Scholars, wittingly or not, have incorporated attributes connected to *uti possidetis de facto* in assessing Russian sovereign claims. For instance, Michael Byers argued that the Vilkitsky, Shokalsky, Dmitry Laptev, and Sannikov Straits "are almost certainly Russian internal waters, having been closed off given the absence of any nonconsensual transits by foreign surface vessels and the fact that only one country has expressly opposed the Russian position."[273] Miaojia Liu and Jacob Kronbak labeled the Northern Sea Route "primarily an 'internal' Russian shipping route,"[274] and have noted its future commercial attractiveness depends on Russia's economic and political development.[275] Claes Lykke Ragner noted commercial transit navigation absent assistance was unrealistic;[276] Irina Nossova asked whether the Northern Sea Route, as a *"historically formed national transportation route … should be understood as* [an] extension of Russian sovereignty."[277] Dismissing territorial analysis *strictu sensu*, Nossova and others nevertheless noted a litany of *effectivités* demonstrating Russia's supreme control over the route: No other state has the power to enact legislation on the route (which the Russians have accomplished); foreign (presumably surface) vessels are obliged to submit to Russian jurisdiction (and do so willingly);[278] Russia is appropriating the economic benefits from this traffic and its conduct has been accepted by the largest part of the world community. Indeed, Russia is the only country able to provide navigational

---

[272] My thought here is a bit more cautious than the Chamber's application of *uti possidetis* in the Land, Island dispute over the Gulf of Fonseca between El Salvador and Honduras. In that case, the Chamber contemplated a *sui generis* situation, referencing the historical background, and, curiously, bestowed on three states simultaneously rights of a coastal state over a common territorial sea, which introduced the concept of a pluri-state historic bay. Land, Island and Maritime Frontier Dispute (El Sal./Hond.: Nicar. Intervening), Judgment, 1992 I.C.J. 351, 593, 605. Judge Oda appended a robust dissenting opinion, arguing the concept "has *no* existence as a *legal* institution." *Id.* at 733 (dissenting opinion of Judge Oda). But the point recognized here is that the seaward extension of the principle arose over a unique situation, not unlike the speed with which international law is attempting to adapt to global warming, as a resourceful solution to an emerging *lacuna* in the law.

[273] Byers, *supra* note 80, at 148–149.

[274] Miaojia Liu & Jacob Kronbak, *The Potential Economic Viability of Using the Northern Sea Route (NSR) as an Alternative Route between Asia and Europe*, 18 J. Transp. Geography 434, 435 (2010).

[275] *See id.* at 435.

[276] Ragner, *supra* note 82, at 119.

[277] Nossova, *supra* note 99, at 149.

[278] Brubaker & Østreng, *supra* note 79, at 318 (noting, other than the incidents in the 1960s, "all recent commercial shipments with foreign elements have been made in compliance with the Russian regime[,]" including US research vessels).

charts, lighthouses, and beacons, in addition to being one of two countries geographically positioned to provide[279] ports of refuge, weather and ice fore-casting, search and rescue assistance, police and environmental controls, and icebreaker escort – all of which are essential to safe transit.[280] Absent Russian approval, licensing procedures, and administrative assistance, insurance com-panies likely would dare not provide coverage against liability for commer-cial accidents, or seizure of cargo.[281] Additionally, as evidence of its claim of *animus occupandi*, the Russians have been maintaining and almost singularly utilizing this waterway as its intercoastal highway since 1932.[282] The peculiar conditions of the Arctic region and Russia's long-standing cabotage system underscore significantly the primary teaching of *uti possidetis*: As you possess, so you may possess.

Scholars have emphasized the simple reality that the Northern Sea Route functionally remains Russia's internal navigation passage.[283] Margaret Blunden recognizes that other interested states are not currently challenging Russia's claim; to the contrary, they are collaborating as their interests dictate.[284]

---

[279] Norway, Finland, and the United States have assisted Russia in replacing radioisotope ther-moelectric generators in lighthouses and beacons along its Arctic coast due to the radioactive security and environmental threats posed if radioactive material is stolen, diverted, or damaged from the appliances. *See* Charles Digges, *Norway and Finland Ink Deal to Remove Radioactive Batteries from Russia's Baltic Sea Region*, BELLONA (Nov. 12, 2009), www.bellona.org/articles/ articles_2009/saudi_arabia; *see also* Thomas Nilsen, *Nuclear Lighthouses to be Replaced*, BELLONA (Feb. 2, 2003), www.bellona.ru/bellona.org/english_import_area/international/russia/ nuke-weapons/nonproliferation/28067 (noting US aid to replace Russia's nuclear lighthouses in the Arctic).

[280] Byers, *supra* note 80, at 139.

[281] *See* Valery Musin, *Marine Insurance for the Northern Sea Route* (INSROP working paper No. 98–1998, IV.3.3), *available at* www.arctis-search.com/Marine+Insurance+for+the+ Northern+Sea+Route. Already, insurers charge two to three times the open-water rate for ships using the Northern Sea Route. *See* Franklyn Griffiths, *New Illusions of a Northwest Passage*, *in* INTERNATIONAL ENERGY POLICY, THE ARCTIC AND THE LAW OF THE SEA, *supra* note 20, at 303, 310. Rupert Herbert-Burns has noted that the Russians require "special and expensive" insurance and icebreaker escort given their *de facto* "if not endemic *de jure*" military control. RUPERT HERBERT-BURNS, STIMSON CTR., ARCTIC COMMERCIAL SHIPPING AND THE STRATEGIC SIGNIFICANCE OF THE NORTHERN SEA ROUTE (2013), *available at* www.stimson.org/images/ uploads/Arctic-Rupert.pdf.

[282] *See* Horensma, *supra* note 163, at 163. Scholars note, however, the disintegration of the Soviet Union resulted in the degeneration of the Northern Sea Route infrastructure, prompting concerted efforts by the Russian government to regain control over the admin-istrative regime of the Northern Sea Route. *See* KATRI PYNNÖNIEMI, FINNISH INST. OF INT'L AFFAIRS, BRIEFING PAPER 81, MUCH ADO ABOUT NOTHING: THE EU'S TRANSPORT DIALOGUE WITH RUSSIA 8 (2011), *available at* www.isn.ethz.ch/Digital-Library/Publications/Detail/ ?ots591=0c54e3b3-1e9c-be1e-2c24-a6a8c7060233&lng=en&id=131365.

[283] Golts, *supra* note 91, at 50.

[284] Blunden, *supra* note 55, at 129.

R. Douglas Brubaker and Willy Østreng find that the Russian's claim enjoys proactive support.[285] Michael Byers' assessment of Russian sovereignty was cemented in the 1960s, when the Soviets blocked passage of the USS *Burton Island* and USCGC *Northwind* through the Vilkitsky Strait.[286] He claimed these incidents crystallized the dispute and provide, much as *uti possidetis* emphasizes, the critical date "when the different positions became clear and subsequent attempts to bolster them became inconsequential to the legal analysis."[287] Byers' borrowing of the inter-temporal feature of *uti possidetis* – the critical date – has an established history in international jurisprudence, with obvious connection to the ICJ's judgment in *Pedra Branca/Pulau Batu Puteh*,[288] *Nicaragua/Honduras*,[289] and *Minquiers and Ecrehos*.[290] In such cases, jurists searched for a temporal trigger to determine the historical moment sovereign rights had been exercised "to an extent sufficient to constitute a valid title."[291] International courts and tribunals look to the critical date to "distinguish *effectivités* admissible *in casu* from other possible alleged *effectivités*."[292]

The Russians and their Soviet predecessors adamantly maintain that the Northern Sea Route has never been used for international shipping. Moreover, they claim the majority of the straits in the route overlap with other pelagic regimes, including the territorial sea, internal waters, and Russia's EEZ; and that transit corridors seaward or between islands dotting the route present no more convenient means of navigation.[293] They lay specific and historic claim to the Vilkitsky, Shokalsky, Dmitry Laptev, and Sannikov straits, and boldly note that the integral nature of the Northern Sea Route as a transport route is not affected by the fact that individual portions of it may pass into the high

---

[285] *See* Brubaker & Østreng, *supra* note 79, at 318.

[286] Byers, *supra* note 80, at 149.

[287] *Id.*

[288] Sovereignty over Pulau Ligitan and Pulau Sipadan (Indon./Malay.), Judgment, 2002 I.C.J. 625, 682 (observing "that [the I.C.J.] cannot take into consideration acts having taken place after the date on which the dispute … crystallized unless such acts are a normal continuation of prior acts").

[289] *See* Territorial and Maritime Dispute between Nicaragua and Honduras in the Caribbean Sea, Judgment, 2007 I.C.J. 659, 697–698 (referring to the critical date on which the dispute crystallized as significant in terms of distinguishing between those acts which should be taken into consideration for the purpose of establishing or ascertaining sovereignty and those acts occurring after such date, "which are in general meaningless for that purpose").

[290] The Minquiers and Ecrehos Case (Fr./U.K.), Judgment, 1953 I.C.J. 85, 105 (individual opinion of Judge Carneiro).

[291] *Id.* at 85.

[292] Maritime Delimitation and Territorial Questions between Qatar and Bahrain, Judgment, 2001 I.C.J. 257, 286 (dissenting opinion of Judge Torres Bernárdez).

[293] There is "no right of transit passage through a strait that contains a route through the high seas or EEZ that is of similar convenience as the strait. This corollary to the general rule of transit

seas.[294] This extended claim is dubious,[295] and the historic claim is arguably too recent to count as a historic claim.[296] But the *effectivités* associated with control over the chokepoints have legal support. The international community, save for the US Navy, has seemingly acquiesced to Russia's administration and control over the route. China has yet to weigh in on the matter,[297] but its joint oil and gas ventures with Russia suggest a developing economic relationship more important than tussling over the Northern Sea Route. Additionally, China's pragmatic acceptance of Russian sovereignty over pelagic space in the High Arctic might stimulate, or expect to stimulate, Russian quiescence over China's boisterous moves to territorialize the East China and South China Seas.

Furthermore, the Russians argue that the Northern Sea Route is a coastal transport route, similar to Norway's *Indreleia*, which the ICJ treated in the *Anglo-Norwegian Fisheries* case (1951) as a navigational route under the complete control and administration of Norway, regardless of whether parts fell within internal and territorial waters.[298] In that case, Norway employed forty-seven straight baselines to measure its territorial sea, generating complaint by Great Britain of that practice and the Norwegian claim that sea space on the landward side of these straight lines (called the *Indreleia*, which contained several passages) were part of its internal waters.[299] The Court sided with Norway and referred to the *Indreleia* not as a strait, "but rather a navigational route prepared as such by means of artificial aids to navigation."[300] The

passage is referred to as the 'Messina exception.'" James Kraska, Maritime Power and the Law of the Sea: Expeditionary Operations in World Politics 127 (2011); *see also* UNCLOS arts. 36 and 38(1) (failing to provide such a right of transit).

[294] As mentioned earlier, the Northern Sea Route is not a fixed route; its sea-lanes may move to different latitudes depending on sea ice conditions. "The fact that some areas of the transportation route lie within the high seas does not, in Russian opinion, influence the integrity of this transport communication, as the vessel sailing the [Northern Sea Route] cannot get to the high seas without previous passage through Russian waters." Nossova, *supra* note 99, at 26.

[295] *See* Rothwell, *supra* note 108, at 202 (criticizing the claim vis-à-vis its extension into high seas areas and also as applied to internal waters, but admitting with regard to the latter that the subject is "clouded by uncertainty").

[296] *See* Lalonde & Lasserre, *supra* note 79, at 38–39 (noting the Soviet Union began considering the waters around its Siberian archipelagos as Soviet internal waters as early as the 1940s).

[297] *See* Michael Byers, *How the Arctic Ocean Could Transform World Trade*, Al Jazeera (Aug. 27, 2013,), www.aljazeera.com/indepth/opinion/2013/08/201382273357893832.html (noting "no evidence ... so far" of China's position on the status of the Northern Sea Route).

[298] *See* Fisheries Case (U.K. v. Nor.), Judgment, 1951 I.C.J. 116, 132.

[299] Ruth Lapidoth, *The Reopened Suez Canal in International Law*, 4 Syracuse J. Int'l L. & Com. 1, 5 (1976–1977).

[300] Fisheries Case (U.K. v. Nor.), 1951 I.C.J. at 132. During pleadings, the Norwegians persuasively were able to show that the *Indreleia* passed through ports and harbors, including the

Court observed Norway's claim attained legal validity by way of "historical consolidation,"[301] which perfected a title originally lacking but now opposable to the world.[302] Importantly, however, the Court noted Norway "exercised the necessary jurisdiction over them for a long period without opposition from other states, a kind of *possessio longi temporis*."[303]

The Soviet Union assertively sought to establish historic title to internal waters in 1985, when it adopted straight baselines connecting the island groups of Novaya Zemlya, Severnaya Zemlya, and the New Siberian Islands to the mainland.[304] It did so in order to base its claims of straight baselines and historic title on customary international law, rather than the more restrictive requirements of UNCLOS, which it had signed but not yet ratified.[305]

Russia continues to express its will to act as a sovereign (*à titre de souverain*); it accepts the responsibility to protect life and property. Like Canada and the United States, Russia extends its jurisdiction over internal environmental issues through domestic legislation[306] as it resists external interference. Moreover, *les effectivités* relating to key chokepoints over the Northern Sea Route underscore the pragmatic considerations identified by Charles De Visscher:[307] The orderly territorialization of the international legal world demands practicality, stability, certainty, continuity, and finality[308] – pragmatic considerations all seemingly satisfied by the route's increasing appeal as a commercial artery, an appeal that would not exist absent Russia's possessory capacity. As Russia possesses, so it may possess.

---

major port of Tromsø. *See* Jens Evensen, *The Anglo-Norwegian Fisheries Case and Its Legal Consequences*, 46 AM. J. INT'L L. 609, 620 (1952).

[301] Fisheries Case (U.K. v. Nor.), 1951 I.C.J. at 138.

[302] Schwarzenberger, *supra* note 264, at 310.

[303] Fisheries Case (U.K. v. Nor.), 1951 I.C.J. at 130.

[304] *See* Byers, *supra* note 80, at 146–147.

[305] *Id.* at 147.

[306] *See*, e.g., Oil Pollution Act of 1990, Pub. L. No. 101–380, 104 Stat. 484 (1990) (codified as amended at 33 U.S.C. §§ 2701–2761 (1994 & Supp. III 1997)); Arctic Waters Pollution Prevention Act, R.S.C. 1985, c. A-12 (Can.); Russian Federation Federal Law N 132-Ф3, On Amendments to Specific Legislative Acts of the Russian Federation Related to Governmental Regulation of Merchant Shipping in the Water Area of the Northern Sea Route, adopted by the State Duma July 3, 2012, approved by the Federation Council July 18, 2012, signed into law July 28, 2012, *available at* www.arctic-lio.com/docs/nsr/legislation/federal_law_nsr.pdf. (English translation of Russian law). *See also* Brubaker & Østreng, *supra* note 79, at 313.

[307] *See generally* CHARLES DE VISSCHER, LES EFFECTIVITÉS DU DROIT INTERNATIONAL PUBLIC (1967) (discussing the various means by which particular social facts are incorporated into international law).

[308] *See id.* at 153.

CONCLUSION

International law requires a stopgap tool to settle territorial disputes. Historically, these disputes have been rooted in overlapping claims arising out of assertions of *terra nullius* or the disintegration of power structures. *Uti possidetis* has provided this stopgap feature for international law. Changing circumstances – whether prompted by climate change or technological advances that locate or unlock hidden resources of the global commons – prompt renewed consideration of *uti possidetis*. Decolonization may have ended, but territorial temptation continues.

Despite its close association with the colonial period, the principle of *uti possidetis* is not *passé*. Its analogous application to the Northeast Passage – particularly its emphasis on factual circumstances involving possessory interests, *les effectivités* – demonstrates its timeless utility. Certainly, *uti possidetis* is not without controversy. *Uti possidetis'* elevation to international law conflicts with the right of self-determination. Its applications as palliative and prophylactic tools to address gross human rights abuses have drawn complaints that it is more of a blunt political instrument than a refined legal principle. But these criticisms, endemic as they may be to the modern application of *uti possidetis*, overlook the importance of pragmatic *effectivités* hewn from centuries-long development in domestic systems. Reconnecting *uti possidetis* to its doctrinal mooring lines, emphasizing *à titre de souverain* as demonstrated by *effectivité*, sidesteps much of this doctrinal debate and lends support to its growing significance in pelagic space. These considerations buttress the strong Russian claim that the route, at a minimum, passes through key geographical strictures that historically and practically have been nationalized by Russia.

Consideration of *uti possidetis'* attributes best explains how the commercial exploitation of the Northern Sea Route progresses in the face of substantial uncertainty and gaps in the international law of the High Arctic. UNCLOS Part III made important strides to progressively develop the international law of straits, but questions remain. For example, Russia signed the treaty but was mindful to declare straight baselines and formally internalize its historic title to these straits before ratifying the treaty. *Dicta* from the ICJ in the *Corfu Channel Case* and scholarly discourse leave open questions about whether international straits require a minimum volume of traffic.[309] UNCLOS Article 234 clearly preferences coastal state police powers in the Northern Sea Route's ice-covered region, but its interactions with Part III provisions remain

---

[309] *See supra* text accompanying notes 162–164.

sublimely unclear, and, of course, do nothing to quiet Russia's historic title to sovereignty.

Factors associated with *possessio longi temporis* – such as a critical date cementing Russia's assertion of sovereignty – remain important factual determinants to establish title to territory. These factors emphasize the temporal ingredient that is part of *uti possidetis*' intellectual pedigree. They are no doubt contested items between Russia and the United States. However, to paraphrase the ICJ in *Eritrea v. Yemen*, references to history, particularly involving title to territory, can be voluminous in quantity, yet sparse in useful content.[310] No other country has expressly joined in the United States' persistent objection to Russia's claim of sovereignty over the Northern Sea Route, and certainly not to the key straits mentioned here. In fact, it is not likely that other countries would object, given the administrative *effectivités* that contribute to Russia's claim of ownership. The commercial opportunities suggested by the opening up of a new, safe, corridor across the top of the world are powerful practical inducements favoring Russia's claim in a resource-hungry world. The glint of *emporia* from the East is an attraction as old as the *Travels of Marco Polo*.[311] The surging demand for energy worldwide is no greater than in Asia, and no more important to any country's domestic policy planning than Russia's. The Putin Administration has identified High Arctic energy supply as the engine to return Russia to Great Power status following the collapse of the Soviet Union. The Northern Sea Route is a principal means to secure that end – were it only navigable.

Some scholars have posited that interest in the Northern Sea Route as a competitor to southern routes may be predicated more on Russian aspiration than on reality. It is an interesting question: "Why does Russia attempt to legally secure straits as internal waters that are largely unusable to itself[?]"[312] The shallow seas and straits of the Northern Sea Route, compounded by a still relatively short sailing season – notwithstanding claims of global climate change – and costs associated with mandatory pilotage or icebreaker escort, may negate any commercial benefit presented by increasing ice-free access through the route. Moreover, Putin's almost singular focus on establishing the economic viability of the Northern Sea Route may neglect the prospect of an even more enticing geopolitical consequence of global warming – the possible appearance of an ice-free Transpolar Sea

---

[310] *See supra* note 251 and accompanying text.
[311] *See generally* TRAVELS OF MARCO POLO: A MODERN TRANSLATION (Teresa Waugh & Maria Bellonci, trans., 1984) (discussing the adventures to the East and back by the thirteenth-century Italian explorer).
[312] Brubaker & Østreng, *supra* note 79, at 323.

Route across, or nearly across, the top of the world. Such a conduit would connect Asian, European, and North American commerce even more directly than the Northeast or Northwest Passages. It would circumvent bottlenecks and the attending Russian and Canadian sovereign claims associated with straits in both waterways and make full use of the traditional high seas freedom of navigation in the Arctic Ocean. A Transpolar Sea Route is not a fanciful idea. Its prospect has been associated directly with China's emerging interest in Arctic shipping and its growing economic relationship with Iceland, which could (along with Norway) emerge as a major transpolar port of call.[313]

Perhaps Russia harbors a hidden motive: to restrict the suspected presence of foreign submarines, principally (and presumably) US vessels, from operating so close to Russia's Arctic coast. This motivation might be linked to the US insistence that the route forms part of an international strait – a claim that maximizes US navigational and security interests connected to the submerged transit passage of its submarine fleet.

Distinct from the many *effectivités* supporting Russian *de facto* control over the Northern Sea Route is the significantly overvalued military-strategic significance of the route as a staging point for war. Russia's once proud Northern Fleet, recently rebuilt following the collapse of the Soviet Union but still suffering from the loss of Baltic ports belonging now to Lithuania, Latvia, and Estonia, remains based on the Kola Peninsula.[314] Using the Northern Sea Route to shuttle surface warships between its Northern and Pacific fleets has been shown to "reduce, rather than enhance [Russia's] overall naval effectiveness and military preparedness."[315] Russia's "[s]urface warships are designed solely for blue water operations" and, thus, Russia makes little use of the

---

[313] *See generally* Malte Humpert & Andreas Raspotnik, *The Future of Arctic Shipping Along the Transpolar Sea Route*, in ARCTIC Y.B. 281 (Lassi Heininen, ed., 2012) (discussing climatic, economic, and political factors in the future development of a Transpolar Sea Route with emphasis on China's emerging interest). Although "a late comer to the Arctic," China now operates a research center in Svalbard and conducts substantial research on icebreakers. CANADIAN INT'L COUNCIL ET AL., INTERESTS AND ROLES OF NON-ARCTIC STATES IN THE ARCTIC, BACKGROUND BRIEF 4 (Oct. 2011), *available at* www.gordonfoundation.ca/sites/default/files/publications/Arctic%20Seminar%20Background%20Brief_1.pdf. In 2013, the Arctic Council granted China permanent observer status (along with India, Italy, Japan, South Korea, and Singapore). *A Warmer Welcome: The Arctic Council Admits its First Permanent Asian Observers*, ECONOMIST (May 18, 2013), www.economist.com/news/international/21578040-arctic-council-admits-its-first-permanent-asian-observers-warmer-welcome.

[314] Brubaker & Østreng, *supra* note 79, at 303–304. For an assessment of Russia's interest in restoring its naval presence, *see* Kraska, *supra* note 293, at 421–423.

[315] *See* Brubaker & Østreng, *supra* note 79, at 305 (discussing USSR attempts to utilize the Northern Sea Route).

Northeast Passage.[316] Surveilling the route to possibly interrupt this activity yields limited results for American military planners.

Furthermore, Russia cannot even use its own submarines in the Northern Sea Route for strategic purposes. Russia's Typhoon and Delta class nuclear ballistic submarines (SSBNs) are too large to operate in most areas of the Northern Sea Route. As high as a twelve-story building and as big as the largest battleships of World War II, Typhoons and the smaller Deltas operate in deep troughs that commingle ice and open water, known as Marginal Ice Zones (MIZ).[317] Only the MIZ in the Laptev Sea could accommodate these behemoths, which would localize their presence and make that area of obvious interest to US antisubmarine-warfare planners. Operating in this area also involves the dangers of submerged icebergs, a problem known to be more severe in eastern stretches of the Northern Sea Route such as the Laptev Sea than in western parts.[318] The deep Artic MIZ and the Central Arctic Basin have been identified as the far safer and more likely havens for lurking Russian submarines.[319] And it is here, along with the so-called GIUK gap (an acronym for the northern Atlantic Ocean sea-spaces between Greenland/ Iceland, and Iceland/United Kingdom), where US forces concentrate their antisubmarine warfare in the North.[320] The US submarine fleet has no need to enter the Northern Sea Route to preserve its second-strike capability;[321] and generally, the military-security value of the route is low.[322] Nevertheless, the question is interesting: Why does the United States "claim but rarely enforce transit passage through straits of such minor 'indispensability'?"[323] R. Douglas Brubaker and Willy Østreng have likely identified the answer: For the United States, "freedom of navigation globally is of supreme consideration to the US military, and deviations will simply not be permitted anywhere."[324]

Thus, it is likely Russia's possessory interest in key chokepoints along its Northern Sea Route will remain secure and unchallenged, most practically because *uti possidetis'* time-tested domestic law emphases on factual

---

[316] *Id.* at 306.

[317] *See id.* at 304, 306, noting that the tower of a Typhoon submarine would "protrude above the surface of the ocean" when resting on the sea floor in extensive parts of the Kara, East Siberian, and Chukchi Seas. *See id.* at 306. Russia's Delta class SSBNs are smaller, but face the same maneuverability problems. *See id.*

[318] *See* Brubaker & Østreng, *supra* note 79, at 307.

[319] *See id.* at 310.

[320] *See id.* at 302, 316.

[321] *See id.* at 309.

[322] *See id.* at 311.

[323] *See* Brubaker & Østreng, *supra* note 79, at 323.

[324] *Id.* at 324.

circumstances – *effectivités* – create effective title (*à titre de souverain*). The United States will likely persistently and solely object, motivated by the unarticulated rationale of preserving navigation freedoms and security interests elsewhere, and not out of an interest in returning to the Arctic brinkmanship days of the Cold War. In this particular geo-spatial and pelagic area of the world, *uti possidetis de facto* and the Grotian tendency are at work providing powerful practical and legal justifications that allow Russia to territorialize and eat its Northern Sea Route cake, if only it can have it too.

4

Terra Nullius and the "Unique" International Problem of Svalbard

In April 2015, Russia's deputy prime minister, Dmitry Rogozin, paid an unscheduled visit to Norway's High Arctic archipelago, Svalbard. His presence sparked an angry response from Norway, whose Foreign Ministry had been caught unaware. Norway, like other western countries, had banned him from entry as a personal punishment for his role in Russia's annexation of Crimea and destabilization of Eastern Ukraine.[1]

Russia's Foreign Ministry lampooned the Norwegian sanction as inexplicable and absurd.[2] Although sovereign states are free to engage in such a retorsion, Norway's sovereignty over Svalbard fell into a special category established by the 1920 Svalbard Treaty (Spitsbergen Treaty).[3] Unlike other unclaimed territories, which historically have been acquired by discovery, effective or symbolic occupation,[4] or by

---

[1] *See* Thomas Nilsen, *Strong Norwegian Reaction to Rogozin's Svalbard tour*, BARENTS OBSERVER (Apr. 18, 2015), http://barentsobserver.com/en/politics/2015/04/strong-norwegian-reaction-rogozins-svalbard-tour-18-04.

[2] *See "Inexplicable and Absurd" – Russia Blasts Norway's Overreaction on Official Svalbard visit*, RT (Moscow) (Apr. 20, 2015), http://rt.com/politics/251209-russia-rogozin-svalbard-ministry/; Trudde Pettersen, *Norway Has No Right to Stop Anyone from Visiting Svalbard*, BARENTS OBSERVER (Apr. 21, 2015), http://barentsobserver.com/en/politics/2015/04/norway-has-no-right-stop-anyone-visiting-svalbard-21-04.

[3] Treaty between Norway, The United States of America, Denmark, France, Italy, Japan, the Netherlands, Great Britain and Ireland and the British overseas Dominions and Sweden concerning Spitsbergen signed in Paris February 9, 1920, www.sysselmannen.no/Documents/Sysselmannen_dok/English/Legacy/The_Svalbard_Treaty_9ssFy.pdf [hereinafter The Svalbard Treaty]. Prior to 1920, when the treaty was signed, the archipelago was commonly referred to as Spitsbergen; when the treaty came into effect in 1925, the King of Norway proclaimed the islands as Svalbard. Mindful of the political sensitivity associated with the name applied to the archipelago, for practicality's sake, I maintain that distinction and refer to the archipelago as Spitsbergen when discussing events prior to 1920/1925 and Svalbard when discussing events after 1925.

[4] *See generally* James Simsarian, *The Acquisition of Legal Title to Terra Nullius*, 53 POL. SCI. Q. 111 (1938) (discussing transition from symbolic to occupational claims of title to *terra nullius*).

force,[5] Norway's sovereignty over Svalbard was conferred on it by this treaty. The treaty contained "equal enjoyment" and "equal liberty of access" provisions for nationals of states parties to the convention,[6] which includes Russia.[7] These provisions restricted Norway's sovereignty, and the ideas of conferring and restricting sovereignty are the treaty's most unusual features.

Rogozin said bad weather prompted his unannounced stopover, but he easily could have claimed, as head of the State Commission for Arctic Development, that he wanted to visit the historical Russian mining community at Barentsburg,[8] not that Russia conceded he needed any reason to visit.[9] Others sensed a more troubling explanation. Analysts called it a deliberate provocation,[10] obliquely reinforced by Rogozin's statement that "the Arctic is a Russian Mecca."[11] Rogozin set foot on turf that Russia once claimed as a preferential interest. But Bolshevik predecessors traded away any future sovereign

---

[5] *See* WILLIAM BLACKSTONE, COMMENTARIES Bk. 1 INTRODUCTION, § IV, vol. 1, 1765 p. 105, http://avalon.law.yale.edu/18th_century/blackstone_intro.asp [Of the countries subject to the laws of England] (discussing acquisition of conquered or ceded colonies that were unclaimed but inhabited).

[6] *See* Svalbard Treaty, *supra* note 3, art. 2 ("Ships and nationals of all the High Contracting Parties shall enjoy equally the rights of fishing and hunting in the territories specified"), and art. 3 ("The nationals of all the High Contracting Parties shall have equal liberty of access and entry for any reason").

[7] Fourteen states were original signatories. The Soviet Union and Germany signed the agreement in 1924 and 1925, respectively. Currently, forty-two states have ratified the treaty. They include Afghanistan, Albania, Argentina, Australia, Austria, Belgium, Bulgaria, Canada, Chile, China, the Czech Republic, Denmark, Dominican Republic, Egypt, Estonia, Finland, France, Germany, Greece, Hungary, Iceland, India, Italy, Japan, Lithuania, Monaco, the Netherlands, New Zealand, Norway, Poland, Portugal, Romania, Russia, Saudi Arabia, South Africa, Spain, Sweden, Switzerland, Ukraine, United Kingdom, United States, and Venezuela.

[8] *See* Eirik Palm, *'I am not in the least going around worrying'*, SVALBARDPOSTEN (May 22, 2015), http://svalbardposten.no/index.php?page=vis_nyhet&NyhetID=5927 (bad weather). *See also Pettersen, supra* note 2 (noting the Russian consulate in the mining community of Barentsburg).

[9] *See* Pettersen, *supra* note 2, http://barentsobserver.com/en/politics/2015/04/norway-has-no-right-stop-anyone-visiting-svalbard-21-04 (quoting Russian Foreign Ministry view that Oslo has "no legal grounds" against Rogozin's visit).

[10] Kjetil Malkenes Hovland, *Norway Summons Ambassador after Banned Russian Visits Svalbard*, WALL ST. J. (Apr. 20, 2015), www.wsj.com/articles/norway-summons-ambassador-after-banned-russian-visits-svalbard-1429536060 (citing Norwegian foreign policy researcher, Jakub Godzimirski); Eirik Palm, *Ædda bædda fra Rogozin*, SVALBARDPOSTEN (Norway) (Apr. 19, 2015), www.svalbardposten.no/index.php?page=vis_nyhet&NyhetID=5799 (citing Nansen Institutt's Jørgen Holten Jørgensen's view the Russians were probing Norway's reaction to see how far they could go).

[11] Steffen Pedersen Øberg, *Rogozin: "Arktis er det russiske Mekka*," AFTENPOSTEN (Norway) (Apr. 20, 2015), www.aftenposten.no/nyheter/iriks/Rogozin-Arktis-er-det-russiske-Mekka-7987876 .html (quoting Rogozin).

claim during the Soviet Union's turbulent formative years in the 1920s.[12] Perhaps Rogozin wanted to spitefully grudge Norway what Russia could not itself secure.[13] Or worse, perhaps his unannounced presence suggested an interest in Svalbard that Russia never fully relinquished: "Russia has begun to understand its place, its borders and its interests," Rogozin said after the visit; referencing Crimea's annexation in 2014, he continued: "We saw something historic take place last year. Russia's territorial integrity was restored. This year, we are casting our glance elsewhere. We are taking a closer look at the development of the Arctic. The two things are the same."[14]

Rogozin's reputation for bluster[15] is more easily set aside than the timing of his visit: the month before, Russia's Ambassador to Norway filed a sharp diplomatic protest when Norway began soliciting bids to develop areas of the Barents Sea adjacent to Svlabard's territorial waters for energy exploration.[16] Russia claimed Norway's solicitation violated the peculiar conditions placed on sovereign rule by the Svalbard Treaty.[17] Implicit in the Russian view is Norway's provocation, which upsets a relatively quiet status quo arrangement in a bid to territorialize new resources that changing circumstances now allow.[18]

---

[12] Official Soviet accession to the treaty "without any conditions and reservations," including Norway's sovereignty over Bear Island, occurred on May 7, 1935, although the Soviet pledge "not to advance objections" was recorded on February 16, 1924. *See* A. N. VYLEGZHANIN & V. K. ZILANOV, SPITSBERGEN: LEGAL REGIME OF ADJACENT MARINE AREAS 25 and 24 (W. E. Butler, ed. and trans., 2007) [hereinafter Vylegzhanin & Zilanov].

[13] Recalling Aesop's fable, The Dog in The Manger. *See The Dog in The Manger*, FABLES OF AESOP: A COMPLETE COLLECTION, http://fablesofaesop.com/the-dog-in-the-manger.html (noting the moral to the story is: people often begrudge others what they cannot enjoy themselves).

[14] Erik Lund, *When Dmitry Rogozin Speaks, People Worry*, THE ARCTIC JOURNAL (May 7, 2015), http://arcticjournal.com/politics/1562/when-dmitry-rogozin-speaks-people-worry (quoting Rogozin).

[15] *See* Clifford J. Levy, *Russia's NATO Envoy, Big on Bluster, Modifies His Tone*, N.Y. TIMES (Aug. 27, 2008), www.nytimes.com/2008/08/27/world/europe/27iht-moscow.4.15691237 .html?pagewanted=all&_r=0 (labeling Rogozin blustery); Emily Gertz, *Russian Bluster Aside, What Will Become of the ISS*, POPULAR SCIENCE (May 19, 2014) (citing Rogozin's threat to end cooperation on the International Space Station); Roger McDermott, *Russian Military Modernization: Rogozin Promises a "Nuclear Surprise,"* EURASIA DAILY MONITOR (Oct. 7, 2014), www.jamestown.org/programs/edm/single/?tx_ttnews%5Btt_news%5D=42926&cHash= 419d2173f0771cbff161b9709d5a39a7#.VXG6vc9Viko (noting Rogozin's "nuclear surprise" for adversaries following military modernization).

[16] *See* Rolf Stange, *Russia Protests against Norwegian Oil Development in the Barents Sea*, SPITSBERGEN/SVALBARD ARCTIC BLOG (May 12, 2015), www.spitsbergen-svalbard.com/2015/05/ 12/russia-protests-against-norwegian-oil-development-in-the-barents-sea.html?lang=en.

[17] *See* Alf Bjarne Johnsen, *Russland protesterer mot oljeboring i Svalbard-sonen: UD mottok skarp note fra Moskva*, VG NYHETER (Norway) (May 2, 2015), www.vg.no/nyheter/innenriks/norsk-politikk/russland-protesterer-mot-oljeboring-i-svalbard-sonen/a/23444540/.

[18] *See* Katarzyna Bozena Zysk, *Russian Military Power and the Arctic*, EU-RUSSIA CENTRE 82 (2008), www.isn.ethz.ch/Digital-Library/Publications/Detail/?lang=en&id=99789 (discussing

Rapid ice melt and conditions of global warming, together with technological advances and increasingly accessible resources, have awakened competing interests over the legal regime that both confers on Norway full and absolute sovereignty and limits that sovereignty by establishing equal access and non-discrimination rights for all states parties to the treaty. Understanding how this paradoxical arrangement came about, bearing some similarity to the Mandates System under the League of Nations,[19] better informs of the challenges facing its application and High Arctic governance in the unfolding age of rapidly receding ice. With technological changes making more accessible and safe offshore oil development, pressure increases to open up new unexplored areas to replace barren North Sea oil fields; with rapid ice melt, prospects enhance to explore and exploit the High Arctic's massive oil and gas reserves;[20] with commercial fishing fleets competing worldwide for diminishing stocks, Svalbard's bountiful waters present an enticing lure. These factors, taken together, present obvious territorial temptations.[21]

Discussions about the complexities of Svalbard's sovereignty are not new, but they tend to focus, and properly so, on the applicability of that regime structure to the geographical regions beyond Svalbard's territorial waters and not on the treaty's antecedents. These antecedents add texture and meaning to the peculiar and paradoxical shared resource arrangement the Svalbard Treaty created. They help to explain why current differences regarding the treaty's seaward extension will not be resolved easily, and probably not without Norway's further accommodation of competing interests. They also shed light on state practices that arise in status quo arrangements and how those practices

a widespread Russian conviction that Norway's Svalbard policy aims to drive Russia away from the archipelago and adjacent waters).

[19] See GEIR ULFSTEIN THE SVALBARD TREATY: FROM TERRA NULLIUS TO NORWEGIAN SOVEREIGNTY 50 (1995) [hereinafter ULFSTEIN, THE SVALBARD TREATY]; Torkel Opsahl, *Norwegian Dependencies, Particularly Spitsbergen and the European Communities, in* LEGAL PROBLEMS OF AN ENLARGED EUROPEAN COMMUNITY 179 (M. E. Bathurst et al., eds., 1972).

[20] See *90 Billion Barrels of Oil and 1,670 Trillion Cubic Feet of Natural Gas Assessed in the Arctic,* US GEOLOGICAL SURVEY (July 23, 2008), www.usgs.gov/newsroom/article.asp?ID=1980# .VbJqDvlViko (projecting undiscovered, technically recoverable energy reserves above the Arctic Circle).

[21] A giant 2011 discovery of oil and gas deposits in the Johan Castberg sector of Norway's Barents Sea continental shelf has turned "this huge area into a hotspot" for exploration; several dry wells in the Norwegian Sea have diverted oil company attention and enthusiasm elsewhere, certainly toward the High North; reports of diminishing expectation for oil recovery in the North Sea abound, but supergiant strikes on the Utsira High in 2010 and 2011 (renamed Johan Sverdrup), a mature part of the North Sea, may rank as Norway's largest discovery ever, focusing renewed interest in Norwegian North Sea oil prospects. *See* Halfdan Carstens, *Small Is Also beautiful,* 10 GEOExPRO (2013), *available at* www.geoexpro.com/articles/2014/01/small-is-also-beautiful.

provide second-best rewards when not interpreted as creeping jurisdictional threats to secure sovereign control. By delving into the history of Svalbard, a deeper understanding of Svalbard's constructed *terra nullius* status is obtained along with the vagaries of that phrase, which also help to explain the peculiar equivocations reflected in the Svalbard Treaty. Placing current discussions in a more global and historical context also enhances the assertion that capable states have long displayed territorial temptations regarding the resources of the archipelago when they have become apparent and accessible. But when not able to assert sovereignty over this harsh land void of indigenous population, history reveals that states created their own *de facto* course of dealing – which maximize parochial interests regarding resource extraction – sometimes in the name of common use, sometimes in the form of a *quasi*–condominium arrangement – if only to preclude any other individual state's perfection of sovereign interests over Svalbard. Preclusive interests again are on display as Norway seemingly seeks to test the limits of its ultimate parochial design to perfect its sovereignty over resources adjacent to Svalbard's territorial sea. Its efforts give rise to the central question: does Norway's grant of sovereignty in the 1920 Svalbard Treaty extend to the modern maritime zones adjacent to Svalbard's territorial sea?

INCREASING TENSIONS OVER RESOURCES AND THE DYNAMIC INTERPRETATION OF THE SVALBARD TREATY

The seaward extension of the territorial rule allowing for control over resources conforms to a basic principle of the law of the sea: the land dominates the sea.[22] Sovereignty over the riches of an archipelago's continental shelf is legally "an emanation from and an automatic adjunct of the territorial sovereignty of the coastal State."[23] Norway claims it owns Svalbard's continental shelf because it reigns over Svalbard; Russia claims Svalbard's sovereignty is conferred by mutual agreement and that the unusual equitable and nondiscriminatory provisions bestowed by that authority extend to the administration, ownership, and exploitation of resources off Svalbard's coast, which (presumably) also must be equally beneficial to the states parties to the Svalbard Treaty. Scholars deem this interpretation dynamic; this dynamism views the treaty as an all-encompassing package solution, whereby Norway's sovereignty hinged

---

[22] Grisbardana Case (Nor. v. Swe.), Arbitral Award of October 23, 1909, R.I.A.A. XI 155, 159 (noting the fundamental principle *"tant ancient que modern"* that *"le territoire maritime est un dépendance necessaire d'un territoire terrestre"*); North Sea Continental Shelf Cases (FRG/ Den.; FRG/Neth.), Judgment, 1969 I.C.J. 3, 51, ¶ 96 (the "land dominates the sea").

[23] Aegean Sea Continental Shelf (Gr. v. Turk.), Judgment, 1978 I.C.J. 3, 36, ¶ 86.

originally on the understanding that other states parties "retained certain *terra nullius* rights."[24] If Norway's treaty-conferred rights were to expand, other parties' rights would too.

SIGNS OF COOPERATION

Svalbard's maritime surroundings have been disputed for decades, although the two principal stakeholders – Norway and Russia – have been fairly content to avoid direct confrontation over the treaty's long reach,[25] absent a pressing need to resolve ambiguities and contested interpretations,[26] until now.

Although vastly different in terms of size, population, and military strength, Norway and Russia closely compete in oil and gas industries. Both countries are among the world's largest net exporters of energy; and both have major stakes in Europe: Norway supplies 21 percent of Europe's natural gas; Russia is the European Union's leading supplier of oil and gas. A Norwegian concession was the first to strike offshore oil in 1969 and production has since that time moved from the North Sea into the Norwegian Sea, off the midsection of the country, and most recently into the High North reaches of the Barents Sea.[27] Russia historically focused oil production on land but shifted policy in the mid-1980s and now decidedly is rotating its industry into High North waters.[28] Despite its smaller size, Norway benefits from extensive experience in offshore production and a more coherent policy,[29] making it a formidable and enviable competitor. Moving geographically in clockwise and counterclockwise

[24] *See, e.g.,* Sarah Wolf, Svalbard's Maritime Zones, Their Status under International Law and Current and Future Dispute Scenarios 2, 18 (Stiftung Wissenschaft und Politik, Working Paper FG. 2013 No. 02, 2013), *available at* www.swp-berlin.org/fileadmin/contents/products/arbeitspapiere/WP_Wolf_2_2013.pdf

[25] *See generally* Peter T. Ørebech, *The "Long-Arm" Reach of the Svalbard Treaty?* (July 2015), http://works.bepress.com/cgi/viewcontent.cgi?article=1000&context=peter_orebech

[26] *See* Robin Churchill & Geir Ulfstein, *The Disputed Maritime Zones Around Svalbard, in* Changes in the Arctic Environment and the Law of the Sea 593(Myron H. Nordquist, Tomas H. Heidar, & John Norton Moore, eds., 2010) [hereinafter Churchill & Ulfstein].

[27] *Norway Claims First Strike* OilCity, www.oilcity.co.uk/home/article.asp?pageid=470 (detailing the Ocean Viking strike by Phillips Petroleum in the Ekofisk field on December 23, 1969). *See also Norway Supplies More than 20% of Europe's Natural Gas Needs,* US Energy Information Administration (May 16, 2014), www.eia.gov/todayinenergy/detail.cfm?id=16311 (citing Norway supplies 21 percent of total European natural gas); and Energy production and imports, Eurostat, May 2015, http://ec.europa.eu/eurostat/statistics-explained/index.php/Energy_production_and_imports (citing in table 3 Russia as the EU's main supplier of crude oil and natural gas (and solid fuels)).

[28] *See* Arlid Moe, *Russian and Norwegian Petroleum Strategies in the Barents Sea,* 1 Arctic Rev. on Law & Pol. 225–226 (2010).

[29] *See id.*

directions across the northern expanse, these energy-producing titans are increasingly setting sights on availing but formerly out-of-reach resources surrounding Svalbard.

For forty years, an offshore border dispute in the Barents Sea between the island chains of Svalbard and Novaya Zemlya (the so-called "Loop Hole") complicated Norwegian-Russian relations. Where and how to draw that line stymied development of an area of open sea the size of Florida, containing under its subsoil an estimated thirty-nine billion barrels of oil.[30] But in 2010, the countries came to terms on a compromise delimitation, opening up the prospect of offshore development.[31] Russia emphasized, however, that the accord did not resolve the two countries' disagreement over the waters around Svalbard.[32] The dispute was not purely bilateral. Voices in the European Parliament questioned whether the delimitation improperly divvied up a portion of Svalbard's fishery resource belonging to neither state.[33]

A DRAMATIC DETERIORATION

Despite long-standing cooperation in the Norwegian and Barents Seas through the Russian-Norwegian Fisheries Commission, and more recent ventures, including a 2012 agreement to explore jointly frontier areas, and a Russian stake in a license in the Barents Sea operated by Norway's state-owned Statoil, relations deteriorated dramatically when Norway offered its twenty-third licensing round in January 2015.[34] This round opened up fifty-seven blocks for exploration, thirty-four of which were in formerly disputed

---

[30] *See* Andrew E. Kramer, *Russia and Norway Agree on Boundary*, N.Y. TIMES (Sept. 15, 2010), www.nytimes.com/2010/09/16/world/europe/16russia.html?_r=0.

[31] *See* "Treaty between the Kingdom of Norway and the Russian Federation Concerning Maritime Delimitation and Cooperation in the Barents Sea and the Arctic Ocean," Nor.–Russ. (Sept. 15, 2010), *available at* www.regjeringen.no/globalassets/upload/UD/Vedlegg/Folkerett/avtale_engelsk.pdf.

[32] *See* Lotta Numminen, A *History and Functioning of the Spitsbergen Treaty, in* THE SPITSBERGEN TREATY: MULTILATERAL GOVERNANCE IN THE ARCTIC 7, at 13 (Diana Wallis & Steward Arnold, eds., 2011).

[33] *See* Andreas Raspotnik & Andreas Østhagen, *From Seal Ban to Svalbard-The European Parliament Engages in Arctic Matters*, THE ARCTIC INSTITUTE (Mar. 10, 2014), www.thearcticinstitute .org/2014/03from-seal-ban-to-svalbard-european.html (noting a Polish parliamentarian's inquiry about a European Commission claim for compensation). The European Union is not party to the treaty but bases its interests on the principle of "conferral of competence" owing to certain shared competences some of its member states have involving Svalbard. *See id.*

[34] Exclusive rights extended to companies for oil licenses is regulated by a designate block system operated by the Norwegian Petroleum Directorate. *See generally* "Exploration Policy, Norwegian Petroleum," www.norskpetroleum.no/en/exploration/exploration-policy/ (detailing licensing position for the Norwegian continental shelf as of April 2015).

waters with Russia,[35] including, controversially, three blocks in waters offshore from Svalbard.[36] Russia reiterated long-simmering objections pertaining to these waters: it claimed Norway violated the Svalbard Treaty by offering drilling opportunities in those three blocks; that Svalbard has its own continental shelf subject to inter-temporal interpretations of the nondiscrimination provisions of the 1920 treaty; and that Norway obdurately refused to negotiate.[37] Spain and Iceland share the view that the equal access and nondiscrimination provisions of the treaty restrict Norway's sovereign rights off Svalbard's coast, and periodically have indicated they will refer the question to the ICJ.[38] Norway, in turn, claimed Svalbard has an undifferentiated continental shelf (notwithstanding the general legal view that islands, save for uninhabitable rock outcroppings, generate their own continental shelves);[39] that it extends from its mainland and around and past Svalbard,[40] save for the treaty's exception of Svalbard's territorial waters;[41] that Norway does not need to negotiate rights with any country as its rights are secured under the 1958 Continental Shelf Convention;[42] and that the Svalbard Treaty's equal treatment provisions

---

[35] *See* Atle Staalesen, *Norway Offers 34 Arctic Blocks Along Russian Border*, BARENTS OBSERVER (Jan. 20, 2015), http://barentsobserver.com/en/energy/2015/01/norway-offers-34-arctic-blocks-along-russian-border-20-01.

[36] *See* Trude Pettersen, *Russia Protests Drilling in Svalbard Zone*, BARENTS OBSERVER (May 5, 2015), http://barentsobserver.com/en/energy /2015/05/russia-protests-drilling-svalbard-zone-05-05.

[37] *See id.*

[38] *See* TORBJØRN PEDERSEN, CONFLICT AND ORDER IN SVALBARD WATERS 187 (dissertation, University of Tromsø, 2008) [hereinafter PEDERSEN, CONFLICT AND ORDER] (noting Spain's 1986 and Iceland's 1994 indications to refer the question to the ICJ); Torbjørn Pedersen, *The Svalbard Continental Shelf Controversy: Legal Disputes and Political Rivalries*, 37 OCEAN DEV. & INT'L L. 339, 345 (2006) [hereinafter Pedersen, *Svalbard Continental Shelf Controversy*] (noting Iceland and Russia most vigorously object to Norway's view); and Nkeiru Scotcher, *The Sovereignty Dilemma, in* THE SPITSBERGEN TREATY: MULTILATERAL GOVERNANCE IN THE ARCTIC 21 at 22 (Diana Wallis & Stewart Arnold, eds., 2011).

[39] Churchill & Ulfstein point out that UNCLOS art. 121 regards every island, apart from uninhabitable rocks, as having a continental shelf. *See* Churchill & Ulfstein, *supra* note 26, at 567.

[40] *See* Pedersen, *Svalbard Continental Shelf Controversy, supra* note 38, at 344 (summarizing the Norwegian view that the continental shelf of Svalbard is "physically and inherently one continuous seabed adjacent to the Norwegian coastline"). The Norwegian Foreign Ministry compares Svalbard's geological situation to the Shetland Islands on Great Britain's continental shelf, or Novaya Zemlya and Franz Josef Land on Russia's continental shelf. *See The Continental Shelf- Questions and Answers* 6, UTENRIKSDEPARTEMENTET, REGJERINGEN.NO, Retningslinjer, Oct. 30, 2009, *available at* www.regjeringen.no/no/dokumenter/the-continental-shelf–questions-and-an/id583774/ [hereinafter UTENRIKSDEPARTEMENTET].

[41] *See* The Svalbard Treaty, *supra* note 3, art. 2 ("Ships and nationals of all High Contracting Parties shall enjoy equally the rights of fishing and hunting in the territories specified in Article 1 and in their territorial waters").

[42] *See* Pettersen, *supra* note 36.

have no applicability beyond the treaty's original scope,[43] which limits the treaty's application solely to the land and territorial waters.[44] In line with the famous *S.S. Lotus dictum*, Norway argues that restrictions on its sovereignty are not to be presumed;[45] and that restricting sovereignty conferred by treaties must conform to the literal and ordinary meaning of the treaty, which has no ambulatory, dynamic, or inter-temporal significance.[46] Instead, the treaty set in stone only those legal interests secured by its express terms and cannot be enlarged imaginatively to trump subsequent developments in the law of the sea even though its fundamental intent and purpose was to secure an equitable regime for peaceful utilization based on equal enjoyment and nondiscrimination.[47] In line with Lord Asquith's reasoning in the famous *Abu Dhabi Arbitration* (1951), "it would be a most artificial refinement to read back into [an agreement] the implication of a doctrine" not established at the time of its creation.[48]

Some experts think there is too much at stake not to settle the dispute, others see Russia and Norway on a collision course.[49] Either way, the waters off Svalbard highlight increasing tensions regarding the legal status of the archipelago and its surroundings, making it an emerging centerpiece of a new global power race for influence and resources.[50] "For anyone interested in

[43] Øystein Jensen & Svein Vigeland Rottem, *The Politics of Security and International Law in Norway's Arctic Waters*, 46 POLAR RECORD 73, 79 (2010).

[44] See D. H. Anderson, *The Status under International Law of the Maritime Areas around Svalbard*, 40 OCEAN DEV. & INT'L L. 373, 374 and 380 (2009) (noting they are the only two spaces mentioned in the Treaty).

[45] See *id.* at 379 (citing the 1999 Norwegian Ministry of Justice White Paper); *see also* Churchill & Ulfstein, *supra* note 26, at 565–566 (noting the opinion of Norwegian Foreign Ministry consultant Carl August Fleischer).

[46] See UTENRIKSDEPARTEMENTET, *supra* note 40, at 7 (rejecting any connection between Norway's outer continental shelf submission and the Svalbard Treaty). *See also* Anderson, *supra* note 44, at 380 (summarizing Norway's view, which differs from the author's view).

[47] See preamble and art. 1, The Svalbard Treaty, *supra* note 3.

[48] Petroleum Development Ltd. v. Sheikh of Abu Dhabi, 18 ILR 1951, 141 at 152. The case concerned a petroleum concession contract allowing for exclusive rights to drill for oil in the whole of the lands, islands, and sea which belong to the Ruler of Abu Dhabi. The question was whether the concession also extended to the area of the continental shelf. Lord Asquith's award held the continental shelf had not attained legal status as a matter of customary law at that time.

[49] See Patrick McLoughlin, *Norway, Russia on Collision Course over Arctic Oil Drilling*, PLATTS (May 27, 2015), www.platts.com/latest-news/oil/london/norway-russia-on-collision-course-over-arctic-26102429 (quoting oil industry expert stating that an agreement is likely because too much is at stake; noting neither side is backing down).

[50] Elisabeth Braw, *The Tip of the Iceberg: Arctic Island Svalbard Is at the Center of a New Global Power Race - for Influence, and Oil*, POLITICO (May 17, 2015), www.politico.eu/article/svalbard-iceberg-tourism-travel-ban/.

geopolitics," noted the president of the Norwegian Scientific Academy for Polar Research, "this is the region to follow in years to come."[51]

COORDINATED OPPOSITION TO NORWAY

Russia's objection to the status quo is long-standing. Soviet Foreign Minister Molotov thought the treaty should have been "thrown in the trashcan" in the 1940s; that sovereignty over the southernmost island in the archipelago, Bear Island (Bjørnøya), more properly (that is, historically) belonged to Russia anyway, and that a Russo-Norwegian condominium should administer the remainder.[52]

Coordinated opposition to Norway extends beyond Russia's historical view, signaling that multiparty disputes are consolidating around the binary positions of Norway and other Arctic stakeholders:[53] In 2004, the European Union delivered an "unprecedented and hostile" *note-verbale* demanding Norway halt enforcement policies in Svalbard's waters;[54] in 2005, Finland withdrew its support of Norway during a Barents Euro-Arctic Council session;[55] Spain and Iceland have protested Norway's fishing restrictions off Svalbard;[56] and in 2006, Great Britain hosted the United States, Canada, Denmark, France, Germany, Iceland, the Netherlands, Russia, and Spain in discussions about Svalbard's continental shelf. Norway was not invited.[57] The United States once described Norway's interpretation of sovereign rights off Svalbard's continental shelf and superjacent water as "wishful thinking,"[58] and has since 1974 steadfastly reserved its rights with regard to the problematic interpretation of the Svalbard Treaty, thus preserving its option to oppose Norway while keeping open strategic and economic options vis-à-vis Russia.[59]

---

[51]   Andrew Higgins, *A Rare Arctic Land Sale Stokes Worry in Norway*, N.Y. Times (Sept. 27, 2014), www.nytimes.com/2014/09/28/world/europe/a-rare-land-sale-stirs-concerns-in-norway.html?_r=0 (quoting Willy Østreng).

[52]   *See* Torbjørn Pedersen, *The Dynamics of Svalbard Diplomacy*, 19 Diplomacy & Statecraft 237 (2008).

[53]   *See* Pedersen, Conflict and Order, *supra* note 38, at 204.

[54]   *See* Pedersen, *Dynamics of Svalbard Diplomacy*, *supra* note 52, at 250.

[55]   *See id.* at 251.

[56]   *See id.* at 250.

[57]   *See* Torbjørn Pedersen, *International Law and Politics in US Policymaking: The United States and the Svalbard Dispute*, 42 Ocean Dev. & Int'l L. 120, 131 (2011) [hereinafter Pedersen, US Policymaking].

[58]   *See id.* at 124 (quoting a 1974 statement by US Ambassador to Norway, Thomas Byrne).

[59]   *See id.* at 120 and 131.

ORIGINS OF THE CURRENT DISPUTE

The current dispute dates to 1970, one year before Norway ratified the United Nations Continental Shelf Convention. In that year Norway prescribed straight baselines around the archipelago, defining inland waters and territorial waters, which it asserted extended four nautical miles from shore.[60] The Svalbard Treaty confirmed that Svalbard had a maritime zone because it specifically mentions Svalbard's territorial waters. But it was the only zone mentioned in the treaty. It was the only zone aside from high seas, and perhaps historic bays,[61] that existed at that time. The contiguous zone, the continental shelf, extended continental shelf assertions, exclusive fishing zones (EFZ/FPZ – Fisheries Protection Zones), and EEZ mark developments in the law of the sea that postdate the Svalbard Treaty. Deep divisions exist among parties to the treaty as to whether the treaty applies beyond the territorial sea.[62] Legal opinions divide[63] or equivocate[64] on this question, but it seems the prevailing view supports the proposition that recognizes Norway's sovereignty and jurisdiction in maritime areas adjacent to Svalbard's territorial waters while also acknowledging the application of Svalbard's nondiscrimination treaty provisions.[65]

---

[60] *See* Royal Decree of September 25, 1970 concerning the Delimitation of the Territorial Waters of Parts of Svalbard, www.un.org/depts/los/LEGISLATIONANDTREATIES/PDFFILES/NOR_1970_DelimitationDecree.pdf; *See* Anderson, *supra* note 44, at 373–376.

[61] *See* Land, Island and Maritime Frontier Dispute (El Sal./Hodn.; Nicar. Intervening), Judgment, 1992 I.C.J. 351, 733, ¶ 11 (dissenting opinion of Judge Oda) (noting the term "historic bay" arose around 1910). *See also* Christopher R. Rossi, *Jura Novit Curia? Condominium in the Gulf of Fonseca and the "Local Illusion" of a Pluri-State Bay*, 37 Hous. J. Int'l L. 793, 801 (2015).

[62] *See* The Norwegian Government's High North Strategy 17 (Norwegian Ministry of Foreign Affairs, 2006), www.regjeringen.no/globalassets/upload/ud/vedlegg/strategien.pdf (acknowledging, for instance, disputes with Spain, Iceland, and Russia over Norway's Fisheries Protection Zone and continental shelf). *See also* Odd Gunnar Skagestad, The "High North": An Elastic concept in Norwegian Arctic Policy 12 (Fridtjof Nansens Institutt, 2010) (noting various challenges to the Fisheries Protection Zone around Svalbard).

[63] Norway's position has been supported ardently by Carl August Fleischer. *See*, e.g., "The New International Law of the Sea and Svalbard. Norwegian Academy of Science and Letters 150th Anniversary Symposium," Jan. 25, 2007, 1–15; for the opposite view, *see generally* Wolf, *supra* note 24; Robin Churchill & Geir Ulfstein, Marine Management in Disputed Areas: The Case of the Barents Sea (1992) (especially ch. 2). The US State Department Legal Adviser once opined that the treaty does provide resource rights to non-Norwegians beyond Svalbard's territorial sea; but the general counsel to the US Department of Defense concluded Norway's claim was strongest. *See* Pedersen, *US Policymaking, supra* note 57, at 129 (footnotes omitted).

[64] *See* Churchill & Ulfstein, *supra* note 26, 593 (concluding it is "not possible to reach a clear-cut and unequivocal conclusion as to the geographical scope of the non-discriminatory right of all parties to the Svalbard Treaty to fish and mine in the waters around Svalbard.").

[65] *See* Wolf, *supra* note 24, at 18 (citing R. R. Churchill's and G. Ulfstein's views). Denmark shifted toward this view in the early 1980s, when Danish fleets moved into Svalbard waters after

A Norwegian intelligence report indicated that the purpose of demarcating the territorial sea around Svalbard in 1970 was to lay the formal foundation for Norway's long-term plan: to claim *unrestricted Norwegian jurisdiction* over the seabed from North Cape (near the northernmost tip of Europe) to Svalbard as well as around Svalbard *except from* the areas within the four mile limits, which would be subject to Svalbard Treaty provisions.[66] In 2004, to conform to UNCLOS, the territorial limit was extended from four to twelve nautical miles.[67] Anticipating that treaty, Norway established a 200 nautical mile EEZ in 1976 off its mainland coast.[68] Norway aimed at establishing an EEZ around Svalbard, but other states objected based on the equal enjoyment provision of the Svalbard Treaty.[69] Seeking "to avoid outright confrontation,"[70] Norway chose not to press its claimed exclusive rights in the area.[71] Instead, by Royal Decree in 1977, Norway proclaimed – "for the time being"[72] – a 200 mile FPZ around Svalbard to regulate non-Norwegian fishing vessels.[73] Several observers interpret Norway's approach as a long-range means of institutionalizing its management claim by minimizing "attention to conflicting interests in the Svalbard offshore area."[74] Access would be shared by all nationals of those countries that had an established record of fishing in these waters in a ten-year period prior to the decree[75] – a framework meant to accord with the nondiscriminatory spirit of the Svalbard Treaty.[76]

---

depleting fishing stocks elsewhere. *See* T. Pedersen, *Denmark's Policies toward the Svalbard Area*, 40 OCEAN DEV. & INT'L L. 319 at 329 [hereinafter Pedersen, *Denmark's Policies*].

[66] *See* Pedersen, *Svalbard Continental Shelf Controversy, supra* note 38, at 343.

[67] *Id.* at 344.

[68] *See* Act No. 91 of December 17, 1976 relating to the Economic Zone of Norway, *available at* www.un.org/depts/los/LEGISLATIONANDTREATIES/PDFFILES/NOR_1976_Act.pdf; *see also* Anderson, *supra* note 44, at 376. In the first year of UNCLOS' negotiation, the USA and USSR were quick to signal to others they would support the concept of a 200 nautical mile EEZ. *See* Rachel Tiller & Elizabeth Nyman, *Having the Cake and Eating It Too: To Manage or Own the Svalbard Fisheries Protection Zone*, 60 MARITIME POL'Y 141, 144 (2015).

[69] *See* The Svalbard Treaty, *supra* note 3, art. 2; *see also* Wolf, *supra* note 24, at 13–14.

[70] Tiller & Nyman, *supra* note 68, at 143.

[71] *See* Torbjørn Pedersen, *The Constrained Politics of the Svalbard Offshore Area*, 32 MARITIME POL'Y 913, 916 (2008).

[72] *See id* ("for the time being"); *see also* www.regjeringen.no/en/find-document/dep/UD/reports-to-the-storting/20042005/report_no-30_to_the_storting_2004-2005/3/id198409/ (rephrasing as "until further notice").

[73] Pedersen, *Svalbard Continental Shelf Controversy, supra* note 38, at 344. The Norwegian government, nevertheless, justified the establishment of the FPZ on the basis of UNCLOS and its grant to coastal states a 200 nautical mile EEZ. *See* Numminen, *supra* note 32, at 14.

[74] PEDERSEN, CONFLICT AND ORDER, *supra* note 38, at 202 (summarizing the "attention cost" sensitivity small-state Norway cultivates to stabilize the regime in maritime areas adjacent to Svalbard); *see also* Tiller & Nyman, *supra* note 68, at 143.

[75] *See* Pedersen, *US Policymaking, supra* note 57, 127.

[76] Pedersen, *Denmark's Policies, supra* note 65, at 322 and 323–324 (2009).

The FPZ problematized Norway's position, however, generating criticism that Norway denies Svalbard has its own continental shelf and yet claims Svalbard generates a 200 nautical mile FPZ.[77] While Norway did not exclude nonnationals from fishing in the zone, it maintains the right to do so;[78] in 1986 it issued cod quotas, which were extended in 1996 to shrimp,[79] and periodically has skirmished with nonnational vessels to enforce its restrictions.[80] And yet, when Norway delimited a boundary with Denmark in 2006, it derived basepoints using markings from the headlands and outermost islands of the two opposing sides, which is a normal means of constructing a provisional equidistance line.[81] The Norwegian basepoints, however, did not lie on the mainland of Norway but between the nearest basepoints between Greenland and Svalbard, which necessarily suggested that Svalbard must have a continental shelf.[82] Moreover, Norway's formulation of an application to extend the continental shelf north of Svalbard, in its submission to the CLCS,[83] demarcated an area as "Continental Shelf beyond 200 miles" – as measured from Svalbard. "But if Svalbard has no continental shelf the 'Continental Shelf beyond 200 miles' would have to be delimited from the Norwegian mainland, not Svalbard."[84]

It appears Norway has sought to make good use of the Svalbard Treaty and Svalbard's lack of a continental shelf to emphasize issues of sovereignty, natural prolongation of the continental shelf from its mainland, and Norwegian

---

[77] *See* Pedersen, *Svalbard Continental Shelf Controversy*, *supra* note 38, at 346; Churchill & Ulfstein, *supra* note 26, at 567–568; *see also* Numminen, *supra* note 32, at 12.

[78] As implied by the language employed by the 1977 Royal Decree (for the time being); *see* Pedersen, *Svalbard Continental Shelf Controversy*, *supra* note 38, at 346.

[79] *See* Wolf, *supra* note 24, at 23.

[80] *See* Pedersen, *Svalbard Continental Shelf Controversy*, *supra* note 38, at 346 (discussing conflicts over Norway's Fisheries Protection Zone); Numminen, *supra* note 32, at 13 (citing specific skirmishes with Spanish and Russian trawlers); Kristian Åtland & Kristin Ven Bruusgaard, *When Security Speech Acts Misfire: Russia and the Elektron Incident*, 40 SECURITY DIALOGUE 333 (2009) (discussing the hot pursuit of the Russian trawler *Elektron*, which refused arrest for illegal fishing in the FPZ, and headed for Russian territorial waters with two Norwegian coast guard inspectors on board). In 2004, the arrest of two Spanish trawlers in Svalbard's FPZ prompted a suit settled in favor of Norway by the Norwegian Supreme Court. The applicability of the Svalbard Treaty was argued but not a basis for the decision, which, instead, highlighted the nondiscriminatory application of the FPZ. *See* Tiller & Nyman, *supra* note 68, at 143.

[81] *See* Anderson, *supra* note 44, at 377.

[82] Numminen, *supra* note 32, at 12 ("Svalbard cannot provide basepoints for determining an equidistant line if it does not have a continental shelf"); *see also* Churchill & Ulfstein, *supra* note 26, at 567.

[83] *See* UNCLOS, art. 76 (establishing the Commission).

[84] Numminen, *supra* note 32, at 12; *see also* Churchill & Ulfstein, *supra* note 26, at 568.

ownership of resource exploration and exploitation rights in portions of the
Barents Sea. But where it has been beneficial for Norway to rely on Svalbard's
own continental shelf – to delimit boundaries with Denmark, and to present to
the CLCS continental shelf extension considerations northward of Svalbard –
it displays the Grotian tendency to seek control over previously unsecured
resources because it is in an enviable position to do so.[85] This tendency has
a firm basis in the history of the law of the sea.[86] But D. H. Anderson argued
Norway cannot have it both ways: it cannot interpret its sovereignty in an
ambulatory (inter-temporal/dynamic) way to maximize control over its land
and original waters, but also to the extended territorial sea, the continental
shelf, and fisheries zone, while at the same time "interpret[ing] the reference
to other states' rights strictly so that [their] rights were confined to the land and
the original territorial sea."[87] It appears beneficiary countries of Norway's FPZ
seemingly are wanting it both ways, as well. While some reserve their rights
to declare the Svalbard Treaty's geographic applicability to the continental
shelf adjacent to Svalbard's territorial waters, and others dispute Norway's
claim to both the continental shelf and the FPZ, all benefit from Norway's
inclusion of their nationals' fishing interests in the resource-rich waters within
the zone[88] and the exclusion of other national fleets that had no traditional
fishing presence there ten years prior to Norway's enclosure of that fishing
zone.[89] Additionally, all benefit as free riders as management costs are borne
by Norway alone. For this reason, many of the conservation measures undertaken in the FPZ are respected,[90] less so its enforcement measures, however.[91]

---

[85] *See generally* Christopher R. Rossi, *A Particular Kind of Dominium: The Grotian Tendency and
the Global Commons in a Time of High Arctic Change*, 11 J INT'L L. & INT'L REL. 1 (2015).

[86] *See generally id*; PETER BORSCHBERG, HUGO GROTIUS, THE PORTUGUESE AND FREE TRADE IN
THE EAST INDIES (2010); and MARTINE JULIA VAN ITTERSUM, PROFIT AND PRINCIPLE: HUGO
GROTIUS, NATURAL RIGHTS THEORIES AND THE RISE OF DUTCH POWER IN THE EAST INDIES
(1595–1615) (2006).

[87] Anderson, *supra* note 44, at 381. If the equitable treatment provisions of the Svalbard Treaty
were deemed to cover activity on the continental shelf of Svalbard, ancillary issues would arise
regarding the Svalbard Treaty's tax provision (which limits Norway's imposition of higher taxes
strictly to what is required for administration of the archipelago, thus serving as a boon for oil
companies) and Mining Code (and whether its mining provision on Svalbard's land and in
territorial waters extends by analogy to petroleum and gas operations on the continental shelf).

[88] The zone is particularly rich in cod, haddock, and capelin, with 25 percent of cod catches in
the Barents Sea coming from the zone and 18 percent of Norway's total fish catch coming from
the Svalbard zone. *See* Churchill & Ulfstein, *supra* note 63, at 100.

[89] *See* Numminen, *supra* note 32, at 14–15; *see also* Anderson, *supra* note 44, at 374.

[90] *See* Olav Achram Stokke, *The Struggle over Illegal, Unreported and Unregulated Fishing in
the Barents Sea*, AFTENPOSTEN (Norway) (Oct. 22, 2005), available (in English) at www.fni.no/
doc&pfd/oss-kronikk-eng.PDF.

[91] *See generally* Geir Hønneland, *Fisheries in the Svalbard Zone: Legality, Legitimacy and
Compliance, in* THE LAW OF THE SEA AND POLAR MARITIME DELIMITATION AND JURISDICTION 317

It appears Canada and Finland supported for a time Norway's view that the treaty does not apply seaward of Svalbard's territorial sea, but these views have changed.[92] Iceland and Russia vociferously dispute that claim, as does the Netherlands, Spain, and the United Kingdom. Other states parties to the treaty have reserved their positions or have not made them known publicly.[93] Relevant international case law is modest and inconclusive, but portions of one case support Norway's opponents. In the *Aegean Sea Continental Shelf* case,[94] Greece asked the ICJ to adjudicate a continental shelf dispute with Turkey. Greece had made a reservation to the ICJ's jurisdiction long before the continental shelf doctrine existed; the reservation exempted from the ICJ's purview disputes "relating to the territorial status of Greece." Greece attempted unsuccessfully to argue its reservation could not be used against it to excuse judicial review because it was not made in contemplation of the zone in dispute. But the Court found it applicable, holding that Greece intended the reservation pertaining to the "territorial status of Greece" as a generic term that had ambulatory significance: "Its meaning was intended to follow the evolution of the law and to correspond with the meaning attached to the expression by the law in force at any given time." Robin Churchill and Geir Ulfstein have argued that this case parallels the Svalbard situation: if Greece's "maritime rights had changed over time to include the continental shelf, so had there been a corresponding change in the scope of Greece's acceptance of jurisdiction."[95] Likewise, if Norway's right to sovereign claims over Svalbard has increased over time, "so, it can be argued, there has been a corresponding increase in the limitations on that sovereignty" as expressed in Articles 2 and 3, the equal enjoyment and equal liberty of access provisions.[96]

THE MEANING OF FULL AND ABSOLUTE SOVEREIGNTY

The 1920 Svalbard Treaty conferred "full and absolute sovereignty" on Norway over Svalbard.[97] But not in accordance with the ordinary and plain

---

(Alex G. Oude Elferink & Donald R. Rothwell, eds., 2001). *See also* Wolf, *supra* note 24, at 23. There are some complaints that Norway has turned something of a blind eye to Russian laxity with regard to its reported catch. *Id.* at 25. Russian authorities refuse to accept Norwegian managerial sovereignty in the Svalbard zone and refuse to submit and sign inspection reports to the Norwegian Fisheries Directorate in Bergen. *See* Tiller & Nyman, *supra* note 68, at 145–146. For tabulated instances of Russian challenges to Norwegian sovereignty in the Svalbard FPZ, *see id.* at 146.

[92] *See* Churchill & Ulfstein, *supra* note 26, at 564–565.
[93] *See id.,* 565.
[94] *See supra* note 23.
[95] Churchill & Ulfstein, *supra* note 26, at 578.
[96] *Id.*
[97] Treaty between Norway, The United States of America, Denmark, France, Italy, Japan, the Netherlands, Great Britain and Ireland and the British overseas Dominions, and Sweden

meaning of that phrase.[98] Conditions attached to Norway's sovereignty obligating Norwegian authorities to respect certain restrictions as the *quid pro quo* for international recognition of it rule.[99] Fundamental to the treaty are the principles of nondiscrimination and equal enjoyment. Citizens and companies from all treaty nations enjoy equally the same right of access to and residence in Svalbard. Rights to fish, hunt, or undertake any kind of maritime, industrial, mining, or commercial enterprises on land and in the territorial waters are granted to them all on equal terms. While Norway is granted allowance to maintain suitable environmental controls, such protections must apply equally to all. All parties have equal liberty of access to the islands' waters, fjords, and ports. Nationality accords no preferential treatment among signatories. On matters of international trade, the nationals of all parties to the agreement shall not be subject to any charge or restriction not borne by the nationals to whom Norway grants most favored nation status. Property rights, including mineral rights, are granted to all nationals of parties to the agreement on the basis of complete equality. Taxes collected on Svalbard may only benefit Svalbard, not the mainland, and the islands must remain demilitarized.[100]

The curious and qualified meaning of Norway's full and absolute sovereignty over Svalbard and its territorial waters are at the heart of this dispute, as is the idea of limiting sovereignty over previously uncontemplated but newly accessible resources. Qualified yet full and absolute sovereignty has the ring of an oxymoron. But surprisingly, it has an involved history that predates the Svalbard Treaty; the problematic phrase can better be understood within the context of Svalbard's four hundred year human history. Even in this context, a definitively clear understanding remains elusive, perhaps because states historically reaped delicate territorializing rewards by maintaining an artifice of temporary sovereignty. Svalbard's history presents a tidal flow of equivocating interest in the archipelago, rising and receding with estimates of its economic potential. Void of an indigenous population, the region nevertheless bears the imprint of the human hand; commonly called a no man's land, it never unequivocally embraced the meaning of a *terra nullius*, a term that escapes a single, precise, and agreed upon

---

concerning Spitsbergen signed in Paris February 9, 1920, www.sysselmannen.no/Documents/Sysselmannen_dok/English/Legacy/The_Svalbard_Treaty_9ssFy.pdf.

[98] *See* Barbara Kempen, Der völkerrechtliche Status der Inselgruppe Spitzbergen 54–71 (1995).

[99] *See* Wolf, *supra* note 24, at 9 (noting Norway's sovereignty was recognized in conjunction with other states parties' nondiscriminatory rights *ab initio*).

[100] *See* The Svalbard Treaty, *supra* note 3, arts. 1–9; Hilo Neumann, Die norwegische Arktis im Völkerrecht: Landgebiete-Seegebiete-Granzgebiete 66–73 (2013).

meaning.[101] The ICJ defined *terra nullius* as a "territory belonging to no one,"[102] where, as Peter Ørebech claimed, the term's core characteristic is lack of governmental regulation.[103] And yet states historically have proposed various schemes for the international administration of the archipelago while acknowledging that it should remain a *terra nullius*.[104]

THE POVERTY OF COMPETING HISTORICAL NARRATIVES

National historical traditions contribute to multiple and competing narratives regarding the colonization of Spitsbergen, including one hypothesis dating to the Stone Age.[105] These narratives are legally significant. They play an important, sometimes essential, role in showing how title to territory has been interpreted in practice.[106] Judges and arbitrators refer to them as *effectivités*, the importance of which we have seen in relation to *uti possidetis*. Decision-makers seek them out where definitive legal or historic title is lacking, as they may provide concrete considerations leading to determinations of good title. But again, they cannot upend the status quo if good title already exists. Much is made of them from national perspectives to buttress competing claims of first-finder or first-occupier, but they can become all-consuming,[107] and

[101] *See generally* MICHAEL CONNOR, THE INVENTION OF TERRA NULLIUS: HISTORICAL AND LEGAL FICTIONS ON THE FOUNDATIONS OF AUSTRALIA (2005). Blackstone's COMMENTARIES, *supra* note 5, Bk. 1, Ch. 4, 106–108, makes reference to "deserted" or "uncultivated" or "uninhabited" land, but never uses the term; other usages relate to inhabited but undeveloped land. Geoffrey Partington notes Blackstone never used the term *terra nullius*. Geoffrey Partington, *Thoughts on Terra Nullius*, 19 PROCEED. OF THE NINETEENTH CONF. OF THE SAMUEL GRIFFITH SOC'Y 96, at 96 (2007), *available at* www.samuelgriffith.org.au/papers/html/volume19/v19chap.11.html. *See also* PHILIP E. STEINBERG ET AL., CONTESTING THE ARCTIC: POLITICS AND IMAGINARIES IN THE CIRCUMPOLAR NORTH 31 (2015) (noting the nebulous image of the Arctic as terra nullius).
[102] Western Sahara, Advisory Opinion, 1975 I.C.J. 12, 38, ¶ 79.
[103] Ørebech, *supra* note 25, at 9.
[104] *See id.* at 9 (noting Norway's stance at the beginning of World War I "that Spitsbergen should remain a no man's land (*terra nullius*) and that the management of the archipelago should become international").
[105] *See generally* Thor B. Arlov, *The Discovery and Early Exploitation of Svalbard. Some Historiographical Notes*, 22 ACTA BOREALIA 3 (2005) (discussing Svalbard's controversial historiography relating to its discovery, including the possibility of a Stone Age settlement); S. E. Albrethsen & T. B. Arlov, *The Discovery of Svalbard – A Problem Reconsidered*, FENNOSCANDIA ARCHAEOLOGICA V, 105–110 (1988) (reviewing Stone Age, Viking twelfth/thirteenth-century, Russian Pomor 16th century and Barents hypotheses); Edwin O. Okhuizen, *Dutch Pre-Barents Maps and the Pomor Thesis about the Discovery of Spitsbergen*, 22 ACTA BOREALIA 21–41 (2005) (surveying archaeological investigations favoring and disfavoring the Pomor thesis on Spitsbergen's discovery).
[106] Frontier Dispute, 1986 I.C.J. 587; cf. Maritime Delimitation and Territorial Questions between Qatar and Bahrain (Qatar/Bahrain), Judgment of March 16, 2001, 2001 I.C.J. 212, at 219 (separate opinion of Judge Al-Khasawneh).
[107] *See, e.g.*, ROBERTO C. LAVER, THE FALKLANDS/MALVINAS CASE: BREAKING THE DEADLOCK IN THE ANGLO-ARGENTINE SOVEREIGNTY DISPUTE (2001) (detailing withering historical and legal

should be received with indulgence.[108] The important early-twentieth-century American legal authority, James Brown Scott, animated by the conquest of the North Pole in 1909, took up the *terra nullius* implications of Arctic exploration and international law, but promptly "disregarded" *les effectivités* of early (premodern) Arctic expeditions, "just as the predecessors of Columbus are ordinarily passed over in considering the discovery of America."[109] According to Scott, they lacked the jarring impetus and incentive to stimulate "conflict and controversy" and the need for legal regulation.[110]

This was a selective recourse to history, perhaps, but an observation of relevance to subjective application of *effectivités* in charting the human history of Spitsbergen. Russian hunters of the high northwest (the Pomors) are said to have referred to the islands, which they called Grumant, since medieval times; a leading Russian monograph concludes Russian discovery rights to Spitsbergen are persuasive;[111] the Vikings mentioned it in Icelandic sagas (the *Landnámabók*) in 1194,[112] supporting the prevailing Norwegian theory that Norsemen discovered the islands;[113] the Danes were said to frequent the archipelago by the sixteenth century, and claimed them under a mistaken identity;[114] England asserted Sir Hugh Willougby made the discovery in 1553 before perishing in a tempest off Norway;[115] but most credit the Dutch explorer, Willem Barents, with the discovery in 1596. On a third voyage in search of the elusive Northeast Passage to Cathay, piloting ships commanded by Jacob van Heemskerck (who was involved in the taking of the

disputes between Argentina and Great Britain over competing sovereignty claims to Falkland/Malvinas islands). Thilo Neumann argues in the case of Svalbard, the question of its first discoverer is meaningless ("*ohne Bedeutung*"). NEUMANN, *supra* note 100, at 48.

[108] Award of the Arbitral Tribunal in the First Stage of Proceedings between Eritrea and Yemen (Territorial Sovereignty and Scope of the Dispute) (Eritrea/Yemen), 22 R.I.A.A. ¶ 239, 268 (Perm. Ct. Arb, 9 October 1998). Disputed features in the South China Sea, doubtless, have and will give rise to extensive and competing claims of historical title, the legal significance of which remains to be seen.

[109] James Brown Scott, *Arctic Exploration and International Law*, 3 AM J. INT'L L. 928, 928 (1909).

[110] *Id.* at 928–929.

[111] *See* Vylegzhanin & Zilanov, *supra* note 12, 1–2.

[112] *See* II FRIDTJOF NANSEN, IN NORTHERN MISTS: ARCTIC EXPLORATION IN EARLY TIMES 166 (Arthur G. Chater, trans., 1911) (noting "*Svalbaros furdr*" [Svalbard discovered] "surely no great geographical discovery has ever been more briefly recorded in literature").

[113] *See* ULFSTEIN, THE SVALBARD TREATY, *supra* note 19, at 33 (1995). *See also* WILLY ØSTRENG, POLITICS IN HIGH LATITUDES: THE SVALBARD ARCHIPELAGO 2 (R. I. Christophersen, trans., 1978).

[114] Danish king Christian IV also claimed them in his capacity as king of Norway owing to the general sovereignty over the Northern Sea that this title bestowed. *See* THOR B. ARLOV, A SHORT HISTORY OF SVALBARD 18 (1989) [hereinafter ARLOV, SHORT HISTORY].

[115] *See* RICHARD HAKLUYT, THE PRINCIPALL NAVIGATIONS, VOIAGES AND DISCOVERIES OF THE ENGLISH NATION, MADE BY SEA OR OVER LAND, TO THE MOST REMOTE AND FARTHEST DISTANT QUARTERS OF THE EARTH AT ANY TIME WITHIN THE COMPASSE OF THESE 1500. YEERS: DEVIDED

Santa Catarina) and Jan Cornelisz Rijp, Barents spied a land consisting only of mountains and pointed hills, and named it Spitsbergen,[116] mistaking it for a part of Greenland.[117] In the early twentieth century, the Dutch attempted to attach priority to Barents' name as the sole discoverer of Spitsbergen.[118] Aside from conflicting historical narratives, Spitsbergen indisputably forms the largest island in the archipelago now called Svalbard, an Old Norse term meaning "cold coast."[119]

With Barents' sighting, conflict and controversy followed. Henry Hudson, looking for the elusive Northwest Passage in service of the Dutch East India Company (VOC), caught sight of numerous whales off Spitsbergen in 1607. Buttressed by additional pod sightings in 1611, a robust whaling industry commenced.[120] By the late seventeenth century, the Spitsbergen area hosted two hundred to three hundred whaling ships carrying upward of twelve thousand men.[121] The Dutch alone caught one thousand one hundred whales in 1722, but already the industry's take probably exceeded the replenishment of stock.[122] This industry first attracted Englishmen, then embittered Dutchmen, whose maritime interests were caught in a vice: by royal decree in 1609,[123]

INTO THREE SEVERALL PARTS, ACCORDING TO THE POSITIONS OF THE REGIONS WHEREUNTO THEY WERE DIRECTED 263–280 (1589) (discussing Willougby's voyages and discoveries); ULFSTEIN, THE SVALBARD TREATY, *supra* note 19, at 34 (noting that the claim has been rejected).

[116] *See generally* V. F. Starkov, *Russian Arctic Seafaring and the Problem of the Discovery of Spitsbergen*, FENNOSCANDIA ARCHAEOLOGICA III, 67 (1986). *See* III-IV SAMUEL PURCHAS, PURCHAS HIS PILGRIMES IN FIVE BOOKES (The Third, Voyages and Discoveries of the North parts of the World, by Land and Sea, in Asia, Europe, the Polare Regions, and in the Northwest of America) 473–482 (1625) (presenting an account of the first and second navigations of William Barents into the North Sea, behind Norway, Muscouia, and Tartaria; written by Great de Veer) and The Fourth (English Northerne Navigations, and Discoveries: Relations of Greenland, Groenland, the North-west passage, and other Arcticke Regions, with later Ruffian Occurrents).

[117] *See* MARTIN CONWAY, NO MAN'S LAND: A HISTORY OF SPITSBERGEN FROM ITS DISCOVERY IN 1596 TO THE BEGINNING OF THE SCIENTIFIC EXPLORATION OF THE COUNTRY 14 (2011) [1906].

[118] *See* Elen C. Singh & Artemy A. Saguirian, *The Svalbard Archipelago: The Role of Surrogate Negotiators*, *in* POLAR POLITICS: CREATING INTERNATIONAL ENVIRONMENTAL REGIMES 54, at 61 (Oran R. Young & Gail Oserenko, eds., 1993).

[119] NANSEN, *supra* note 112, at 166.

[120] *See* Louwrens Hacquebord, Frits Steenhuisen & Huib Waterbolk, *English and Dutch Whaling Trade and Whaling Stations in Spitsbergen (Svalbard) before 1660*, 15 INT'L J. MARIT. HIST. 117, 117 (December 2003). Apparently, the earliest English whalers set sights first on herds of walruses, which were plentiful on the west coast of Spitsbergen. *See 17th Century Whaling, History of Spitsbergen, Spitsbergen*, www.spitsbergen-svalbard.com/spitsbergen-information/ history/17th-century-whaling.html; *see also* Conway, *supra* note 117, at 20ff. (discussing commencement of walrus hunting in 1603–1604).

[121] *See* ARLOV, SHORT HISTORY, *supra* note 114, at 25.

[122] *See id.* at 32–33.

[123] *By the King, A Proclamation Touching Fishing*, Westminster, May 6, 1609, James I: Volume 45, May, June, 1609, *in* Calendar of State Papers Domestic: James I, 1603–1610, 507–523

English king James I had blocked them from fishing herring off England's coast; and Spain and Portugal had since 1598 blockaded Dutch access to the Mediterranean Sea. In response, Grotius published his famous tract on *Mare Liberum* (The Free Sea, 1609),[124] and a year later, the Dutch articulated the cannon shot rule, to reclaim control over waters encroached on by England. This claim reformulated a 1598 Danish decree establishing an exclusive two-league fishing belt around Iceland's waters, owing to Denmark's functional inability to assert broader sovereign interests over the Northern Sea. The Dutch claimed no sovereign could control more of the sea than he could command with a cannon, a distance from the shore of three nautical miles.[125] The Dutch publicist, Cornelius van Bynkershoek, later crystallized this famous cannon-shot rule in doctrinal form, establishing the territorial extension of sovereignty into the seas.[126] The seafaring seventeenth century soon enough would belong to the Low Countries, but at the beginning of that century, excluded from the North and Mediterranean Seas, they had to set sail farther north in search of fish and a wishful passageway to eastern emporia.

Their sea roving led to Spitsbergen, where they established an onshore flensing camp at Smeerenburg (Blubbertown), on the northwest tip of the island. The English, shortly before, had set up camp in the southwestern Bell Sound near Bottle Cove.[127] At these stations and others, hunters harvested seal, walrus tusks, baleen, and blubber to trade with the rest of Europe. Baleen is the comb-like filtration system found in the upper jaw of baleen whales that Europeans transformed into parts for parasols, furniture, wagons, and corsets. At times its price was so high that whales were caught exclusively to acquire it.[128] Blubber was rendered into oil for lamps, lubricants for industry, tanning fats for hides, soap – and good money. Its most

---

(Mary Anne Everett Green, ed., 1857), *available at* BHO/British History Online, www.british-history.ac.uk/cal-state-papers/domestic/jas1/1603–10/pp.

[124] Grotius withheld publication of the pamphlet, the re-worked 12th chapter of a much larger, never published work (*De Jure Praede*), on the instruction of his mentor, the Land Advocate of the rebellious Dutch Republic, Johan van Oldenbarnevelt, who at that time was involved in delicate negotiations with Spain, which resulted in the Twelve Years' Truce, easing Dutch access into the Mediterranean. *See* Rossi, *supra* note 85, at 20–21.

[125] *See* H. S. K. Kent, *The Historical Origins of the Three-Mile Limit*, 48 AM. J. INT'L L. 537, at 538–539, and accompanying notes 6–9 (1954).

[126] *See generally* CORNELIUS VAN BYNKERSHOEK, DE DOMINIO MARIS DISSERTATIO (Ralph Van Deman Magoffin trans, 1923) [1744 edn.].

[127] *See* Hacquebord et al., *supra* note 120, at 117–119; *Bowhead Whale*, NOAA Fisheries Office of Protected Resources, www.nmfs.noaa.gov/pr/species/mammals/cetaceans/bowheadwhale.htm (up to 50 cm layer of blubber).

[128] J. N. TØNNESSEN & A. O. JOHNSEN, THE HISTORY OF MODERN WHALING 6 (R. I. Christophersen, trans., 1982).

prized and pursued supplier was the Bowhead (Right)[129] whale, layered in up to fifty centimeters (1.6 feet) of blubber.[130] Its population estimate "prior to the beginning of commercial exploration in the early sixteenth century was a minimum of fifty thousand, of which almost half (twenty-four thousand) were in the Spitsbergen stock of the Greenland Sea."[131] Captain Ahab plied the nineteenth-century South Sea in vengeful pursuit of one Sperm whale, *Moby Dick*, but the novel's author, Herman Melville, drew real-life inspiration from the English Arctic whaler, William Scoresby, who attracted fame from ventures in the Greenland Sea; his firsthand accounts of the Arctic whale trade[132] attained a kind of canonical status among mariners.[133] Melville cited Scoresby's accomplishments in his great novel's curious thirty-second chapter. There, Melville diverted the narrative account of the *Pequod's* impending doom "to attend to a matter almost indispensable" – cetology.[134] The book's narrator praises Captain Scorseby as the supreme exemplar of the harpooner and whaler, the "best existing authority" on the Greenland (Right) [Bowhead] whale; the narrator's only criticism of Scoresby is his ignorance that "the great sperm whale now reigneth!," not the "Greenland or right-whale."[135]

French sea hunters followed the Dutch to Spitsbergen, with Basque masters on board to school them in the craft of harpooning.[136] Scandinavians from the united kingdom of Denmark-Norway appeared, as did Germans,[137] and a two-hundred-and-fifty-year enterprise began. This industry waned in

---

[129] Called the "Right" whale because it was the right whale to hunt. *See Right Whales*, NOAA FISHERIES, www.afsc.noaa.gov/nmml/education/cetaceans/right.php.

[130] *See* ARLOV, SHORT HISTORY, *supra* note 114, at 22.

[131] 1 THE ARCTIC WHALING JOURNALS OF WILLIAM SCORESBY THE YOUNGER: THE VOYAGES OF 1811, 1812 AND 1813, xxxviii (C. Ian Jackson, ed., 2003) [hereinafter SCORESBY]. Regulatory protections of the Bowhead whale date to the 1931 League of Nations Covenant, but the Spitsbergen stock never recovered from whaling epoch. They currently number less than one hundred in these waters and remain "endangered" in this area.

[132] *See generally* AN ACCOUNT OF THE ARCTIC REGIONS WITH A HISTORY AND DESCRIPTION OF THE NORTHERN WHALE-FISHERY, vols. I and II (1968/1969) [1820].

[133] *See* GORDON JACKSON, BRITISH WHALING TRADE xi (2005) (concluding, "any work on the traditional whaling trade must be deeply indebted to William Scoresby"); Sir Alister Hardy, *Introduction*, AN ACCOUNT OF THE ARCTIC REGIONS WITH A HISTORY AND DESCRIPTION OF THE NORTHERN WHALE-FISHERY I [no page number] (1968) [1820] (citing volume I as a "classic" and "one of the most remarkable books in the English language," and volume II as "the finest account of Arctic whale fisheries ever written").

[134] HERMAN MELVILLE, MOBY DICK, OR, THE WHALE Ch. 32, 133 (1979) [1851].

[135] *Id.* at 134.

[136] *See* Philippe Henrat, *French Naval Operations in Spitsbergen during Louis XIV's Reign*, 37 ARCTIC 544, 544 (Dec. 1984).

[137] *See* KEMPEN, *supra* note 98, at 14.

the mid-seventeenth century due to the development of open-sea flensing techniques, which contributed to overfishing; this development diminished the need for *terra firma* whaling stations, provided more time at sea to hunt, and pushed fleets farther west into unadulterated waters of the Greenland Sea. By the 1870s, massive overexploitation[138] and commercial substitutes for whale oil[139] took their toll and ended the commercial trade. But from the moment of its discovery in the modern age, the history of Spitsbergen became associated with the exploitation of natural resources;[140] denuded of its cetological economy, human interest in Spitsbergen was swept away, along with the detritus left by flensers at the water's edge.

THE PROTO-COMMONS AGREEMENT OF 1872

By 1872, following a forestalled effort by a united Sweden-Norway to claim sovereignty,[141] an unusual reversal of territorial temptation took place: through a diplomatic exchange of notes, Russia and Sweden-Norway declared Spitsbergen to be a *terra nullius* – commonly called a no-man's-land,[142] thought to be valueless except to occasional Russian and Norwegian fur trappers,[143] whose numbers already had diminished by then due to scurvy, murder, and privation.[144]

---

[138] *See* Pedersen, *Svalbard Continental Shelf Controversy, supra* note 38, at 341. Data from Dutch, German, and British sources suggest depredations in stock upwards of ten thousand per decade in the late seventeenth century. *See* 1 Scoresby, *supra* note 131, at xxxviii.

[139] *See* John R. Bockstoce & John J. Burns, *Commercial Whaling in the North Pacific Sector, in* THE BOWHEAD WHALE 563, 570 (John J. Burns, J. Jerome Montague & Cleveland J. Cowles, eds., 1993) (noting negative price effect by the 1880s).

[140] Dag Avango, *Svalbard Archaeology* (Royal Institute of Technology, Stockholm, 2005), *available at* www.svalbardarchaeology.org/history.html.

[141] Denmark ceded Norway to Sweden in 1814 (the Treaty of Kiel), and the United Kingdoms of Sweden and Norway lasted until 1905, when Norway formed its own constitutional monarchy. On Russia's opposition to Sweden-Norway's brief 1871 attempt to claim sovereignty, *see* KEMPEN, *supra* note 98, at 14.

[142] *See* R. N. Rudmose Brown, SPITSBERGEN IN 1914, 46 THE ROYAL GEOGRAPHICAL SOC'Y (WITH THE INSTITUTE OF BRITISH GEOGRAPHERS), 10, 15 (1915); Neumann, *supra* note 100, at 59–60.

[143] *See* Pedersen, *Svalbard Continental Shelf Controversy, supra* note 38, at 341. *See also* Conway, *supra* note 117, at 3. Norwegian fur traders first appeared in 1795. *See* Vylegzhanin & Zilanov, *supra* note 12, at 5.

[144] *See* Vylegzhanin & Zilanov, *supra* note 12 at 4; Marek E. Jasinski, *Russian Hunters on Svalbard and the Polar Winter*, 44 ARCTIC 156, 156 (1991) (noting that Russian trappers left the archipelago completely by around the middle of the nineteenth century). For an interesting discussion of the relationship between *terra nullius* and thinly populated, nongoverned territories, *see* Peter Thomas Ørebech, *Terra nullius, Inuit Habitation and Norse Occupation – With Special Emphasis on the 1933 Eastern Greenland Case*, 7 ARCTIC REVIEW ON LAW AND POLITICS 20–41 (2016).

A DIFFERENT KIND OF NO-MAN'S-LAND

But the Russo/Swedish-Norwegian Agreement of 1872 established a different kind of no-man's-land. The agreement employed the term *terra nullius* but did not construe Spitsbergen as a landmass void of overarching law.[145] Rather, the agreement – as between the two countries – consolidated their preferential rights to clarify the emerging legal status of Spitsbergen on behalf of the international community – a preferential movement toward a special kind of condominium whereby "Spit[s]bergen was regarded as a territory which could not be the object of exclusive possession by any State."[146] The binding implications of this exchange of notes would be revisited in the early twentieth century in line with the principle of *pacta tertiis*, which precludes the application of agreements against the rights of third parties absent their consent.[147] But the 1872 diplomatic exchanges marked an important historical first step in Spitsbergen's legal development, conceptualizing it more as a *res communis* – at least in terms of subjecting its administration to common oversight by two self-deputized stewards – rather than as a *terra nullius*. As noted by Geir Ulfstein, "[t]he legal difference between the two concepts is that sovereignty over *terra nullius* may be acquired by occupation (equating the notion of *terra nullius* with *res nullius*[148]), whereas *res communis* cannot be the object of occupation."[149] Important Russian legal scholars support the contention that the 1872 diplomatic exchanges meant Spitsbergen could no longer be considered a *terra nullius*, if interpreted as a land subject to any state's sovereign claim.[150]

---

[145] Vylegzhanin & Zilanov, *supra* note 12, at 10.

[146] *Id.* at 9 (quoting Dekanozov's interpretation of the 1872 exchange of notes). Responding to Sweden-Norway's query whether Russia would object to the former's assertion of sovereignty over Spitsbergen, the Russians responded in its diplomatic note 15 of May 27, 1871 with "the more practical proposal to maintain by tacit agreement that this group of islands remain as an area accessible to all" ("*Ill nous paraîtrait dès lors plus pratique de ne point les aborder et de nous borner à la situation de fait maintenue jusqu'ici par un accord tacite entre les Gouvernements et qui fait considerer ce groupe d'îles comme un domaine indécis accessible à tous le Etats*"). See ULFSTEIN, THE SVALBARD TREATY, *supra* note 19, at 37 n. 53.

[147] *See*, e.g., the perspectives added following the 1914 Conference on Spitsbergen, *infra*, text accompanying, nn. 219–222.

[148] *Res nullius*: A thing that has no owner, in which case it may be appropriated by the first finder. *See generally* F. S. Ruddy, *Res Nullius and Occupation in Roman and International Law*, 36 UMKC L. REV. 274 (1968).

[149] ULFSTEIN, THE SVALBARD TREATY, *supra* note 19, at 37.

[150] *See* Vylegzhanin & Zilanov, *supra* note 12, at 10–11, and accompanying notes (citing Dekanozov, Buromenskii, and Timchenko, and attributing the inaccuracy to Oreshenkov's reading of Bekiashev's PUBLIC INTERNATIONAL LAW (3rd edn., 2004)). The authors also claim that the diplomatic exchange of notes did not renounce Russia's historical rights to the archipelago. *See id.* at 10. The important American international law scholar and practitioner,

THE HISTORICAL DIFFICULTY WITH SPITSBERGEN'S COMMON ADMINISTRATION: CONTESTED CLAIMS

The proto-commons administration idea stood in opposition to the early seventeenth-century mind-set. Disputes about title to Spitsbergen arose almost immediately after human colonization – on land and in the blubber-rich western waters off Spitsbergen. English whalers removed the Dutch marker set up by Barents,[151] contesting whatever implications of *dominium* it might imply. English and Dutch commanders secured an uneasy peace by mutually agreeing to exclusive whaling grounds in 1614, but the peace would not hold.[152] Denmark-Norway dispatched warships to collect tribute from interloping whalers;[153] camps were raided and destroyed;[154] vessels were seized; the Dutch belligerently penetrated Bell Sound and in 1617 dispatched a fleet of twenty-three men-of-war to respond to provocation and to intimidate the English.[155] Motivated by the lingering belief Spitsbergen formed part of Danish-Norwegian Greenland, king James I offered to purchase the islands in 1613. Failing a reply from the union's king, Christian IV, he claimed them for England in 1614.[156] Christian IV responded by sending warships north and intermittently continued to do so as late as 1643, still defending the mistaken belief that Spitsbergen formed part of Danish-owned Greenland. In a demonstration of its astonishingly rapid rise as the century's maritime super-power, the United Provinces asserted military and seamanship superiority over the English hunting fleet in 1618, effectively securing for its fleet access to Spitsbergen's whaling rewards.[157]

The waning of the whaling industry gave way to a late-eighteenth to mid-nineteenth-century period of commercial quietude – turning Spitsbergen into a *de facto terra nullius*; but twentieth-century economic pursuits, this time mineral pursuits, brought renewed human interest in the archipelago.

James Brown Scott, also mischaracterized the conclusion of the diplomatic exchanges. *See* Scott, *supra* note 109, at 941 (finding "the two governments agreed formally that the region should remain as it had been, no man's land (*terra nullius*))."

[151] Pedersen, *Svalbard Continental Shelf Controversy, supra* note 38, at 341.

[152] Hacquebord et al., *supra* note 120, at 120.

[153] ARLOV, SHORT HISTORY, *supra* note 114, at 18.

[154] *See* ULFSTEIN, THE SVALBARD TREATY, *supra* note 19, at 34.

[155] Hacquebord et al., *supra* note 120, at 120.

[156] Pedersen, *Svalbard Continental Shelf Controversy, supra* note 38, at 341; Rudmose Brown, *supra* note 142, at 15 (noting England's proxy authority to claim the land as "King James his New Land" was given to ships operating under the authority of the English Muscovy Company, which was created for trade with Russia. *See* Vylegzhanin & Zilanov, *supra* note 12, at 3).

[157] *See* Pedersen, *Svalbard Continental Shelf Controversy, supra* note 38, at 341.

A four-hundred-million-year succession of metamorphic geology layered Spitsbergen's fifteen-thousand-meter-thick sedimentary bedrock with coal.[158] Norwegians commenced the first commercial mining operation in 1899 and British-Norwegian, American-Norwegian, Russian, Swedish, and Dutch mining towns sprouted up before World War I,[159] establishing a human presence that continues to this day. Svalbard's main city, Longyearbyen, bears the name of the American head of the Arctic Coal Company, John M. Longyear, whose company, chartered in West Virginia,[160] established the settlement in 1906.

The commingling of mining nationalities soon created conflicts. But Spitsbergen's location presented a strategic problem too. Both the United States and Russia recognized the military importance of the archipelago.[161] In 1899, Russia dispatched the naval vessel *Svetlana* to Bear Island, the southern-most island of the archipelago, to counter a German presence and to preempt its possible claim of sovereignty.[162] Russian foreign policy archivists regarded Bear Island as a station on its maritime route from the Baltic Sea to its Far North and to Siberia.[163] Connecting Spitsbergen to the maritime route to Siberia implies its connection to the Northern Sea Route, the intercoastal route established to develop and extract resources from Russia's High Arctic interior.[164] The US Foreign Office briefly entertained the thought of making Spitsbergen an American protectorate in 1909.[165] Establishing strategic refueling stations for far-flung naval fleets was a major preoccupation for maritime powers at this time, and posturing for port access to well-placed coaling stations stimulated keen competition among US, European, and Japanese navies in Caribbean and Pacific waters surrounding the soon-to-be open Panama Canal.[166] The US Navy's surprisingly successful use of colliers for refueling during its world cruise of 1907–1909 soon would lessen the importance of this

---

[158] *See* Ole Humlum, *A Geographical-Historical Outline of Svalbard*, www.unis.no/35_staff/staff_webpages/geology/ole_humlum/SvalbardOutline.htm.

[159] *See id.*

[160] ELEN C. SINGH, THE SPITSBERGEN (SVALBARD) QUESTION: UNITED STATES FOREIGN POLICY, 1907–1935, at 12 (1980).

[161] For Russia's view, *see* KEMPEN, *supra* note 98, at 18 ("*Russland erkannte die militärstrategische Bedeutund des Archipels*"); for the US view, *see infra*.

[162] *See* ULFSTEIN, THE SVALBARD TREATY, *supra* note 19, at 38.

[163] *See* Vylegzhanin & Zilanov, *supra* note 12, at 22 (footnote omitted).

[164] This cabotage system would play an important military role for the Soviets in World War II.

[165] *See* Rudmose Brown, *supra* note 142, at 15.

[166] The competition was a motivation behind the August 1914 Bryan-Chamorro Treaty between the USA and Nicaragua. Art. II granted the USA an exclusive and renewable 99-year lease on a naval base on islands in the Gulf of Fonseca. *See generally* Interoceanic Canal (Bryan-Chamorro Treaty), 10; C. BEVANS, TREATIES AND OTHER INTERNATIONAL AGREEMENTS OF THE UNITED STATES OF AMERICA, 1776–1949, 379 (1968–1976).

imperial temptation, perhaps diverting military but not economic attention away from High Arctic waters.[167]

THE PROBLEMATIC RISE OF THE TERM *TERRA NULLIUS*

But in 1906, a nonmilitary matter arose: Norwegian coal miners, employed extensively among the foreign mining companies at varying wages, went on strike.[168] The strike presented Spitsbergen's first dangerous development given the land's lack of legal authority.[169] At one point, mounting tensions prompted an English mining company to petition for Royal Navy support to quell labor strife at a camp called Advent City.[170] Labor unrest would persist in Spitsbergen until 1920,[171] the year Norway undertook to draft a Mining Code in anticipation of achieving sovereign rights over Spitsbergen (which it would later rename Svalbard).[172]

It was specifically within this Arctic context that the problematic term *terra nullius* again came to prominence, appearing in the pages of the *Revue générale de droit international public* and in the writings of Camille Piccioni, James Brown Scott, Ernest Nys, and Franz Depagnet.[173] But what did *terra nullius* mean in Spitsbergen's twentieth-century context? Did it preclude possession by states as a confused or commingled expression of *res communis*? Did it imply a condominium arrangement among interested parties? Did it require formal multilateral legal administration through treaty creation? Or did it express a beachcomber's delight, bestowing treasures on privateers who were lucky or capable enough to fall first into possession of ownerless property? Each of these usages attached to the meaning of *terra nullius* in Spitsbergen's history. But the term also faded from the lexicon alongside periods of Spitsbergen's diminishing economic appeal. But with the return of Spitsbergen's economic potential, legal views began to reformulate applications of the *terra nullius* term.

ROBERT LANSING'S VIEW

None of these reformulations exceeded the significance of Robert Lansing's views. Lansing served as US State Department Legal Advisor and then as US

---

[167] *See* Rossi, *supra* note 61, at 833–834.

[168] *See* KEMPEN, *supra* note 98, at 17.

[169] *See id.* at 17 (noting *"die ersten gefärlichen Folgen"*).

[170] *See* ARLOV, SHORT HISTORY, *supra* note 114, at 58.

[171] *See id.* at 58.

[172] Art. 8 Treaty Relating to Svalbard (requiring Norway to undertake mining regulations); *See* ØSTRENG, *supra* note 113, at 16–18 (discussing the origins of the Mining Code).

[173] *See* Andrew Fitzmaurice, *The Genealogy of Terra Nullius*, 38 (129) AUSTRALIAN HISTORICAL STUDIES 1, 2–4, and accompanying notes (2007).

President Woodrow Wilson's Secretary of State in World War I through the Paris Peace Conference. He distinguished himself as the leading US authority on High North affairs, representing US interests in the 1892–1893 Bering Sea Arbitration, the 1896–1897 Bering Sea Claims Commission, the 1903 Alaskan Boundary Tribunal, the 1910 North Atlantic Fisheries Arbitration, and the North Atlantic Fisheries and Fur Seals Conferences in 1911.[174] By 1914, "he had served on more international arbitrations than any other living American."[175] In 1911, he drafted two memoranda that helped shape the evolving discussion about staking claims in the ownerless land of Spitsbergen, distinguishing political sovereignty ("the exclusive exercise of sovereignty over particular persons without regard to the place of such exercise") from territorial sovereignty ("the exclusive exercise of sovereignty within a defined special sphere").[176] His main point was that a governance regime presiding over a *terra nullius* was possible because "the right of sovereignty [was] not uniformly dependent upon a special sphere [i.e., a state] for its exercise."[177] In effect, Lansing's view cleaved sovereignty from its post-Westphalian identification with the territorial state – a view that had antecedents in the idea of agency or divided sovereignty as discussed by Grotius in his *Mare Liberum* defense of Dutch colonial interests in Asia.[178] It seems Lansing intended to articulate a variant of sovereignty to preside over *terra nullius* to protect, even temporarily, "established interests"[179] – a reference doubtless to extant US mining interests in Spitsbergen.

The subject preoccupied Lansing and he reformulated his thoughts in an article published in 1917 in the *American Journal of International Law*. According to Lansing's common but somewhat misleading assessment, Spitsbergen fast presented "a unique international problem;" overlooking its modern history, much as James Brown Scott did, he wrote: "No nation

---

[174] *See* Daniel M. Smith, Robert Lansing and American Neutrality, 1914–1917, at 1 (vol. 59, 1958). *See also Biographies of the Secretaries of State: Robert Lansing*, US Dep't of State Office of the Historian, https://history.state.gov/departmenthistory/people/lansing-robert.

[175] Smith, *supra* note 174, at 1.

[176] Singh & Saguirian, *supra* note 118, at 85, and accompanying note 58 (quoting Lansing's 1911 "Note: Government over persons within *terra nullius* – General Principles"). Lansing's other memorandum was: "General Statement of Conventional Plan for Government in Spitzbergen," which circulated in February 1911. *See id.* at 85 n. 60. The distinction between political and territorial sovereignty extended his division between the political and territorial state, which he detailed in 1907. *See* Robert Lansing, *Notes on Sovereignty in a State*, 1 Am. J. Int'l L. 105, 109 (1907).

[177] Singh & Saguirian, *supra* note 118, at 85 (quoting Lansing's "Note: Government over persons within *terra nullius* – General Principles").

[178] *See generally* Edward Keene, Beyond the Anarchical Society: Grotius, Colonialism and Order in World Politics (2002) (discussing the prevalence of divisible sovereignty).

[179] Singh & Saguirian, *supra* note 118, at 85 n. 59.

has ever considered it worth its while to occupy them or to assert sovereignty over them;" "[t]hus the archipelago remained unoccupied, and it became generally recognized that Spit[s]bergen was *terra nullis*, a 'no man's land.'"[180] But it was ownerless property in the unusual sense that states were maneuvering to preclude any state's sole title to this territory that nevertheless had become enmeshed in conflicting multinational private property disputes. If no one state could perfect its sovereign interest over Spitsbergen, the archipelago's *terra nullius* status meant no other state should perfect such an interest either. More correct was Lansing's sense of the Grotian tendency, at least as reflected between the whaling and mining epochs: "the intense cold and the long period of the year when [the islands] are ice-bound necessarily made an attempt to develop their resource extremely difficult, so that they seemed to be an undesirable possession, a probable source of expense rather than a source of profit."[181] He correctly noted that this view changed in recent years in view of its possible mineral wealth.[182]

Interestingly, even from Lansing's icebound vantage point, Spitsbergen's ambiguous *terra nullius* characterizations – evolving as they were – had a Polynesian analog, making his estimation of the problem, if unique, also comparable to the issue presented for legislative solution by the 1856 Guano Islands Act.[183]

GUANO

Guano – bird droppings – was a fertilizer known for its potency due to the inquisitive mind of the German naturalist and explorer, Alexander von Humboldt. He collected a sample while sojourning in Peru, took it back to Europe in 1804, and had it chemically analyzed.[184] Its phosphate-rich properties circulated in French and then American and British chemical journals.[185] By mid-nineteenth century, American farmers in the Chesapeake basin were touting its "magical influence on the soil," prompting an almost insatiable

---

[180] Robert Lansing, *A Unique International Problem*, 11 Am. J. Int'l L. 763, 764 (1917).

[181] *Id.* at 764.

[182] *See id.* at 764.

[183] The Guano Islands Act (11 Stat. 119, enacted August 18, 1856, codified at 48 U.S.C. Ch. 8 §§1411–1419).

[184] Alexander de Humboldt, Personal Narrative of Travels to the Equinoctial Regions of the New Continent, during the years 1799–1804 xiii n*(Helen Maria Williams, trans., 1815) (noting "the guano of the islands of Peru" as one of the substances brought from America and submitted to chemical analysis).

[185] *See* Richard A. Wines, Fertilizer in America: From Waste Recycling to Resource Exploitation 34–35 (1985).

demand.[186] Guano island mania ensued, sparking keen competition in British and American agriculture markets for the product.[187] Its supply was traced to mines long established on Peru's three Chincha Islands.[188] As its principal export and source of foreign currency, Peru tightly controlled its excavation, elevating its price to one-quarter of the price of gold.[189] A worldwide search for alternatives uncovered hundreds of potential repositories on islands off Mexico, in the Caribbean, and later on the west coast of Australia and the East Indies.[190] But speculative pursuit in the crowded waters of the Americas provoked "numerous [and] protracted diplomatic disputes."[191] British and American prospectors clashed with Peruvian officials on the Lobos Islands in 1852 – there, military threats rose to the highest diplomatic levels and the issue occupied several paragraphs in US President Millard Fillmore's 1852 State of the Union Address.[192] Venezuela expelled Baltimore merchants from the Los Monjes islands; Mexico ejected foreigners from the Alacranes islands off the coast of Yucatan; and in the so-called Aves Affair – involving prospectors' claim-jumping – the Venezuelan Navy expelled both claimants and staked its own tenuous claim of sovereignty.[193]

A grander opportunity to circumvent Peru's monopoly control over production arose in the expansive Pacific. Since the 1820s, American and British whalers had plied the waters of the central Pacific; their observations prompted rumors of Guano islands. Speculators had interviewed these whalers and had drawn up a list of islands for the US Navy to reconnoiter.[194] The massive US Surveying and Exploration Expedition – a fully equipped six-vessel flotilla of weather men, vegetation specialists, naturalists, cartographers, artists, scientists, and military men under the captaincy of Charles Wilkes[195] – set sail between 1838 and 1842. Wilkes' thickly descriptive narrative of the expedition's encounters, including

---

[186] *Id.* at 40.

[187] *See id.*, at 54–70.

[188] *See* Christina Duffy Burnett, *The Edges of Empire and the Limits of Sovereignty: American Guano Islands*, 57 Am. QUARTERLY 782–783 (2005); WINES, *supra* note 185, 42–47.

[189] Dan Vergano, *Bird Droppings Led to U.S. Possession of Newly Protected Pacific Islands*, NAT'L GEOGRAPHIC, September 28, 2014, http://news.nationalgeographic.com/news/2014/09/140926-pacific-island-guano-national-monument-history/.

[190] *See* WINES, *supra* note 185, at 58–68.

[191] *Id.* at 54.

[192] *See* Millard Fillmore, 1852 State of the Union Address (Dec. 6, 1852), www.presidentialrhetoric .com/historicspeeches/fillmore/stateoftheunion1852.html (discussing the Lobos Island guano dispute with Peru). President Fillmore also noted the rapidly increasing commercial inter-course involving American whalers and the Arctic Sea. *Id.*

[193] *See* WINES, *supra* note 185, 56–60.

[194] *See id.* at 61.

[195] *See id.* Wilkes narrative account of his Polynesian encounters apparently inspired Melville's description of the tattooed Rokovoko harpoonist, Queequeg. *See* Nathaniel Philbrick, *The*

dutifully recorded track records of the voyage, clearly document the expedition's crisscrossing of many uninhabited islets teeming with guano deposits.[196] Jarvis, Howland, and Baker Islands on the equator, and Kingman Reef, the fifty-island Palmyra Atoll, and the Johnston Atoll slightly southwest of Hawaii – islands broadly falling within what now comprises the largest marine conservation area in the world[197] – became the object of congressional attention. Estimates throughout the central Pacific were staggering: some deposits measured as much as one hundred and fifty feet deep,[198] inciting a Klondike-like fever among privateers, who set out to extract an estimated twelve million tons of Polynesian white gold[199] to take to British and North American markets.

With military threats and claim-jumping disputes heating up in the Gulf of Mexico and Caribbean, increasing demands were put on US legislators by powerful agricultural lobbyists to secure the resource. Agriculture employed four-fifths of the working population in the United States in the early 1850s.[200] American warships were dispatched to Baker and Jarvis islands to procure guano samples.[201] US Senator William Seward, later derided for arranging, as Secretary of State, the US purchase of Alaska from Russia, drafted legislation that would ultimately become the Guano Islands Act, establishing US sovereign control over area in the Pacific now encompassing territory three times the size of California.[202] Like the later Russo/Swedish-Norway Agreement of

Scientific Legacy of the U.S. Exploring Expedition, Smithsonian Libraries (Jan. 2004), www .sil.si.edu/digitalcollections/usexex/learn/Philbrick.htm. Wilkes would be court-martialed and materially acquitted for a massacre that would take place in Fiji (Tahitians had forewarned that he should "go to your own land; this belongs to us and we don't want anything to do with you)." [vol. 1 p. 312].

[196] *See generally* CHARLES WILKES, NARRATIVE OF THE UNITED STATES EXPLORING EXPEDITION DURING THE YEARS 1838, 1839,1840, 1841, 1942 (1845). Sina Najafi & Christina Duffy Burnett, *Islands and the Law: An Interview with Christina Duffy Burnett,* 38 CABINET (Summer 2010), www .cabinetmagazine.org/issues/38/najafi_burnett.php.

[197] *See* Title 3, The President, Proclamation 9173-Pacific Remote Islands Marine National Monument Expansion, Sept. 25, 2014, vol. 79, no. 188 Federal Register, www.fws.gov/uploadedFiles/Region_ 1/NWRS/Zone_1/Pacific_Remote_Islands_Marine_National_Monument/Documents/ Presidential%20Proclamation%209173.pdf (expanding the monument to create the largest marine reserve in the world).

[198] *See* Matt Rosenberg, *Guano Island Act, About Education,* http://geography.about.com/od/ politicalgeography/a/guanoisland.htm.

[199] *See* WINES, *supra* 185, at 54; *see also The Great Peruvian Guano Bonanza: Rise, Fall, and Legacy,* Council on Hemispheric Affairs (July 13, 2011), www.coha.org/the-great-peruvian-guano-bonanza-rise-fall-and-legacy/ (12 million tons); Vergano, *supra* note 189 ("White Gold").

[200] Four-fifths of Americans were employed in the cultivation of the soil in 1851. *See* Millard Filmore, "1851 State of the Union Address (Dec. 2, 1851), Presidential Rhetoric," www .presidentialrhetoric.com/historicspeeches/fillmore/stateoftheunion1851.html

[201] WINES, *supra* note 185, at 62.

[202] Obama establishes world's largest marine preserve, CBSNEWS (Sept. 25, 2014), www.cbsnews .com/news/obama-establishes-worlds-largest-marine-preserve/.

1872, the Guano Islands Act reworked the concept of sovereignty to avoid provoking a backlash.

The act allowed any US citizen to take peaceable possession of any island, rock, or key not within the lawful jurisdiction of any government and claim it, at the discretion of the President, as *appertaining* to the United States.[203] The Act "virtually assigned ownership of unclaimed islands to the United States," and John Longyear unsuccessfully lobbied State Department officials to amend the act to cover coal, thereby making it applicable to Spitsbergen.[204] But Congress, sensitive to anti-imperialism charges at home and abroad, produced a solution that allowed the United States to territorialize its interests and yet avoid criticisms of flagrant annexation that could provoke conflict. Certain provisions allowed the United States to defend these claims through military force;[205] but other provisions allowed the United States to relinquish claims once the resource was removed.[206] The acquisition of territory and the projection of power accompanied a provision to disclaim sovereignty and deny territorial *dominium*.[207] Earlier drafts of the bill excised references to the United States' "sovereignty," "territory," and "territorial domain" over guano islands,[208] substituting the term "appertaining to," which became law.

An exhaustive analysis of the legal status of the American Guano Islands prepared by the State Department in 1931–1932 summed up an eighty-year history of efforts to make sense of the Guano Islands Act with the remark that "the only conclusion which can fairly be drawn from [these efforts] is that no one knew what the Guano Act really meant." In particular, no one understood precisely what it meant to say that a guano island could "be considered as appertaining" to the United States.[209]

It meant that the United States intended to protect the interests of its privateers, and ambiguously claim title while preserving an option of disavowing ownership so as to not incite anti-expansionist sentiment at home or counterclaims from abroad. Establishing a governance regime closely approximating, but not necessarily dependent on, state sovereignty would later inform

---

[203] *See* 48 U.S.C. §1411.

[204] SINGH, *supra* note 160, at 37–38.

[205] *See* 48 U.S.C. §1418 (The President is authorized, at his discretion, to employ the land and naval forces of the United States to protect the rights of the discoverer or of his widow, heir, executor, administrator, or assigns).

[206] §1419. Nothing in this chapter contained shall be construed as obliging the United States to retain possession of the islands, rocks, or keys, after the guano shall have been removed from the same.

[207] *See* Burnett, *supra* note 188, at 781.

[208] *Id.* at 785.

[209] *Id.* at 786.

Lansing's view, which conformed to the concept of *terra nullius* to territorial temptation but only so long as necessary to secure parochial interests of nationals. This perspective expresses a recurring equivocating sentiment in Spitsbergen's legal history, and parallels a mid-to-late-nineteenth-century practice whereby imperial European powers pursed fictive sovereignty to maintain influence, exercise control, promote trade, and project power over colonial holdings without assuming the burdens of formal sovereignty.[210]

Interestingly, the problem of claim jumping in the Caribbean guano islands would foreshadow claim jumping in High Arctic coal mining operations.[211] Recognizing the improbable challenges presented by labor and territorial unrest in a no-man's-land located 78° North, in addition to crafting a governance regime divorced from the concept of statehood, Norway began to reformulate ideas for a shared-sovereignty arrangement.[212]

THE CONDOMINIUM DISCUSSIONS OF 1910, 1912, AND 1914

In 1910, the first of three conferences on Spitsbergen was convened. Norway (now a constitutional monarchy), Sweden, and Russia held *pourparlers* in Christiania (renamed Oslo in 1924) and agreed on additional discussions to create a supreme public authority for legal and administrative authority in Spitsbergen.[213] The nationality principle of jurisdiction emerged as a starting point for resolving conflicts or matters of island administration. This principle held that relative rights of persons residing in Spitsbergen vested in the authority nations have over their nationals wherever they may be found.[214] Based on its perceived application, additional international conferences convened in Christiania in 1912 and 1914 to "frame an international administration for the archipelago."[215] The 1912 conference contemplated establishment of a joint administration agreement – a condominium arrangement – whereby the

---

[210] This point is extensively discussed in Ch. 2 of Martti Koskenniemi's Gentle Civilizer of Nations: The Rise and Fall of International Law 1870–1960 (2004).

[211] *See* Singh & Saguirian, *supra* note 118, at 64.

[212] *See* Kempen, *supra* note 98, at 17 ("*In dieser Situation schlug die norwegische Regierung vor, dass die Inselgruppe entweder von Norwegen als Mandat im Namen der interessierten Staaten oder aber durch sämtlichen Mächte gemeinsam verwaltet warden sollte*").

[213] *See id.* at 18; Ulfstein notes a draft commission proposal consisting of the three conference attendees that produced German and US objections after circulation for comments. *See* Ulfstein, The Svalbard Treaty, *supra* note 19, at 39.

[214] *See* Fred K. Nielsen, *The Solution of the Spitsbergen Question*, 14(1–2) Am. J. Int'l L. 232, 232–33 (1920). *See also* Lansing, *supra* note 180, at 766 ("wherever such persons may be, they are under the regulation of the sovereign power").

[215] Nielsen, *supra* note 214, at 232. Norway hosted all conferences in its capital. The second conference was convened in May 1912 and included Norway, Sweden, and Russia. *See* Rudmose

territory would remain neutral and open to all nations but administered by Sweden, Norway, and Russia.[216] That idea was fleshed out in terms of establishing an international police force, a self-financing tax structure based on mining claims, and explorations of scientific and environmental issues. Struggling still with the concepts of *terra nullius* and common use, Article 1 of the draft proposal conflated these usages, holding that Spitsbergen should remain a *terra nullius* and should not be subject to annexation.[217] J. H. W. Verzijl coined this provision as an "artificial *terra nullius*,"[218] akin to the US Congress' claim that Guano islands "appertained to" but did not belong to the United States. Other proposals were submitted for ratification at the 1914 conference, which added representatives from Germany, Belgium, the United States, Denmark, France, Great Britain, and the Netherlands, whose nationals had established historical connections to the islands.[219] There, Norway favored joint management among all powers doing business in Spitsbergen; Sweden favored joint management with Russia and Norway; the United States sought a veto power to preserve economic claims but mostly advocated in favor of Sweden's position;[220] while Germany advocated enlargement of the administrative commission to include its representative, which Russia and Sweden opposed.[221] It appears the composition of the administrative commission, and not the idea of condominium, became the major sticking point.[222] Willy Østreng concluded that these attempts may have exacerbated disagreement between the discussants.[223] There would be no resolution; the conference set a date for reconvening in February 1915, then adjourned days before the outbreak of World War I. It was the "last occasion on which direct negotiations took place among all of the powers most concerned with resolving the Spitsbergen question."[224]

Brown, *supra* note 142, at 15. The third conference took place in June 1914 and was attended by representatives of Germany, USA, Denmark, France, Great Britain, Norway, the Netherlands, Russia, and Sweden. *See* Nielsen, *supra* note 214, at 232; Neumann, *supra* note 100, at 60–66.

[216] Rudmose Brown, *supra* note 142, at 15.
[217] *See* ULFSTEIN, THE SVALBARD TREATY, *supra* note 19, at 39.
[218] *See id.* at 40 n. 68 (quoting volume IV of VERZIJL'S INTERNATIONAL LAW IN HISTORICAL PERSPECTIVE).
[219] The third conference took place in June 1914. *See* Nielsen, *supra* note 214, at 232.
[220] *See* KEMPEN, *supra* note 98, at 19.
[221] *See* Singh & Saguirian, *supra* note 118, at 65.
[222] *See* ULFSTEIN, THE SVALBARD TREATY, *supra* note 19, at 41. Ulfstein reduced the main dispute to US and German bids to participate in the governance of the islands and Russia's opposition to both. *Id.* at 40. *See also* Singh & Saguirian, *supra* note 118, at 76 (noting from a review of the draft treaties that the "veil of uncertainty was not thick" surrounding the idea of granting all parties open access).
[223] ØSTRENG, *supra* note 113, at 2.
[224] Singh & Saguirian, *supra* note 118, at 65.

THE PARIS PEACE CONFERENCE

A markedly changed political landscape after World War I led to a break-through following the 1919 Paris Peace Conference: "The Allied Supreme Council granted Norway 'full and unqualified' sovereignty over Svalbard, though with provisions for international activity in the islands, resulting in the 1920 Treaty Concerning the Archipelago of Spitsbergen."[225] This extension of sovereign rights to Norway, albeit qualified to allow signatories the right of economic activity on an entirely equal footing with Norwegian nationals,[226] marked the principal change and was the result of a combination of factors.

Twenty-seven nations attended the Paris Peace Conference, but Russia and Germany were not invited. Russia fought with the Allies until 1917, but hast-ily withdrew from the war to attend to internecine problems caused by the Bolshevik Revolution. In 1918, the Bolsheviks signed the separate and pun-ishing 1918 Brest-Litovsk peace agreement with the Central Powers.[227] Their repudiation of foreign debt owed to Allied powers and disclosure of secret agreements relating to postwar plans provoked the Allies into adopting a pol-icy of nonrecognition against the Soviet state. Germany, as one of the defeated Central Powers (together with Austria-Hungary, Turkey, and Bulgaria), was in no position to negotiate. The product of the peace conference, the Treaty of Versailles, bears this point out. It extracted punitive measures from Germany, forcing it to cede all overseas possessions, 10 percent of its prewar European territory, the coal-rich Saarland, its Baltic Sea port of Danzig (now Gdansk), and to accept armament restrictions, responsibility for initiating and conduct-ing the war, and massive demands for reparations. Neutral countries, such as Belgium, the Netherlands, Sweden, and Norway, technically did not partici-pate at the conference, but could make their voices heard.

A provision in the Brest-Litovsk Treaty contemplated placing Russia and Germany "on an equal footing" in the settlement of the Spitsbergen question and called on Norway to host a continuation of the conference on the subject.[228] The Bolsheviks meant this provision to preserve their historic claim in the archi-pelago, but that treaty was repudiated by Germany's defeat; and Norway, in view

---

[225] *See* Adam Grydehøj, Anne Grydehøj & Maria Ackrén, *The Globalization of the Arctic: Negotiating Sovereignty and Building Communities in Svalbard, Norway*, 7 ISLAND STUD. J. 99, 101 (2012).

[226] *See* ØSTRENG, *supra* note 113, at 26.

[227] The Brest-Litovsk Treaty of March 3, 1918 ended Soviet Russia's participation in World War I. *See generally* Peace Treaty of Brest Litovsk, *available at* The Avalon Project, Yale Law School, http://avalon.law.yale.edu/20th_century/bl34.asp#art33a.

[228] *See id.*, art. 33.

of changed circumstances, had moved beyond the proto-condominium idea suggested by the 1872 diplomatic exchanges and the work product of the three Spitsbergen prewar conferences. This latter point weighs heavily on Russia's collective legal and political memory,[229] and may account for Russian politicians' buyers' remorse (and Rogozin's irredentist lament[230]), when contemplating the Bolsheviks' accession to the 1920 treaty.

Anticipating a reward as a "neutral ally,"[231] the Norwegian Storting's Foreign Affairs Committee met in closed session shortly before the Paris Peace Conference and set upon a plan to acquire the islands.[232] Norway's particularly able ambassador in Paris, F. Wedel-Jarlsberg,[233] acutely interested in obtaining Spitsbergen to make Norway self-sufficient in coal production,[234] portaged the request to the conference's Council of Heads of Delegations,[235] where it gained traction. The Americans already may have been inclined toward the idea of Norway's ownership; Robert Lansing, by this time promoted to US Secretary of State, had expressed that view privately to Norway's Foreign Minister,[236] as the State Department had no direct American proprietary interest to represent diplomatically when in 1916 all four American mining tracts were sold to a Norwegian banking syndicate.[237]

And then there was the question of Norway's war reward. Of all the neutrals, Norway most beneficially qualified its neutrality toward the Allied camp.[238] Its pro-Entente sentiment aside, Norway had to manage a delicate geostrategic situation. Despite Norway's profitable early rewards as a neutral – massive foreign capital accumulation through trade with both belligerent camps[239] – Great

---

[229] *See* Vylegzhanin & Zilanov, *supra* note 12, at 25 (noting the 1872 Agreement with Sweden-Norway secured "materially greater" rights for Russia).

[230] *See supra* text accompanying note 14.

[231] *See generally* Olav Riste, THE NEUTRAL ALLY: NORWAY'S RELATIONS WITH BELLIGERENT POWERS IN THE FIRST WORLD WAR (1965).

[232] *See* ULFSTEIN, THE SVALBARD TREATY, *supra* note 19, at 41 (discussing the Storting Committee's closed meeting of November 8, 1918).

[233] Several scholars credit Wedel-Jarlsberg's diplomatic acumen for Norway's acquisition of sovereignty over Svalbard. *See* ARLOV, SHORT HISTORY, *supra* note 114, at 66; Singh & Saguirian, *supra* note 118, at 64 n. 56 and 86–89.

[234] *See* Singh & Saguirian, *supra* note 118, at 87.

[235] *See id.* at 66.

[236] *See id.* at 63 (noting US Secretary of State Robert Lansing's telegram of May 6, 1917 to Norway's Foreign Minister Helmer Bryn expressing the view the islands should belong to Norway).

[237] *See* Singh, *supra* note 160, 84–89.

[238] Olav Riste claims Norway's policy of neutrality was "without question overwhelmingly pro-Entente," noting as well that losses to its merchant fleet amounted to about half of its tonnage at a cost of two thousand merchant mariners. Riste, *supra* note 231, at 226.

[239] *See* Jan Normann Knutsen, *Norway in the First World War*, 5 FOLIA SCANDINAVICA POZNAŃ 43, 57 (1999).

Britain exercised a commanding stranglehold over Norway's huge merchant marine fleet, measured in terms of Great Britain's worldwide control over supply lines and access to bunker stations.[240] It made good use of this leverage, particularly in the second half of the war, which fiendishly complicated commercial transit through the introduction of unrestricted submarine warfare on January 9, 1917.[241] According to Olav Riste, the unequal belligerent control over Norway's neutrality meant that Germany found advantage in the barest minimum of Norway's economic concessions, "whereas the Entente was only satisfied with a neutrality from which a maximum of benefits could be derived."[242] At the war's end, Norway was acknowledged as having provided good service to the Allied cause – committing eight hundred ships and one thousand two hundred of its merchant mariners in support of British and French interests;[243] other estimates were more exacting: Norway "suffered more civilian losses at sea than any other country," about half the tonnage of its merchant fleet and two thousand sailors.[244] Adopting a more "introspective attitude" and a "more active foreign policy," Norway "deliberately attempted to profit from the goodwill with the victorious Western powers which Norway's contributions during the war had created. Norwegian sovereignty over Svalbard, enlarging its territory by one-fifth,[245] was the most notable achievement of this policy."[246]

Spitsbergen's legal status did not preoccupy the Allied powers, but it was a central foreign policy focus for Norway.[247] French Premier Georges Clémenceau, the host of the Paris Peace Conference, may have been inclined toward Norway's position due to well-established French animus toward Germany, suspicions regarding Bolshevik Russia, and a desire to provide a reward to Norway in lieu of exciting Norwegian compensation claims for wartime losses to its merchant marine.[248] A Spitsbergen Commission consisting of representatives from the United States, France, United Kingdom, and Italy was appointed in July 1919 following the Versailles Treaty. Norwegian diplomats also were actively working behind the scene. In 1919, Norwegian

---

[240] *See id.* at 51.

[241] *See* Smith, *supra* note 174, at 152–153.

[242] Riste, *supra* note 231, at 227.

[243] *See* Vylegzhanin & Zilanov, *supra* note 12, at 22 (citing an August 1919 correspondence of British Foreign Secretary Balfour ("good service") and merchant marine statistics).

[244] Knutsen, *supra* note 239, at 57 (1999); Riste, *supra* note 231, at 226.

[245] *See* Arlov, Short History, *supra* note 114, at 68.

[246] Knutsen, *supra* note 239, at 57.

[247] *See* Singh & Saguirian, *supra* note 118, at 79 (noting that Norway viewed the resolution of the Spitsbergen question as a high priority, but it was not a high priority for France, Great Britain, Italy, or the USA).

[248] *See id.* at 83.

Foreign Minister Ihlen twice secured from Denmark its pledge recognizing Norway's sovereignty over Spitsbergen in exchange for Norway's recognition of Denmark's claim of sovereignty over Greenland;[249] the binding effect of Ihlen's later unilateral declaration respecting Danish sovereignty was contested by Norway but upheld by the PCIJ in its famous decision on the *Legal Status of Easter Greenland* case.[250]

The Soviets, desperate to secure international legal personality, dropped their opposition to the treaty, which it had protested on several occasions,[251] and in 1924 agreed to recognize Norway's sovereignty over Svalbard in exchange for Norway's recognition of the USSR.[252]

CONCLUSION

Deep-seated resentment about the condition of weakness[253] surrounding Russia's accession to the Svalbard Treaty frames perspectives of Russian foreign policy leaders from Molotov to Rogozin. Failing to secure its historical interests in a provision of the punishing, subsequently rescinded, Brest-Litovsk Pact saddled Russia with a residual status as a coparcener over territory historically and psychologically regarded as belonging to it. The Soviets' official news agency, *Tass*, once referred to Bear Island as a *"de facto* Russian island."[254] Its location at the gateway to the Kola Peninsula, home to Russia's Northern Fleet, makes it strategically significant, as is Svalbard's general geographic station in the military-strategic landscape of the High North.[255] Sharing the island and indeed the archipelago with numerous NATO allies has generated deep suspicion in Russian political and military circles: "Russians have repeatedly pointed to a number of 'dual purpose' installations on Svalbard, mainly monitoring and surveillance systems, which could allegedly be used by the United States and NATO for military purposes,"[256] notwithstanding the Svalbard Treaty's nonmilitarization provision. The former vice president of the European Parliament's Northern Dimension policy labels the current dispute

---

[249] *See* Vylegzhanin & Zilanov, *supra* note 12, at 21.
[250] *See* Legal Status of Eastern Greenland (Norway v. Denmark), 1933 P.C.I.J. Ser. A/B., No. 53, at 71 (ending Norway's illegal occupation of East Greenland).
[251] *See* ARLOV, SHORT HISTORY, *supra* note 114, at 71; Vylegzhanin & Zilanov, *supra* note 12, at 23–24.
[252] Vylegzhanin & Zilanov, *supra* note 12, at 23.
[253] *See id.* at 81.
[254] *On the Question of Spitsbergen*, TASS (Jan. 15, 1947), *reprinted in* Vylegzhanin & Zilanov, *supra* note 12, Annex 12, at 136.
[255] *See* Zysk, *supra* note 18, at 80.
[256] *Id.* at 83.

over Svalbard's waters a stalemate.[257] But the political and legal Norwegian-Russian backdrops, in addition to economic considerations, indicate this stalemate is potentially far more volatile than static.

The dynamic, inter-temporal interpretation of the Svalbard Treaty, with its preamble specifying the creation of an equitable regime to "assure … development and peaceful utilization," has not been secured. Norway opposes this interpretation, but its stratagem of avoiding outright confrontation while incrementally attempting to secure managerial control, first in the FPZ, and now in oil exploration blocks of Svalbard's contested continental shelf, has of late generated a great deal of unwanted attention. The geographical reach of the Svalbard Treaty and its problematic pairing of Norway's full and absolute sovereignty with states parties' equal enjoyment once again are focal points of attention. Norway's goal of limiting the treaty's application to the strict textual terms of the 1920 treaty now runs counter to the weight of political opinion, particularly the opinions of interested and capable states operating in the High Arctic.

And yet these two countries – Norway and Russia – have created a nuanced course of dealing: Rachel Tiller and Elizabeth Nyman have noted that Russia has been content to cede to Norway *de facto* control over fisheries management because it is able to maintain that this control is illegal without having to face the consequences of a total lack of management that the realization of its objections would produce.[258] Moreover, the status quo has produced "a relatively stable regime based on unofficial cooperation and understanding" between Norway and Russia, notwithstanding the ostensible objections each professes in their opposing management regimes:[259] "Both are able to share the resources without much interference or complaint from third parties."[260] For this reason, they have successfully maintained the delicate "balancing act of official diplomatic protest and unofficial cooperation and acceptance."[261] Lotta Numminen agrees that Norway has been able to manage resources in the FPZ while avoiding major conflicts, but she, like Tiller and Nyman,[262] predicts trouble ahead, particularly "if Norway is to open the Svalbard continental shelf for oil and gas exploration."[263]

---

[257] Diana Wallis, *Introduction, in* THE SPITSBERGEN TREATY: MULTILATERAL GOVERNANCE IN THE ARCTIC 7, at 6 (Diana Wallis & Steward Arnold, eds., 2011).

[258] *See* Tiller & Nyman, *supra* note 68, at 147.

[259] *Id.*

[260] *Id.*

[261] *Id.*

[262] *See id.* at 147 (noting Norway and Russia currently are eating their cake and having it too, "but probably not forever").

[263] Numminen, *supra* note 32, at 14.

Alyson Bailes argues that the Svalbard Treaty is outdated, a victim of the passage of time and unanticipated developments now producing ambiguities in its application.[264] Similar claims have been sounded about UNCLOS' perceived shortcomings and the need for a region-specific Arctic treaty. Indeed, the contraposition of Norway's claim of ownership over resources extending from Svalbard's coast, and other states' rejoinders that they must be shared, creates ambiguities that play into some states' interest to negotiate anew. But Bailes makes a good point: settlement of sovereignty and ownership issues will not obviate the need for good governance of the Arctic. If the Arctic is trending toward treatment as a global commons, it will be "hard to reject global involvement" over matters of sustainable fishing, fisheries protection, nuclear pollution, and accidents.[265]

But is the Arctic trending toward treatment as a global commons? Canada and Russia make mirror image sovereign claims concerning vast waterways atop their respective land masses;[266] a "flurry of territorial claims on the Arctic seabed" have been presented to the CLCS, which if perfected will substantially reduce what formerly was regarded the Common Heritage of Mankind.[267] In 2008, five circumpolar states issued the Ilulissat Declaration,[268] which asserts their "unique position" to safeguard issues affecting the Arctic environment. Three other Arctic stakeholders – Iceland, Sweden, and Finland – were excluded from that meeting, and a 2010 follow-up meeting in Chelsea, Quebec, sparking a movement to globalize Arctic issues in the newly formed Arctic Assembly.[269]

A closer look at Svalbard's history indicates that the treatment of the archipelago as a global commons does not precisely summarize the intentions of those states that share propinquity to the Arctic. A revised Svalbard Treaty with this intention in mind, however noble, does not seem likely, absent the political will of interested parties. Instead, from a historical perspective, ambiguities have allowed a small number of states access to Svalbard's living and

---

[264] *See* Alyson Bailes, *Spitsbergen in a Sea of Change in The Spitsbergen Treaty, in* THE SPITSBERGEN TREATY: MULTILATERAL GOVERNANCE IN THE ARCTIC 34, 35–36 (Diana Wallis & Steward Arnold, eds., 2011).

[265] Bailes, *supra* note 264, at 35–36.

[266] *See* M. Byers, *Toward a Canada-Russia Axis in the Arctic*, GLOBAL BRIEF (February 6, 2012), globalbrief.ca/blog/2012/02/06/toward-a-canada-russia-axis-in-the-arctic/.

[267] Scott J. Shackelford, *Tragedy of the Common Heritage of Mankind*, 28 STAN. ENVTL. L.J. 109, 130 (2009).

[268] The Ilulissat Declaration, Arctic Ocean Conference, Ilulissat, Greenland (May 28, 2008), www.oceanlaw.org/downloads/arctic/Ilulissat_Declaration.pdf (involving Canada, Denmark, Norway, Russia, and the USA).

[269] *See* Address of Olafur Grímsson, President of Iceland, National Press Club (Apr. 15, 2013), http://press.org/sites/default/files/20130415_grimsson.pdf

mineral resources while maintaining loosely constructed definitions of *terra nullius* – definitions that facilitate resource extraction while precluding claims of state-sponsored ownership. A fundamental consequence (as opposed to purpose) of the legal regime has been to facilitate territorializing temptations under a soft law arrangement while maintaining a hard law treaty artifice. As paradoxical as the Svalbard Treaty's full and absolute sovereignty and equal enjoyment and access provisions seem, it has kept the peace and facilitated resource extraction through an unusual variant of the notion of divisible sovereignty. Corporate agents, dating certainly to the whaling epoch of the seventeenth century, were able to secure resources in line with state objectives. During the mining epoch and moving forward into the period of Norway's articulation of its FPZ, overt confrontations largely have been avoided, although infringements are closely recorded rather than uniformly enforced. The fundamental objective of a Robert Lansing-type understanding of *terra nullius* was to promote parochial and extant economic interests involving resource extraction, which accounted for a peculiar type of claim jumping: claimants took hold of territory in the archipelago before overarching interests of any sovereign or condominium arrangement could. The proto-condominium arrangements discussed in the 1870s and immediately preceding World War I attempted to conform the concept of condominium to parochial interests – and not the other way around – principally because no individual state was capable enough to secure or perfect its own economic security interest. To secure resources *appertaining to* the interests of states without engendering political risks associated with outright annexation, early-twentieth-century powers engaged in a dalliance with the idea of condominium – not for purposes of creating a global commons, but for purposes of securing temporary interests of the limited number of states by precluding access to others. The concept of *terra nullius* was constructed to afford virtually assigned ownership while skirting perceptions of state-based ownership by occupation.

The Svalbard Treaty may have created a sovereign arrangement that no state party to the agreement can perfect, presenting, as Robert Lansing once wrote, a unique international problem. Co-mingling full and absolute sovereignty with a notion of divisible sovereignty in forms of equal enjoyment and access is in fact an imperfect negation of territorial temptation. It provides a suitable alternative to the exercise of *dominium* by creating a virtual or artificial *terra nullius* that allows for resource exploitation and management so long as the geospatial regime remains incapable of appropriation by any one state. Norway seeks at this juncture to end the virtual legal reality relating to Svalbard's contested continental shelf. Whether Norway will be able to portage its sovereign interests to this geographical region (which certainly will call into question Norway's Royal Decree pertaining to the FPZ as well), through its restrictive interpretation of the reach of the Svalbard Treaty, remains to be seen. The political climate suggests Norway has overplayed its hand; that it will – for the time being – diplomatically and indefinitely delay acceptance of bids to open up resource exploration. But what is clear from the long human history of Svalbard is that the territorial temptation to secure its resources lurks ever so close to the resource-rich offerings of its continental shelf and exclusive economic zone (EEZ), despite the shared sovereignty arrangement of the legal regime of the Svalbard Treaty.

5

Problems of Governance: The Arctic and the Club Within the Club

In 2008, five circumpolar states – Canada, Denmark, Norway, Russia, and the United States – issued the Ilulissat *Declaration*,[1] an eight paragraph soft-power statement on Arctic Ocean management with *Realpolitik* implications.[2] Reinforcing the theme that the land dominates the sea,[3] the declaration asserted the unique position of these coastal states – the so-called Arctic 5 – to safeguard issues affecting the Arctic environment, indigenous communities, and natural resource exploitation.[4]

The countries claimed that their stewardship over ocean issues[5] obviated any "need to develop a new comprehensive international legal regime to govern the

[1] The Ilulissat Declaration, Arctic Ocean Conference, Ilulissat, Greenland (May 28, 2008), www.oceanlaw.org/downloads/arctic/Ilulissat_Declaration.pdf.

[2] "Soft power" is a term coined by Joseph S. Nye, Jr. He defines it as "the ability to get what you want through attraction rather than coercion or payments." JOSEPH NYE, SOFT POWER: THE MEANS TO SUCCESS IN WORLD POLITICS x (2004). "Hard power," in a political sense, means military or economic might; in a legal sense, "hard law" can be defined as "legally binding obligations that are precise ... and that delegate authority for interpreting and implementing the law." Kenneth W. Abbott & Duncan Snidal, *Hard and Soft Law in International Governance*, 53 INT. ORG. 421 (2000). In an important sense, the entire discussion may trace to Lord McNair, who is credited with introducing the idea of "soft law" into legal discourse. *See* G. Abi-Saab, *Cours Général de Droit International Public*, 207 RECUEIL DES COURS 132 (1987) ("*C'est ce processus qui a été décrit par lord McNair comme le passage de la soft law à la hard law, termes qu'il a utilisés à l'origine pour designer respectivement le droit en forme de principes abstraits*"); *see also* Lászlo Blutman, *In the Trap of a Legal Metaphor: International Soft Law*, 59 INT'L & COMP. L.Q. 606 (2010).

[3] *See* North Sea Continental Shelf Cases (Ger./Den.; Ger./Neth.), 1969 I.C.J. 3, 51; Aegean Sea Continental Shelf Case (Gr/Turk), 1978 I.C.J. 3, 36; Case Concerning Maritime Delimitation and Territorial Questions between Qatar and Bahrain (Qatar/Bahr.), 2001 I.C.J. 40, 97; Maritime Delimitation in the Black Sea (Rom./Ukr), 2009 I.C.J. 61, 89 (juridically supporting the theme).

[4] *Supra* note 1.

[5] *Id.* (including matters relating to freedom of navigation, scientific research, settlement of overlapping claims, tourism, search and rescue, and disaster response).

Apologies to HERNANE TAVARES DE SÁ, author of THE PLAY WITHIN THE PLAY: THE INSIDE STORY OF THE UN (1966).

Arctic Ocean," akin to the established treaty system that governs Antarctica.[6] This assertion sought to cut off discussions advocating creation of an Arctic treaty and to counter voices in the international environmental movement claiming the Arctic needed to be "saved" from sovereign politics.[7] Both criticisms implied the Arctic had been "caught up in a legal void"[8] and that the existing framework inadequately addressed rapidly changing circumstances. But the Ilulissat signatories stressed that the international legal framework, principally crafted around UNCLOS, provided sufficient support for resolution of Arctic issues; they argued that no supplementation was needed, even though the treaty omits any direct reference to the mostly landless Arctic and its vastly land-like, ice-covered expanse.[9]

Pledging strengthened trust, cooperation, and transparency in the region, the Ilulissat signatories affirmed their close collaboration with the extant Arctic Council,[10] the high-level membership forum to which each signatory already belonged.[11] But the public rhetoric did not match private perceptions: these self-declared unique Arctic stewards, convening in a small town in

---

[6] *Id.* The Antarctic Treaty system is hardly analogous to the situation in the Arctic, however. The Antarctic Treaty suspended claims of sovereignty on a continent far removed from continental surroundings, partially to promote peaceful scientific research; the Arctic region is mostly pelagic space, much of which is subject to international rules relating to the law of the sea. *See also* Klaus Dodds, *The Ilulissat Declaration (2008): The Arctic States, "Law of the Sea," and Arctic Ocean*, 33 SAIS REVIEW 45 (2008) (noting the Ilulissat Declaration "marginalized alternative governance proposals, such as the Arctic Treaty"). It might be best to recall Stephen Krasner's definition of "regimes." Accordingly, regimes "are defined as principles, norms, rules, and decision-making procedures around which actor expectations converge in a given issue area." Stephen D. Krasner, *Structural Causes and Regime Consequences: Regimes as Intervening Variables, in* INTERNATIONAL REGIMES 1 (Stephen D. Krasner, ed., 1983).

[7] Dodds, *The Ilulissat Declaration, supra* note 6, at 49 (noting calls for a new treaty in the European Parliament and efforts from environmental groups such as Greenpeace). *See also* Brooks B. Yeager, "The Ilulissat Declaration: Background and Implications for Arctic Governance" (Remarks prepared for the Aspen Dialogue and Commission on Arctic Climate Change, November 5, 2008), www.arctic-report.net/wp-content/uploads/2012/01/2008.11-Ilulissat-Background-and-Implications.pdf (discussing various interpretations of the Declaration).

[8] Dodds, *The Ilulissat Declaration, supra* note 6, at 49.

[9] Article 234 of the treaty indirectly touches on the Arctic by reference of enhanced police powers of coastal states to regulate in nondiscriminatory ways ice-covered areas. For a discussion of the idiosyncratic qualities of the region of the Arctic due to its status as a semi-enclosed ocean, its "fuzzy" boundaries separating ice and land, contested sovereignties, and falling in an area of historically limited political agenda, *see generally* Sebastian Knecht, *Arctic Regionalism in Theory & Practice: From Cooperation to Integration?, in* ARCTIC Y.B. 164 (2013).

[10] *See* Joint Communiqué and Declaration of the Establishment of the Arctic Council, issued in Ottawa, Canada, September 19, 1996, *reprinted in* ILM 35 (1996): 1382 [the Ottawa Declaration]. The Ilulissat signatories also pledged continuing cooperation with another Arctic forum, the Barents Euro-Arctic Region (BEAR), which has its secretariat located in Kirkenes, Norway.

[11] *Id.* art. 2.

western Greenland, excluded Sweden, Finland, and Iceland, the three other permanent and founding Arctic Council members.[12] Indigenous communities, led by the Inuit Circumpolar Council, also were excluded. Asked why there was a need to meet at all, given the unity professed by all Ilulissat participants and the Arctic Council, Denmark's foreign minister said it was important for Arctic coastal states to clarify shared views and commitments; unconvinced, the ICC issued its own circumpolar declaration on sovereignty in the Arctic, which accused the Ilulissat signatories of neglect.[13]

These exclusions suggested a club had formed within the Arctic Council and that the Arctic 5 had become an informal niche governance association based on coastal state authority above the Arctic Circle.[14] Although the Arctic Council often is lauded for its work in common areas,[15] and has directly contributed to two recent binding international agreements (Search and Rescue, 2011; Oil Pollution, Preparedness and Response, 2013),[16] the Arctic 5 share a

---

[12] See *Finland, Sweden, Iceland left out*, SIKU NEWS (May 5, 2008), http://archive.is/mwj95.

[13] See ¶ 20, Deputy Secretary's Participation at Arctic Ocean Conference in Greenland (Cain), June 6, 2008, https://wikileaks.org/plusd/cables/08COPENHAGEN321_a.html. For the reaction of the Inuit Circumpolar Council, *see* art. 2 (2.6), A Circumpolar Inuit Declaration on Sovereignty in the Arctic, April 2009, www.itk.ca/publication/circumpolar-declaration-sovereignty-arctic. *See also* Sophie Theriault, *Northern Frontier, Northern Homeland: Inuit People's Food Security in the Age of Climate Change and Arctic Melting*, 15 Sw. J. INT'L L. 243 n. 90 and accompanying text (2009) (discussing the meeting in Nunavik leading up to the Declaration).

[14] Niche governance regimes are specialized structures within a larger institutional complex. Applied to the Arctic, they conduct generic tasks of governance, concentrating on building knowledge, strengthening norms, enhancing problem-solving, or enforcing rule compliance. *See generally* Olav Schram Stokke, *Regime Interplay in Arctic Shipping Governance: Explaining Regional Niche Selection*, 13 INT'L ENVIRON AGREEMENTS, POL. L. & ECON. 65–85 (2013).

[15] *See generally* Oran R. Young, *Institutional Linkages in International Society: Polar Perspectives*, 2 GLOBAL GOVERNANCE 1–24 (1996) (discussing institutional linkages and polar regions); ORAN R. YOUNG, CREATING REGIMES: ARCTIC ACCORDS AND INTERNATIONAL GOVERNANCE (1998) (discussing programmatic aspects of regime formation and the emergence of the Arctic as a distinct regime); OLAV SCHRAM STOKKE & GEIR HØNNELAND, eds., INTERNATIONAL COOPERATION AND ARCTIC GOVERNANCE: REGIME EFFECTIVENESS AND NORTHERN REGION BUILDING (2007) (essays focusing on the Arctic Council, the Barents Euro-Arctic Region and the Council of the Baltic Sea States); Njord Wegge, *The Political Order in the Arctic: Power Structures, Regimes and Influence*, 47 POLAR RECORD 165–176 (2011) (analyzing the Arctic region as a system in its own right).

[16] Agreement on Cooperation on Aeronautical and Maritime Search and Rescue in the Arctic, May 12, 2011, reprinted in 50 ILM 1119 (2011); Agreement on Cooperation on Marine Oil Pollution Preparedness and Response in the Arctic, May 15, 2013, Arctic Council, Emergency Prevention, Preparedness and Response, www.arctic-council.org/eppr/agreement-on-cooperation-on-marine-oil-pollution-preparedness-and-response-in-the-arctic/ (multilingual versions of both treaty and appendices). *See also* US Dep't of State, Fact Sheet: Agreement on Cooperation on Marine Oil Pollution Preparedness and Response in the Arctic (May 15, 2013), (English language treaty without appendices) www.state.gov/r/pa/prs/ps/2013/05/209406.htm.

deeper common denominator: they share creeping jurisdictional interests that only an Arctic coastline can provide.

This chapter investigates the relationship between the Arctic Council and the Arctic 5, questioning whether the less formal, subregional structure of the Arctic 5 facilitates territorializing interests among the Arctic littoral powers in ways that complicate the status of the Arctic Council, prompting alternative and increasingly global calls for a new governance regime for the Arctic.

THE ARCTIC 5: A NICHE GOVERNANCE ASSOCIATION?

Classified diplomatic cables, summarizing discussions among some Arctic 5 members, support the view that the Arctic 5 has developed into an informal niche governance association. Leaked as part of the Wikileaks Cablegate scandal in 2010–2011, they reveal concerns about the Arctic Council's "unwieldy" political nature, the need for "a smaller group," and the need to make the Arctic Council "more political, in the right sense of the word."[17] Vague perhaps, but remarks attributed to Denmark's foreign minister, Per Stig Møller, provided coloration: the more closely-knit Arctic 5 format was necessary "to determine ... extended continental shelves and settle maritime disputes" – in other words, to stake enlarging claims over resources on and under the ocean floor; a subordinate purportedly noted the Ilulissat conference was convened to "prevent tensions from emerging over the extended continental shelf claims process;" another cable claimed that Greenland's Premier said the Ilulissat meeting was about the Arctic 5's pursuit of resources and exercise of sovereignty.[18] Such comments square with an assessment of Russia's position, which favors "resolving Arctic problems within the narrower group of littoral states." These views indicate the Arctic 5 has formed into an expedient for coordinated and expanded control over continental shelf resources.[19]

---

[17] Torbjørn Pedersen, *Debates over the Role of the Arctic Council*, 43 OCEAN DEV. & INT'L L. 146, 151 (2012) (quoting a US diplomatic cable's summary of its own Deputy Secretary of State [Negroponte]'s and Assistant Secretary McMurry's view ["unwieldy/smaller group" attributed to McMurry] and of Norway's Foreign Minister [Stoere]'s view ["right sense of the word"]). (Elsewhere, Pedersen claims Denmark's Foreign Minister Møeller called the smaller group "necessary;" and that Russia's Foreign Minister Lavrov said "the Five Arctic Littoral States should show leadership in the Arctic Council." *Id.* at 150 and 152).

[18] *Id.* at 150 (quoting a US diplomatic cable's summary of the Danish Foreign Minister's view). *See also* ¶ 9, statement of Danish Ministry of Foreign Affairs Political Director, Carsten Damsgaard, as quoted in US diplomatic cable, "Norway Hosts Informal Arctic Meeting" (Oct. 21, 2008), https://cablegatesearch.wikileaks.org/cable.php?id=08STATE111997&q=ilulissat; and ¶ 8, "Ambassador Fulton Meets Greenland Premier" (Aug. 18, 2009), https://cablegatesearch .wikileaks.org/cable.php?id=09COPENHAGEN356&q=ilulissat (on cable paraphrasing Greenland's Premier, Kuupik Kleist).

[19] Pavel K. Baev, *Russia's Arctic Ambitions and Anxieties*," 112 CURRENT HISTORY 268 (2013). Baev also concludes "Moscow seeks to convince the littoral states ... of the benefits of dividing the

Complaints arose again in late March 2010 when Canada hosted a second Arctic 5 summit in Chelsea, Quebec. Outsider suspicions of an Arctic clique sounded when Sweden, Finland, and Iceland again were excluded along with representatives of the Inuit Circumpolar Council.[20] Despite continuing diplomatic assurances of the Arctic Council's preeminence,[21] it appeared that overarching maritime jurisdiction and security issues prompted the coastal Arctic 5 to initiate "a dialogue among themselves regarding issues deemed unsuitable for treatment within the setting" of the Arctic Council.[22] Again, the unique position of Arctic Ocean coastal states served as justification for the exclusion.[23] In a rare public rebuke of its Canadian ally, which convened Ilulissat II, as it is sometimes known, US Secretary of State Hillary Clinton noted the absence of key stakeholders and underscored the need to cooperate, "not create new divisions"[24] – a declaration that rhetorically indicated a US policy preference for the Arctic Council forum, notwithstanding indications to the contrary and its long-standing refusal to ratify UNCLOS.

THE ARCTIC COUNCIL CLUB

There is irony here. The Arctic Council long has been criticized for its own club-like behavior. It is the subject of a withering litany of complaints:[25] Its

Arctic Ocean's continental shelf among them by legitimizing claims for expanding 'exclusive economic zones' beyond the standard 200 nautical mile limit." *Id.* at 267. *See also* ¶ 5, Denmark Resets Relationship with Russia (Nov. 6, 2009), https://cablegatesearch.wikileaks .org/cable.php?id=09COPENHAGEN494&q=ilulissat.

[20] PETER HOUGH, INTERNATIONAL POLITICS OF THE ARCTIC: COMING IN FROM THE COLD 108 (2013); *see also* Piotr Graczyk, *The Arctic Council Inclusive of non-Arctic Perspectives: Seeking a New Balance, in* THE ARCTIC COUNCIL: ITS PLACE IN THE FUTURE OF ARCTIC GOVERNANCE 280 (Thomas S. Axworthy, Timo Koivurova, & Waliul Hasanat, eds., 2012) [hereinafter AXWORTHY, THE ARCTIC COUNCIL].

[21] Office of the Spokesman, US Dep't of State Media Note, (May 12, 2011), (Department of State Announces Successful Conclusion to Arctic Council Ministerial), www.state.gov/r/pa/prs/ps/ 2011/05/163283.htm.

[22] Paula Kankaanpää & Oran R. Young, *The Effectiveness of the Arctic Council*, 31 POLAR RESEARCH 12 (2012).

[23] Press statement, Canadian Ministry of Foreign Affairs, Trade and Development (Feb. 3, 2010), www.international.gc.ca/media/aff/news-communiques/2010/54.aspx?lang=eng (statement of Lawrence Cannon, Minister of Foreign Affairs, announcing the 29 March meeting of Arctic Ocean coastal states).

[24] Pedersen, *supra* note 17, 152 (footnote omitted); and 153 (Ilulissat II).

[25] *See* Peter Worden, *Arctic Circle Takes Shape*, NORTHERN NEWS SERVICE ONLINE (May 6, 2013), www.nnsl.com/frames/newspapers/2013-05/may6_13ac.html (labeling the Arctic Council "notoriously exclusive"); *A Warmer Welcome: The Arctic Council Admits Its First Permanent Asian Observers*, THE ECONOMIST (May 18, 2013), www.economist.com/news/international/21578040-arctic-council-admits-its-first-permanent-asian-observers-warmer-welcome (calling the Arctic Council a "cozy club" since its 1996 inception).

membership is permanently limited to Arctic States,[26] defined in terms of geographic proximity to the Arctic Ocean;[27] indigenous groups are granted Permanent Participant status[28] – a neologism introduced in the Arctic Council's founding document[29] – but are not allowed to outnumber the members;[30] the Council permits secret meetings,[31] with working groups and Senior Arctic Officials often meeting behind closed doors;[32] the private sector complains of a lack of involvement;[33] the Council tightly controls and accredits observers, but precludes their participation in discussions;[34] major non-governmental environmental groups, such as Greenpeace, long have been

[26] Revised Arctic Council Rules of Procedure as adopted by the Arctic Council at the First Arctic Council Ministerial Meeting, September 17–18, 1998, Iqaluit, Canada; revised by the Arctic Council at the Eighth Arctic Council Ministerial Meeting, May 15, 2013, Kiruna, Sweden, Part I, art. (1). www.arctic-council.org/index.php/en/document-archive/category/4-founding-documents.

[27] The Arctic Council grew out of a meetings held in Rovaniemi, Finland, in 1989 and 1991, where eight Arctic countries – USSR, USA, Sweden, Norway, Iceland, Finland, Denmark, and Canada – met to prepare a strategy to protect the Arctic environment. Their work product resulted in the Arctic Environmental Protection Strategy (AEPS), reprinted in ILM 30 (1991): 1624. Signatories soon recognized that AEPS' terms of reference needed substantial revision to cover "common Arctic issues," including sustainable development. A second phase of Arctic administration developed, culminating in the establishment of the Arctic Council. *See* Timo Koivurova & David L. Vanderzwaag, *The Arctic Council at 10 Years: Retrospect and Prospects*, 40 U. BRIT. COLUMBIA L. REV. 123 and 129 (2007) (discussing the historical development of the Arctic Council).

[28] Ottawa Declaration, art. 2. The indigenous peoples' organizations consist of approximately five hundred thousand persons out of a total of four million inhabitants of the Arctic. Indigenous organizations represented as permanent participants of the Arctic Council (with full consultation rights in connection with Council negotiations and decisions) include the Arctic Athabaskan Council, the Aleut International Association, the Gwich'in Council International, the Inuit Circumpolar Council, the Saami Council, and the Russian Association of Indigenous Peoples of the North. *See* Arctic Council Permanent Participants, www.arctic-council.org/index.php/en/about-us/permanent-participants/123-resources/about/permanent-participants.

[29] *See History of the Arctic Council Permanent Participants*, ARCTIC COUNCIL (last updated, Aug. 28, 2015), www.arctic-council.org/index.php/en/environment-and-people/arctic-peoples/indigenous-peoples-today/568-history-of-the-arctic-council-permanent-participants.

[30] *Id*. art. 2(b).

[31] *Id*. pt. II, art. (6).

[32] *See* Kankaanpää & Young, *supra* note 22, at 9.

[33] *See id.* at 8. The Arctic Council appears to be addressing this issue through its creation of the Task Force to Facilitate a Circumpolar Business Forum. The task force held its first meeting in September 2013. For more information, *see* www.arctic-council.org/index.php/en/about-us/working-groups/task-forces.

[34] *See* Ólafur Grímsson, President of Iceland, Address to the National Press Club, April 15, 2013, http://press.org/sites/default/files/20130415_grimsson.pdf (noting former French Prime Minister Michael Rocard's frustrations with permanent observer protocol restrictions on participation at Arctic Council meetings). Observers may, however, present documents and make statements at the discretion of the Council chair. *See* Pedersen, *Debates over the Role of the Arctic Council, supra* note 17, at 148. *See also* Oran R. Young, *Whither the Arctic? Conflict or*

denied observer status;[35] and China's permanent observer applications were denied three times before being granted along with five others at the 2013 Kiruna ministerial meeting.[36] Japan's application also had been held up notwithstanding its fifty-five-year history of polar research;[37] Brazil's bid was recently turned down; and the Council continues to defer the European Union's similar observer-status request due to Canadian objections over a European Union's import ban of Canadian seal products.[38] European officials, with their developing interest in a Northern Dimension policy,[39] privately complain about the Arctic Council's resistance to broadening the forum,[40] yet Greenland boycotted the Kiruna meeting when the Council's forum was further narrowed down: Denmark's commonwealth territories (Greenland and the Faroe Islands) were refused seats at the principals' table.[41] Indigenous groups now voice concerns about *enhancing* the role of observers – leery aboriginal influence will dilute if weighty observers such as the European Union

---

Cooperation in the Circumpolar North, 45 POLAR RECORD 80 (2009) (noting frustrations that outside actors have had with the Arctic Council).

35 Klaus Dodds, *After Kiruna: The Arctic Council and Arctic Futures*, RUSI (June 24, 2013), www.rusi.org/publications/newsbrief/ref:A51C855CD4C0C4/. The Council's founding document, the Ottawa Declaration, allows for nongovernmental organization observers. The Ottawa Declaration, art. 3(c). Its Rules of Procedures limits observer status to organizations "that the Council determines can contribute to its work." Revised Arctic Council Rules of Procedure, art. 36(c). Eleven nongovernmental organizations have been granted observer status, some with apparent environmental agendas. Official observers include Advisory Committee on Protection of the Seas, Arctic Cultural Gateway, Association of World Reindeer Herders, Circumpolar Conservation Union, International Arctic Science Committee, International Arctic Social Sciences Association, International Union for Circumpolar Health, International Work Group for Indigenous Affairs, Northern Forum, University of the Arctic, and the World Wildlife Fund. For more information, *see* www.arctic-council.org/index.php/en/about-us/arctic-council/observers.

36 *See A Warmer Welcome: The Arctic Council Admits Its First Permanent Asian Observers*, THE ECONOMIST (May 18, 2013), www.economist.com/news/international/21578040-arctic-council-admits-its-first-permanent-asian-observers-warmer-welcome. In addition to China, those granted permanent observer status were South Korea, Japan, Singapore, Italy, and India, joining France, Great Britain, The Netherlands, and Spain.

37 Italy's and South Korea's applications also were turned down in 2009.

38 Matt McGrath, *China Joins Arctic Council but a Decision on the EU Is Deferred*, BBC NEWS (May 15, 2013), www.bbc.com/news/science-environment-22527822. An emerging dispute over EU oil imports extracted from Alberta tar sands may further complicate EU's deferral. *Id.*

39 *See generally* PAMI AALTO, HELGE BLAKKISRUD, & HANNA SMITH, THE NEW NORTHERN DIMENSION OF THE EUROPEAN NEIGHBOURHOOD (2009) (examining regional cooperation in the North ad European Union external relations).

40 Andrew Willis, *EU Gets Cold Shoulder in the Arctic*, EU OBSERVER (May 13, 2011), http://euobserver.com/foreign/32331.

41 *See Greenland's Premier Boycotts the Arctic Council in "Drastic Protest,"* NUNATSIAQ ONLINE (May 15, 2013), www.nunatsiaqonline.ca/stories/article/65674greenland_walks_away_from_the_arctic_council/.

are included.[42] Now, crosscutting influences inside and outside the Arctic Council, amplified by the *sui generis* implications of the Ilulissat declarants – given their self-professed unique position to safeguard interests – call into question not only whether an Arctic forum's center will hold but where it will be.

DUELING ARCTIC FORA?

At its 2011 Ministerial Meeting in Nuuk, Greenland, the Arctic Council agreed to establish a standing secretariat in Tromsø, Norway.[43] But recently a movement has emerged to create a new, transparent, and roving Arctic forum. Sensing a need "to enhance [the Arctic] dialogue, and to bring more people, more effectively and more productively, together," Iceland's president, Ólafur Ragnar Grímsson, appeared before the National Press Club in Washington, DC, on April 15, 2013, and called for the creation of a new organization, The Arctic Circle.[44] Discarding distinctions of protocol – a veiled reference to the Arctic Council – Grímsson sketched out an "open tent" approach to Arctic dialogue involving states, corporations, and organizations.[45] Although Grímsson diplomatically noted the new forum was not meant to replace the Arctic Council, reports suggest a rivalry was under way.[46] Grímsson explicitly projected a global understanding of the Arctic by distancing his view from the geographic definition that inherently preferences circumpolar state interests. "What we thought was our Arctic," he stated in reference to Northern countries, has become "the global Arctic, with countries in faraway places wanting to have a seat at the Arctic table."[47]

---

[42] *See* Klaus Dodds, *Anticipating the Arctic and the Arctic Council: Pre-emption, Precaution and Preparedness, in* AXWORTHY, THE ARCTIC COUNCIL, *supra* note 20, 24.

[43] Nuuk Declaration, On the occasion of the Seventh Ministerial meeting of The Arctic Council, May 12, 2011, Nuuk, Greenland, http://arctic-council.npolar.no/accms/export/sites/default/en/meetings/2011-nuuk-ministerial/docs/Nuuk_Declaration_FINAL.pdf.

[44] Grímsson, Address to the National Press Club.

[45] *Id.* For a list of 2013 corporate supporters, including Google, as represented by its CEO, *see* www.state.gov/r/pa/prs/ps/2011/05/163283.htm.

[46] *See* Paul Koring, *New Arctic Group Gives Canada Political Competition,* THE GLOBE AND MAIL (Apr. 15, 2013), www.theglobeandmail.com/news/politics/new-arctic-group-gives-canada-political-competition/article11243970/ (claiming the new circumpolar forum "seems certain to irk some northern nation"). Mia Bennett, *Iceland President Says Arctic Lacks "Effective Governance"; Launches Arctic Circle,* FOREIGN POL'Y ASSOC. (Apr. 25, 2013), http://foreignpolicyblogs.com/2013/04/25/iceland-president-says-arctic-lacks-effective-governance-launches-arctic-circle/ (noting the "subtle swipe at the Arctic Council"). Questions about the Arctic Council being supplanted by another type of governance forum predate Grímsson's speech. *See, e.g.,* Timo Koivurova, *Limits and Possibilities of the Arctic Council in a Rapidly Changing Scene of Arctic Governance,* 46 THE POLAR RECORD 146 (2010).

[47] Grímsson, Address to the National Press Club.

Not since Arvid Pardo's 1967 Common Heritage of Mankind address to the United Nations,[48] which proposed that the resources of the seabed and ocean floor beyond national jurisdiction be shared by all countries, has the pelagic world heard such galvanizing words. Within months, one thousand two hundred delegates from forty nations gathered in Reykjavik, Iceland, to launch the world's largest ever gathering on Arctic issues, giving birth to the Arctic Circle Assembly.[49]

THE GLOBAL ARCTIC

The concept of a global Arctic, embraced by the Arctic Circle Assembly, underscores changing polar dynamics in the second decade of the twenty-first century, dynamics that increasingly affect the *raison d'être* of the Arctic Council: China now describes itself as a near Arctic state;[50] the European Union claims it is an Arctic entity;[51] Singapore has an Arctic Ambassador;[52] South Korea's icebreaker plies Arctic waters;[53] and climate conditions below the snow-packed surface of the Himalayas (in the subnival altitude

---

[48] Maltese Ambassador Arvid Pardo, Remarks on the Declaration and Treaty Concerning the Reservation Exclusively for Peaceful Purposes of the Seabed and of the Ocean Floor, Underlying the Seas Beyond the Limits of Present National Jurisdiction, and the Use of Their Resources in the Interests of Mankind, UN Doc. A/AC.105/C.2/SR.75 (Aug. 17, 1967); for more information on Pardo's promotion of the Common Heritage idea, *see* A. PARDO, THE COMMON HERITAGE: SELECTED PAPERS ON OCEANS AND WORLD ORDER 1967–1974 (1975).

[49] *Arctic Assembly: Iceland Prepares for Historic Summit*, THE ARCTIC JOURNAL (Oct. 11, 2013), http://arcticjournal.com/politics/arctic-assembly-iceland-prepares-historic-summit. The inaugural meeting of the Arctic Circle took place in Reykjavik on Oct. 12–14, 2013. *See The Inaugural Meeting of The Arctic Circle*, ARCUS, www.arcus.org/events/arctic-calendar/19870. *See also* Arctic Circle, www.arcticcircle.org/about (listing statistics about the 2013 Assembly). The 2014 Assembly was held in Reykjavik during Oct. 30–Nov. 2. *See* 2014 Assembly Program, http://arcticcircle.org/sites/arcticcircle/themes/ac/pdf/2014%20Program%20October%2030.pdf (Dec. 8, 2014).

[50] *China Seeks Pragmatic Ties with Arctic Countries*, CHINADAILY.COM (Feb. 11, 2014), www.chinadaily.com.cn/china/2014-11/02/content_18844643.htm.

[51] Interests and Roles of Non-Arctic States in the Arctic: Background Brief 7 (National Capital Branch of the Canadian International Council and the Munk-Gordon Arctic Security, Program, 2011), www.gordonfoundation.ca/sites/default/files/publications/Arctic%20Seminar%20Background%20Brief_1.pdf.

[52] MFA Press Statement: Presentation of Credentials of Singapore's Plenipotentiary Representative to the Caribbean Community, Ministry of Foreign Affairs, Singapore (Mar. 16, 2012), www.mfa.gov.sg/content/mfa/media_centre/press_room/pr/2012/201203/press_20120316.printable.html?status=1 (referencing Ambassador Kemal Siddique's current appointment as Special Envoy for Arctic Affairs).

[53] *Agreement: South Korean Icebreaker Can Explore Canada's Arctic*, ALASKA DISPATCH (May 17, 2012), www.alaskadispatch.com/article/agreement-south-korean-icebreaker-can-explore-canadas-arctic.

above fifteen thousand feet) are demonstrably related to polar conditions, thus informing Arctic scientific discussions.[54] Ten countries operate permanent research stations at Ny-Ålesund, Svalbard, the island midway between Norway and the North Pole;[55] and both the United States and Russia have designated the Arctic a paramount national security issue.[56] Canada, which ceased patroling the Arctic by 1990, has returned its navy to its third ocean,[57] a region it labels fundamental to its national identity and new Northern Strategy;[58] and Iceland, which considers itself a forsaken Arctic coastal state in the context of Arctic 5 discussions,[59] signed a free-trade agreement with China on the same date its president announced the Arctic Circle initiative,[60] a circumpolar move implicitly associated with long-term Chinese interests in the region[61] and with Icelandic pique with the status quo.

[54] Falk Huettmann & Ashok K. Roy, *Three Poles: The Arctic, Antarctic and Himalayas All Connect*, DAILY NEWS MINER (June 2, 2013), www.newsminer.com/opinion/community_perspectives/three-poles-the-arctic-antarctic-and-himalayas-all-connect/article_8a954e96-ca8d-11e2-97b5-0019bb30f31a.html. The Hindu Kush Himalaya region is spread over eight countries: Afghanistan, Bangladesh, Bhutan, China, India, Myanmar, Nepal, and Pakistan. *See* The International Center for Integrated Mountain Development, www.icimod.org/?q=1. For more on India's emerging engagement with the Arctic, *see* Sanjay Chaturvedi, *Geopolitical Transformations: "'Rising' Asia and the Future of the Arctic Council,"* in Axworthy, THE ARCTIC COUNCIL, *supra* note 20, 233–237.

[55] The ten Svalbard research stations are operated by Germany, France, Italy, Great Britain, South Korea, Norway, The Netherlands, China, Japan, and India. *See Research Stations, in* Ny-ÅLESUND, KINGS BAY, http://kingsbay.no/research/research_stations/.

[56] The Free Trade Agreement between the Government of Iceland and the Government of the People's Republic of China, signed in Beijing, Apr. 15, 2013, Icelandic Ministry of Foreign Affairs, www.mfa.is/foreign-policy/trade/free-trade-agreement-between-iceland-and-china/.

[57] Rob Huebert, *Canadian Arctic Maritime Security: The Return to Canada's Third Ocean*, CAN. MIL. J. (2009), www.journal.forces.gc.ca/vo8/no2/huebert-eng.asp#skiplink.

[58] Statement on Canada's Arctic Foreign Policy: Exercising Sovereignty and Promoting Canada's Northern Strategy Abroad, modified Nov. 25, 2013; www.international.gc.ca/arctic-arctique/council-conseil.aspx?lang=eng. For information on Canada's Northern Strategy, announced in 2007 by Canadian Prime Minister Stephen Harper, *see* Canada's Northern Strategy, www.pm.gc.ca/eng/news/2013/08/16/canadas-northern-strategy. As a measure of its Arctic identity, reference to the "True North" is contained in the Canadian National Anthem, "*O Canada.*"

[59] Grimsey Island, lying approximately 25 miles north of Iceland's mainland, is an inhabited rockscape (population: 85) belonging to Iceland; it is the only part of Iceland, aside from several rock outcroppings, above the Arctic Circle.

[60] Ministry of Foreign Affairs, Iceland, Free Trade Agreement between Iceland and China, Apr. 15, 2013, www.mfa.is/foreign-policy/trade/free-trade-agreement-between-iceland-and-china/.

[61] *See* Irene Quaile, *All Eyes on the Arctic Council*, DEUTSCHEWELLE (May 16, 2013), www.dw.de/all-eyes-on-the-arctic-council/a-16811193; Frédéric Lasserre, *China and the Arctic: Threat or Cooperation Potential for Canada* 5 (China Papers No. 11, Canadian International Council; Center of International Relations, University of British Columbia, 2010) (citing Robert Wade's 2008 study).

Much of this interest in the global Arctic is driven by the diminishment of sea ice and the emergence of a new Arctic environment and the economic opportunities it presents.[62] At the forefront of consideration are estimates that vast quantities of resources are located in recoverable areas north of the Arctic Circle.[63] But other issues are pressing, as well, suggesting, despite the sanguine reassurance of the Ilulissat Declaration, that the current Arctic legal framework is either too weak to withstand or too accommodating to resist territorial temptation.

GAPS IN GOVERNANCE

Gaps have appeared in the governance structure of the Arctic, prompting discussions about reforms.[64] The recent additions to Arctic Council observership (known to have generated robust debate in the Council),[65] the establishment of a permanent secretariat in Tromsø, the creation of a Task Force for Institutional Issues and new communication outreach guidelines,[66] and current discussions on facilitating a Circumpolar Business Forum[67] are meant to strengthen the organization, but also are seen as far from optimal fixes.[68] Calls for a region-specific Arctic treaty,[69] animated by the perceived shortcomings of

[62] *See* National Strategy for the Arctic Region 1–11 (May 2013); The White House, Washington, DC, May 10, 2013, www.whitehouse.gov/sites/default/files/docs/nat_arctic_strategy.pdf (cover letter citing reasons for articulating the Arctic Region as a strategic priority); *see also* Dodds, *Anticipating the Arctic*, 2.

[63] *Circum-Arctic Resource Appraisal: Estimates of Undiscovered Oil and Gas North of the Arctic Circle*, US Geological Survey Fact Sheet (2008), http://pubs.usgs.gov/fs/2008/3049/.pdf.

[64] *See* E. J. Molenaar, *Current and Prospective Roles of the Arctic Council System within the Context of the Law of the Sea*," 27 INT'L J. MARINE & COASTAL L. 553 (2012) (noting wide support for strengthening the international Arctic governance regime); Alyson J. K. Bailes, *Understanding the Arctic Council: A "Sub-Regional" Perspective*, 15 J. MIL. & STRAT. STUD. 32 (2013) (noting gaps in Arctic governance); Timo Koivurova & David L. Vanderzwaag, *The Arctic Council at 10 Years, supra* note 27 (assessing the need for Arctic Council reforms on the 10th anniversary of its creation); Donald Rothwell, *The Arctic in International Affairs: Time for a New Regime?*, 15 BROWN J. WORLD AFF. 241, 248 (2008/2009) (noting the Arctic is facing considerable management challenges that individual Arctic states do not want to address); IOANA GEORGESCU, ARCTIC GEOPOLITICS – TIME FOR A NEW REGIME 90 (master's thesis, Institut Europeen Des Hautes Etudes Internationals, Nice, 2010), www.trunity.net/files/150601_150700/150650/georgescu.pdf (concluding a need for new clear and unambiguous legal and regulatory Arctic regime).

[65] Bailes, *Understanding the Arctic Council, supra* note 64, at 46–47.

[66] Molenaar, *Current and Prospective Roles of the Arctic Council System, supra* note 64, at 554.

[67] *Supra* note 33.

[68] Graczyk, *The Arctic Council Inclusive of non-Arctic Perspectives, supra* note 20, at 280; *see also* Molenaar, *Current and Prospective Roles of the Arctic Council System, supra* note 64, at 554.

[69] *See, e.g.,* LEONID D. TIMCHENKO, QUO VADIS ARCTICUM?: THE INTERNATIONAL LAW REGIME OF THE ARCTIC AND TRENDS IN ITS DEVELOPMENT (1996) (an early treatment of the necessity of a new Arctic regime).

UNCLOS[70] or the analogous success of the Antarctic Treaty,[71] face resistance from dominant Arctic coastal powers, which reject the need and lack the will to implement a formal rule-making process, rendering stillborn all calls for an Arctic treaty.

Bids to reform the Council from within also encounter institutional obstacles: Alyson Bailes noted the unusual international architecture of the circumpolar region, with its strong Euro-Atlantic nexus. All Nordic countries belong to bodies like the Organization for Security and Cooperation in Europe (OSCE), and they excel in consultative discussions on environmental, societal, civilian safety, and scientific issues; but unlike the OSCE, the Arctic Council is explicitly "self-debarred" from addressing military issues; it does not discuss arms control and disarmament.[72] The Ottawa Declaration ensures this prohibition, owing to the steadfast views of the United States and Russia. It stipulates the Council should deal with common Arctic issues unrelated to military security.[73]

Institutionally, the Council lacks a *politically* oriented dispute management tradition, and, consequently, a track record of cooperation in such matters.[74] Part of this explanation stems from its history, which emphasized functional issues. The Arctic Council developed from the 1991 Arctic Environmental Protection Strategy (AEPS), and it was established in 1996 as a forum for Arctic discussion and cooperation.[75] The four initial working groups of the AEPS were integrated into the work of the Council, indicating a continuation of a broad environmental focus.[76] The Council was initially designed as a region-building

---

[70] *See* Donald R. Rothwell & Stuart Kaye, *Law of the Sea and the Polar Regions: Reconsidering the Traditional Norms*, 18 MARINE POL'Y 41 and 58 (1994) (noting difficulties in applying traditional law of the sea concepts and UNCLOS to the polar region).

[71] *See* E. C. H. KESKITALO, NEGOTIATING THE ARCTIC: THE CONSTRUCTION OF AN INTERNATIONAL REGION 72 (2004) (noting Antarctic Treaty discussions as a model for the Arctic).

[72] Bailes, *Understanding the Arctic Council, supra* note 64, at 32. Nordic countries such as Sweden and Finland have also kept their distance from other organizations connected to regional military or arms control issues, for instance, the 1990 Treaty on Conventional Armed Forces in Europe.

[73] Art. 1(a) and accompanying footnote, Ottawa Declaration.

[74] *See* Rothwell, *The Arctic in International Affairs, supra* note 64, at 242 (noting the 1973 Polar Bear Agreement as a notable exception).

[75] Koivurova, *Limits and Possibilities of the Arctic Council, supra* note 46, at 146–147; Evan T. Bloom, *Establishment of the Arctic Council*, 93 AM. J. INT'L L. 712 (1999).

[76] Koivurova, *Limits and Possibilities of the Arctic Council, supra* note 46, at 149. The four AEPS working groups were Cooperation, Conservation of Arctic Flora and Fauna (CAFF); the Protection of the Arctic Marine Environment (PAME); Emergency Prevention, Preparedness, and Response (EPPR); and the Arctic Monitoring and Assessment Program (AMAP). The Sustainable Development Working Group (SDWG) was established at the 1998 Ministerial Meeting in Iqaluit, Nunavut, Canada; the Arctic Contaminants Action Program (ACAP)

initiative dealing with these *foci*. Its early aim was to strike a balance between issues of utilization and conservation, and demands of indigenous communities.[77] Since 1996, the Arctic Council has served as a meeting ground for environmental protection and sustainable development discussions in the region. Never intended as a formal international organization, the Arctic Council has no official legal standing or law-making capacity.[78] Denuded of the European Union's personality, it lacks competence to regulate economics, finances, private sector development, and investment.[79] Configured as such, it accomplishes important functional objectives through *ad hoc* expert groups,[80] six scientific working groups,[81] issue-specific task forces,[82] and its Arctic Economic Council.[83] Acting as an epistemic community[84] – which is a group that speaks a common, usually scientific, language directed toward achievement of commonly understood, nonpolitical, goals – and borne out of functional environmental concerns that resemble the Mediterranean Action Plan of the mid-1970s,[85] it has developed international law in the Arctic in a *quasi*-official

was granted working group status at the 2006 Ministerial Meeting in Salekhard, Russia. For detailed histories and activities of the working groups, *see* www.arctic-council.org/index.php/en/about-us/working-groups.

[77] KESKITALO, NEGOTIATING THE ARCTIC 69 and 74 (2004) (noting strongly politicized perspectives).

[78] *See* Pedersen, *Debates over the Role of the Arctic Council, supra* note 17, 149; Nele Matz-Lück, *Planting the Flag in Arctic Waters: Russia's Claim to the North Pole*, 1 Gö J. INT'L L.TTINGEN JOURNAL OF INTERNATIONAL LAW (2009); Molenaar, *Current and Prospective Roles of the Arctic Council System, supra* note 64, at 571.

[79] Bailes, *Understanding the Arctic Council, supra* note 64, at 32–33.

[80] *See, e.g.*, *EBM Experts Group (Ecosystem-Based Management Experts Group)*, ARCTIC COUNCIL (May 7, 2015), www.arctic-council.org/index.php/en/about-us/working-groups/expert-groups.

[81] For the list of working groups, *see supra* note 76.

[82] Task forces are appointed at ministerial meetings and are bounded by specific issues and a limited time frame, after which they become inactive. Four task forces are currently active in the Arctic Council: Task Force on Arctic Marine Oil Pollution Prevention (TFOPP), Task Force on Black Carbon and Methane (TFBCM), Scientific Cooperation Task Force (SCTF), and the Task Force to Facilitate the Circumpolar Business Forum (TFCBF). For descriptions of current and past task forces, *see* www.arctic-council.org/index.php/en/about-us/working-groups/task-forces.

[83] A Senior Arctic Official's Report to Ministers at the Nuuk ministerial meeting (2011) identified the working groups as the principal means for advancing the Council's substantive work. *See* Belén Sánchez Ramos, *Strengthening the Capacity of the Arctic Council: Is the Permanent Secretariat a First Step?, in* THE ARCTIC Y.B. 270–271 (2013).

[84] According to Peter Haas, an epistemic community is a term that germinates "in the literature on the sociology of knowledge and has been adapted for use in international relations to refer to a specific community of experts sharing a belief in a common set of cause-and-effect relationships as well as common values to which policies governing these relationships will be applied." Peter M. Haas, *Do Regimes Matter? Epistemic Communities and Mediterranean Pollution Control*, 43 INT. ORG. 377, 384 n. 20 (1989). *See generally* Peter M. Haas, ed., *Knowledge, Power, and International Policy Coordination*, 46 INT. ORG. (1992) (essays on epistemic communities).

[85] In 1975, sixteen Mediterranean countries and the European Community adopted the Mediterranean Action Plan, a first ever "Regional Seas Program" operated by the United

decision-shaping, but not decision-making, capacity.[86] It is widely regarded as a soft law institution and in this sense takes its place among leading science-oriented knowledge structures that inform international policy.[87] But like all other Euro-Atlantic institutions, it has barely dealt with the new issues created by the opening up of the region due to melting ice, which may soon require decision-making,[88] prompting the question: "What does this powerful group of Arctic nations want to use the Arctic Council *for*?"[89]

THE FUNCTION OF SOFT LAW

A related and perhaps more apt question might address the intentions of the Arctic 5. If the Council suffers from concerns relating to its vision or purpose in the global Arctic age, unable to undertake responsive political reforms, it is helpful to review broadly reasons why such soft law institutions are created.

Literature on soft law institutions implicitly or explicitly relate to hard law institutions and the way law comes into being. It distills broadly into three theoretical perspectives or schools of thought – the views of positivists, rationalists/institutionalists, and constructivists.[90] Positivists preference rules and rule-making, and view hard law and soft law as opposite, or, binary instruments.[91]

Nations Environment Program, to control marine pollution and develop common managerial policies to protect the socioeconomic development of the Mediterranean basin. For more information, *see* United Nations Environment Program, Mediterranean Action Plan for the Barcelona Convention, www.unepmap.org/index.php?module=content2&catid=001001002. *See also,* GABRIELA KÜTTING, ENVIRONMENT, SOCIETY AND INTERNATIONAL RELATIONS: TOWARDS MORE EFFECTIVE INTERNATIONAL ENVIRONMENTAL AGREEMENTS 62–82 (2000) (discussing the history of the Mediterranean Action Plan).

[86] O. R. Young, *Building an International Regime Complex for the Arctic: Current Status and Next Steps*, 2 POLAR JOURNAL 391, 401–402 (2012).

[87] *See generally* Paula Kankaanpää, *Knowledge Structures of the Arctic Council for Sustainable Development, in* AXWORTHY, THE ARCTIC COUNCIL, *supra* note 20, 84 (detailing the boundary-spanning development of the Arctic Council in science and policy discussions); Olav Schram Stokke, *A Legal Regime for the Arctic?: Interplay with the Law of the Sea Convention*, 31 MARINE POLICY 402–408 (2007) (discussing the Arctic Council's strong environmental governance record as the best approach to circumpolar norm-building while acknowledging its "soft law" status).

[88] Bailes, *Understanding the Arctic Council, supra* note 64, at 31.

[89] *Id.*

[90] Gregory C. Shaffer & Mark A. Pollack, *Hard vs. Soft Law: Alternatives, Complements, and Antagonists in International Governance*, 94 MINN. L. REV. 706, 707–708 (2009/2010); *see also* Prosper Weil, *Towards Relative Normativity in International Law,"* 77 AM. J. INT'L L. 413, 414 (1983) (defining hard law as "norms creating precise legal rights and obligations" and soft law, less charitably, as "norms whose substance is so vague, so uncompelling").

[91] Jean d'Aspremont, *Softness in International Law: A Self-Serving Quest for New Legal Materials,"* 19 EUR. J. INT'L L. 1075, 1076 (2008). For positivists' criticism of soft law, *see id.* at 1077–1081.

Hard law refers to formal legal obligations that give rise to binding expectations; soft law is seen as the opposite – norms, procedures, or instruments that are informal and nonbinding but can possibly lead to hard law.[92] Rationalists/institutionalists view lawmaking from perspectives of administrative economy and governance, focusing on the distinct attributes of each that states choose to employ under different contexts. Constructivists downplay law's precision and formality, particularly as portrayed by positivists; they consider these traits distractions for how law really works. They regard state interests and decisions as products of an interactive process, which hard and soft law instruments can help shape.[93]

Taken together, these perspectives shape much of the literature on institutionalization and legalization. In a proactive light, they highlight the notion that informal structures constitute a device for minimizing impediments to cooperation.[94] They form part of the "complex architecture of international agreements"[95] where states may prefer informal institutions to avoid formal, visible pledges of fully legalized institutions.[96] They may be created intentionally to promote "calculated ambiguity,"[97] or take on "creative or generative" capacities which inform of a richer view of international law.[98] International actors "often deliberately choose softer forms of legalization as superior institutional arrangements," particularly when the actors are states that are "jealous of their autonomy"[99] or when dealing with conditions of uncertainty or rapidly changing circumstance.[100] Such a characterization makes sense in light of the intercepted diplomatic cables of the Arctic 5. Soft legalization

---

[92] *See* Abbott & Snidal, *Hard and Soft Law, supra* note 2, at 421; Shaffer & Pollack, *Hard vs. Soft Law, supra* note 90, at 707.

[93] Shaffer & Pollack, *Hard vs. Soft Law, supra* note 90, at 708.

[94] Charles Lipson, *Why Are Some International Agreements Informal?* 45 Int'l. Org. 495, 500 (1991).

[95] Kal Raustiala, *Form and Substance in International Agreements*, 99 Am. J. Int'l L. 581, 581 and 582 (2005).

[96] *See* Judith Goldstein, Miles Kahler, Robert Keohane, & Anne-Marie Slaughter, *Introduction: Legalization and World Politics*, 54 Int'l Org. 385, 396 (2000) (associating fully legalized institutions with high levels of obligation, precision, and delegation). *See also* Raustiala, "Form and Substance," 581ff (differentiating contracts and pledges and binding and nonbinding accords).

[97] Oscar Schachter, *The Twilight Existence of Nonbinding International Agreements*, 71 Am. J. Int'l L. 296, 297 (1977).

[98] *See* Martha Finnemore & Stephen J. Troope, *Alternatives to "Legalization": Richer Views of Law and Politics*, 55 Int'l. Org. 743, 744–745 (2001) (discussing limited views of law based on formal notions of legalization).

[99] Abbott & Snidal, *Hard and Soft Law, supra* note 2, at 423.

[100] *See id.* at 441–444 (discussing how soft power arrangements can provide a rational adaptation to uncertainty and incomplete knowledge); C. M. Chinkin, *The Challenge of Soft*

also may mitigate cost and allow states to maintain future control if adverse circumstances arise.[101] As a source of institutional strength, soft law structures are more flexible[102] and more adaptable to modification; they may make fewer informational demands on parties; and they are "pre-eminently suitable" for avoiding adjudication and promoting self-regulation.[103] Because of their lower profile, they are less exposed to outsider intrusions, can be controlled more tightly by governments,[104] and they may be more available or open to non state and sub state actors.[105]

But for many of the same reasons, soft law institutions can be problematic. A substantial debate surrounds the meaning and utility of the soft law concept.[106] Prosper Weil warned of the growing use of soft law instruments, which potentially can relativize and destabilize international law norms and turn the legal system into an instrument no longer able to manage sovereign relations.[107] Others find the concept redundant, because it forces a false dichotomy with hard law,[108] or find it unhelpful, because hard law instruments also may fall prey to soft law problems.[109] Some scholars view the hard law/soft

---

Law: Development and Change in International Law, 38 INT'L & COMP. L.Q. 850, 852–853 (1989) (facilitating flexibility and freedom to maneuver where changing circumstances require).

[101] *Id.* at 435.

[102] Chinkin, *supra* note 100, 852.

[103] *Id.* at 862.

[104] Lipson, *supra* note 94, 500–501.

[105] Shaffer & Pollack, *Hard vs. Soft Law*, *supra* note 90, at 719 (footnote omitted).

[106] *See* D. Thürer, *Soft Law*, *in* IV ENCYCLOPEDIA OF PUBLIC INTERNATIONAL LAW 454 (2000) (concluding that the term has no clearly defined content (R. Bernhardt, ed., 2000); *see also* Blutman, *supra* note 2, at 606 (citing the work of Thürer, *id.*, and A. Aust, HANDBOOK OF INTERNATIONAL LAW), and separating the concept of soft law into norms that do not take the shape of a recognized international law but have legal relevance, and norms that are recognized by international law but are not enforceable owing to their generality) (internal footnote omitted).

[107] Weil, *Towards Relative Normativity in International Law*, *supra* note 90, at 423.

[108] Raustiala, "Form and Substance," 586; Richard Bilder, *Beyond Compliance: Helping Nations Cooperate*, *in* COMMITMENT AND COMPLIANCE: THE ROLE OF NON-BINDING NORMS IN THE INTERNATIONAL LEGAL SYSTEM 72 (2000) (calling the concept of soft law "inappropriate and unhelpful" in that it "deprecate[s] the currency of law;" Hartmut Hilgenberg, *A Fresh Look at Soft Law*, 10 EUR. J. INT'L L. 499, 500 (1999) (calling "soft law" a contradiction in terms); Jan Klabbers, *The Redundancy of Soft Law*, 65 NORD. J. INT'L L. 168 (1996) (preferencing the binary distinction).

[109] H. L. A. HART, THE CONCEPT OF LAW (1961) (noting the indeterminacy of rules stemming from norms of international law); Schachter, *supra* note 97, at 228 (noting imprecision and generalities are known qualities of treaties of unquestioned legal force). The point is also well recognized by Weil, a critic of soft law approaches. He notes "numerous treaty provisions whereby the parties undertake merely to consult," or where agreement is based purely on "hortatory or exhortatory provisions." Weil, *Towards Relative Normativity in International Law*, *supra* note 90, at 414.

law interplay as nuanced options available to states that employ them in complementary and antagonistic ways.[110] Jan Klabbers, more directly, regards soft law as a "smokescreen" that enables the powers that be "to strengthen their own position to the detriment of others."[111]

Klabbers' view is worth considering with regard to Arctic Council's identity issues. Caught between emerging issues caused by rapid ice melt and established, crosscutting interests of the subregional Arctic 5, the Arctic Council, like never before, lacks a common vision for the future.[112] If the Council now exists in a state of institutional purgatory, has it been intentionally placed there? Its functional orientation and founding document create a structural firewall protecting against consideration of political and security issues. Diplomatic courtesy may prompt continuing reference to it as the preeminent Arctic forum, but this designation seems increasingly like a rhetorical smokescreen in light of emerging lacunae in Arctic governance issues, which appear serious, structural, and increasingly obvious.

Governance issues abound in the Arctic Ocean. They are growing and migrating beyond the environmental and sustainable development realms where the Arctic Council has long excelled.[113] And they involve, from the perspective of the United States, the world's leading maritime power, numerous national security concerns.[114]

But as these issues develop, the most critical of which involve the territorializing impulses of coastal states, the Arctic Council continues to eschew creation of a firmer legal governance regime or internal procedural reforms, while the Ilulissat signatories assert parochial and exclusive oversight based on a notion of *sui generis* stewardship. While there is outsider recognition that the Council needs to open up its forum, and some internal signs indicating the same,[115] the status quo station of the Arctic Council as a soft law regime remains intact – as originally intended – and facilitates a calculated ambiguity that allows circumpolar members to pursue their primary jurisdictional

---

[110] *See*, e.g., Shaffer & Pollack, *Hard vs. Soft Law, supra* note 90, at 708–709.

[111] Klabbers, *The Redundancy of Soft Law, supra* note 108, at 391 and 387. *See also* Shaffer & Pollack, *Hard vs. Soft Law, supra* note 90, at 744 (arguing: "individual states (or other actors) may deliberately use soft-law instruments to undermine hard-law rules to which they object").

[112] Graczyk, The Arctic Council Inclusive of non-Arctic Perspectives, *supra* note 20, at 276.

[113] See Annika E. Nilsson, Knowing the Arctic: The Arctic Council as a Cognitive Forerunner, in AXWORTHY, THE ARCTIC COUNCIL, *supra* note 20, 192 (claiming scientific studies such as the Arctic Climate Impact Assessment are the Arctic Council's most effective products).

[114] *See* Remarks of United States Secretary of State John Kerry on the establishment of a Special Representative for the Arctic Region, US Dep't of State Press Statement, Feb. 14, 2014, www .state.gov/secretary/remarks/2014/02/221678.htm.

[115] Search and rescue ... stemming from the Council's 2009 Arctic Marine Shipping Assessment.

interests elsewhere. This circumstance prompts consideration of an intriguing prospect – a challenge to Arctic governance and the rhetorical preeminence of the Arctic Council forum by the upstart Arctic Circle Assembly. Given the closed nature of the Council, and the even more tightly bound interests of the club-within-the-club, the Arctic 5, could the genesis of the Arctic Circle Assembly represent a growing consensus among excluded and non-circumpolar third parties that the governing Arctic regional regime insufficiently accommodates globalizing concerns? If so, a potential challenge to Arctic governance could emerge from the Arctic Circle Assembly movement – itself a soft law variant of the *pacta tertiis* principle. *Pacta tertiis*[116] derives from Roman law; it supports the consensual nature of international law and holds – absent consent – that agreements neither confer rights nor impose obligations on third parties. It is a codified rule of treaty law,[117] but it is widely regarded as a general (customary) principle of law, as well.[118] The general course of dealing in Arctic affairs, governed by the interplay between the Arctic Council and the Arctic 5, does not appear to satisfy global interests. The tenor of a coming discourse on Arctic governance might begin to reflect the view that the soft law stewardship of the Arctic Council, which enables *Realpolitk* extensions of resource claims by the Arctic 5, does not embrace an emerging global conception of the Arctic. It remains to be seen whether the reflected rays of the *pacta tertiis* principle begin to shine light on the prospect of an alternative form of Arctic governance based on the inability of the status quo to satisfy expanding state interests. Will a coming global Arctic age make *passé* stewardship claims based on geographic propinquity to the pole?

If the Arctic region is caught in a legal void, it is a void of the Arctic 5's making. In the aggregate, the Arctic Council's kept status as a *quasi*-organization (or, as self-described, "a high level intergovernmental forum") helps the Arctic 5 enact its loosely knit subregional agenda to turn major portions of the Arctic Ocean into a *de facto mare clausum*,[119] spurring an excluded third-party reform

---

[116] The principle in full reads *pacta tertiis nec nocent nec prosunt.*

[117] Vienna Convention on the Law of Treaties, May 23, 1969, art. 39, 1155 U.N.T.S. 331 (entered into force on January 27, 1980); Case Concerning Certain German Interests in Polish Upper Silesia, 1925 P.C.I.J. Ser. A, No. 7, 28–29; Case Concerning the Factory at Chorzów, 1928 P.C.I.J. Ser. A, No. 17, 45; LORD MCNAIR, THE LAW OF TREATIES (1961): 309.

[118] *See* Erik Franckx, Pacta Tertiis *and the Agreement for the Implementation of the Straddling and Highly Migratory Fish Stocks Provisions of the United Nations Convention on the Law of the Sea*, 8 TUL. J. INT'L & COMP. L. 49 (2000) (arguing the rule's general acceptance today and noting also its reflection in persistent objector theory).

[119] Alyson Bailes correctly identifies the extant structure of the Arctic Council, with its "inner Five" machinations, as a political weakness of the Arctic Council specifically, and a problem for subregional institutions generally. Bailes, *Understanding the Arctic Council, supra* note 64,

movement in the form of the Arctic Circle Assembly and other demands for more rule-oriented governance in the Arctic. A word of caution is necessary here. The notion of a *mare clausum* historically conjures up images of exclusive control over navigation and fishing. The Romans were bold enough to assert such a claim in the Mediterranean, which they referred to as *mare nostrum* (our sea). Venetians asserted such a claim over the Aegean from the twelfth to fifteenth centuries, and other bolder and broader claims were to follow. But mention of the notion of a *de facto mare clausum* here is not meant to suggest impingement on established high seas freedoms of navigation and fishing, but rather on the resource exploitation designs of extended continental shelf claims.

THE CREEPING COASTAL STATE AGENDA

Since the dawn of the state system, coastal states have been projecting territorial rule into pelagic space, adding new dimensions to the concept of freedom of the seas. We have seen how key regimes such as the territorial sea, the contiguous zone, the Truman Proclamations and the development of the patrimonial sea and continental shelf doctrines, and the exclusive economic zone (EEZ) attest to the resurgence of coastal state jurisdictional interests in the twentieth century alone. Added to these examples of creeping coastal state interest are the array of piecemeal or ad hoc jurisdictional claims currently presented by coastal states: key among them is the question of extended continental shelf claims, which will redefine and enlarge outward maritime boundary delimitations over mineral resources.[120] A variety of extended continental shelf claims are in the works or have been reviewed by the CLCS potentially territorializing huge swaths of Arctic Basin seabed and subsoil;[121] Norway already has staked and settled its 235,000 square kilometer claim.[122] In late 2013, Canada made a partial

---

at 39. Without reform, she admits "the temptation" for a co-optation of the Council's agenda by the "5 littoral states will never fade." *Id.* at 45–46.

[120]   *See* Kankaapää & Young, *The Effectiveness of the Arctic Council,* POLAR RESEARCH 11.

[121]   *See generally* Scott J. Shackelford, *Was Selden Right: The Expansion of Closed Seas and Its Consequences,"* 47 STAN. J. INT'L L. 1 (2011).

[122]   *See* United Nations Convention on the Law of the Sea, Annex VI, Commission on the Limits of the Continental Shelf, Summary of the Recommendations of the Commission on the Limits of the Continental Shelf in Regard to the Submission made by Norway in Respect of Areas in the Arctic Ocean, the Barents Sea, and the Norwegian Sea on November 27, 2006, www.un.org/depts/los/clcs_new/submissions_files/nor06/nor_rec_summ.pdf; Utenriksdepartementet, The Continental Shelf – Questions and Answers, November 30, 2009, www.regjeringen.no/nb/dep/ud/dok/lover_regler/retningslinjer/2009/the-continental-shelf–questions-and-an.html?id=583774; *see also* Dodds, *The Ilulissat Declaration, supra* note 6, at 50.

submission regarding its continental shelf in the Atlantic Ocean (covering the Labrador Sea, the Grand Banks, and Nova Scotia regions).[123] It and Russia continue to hone applications relating to respective extended Arctic continental shelves. Denmark submitted a claim in November 2013 regarding the Northeastern Continental Shelf of Greenland, and the CLCS endorsed its 87,792 square kilometers submission pertaining to extended continental shelf North of the Faroe Islands in March 2014;[124] The United States is not party to UNCLOS, which, in accordance with Articles 76 and 77, allows for extended continental shelf claims to 350 nautical miles, or substantially farther, depending on technical details.[125] The Obama Administration, without articulating any legal basis, noted that the United States' extended continental shelf claim could extend for hundreds of miles from the north coast of Alaska.[126]

Continental shelf extension claims are based on an estimated $1.2 trillion in resources contained in what formerly was regarded as a common area.[127] The extension of sovereign rights in the EEZ out to 200 nautical miles did not satiate the territorial temptation for control over more offshore resources, notwithstanding evidence most proven resources are located within the EEZs of Arctic States.[128] Where the EEZ and the continental shelf overlap, up to a distance of 200 nautical miles, the two sets of sovereign rights too overlap. But under Article 76 of UNCLOS, the outer limits of the continental shelf involve yet another kind of delimitation to determine where the high seas actually begin. This determination is not straightforward;[129] rather, it involves "wild card" assessments[130] of exceptional complexity and expense, involving measurements gathered and submitted by the petitioning coastal state,[131] legal terms

---

[123] *See* Commission on the Limits of the Continental Shelf (CLCS). Outer limits of the continental shelf beyond 200 nautical miles from the baselines: Submissions to the Commission: Partial Submission by Canada, United Nations Division for Ocean Affairs and the Law of the Sea, www.un.org/depts/los/clcs_new/submissions_files/submission_can_70_2013.htm.

[124] *See* The Continental Shelf Project, News of Nov. 27, 2013 and Mar. 25, 2014, http://a76.dk/lng_uk/main.html.

[125] UNCLOS, art. 76(5) (up to 100 nautical miles beyond the 2500 meter isobaths).

[126] *See* National Strategy for the Arctic Region, *supra* note 62, at 9.

[127] *Law of the Sea – Outer Limits of the US Continental Margins*, USGS (Dec. 1, 2011), http://walrus.wr.usgs.gov/research/projects/lawofsea.html#overview.

[128] A Danish study cited by Russia's Ambassador-at-Large to the Arctic Council claims that up to 97 percent of proven resources are located within EEZs of Arctic States, suggesting the "race" to recover resources is mostly moot because "there's nothing to divide, everything has been already divided." Anton Vasiliev, *The Arctic, Our Home and Future*, ARCTIC INFO, (undated) www.arctic-info.com/ExpertOpinion/Page/the-arctic–our-home-and-future.

[129] *See* Philip Allot, *Power Sharing in the Law of the Sea*, 77 AM. J. INT'L L. 14 (1983).

[130] Ron Macnab, *Submarine Elevations and Ridges: Wild Cards in the Poker Game of UNCLOS Article 76*, 39 OCEAN DEV. & INT'L L. 223 (2008).

[131] *See* Allot, *supra* note 129, at 17–18. *See also* Vladimir Jares, *The Continental Shelf beyond 200 Nautical Miles: The Work of the Commission on the Limits of the Continental Shelf and the*

of art, problems of administrative law, complicating factors of confidentiality, and reliance on bathymetric and seismic data derived from ice-covered areas presented to commissioners serving in their private capacities,[132] for a mechanism that may or may not have final decision-making authority.[133] Doubt and ambiguity shroud the current closed Article 76 process for extended continental shelf submissions, raising the threat that its recommendations for outer continental shelf delimitations "may be greeted with skepticism by states whose interests are affected, or with concern by other coastal states with comparable continental shelf aspirations."[134]

In principle, each delimitation of the outer limits of the continental shelf is subject to four possible outcomes[135] involving a mix of five criteria.[136] Moreover, "a plethora of ambiguities"[137] creates uncertainty as to whether the coastal state, the CLCS, or some other third-party dispute settlement mechanism makes the final determination about the outer limit.[138] Current claims exploit these ambiguities and portend to shrink the oceanic

---

    Arctic, 42 VAND. J. TRANSNAT'L L. 1265, 1272–1276 (2009); and John E Noyes, *Judicial and Arbitral Proceedings and the Outer Limits of the Continental Shelf*, 42 VAND. J. TRANSNAT'L L 1211, 1227 (2009).

[132] Ron Macnab, *The Case for Transparency in the Delimitation of the Outer Continental Shelf in Accordance with UNCLOS Article 76*, 35 OCEAN DEV. & INT'L L. 1, 10 (2004). See Charles K. Ebinger & Evie Zambetakis, *The Geopolitics of Arctic melt*, 85 INT'L AFFAIRS 1215, 1224–1226 (2009) (discussing the United Nations' lack of institutional capacity to handle continental shelf extension claims). The point is reinforced by Norwegian Foreign Minister Stoere's purported comment, leaked as part of a confidential cable following the Ilulissat meeting, June 22, 2008: "FM Stoere said it is for states, not the commission, to settle overlapping claims by negotiation," at ¶ 5; Deputy Secretary's meeting with Norwegian FM Stoere in Greenland, June 11, 2008, https://cablegatesearch.wikileaks.org/cable.php?id=08COPENHAGEN337&q=ilulissat.

[133] *See* Mcnab, *supra* note 133, at 11 (noting the CLCS shall consider information submitted by the coastal state and make recommendations on the establishment of the outer limits); *see also* Michael Sheng-ti Gau, *The Commission on the Limits of the Continental Shelf as a Mechanism to Prevent Encroachment upon the Area*, 10 CHINESE J. INT'L L. 6 (2011) (arguing that existing international rules and mechanisms cannot sufficiently address the problem of coastal state encroachment).

[134] *Id.* at 15.

[135] Depending on the scientific evidence, the outer limits to the continental shelf may be drawn at 200 nautical miles, at the outer edge of the continental margin; at 350 nautical miles, which is the general cutoff point established in Article 75(5); or at 100 miles from the 2,500-meter isobath. See Allot, *supra* note 129, at 18.

[136] The criteria include consideration of natural prolongation, the continental margin, determination of the outer edge of the continental margin, consideration of the continental slope, and analysis of submarine ridges. *See id.*, *supra* note 129, at 17–18.

[137] Macnab, *supra* note 132, at 1.

[138] Established according to Article 76 of UNCLOS, and its Annex II, the CLCS shall consider information submitted by the coastal state and make recommendations on the establishment of the outer limits. See UNCLOS, *supra* note 17, art 76(8) and art 3(1) (1) of Annex II. *See also* Macnab, *supra* note 132, at 11.

commons "by more than 40 percent," significantly redefining the seabed as a resource of national, not supranational, control.[139]

Such claims have an especially profound and diminishing effect on the global commons in the Arctic Ocean. This ocean consists almost entirely of continental shelf, meaning most of the Arctic Basin seabed could fall under the national jurisdiction of one of the five adjacent Arctic States (Canada, the United States, Russia, Norway, and Denmark (via its territory, Greenland)).[140] Russia alone claims almost one-half the Arctic area based on the 1,240-mile underwater Lomonosov Ridge as an extension of its Siberian continental margin.[141] This claim overlaps with a Canadian claim to part of the Lomonosov Ridge, and a likely Danish claim.[142] The Canadian claim, in turn, overlaps with a projected US claim in the Beaufort Sea;[143] the United States, which is not a party to the Convention, nevertheless initiated its own data-gathering study, which projects an extended continental shelf from the

---

[139] *Supra* note 121, at 23. *See also* Gau, *The Commission on the Limits of the Continental Shelf as a Mechanism to Prevent Encroachment Upon the Area, supra* note 133, at 6 (noting that existing international rules and mechanisms cannot sufficiently address the problem of coastal state encroachment).

[140] This outcome appears likely if circumpolar states maximize the extent to which the outer limits can be measured. *See* Mel Weber, *Defining the Outer Limits of the Continental Shelf across the Arctic Basin: The Russian Submission, States' Rights, Boundary Delimitation and Arctic Regional Cooperation,* 24 INT'L J. MARINE & COASTAL L. 653, 656–657 (2009); Shackelford assertively claims, "eventually the entire Arctic Ocean [continental shelf] save for a one hundred square-mile area around the North Pole" will fall under national jurisdiction, *supra* note 121, at 3; Øystein Jensen estimates that a maximum measurement of outer continental shelf would leave "only two relatively small enclaves" as part of the international seabed area: the Gakkel Ridge and a smaller seabed area in the Canadian Basin. Øystein Jensen, *Limits of the Continental Shelf in the Arctic Ocean,* 2 ESIL REFLECTIONS (Apr. 25, 2013), at 2, www.esil-sedi .eu/sites/default/files/Jensen%20-%20ESIL%20Reflection.pdf.

[141] Paul Reynolds, *Russia Ahead in Arctic "Gold Rush"* BBC News Special Reports (Aug. 1, 2007), BBC News, http://news.bbc.co.uk/2/hi/6925853.stm.

[142] Colin Sullivan, *Is the U.S. Napping Through the Arctic Thaw?* National Tribal Air Association (Mar. 13, 2012), www.ntaatribalair.org/index.php?option=com_content&view=article id=1309:jeny&catid=24:climate-change (noting Denmark "is expected to file a claim that the Lomonosov Ridge is a natural prolongation of Greenland"). For a map and discussion of overlapping Danish, Canadian, and Russian claims involving the Lomonosov Ridge, *see "Territorial Claims" The Right Arctic,* http://arcticcontroversy.weebly.com/territorial-claims.html and *Evolution of Arctic Territorial Claims and Agreements: A Timeline (1903-Present),* Stimson (Apr. 15, 2013), www.stimson.org/infographics/evolution-of-arctic-territorial-claims-and-agreements-a-timeline-1903-present/.

[143] *See* John Abrahmason, *Joint Development of Arctic Ocean Oil and Gas Resources and the United Nations Convention on the Law of the Sea, in* International Boundaries Research Unit Conference–The State of Sovereignty (2009), slide 41 www.dur.ac.uk/resources/ibru/conferences/sos/john_abrahamson_powerpoint.pdf.

north coast of Alaska[144] – a distance of keen interest to oil companies and Alaska politicians.[145]

Furthermore, UNCLOS Article 234 grants coastal states unilateral rights to enforce nondiscriminatory regulations in EEZs where severe climate conditions and ice coverage create exceptional hazards. The article is an important achievement of Russian and Canadian pelagic diplomacy;[146] together, these countries occupy 75 percent of the Arctic Ocean's coastline.[147] Additionally, Russia has passed domestic legislation claiming sovereignty over its intercoastal (cabotage) route, asserting historic title to a 5,400 kilometer stretch of the Northeast Passage, known as the Northern Sea Route, leading some Russian authorities to put forward extended and tendentious sovereignty claims based on the Route's "integral nature" stretching even beyond its 200 nautical mile EEZ.[148] In mirror-image fashion, Canada has claimed historic title to the waters of the fabled Northwest Passage, the nineteen-thousand-island archipelago system uniting the Atlantic and Pacific Oceans atop the North American landmass.[149] Russia's touting of a new seafaring commercial corridor across the Eurasian waterway enthusiastically (although unrealistically) has been portrayed as a soon-to-be Arctic rival to the Suez and Panama canals.[150]

---

[144] *National Strategy for the Arctic Region, supra* note 62, at 9; *see also* "ECS Data Management – U.S. Extended Continental Shelf Project," *National Oceanic and Atmospheric Administration (NOAA) National Geophysical Data Center*, National Geophysical Data Center, www.ngdc .noaa.gov/mgg/ecs/.

[145] *See* David J Bederman, *The Old Isolationism and the New Law of the Sea: Reflections on Advice and Consent for UNCLOS*, 49 Harv. Int'l L. J. 21, 25 (2008).

[146] *See* Rothwell, *The Arctic in International Affairs, supra* note 64, at 242.

[147] Ariel Cohen, *Russia in the Arctic: Challenges to U.S. Energy and Geopolitics in the High North, in* RUSSIA IN THE ARCTIC 13 (Stephen J. Blank, ed., 2011).

[148] Cl. 5.1, Navigation in the Water Area of the Northern Sea Route, Russian Federation, Federal Law N 132-ФЗ, On Amendments to Specific Legislative Acts of the Russian Federation Related to Governmental Regulation of Merchant Shipping in the Water Area of the Northern Sea Route, adopted by the State Duma, July 3, 2012; approved by the Council of Federation, July 18, 2012, signed in Moscow, July 28, 2012 by V. Putin, President of The Russian Federation, www. arctic-lio.com/docs/nsr/legislation/federal_law_nsr.pdf. Katarzyna Zysk quotes several Russian authorities in support of the legally tenuous assertion that the "integral nature of the [Northern Sea Route] ... is not affected by the fact that individual portions of it ... may pass into the high seas" – and may, thus, include sea lanes running beyond Russia's EEZ. Katarzyna Zysk, *Russia's Arctic Strategy: Ambitions and Constraints*, 57 JOINT FORCE QUARTERLY 107 (2010) (footnote omitted).

[149] Canadian Order-in Council, September 10, 1985; Territorial Sea Geographical Coordinates (Area 7) Order, SOR/85–872, www.canlii.org/en/ca/laws/regu/sor-85-872/latest/sor-85-872 .html?searchUrlHash=AAAAAQATVGVycmlob3JpYWwgU2VhIEFjdAAAAAB (affirming "Canada has long maintained and exercised sovereignty over the waters of the Canadian Arctic Archipelago").

[150] *See* Gleb Bryanski, *Russia's Putin Says Arctic Trade Route to Rival Suez*, REUTERS CAN. (Sept. 22, 2011), www.reuters.com/article/2011/09/22/us-russia-arctic-idUSTRE78L5TC20110922.

Meanwhile, other specialized regulatory regimes are at work outside the ambit of the Arctic Council: the International Maritime Organization is developing a Polar Code set of binding rules for ships traversing ice-covered waters;[151] the North East Atlantic Fisheries Commission is addressing management issues in the Norwegian Sea; the US Arctic Research Commission has called for a commercial fishing ban in increasingly ice-free Arctic waters to survey stock to forestall catastrophic overfishing;[152] and the International Union on Circumpolar Health is "operating under broad mandates articulated by the World Health Organization."[153] A global Arctic age is spreading institutionally, geographically, politically, and rapidly; and the extant Arctic governance structure may not be prepared for it. The challenge for the Arctic Council will be to match its rhetorical assertion of premier status against the informal structural and preferred arrangements that preference the territorializing interests of its subset: the powerful and capable Arctic coastal states.

Despite some interest in crafting a new agenda for the Arctic Council, it appears the Arctic 5 intends it to remain in its current state of institutional purgatorium. Its good work as a functional, neighborly organization will progress in environmental, scientific, and sustainable development maters, but it will not meet its fullest expression as the preeminent Arctic forum – as the rise of the Arctic Circle Assembly suggests – until the territorializing temptations of the Arctic coastal club no longer need the ambiguities of a soft law regime structure to accomplish primordial sovereign objectives.

---

[151] For information on the International Maritime Organization's draft Polar Code, *see* www.imo .org/MediaCentre/HotTopics/polar/Pages/default.aspx. It is important to note that the decision to develop the Polar Code was shaped considerably by the Council's Arctic Marine Shipping Assessment. *See* Molenaar, *Current and Prospective Roles of the Arctic Council System, supra* note 64, at 571.

[152] Alex Kirby, *U.S. Calls for Commercial Fishing Ban in Arctic as Sea Ice Melt Opens International Waters*, EcoNews (Feb. 25, 2014), http://ecowatch.com/2014/02/25/fishing-ban-in-arctic-sea-ice-melt-opens-international-waters/.

[153] Young, *Whither the Arctic?, supra* note 34, at 77.

6

Sharing Sovereignty: *Jura Novit Curia?* and the Gulf of Fonseca

The concept of sovereignty as an indivisible building block of the state system commonly but imprecisely dates to the Peace of Westphalia in 1648.[1] A doctrinal formulation introduced earlier by Bodin[2] distilled to the "absolute, and perpetual power" of an individual to rule over subjects and territory.[3] This personification of the individual as ruler found artistic and iconic expression on the copperplate engraving adorning the title page of the first English language edition of Hobbes' *Leviathan* (1651).[4] The inscription at the top of the copperplate, serving as the motto of the sovereign, derives from the *Book of Job* (41:24): *Non est potestas super terram quae compareteur ei*: "Upon earth, there is not his like." The uniqueness of the sovereign, the *magnus homo*,[5] meant he had no earthly counterpart

---

[1] *See generally* Derek Croxton, *The Peace of Westphalia of 1648 and the Origins of Sovereignty*, 21 INT'L HIST. REV. 569, 591 (1999) (explaining the origins of the concept of sovereignty).

[2] See Jacques Maritain, *The Concept of Sovereignty*, 44 AM. POL. SCI. REV. 343, 344 (1950) (introducing the doctrinal formulation of sovereignty).

[3] JEAN BODIN, SIX BOOKS OF THE COMMONWEALTH 25 (M. J. Tooley, trans., 1955) (translating JEAN BODIN'S DE LA RÉPUBLIQUE, Bk. I, Ch. 8: "*La souveraineté est la puissance absolue et perpétuelle d'une République*"); *see also* Maritain, *supra* note 2, at 346 (noting that Bodin conceived the sovereign as ruling over the entire body politic).

[4] *See* THOMAS HOBBES, LEVIATHAN, OR THE MATTER, FORME, & POWER OF A COMMON-WEALTH ECCLESIASTICALL AND CIVILL (1651); CARL SCHMITT, THE LEVIATHAN IN THE STATE THEORY OF THOMAS HOBBES: MEANING AND FAILURE OF A POLITICAL SYMBOL 17–18 (1996) (displaying the copper-plate engraving).

[5] *Id.* at 19. Schmitt noted that the realistic interpretation of the significance of the illustration would disappoint readers expecting a depiction of a dragon or sea monster or creature resembling a whale, in the sense depicted in the Hebrew Bible. *Id.* at 18. Hobbes' modern Leviathan, representing *civitas* or *res publica* (which Hobbes references at the beginning of Leviathan) is the *magnus homo*, or huge man. *Id.* at 18–19.

with whom to divide or share power; as French king Louis XIV (1638–1715) purportedly quipped, *"L'État c'est moi."*[6] Carl Schmitt, Hobbes' twentieth-century admirer, interpreted the *Leviathan* engraving as contributing powerfully to the evocative effect of the book,[7] and, doubtless, to the enduring significance of the concept of undivided sovereignty. Few concepts in international law have endured as long or have been subject to as much scrutiny and diatribe.[8]

In an age where this "dogma of sovereignty" still influences international legal discussion,[9] how curious is it to consider the prospect of an amalgam of sovereignties presiding indivisibly over joint property, where states are granted a *jus prohibendi*, enjoining "one joint owner from doing anything" harmful to the interests of other *socii* (associates)?[10] And how more curious is it to consider the extension of this essentially territorial concept seaward, to a realm once thought by Grotius so immense it could never be possessed?[11] Analogized from private property concepts of Roman law (*pro indiviso communis*),[12] these curious adaptations resulted not by international agreement among states, but by the judgment of the Chamber of the International Court of Justice (ICJ) in the historically complicated case involving the Gulf of Fonseca and the 1992 *Land, Island and Maritime Frontier Dispute between El Salvador and Honduras, with Nicaragua Intervening* [*Gulf of Fonseca* case].[13] There, the

---

[6] *Louis XIV (1638–1715)*, BBC NEWS, www.bbc.co.uk/history/historic_figures/louis_xiv.shtml (last visited Feb. 26, 2015). *See generally* Herbert H. Rowen, *"L'État c'est à moi": Louis XIV and the State*, 2 FRENCH HIST. STUD. 83–98 (1961) (discussing Louis XIV's views on sovereignty).

[7] SCHMITT, *supra* note 4, at 18.

[8] *See* Croxton, *supra* note 1, at 569 (listing descriptions of sovereignty as defiled, cornered, eroded, extinct, anachronistic, and more).

[9] Hans Kelsen coined the phrase "dogma of sovereignty." Hans Kelsen, *Absolutism and Relativism in Philosophy*, 42 AM. POL. SCI. REV. 906, 910 (1948). *See generally* Brad R. Roth, *Enduring Significance of State Sovereignty*, 56 FLA. L. REV. 1017 (2004) (explaining the significance of the dogma of sovereignty).

[10] P. Van Warmelo, *Aspects of Joint Ownership in Roman Law*, 25 TIJDSCHRIFT VOOR RECHTSGESCHIEDENIS 125, 125 (1957); *see also* 1 G. H. HACKWORTH, DIGEST OF INTERNATIONAL LAW 615–616 (1940–1944) (involving 1923 German Court of Criminal Appeals holding *jus prohibendi* principle applicable to Lake Constance and riparian interests of Germany, Switzerland, and Austria).

[11] *See generally* Chapter 2.

[12] Van Warmelo notes the term *condominium* was not known to Roman jurists and probably arises around the fourteenth and fifteenth centuries. Van Warmelo, *supra* note 10, at 125. The concept was understood in variegated form, however; employed but "not very much" favored, and "widely scattered" throughout Justinian's *Digest* ("compilation"). *Id.* at 127; *see also* Vincent P. Bantz, *International Legal Status of Condominia*, 12 FLA. J. INT'L L. 77, 79 (1998) (explaining the evolution of the concept of condominium).

[13] Land, Island and Maritime Frontier Dispute (El Sal./Hond.; Nicar. intervening), Judgment, 1992 I.C.J. 351.

Chamber gave juridical expression to the pelagic adaptation of the concept of condominium.[14]

This chapter investigates the legal and historical bases for this application of condominium, which found expression in the Chamber's determination that the maritime space in dispute – the Gulf of Fonseca – constitutes "a condominium" of "co-ownership";[15] not simply of "an historic bay,"[16] but of "an enclosed pluri-state bay";[17] it characterized the Gulf as a "closed sea,"[18] but "subject to a joint sovereignty of ... three coastal states";[19] having "internal waters," but "subject to a special and particular regime *not only* of [threefold][20] joint sovereignty but of rights of passage."[21]

In judicial administration, the presumption of *jura novit curia* reigns: "The court knows the law," which it may apply *ex officio*, that is, independent of the legal arguments of the parties in dispute.[22] But in this case, did the Chamber know its facts? And after wending its way through land, island, and maritime geo-space regimes, involving, by its own estimation, "a kind of bay for which ... there are notoriously no agreed and codified rules,"[23] where did the Chamber find this curious law about sharing sovereignty?

CONDOMINIA IN INTERNATIONAL LAW

Condominium arrangements arise when two or more states exercise joint sovereignty over a territory.[24] The concept "is not common in the relations among nations," but its appearance is "not an inconceivable or an isolated fact."[25] Such arrangements resemble the "community of interest" standard governing

---

[14] *Id.* ¶ 412 ("the waters of the Gulf [being] the subject of the condominium or co-ownership").

[15] *Id.*

[16] *Id.* ¶ 432.

[17] *Id.* ¶ 395 and ¶ 412 ("pluri-state historic bay").

[18] Land, Island, and Maritime Frontier Dispute, 1992 I.C.J. ¶ 395.

[19] *Id.* ¶ 404.

[20] *Id.* ¶ 418.

[21] *Id.* ¶ 412 (emphasis added).

[22] *See* Military and Paramilitary Activities in and Against Nicaragua (Nicar. v. USA), 1986 I.C.J. 14, ¶ 29 ("the principle *jura novit curia* signifies that the court is not solely dependent on the argument of the parties before it with respect to the application of law"); *see also* Fisheries Jurisdiction (U.K. v. Ice.) 1974 I.C.J. 3, 9 (discussing the court's ability to bring its own legal arguments); S.S. Lotus (Fr. v. Turk), 1927 P.C.I.J. Ser. A., No. 10, 31 (discussing the court's ability to bring its own legal arguments).

[23] Land, Island, and Maritime Frontier Dispute, 1992 I.C.J. ¶ 384.

[24] I. L. Oppenheim, International Law: A Treatise 220 (Peace 1905) (noting that this type of joint tenancy is an apparent but not real exception to his view that "on one and the same territory can exist one full-Sovereign State only." Id).

[25] El Salvador v. Nicaragua, C.A.C.J., Judgment of Mar. 9, 1917, 11 Am. J. Int'l L. 674, 712 (1917).

riparian relations, where the interest in a navigable river becomes "the basis of a common legal right."[26] Although often confused with other postwar or postcolonial administrative arrangements, such as mandates, trusts, non-self-governing territories, and protectorates, condominia retain their significance because their purpose and scope attach to the administering powers rather than to third parties, and they are intended to be long-standing, if not permanent, arrangements.[27]

There is some doctrinal variance. Hans Kelsen, for example, wrote of condominium in the proposed rule over post-Nazi Germany,[28] and again when the United States, Soviet Union, Great Britain, and the Provisional Government of the French Republic signed the Berlin Declaration of June 5, 1945.[29] In his construction, the temporal element was less important than the special quality the new political order created: he employed the concept in the postwar German context given what he considered to be a *sui generis* circumstance: all continuity with the previous political order was to be destroyed through its application, and the "new constitution of sovereign Germany would not be the result of a constitutional or revolutionary change" from within.[30] In contrast, the Chamber in the *Gulf of Fonseca* case "relied on principles of state

---

[26] Territorial Jurisdiction of the International Commission of the River Oder (U.K. v. Pol.), 1929 P.C.I.J. (ser. A.), No. 23, at 27; *see also* Land, Island, and Maritime Frontier Dispute, 1992 I.C.J. ¶ 407 ("That there is a community of interest of the three coastal states of the Gulf is not open to doubt"). The Chamber puzzled over Honduras' claim that application of the "community of interest" standard *requires* a delimitation of the waters. *See id.* ¶ 372 (noting that Honduras' claim seemed misguided). A condominium arrangement (*communauté de patrimoines*), however, would be incompatible with a delimitation. *Id.* ¶ 408. According to the Chamber: "It seems odd ... to postulate a community of interest regime as an argument against a condominium regime; for a condominium is almost an ideal juridical embodiment of the community of interest's requirement of perfect equality of user." *Id.* ¶ 407.

[27] *See* Joel H. Samuels, *Condominium Arrangements in International Practice: Reviving an Abandoned Concept of Boundary Dispute Resolution*, 29 Mich. J. Int'l L. 727, 758–767 (2008) (discussing how condominiums retain their significance).

[28] *See* Hans Kelsen, *The International Legal Status of Germany to be Established Immediately Upon Termination of the War*, 38 Am J. Int'l L. 689, 692–694 (1944) (discussing the idea of condominium in relation to post-Nazi Germany).

[29] *See generally* Hans Kelsen, *The Legal Status of Germany According to the Declaration of Berlin*, 39 Am J. Int'l L. 518, 518–526 (1945) (assuming "supreme authority" over the territory of the German Reich and the division of allied-occupied Germany into four zones in accordance with understandings reached at the February 1945 Yalta Conference). Kelsen understood that the condominium could be terminated, but employed the concept, nonetheless, because all vestiges of the previous political order would have been destroyed permanently through its application: "No continuity between the destroyed Nazi state and the new democratic Germany would exist;" and the "new constitution of sovereign Germany would not be the result of a constitutional or revolutionary change" from within. Kelsen, *supra* note 28, at 693.

[30] Kelsen, *supra* note 28, at 689.

succession"[31] and detailed references to historical continuity to validate its application – the opposite of Kelsen's formulation. But the Chamber, nevertheless, "found it sensible to regard the waters of the Gulf and the subject of the condominium of ownership, as *sui generis.*"[32]

Despite notable historical examples,[33] recourse to the concept has been limited and generally "dismissed" both as a means of dispute settlement and territorial administration.[34] A leading international legal treatment of the concept calls it "incompatible" with modernity, a "historical relic from the feudal age," and a "patently inadequate anomaly" that has never established itself in modern international law as anything more than an exigent stopgap measure of last resort.[35]

J. H. W. Verzijl referred to it as "peculiar and exceptional," citing the provisional condominium created in 1920 with the Free City of Danzig and surrounding communities.[36] Others have investigated its provisional application: for example, as between the United States and Great Britain and their joint control over the Oregon Country/Columbia District of the Pacific Northwest from 1815 to 1846;[37] in the Atacama desert region of Bolivia/Chile/

---

[31] Iain Scobbie, *The ICJ and the Gulf of Fonseca: When Two Implies Three but Entails One*, 18 Marine Pol'y 249, 255 (1994).

[32] Land, Island and Maritime Frontier Dispute, 1992 I.C.J. ¶ 412.

[33] Kelsen's list of well-known examples of condominium include Austria's and Prussia's joint rule over Schleswig-Holstein and Lauenburg (1864–1866); Great Britain's and Egypt's condominium over the Sudan (ongoing since 1898 to the date of Kelsen's writing, but ending in 1955); British and French joint sovereignty over the New Hebrides (1914–[1980], although others date the condominium beginning in 1906); and Austria's and Hungary's condominium over Bosnia and Hercegovina (1909–1918). *See* Kelsen, *supra* note 29, at 524 (discussing different times, the possibility of condominium has been entertained); *Anglo-Egyptian Condominium*, Encyclopaedia Britannica, www .britannica.com/EBchecked/topic/25025/Anglo-Egyptian-Condominium (last visited Feb. 26, 2015) (noting the end of the British condominium over Sudan); *Republic of Vanuatu*, Nations Online Project, www.nationsonline.org/oneworld/vanuatu.htm (last visited Feb. 26, 2015) (discussing the end of the British and French condominium over New Hebrides and the country's name change to Vanuatu, along with the argument that the condominium began in 1906). There are numerous other examples of condominium attempts throughout history. *See generally* Samuels, *supra* note 27, at 727–776 (explaining prior attempts at condominium).

[34] *See* Samuels, *supra* note 27, at 728–730 (dismissing condominium as a workable concept).

[35] Peter Schneider, *Condominium, in* 10 Encyclopedia of Public International Law 58, 59 (1987).

[36] J. H. W. Verzijl, 6 International Law in Historical Perspective 69 (1973).

[37] *See generally* Joseph Schafer, *British Attitude Toward the Oregon Question, 1815–1846*, 16 Am. Hist. Rev. 273, 273–299 (1911) (discussing the question of whether the United States or Great Britain "would succeed in establishing its sovereignty over the region west of the Rocky Mountains").

Peru;[38] in the 1910/1912 trilateral conferences among Norway, Sweden, and Russia on the High Arctic administration of Spitsbergen (Svalbard);[39] or in regard to the historical oddity of tiny Andorra, which from 1278 to 1993 was administered jointly by France and the Catalan Bishop of Urgell.[40] Part of this exceptional treatment stems from the condominium's incompatible relation to sovereignty, as classically construed above. Another part relates to a perceived lack of need for the concept. Hersch Lauterpacht thought it practical only where "an atmosphere of understanding or co-operation" prevails between two states, "in which case solutions more simple than a condominium will be found in the first instance."[41] The Chamber in the *Gulf of Fonseca* case seemingly agreed, noting it would be "difficult to see how such a structured system of joint government could be created" absent agreement.[42] Problematically, the Chamber went on to apply the concept over the objections of two of the three parties involved.[43]

Notwithstanding its rare appearance in modern relations, the concept intrigues international legal scholars, who periodically revisit its prospects in disputed boundaries, including Gibraltar, Brčko in the former Yugoslavia, the West Bank and Gaza, the Caspian Sea, and in pelagic spaces such as the Barents Sea, the Baie du Figuier, possessed jointly by France and Spain, and Lake Constance, located on the adjoining shores of Germany, Switzerland, and Austria.[44] It has received an indirect boost in attention from the work of Elinor Ostrom and common-pool resource theorists.[45] These theorists investigate the often informal but enduring joint management rules regarding

---

[38] *See generally* Ronald Bruce St. John, *The Bolivia-Chile-Peru Dispute in the Atacama Desert*, 1 Boundary & Territory Briefing 1, 1–32 (1994) (discussing the dispute between Bolivia, Chile, and Peru over the Atacama Desert on the central-west coast of South America).

[39] *See* Chapter 7.

[40] *See* Jordie Saperia, *Jerusalem: Legal Status, Condominium and Middle East Peace*, 3 J. E. Asia & Int'l L. 175, 184 (2010).

[41] 1 International Law: Being the Collected Papers of Hersch Lauterpacht 371–372 (E. Lauterpacht, ed., 1970).

[42] Land, Island and Maritime Frontier Dispute, 1992 I.C.J. ¶ 399.

[43] *Id.* ¶ 398 (noting both Honduras and Nicaragua opposed the condominium solution).

[44] *See* Samuels, *supra* note 27, at 729, 753 n. 157 (discussing areas in dispute); *see also* Land, Island and Maritime Frontier Dispute, 1992 I.C.J ¶ 401 (citing the Baie du Figuier as an "instance" of condominium).

[45] *See generally* Elinor Ostrom, Governing the Commons: The Evolution of Institutions for Collective Action (1990) (proposing solutions to governance of natural resources used by many individuals in common); *see also* Samuels, *supra* note 27, at 772–776 (describing "principles for a model condominium drawn from Ostrom's work on common pool resources combined with lessons derived from past condominia"); Jack McNeily, *A Condominium Approach to Abyei*, 13 Chi. J. Int'l L. 265, 280–281 (2012) (discussing Ostrom's baseline design principles).

natural or human made resources deemed too large to exclude beneficiaries from use.[46] The concept of condominium is not far removed from proposals involving joint administration of the global commons, making its significance more important than is perhaps appreciated.

But its controlling appearance in the *Gulf of Fonseca* case stands out and is almost alone in the jurisprudence. In dissent, the erudite and meticulously systematic Judge Shigeru Oda[47] rebuked the Chamber for its application of *jura novit curia.* Judge Oda intimated that the Chamber engaged in a perilous form of judicial innovation, claiming the Chamber's condominium articulation of a historic, pluri-state bay had no basis in law.[48] He had problems with the Chamber's usage of the term "historic bay," which found hardly any legal support prior to 1910,[49] and could not be granted legal status *sua sponte* as a *sui generis* regime;[50] he had problems with the notion that a bay, regardless of its description geographically or historically, could be accorded special legal status as one united area as between two or more riparian states;[51] he had problems with the conflated treatment of the waters within the bay as "internal waters" and as "territorial sea." He argued that sea waters adjacent to the coasts of states admit to one of two conjoined legal descriptions:[52] they are either territorial seas, which provide for a right of innocent passage, or internal waters, which do not.[53] The Chamber, relying on the findings of an earlier court decision,[54] recognized this conjoined tension, but dismissed it because such analysis was not necessarily appropriate to discussions involving a pluri-state bay.[55] And Judge Oda had problems with establishing an inner littoral maritime belt along the coastlines of the three states in relation to establishing a closing line between the bay and the Pacific Ocean. The Chamber seemingly recognized that "if the waters internal to that bay are subject to a threefold joint sovereignty, it is the *three* coastal states that are entitled to territorial sea

---

[46] *See* Elinor Ostrom et al., Rules, Games, & Common-Pool Resources 4–5 (1994) (discussing research done on rules enabling individuals to utilize resources over long periods of time).

[47] *See* Michael Reisman, *Judge Shigeru Oda: A Tribute to an International Treasure,* 16 Leiden J. Int'l L. 57, 61 (2003) (describing Judge Oda's characteristics).

[48] Land, Island and Maritime Frontier Dispute 1992 I.C.J. ¶¶ 2 and 24 (dissenting opinion of Judge Oda).

[49] *Id.* ¶ 11.

[50] *Id.* ¶¶ 4 and 46.

[51] *Id.* ¶ 13.

[52] *Id.* ¶ 24.

[53] Land, Island and Maritime Frontier Dispute, 1992 I.C.J. ¶¶ 26, 44, and 51 (dissenting opinion of Judge Oda).

[54] *See generally* El Salvador v. Nicaragua, 11 Am. J. Int'l L. 674 (1917) (opinion and decision of the Central American Court of Justice in the case involving those two countries).

[55] *See* Land, Island and Maritime Frontier Dispute, 1992 I.C.J. ¶ 393.

[outside] the bay."[56] Aside from implications involving condominium over the territorial sea (or involving the continental shelf and EEZs),[57] such a formulation gave rise to a tension recognized, but not completely answered,[58] by the Chamber: "a state cannot have two territorial seas off the same littoral" coast.[59] This confusing prospect prompted Judge Oda to wonder what the judgment did to the concept of the three-mile coastal belt.[60] The Chamber, he concluded, employed concepts to denominate the legal status of Fonseca's waters in ways that were "extraneous" to the historical and current understanding of the law of the sea.[61]

Moreover, Judge Oda pinpointed the source of the legal fiction, the Central American Court of Justice's (CACJ) 1917 judgment, on which the ICJ Chamber heavily relied.[62] "[N]ot until the rendering of that [j]udgment," wrote Judge Oda, had the legal status of the Gulf of Fonseca ever been "clothed as 'a[n] historic bay.'"[63] Indeed, the concept of the historic bay had arisen in the context of limited and long-standing usages,[64] as recognized by the 1910 Award of the Permanent Court of Arbitration in the *North Atlantic Coast Fisheries*

[56] *Id.* ¶ 418 (emphasis in the original).
[57] *See id.* ¶ 420 ("Since the legal situation on the landward side of the closing line is one of joint sovereignty, it follows that all three of the joint sovereigns must have entitlement outside the closing line to territorial sea, continental shelf and exclusive economic zone").
[58] By special agreement the Chamber was tasked "to determine the legal situation of the maritime spaces"; the Chamber ruled this charge did not confer jurisdiction to effect any delimitation of those maritime spaces within or outside the Gulf, but reminded the parties that any such delimitation would have to be effected by agreement on the basis of international law. *Id.* ¶ 432(2)–(3).
[59] *Id.* ¶ 416.
[60] Land, Island and Maritime Frontier Dispute, 1992 I.C.J. ¶ 40 (dissenting opinion of Judge Oda). Judge Oda also argued Honduras' geographical situation, "bottled up" as it is in the Gulf, precluded its offshore claim to areas of the Pacific coast outside the Gulf, except, possibly, in line with rights of geographically disadvantaged nations as contemplated in the 1982 United Nations Convention on the Law of the Sea. *See id.* ¶ 6 ("bottled up"); *id.* ¶ 55 (geographically disadvantaged). He reminded the Chamber that geographical realities of nature cannot be refashioned by judicial administration. *Id.* ¶ 53. None of the three Central American states was party to the 1982 Convention on the Law of the Sea. *Id.* ¶ 383.
[61] Land, Island and Maritime Frontier Dispute, 1992 I.C.J. ¶ 5 (dissenting opinion of Judge Oda).
[62] *Id.* ¶ 38.
[63] *Id.* ¶ 27.
[64] These claims pertained to geographical bays considered internal waters by single coastal state claimants that historically had exercised jurisdiction beyond the range of cannon shot – for example, the Delaware and Chesapeake Bays on the Atlantic seaboard of the United States, part of the Bristol Channel, and Conception Bay in Newfoundland. *Id.* ¶¶ 10 and 32; N. Atl. Coast Fisheries (U.K. v. US), 11 R.I.A.A. 167, 197, 205 (Perm. Ct. Arb. 1910) (explaining the "cannon-shot" rule); cf. Donat Pharand, *The Arctic Waters and the Northwest Passage: A Final Revisit*, 38 OCEAN DEV. & INT'L LAW 3, 5 (2007) (discussing historic title as a basis for internal waters).

Case;[65] but Judge Oda argued the term had been misapplied to the Gulf of Fonseca (which was enclosed by more than one littoral state),[66] asserted unanimously as true by the CACJ on the basis of a questionnaire formulated by that Court,[67] and, in turn, affirmed by a litany of established doctrinal authorities, who echoed and validated the 1917 judgment, thus providing the Chamber a faulty basis for concluding that "commentators generally, are agreed that [the Gulf of Fonseca] is an historic bay, and that the waters of it are accordingly historic waters."[68] Judge Oda identified Oppenheim's third edition of *International Law* (1920) as the doctrinal source of this faulty shift in thinking, with Fauchille, Jessup, Wheaton, Gidel "and others" dutifully affirming in succession.[69] "[But they] never presented any justification for this label," according to Judge Oda, "outside the fact that the 1917 Judgment had so styled the Gulf."[70]

Judge Oda's dissent can be read as a sublime critique of the historiography of international law and the various legal authorities who, in treatise form, uncritically take for granted "local illusions" of law and historical fact.[71] Once misrepresented by a court, these illusions thereby facilitate the reception of these false conclusions into the corpus of international law.[72] Judge Oda's opinion carries considerable weight given his professorial reputation as a leading law of the sea scholar and specialist.[73] The Chamber found it "clearly

---

[65] North Atlantic Coast Fisheries, 11 R.I.A.A. at 206; *see also* Land, Island and Maritime Frontier Dispute, 1992 I.C.J. ¶ 27 (dissenting opinion of Judge Oda) (discussing the term "historic bay").

[66] Land, Island and Maritime Frontier Dispute, 1992 I.C.J. ¶ 33 (dissenting opinion of Judge Oda).

[67] *See* El Salvador v. Nicaragua, 11 AM. J. INT'L L. at 693 ("Taking into consideration the geographic and historic condition, as well as the situation, extent and configuration of the Gulf of Fonseca, what is the international legal status of the Gulf?"); *see also* Land, Island and Maritime Frontier Dispute, 1992 I.C.J. ¶ 390 (quoting the ninth question of the CACJ Judgment). The judges answered unanimously that the Gulf is a historic bay possessed of the characteristics of a closed sea, but provided no basis for its conclusion. *See id.* ¶ 32 (dissenting opinion of Judge Oda) (questioning the unanimous decision). In a thinly veiled critique of *juria novit curia,* Judge Oda wrote: "[I]t seems a needless self-restriction on the part of the Chamber to have refrained from any critical inspection of [this point]." *Id.* ¶ 34.

[68] Land, Island and Maritime Frontier Dispute, 1992 I.C.J. ¶ 383.

[69] *Id.* ¶ 28 (dissenting opinion of Judge Oda).

[70] *Id.*

[71] Judge Oda's actual words were: "It appears to me that the 1917 Judgment [on which the ICJ "heavily" relied] was based upon a local illusion as concerns the historical background of law and fact." Land, Island and Maritime Frontier Dispute, 1992 I.C.J. ¶ 39, at 754 (dissenting opinion of Judge Oda).

[72] *Id.* ¶¶ 27 and 28.

[73] Oda's doctoral dissertation, supervised by Myers McDougal at Yale Law School, took up the subject of the law of the sea; he served as a member of the Japanese delegation to the United Nations' First and Third Law of the Sea Conferences in 1958 and 1974; and he served on the United Nations Seabed Committee when it formed in 1968 and joined the German legal team before the ICJ in the *North Sea Continental Shelf Cases.* Reisman, *supra* note 46, at

necessary" to "investigate the particular history of the Gulf of Fonseca" to arrive at its conclusion.[74] Indeed.

THE HISTORICAL SETTING

The Gulf of Fonseca is a small bay fronting the Central American countries of El Salvador, Honduras, and Nicaragua. El Salvador's Cape Amapala, to the northwest, and Nicaragua's Cape Cosiguina, to the southeast, pinch the 19.75-mile-wide entrance of Pacific Ocean waters into its basin, which penetrates thirty to thirty-two nautical miles landward.[75] Honduras lies between the two countries, with its outlet to the sea "bottled up" by the impinging coastlines adjacent to its shore.[76] Christopher Columbus identified the entire region for future European exploit on his fourth voyage to the New World in 1502.[77] Two decades later, explorer Andrés Niño, specifically in search of an interoceanic route,[78] sailed into the Gulf, "encountered a complex, interrelated socioecological zone inhabited by multiple ethnic" and linguistic groups,[79] and claimed it on behalf of Spanish monarchs, naming it after the expedition's patron, Juan Rodríguez de Fonseca, Bishop of Burgos,[80] overseer of Spanish colonial interests in the New World,[81] and Columbus' Andalusian rival.[82]

PRE-INDEPENDENCE: 1522–1821

For almost three hundred years, the Crown of Castile administered this region of the Spanish Indies through the viceroyalty of New Spain (Mexico),[83] which

---

60, 62; Judge Shigeru Oda and the Path to Judicial Wisdom: Opinions (Declarations, Separate Opinions, Dissenting Opinions) on the International Court of Justice, 1993–2003, at 7–11 (Edward McWhinney & Mariko Kawano, eds., 2006).

[74] Land, Island and Maritime Frontier Dispute, 1992 I.C.J. ¶ 384, at 589.

[75] *Id.* ¶ 382.

[76] *Id.*; Land, Island and Maritime Frontier Dispute, 1992 I.C.J. ¶ 6 (dissenting opinion of Judge Oda).

[77] Linda A. Newson, Indian Survival in Colonial Nicaragua 92 (1987).

[78] Esteban Montes Gomez, Archaeology of the Colonial Period Gulf of Fonseca, Eastern El Salvador, 42 (2010) (unpublished PhD dissertation, University of California Berkeley) (on file with UC Berkeley Electronic Theses and Dissertations).

[79] *Id.* at 37.

[80] Land, Island and Maritime Frontier Dispute, 1992 I.C.J. ¶ 385. The expedition was organized by Captain Gil González Dávila. *Id.*

[81] Felipe Fernández-Armesto, Columbus 101 (1991).

[82] *Id.* at 148.

[83] John A. Booth et al., Understanding Central America: Global Forces, Rebellion, and Change 43 (4th edn., 2006). The viceroy of Mexico dispatched the brigantine *El Activo* in 1794 to survey the Gulf of Fonseca. The expedition mapped the gulf but its chart, the

included the Captaincy-General of Guatemala,[84] consisting of the provinces of Chiapas, Guatemala, San Salvador, Honduras, Nicaragua, and Costa Rica.[85] But the Spanish conquest of this region met with varied,[86] sometimes difficult and persistent, resistance,[87] and was not as placidly uninterrupted as the Chamber's historical reading suggests.[88] The early development of the Gulf of Fonseca as an interoceanic port connecting the Pacific to the Caribbean stalled under the weight of imperial demands elsewhere;[89] the region's high population density became the object of the Crown's enslavement needs for mining operations in Honduras and South America.[90] Spanish slave laws, imprecisely applied, difficult to generalize,[91] but brutally depicted by the Spanish Dominican's, Bartolomé de las Casas' (c. 1484–1566) accounts,[92]

Carta Esférica, was lost and later recovered after the 1992 judgment, launching a claim by El Salvador to revisit the judgment based on a perceived avulsion to the Goascorán River. G.A. Res. 58/4, ¶ 235–239, U.N. Doc. A/RES/58/4 (Oct. 29, 2003); Application for Revision of the Judgment of September 11, 1992 in the Case Concerning the Land, Island and Maritime Frontier Dispute (El Sal./Hond.: Nicar. intervening) (El. Sal. v. Hond.) 2003 I.C.J. 392, ¶¶ 25 and 26. For an early English language presentation of Spanish holdings and conquests in the New World, *see* JOHN OGILBY, AMERICA: BEING THE LATEST, AND MOST ACCURATE DESCRIPTION OF THE NEW WORLD: CONTAINING THE ORIGINAL OF THE INHABITANTS, AND THE REMARKABLE VOYAGES THITHER: THE CONQUEST OF THE VAST EMPIRES OF MEXICO AND PERU, AND OTHER LARGE PROVINCES AND TERRITORIES, WITH THE SEVERAL EUROPEAN PLANTATIONS IN THOSE PARTS: ALSO THEIR CITIES, FORTRESSES, TOWNS, TEMPLES, MOUNTAINS, AND RIVERS: THEIR HABITS, CUSTOMS MANNERS, AND RELIGIONS: THEIR PLANTS, BEASTS, BIRDS, AND SERPENTS: WITH AN APPENDIX CONTAINING, BESIDES SEVERAL OTHER CONSIDERABLE ADDITIONS, A BRIEF SURVEY OF WHAT HATH BEEN DISCOVER'D OF THE UNKNOWN SOUTH-LAND AND THE ARCTICK REGION (1671); and ANTONIO DE SOLIS, THE HISTORY OF THE CONQUEST OF MEXICO BY THE SPANIARDS (Thomas Townsend, 1724).

84 Mary Wilhelmine Williams, *The New Central America*, 214 N. AM. REV. 297, 297 n. 790 (1921).
85 Charles L. Stansifer, *United States-Central American Relations, 1824–1950, in* UNITED STATES-LATIN AMERICAN RELATIONS, 1800–1850, at 25, 27 (T. Ray Shurbutt, ed., 1991).
86 The conquest of Pacific Nicaragua was "relatively easy" although Spanish fortifications had to be built in the urban centers of León and Granada; coordinated resistance arose in Honduras and aboriginal resistance to Spanish colonizers "persisted throughout the colonial period" in eastern Nicaragua. Newson, *supra* note 77, at 92.
87 Montes, *supra* note 78, at 49.
88 *See* Land, Island and Maritime Frontier Dispute, 1992 I.C.J. ¶ 385.
89 *See* Montes, *supra* note 78, at 40–41 (noting that the prospect of developing the Gulf was abandoned after the settlers realized the land was "unprofitable").
90 *Id.* at 41–42.
91 Spanish slave laws dated to the thirteenth century *Siete Partidas* of Alonso X, "*el Sabio*" (1221–1284), and were meant by Queen Isabella's *royal cédula* in 1503 to apply only to "hostile" *indios*, a practice later abandoned until reinstated in 1534. Gomez, *supra* note 77, at 45; *see also* CLIFFORD L. STATEN, THE HISTORY OF NICARAGUA 16 (2010) (discussing the Crown's laws after 1542 to protect indigenous populations from abuse).
92 *See generally* BARTOLOMÉ DE LAS CASAS, AN ACCOUNT, MUCH ABBREVIATED, OF THE DESTRUCTION OF THE INDIES, WITH RELATED TEXTS (Franklin W. Knight, ed., Andrew Hurley, trans., 2003) (describing in lengthy detail the violence and mistreatment the indigenous people suffered at

sparked rebellions from Fonseca's Lenca-speaking island inhabitants[93] and other indigenous peoples throughout the region.[94] The Crown's administration of tribute (the *encomienda*)[95] created fierce intramural rivalries among competing Spanish *encomenderos*,[96] inducing some to circumvent colonial regulation.[97] Between 1522 and 1531, the governors of Nicaragua and Guatemala "jockeyed for control in the area," which "functioned under separate royal orders,"[98] precipitating armed conflicts and diplomatic disputes between the governorships until 1543,[99] when jurisdiction over the islands and Gulf consolidated with the *encomienda* awarded to Guatemala under Melchor Hernandez.[100] Astonishingly, European diseases, which were carried south from their landward entry point in Mexico, preceded the arrival of Spaniards in the region of the Bay of Fonseca, killing up to 50 percent of the indigenous populations before the conquistadors' campaign launched in 1524.[101] This demographic, estimated to have reduced the original native numbers from around one million to tens of thousands within a few decades, stands as perhaps the most consequential and tragic result of Europeans' immediate encounter with the New World,[102] and may suggest the placid waters off Fonseca's coast were due to viral decimation interpreted centuries later as pelagic accord.

the hands of the Spaniards); Helen Rand Parish & Harold E. Weidman, *The Correct Birthdate of Bartolome de las Casas*, 56 Hisp. Am. Hist. Rev. 385, 385–386 (1976) (discussing de las Casas' life). An object of de las Casas' moral complaint, "the great tyrant captain," Pedro de Alvarado, provided accounts of his own incursion into Guatemala, in letters sent back to his superior, Hernando Cortes. An Account of the Conquest of Guatemala in 1524 by Pedro de Alvarado 9, 125 (Sedley J. Mackie, ed., 1924).

[93] *See* Montes, *supra* note 78, at 48 (discussing how the Lenca-speaking people resisted the Spanish to defend their lands).

[94] *See* Linda A. Newson, The Cost of Conquest: Indian Decline in Honduras Under Spanish Rule 96 (1986) (attributing problems of conquest to large numbers of independent indigenous groups).

[95] *See* Montes, *supra* note 78, at 42 (discussing the *encomienda*).

[96] *See* Christopher M. White, The History of El Salvador 32 (2009) (noting, for instance, competition in the 1520s between conquistador factions controlled by Davila, Cortez and de Alvarado).

[97] *See* Montes, *supra* note 78, at 42 (noting that colonial involvement incentivized some individuals to hide their acquisitions to avoid paying royalty taxes on them).

[98] *Id.*

[99] *Id.* at 49.

[100] *Id.* at 43.

[101] White, *supra* note 96, at 32.

[102] *See* Thomas W. Walker & Christine J. Wade, Nicaragua: Living in the Shadow of the Eagle 8–9 (5th edn., 2011); Victor Perera, Unfinished Conquest: The Guatemalan Tragedy 4–5 (1993) (noting diseases "unknown in the New World killed several times more Mayas than the most sanguinary of conquistadores ever intended to").

Although non-Spaniards had been excluded officially from the Indies in 1501,[103] by the 1560s and 1570s, the circum-Caribbean region became the focal point of pirating expeditions,[104] with buccaneers "swarming through the Caribbean between the 1650s and the 1680s."[105] Elizabethan sea interests, ambitious but still no match for other European powers, developed a seaborne "cold war" strategy against the Castilian Crown, which focused on raiding its burgeoning silver trade in the Americas as a means of "waging war on the cheap."[106] This predation also took place in Pacific waters up and down the west coast of the Americas – the so-called Spanish South Sea – reaching its damaging apex in the 1680s,[107] but extending well into the eighteenth century.[108]

In the 1570s, Dutch sea rovers, or Sea Beggars, also began plying the waters of the Spanish Caribbean, raiding Luso-Castilian shipping and settlements when not in search of salt.[109] Historians will recall Grotius' *Mare Liberum* (The Free Sea, 1609) was commissioned to validate the actions of these private auxiliaries (in the form of the Verenigde Oostindische Compagnie: VOC, operating, albeit, in East Asian waters)[110] as a means of making just war against transgressors of the natural order and the right of the Low Countries to engage in trade.[111] Labeled pirates by Philip II (1527–1598), their depredations against the Crown in the New World were an outgrowth of a generalized state of war.[112] In 1614 a fleet sponsored by the rebellious States-General and its corporate agent, the VOC, crossed the Atlantic, rounded South America and "wreak[ed] havoc" in the Spanish South Sea, searching to abduct the newly appointed viceroy of Peru while cruising from Chile to Mexico; it reconnoitered the

---

[103] Paul E. Hoffman, *Diplomacy and the Papal Donation 1493–1585*, 30 AMERICAS 151, 154 n. 2 (1973).

[104] KRIS E. LANE, PILLAGING THE EMPIRE: PIRACY IN THE AMERICAS 1500–1750, at 40–41 (1967).

[105] J. H. ELLIOTT, EMPIRES OF THE ATLANTIC WORLD: BRITAIN AND SPAIN IN AMERICA 1492–1830, at 224 (2006).

[106] PAUL KENNEDY, THE RISE AND FALL OF THE GREAT POWERS: ECONOMIC CHANGE AND MILITARY CONFLICT FROM 1500–2000, at 61 (1987); *see also, id.* at 53–55 (describing how the Crown seized American silver imported for its people, and forced them to accept government bonds in exchange).

[107] *See* LANE, *supra* note 104, at 153–154 (describing the journey of the pirates through the Spanish sea, traveling through various parts of the Americas).

[108] *See* Simon Smith, *Piracy in Early British America*, 46 HIST. TODAY 29, 30 (1996) (noting that piracy experienced a "golden age" at the start of the eighteenth century).

[109] LANE, *supra* note 104, at 62, 64–65.

[110] Grotius was hired to justify the Dutch seizure and condemnation in an Amsterdam admiralty court of the Portuguese carrack, *Santa Catarina*, captured off the coast of Singapore in 1603. *See* Chapter 2 (this volume).

[111] HUGO GROTIUS, MARE LIBERUM 1609–2009, at 153, 155 (Robert Feenstra, trans., 2009).

[112] LANE, *supra* note 104, at 62.

Gulf of Fonseca [Amapala Bay] before eventually crossing the Pacific to Manila and the Moluccas to plunder again, this time against Spain's Asian holdings and Portugal's *Estado da Índia* (colonial empire).[113] The voyage was a "watershed" awakening for Spanish South Sea defense strategy, compelling the viceroy to order construction of fixed garrisons and increase taxes on an increasingly burdened merchant class,[114] all in support of an overstretched imperium. European privateers, empowered by loosely administered and widely abused letters of marque and reprisal, began populating the island chain of the Antilles by the 1620s – Barbados, St. Kitts, Martinique, and Guadeloupe – using them as staging ports for raids against the Crown at sea, on the northern coast of Hispaniola,[115] and certainly throughout the Spanish Main.[116] The island of Tortuga became central to French Huguenot operations; Jamaica's Port Royal – the "wickedest town in America" – became the base of Oliver Cromwell's "Western Design," prompting the Anglo-Spanish War (1654–1660) to establish a "Protestant empire in the Indies."[117]

By the latter part of the seventeenth century, freebooting and privateering had turned the Spanish Main into a "paradise for ... adventurous robber[s]," who operated on a scale "almost unbelievable."[118] And yet, notwithstanding the fractious intramural and international problems of Spanish rule in the

---

[113] *Id.* at 79–83; *see* KEVIN JOSEPH SHEEHAN, IBERIAN ASIA: THE STRATEGIES OF SPANISH AND PORTUGUESE EMPIRE BUILDING, 1540–1700, at 5, 287–289 (2008) (dissertation, University of California, Berkeley) (noting Manila was controlled by Spain and the Moluccas were controlled by Portugal).

[114] *Id.* at 83–84.

[115] *See* PETER EARLE, THE PIRATE WARS 90 (2003) (discussing the origins of buccaneers); David J. Bederman, *Privateering, in* VIII ENCYCLOPEDIA OF PUBLIC INTERNATIONAL LAW 475, 476 (Rüdinger Wolfrum, ed., 2012) (discussing abuse of letters of marque and reprisal); *English Letters of Marque Against Spain, James I, 1625,* CONSTITUTION SOC'Y (Feb. 16, 2015), www .constitution.org/mil/lmr/1625engl.htm (granting actions against the Spanish Crown).

[116] EARLE, *supra* note 115, at 90. Broadly defined, the Spanish Main came to designate the entire Caribbean Sea and the southern half of the Gulf of Mexico; more narrowly, it was intended to denote the Spanish "Mainland," or *tierra firme,* stretching from the northern coast of South America from Panama to the Florida Gulf coast and on the east to Trinidad. PHILIP AINSWORTH MEANS, THE SPANISH MAIN: FOCUS OF ENVY 1492–1700, vii (1935).

[117] EARLE, *supra* note 115, at 91; *see* Gérard Lafleur & Lucien Abénon, *The Protestants and the Colonialization of the French West Indies, in* MEMORY AND IDENTITY: THE HUGUENOTS IN FRANCE AND THE ATLANTIC DIASPORA 267 (Bertrand Van Ruymbeke & Randy J. Sparks, eds., 2003) (discussing a Huguenot republic on the island of Tortuga); Matthew Craig Harrington, "The Worke Wee May Doe in the World": The Western Design and the Anglo-Spanish Struggle for the Caribbean, 1654–1655, at 5 (May 26, 2004) (unpublished MA thesis, Florida State University) (The Anglo-Spanish War was "sparked by the Western Design."); WILLIAM EDMUNDSON, A HISTORY OF THE BRITISH PRESENCE IN CHILE: FROM BLOODY MARY TO CHARLES DARWIN AND THE DECLINE OF BRITISH INFLUENCE 5 (2009) (discussing the Anglo-Spanish War).

[118] *Id.* at 93–94.

New World, the ICJ Chamber concluded, with scant historical evidence,[119] that on these shores of the South Sea, "[i]t appears that the Spanish Crown ... exercised continuous and peaceful sovereignty over the waters of the Gulf [of Fonseca], without serious or more than temporary contestation," for almost three hundred years.[120]

How so? Judge Oda recognized the fundamental circumstances of topography and history prior to decolonization: "the Gulf of Fonseca was surrounded by the territory of Spain, as a single state."[121] But for him "there is no ground for believing [at that time the Spanish Crown] had any control in the sea-waters beyond the traditionally accepted rule of the range of cannon-shot in the Gulf."[122] Moreover, both the CACJ and ICJ judgments "depend[ed] on the hidden assumption that the maritime area in question" was not only "single and undivided" but *"in its entirety* ... within the territorial jurisdiction of a single riparian State" – "overlook[ing] the basic fact that [no such legal conception of a bay existed at that time]."[123]

After 1522, only a "few available documents ... comment on the Gulf of Fonseca," save for notable late-sixteenth-century accounts by administrators and Franciscans.[124] But more general, less serene, matters are known: Sir Francis Drake (c. 1539/1543–d. 1596) reconnoitered the Gulf in 1579[125] and allegedly used the island El Tigre as a launching point for raids. He plundered many Spanish vessels, most importantly one that was two leagues off the coast of Nicaragua near the Gulf of Fonseca, which provided sea charts of inestimable value, opening up the coasts of Mexico and California and showing a route to him of the Indies to the Cape of Good Hope,[126] contributing doubtless

---

[119] *See* Montes, *supra* note 78, at 43 ("After 1522 there are few available documents that comment on the Gulf of Fonseca").

[120] Land, Island and Maritime Frontier Dispute, 1992 I.C.J. ¶ 385.

[121] *Id.* ¶ 37 (dissenting opinion of Judge Oda).

[122] *Id.*

[123] *Id.* (emphasis in original).

[124] Montes, *supra* note 78, at 43; *see also id.* at 39 (noting these rare recordings "are considered canonical documents" among scholars of Central American, pre-Colombian, and Latin American colonial studies).

[125] *See* Harry Kelsey, Sir Francis Drake: The Queen's Pirate 165 (1998) ("seeing the volcanos of Honduras and Guatemala"). Drake was born on "a date no earlier than 1539 or later than 1543" and died in 1596. *Id.* at 396, 412–413. *See* II E. G. Squier, Nicaragua; Its People, Scenery, Monuments, and the Proposed Interoceanic Canal 168, 243 (1856) ("Drake had his headquarters on the island of Tigre" during his operations in the Pacific Ocean and the South Sea).

[126] George Davidson, *Francis Drake on the Northwest Coast of America in the Year 1579: The Golden Hinde Did Not Anchor in the Bay of San Francisco,* 5 Transactions & Proc. Geographical Soc'y Pac. 1, 35 (1908); *see also* George Davison, *The Discovery of San Francisco Bay,* 4 Transactions & Proc. Geographical Soc'y Pac. 1, 17–18 (1907) (Drake took refuge in a

to his and future predatory incursions in the Americas and around the globe.[127] In 1671, the Welsh buccaneer Henry Morgan laid siege to Panama City after marching across the Isthmus of Darien (Panama);[128] and in the 1680s, English buccaneers led by Bartholomew Sharpe hacked their way across the isthmus again, commandeered the Spanish battleship, *La Santissima Trinidad*, launched an eighteen-month terror campaign on the South Sea, plundered with impunity along the unprotected Pacific shore,[129] captured sea charts and maps of immeasurable military value (that he would later parlay into an amnesty for his campaign),[130] and then "rounded Cape Horn and crept up the South Atlantic."[131] Although not at war with Spain at this time due to the

California harbor he likely learned of from the papers obtained from captured Spanish vessels). *See generally* RICHARD HAKLUYT, THE PRINCIPALL NAVIGATIONS, VOIAGES AND DISCOVERIES OF THE ENGLISH NATION, MADE BY SEA OR OVER LAND, TO THE MOST REMOTE AND FARTHEST DISTANT QUARTERS OF THE EARTH AT ANY TIME WITHIN THE COMPASSE OF THESE 1500. YEERS: DEVIDED INTO THREE SEVERALL PARTS, ACCORDING TO THE POSITIONS OF THE REGIONS WHEREUNTO THEY WERE DIRECTED [twelve page insertion between 643 and 644] (1589) (discussing "The famous voyage of Sir Francis Drake into the South Sea, and there hence about the whole Glob of the Earth, begun in the yeere of our Lord, 1566").

[127] Drake's "enormous haul of booty" inspired a generation of English adventurers, including Thomas Cavendish, who successfully sailed and plundered in Drake's wake in 1588, and others who were less successful in rounding the treacherous Magellan Straits. KENNETH R. ANDREWS, DRAKE'S VOYAGES: A RE-ASSESSMENT OF THEIR PLACE IN ELIZABETHAN MARITIME EXPANSION 84 (1967); *see* THE ROUTLEDGE ENCYCLOPEDIA OF TUDOR ENGLAND 197 (Arthur F. Kinney & David W. Swain, eds., 2001) (Drake's "return to London with a rich haul of plunder inspired imitation, which came with Thomas Cavendish's circumnavigation from 1586 to 1588"). *See generally* HAKLUYT, *supra* note 126, at 809–813 (discussing "The worthy and famous voyage of Master Thomas Candishe *made round about the globe of the earth, in the space of two yeeres* and lesse then two monethes, begun in the yeere, 1586").

[128] *See* PHILIP GOSSE, THE HISTORY OF PIRACY 158–159 (1946) (discussing Morgan's attack in Panama). Morgan and his raiders alone are credited with sacking fifty-seven cities, towns, and villages in New Spain. *See* MARCUS REDIKER, BETWEEN THE DEVIL AND THE DEEP BLUE SEA: MERCHANT SEAMEN, PIRATES AND THE ANGLO-AMERICAN WORLD, 1700-1750, 58 (1987) (discussing Morgan's feats in New Spain). Morgan's exploits are wonderfully recorded by his fellow buccaneer, John Esquemeling. *See* I-II BUCANIERS OF AMERICA: OR, A TRUE ACCOUNT OF THE MOST REMARKABLE ASSAULTS COMMITTED OF LATE YEARS UPON THE COASTS OF THE WEST INDIES, BY THE BUCANIERS OF JAMAICA AND TORTUGA, BOTH ENGLISH AND FRENCH (1684).

[129] *See* PHILIP GOSSE, THE PIRATES' WHO'S WHO 259 (1924) ("eighteen months [of] sacking towns and attacking Spanish ships"); GOSSE, *supra* note 128, at 161–162 (discussing the attack on *La Santissima Trinidad*). An account of "The Dangerous Voyage, and bold Attempts of Capt. Barholomew Sharp, and others, in the South Sea, for two Years, &c." can be found in II ESQUEMELING, BUCCANEERS OF AMERICA, *supra* note 128, pt. IV, ch. I.

[130] A BUCCANEER'S ATLAS: BASIL RINGROSE'S SOUTH SEA WAGGONER: A SEA ATLAS AND SAILING DIRECTIONS OF THE PACIFIC COAST OF THE AMERICAS 1 (Derek Howse & Norman J. W. Thrower, eds., 1992); *see* MARK DONNELLY & DANEIL DIEHL, PIRATES OF VIRGINIA: PLUNDER AND HIGH ADVENTURE ON THE OLD DOMINION COASTLINE 21 (2012) (The maps "were of such strategic importance that when the pirates returned to England, they presented them to Charles II, who granted the crew a full pardon").

[131] GOSSE, *supra* note 128, at 168.

Treaty of Madrid,[132] that peace was understood in practice not to apply in the New World, where maritime lines of amity, once crossed (the meridian of the Azores to the west and the Tropic of Cancer to the south), prompted application of the European code that "there shall be no occasion for complaints and claims for damages," and likewise, "No Peace Beyond the Line."[133]

In the 1680s, English buccaneers sojourning in the Bay of Fonseca contracted tropical fever; they decamped but were replaced by French corsairs, who used the bay as a staging ground for raids against settlements to the northwest before trekking overland to the Caribbean and back to their island retreat of Tortuga.[134] Such episodes on the Spanish South Sea strike against the claim of peaceful and uninterrupted Spanish rule as evidence of the colonial *effectivité* demonstrating effective exercise of territorial jurisdiction,[135] without opposition and with *possessio longi temporis.*[136] Interestingly, the Chamber came to the important conclusion that the terrestrial principle of *uti possidetis* should apply to the waters of the Gulf of Fonseca as well as the land,[137] but the presumption of peaceful and uninterrupted control of what was not contemplated as a "single-state" bay under the sole sway of the Spanish Crown suffers in light of the specific (albeit sketchy) historical record involving the Gulf of Fonseca and the general and known mayhem taking place on the Spanish Main and on the South Sea due to the onslaught of piracy and freebooting.

---

[132] *See generally* Donald Grunewald, *The Anglo-Guatemalan Dispute over British Honduras,* 5 CARIBBEAN STUD. 17–44 (1965) (discussing centuries of conflict in British Honduras).

[133] Garrett Mattingly, *No Peace Beyond What Line?,* 13 TRANSACTIONS ROYAL HIST. SOC'Y 145, 149 (1963). The agreement stemmed from the Treaty of Vervins (1598) between Henry IV of France and Philip II of Spain. DAVID HACKETT FISCHER, CHAMPLAIN'S DREAM 67–68 (2008). European amity ended for those who ventured west and south of the line; it was the "maxim that governed both the official action and private conduct of all Englishmen (Frenchmen, Dutchmen, and Spaniards too)" through the seventeenth century. CARL & ROBERTA BRIDENBAUGH, NO PEACE BEYOND THE LINE: THE ENGLISH IN THE CARIBBEAN, 1624–1690, 3 (1972).

[134] LANE, *supra* note 104, at 147, 153–154.

[135] *See* Land, Island and Maritime Frontier Dispute, 1992 I.C.J. ¶¶ 45 and 385 (discussing "title" to the contested areas and finding that the "Spanish Crown thereafter claimed and exercised continuous and peaceful sovereignty over the waters of the Gulf, without serious or more than temporary contestation, until … 1821"); Frontier Dispute (Burk. Faso/ Mali), 1986 I.C.J. 554, ¶ 63 (Dec. 22) (defining "colonial *effectivités*" as "the conduct of the administrative authorities as proof of the effective exercise of territorial jurisdiction in the region during the colonial period").

[136] Fisheries Case (U.K. v. Nor.), 1951 I.C.J. 116, 130 (*possessio longi temporis* can justify a claim that "waters are territorial or internal on the ground that [a country] has exercised the necessary jurisdiction over [the waters] for a long period of time without opposition from other states").

[137] Land, Island and Maritime Frontier Dispute, 1992 I.C.J. ¶ 386.

In the late seventeenth century, piracy (not Spanish colonial rule) forced the Lenca off the islands of the Gulf of Fonseca,[138] again countering the conclusion of effective, peaceful, and unopposed Castilian control of these waters.

POST-INDEPENDENCE: 1821–1917

Postindependence politics in the region were equally turbulent. In 1821, the provinces gained independence.[139] Following a brief period of annexation to Mexico, five of the six former colonies attempted a union as the Federal Republic of Central America, with Chiapas choosing to remain with Mexico.[140] But fractious problems stood in the way, foreshadowing the violent century to follow: a structural arrangement denied densely populated Guatemala majority control in the federation assembly; indigenous populations remained unassimilated; ethnic homogeneity did not exist; postcolonial differences emerged on the role of the church;[141] provincial dependencies formed in proximity to the central administration in Guatemala; rivalries arose between liberal and conservative elites;[142] and a movement began in El Salvador to cleave the western highlands from Guatemala to diminish Guatemalan power in any future federation.[143] After the federation's failure in 1838, and despite fitful attempts to reestablish the union reaching into the twentieth century,[144] Costa Rica, Salvador, Guatemala, Honduras, and Nicaragua began reorganizing as individual republics.[145]

The Chamber concluded that sovereign control of the Gulf seamlessly passed from the Crown to the federation and ultimately to the respective individual republics.[146] This seamless transfer is of critical importance to a major aspect of the *Gulf of Fonseca* case – the application of *uti possidetis*. This

---

[138] *Gulf of Fonseca*, U.N. Educ., Sci. & Cultural Org. (Sept. 21, 1992), http://whc.unesco.org/en/tentativelists/206/.

[139] Stansifer, *supra* note 85, at 27.

[140] *See id.* at 28 (discussing early postindependence Central American history).

[141] *Id.*

[142] Booth et al., *supra* note 83, at 43–44.

[143] Wayne M. Clegern, Origins of Liberal Dictatorship in Central America: Guatemala, 1865–1873, at 1–2 (1994).

[144] Attempts at union were made in 1835, 1842, 1847, 1852, 1889, 1895, and 1921. *See* Manley O. Hudson, *The Central American Court of Justice*, 26 Am. J. Int'l L. 759, 759 (1932) (discussing attempts at unions among Central American states); *see also* James Brown Scott, *The Central American Peace Conference of 1907*, 2 Am. J. Int'l L. 121, 122–124 (1908) (discussing efforts to form a union among Central American countries).

[145] *See* Scott, *supra* note 144, at 122 ("[T]he various states ... set up independent governments ... and national constitutions"); *see also* El Salvador v. Nicaragua, 11 Am. J. Int'l L. at 700 (discussing the right of exclusive ownership in the Gulf of Fonseca).

[146] *See* Land, Island and Maritime Frontier Dispute, 1992 I.C.J. ¶ 385 (reviewing the history of the control of the bay from the time of Spanish rule).

Roman law concept specifically was imported into international law to ensure that questions of sovereignty were never held in abeyance, and to forestall recrudescent claims of *terra nullis* that would provoke postcolonial landgrabs and war.[147] But the extension of this historically terrestrial concept of *uti possidetis juris* to pelagic space, to avoid the problem of *terra nullius*, created logical incongruities, as recorded by Judge Oda in his dissent:

> [I]f the assumption of unitary status for the entire waters in the Gulf had been correct [at the time of independence or after the failure of federated union], why should the 1917 Judgment and the [Chamber] Judgment not have preferred the far more natural interpretation that, once the territory over which a single state, Spain, and later the Federal Republic of Central America, had sovereignty was divided into five States as a result of their independence, the authority over and control of the offshore waters (which had always been considered as appurtenances of the land) might have been divided correspondingly to the divided territories of those newly independent States, and that the three riparian States of El Salvador, Honduras and Nicaragua each inherited authority over and control of their respective offshore waters of their own land territory in the Gulf of Fonseca?[148]

His answer, stated elsewhere, was that the 1917 Judgment was not really about the legal status of the Gulf waters or the historically unknown equation that "historic bay = condominium."[149] That latter idea may indeed have been an invention of El Salvador to parry an imperial initiative by the United States and its then amenable ally, Nicaragua, to militarize the region and control trade routes.[150]

CONDOMINIUM AND OUTSIDE INTERESTS; CONDOMINIUM AND HARMONY OF INTERESTS

The transition from colonial rule to independence stoked preexisting hostilities throughout Central America, vexing relations throughout the nineteenth and early twentieth centuries.[151] A boundary dispute between Guatemala and Honduras, stemming from the Gulf of Fonseca to the Gulf of Honduras,

---

[147] *See* Giuseppe Nesi, L'Uti Possidetis Iuris nel Diritto Internazionale 3 (1996) (defining *uti possidetis* as an instrument for preventing neocolonial land grabs).

[148] Land, Island and Maritime Frontier Dispute, 1992 I.C.J. ¶ 38 (dissenting opinion of Judge Oda).

[149] *Id.* ¶ 34.

[150] *See id.* (discussing the idea of "historic bay = condominium" in relation to El Salvador's opposition to the building of a US naval base on Nicaraguan territory).

[151] *See* Scott, *supra* note 144, at 121–128 (reviewing postindependence political turmoil and attempts at peace in Central America).

embittered relations for nearly one hundred years.[152] Disputes over Fonseca's islands first arose in 1854, and land disputes followed in 1861.[153] An economic world of "Banana men" and transport barons also began to complicate the region in the mid part of the nineteenth century;[154] this world was dominated by North American adventurers, financiers, filibusters, and mercenaries[155] in pursuit of the United States' "Manifest Destiny."[156] But not exclusively. European "metropole countries" – Great Britain, Italy, Germany, France, Belgium, Holland – which dominated worldwide production and distribution – also began to compete for access to raw materials and communication routes in the region.[157] After independence, and particularly by the mid-nineteenth century, "fledgling Central American republics were shunted aside by the superpowers, Great Britain and the United States," which dealt with isthmian political questions "with little or no regard for Central American interests."[158]

---

[152] *See* F. C. Fisher, *The Arbitration of the Guatemalan-Honduran Boundary Dispute*, 27 AM. J. INT'L L. 403, 403 (1933) (summarizing the resolution of a boundary dispute between Guatemala and Honduras in 1933). This boundary dispute preceded independence; in 1812 a Hondureñan claim to the eastern part of present-day El Salvador was presented to the King of Spain. Memorial of the Republic of El Salvador, Land, Island, and Maritime Frontier Dispute (El Sal./Hond.), 1988 I.C.J. 1, ¶ 7.11 (June 1), www.icj-cij.org/docket/files/75/6581.pdf.

[153] Malcolm N. Shaw, *Case Concerning the Land, Island and Maritime Frontier Dispute (El Salvador/ Honduras: Nicaragua intervening), Judgment of 11 September 1992*, 42 INT'L & COMP. L.Q. 929, 930 (1993); *see also* Land, Island and Maritime Frontier Dispute, 1992 I.C.J. ¶¶ 30 and 31 (discussing El Salvador's objection to a proposal by the United States to purchase land from Honduras in 1854 and El Salvador's note to Honduras marking the beginning of a land dispute in 1861).

[154] *See* LESTER D. LANGLEY & THOMAS SCHOONOVER, THE BANANA MEN: AMERICAN MERCENARIES AND ENTREPRENEURS IN CENTRAL AMERICA, 1880–1930, at 6–7 (1995) (noting the intervention of US filibusters in Central America during the 1850s).

[155] *Id.* at 6. At that time, a filibuster referred to a "non-authorized military incursion into another country for the purpose of seizing power." Staten, *supra* note 91, at 23. *See generally* WILLIAM O. SCROGGS, FILIBUSTERS AND FINANCIERS: THE STORY OF WILLIAM WALKER AND HIS ASSOCIATES (1916) (detailing the activities of William Walker and other filibusters in Central America).

[156] *See* JOHN E. FINDLING, CLOSE NEIGHBORS, DISTANT FRIENDS: UNITED STATES-CENTRAL AMERICAN RELATIONS 26–27 (1987) (connecting filibusterism to American attitudes concerning Manifest Destiny).

[157] *See* LANGLEY & SCHOONOVER, *supra* note 154, at 8–11 (providing an overview of the intervention of industrializing countries, including European metropole countries); *see also* Thomas Schoonover, *Metropole Rivalry in Central America, 1820s to 1929: An Overview*, in CENTRAL AMERICA: HISTORICAL PERSPECTIVES ON THE CONTEMPORARY CRISES 21, 21–46 (Ralph Lee Woodward, Jr., ed., 1988) (providing information on the competition between metropole countries and its effect on Central America); THOMAS SCHOONOVER, THE FRENCH IN CENTRAL AMERICA: CULTURE AND COMMERCE, 1820–1930, at 1–46 (2000) (providing an account of French intervention in Central America in the mid-nineteenth century); THOMAS SCHOONOVER, GERMANY IN CENTRAL AMERICA: COMPETITIVE IMPERIALISM, 1821–1929, at 12–54 (1998) (providing general information about Germany's intervention in Central America during the nineteenth century).

[158] Stansifer, *supra* note 85, at 38–39.

Prompted by continuous intra-American strife, the United States and Mexico organized the 1907 Central American Peace Conference, convened in Washington, DC. It produced eight conventions, including the establishment of the CACJ,[159] which rendered the 1917 judgment of decisive import to the Chamber in the *Gulf of Fonseca* case.[160] But by this time, decolonization had registered particularly disruptive effects on relations between small but densely populated El Salvador and large but sparsely populated Honduras, which disputed ill-defined portions of frontier boundary dating from the time of independence.[161] Honduras' central station became a political center of gravity and launching point for belligerent activity across the isthmus, making its future and permanent neutrality a major focus of Salvadoran diplomacy and result of the 1907 Conference.[162]

But during the period dating from independence up to the 1917 CACJ judgment, the CACJ found that successive authorities had affirmed notorious and peaceful ownership of the Gulf, "without protest or contradiction by any nation whatsoever."[163] The Chamber found no evidence there was for the waters "anything analogous" to the disputes associated with the land boundary;[164] and it concluded the 1917 Judgment had to be taken into consideration for its examination of an important part of the Gulf's history.[165] But according to Iain Scobbie, the Chamber "did no more than repeat and affirm the conclusions reached by the [CACJ]"[166] by holding: "The essence

---

[159] Scott, *supra* note 144, at 133. The Conference convened from November 14 through December 20, 1907. *See id.* at 127–143 (summarizing relevant articles, and preparatory statements of US Secretary of State Elihu Root and Mexican Ambassador Extraordinary and Plenipotentiary to the United States, Don Enrique C. Creel).

[160] *Infra.*

[161] *See* Jeffrey J. Smith, *Notre Mer? An Independent Québec's Maritime Claims in the Gulf of St. Lawrence and Beyond*, 35 Can. Y.B. Int'l L. 113, 172 (1997) (revealing that the history of conflict between Honduras and El Salvador began soon after independence). Fractious immigration, political, and economic issues resulted in belligerent relations in the 1960s, resulting in a brief but damaging 100-Hour War between the two countries in 1969 (also known as the Football War). *See* Vincent Cable, *The "Football War" and the Central American Common Market*, 45 Int'l Aff. 658, 659–662 (1969) (summarizing the events surrounding the Football War).

[162] *See* Salvador Rodríguez González, *The Neutrality of Honduras and the Question of the Gulf of Fonseca*, 10 Am. J. Int'l L. 509, 509 (1916) (discussing the purpose of the 1907 conference and the geographical and political status of Honduras); *see also* Scott, *supra* note 143, at 135 (referencing art. III of the 1907 General Treaty of Peace and Amity: "Honduras declares from now on its absolute neutrality in any conflict between the other republics").

[163] El Salvador v. Nicaragua, 11 Am. J. Int'l L. at 700–701; *see also* Land, Island and Maritime Frontier Dispute, 1992 I.C.J. ¶ 394 (discussing consensus that the Gulf of Fonseca is a historic bay).

[164] Land, Island and Maritime Frontier Dispute, 1992 I.C.J. ¶ 386.

[165] *Id.* ¶ 387.

[166] Scobbie, *supra* note 31, at 252.

of the 1917 decision … was … that these historic waters were then subject to a 'co-ownership' ('*condominio*') of the three coastal States."[167] Again, that factual conclusion warrants closer attention, as it is based on a convenient distinction between the asserted placid waters of the bay and long-standing terrestrial hostilities among its littoral powers. The CACJ judgment did take judicial notice of the "repeated and dangerous controversies" in the region between the United States and Great Britain.[168] These controversies led to the Clayton-Bulwer Treaty,[169] which attempted to quiet mid-nineteenth-century rivalry over control of possible trade routes.[170] But in view of this competition, the CACJ adopted the sanguine perspective that, "whatever may have been the motives" behind concluding the treaty, it "consecrated a principle of justice – of honorable respect for the sovereignty and independence of the weak Central American nations."[171] Moreover, the CACJ's treatment of Great Power interest in the region comes across as starkly Pollyannaish, certainly dismissive of the filibuster campaigns and practices of the Banana men and dueling transit barons.[172] Salvador's Minister to the United States, in a 1913 letter to the US Secretary of State, bluntly reinforced this point, protesting the repeated interferences of "filibustering hordes" that preyed on Central American coastlines with the intention of "work[ing] their way up to the heart of the [G]ulf [of Fonseca] in their intention to settle on Tigre Island."[173] According to the CACJ, however, though "the diplomatic history of certain Powers shows that for more than half a century they have been seeking to establish rights of their own in the Gulf for purposes of commercial policy," such machinations were done "always on the basis of respect for the ownership and possession which the States have maintained by virtue of their sovereign authority."[174]

---

[167] Land, Island and Maritime Frontier Dispute, 1992 I.C.J. ¶ 398.
[168] El Salvador v. Nicaragua, 11 AM. J. INT'L L. at 701.
[169] *Id.*
[170] *See* Thomas M. Leonard, *"Keeping the Europeans Out": The United States and Central America since 1823, in* CENTRAL AMERICA: HISTORICAL PERSPECTIVES ON THE CONTEMPORARY CRISES 5, 7 (Ralph Lee Woodward, Jr., ed., 1988) (providing an overview of the Clayton-Bulwer Treaty).
[171] El Salvador v. Nicaragua, 11 AM. J. INT'L L. at 701.
[172] Note, for example, the US adventurer and filibuster, William Walker, who, with a band of transport-financed mercenaries, formed a coalition with Nicaraguan Liberals, and overthrew the government in 1855, receiving recognition from US President Franklin Pierce's administration. For an account of his filibusterism and its consequences in the region, *see* FINDLING, *supra* note 156, at 26–33.
[173] Letter from Francisco Dueñas, the Minister of Salvador, to the Secretary of State (Oct. 21, 1913) (on file at Papers Relating to the Foreign Relations of the United States 1913–1915, File No. 817.812/49, at 1028), http://images.library.wisc.edu/FRUS/EFacs/1913/reference/frus.frus1913.i0028.pdf.
[174] El Salvador v. Nicaragua, 11 AM. J. INT'L L. at 701.

Although the CACJ was aware of police powers exercised in the Gulf by El Salvador, Honduras, and Nicaragua,[175] no support was proffered suggesting that police powers amounted to the establishment of condominium. To the contrary, the CACJ glossed over the fact that Honduras and Nicaragua attempted to "[fix] a divisionary line between the two ... in the waters of the Gulf" in 1900,[176] as did El Salvador and Honduras in 1884.[177] In support of a supposed "cordial harmony" of interests,[178] the CACJ relied on a detailed description of the Gulf by the American geographer and former US Chargé d'Affaires for Central American States, George Squier,[179] who noted the Bay of Fonseca was not simply valuable for its "admirable ports,"[180] but even more valuable "to us" considering its inevitable geopolitical position as the "inevitable terminal, in the Pacific, of a railway between the two oceans."[181] Furthermore, it should be recalled that the Central American War of 1907 served as the immediate prompt for the 1907 Peace Conference,[182] a conference described as a three-way mediation between the belligerent states of Salvador, Honduras, and Nicaragua.[183] The

---

[175] *Id.* at 700–701.

[176] *Id.* at 678 and 710.

[177] *See id.* at 710 (noting that the Honduran Congress rejected the demarcation convention).

[178] *Id.*

[179] *Id.* at 702–704.

[180] El Salvador v. Nicaragua, 11 AM. J. INT'L L., at 704.

[181] *Id.*

[182] *See* LANGLEY & SCHOONOVER, *supra* note 154, at 62–67 (discussing the Central American War of 1907). Nicaragua invaded Honduras after Honduras had overthrown Nicaragua's political ally. *See id.* at 64 (discussing the Nicaraguan invasion of Honduras in February 1907). Nicaragua attacked Honduras' northwestern frontier, seized the city of San Marcos, and set sail against major Atlantic Ocean ports on the Honduran north coast, where Honduras drew its revenue from US concessionaires and banana companies. *See id.* (examining the main front of the Nicaraguan invasion, which took San Marcos). US marines and bluejackets intervened to protect nationals and interests but did not act to halt the invasion. *See id.* at 65 (noting the United States sent marines ashore to police seaports). Guatemala began arming Salvador, which had an alliance with Honduras. *See id.* at 64 (noting that Guatemala sent arms to the president-elect of El Salvador and the existence of a Hondurian-Salvadoran treaty). On March 17, 1907, Honduran and Salvadoran troops were decimated at the battle of Namasigüe, due in part to the introduction in Central America of Maxim machine guns. *See id.* at 66 (describing the battle of Namasigüe). In terms of the number killed in proportion to the number engaged, Namasigüe holds the grim distinction of the bloodiest battle in history. *Id.* Shortly after the creation of the CACJ, the President of Costa Rica, using his good offices, convinced Honduras, Nicaragua, Guatemala, and El Salvador to address grievances in the CACJ, but a judgment secured the signatures of only three of the four judges, in violation of art. 24 of the Convention establishing the Court, thus calling into question the judgment's validity. *See* Hudson, *supra* note 144, at 768–769 (discussing the resort to the Court to maintain peace and harmony between Guatemala, El Salvador, Honduras, and Nicaragua and the judgment rendered).

[183] *See* Rodríguez, *supra* note 162, at 517 (characterizing El Salvador, Nicaragua, and Honduras as belligerents and describing the conference as a mediation). The assessment of impending

acceptance of a condition of peaceful and conjoined administration of waters on the west coast of these three states – historically riven with rivalry and engaged so recently in a vicious land war that also included Caribbean sea assaults – strains credulity, particularly in light of regional tensions that would arise again almost immediately following the outbreak of World War I.[184] It was in this setting, against a political backdrop of control over a trade route across the isthmus, that international decision-makers asserted the legal idea of condominium.

THE BRYAN-CHAMORRO TREATY AND ITS AFTERMATH

On August 5, 1914, Nicaragua and the United States concluded the Bryan-Chamorro Treaty.[185] Article I of the treaty granted the United States an option to construct and maintain an interoceanic canal using the San Juan River route through Nicaragua.[186] Article II granted the United States exclusive jurisdiction and a renewable ninety-nine-year lease of a naval base on islands in the Gulf of Fonseca.[187]

Although the maiden voyage through the US-constructed Panama Canal was by that time only days away,[188] the United States had reasons to negotiate

---

war is a fair one and is borne out by a barrage of communications among the heads-of-state and their plenipotentiaries. *See generally* Papers Relating to the Foreign Relations of the United States: Part 2, at 606–643 (Wash. Gov't Printing Office 1910) (relating to the diplomatic correspondence leading up to the conclusion of the Central American Protocol of Washington, September 17, 1907).

[184] Austria-Hungary and Germany declared war on Serbia on July 28, 1914. *See* Barbara W. Tuchman, The Guns of August: The Outbreak of World War I, 71 (1962) (noting Austria-Hungary's declaration backed by Germany's "faithful support"); Holger H. Herwig, The First World War: Germany and Austria-Hungary, 1914–1918, at 18 (1997) (noting Kaiser Wilhelm's signed war declaration on the same date).

[185] Interoceanic Canal (Bryan-Chamorro Treaty), Aug. 5, 1914, *in* 10 Charles I. Bevans, Treaties and Other International Agreements of the United States of America, 1776–1949, at 379–381 (1972). The treaty was ratified by the US Senate on February 18, 1916. *Id.* at 379.

[186] *Id.* art. I.

[187] *Id.* art. II. The treaty bears the name of then-US Secretary of State William Jennings Bryan and Nicaragua's Ambassador to the United States, General Emiliano Chamorro. *Id.* at 381; Sara Steinmetz, Democratic Transition and Human Rights: Perspectives on U.S. Foreign Policy 97 (1994); *see Biographies of the Secretaries of State: William Jennings Bryan*, U.S. Dep't. of State, https://history.state.gov/departmenthistory/people/bryan-williams-jennings (last visited Feb. 26, 2015) (showing that William Jennings Bryan was Secretary of State from 1913 to 1915).

[188] *See* Interoceanic Canal (Bryan-Chamorro Treaty), *supra* note 185, at 379 (noting that the treaty was signed August 5, 1914); David McCullough, The Path Between the Seas: The Creation of the Panama Canal, 1870–1914, at 609 (1977) (noting that the first voyage crossing the Panama Canal was on August 15, 1914). The Panama Canal officially opened on August 15, 1914. *See id.*

an option to construct another nearby canal: it wanted to prevent any foreign power of the opportunity to construct a competing interoceanic canal.[189] Other possible canal and transport routes long had been of interest to explorers. As early as 1539–1540, Spanish colonial authorities had charted a transport route connecting the Bay of Honduras in the Caribbean to the Gulf of Fonseca;[190] Squier uncovered Spanish documents from the sixteenth and seventeenth centuries favoring the Honduras route, which apparently was abandoned due to concerns about expense and pirates.[191] The Gulf's "superior advantages," however, and "constellation of ports" made it "the unrivaled terminus on the entire Pacific coast of America," according to Squier's nineteenth-century account.[192] A Nicaraguan route across the isthmus, making use of Lake Nicaragua, also had long intrigued engineers, financiers,[193]

(noting that the *Ancon's* crossing on August 15 and the official declaration of the Canal's opening were not headline news).

[189] *See* George A. Finch, *The Treaty with Nicaragua Granting Canal and Other Rights to the United States,* 10 Am. J. Int'l L. 344, 346 (1916) (discussing the treaty with Nicaragua as only a way to guarantee that nobody else built a competing interoceanic railway).

[190] *See* E. G. Squier, The States of Central America 677–678 (1858) (noting that Spain had charted an interoceanic railway through the Isthmus of Panama). Franciso de Montejo, governor of Honduras, urged in a letter to the emperor in 1539 for construction of a road between Puerto de Caballos and the Gulf of Fonseca, owing to a better climate and pacific inhabitants. C. L. G. Anderson, Old Panama and Castilla Del Oro 309 (1911).

[191] Charles L. Stansifer, *E. George Squier and the Honduras Interoceanic Railroad Project,* 46 Hisp. Am. Hist. Rev. 1, 2 n. 4 (1966).

[192] Squier, *supra* note 190, at 678, 690, 692.

[193] *See generally* Stephen Dando-Collins, Tycoon's War: How Cornelius Vanderbilt Invaded a Country to Overthrow America's Most Famous Military Adventurer (2008) (chronicling Cornelius Vanderbilt's efforts as a financier of the Nicaraguan Route across the Isthmus). Cornelius Vanderbilt, one of the richest Americans, secured rights from Nicaragua to construct a canal along the San Juan River route in 1849, as a means of facilitating a faster US east coast connection to the newly discovered gold mines in California. *See* Noel Maurer & Carlos Yu, The Big Ditch: How America Took, Built, Ran, and Ultimately Gave Away the Panama Canal 37 (2011) (discussing Vanderbilt securing rights to build a canal along the San Juan River). In 1850, he sent his agent, Orville Childs, seasoned by the Erie Canal dig, to scope out a plan, which ultimately fell through because of a lack of financing and concerns about dredging and draft requirements. *See id.* at 37–38 (describing Orville Childs' plan for the canal which ultimately fell through). In 1889, the US Congress granted a charter to the Maritime Canal Company to again develop a San Juan River route, which excavated one and one-half miles of canal and eleven and one-half miles of railroad before running out of money in 1893. *See Central American: Panama Canal: Pre-Canal History,* Global Perspectives, www.cotf.edu/earthinfo/camerica/panama/pctopic2.html (last visited Feb. 17, 2015) (noting that the Maritime Canal Company was charted by the United States to build in Nicaragua on the San Juan River Route, but ran out of funding in 1892 before completing the project); *Canals and Costa Rica,* Power & Money (Oct. 3, 2008), http://noelmaurer.typepad.com/aab/2008/10/canals-and-cost .html (noting the length of canal excavated and railroad built before construction stopped in 1893).

and Nicaragua's profit-sensing elites,[194] as did an interoceanic railroad route through Honduras.[195] Hedging bets, the Spooner Act (1902) authorized the US President to negotiate a canal with Nicaragua should the Panama venture collapse.[196] Maritime and commercial powers naturally gravitated to the region, spawning, most importantly, a rivalry in Central America between the United States and Great Britain dating to the mid-1830s.[197] Although a proto-maritime power at the beginning of the Mexican-American War (1846–1848), the United States made the seizure of Mexican Pacific coast ports from Mazatlán up the California coast to Oregon an almost immediate objective of the war – a stratagem motivated more because of Britain's designs on California rather than grievances with Mexico.[198] At war's outset, the US Navy also opened up a second theatre in the Gulf of Mexico, effectively blockading and then seizing key ports of Veracruz and Tampico in the Yucatan Peninsula. Establishing this two-theatre naval operation in seas 2,500 miles apart by land and 14,000 miles apart by sea had a "revolutionary impact" on burgeoning US seaborne interests and thoughts about spreading Manifest Destiny.[199] In 1846, the United States secured a right of way across Panama in an agreement with New Granada (now Colombia).[200] The British responded by seizing in 1848 the port of San Juan del Norte on the Atlantic coast of Nicaragua in exercise of its protectorate of the Mosquito Nation,[201] but also thinking it to be the "most likely" isthmian

---

[194] *See* MICHEL GOBAT, CONFRONTING THE AMERICAN DREAM: NICARAGUA UNDER U.S. IMPERIAL RULE 28 (2005) (noting the dreams of elite Nicaraguans for a canal).

[195] *See* Stansifer, *supra* note 191, at 1 (noting that beginning in 1850 following a trip by the US Chargé d'Affaires in Central America to the Bay of Fonseca, an interoceanic railway was envisioned).

[196] *See* Edwin C. Hoyt, *Law and Politics in the Revision of Treaties Affecting the Panama Canal*, 6 VA. J. INT'L L. 289, 294 n. 26 (1966) (describing the Spooner Act).

[197] *See* Stansifer, *supra* note 85, at 38 (acknowledging the rivalry between the United States and Great Britain on the isthmus in the mid-1830s in Central America).

[198] *See* K. JACK BAUER, THE MEXICAN AMERICAN WAR, 1846–1848, at 164–166 (1974) (discussing US seizure of ports from Mazatlan up the coast to Oregon and fears about the British that motivated these actions).

[199] *See* K. JACK BAUER, SURFBOATS AND HORSE MARINES: U.S. NAVAL OPERATIONS IN THE MEXICAN WAR, 1846–48, at 239 (1969) (describing the impact of the Mexican-American War on US history).

[200] *See* Treaty of Peace, Amity, Navigation and Commerce with New Granada, Dec. 12, 1846, art. 35, *in* 6 CHARLES I. BEVANS, TREATIES AND OTHER INTERNATIONAL AGREEMENTS OF THE UNITED STATES OF AMERICA 1776–1949, at 868–881 (1971) [the Mallarino-Bidlack Treaty] (holding that the United States "shall enjoy in the Ports of New Grenada ... all the exemptions, privileges, and immunities, concerning commerce and navigation, which are now ... enjoyed by Granadian citizens"). The Mallarino-Bidlack Treaty is named after New Granada Commissioner, Manuel María Mallarino, and US Chargé d'Affaires in Bogotá, Benjamin A. Bidlack. *See id.* at 868 (noting Manuel María Mallarino and Benhamin A. Bidlack agreed to the general treaty of peace).

[201] GEORGE THOMAS WEITZEL, AMERICAN POLICY IN NICARAGUA 6 (1916); *see* Hoyt, *supra* note 195, at 302 (noting that the British seized control of the mouth of the San Juan River in the name of the Mosquito Indians).

canal terminus.[202] In 1849, it seized Tigre Island in the Gulf of Fonseca.[203] "War fever" abated, however, when the two powers agreed to end bids for exclusive control over possible canal sites (the Clayton-Bulwer Treaty (1850–1901)),[204] an agreement the British negotiated to forestall further annexations to its weakening holdings and interests in Central America,[205] which included, in addition to its historical presence on the Mosquito Coast,[206] interests in British Honduras [Belize], and the Bay Islands (off the Atlantic coast of Honduras).[207] Geostrategic posturing continued, notwithstanding the Clayton-Bulwer Treaty,[208] and stoked long-established US suspicions about foreign imperial intentions in the region[209] and hemisphere.[210] These suspicions had been stirred more recently by a 1902 European blockade and British bombardment

---

[202] Stansifer, *supra* note 85, at 40.

[203] WEITZEL, *supra* note 201, at 6.

[204] *See* Stansifer, *supra* note 85, at 44 (discussing the cooling of "war fever"); Treaty with Great Britain for Facilitating and Protecting the Construction of a Ship Canal between the Atlantic and Pacific Oceans, Apr. 19, 1850, *in* 12 CHARLES I. BEVANS, TREATIES AND OTHER INTERNATIONAL AGREEMENTS OF THE UNITED STATES, 1776–1947, at 775 (1974) (discussing neutrality of the Canal) [Clayton-Bulwer Treaty]; abrogated with the Hay-Pauncefote Treaty, Nov. 18, 1901. *See generally* GRAHAM H. STUART & JAMES L. TIGNER, LATIN AMERICAN AND THE UNITED STATES 184–196 (6th edn., 1975) (detailing Anglo-American Isthmian Diplomacy).

[205] *See* Richard W. Van Alstyne, *British Diplomacy and the Clayton-Bulwer Treaty, 1850–60*, 11 J. OF MODERN HIST. 149, 156 (1939) (citing Bulwer's "History of the Mosquito Question"). Van Alstyne considered the treaty an "imperial triumph" of British diplomacy for the concessions agreed to by a vacillating and anxiety-prone US upstart administration. *Id.* at 157. British declarations exempted application with regard to British interests in Belize and the Bay Islands. *See id.* at 160 (discussing Belize and the Bay Islands as outside the scope of the treaty). The treaty was revisited and abrogated in 1901 with the Hay-Pauncefote Treaty, when changing circumstances, prompted by the United States' rise to primacy with its defeat of Spain in the 1898 Spanish-American War, necessitated Britain's political, but not commercial, retirement from the scene. *See id.* at 161 (discussing the abrogation of the Clayton-Bulwer treaty with the Hay-Pauncefote Treaty of 1901).

[206] *See* Robert A. Naylor, *The British Role in Central America Prior to the Clayton-Bulwer Treaty of 1850*, 40 HISP. AM. HIST. REV. 361, 363 (1960) (describing British activities in Central American and the Mosquito Coast). The Mosquito Coast forms part of the eastern seaboard of Nicaragua and Honduras. *Mosquito Coast, in* 1 ENCYCLOPEDIA OF WORLD GEOGRAPHY 634 (R. W. McColl, ed., 2005).

[207] *See* Stansifer, *supra* note 85, at 38.

[208] *See* Leonard, *supra* note 170, at 7 (noting "the ink barely dried on the Clayton-Bulwer Treaty before differences in interpretation surfaced").

[209] *See* ROBERT W. AGUIRRE, 15 INTERNATIONAL STRAITS OF THE WORLD: THE PANAMA CANAL 178–179 (Gerald J. Mangone, ed., 2010) (discussing the US suspicions of European interest in the region).

[210] *See* James Monroe, *Message of the President of the United States at the Commencement of the First Session of the Eighteenth Congress (Dec. 2, 1823), in* AMERICAN STATE PAPERS, FOREIGN RELATIONS 245, 246 (1858) (describing US concerns about British intentions in the hemisphere) [the "Monroe Doctrine"].

of ports on the mouths of Venezuela's sprawling Orinoco River.[211] That crisis began when the destabilized Venezuelan government defaulted on payments to European creditors for development of Venezuela's interior.[212] A veiled threat of naval intervention on Venezuela's behalf by US President Theodore Roosevelt brought the row to a resourceful conclusion through the famous Venezuelan Arbitrations of 1903.[213] Moreover, in 1909, animated in part by German and Japanese canal-construction overtures with Nicaragua's president José Santos Zelaya, US marines were dispatched to Nicaragua, where they remained until 1933.[214] In 1912, following Japanese corporate attempts to secure land in Magdalena Bay in Baja, Mexico, the US Senate adopted the "Lodge Corollary" to the Monroe Doctrine, making non-American ownership or control of ports in the Americas a matter of grave concern to the United States.[215] Thus, the canal option signed with Nicaragua in 1914 and ratified in 1916 (following failed attempts to ratify it in 1911 and 1913)[216] secured long-standing US interests against further meddling: it foreclosed the possibility of a competing non-American-controlled pathway between the oceans.[217]

---

[211] *See* Christopher R. Rossi, *Jus ad Bellum in the Shadow of the 20th Century*,15 N.Y.L. Sch. J. Int'l & Comp. L. 49, 55 (1994) (describing the British naval blockade against five Venezuelan ports on the Orinoco River).

[212] *See id.* at 57 (discussing the events that precipitated the European Blockade and British bombardment).

[213] *See id.* at 56–57 (explaining the events leading to the Venezuelan Arbitrations of 1903); *see also* Jackson H. Ralston & W. T. Sherman Doyle, Venezuelan Arbitrations of 1903 (1904) (chronicling the Venezuelan Arbitrations).

[214] Steinmetz, *supra* note 187, at 98. The United States also severed diplomatic relations with Nicaragua in 1909 due to filibusters' support of revolutionary activity against the Zelaya regime. *See A Guide to the United States' History of Recognition, Diplomatic, and Consular Relations, by Country, since 1776: Nicaragua*, U.S. Dept. of State, http://history.state.gov/counties/ nicaragua (last visited Feb. 5, 2015) (discussing the United States severing diplomatic relations with Nicaragua in 1909). US marines landed in Bluefields soon thereafter. *Id.* Zelaya's regime collapsed in December 1909. *See id.* (noting that Zelaya resigned in December 1909).

[215] Henry Cabot Lodge, Corollary to the Monroe Doctrine (Aug 2, 1912), *in*62 Cong. Rec. 10045 (1912); *see* Donald H. Estes, *Asama Gunkan: The Reappraisal of a War Scare*, 24(3) J. San Diego Hist. 267–299 (1978), www.sandiegohistory.org/journal/1978/july/asama/ (discussing the corollary to the Monroe Doctrine as resulting from Japanese negotiations to purchase Magdalena Bay).

[216] Hudson, *supra* note 144, at 777–778. The third attempt at the convention was signed at Washington on August 5, 1914. *Id.* at 777.

[217] *See* Lawrence Lenz, Power and Policy: America's First Steps to Superpower, 1889–1922, at 176 (2008) (discussing the United States signing the Wertzel-Chamorro Treaty). A French company began construction of the Panama Canal in 1881; but after declaring bankruptcy in 1889, the US Congress authorized purchase in the 1902 Panama Canal Act. *See* Maurer & Yu, *supra* note 193, at 55–76 (discussing the French initiative and the American takeover). Twelve days after declaring independence from Colombia (Nov. 6, 1903), the United States and the Republic of Panama concluded an agreement for the construction of the canal across the Panamanian Isthmus. Convention for the Construction of a Ship Canal, Nov. 18, 1903,

But more was required. Article II of the Bryan-Chamorro Treaty granted the United States a renewable lease of a naval base on islands in the Gulf of Fonseca.[218] Here, US intentions sought to deny Europeans control over the flanks of the proposed isthmian canal, which could provide port access to Haiti, St. Thomas, and the Galápagos Islands, and serve as much needed coaling stations for extended European naval fleets.[219] The Atlantic flank was well protected due to US naval bases at Guantanamo Bay, Cuba, and at San Juan, Puerto Rico.[220] But the Pacific expanse was exposed, presenting a serious threat, with only two options – purchasing the small, isolated, and "bleak" Cocos Island, one hundred miles south of the canal, or Little Corn and Great Corn Islands in the Gulf of Fonseca.[221] The Gulf of Fonseca might have become a site by default, but it also retained interest as a means to stymie German interest in constructing a naval station in the Gulf of Fonseca.[222] Although several hundred miles away from the western terminus of any canal constructed by way of Lake Nicaragua, and 600 miles west and 300 miles north of Panama, Fonseca's waters provided the strategic way station "from which to launch a flank attack upon any unfriendly naval demonstration directed against" the United States' Pacific control over the Panama Canal.[223]

The naval base agreement was negotiated for three million dollars and reworked as forgiveness of debt owed by cash-strapped Nicaragua to the United States.[224] But to the embarrassment of the United States – and most certainly to one of its chief architects of the 1907 Central American peace process, the preeminent international lawyer, Elihu Root[225] – furious protests

---

US-Panama, 10 BEVANS TREATIES AND OTHER INTERNATIONAL AGREEMENTS OF THE UNITED STATES OF AMERICA 1776–1948, at 663. In June 2013, Nicaragua awarded a Chinese company a $40 billion concession to construct a massive waterway between the Atlantic and Pacific to rival the Panama Canal. Bruce Kennedy, *Nicaragua Plans Its Own Panama Canal* CBS MONEYWATCH (Feb. 24, 2014), www.cbsnews.com/news/nicaragua-plans-its-own-panama-canal.

[218] Convention for the Construction of a Ship Canal, *supra* note 217, at 380.
[219] *See* AGUIRRE, *supra* note 209, at 177–180 (discussing the United States not wanting Europeans to have control over the isthmian canal).
[220] PAOLO E. COLETTA, ed., UNITED STATES NAVY AND MARINE CORPS BASES, OVERSEAS 69 (K. Jack Bauer, asst. ed., 1985).
[221] *Id.*
[222] *See* EDWARD S. KAPLAN, U.S. IMPERIALISM IN LATIN AMERICA: BRYAN'S CHALLENGES AND CONTRIBUTIONS, 1900–1920, at 46 (1998); *see also* Robert Freeman Smith, *A Note on the Bryan-Chamorro Treaty and German Interest in a Nicaraguan Canal, 1914*, 9 CARIBBEAN STUD. 63, 63–64 (1969) (discussing Germany's interest in a Nicaraguan canal).
[223] Finch, *supra* note 189, at 347.
[224] *See* HAROLD EUGENE DAVIS ET AL., LATIN AMERICAN DIPLOMATIC HISTORY: AN INTRODUCTION 161 (1977) (noting the United States attempted to help Nicaragua with the treaty that gave Nicaragua three million dollars to meet debt payments); Hudson, *supra* note 144, at 777 (noting that funds from treaty would be used to "rehabilitate [Nicaragua's] depleted treasury").
[225] Root was a leading officer in the American Society of International Law and cofounder of its journal; the American delegate to the 1907 Hague Peace Conference; the first President

erupted throughout the region, fueled by the "considerable secrecy" attending the treaty's negotiation.[226] From Central American perspectives, the treaty embedded designs to render Nicaragua a protectorate of the United States, "mak[ing] forever impossible" any lingering prospect of federation.[227] Indeed, a previous and ultimately forestalled attempt to secure such a treaty (the so-called Weitzel-Chamorro treaty, signed but not ratified on February 8, 1913) contained an article that expressly attempted to extend provisions of the Platt Amendment regarding Cuba to Nicaragua.[228] Moreover, the proposed arrangement complicated regional discussions concluded at the Fourth Central American Conference of 1912, which proposed making extensive use of the Gulf of Fonseca for a new communications network in Central America.[229] But an economic imperative was at work as well, an imperative that cleaved Nicaraguan interests from its neighboring powers in Fonseca's waters. Nicaragua had no port of entry within the Gulf of Fonseca; Salvador and Honduras operated two large ports at La Union and Amapala; both ports contributed considerably to the material well-being of the countries, and worriment arose that a US naval base in the Gulf would strongly and negatively affect the revenue and police powers of Honduras and Salvador.[230]

Protests swept Central America. Colombia reasserted sovereign claims to the islands that Nicaragua purportedly leased to the United

---

of the Carnegie Endowment for International Peace; a member of the Permanent Court of Arbitration; the US Secretary of War (1899–1904); the US Secretary of State (1905–1909); Senator from New York (1909–1915); Ambassador Extraordinary to the Provisional Government of Russia; and 1912 Nobel Peace prize recipient. *See* CHRISTOPHER R. ROSSI, EQUITY AND INTERNATIONAL LAW: A LEGAL REALIST APPROACH TO INTERNATIONAL DECISIONMAKING 100 n. 58 (1993) (footnote omitted) (discussing Root's qualifications and achievements).

[226] Hudson, *supra* note 144, at 777 n. 103.

[227] Finch, *supra* note 189, at 345 (footnote omitted).

[228] J. S. Reeves, *Clearing the Way for the Nicaragua Canal*, 17 AM. J. INT'L L. 309, 311 (1923). The Platt Amendment (to a US Army appropriations bill of March 1901) secured for the United States a right to intervene in Cuban affairs. *See generally* James H. Hitchman, *The Platt Amendment Revisited: A Bibliographical Survey*, 23 AMERICAS 343–369 (1967) (discussing the implications of the Platt Amendment). US Secretary of State, William Jennings Bryan repeatedly lobbied, unsuccessfully, the US Senate Foreign Relations Committee to extend the Platt Amendment provision to Bryan-Chamorro Treaty. *Bryan-Chamorro Treaty*, www.read-facts-about.com/ bryan%E2%80%93chamorro_treaty (last visited Feb. 26, 2015) (stating that the Wilson administration wanted to add an amendment similar to the Platt amendment, but the US Senate opposed it).

[229] *Conventions Adopted by the Fourth Central American Conference*, Managua, 1–11 Jan., 1912, *reprinted in* 7 AM. J. INT'L L. (Supp: Official Documents) 34, at 40 (1913).

[230] Letter of Francisco Dueñas, *supra* note 173, at 1030 (noting the importance of the ports and concern that a US naval base would be a hindrance).

States;[231] Honduras registered objections to the treaty[232] (although possibly because its own, almost identical, loan-forgiveness agreement recently had failed to secure US Senate ratification);[233] Costa Rica complained of the "contemptuous slight,"[234] and El Salvador and Costa Rica – "two states to which America's 'Dollar Diplomacy' had not been applied"[235] – brought suit against Nicaragua before the CACJ. Costa Rica asserted violations of riparian rights on the San Juan River, citing a previous arbitral award and claiming an interoceanic canal across Nicaragua could not be built without affecting riparian interests of Costa Rica.[236] El Salvador claimed the treaty impinged on neutral rights,[237] citing instances of state practice that precluded fortifications of points near neutral waters as a menace to the principle of neutrality.[238] El Salvador's complaint necessarily raised questions about the status of the Gulf of Fonseca's waters, suddenly launching long-standing territorial disputes seaward.

---

[231] Hudson, *supra* note 144, at 778; *see also* The Letter of Francisco José Urrutia, "Minister for Foreign Affairs of Colombia to the Minister for Foreign Affairs of Nicaragua," Dec. 24, 1913, *in Foreign Relations of the United States*, at 1032, http://images.library.wisc.edu/FRUS/EFacs/ 1913/reference/frus.frus1913.i0028.pdf (registering Colombia's claim).

[232] *See* Hudson, *supra* note 144, at 779 (noting the resolution of the Senate referred to objections from Honduras).

[233] *See* Finch, *supra* note 189, at 349 (discussing the loan forgiveness agreement failed to be ratified).

[234] Hudson, *supra* note 144, at 779 n. 108.

[235] "Dollar Diplomacy" characterizes that period of US foreign policy immediately preceding World War I, where the goal of diplomacy was to improve financial opportunities by use of private capital to assist US interests abroad. *See Milestones: 1899–1913*, U.S. Dep't St., Office of the Historian., https://history.state.gov/milestones/1899–1913/dollar-diplo (last visited Feb. 26, 2015) (discussing when Dollar Diplomacy came about and where it was used). The practice was most evident in the Caribbean, Central America, and China. *Id.*

[236] *Costa Rica v. Nicaragua*, C.A.C.J. Judgment of 30 Sept., 1916, 11 Am J. Int'l L. 181 (1917), www.worldcourts.com/cacj/eng/decisions/1916.09.30_Costa_Rica_v_ Nicaragua.htm. Costa Rica alleged that the US agreement with Nicaragua, which it came to learn about through private channels, violated an 1888 arbitral award rendered by US President Grover Cleveland, based on the 1858 Cañas-Jerez Treaty, and the Central American Treaty of Washington. *Id.* at 191–192; *see also* Finch, *supra* note 189, at 347–348 (relating to the impossibility of constructing a Nicaraguan canal without affecting Costa Rican interests). Disputes regarding this border area persist. *See Pending Cases*, Int'l Ct. Just., www.icj-cij.org/ docket/index.php (last visited Mar. 11, 2015) (showing that the proceedings on Certain Activities Carried Out by Nicaragua in the Border Area (Costa Rica v. Nicar.) have been joined with Construction of a Road in Costa Rica Along the San Juan River (Nicar. v. Costa Rica)).

[237] *See* El Salvador v. Nicaragua, 11 Am. J. Int'l L. at 685 (discussing El Salvador's concerns regarding neutral rights).

[238] Finch, *supra* note 189, at 350. Finch cites the Salvadoran contention that the 1858 Treaty of Paris, the 1911 Congo agreement between France and Germany, and a 1904 agreement

THE 1917 DECISION OF THE CACJ AND ITS AFTERMATH

In its petition to the CACJ to enjoin enforcement of the treaty, El Salvador introduced the claim of co-ownership over the waters of the Gulf.[239] Much of the argument seems to have been crafted by Salvador's legation to the United States, whose chief, Francisco Dueñas, simply asserted that "Salvador, Honduras, and Nicaragua's conjoint sovereignty over the Gulf of Fonseca 'ha[d] not ceased, even for a day' since the time of the Spanish discoverers."[240] Salvadoran diplomat and Central American Peace Conference delegate, Don Salvador Rodríguez González,'[241] had fortified this argument one year before the CACJ's judgment in a 1916 journal piece published by the *American Journal of International Law*,[242] and refined subsequently in treatise form.[243] Washington's deal flagrantly violated Honduran neutrality and the rights of co-guarantors of Honduran neutrality; it imperiled nations fronting the Gulf by placing them in range of possible artillery fire; it violated provisions of the 1907 Treaty of Peace and Amity; and it gave rise to legal causes of action. Rodríguez' argument asserted a controlling security interest, rather than an economic one, in pluri-state control over the Gulf of Fonseca,[244] arguing that underlying natural law principles in support of national security interests had imposed indivisible and joint holdings for the three "riparian owners."[245] Drawing on extensive references to the 1830 Belgian revolution against The Netherlands[246] – "perfectly applicable" in his mind to the teachings on the need for permanent neutrality in the Gulf of Fonseca[247] – Rodríguez laid the basis for a *jus prohibendi* argument that would heavily influence the 1917 CACJ judgment. He argued that national security and defense considerations were more suitable for condominium arrangements over gulfs and bays, and that the "indivisible community of property" enjoined any actions by any co-owners that might jeopardize the security or existence of the

---

between France and England regarding the Straits of Gibraltar required that states bordering neutral, navigable waters were obligated not to fortify their coasts. *Id.*

[239] El Salvador v. Nicaragua, 11 Am. J. Int'l L., at 685.

[240] Letter from Francisco Dueñas, *supra* note 173, at 1028.

[241] *See* Minutes of the Central American Peace Conference (preliminary session), November 1907, Papers Relating to the Foreign Relations of the United States Part 2, 685ff (listing Don Salvador Rodríguez González as a delegate).

[242] Rodríguez, *supra* note 162, at 509–542.

[243] *See* El Salvador v. Nicaragua, 11 Am. J. Int'l L., at 725–728 (alleging violations of arts. II and IX).

[244] *See* Rodríguez, *supra* note 162, at 527 (noting the purpose of joint control is for safety and defense).

[245] *Id.*

[246] *Id.* at 515–526.

[247] *Id.* at 523 (as especially applied to Honduras' neutrality, according to González).

others.[248] Part of his argument traced vaguely to Grotius' "common use" argument articulated in *Mare Liberum*: "One cannot appropriate what is common to all" (or to the joint owners in the Gulf), because the natural order – Grotius' immutable primary law of nature – precluded individual appropriations that prejudice the community property interests of others.[249] Reflecting this argument, the CACJ judgment held: "One coparcener cannot lawfully alter, or deliver into the hands of an outsider, or even share with it, the use and enjoyment of the thing held in common, even though advantage might result therefrom to the other coparceners, unless the consent of all is obtained."[250] But Rodríguez' argument of condominium drifted far from Grotius' shore and merely asserted the historical existence of a *jus prohibendi* in the Gulf of Fonseca that should be respected so as to not endanger the peace, or upset the tenuous neutrality of its waters.[251] The legal basis for this *jus prohibendi* argument – the historical *effectivités* – do not appear to be more apparent than the unfolding political interests to forestall a naval agreement with port-development consequences between Nicaragua and the United States.

But the CACJ agreed with Salvador, concluding the Bryan-Chamorro treaty "menaced" its "primordial interests" and national security, and violated its rights of co-ownership in the Gulf,[252] save for the sovereign establishment of a three mile "littoral marine leagues," a proto-contiguous nine-mile zone for police powers; and a right of innocent use for third states in nonlittoral waters.[253] It found Nicaragua's agreement with the United States violated Article II of the General Treaty of Peace and Amity concluded by the Central American Republics in 1907, and ordered Nicaragua to restore the status quo ante to conclusion of the Bryan-Chamorro Treaty.[254] In support of its conclusions, the CACJ referenced the "separate opinion" of the distinguished Argentine jurist, Luis Drago, an arbiter in the 1910 *North Atlantic Coast Fisheries Case*.[255] Yet,

[248] *See id.* at 527 (discussing the impact of joint control).

[249] *See* HUGO GROTIUS, THE FREE SEA 80–81 (David Armitage, ed., Richard Hakyult, trans., 2004) (discussing the sea being common to all); Rodríguez, *supra* note 162, at 528 (discussing the co-ownership of the Gulf).

[250] El Salvador v. Nicaragua, 11 AM. J. INT'L L., at 712.

[251] *See* Rodríguez, *supra* note 162, at 527–530 (discussing the historical rights of all of the countries).

[252] El Salvador v. Nicaragua, 11 AM. J. INT'L L., at 694–696.

[253] *Id.* at 711, 715–716.

[254] *Id.* at 694–695.

[255] *Id.* at 707. I believe the CACJ was referring to Drago's partial dissenting opinion. *See Grounds for the Dissent to the Award on Question V by Dr. Luis M. Drago*, N. Atl. Coast Fisheries, 11 R.I.A.A., at 203–211. Drago wrote: "[I]t may safely be asserted that a certain class of bays, which might be properly called historical bays, such as the Chesapeake Bay and Delaware Bay in North America and the great estuary of the River Plate in South America, form a class distinct and apart and undoubtedly belong to the littoral country." *Id.* at 993. He emphasized the need to show "a continuous and established usage." *Id.* at 992.

as alluded to by Judge Oda in his *Gulf of Fonseca Case* dissent,[256] the 1910 discussion revolved around the subject of a single-state bay and the jurisdictional character of a limited number of gulfs that fell into the category of a historic bay. The CACJ took notice of the "voluminous commentaries" and authorities citied by the eminent Drago to buttress this point,[257] but none actually discussed, much less referenced, condominium.

Historians have written that the CACJ wrote its own obituary by holding that the naval base agreement violated co-ownership rights possessed in the Gulf.[258] Nicaragua ignored the proceedings, declared the decision null and void, and later gave notice to terminate the convention creating the CACJ.[259] Manley O. Hudson observed the court "was doomed to failure from the outset," given the influences of "an overshadowing outside state,"[260] an obvious reference to the United States. So ended the first international court in modern history,[261] "during a period of unusual unrest in Central America,"[262] and over a matter that ultimately never came to pass: the "unexpected success of using colliers for refueling during the Navy's world cruise of 1907–1909" reduced the benefit of constructing a naval station on the islands of the Gulf of Fonseca; the option was never exercised.[263]

But the shadow cast over international judicial integrity would have a long and dark effect on the prospects of third-party dispute settlement. Attempts to recreate the Central American tribunal sputtered and bled over into Honduras' refusal to sign, and Nicaragua's refusal to submit, the Protocol of Signature of December 16, 1920, establishing the PCIJ.[264] In the case of Nicaragua, the

[256] Land, Island and Maritime Frontier Dispute, 1992 I.C.J. ¶ 32 (dissenting opinion of Judge Oda); *see also id.* ¶ 27 ("The Gulf of Fonseca, a bay bordered by the land of the three littoral States, was certainly not uppermost in the minds of the members of the 1910 Arbitral Tribunal").

[257] El Salvador v. Nicaragua, 11 Am. J. Int'l L., at 707.

[258] Nicaragua ignored the proceedings. *See* Davis et al., *supra* note 224, at 162 (claiming the actions by the Court "sounded the court's definitive death knell"). This result provided a historical defeat to the legacy of America's premier proponent of international law, Elihu Root, who played a central role in the creation of the Central American Court. Dana G. Munro, *Dollar Diplomacy in Nicaragua, 1909–1913*, 38 Hisp. Am. Hist. Rev. 209(1958).

[259] Hudson, *supra* note 144, at 777–781. Nicaragua also declared it would not abide by any adverse judgment brought against it in the proceedings initiated by Costa Rica. *Id.* at 775.

[260] *Id.* at 785.

[261] The Court was reestablished in 1991, pursuant to the Protocol of Tegucigalpa and the creation of the Central American Integration System. *Central American Court of Justice*, Int'l Just. Resource Center., www.ijrcenter.org/regional-communities/central-american-court-of-justice/ (last visited Feb. 15, 2015).

[262] Hudson, *supra* note 144, at 785–786.

[263] Coletta, *supra* note 220, at 69–70. I thank Alexandra McCallen of the Navy Dep't Library at the US Naval History and Heritage Command for bringing this point to my attention.

[264] *See* Hudson, *supra* note 144, at 784.

failure to perfect its adherence to the compulsory jurisdiction of the PCIJ became a forgotten point, until raised by the United States decades later, first to escape from the compulsory jurisdiction of the ICJ in preliminary phases of the *Military and Paramilitary Activities in and Against Nicaragua Case*,[265] and then, failing that bid, to assail the institutional integrity of the ICJ for finding that Nicaragua's declaration consenting to compulsory jurisdiction was to be treated as in force though admittedly never in force.[266] This faulty demonstration of *jura novit curia* indicated to the United States the ICJ's predisposition to proceed to the merits of the case notwithstanding its relevant procedural due process objections. The United States withdrew from the proceedings on the heels of its own, illegal, modification to its compulsory jurisdiction clause.[267] Its departure harmed the integrity of the international judicial process as the ICJ turned to the merits of the case – a residual and oblique outcome of the turn of the twentieth-century turmoil in Fonseca's waters.

The ICJ Chamber's finding of condominium provoked yet another round of institutional attacks against the integrity of international decision-making, beginning with the tension recognized but not completely answered by the Chamber's 1992 judgment involving condominium and its seaward extension over the continental shelf and EEZs beyond the Gulf itself. Ironically, it was El Salvador, the progenitor of the condominium concept in Fonseca's waters, that was charged (twice) by Honduras with unjustifiably delaying and disregarding "the letter and the spirit" of the 1992 judgment, first by registering reservations to a joint marine and environmental convention governing Pacific waters,[268] and then again by refusing "to fully observe the right of

[265] United States contended, "Nicaragua never became a party to the Statute of the Permanent Court of International Justice, and that accordingly it could not and did not make an effective acceptance of the compulsory jurisdiction of the Permanent Court." Military and Paramilitary Activities in and Against Nicaragua, Jurisdiction and Admissibility (Nicar. v. US), Judgment, 1984 I.C.J. 392, 400.

[266] *See* Christopher R. Rossi, *A Nicaraguan Feast: Having the Jurisdictional Cake and Eating It Too, in* 1 HISTORIC U.S. COURT CASES: AN ENCYCLOPEDIA 228, 230 (John W. Johnson, ed., 2001) (noting that the United States spotted Nicaragua's weakness in its failure to properly file the signature of protocol to inform the international community that it officially agreed to the compulsory jurisdiction of the ICJ).

[267] On April 6, 1984, US Secretary of State George Schultz deposited with the United Nations Secretary-General a unilateral modification to the US 1946 declaration consenting to the compulsory jurisdiction of the ICJ. The 1946 declaration promised six months prior notice for termination or modification, but the Schultz letter declared the 1946 declaration void effective immediately with regard to any Central American State. Military and Paramilitary Activities in and Against Nicaragua, Jurisdiction and Admissibility, 1984 I.C.J. at 398. Nicaragua filed suit three days after submission of the Shultz letter. *Id.* at 395.

[268] Deputy Permanent Rep. of Honduras, Letter dated 11 March 2002, from the Chargé d'Affaires a.i. of the Permanent Mission of Honduras to the United Nations addressed to the President of the Security Council, U.N. Doc. S/2002/251 (Mar.11, 2002).

joint sovereignty ... in the non-delimited waters" of the Gulf of Fonseca.[269] Honduras directly asserted that El Salvador's failure to execute the judgment "pose[d] a challenge to the authority, validity and binding nature of the decisions of the main judicial organ of the United Nations,"[270] another reminder of the consequences of a judicially prescribed application of condominium.

CONCLUSIONS

If the inscription on *Leviathan's* bookplate encapsulates the "dogma of sovereignty" – *Non est potestas super terram quae compareteur ei* ("Upon earth, there is not his like") – another inscription adorning the main façade of the Peace Palace at The Hague, the seat of the ICJ, might serve as the Leviathan's counterpart: summarizing the "impressive and onerous" task of the decision-maker, it reads: *Pacis tutela apud judicem* ("The fostering of peace is the task of the judge").[271] The latter translation comes from Judge Nagendra Singh, a former president of the ICJ,[272] and embraces a generative quality to the judicial function that an alternate translation, preferred perhaps by Judge Oda, might somewhat downplay. The inscription also could translate to read: "The judge is the guardian of the peace."[273]

To foster or to guard: which is it? Part of the onerous task of judicial administration is differentiating between overly generative and overly autocratic applications of justice. And a comparison of these two inscriptions embraces a central tension in the *Gulf of Fonseca* case: the role and limits of judicial administration in relation to competing sovereign claims. The solution articulated by the ICJ Chamber in the *Gulf of Fonseca* case attempted to diminish, if not negate, any competing claims to the waters of the Gulf while establishing a condominium arrangement over such waters, even mindful of the internecine violence that historically beset and continues to beset the principal Central

---

[269] Minister for Foreign Affairs of Honduras, Annex to the letter dated 22 January 2002 from the Chargé d'Affaires a.i. of the Permanent Mission of Honduras to the United Nations addressed to the President of the Security Council, U.N. Doc. S/2002/108 (Jan. 22, 2002).

[270] *Id.*

[271] GLEN NEWEY, ROUTLEDGE PHILOSOPHY GUIDEBOOK TO HOBBES AND LEVIATHAN 23 (2008); NAGENDRA SINGH, THE ROLE AND RECORD OF THE INTERNATIONAL COURT OF JUSTICE 1 (1989).

[272] Judge Singh served as the presiding judge of the ICJ from 1985 to 1988. *Nagendra Singh, Judge at the World Court*, 74, N.Y. TIMES, Dec. 12, 1988, www.nytimes.com/1988/12/13/obituaries/nagendra-singh-judge-at-the-world-court-74.html.

[273] Ernst-Ulrich Petersmann, *The Doha Development Round Negotiations on Improvements and Clarifications of the WTO Dispute Settlement Understanding 2001–2003: An Overview, in* THE WTO DISPUTE SETTLEMENT SYSTEM 1995–2003, at 3 (Federico Ortino & Ernst-Ulrich Petersmann, eds., 2004).

American countries fronting the Gulf. But the basis for this arrangement in view of history and the *effectivités* borne of Spanish colonial rule appear more as an artifice of the judicial mind than as an application of law grounded in historical fact. There can be no doubt that *jura novit curia* reigns, and that the Court is presumed to know the law. But history tells a complicated story about the degree to which the condominium ruling has been received by the parties involved, underscoring the difficulty of applying a judicially prescribed cohabitation ruling over the objections of some parties involved.

In international jurisprudence, one would be hard-pressed to find a more litigious part of the world than the Central American region surrounding the Gulf of Fonseca; it comprises part of the "long saga" of decisions springing from successor claims to Spanish imperial holdings in the Americas.[274] That complicated and interwoven history alone makes it the unlikely *situs* for an application of condominium, or its continuing hold in the region, particularly in light of a litany of events darkening its more recent history: the four-day 1969 "Football War" that resulted in two thousand Honduran and Salvadoran deaths and a forced repatriation of one hundred thirty thousand Salvadoran migrant workers;[275] a reignition of hostilities again in 1976; intervention by the Organization of American States in 1980 to quell disturbances between the same two countries;[276] the use of Central American proxies for Cold War military and paramilitary activity

---

[274] Shaw, *supra* note 153, at 929 (citing notable South American disputes including the *Argentine/ Chile* case, the *Beagle Channel* case, and the *Arbitral Award of the King of Spain*). The docket of the ICJ today bears witness to the contentious legacy of Central American decolonization. Pending cases before the ICJ include three disputes between Costa Rica and Nicaragua (involving Certain Activities carried out by Nicaragua in the Border Area, the proceedings of which have been joined with a dispute on Construction of a Road in Costa Rica along the San Juan River; and Maritime Delimitation in the Caribbean Sea and the Pacific Ocean); and two disputes involving Nicaragua and Colombia (Question of the Delimitation of the Continental Shelf between Nicaragua and Colombia beyond 200 nautical miles from the Nicaraguan Coast, and Alleged Violations of Sovereign Rights and Maritime Spaces in the Caribbean Sea). *See generally,* List of Contentious Cases By Date of Introduction, INT'L CT. JUST., www.icj-cij.org/docket/index.php? (last visited Feb 16, 2015) (listing cases referred to the ICJ since 1946). In 2002, El Salvador presented a claim before the ICJ that decisive new facts rendered unreliable the documents forming the basis for the Chamber's *ratio decidendi,* which the ICJ Chamber found inadmissible. *See* Application for Revision of the Judgment of 11 September 1992 in the Case Concerning the Land, Island and Maritime Frontier Dispute (El Sal./Hond.: Nicar. Intervening) (El Sal. v. Hond.), Judgment, 2003 I.C.J. 392, 392.

[275] Maura A. Bleichert, *The Effectiveness of Voluntary Jurisdiction in the ICJ: El Salvador v. Honduras, A Case in Point,* 16 FORDHAM INT'L L.J. 799, 813 (1992).

[276] Gideon Rottem, *Land, Island and Maritime Frontier Dispute (El Salvador/Honduras: Nicaragua intervening),* 87 AM. J. INT'L L. 618, 619 (1993). El Salvador and Honduras signed the *General Peace Treaty* after they ceased fire. For the terms of the treaty, *see* General Peace Treaty, El Sal.-Hond., Oct. 10, 1980, 1310 U.N.T.S. 213 (entered into force Dec. 10, 1980).

of the 1980s; the devolution of El Salvador and Guatemala into vicious civil war and documented genocide; the rise of the Gulf of Fonseca as a hotbed of clandestine activity involving gunrunning,[277] drug-trafficking,[278] and surveillance,[279] and of Honduras as the murder capital of the world;[280] the numerous United Nations attempts at peace-seeking in the region[281] culminating in the November 1989 United Nations Security Council decision to send military observers to the Gulf of Fonseca to monitor land, sea, and air borders.[282]

Tensions today in the Gulf of Fonseca oscillate between regional peace initiatives and cooperative economic engagements and flashes of animus punctuated by ruptures in relations. In March 2013, a tripartite attempt to create a Gulf of Fonseca zone of peace collapsed, with Honduras threatening to send gunboats and fighter aircraft into the Gulf to safeguard fishing interests against purported Nicaraguan naval intrusions;[283] in September 2014, the Honduran military provoked El Salvador's ire by raising its national flag over disputed

---

[277] Alan Riding, *U.S. to Put Radar System in Honduras*, N.Y. Times, Mar. 12, 1983, -www.nytimes .com/1983/03/12/world/us-to-put-radar-system-in-honduras.html (citing gunrunning concerns).

[278] *See* Abigail Hernández et al., *Honduras, Nicaragua, El Salvador Protect Gulf of Fonseca*, Diálogo (Oct. 9, 2012), http://dialogo-americas.com/en_GB/articles/saii/ features/main/2012/ 09/10/feature-01 ("Gulf is also serving drug traffickers to transport drugs and gangs in Central America").

[279] *See* Juan Carlos Neves, United Nations Peace-keeping Operations in the Gulf of Fonseca by Argentine Navy Units 5–6 (1993) (noting the Gulf of Fonseca as a supply line for Nicaraguan Sandinista forces, Salvadoran FMLN guerrillas, and Nicaraguan resistance fighters (Contras)); Hernández et al., *supra* note 278 (increased watch on drug smuggling); *see also* Riding, *supra* note 277 (United States to increase surveillance of the area with new radar system).

[280] *Which Countries Have the World's Highest Murder Rates? Honduras Tops the List*, CNN (Apr. 11, 2014, 12:48 PM), www.cnn.com/2014/04/10/world/un-world-murder-rates/ (quoting United Nations Office of Drugs and Crime report and listing Belize, El Salvador, and Guatemala in the top five).

[281] Requests of the United Nations to facilitate peace-seeking, resulting in the establishment of the United Nations Observer Mission to verify the electoral process in Nicaragua (ONUVEN), the International Support and Verification Commission (CIAV), the United Nations Observer Mission in El Salvador (ONUSAL), the United Nations Mission in El Salvador (MINUGUA), and the United Nations Mission for the Verification of Human Rights in Guatemala (MINUGUA). *Central America-ONUCA Background*, United Nations, www .un.org/en/peacekeeping/missions/past/onucabackgr.html (last visited Feb. 16, 2015).

[282] S.C. Res. 644, ¶ 2, U.N. Doc. S/RES/644 (Nov. 7, 1989) (creating the United Nations Observer Group in Central America (ONUCA)). From June 1990 to January 1992, Argentine vessels, flying the United Nations flag, sailed more than 72,000 nautical miles over 6,479 patrol hours to observe on site verification of the 1987 Guatemala Agreement. Neves, *supra* note 279, at ii, 35.

[283] *Tensions in the Gulf of Fonseca*, Nicaraguan Dispatch (Mar. 13, 2013), http://nicaraguadis- patch .com/2013/03/tensions-in-the-gulf-of-fonseca/; Jorge Kawas, *El Salvador: Sovereignty Issues over Gulf of Fonseca*, Pulsa Merica (Mar. 18, 2013), www.pulsamerica.co.uk/2013/03/18/ el-salvador-sovereignty-issues-over-gulf-of-fonseca/.

Conejo Island in the Gulf, stirring nationalist sentiments in both countries dating to the Football War.[284]

Surprisingly, some scholars argue that the judicially prescribed application of condominium in the Gulf of Fonseca has proven successful, notwithstanding these persistent troubles. This alleged success "indicates that sovereign States can share valuable resources without protracted conflict or a tragedy-of-the-commons-type depletion of resources."[285] In specific reference to the Gulf of Fonseca case, the argument has been made that "the Judgment has already been complied with to a considerable extent [even though El Salvador's application for revision has been rejected]" and that "the ICJ Judgment has had a significant, almost outcome-determinative effect on the ground, succeeding in reducing political tensions significantly."[286]

If this is so, then perhaps the condominium concept has proven more useful as a stopgap measure vis-à-vis the strategic and commercial interests of metropole or external powers than as a pelagic expression of Central American patrimony. Could condominium adaptively have been employed to alienate these waters from predatory external incursions while providing the vulnerable, littoral powers the time needed to sort out their historical difference? Construed in the historical setting of the 1917 judgment, this outcome may have been intended by that Court. Placed in the setting of 1992, no such historical consolidation had yet taken place, making Judge Oda's queries as to the illogic of it all seem persuasive.

International law, and its theoretical dynamic in the eyes of constructivists, accommodates a path for the attainment of legal validity of Court pronouncements by way of "historical consolidation,"[287] but such pronouncements were meant to follow the consolidation, and not the other way around. This was the method by which Norway perfected its title to the *Indreleia* – its intercoastal navigation route – in the *Fisheries Case*, a claim which was deficient originally but which subsequently became opposable to the world.[288] The local illusion of a pluri-state bay, fostered as a judicial creation rather than as an astute demonstration of *jura novit curia*, suggests of the dangers of judicial adventurism, particularly when confronting squarely or attempting to reconfigure the dogma of sovereignty.

[284] Christine Wade, *Border Disputes, Political Tensions Threaten Needed Cooperation in Central America*, World Pol. Rev. (Sept. 15, 2014), www. worldpoliticsreview.com/articles/14058/border-disputes-political-tensions-threaten-needed-cooperation-in-central-america.

[285] Samuels, *supra* note 27, at 758.

[286] Aloysius P. Llamzon, *Jurisdiction and Compliance in Recent Decisions of the International Court of Justice*, 18 Eur. J. Int'l L. 815, 828–829 (2007).

[287] Fisheries Case, 1951 I.C.J., at 138.

[288] *Id.*

7

Condominium in the Atacama Desert and a Sovereign Access to the Sea

On April 24, 2013, Bolivia instituted proceedings against Chile before the International Court of Justice (ICJ) concerning Chile's obligation to nego-tiate an agreement granting landlocked Bolivia full sovereign access to the Pacific Ocean.[1] The claim highlights the legal status of the Atacama Desert,[2] one of the world's driest and most forbidding places.[3] It once served as Bolivia's sovereign corridor to the ocean. It also once prompted a major international conflict in nineteenth-century South America,[4] the War of the Pacific, which cost Bolivia sovereignty over its coastline. On September 24, 2015, the ICJ

---

[1] Application Instituting Proceedings filed in the Registry of the Court on 24 April 2013, Obligation to Negotiate Access to the Pacific Ocean (Bolivia v. Chile) 10, www.icj-cij.org/ docket/files/153/17338.pdf; International Court of Justice Press Release, No. 2013/11, 24 April 2013, www.icj-cij.org/docket/files/153/17340.pdf.

[2] The northern tier of the Atacama Desert is near the border of Chile and Peru, stretching nearly 1000km (600 miles) south, covering a land mass about the size of New York State (140,000km squared or 54,000 square miles). *See Atacama Desert*, WINDOWS TO THE UNIVERSE, www .windows2universe.org/earth/atacama_desert.html. The region generally is described as con-sisting of the territorial stretch along the Pacific coast of South America from about latitude 19° South to 25° South. *See* BRUCE W. FARCAU, THE TEN CENTS WAR: CHILE, PERU, AND BOLIVIA IN THE WAR OF THE PACIFIC, 1879–1884, 5 (2000) [hereinafter, FARCAU, THE TEN CENTS WAR].

[3] *See* Tibor J. Dunai, Gabriel A. González López, & Joaquim Juez-Larré, *Oligocene-Miocene Age of Aridity in the Atacama Desert Revealed by Exposing Dating of Erosion-Sensitive Landforms*, 33(4) GEOLOGY 321–324 (2015) (noting that the Atacama Desert's status as a major hyperarid desert "represents an extreme habitat for life on Earth and serves as an analogue for dry conditions on Mars"); *South America (Chile)*, THE WORLD FACTBOOK, last updated Oct. 28, 2015, www.cia.gov/library/publications/the-world-factbook/geos/ci.html (describing it as the driest desert in the world); FARCAU, THE TEN CENTS WAR, *supra* note 2, at 5 (describing its terrain as "some of the least hospitable on earth"); *Deserts of the World*, THE 7 CONTINENTS OF THE WORLD, www.whatarethe7continents.com/deserts-of-the-world/#atacamadesert (attrib-uting hyperaridity of the Atacama Desert (receiving 0.04 inches (1mm) of water per year) to its situation between the moisture blocking Andes and Chilean Coastal mountain ranges).

[4] *See* FARCAU, THE TEN CENTS WAR, *supra* note 2, at 11. *See also* WILLIAM F. SATER, CHILE AND THE WAR OF THE PACIFIC 2 (1986) (noting the War of the Pacific "constituted one of the more significant military and naval encounters of the late nineteenth century").

dismissed Chile's preliminary objection to the Court's jurisdiction,[5] ruling a 1904 Peace Treaty,[6] following an armistice of 1884,[7] did not bar proceeding to the merits.[8]

This chapter assesses the prospect for a shared sovereignty or coparcener solution to the dispute in light of this case. When two or more states exercise joint sovereignty over territory, these types of arrangements – also called condominium arrangements – are established.[9] They require a mutuality of interest and shared decision-making; a kind of ownership that allows for divisible sovereignty but not without predetermined respect for ground rules of co-ownership. Chile and Bolivia once fruitlessly attempted a condominium arrangement in the Atacama; and Chile also proffered territorial exchanges to allow Bolivia sovereign access to the sea. Both prospects may resurface in judicial considerations, should the ICJ render a judgment on the merits. But the Court's consideration of the latter prospect is less likely to affect its judgment. Chile proffered Peru's territory,[10] then territory captured from Peru,[11] making Chile's donative intent unlike O. Henry's parable of mutual sacrifice, *The Gift*

---

[5]   *See* Obligation to Negotiate Access to the Pacific Ocean (Bolivia v. Chile), Preliminary Objection, 24 Sept. 2015, Judgment, 54, 20, www.icj-cij.org/docket/files/153/18746.pdf [hereinafter Obligation to Negotiate Access, Preliminary Objection].

[6]   Treaty of Peace and Amity between Bolivia and Chile, signed at Santiago on 20 October 1904 (the 1904 Peace Treaty) Spanish transcription, English translation, original in Spanish, Annex 10, www.icj-cij.org/docket/files/153/18616.pdf [hereinafter the 1904 Peace Treaty].

[7]   Truce Pact between Bolivia and Chile, signed at Valparaíso on 4 April 1884 (the 1884 Truce Pact) Spanish transcription, English translation, original in Spanish, Annex 2, www.icj-cij .org/docket/files/153/18616.pdf [hereinafter the 1884 Truce Pact]. Peru, a cobelligerent and ally of Bolivia, signed a peace treaty (as opposed to an armistice) with Chile the year before. *See* Treaty of Peace of Ancón between Chile and Peru, signed at Lima on 20 October 1883 (the Treaty of Ancón) (Spanish transcription, English translation), Spanish transcription submitted by Bolivia as Annex 97 to its Memorial, Annex 1, www.icj-cij.org/docket/files/153/18616 .pdf [hereinafter the Treaty of Ancón]. Bolivia and Chile replaced the armistice – the 1884 Truce Pact – and formally ended the war by concluding the 1904 Peace Treaty, *supra* note 6, although Bolivia later denounced it.

[8]   *See* Obligation to Negotiate Access, Preliminary Objection, *supra* note 5, ¶ 50, 19 ("In the Court's view, ... the matters in dispute are matters [not] settled by ... treaties in force on the date of the conclusion of [the Pact of Bogotá, which established the Court's jurisdiction]").

[9]   1 L. OPPENHEIM, INTERNATIONAL LAW: A TREATISE 453 (8th edn., H. Lauterpacht, ed., 1955).

[10] *See infra* text accompanying nn. 211–213.

[11] According to historian Bruce Farcau:

> Successive governments in La Paz have consistently demanded access to the sea, and the Chileans have offered a corridor along the current Chile-Peru border that would answer that demand as well as provide a buffer against a still-hostile and well-armed Peru. However, the Peruvians insist that the land involved in such a deal would have been formerly Peruvian territory and that, if Chile wants to give it to anyone, it should return it to Peru, implying that Bolivia will remain landlocked unless Chile chooses to return all the land it took from Peru first, which seems unlikely.

of the Magi.[12] Chile's donative intent has never factored into the equation for a condominium solution in the Atacama;[13] and Bolivia's internal misrule, compounded by the abject realities of its geostrategic checkmate, have complicated its own attempts to negotiate a solution with either Chile or Peru. Bolivia long ago recognized Chile held the padlock and Peru held the key to Bolivia's postwar quest to regain a blue water port in the Pacific.[14] Nevertheless, Bolivia has revisited bilateral attempts to pick the lock. In 1910, Peru parried an informal Bolivian query about both Peru and Chile renouncing interests in the Tacna and Arica provinces in favor of granting Bolivia a corridor to the sea.[15] Secret talks between Bolivia and Chile, which combined the coastal access issue with a contentious riparian dispute over a proposed diversion of water from the Lauca River,[16] collapsed in 1971 when Bolivia's government was overthrown.[17] A mid-1970s Brazilian proposal to grant Bolivia a corridor to the sea through Arica failed because Peruvian popular opinion opposed ceding to Bolivia territory "rightfully" belonging to Peru.[18] Linking Chilean territorial concessions to a Bolivian offer of liquefied natural gas backfired and contributed to sixty deaths and the demise of Bolivian President Carlos Mesa's

Bruce Farcau, *War of the Pacific (1879–1883), in* III THE ENCYCLOPEDIA OF WAR 1628 (Gordon Martel, ed., 2012). The strip of territory proffered by Chile in exchange is the 18-kilometer band of the Lluta Valley, situated between the Arica-La Paz railway and the border of Chile/Peru.

[12] *See* O. HENRY, THE GIFT OF THE MAGI (with illustrations by Steve Edwards, The Printery: Kirkwood, 2005) (involving Della's sale of her brown cascade of hair to purchase for Jim a platinum fob chain; and Jim's sale of his heirloom gold watch for a bejeweled set of tortoise shell combs for Della).

[13] As an example, Chile proposed a Bolivian corridor north of Arica (involving territory formerly belonging to Peru and possibly including the sale of the Arica-La Paz railway) but offset by territorial compensation from Bolivia "roughly equivalent to the area ceded." Dennis R. Gordon, *The Question of the Pacific: Current Perspectives on a Long-Standing Dispute,* 141(4) WORLD AFF. 321, 325 (1979).

[14] *See id.* at 324 (quoting Bolivian General Carlos Alcoreza Milgarejo).

[15] *See* RONALD BRUCE ST. JOHN, BOUNDARIES, TRADE, AND SEAPORTS: POWER POLITICS IN THE ATACAMA DESERT (program in Latin American Studies occasional paper series no. 28) 22 (1992) [hereinafter ST. JOHN, BOUNDARIES, TRADE, AND SEAPORTS].

[16] Arica's status as a possible bargaining chip was complicated during the 1960s by control over the waters of the Lauca River, a 140-mile long river originating in the Chilean Andes feeding into Bolivia's Lake Coipasa. Lake Coipasa served as a water source for towns on the Bolivian *Altiplano,* igniting a dispute when Chile diverted water to irrigate valleys feeding Arica. *See* Robert D. Tomasek, *The Chilean-Bolivian Lauca River Dispute and the O.A.S.,* 9(3) J. OF INTER-AM. STUD. 351–366 (1967). It has been suggested that Chile's interest in contemplating a trade-off solution (i.e., exchanging formerly Peruvian territory north of Arica for a Bolivian concession of roughly equal territory) was "specifically aimed at securing exclusive and unassailable access to the Rio Lauca." Gordon, *supra* note 13, at 328. The riparian dispute caused a rupture in diplomatic relations in 1962.

[17] *See* ST. JOHN, BOUNDARIES, TRADE, AND SEAPORTS, *supra* note 15, at 27.

[18] *See id.*

regime in 2005.[19] Chile and Bolivia picked up discussions again in 2006 as part of a now-stalled thirteen-point agenda to improve bilateral relations.[20] Chile's former president, Sebastian Piñera, scuttled a plan in 2010 to establish a non-sovereign coastal enclave for Bolivia in Chile's northern region of Tarapacá, contending that migratory, free transit, and administrative and infrastructure privileges would functionally divide Chilean territory in two.[21] In response, Bolivian President Evo Morales and his Peruvian counterpart, Alan García Pérez, signed a deal granting Bolivia a ninety-nine-year extension to a free-trade zone concession on a three-mile stretch of shoreline near Peru's southern port of Ilo – a gesture of symbolic rather than economic significance.[22] Discussions about changing the territorial status of the northern tier of the Atacama Desert involve historical claims of the three Andean states, making bilateral solutions difficult because they upset a tenuous balance of power and sow seeds of suspicion. Any solution farther south involving the Atacama's midsection would cleave Chile in two – a partition it vows will not occur.[23]

A condominium arrangement, therefore, has some appeal. An examination of this idea within this context enhances perspectives on shared sovereignty solutions generally, recalls specifically problems involving the doctrine of the

[19] *See* Leslie Wehner, *From Rivalry to Mutual Trust: The Othering Process between Bolivia and Chile*, GERMAN INSTITUTE OF GLOBAL AND AREA STUDIES 6 (GIGA Research Program No. 135, May 2010), http://giga.hamburg/en/system/files/publications/wp135_wehner.pdf (discussing the failure of the *gas por mar* initiative).

[20] Agenda point six contains the Bolivian maritime claim to establish a sovereign access to the Pacific Ocean. The 13-point agenda includes: (1) Mutual Confidence Building Measures; (2) Border Integration; (3) Freedom of Movement; (4) Physical Integration; (5) Economic Cooperation; (6) Access to the Sea; (7) the Silala River issue and Water Resources; (8) Poverty Alleviation; (9) Security and Defense; (10) Cooperation against Drug Trafficking; (11) Education, Science, and Technology improvements; (12) Culture; (13) Energy Issues. *See id.* at 7 n. 2.

[21] *See Chile Outlines Conditions for a Possible Bolivian Access to the Pacific*, MERCOPRESS, Dec. 7, 2010, http://en.mercopress.com/2010/12/07/chile-outlines-conditions-for-a-possible-bolivian-access-to-the-pacific. The foundation for the accord (known as *Boliviamar*) dated to bilateral discussions commencing in 1992. *See* Tess Bennett, *Bolivia's Long Diplomatic Road to the Coast*, THE ARGENTINA INDEPENDENT (Sept. 25, 2013), www.argentinaindependent.com/currentaffairs/bolivias-long-diplomatic-road-to-the-coast/.

[22] *Who Will Gain as Bolivia Wins Support in an Age-old Border Dispute?* KNOWLEDGE@WHARTON (Jan. 12, 2011), http://knowledge.wharton.upenn.edu/article/who-will-gain-as-bolivia-wins-support-in-an-age-old-border-dispute/. The economic significance of the agreement has been questioned, as the port at Ilo is too far north and lacking in trade links that can accommodate Bolivian commercial needs; Bolivia has had access to the free trade zone at Ilo since 1992 but has done little, if anything, to develop it. Id.

[23] *See Chile Outlines Conditions for a Possible Bolivian Access to the Pacific*, MERCOPRESS, Dec. 7, 2010, http://en.mercopress.com/2010/12/07/chile-outlines-conditions-for-a-possible-bolivian-access-to-the-pacific (citing Chilean Foreign Minister Alfredo Moreno's pledge never to divide the country in two over Bolivia's sea access quest).

pactum de contrahendo (an agreement to negotiate a future agreement)[24] – specifically problems of proof and enforceability – reinforces the limited value of factual circumstances used to untangle competing historical narratives, and provides an important prospect for a solution other than the problematic status quo and historically stillborn efforts to arrive at a bilateral solution within a trilateral context.

International law's track record on shared sovereignty arrangements is not good.[25] Such solutions are thought practical only where a cooperative spirit prevails, in which case simpler solutions might better be pursued.[26] Condominium arrangements in international law are not common,[27] nor compelling,[28] but they are not inconceivable.[29] Such a solution in the Atacama Desert dispute seems pragmatic, even workable, although history reveals a cautionary tale: truculent relations characterize Bolivian-Chilean, and indeed regional, relations.[30] They date to Chile's successful campaign to

[24] *See* Arnold Duncan McNair, The Law of Treaties 27, 29 (2nd edn., 1961) (applying the concept to the good faith obligation to negotiate "in the future with a view to the conclusion of a treaty" but differentiating it from a duty to conclude a treaty); *see generally*, Ulrich Beyerlin, *Pactum de Contrahendo und Pactum de Negotiando im Völkerrecht?* 36 Zeitschrift für Ausländishes Offentliches Recht und Völkerrecht [ZaöRV] 407–443 (1976); Ulrich Beyerlin, *Pactum de Contrahendo, Pactum de negotiando, in* 3 Bernhardt, Encyclopedia of Public International Law 854–858 (1984); Martin A. Rogoff, *The Obligation to Negotiate in International Law: Rules and Realities,* 16 Mich. J. Int'l L. 141–185 (1994).

[25] *See* Christopher R. Rossi, *Jura Novit Curia? Condominium in the Gulf of Fonseca and the "Local Illusion" of a Pluri-State Bay,* 37(3) Hous. J. Int'l L. 793, 796–799 (2015) (noting historical problems with condominum arrangements).

[26] 1 International Law; Being the Collected Papers of Hersch Lauterpacht 370 (E. Lauterpacht, ed., 1970).

[27] *See* El Salvador v. Nicaragua, C.A.C.J., Judgment of Mar. 9, 1917, 11 Am. J. Int'l L. 674, 712 (1917) (noting condominium arrangements are not common in the relations among nations).

[28] *See* Peter Schneider, *Condominium, in* 1 Encyclopedia of Public International Law 732, 734 (Rudolf L. Bernhardt, ed., 1992) (referring to condominium arrangements as a "historical relic from the feudal age); Joel H. Samuels, *Condominium Arrangements in International Practice: Reviving an Abandoned Concept of Boundary Dispute Resolution* 29 Mich. J. Int'l L. 727, 728–730 (2008) (noting problems with the concept as a workable concept); J. H. W. Verzijl, 6 International Law in Historical Perspective 69 (1973) (referring to condominium as "peculiar and exceptional").

[29] *See* El Salvador v. Nicaragua, *supra* note 27, at 712 (noting condominium arrangements are "not an inconceivable or an isolated fact"). Several historical examples of condominium arrangements include the joint US–U.K. control over the Oregon Country from 1815 to 1846, the provisional arrangement in 1920 concerning the Free City of Danzig, the 1910–1913 trilateral conference discussions among Norway, Sweden, and Russia regarding Spitsbergen, and Andorra, which from 1278 to 1993 was administered jointly by France and the Catalan Bishop of Urgell. *See* Rossi, *supra* note 25, at 799. For a problematic pelagic adaptation of the condominium concept involving three Central American countries, *see generally, id.*

[30] *See generally*, Wehner, *supra* note 19 (discussing Bolivia's and Chile's socially constructed culture of rivalry).

disrupt the Peruvian-Bolivian Confederation in the 1830s.[31] The two countries have maintained only consular relations since the failure of the Charaña negotiations of 1978,[32] and they have had no formal diplomatic relations since the early 1960s except between 1975 and 1978.[33] Contested political alignments, shifting allegiances, corrupt governance, and secret agreements overlay a historical map of disputed and indeterminate boundaries regarding territory emergent in resources – gold and silver from the time of Pizarro's sixteenth-century assault on the Inca Empire;[34] fertilizer-rich guano, caliche (sodium nitrate), saltpeter (potassium nitrate), rubber, and copper in the nineteenth century; tin, gas, and oil in the early twentieth century.[35] Control over these resources repeatedly has complicated this dispute as well as Andean relations throughout the Southern Cone.[36] It has challenged the effectiveness of international law's blunt doctrine of *uti possidetis* and has resulted in war, annexation, revolution, and territorial dismemberment. As uncompromising as this border dispute seems,[37] the least popular solution appears the most

[31] *See* Clements R. Markham, The War between Peru and Chile, 1879–1882, 31–34 (1882) (discussing Chilean endeavors to dissolve the Confederation); and Sater, Chile and the War of the Pacific, *supra* note 4, at 2 (noting Chile's triumphant fight against establishment of a Peruvian-Bolivian Confederation during the 1830s).

[32] Chile and Bolivia entered into secret negotiations in 1973 following the rupture in diplomatic relations caused by the Lauca River diversion dispute of 1962. In 1975 Chilean leader Augusto Pinochet and Bolivian President Hugo Banzer met in the Bolivian border town of Charaña, where a forestalled land exchange was discussed. *See infra*, text accompanying n. 274.

[33] *See* Uldaricio Figueroa, La demanda maritime boliviana en los foros internacionales 117–137 (2007) (discussing the resumption of diplomatic relations from 1975 to 1978 and the preceding thaw beginning in 1970).

[34] *See* John Hemming, The Conquest of the Incas 47–48 (1970), and Kim MacQuarrie, The Last Days of the Incas 96 (2007) for astonishing accounts of Francisco Pizarro's third expedition to Peru and his 1532 capture of the Incan nobleman, Atahualpa, and his famous offer of a room full of gold, twice filled over with silver, if his life were to be spared.

[35] Andean countries, Chile and Bolivia particularly, are repositories of the world's largest untapped lithium reserves, a mineral essential to operating computers, batteries, cell phones, and portable electronic devices. *See* Hal Hodson, *Follow the Lithium Dreams Expedition to Chile and Bolivia*, New Scientist (July 22, 2015), www.newscientist.com/article/follow-the-lithium-dreams-expedition-to-chile-and-bolivia/.

[36] Southern Cone countries include Argentina, Brazil, Chile, Peru, Bolivia, Paraguay, Uruguay, and Ecuador. *See* Arie M. Kocowicz, Zones of Peace in the Third World: South America and West Africa in Comparative Perspective 67 (1998).

[37] Indeed, Bolivia's 2009 Constitution declares an "inalienable and imprescriptible" right over the territory giving access to the Pacific Ocean and its maritime space. ["El Estado boliviano declara su derecho irrenunciable e imprescriptible sobre el territorio que le dé acceso al océano Pacífico y su espacio marítimo."] Art. 267 (I) Constitución política del estado Plurinacional de Bolivia, art. 267 (Feb. 7, 2009), www.presidencia.gob.bo/documentos/publicaciones/constitucion.pdf.

obvious,[38] and it has some historical support within the hostile environment of the Atacama Desert.

Woven throughout this complicated history is the recurring problem of territorial temptation – the desire of capable states to control emergent resources, or when not possible, then to share the resources or work to preclude another state's ability to secure them.[39] Territorial temptation and condominium arrangements seem incompatible, unless they inescapably reflect the rational interests of all parties concerned. A solution that reflects these interests seems more tenable than Bolivia's demand for a return of territory as a reparation for Chile's war of aggression,[40] and more practical than an appeal to Chile's sense of international comity or conscience. Perhaps a point of shared interest arises in the northern Atacama Desert and makes the prospect of an accommodation feasible, notwithstanding the overarching historical record: this case marks another stage in a long-standing feud, perhaps the most intractable border dispute in the Americas,[41] and yet another contentious chapter in the centuries-long complications arising from Spain's conquest and colonial rule of the Americas.[42]

A DUTY TO NEGOTIATE WHAT? JUDGE OWADA'S QUESTION

The ICJ's ruling on the preliminary question suggested the subject matter of this dispute may revolve around a question other than that of a condominium arrangement. The ruling focused on a duty to negotiate rather than to grant, much less share, sovereignty.[43] This duty arises to resolve a "mutual problem of common interest," presumably where a state's legal right intersects with another state's right.[44] But this duty begs an important question in this case: *what* must the parties negotiate? The question is more subtle

---

[38] See *Bolivia/Chile Pacific Access*, Council on Hemispheric Affairs (June 24, 2011), www.coha .org/boliviachile-pacific-access/.

[39] See Christopher R. Rossi, *A Particular Kind of Dominium: The Grotian Tendency and the Global Commons in a Time of High Arctic Change*, 11(1) J. Int'l L. & Int'l Rel 26 (2015) (discussing territorial temptation).

[40] See Carlos D. Mesa Gisbert, Presidencia Sitiada: Memorias de mi gobierno 243 (2008).

[41] Waltraud Q. Morales, A Brief History of Bolivia 78 (2nd edn., 2010).

[42] Latin America is the most represented continent in contentious cases before the I.C.J., with eight of thirty suits initiated between 2000 and 2013. Laetitia Rouvière & Latetitia Perrier Bruslé, *Bolivia-Chile-Peru: Sea Access*, in 1 Border Disputes: A Global Encyclopedia (Territorial Disputes) 53 (Emmanuel Brunet-Jailly, ed., 2015).

[43] See Obligation to Negotiate Access, Preliminary Objection, *supra* note 5, 25–36, 12–15.

[44] Rogoff, *supra* note 24, at 148. In the Fisheries Jurisdiction Case, the I.C.J. noted the intersection of Iceland's "preferential fishing rights" and Great Britain's "traditional fishing rights" in a common maritime area, holding a state assumes "its own obligation to take account of the rights of other States" in such circumstances. See Fisheries Jurisdiction Case (U.K. v. Ice.), Merits, Judgment, 1974 I.C.J. 72, 31.

than appearances indicate, prompting Judge Hisashi Owada to ask during oral hearings what did the parties mean by their repeated references to a "sovereign access to the sea[?]"[45]

CHILE'S VIEW

Chile contended the access it agreed to provide to Bolivia in the 1904 Peace Treaty pertained in perpetuity to the "fullest and most unrestricted right of commercial transit in its territory and its Pacific ports" and that the access "Bolivia has a right to is not sovereign access."[46] Chile contended Bolivia aimed to force a negotiation on the transfer of "coastal territory bathed by the Pacific Ocean."[47] It claimed the ICJ lacked jurisdiction to consider this issue because the 1904 Peace Treaty already settled that matter.[48] In Chile's view, Bolivia's plea artificially reframed the fact of Chile's territorial sovereignty and the question of Bolivia's right of access to the sea into a negotiation *only* about the details of Bolivia's sovereign access – that is, how much territory was involved and its location – as if these factors already had not been settled by war and peace. Bolivia's posturing, according to Chile, attempted to secure a judicially predetermined outcome to revise or nullify the 1904 Peace Treaty.[49] Chile argued that re-litigating its history would potentially unravel and destabilize the

[45]   Public sitting held on Friday 8 May 2015, at 3 p.m., at the Peace Palace, President Abraham presiding, in the case concerning Obligation to Negotiate Access to the Pacific Ocean (Bolivia v. Chile) Preliminary Objection, Verbatim Record, CR2015/21, 38–39 International Court of Justice, (question of Judge Owada) www.icj-cij.org/docket/files/153/18648.pdf.

[46]   Letter of Felipe Bulnes, Agent of Chile, to the Registrar of the Court, Obligation to Negotiate Access to the Pacific Ocean (Bolivia v. Chile), Chile's Answer to Judge Owada's question concerning the meaning of "sovereign access to the sea," May 12, 2015, www.icj-cij.org/docket/files/153/18662.pdf (citing art. VI of the 1904 Peace Treaty, in which Chile "recognizes in favour of Bolivia in perpetuity the fullest and most unrestricted right of commercial transit in its territory and its Pacific ports").

[47]   Letter of Felipe Bulnes to the Registrar of the Court, Obligation to negotiate Access to the Pacific Ocean (Bolivia v. Chile), Chile's Answer to Judge Owada's question concerning the meaning of "sovereign access to the sea," May 12, 2015, www.icj-cij.org/docket/files/153/18662.pdf.

[48]   Specifically, Chile claimed pursuant to art. VI of the Pact of Bogotá (1948), to which both parties belonged, that the I.C.J. lacked jurisdiction under Art. XXXI of the Pact (the article establishing compulsory jurisdiction) because the matter was "already settled" and in force at the conclusion of the Pact. *See* Obligation to Negotiate Access, Preliminary Objection, *supra* note 5, ¶¶ 21–22, 10–11.

[49]   *See* Obligation to Negotiate Access, Preliminary Objection, *supra* note 5, ¶¶ 28–33, 13–14. Underscoring its sense of moral outrage, Bolivia has referenced the Realpolitik conclusion of Abraham König, Chile's Minister Plenipotentiary to La Paz, as evidence of Chile's denial of previous commitments to negotiate. In a note dated August 13, 1900, König likened Chile's takeover of the Atacama to Germany's imperial annexation of Alsace and Lorraine: "*Nostro*

continent's borders.[50] At most, Chile acknowledged a duty to negotiate access, which neither implied a duty to reach an agreement nor to grant sovereignty.

BOLIVIA'S VIEW

Bolivia claimed the case was not about the precise modalities for granting a sovereign access to the sea (although they elsewhere asserted a nonnegotiable end result: "Chile must grant Bolivia its own access to the sea with sovereignty"[51]). It claimed "the specific modalities of sovereign access are not matters for the Court but, rather, are matters for future agreement" between the parties; and that the dispute had nothing to do with the 1904 Peace Treaty because "the alleged obligation to negotiate existed independently of and in parallel to, the 1904 Peace Treaty."[52] Bolivia's sovereign entitlement derived "from Chile's own unilateral declarations or its repeated agreements with Bolivia to negotiate sovereign access;"[53] from Chile's declarations preceding and subsequently confirming a 1950 Exchange of Notes;[54] from "agreements, diplomatic practice and ... declarations attributable to [Chile]" extending

---

derechos nacen de la victoria, la ley suprema de las naciones. Que el Litoral es rico y vale muchos millones, eso ya lo sabíamos." EL LIBRO DEL MAR 32 (2nd edn., Ministerio de relaciones exteriores de bolivia, 2014) at 32.

[50] *See* Public sitting held on Thursday 7 May 2015, at 4.30 p.m., at the Peace Palace, President Abraham presiding, in the case concerning Obligation to Negotiate Access to the Pacific Ocean (Bolivia v. Chile) Preliminary Objection, Verbatim Record, CR 2015/20, ¶ 10, 41 (Mr. Koh).

[51] *See* Written reply of Bolivia to the question put by Judge Owada at the public sitting held on the afternoon of 8 May 2015, 13 May 2015, 2 www.icj-cij.org/docket/index.php?p1=3&p2=3&k =f3&case=153&code=bch&p3=10.

[52] Obligation to Negotiate Access, Preliminary Objection, *supra* 5, ¶ 30, 13.

[53] *See Bolivia's Comments on Chile's Reply to Judge Owada's Question,* ESTADO PLURINACIONAL DE BOLIVIA, EMBAJADA LA HAYA – PAÍSES BAJOS, ¶ 4, www.icj-cij.org/docket/files/153/18664.pdf

[54] Bolivia contends a 1950 Note of the Chilean Minister of Foreign Affairs on June 20, 1950 expressly recognized prior agreements "aimed at finding a formula that will make it possible to give to Bolivia a sovereign access to the Pacific Ocean of its own." The Note recognized: "the 1895 Transfer Treaty, the 1920 Act [between Bolivian and Chilean foreign ministries, which considered Bolivian sovereign access to the sea through Arica], Chile's Note of 1923, the 1926 Kellogg proposal and Matte Memorandum [a U.S. proposal favorable to Bolivia],"declarations of the Chilean President between 1946 and 1949, Chile's Memorandum of July 10, 1961 [repeating and subsequently confirming the 1950 Exchange of Notes], and various resolutions of the Organization of American States unanimously calling for "a formula for giving Bolivia a sovereign outlet to the Pacific Ocean, on bases that take into account mutual conveniences, rights and interests of all parties involved." *See* Comments in writing of Chile on the written reply of the Bolivian Government to the question put by Judge Owada at the public sitting held on the afternoon of 8 May 2015, ¶¶ 3–6, www.icj-cij.org/docket/index .php?p1=3&p2=3&case=153&code=bch&p3=10.

more than a century,[55] reaching to Chile's highest-level representatives,[56] and existing independently from the 1904 Peace Treaty,[57] and ultimately breached by Chile when it denied its obligation to negotiate in 2011 and 2012.[58] Bolivia argued the teleological implications of the obligation to negotiate required an agreement, the precise form to be determined by future negotiations.[59]

THE ICJ'S VIEW

The ICJ agreed with Bolivia, holding that previous agreements did not bar the Court from proceeding, although it held certain claims in abeyance. It ruled the case at this juncture was not about affirming Bolivia's sovereign access to the sea, nor about pronouncing on the legal status of the 1904 Peace Treaty;[60] these contentions, assuming *arguendo* the ICJ were to find them valid, are subjects of future consideration.[61] The subject-matter of the dispute "is whether Chile is obligated to negotiate in good faith Bolivia's sovereign access to the Pacific Ocean and, if such an obligation exists, whether Chile has breached it[?]"[62] This issue pertains to the duty to negotiate sovereignty, not determine sovereignty. Similar to its limited charge in the *North Sea Continental Shelf Cases*, the drawing of a new border line appears to be overtaken by the ICJ's explication of principles the parties must themselves apply.[63] As *that* matter has not been "already settled" pursuant to the jurisdictional requirement of Article VI of the Pact of Bogotá,[64] the case proceeds.[65]

---

[55] International Court of Justice, Press Release No. 2015/23, 24 September 2015, www.icj-cij.org/ docket/files/153/18756.pdf (quoting Bolivian memorial).

[56] Obligation to Negotiate Access, Preliminary Objection, *supra* note 5, ¶ 31, 14–15.

[57] *Id.* at ¶ 31, 14.

[58] *Id.*

[59] *See* Public sitting held on Friday 8 May 2015, at 3 p.m., at the Peace Palace, President Abraham presiding, in the case concerning Obligation to Negotiate Access to the Pacific Ocean (Bolivia v. Chile), Preliminary Objection, Verbatim Record, CR 2015/21, ¶ 7, 32 ("What matters is that it would be an agreed solution, and not an imposed solution") (Mr. Akhavan).

[60] *See* Obligation to Negotiate access, Preliminary Objection, *supra* note 5, ¶ 33, 14 ("[T]he Court recalls that Bolivia does not ask the Court to declare that it has a right to sovereign access to the sea or to pronounce on the legal status of the 1904 Peace Treaty").

[61] *See id.* at ¶ 33, 14 ("it would not be for the Court to predetermine the outcome of any negotiation").

[62] *Id.* at ¶ 34, 14.

[63] By Special Agreement, parties in the North Sea Continental Shelf Cases limited the Court to decide "[w]hat principles and rules of international law are applicable to the delimitation as between the Parties." North Sea Continental Shelf (F.R.G. v. Den.; F.R.G. v. Neth.), Judgment, 1969 I.C.J. 3, 6.

[64] *See* Obligation to Negotiate Access, Preliminary Objection, *supra* note 5, ¶¶ 37–53, 15–19.

[65] *Id.* at ¶54, 20.

DISTINCTIONS WITH DIFFERENCES: THE DUTY TO NEGOTIATE SOVEREIGNTY AND THE DUTY TO SHARE SOVEREIGNTY

Judge Owada's query about the meaning of a sovereign access to the sea raised subtle issues about a duty to negotiate, a subject he is thoroughly familiar with as an academic and diplomat.[66] His question followed Bolivia's oral argument about "obligations arising from" *pacta de contrahendo, negocio [negotiando]* and estoppel,[67] elsewhere reformulated in terms of unilateral declarations.[68]

PACTA DE CONTRAHENDO AND NEGOTIANDO AND UNILATERAL DECLARATIONS

A *pactum de contrahendo* obligates parties to conclude a future agreement; a *pactum de negotiando*, equally binding although less demanding in substance, obligates parties to enter into future negotiations but does not "[bind] the parties to arrive at an agreement."[69] Unilateral statements made by authorized officials have legal effect and can work as an estoppel.[70] They have been held binding

---

[66] *See* HISASHI OWADA, STUDY ON TREATY RESERVATIONS AND DECLARATIONS, INTERNATIONAL LAW, UN AND JAPAN. TOKYO FESTSCHRIFT TAKANO (1988), 361–384. Owada served as Japan's permanent representative to the United Nations and as the director general of the Treaties Bureau (principal legal advisor) for the Japanese Foreign Ministry, and taught at Tokyo University, Harvard, Columbia, and New York University. *See United Nations Foundation, Who We Are: Hisashi Owada (Japan)*, www.unfoundation.org/who-we-are/board/hisashi-owada-japan.html?referrer= https://www.google.com/.

[67] *See* Public sitting held on Friday 8 May 2015, at 3 p.m., at the Peace Palace, President Abraham presiding, in the case concerning Obligation to Negotiate Access to the Pacific Ocean (Bolivia v. Chile), Preliminary Objection, Verbatim Record, CR 2015/21, ¶ 6, 32 (Mr. Akhayan).

[68] Public sitting held on Wednesday 6 May 2015, at 10 a.m., at the Peace Palace, President Abraham presiding, in the case concerning Obligation to Negotiate Access to the Pacific Ocean (Bolivia v. Chile), Preliminary Objection, Verbatim Record, CR 2015/19, ¶ 6, 52 (Mr. Akhavan).

[69] *See* Hisashi Owada, *Pactum de Contrahendo, Pactum de Negotiando*, in MAX PLANCK ENCYCLOPEDIA OF PUBLIC INTERNATIONAL LAW 18–19 (2008). *See also* Antonio Cassese, *The Israel-PLO Agreement and Self-Determination*, 4 EUR. J. INT'L L. 564, 566–568 (1993) (distinguishing *pacta de contrahendo* from the "more tenuous" *pacta de negotiando*). In the North Sea Continental Shelf Cases, the I.C.J. (citing P.C.I.J.'s Advisory Opinion in the case of Railway Traffic between Lithuania and Poland) recognized "the obligation [to negotiate] was 'not only to enter into negotiations but also to pursue them as far as possible with a view to concluding agreements,' even if an obligation to negotiate did not imply an obligation to reach agreement." North Sea Continental Shelf cases, *supra* note 63, ¶87, 47–48.

[70] *See generally* D. W. Bowett, *Estoppel Before International Tribunals and its Relation to Acquiescence*, 33 BRIT. Y.B. INT'L L. 176 (1957); W. Michael Reisman and Mahnoush H. Arsanjani, *The Question of Unilateral Governmental Statements as Applicable Law in Investment Disputes*, 19(2) ICSID REVIEW 339–340 (2004) (noting the doctrine of estoppel's place in discussions of unilateral statements and its requirement of detrimental reliance).

against the interests of the declarant state in territorial disputes,[71] questions of jurisdiction,[72] and in general statements opposable to the world (*erga omnes*).[73]

Although *pacta de contrahendo* and *negotiando* share legal characteristics, arise in treaty and general international law, and at times are "nearly imperceptible" in terms of difference, they express different understandings of parties' intent to be bound.[74] Judge Charles De Visscher found them almost indistinguishable when the object of negotiations "is only to apply in practice principles forming part of a pre-established" agreement.[75] Even so, an obligation to negotiate does not mean an obligation to agree.[76] The parties' intent also distinguishes the *pacta* from nonbinding agreements[77] and other forms of dispute settlement, such as conciliation and mediation.[78] Importantly, both principles impose obligations that cannot be changed by the will of one party (*non si voluero*), and both are distinguished from unaccepted offers, aspirations, guidelines, or so-called pollicitations (*punctationes*), which are not enforceable.[79] They have arisen in the interpretation of important and familiar treaties, including the Camp David Accords,[80] UNCLOS;[81] the

---

71 *See* Legal Status of Eastern Greenland (Den. v. Nor.), Judgment, 1933 P.C.I.J., Ser. A/B, No. 53, at 36, 57, and 71 (Apr. 5) (holding Norway Foreign Minister Ihlen's pledge, that Danish sovereignty over Greenland "would meet with no difficulties on the part of Norway," was binding) [the Ihlen Declaration]; and Case Concerning the Arbitral Award made by the King of Spain on 23 December 1906 (Hon. v. Nic.), Judgment, 1960 I.C.J. at 210 (involving a telegram sent by the President of Nicaragua to the President of Honduras recognizing as a binding acceptance a territorial award made by the King of Spain).

72 Case Concerning the Temple of Preah Vihear (Camb. v. Thai.), Preliminary Objections, Judgment, 1961, I.C.J., at 17 (May 26) (involving acceptance of the Court's jurisdiction).

73 *See* Nuclear Test Case (Aus. & NZ v. Fr.), Judgment, 1974, I.C.J. ¶¶ 44–46 (noting France's unilateral declaration to cease atmospheric nuclear tests was binding against France, although issued as a general statement).

74 Owada, *supra* note 69, at 19; MᴄNᴀɪʀ *supra* note 24, at 29 (referencing *pactum de contrahendo's* misleading association with the obligation to negotiate in good faith).

75 International Status of South West Africa, Advisory Opinion, 1950 I.C.J. 186, 188 (Dissenting opinion of Judge De Visscher).

76 Stephen L. Kass, *Obligatory Negotiations in International Organizations*, Cᴀɴ. Y.B. Iɴᴛ'ʟ L. 36, 38 (1965).

77 Beyerlin, *Pactum de Contrahendo und Pactum de Negotiando im Völkerrecht?*, *supra* note 24, at 412 ("Der rechtliche Bindungswille der Parteien liefert somit das maßgebliche Kriterium für die Abgrenzung zwischen einem pactum und einer rechtlich unverbindlichen Abrede.").

78 Rogoff, *supra* note 24, at 148 (distinguishing the obligation to negotiate from other forms of dispute settlement such as conciliation, mediation, inquiry, arbitration, and more).

79 1 L. Oᴘᴘᴇɴʜᴇɪᴍ, Iɴᴛᴇʀɴᴀᴛɪᴏɴᴀʟ Lᴀᴡ: A Tʀᴇᴀᴛɪsᴇ, Pᴇᴀᴄᴇ 660–661 (3rd edn., Ronald F. Roxburgh, ed., 1920).

80 Owada, *supra* note 69, at 22.

81 *See* Article 283, United Nations Convention on the Law of the Sea, done Dec. 10, 1982, U.N.Doc. A/Conf.62/122 (entered into force Nov. 16, 1994) (requiring that disputes "proceed

Non-Proliferation Treaty;[82] the 1993 Declaration of Principles on Interim Self-Government Arrangements signed by Israel and the PLO;[83] and in numerous nonbinding instruments.[84]

PROBLEMS WITH *PACTA DE CONTRAHENDO* AND *NEGOTIANDO*: ARTICULATING AND ENFORCING AN OPERATIONAL STANDARD

As weighty as these aforementioned references appear, *pacta de contrahendo* and *negotiando* are sometimes employed by hostile parties to avoid any claim of "premature substantive agreement,"[85] or to postpone agreement over substantive content.[86] They establish the lowest common denominator of agreed upon procedures on which future discussions can build,[87] and at times provide much needed breathing space for "states to order their conduct on the basis of general agreements while adjusting details" as developing circumstances dictate.[88] Case law suggests that if a *pactum de contrahendo* or *negotiando* exists between the parties, the intent to be bound should be expressed in positive rather than inferential terms;[89] but "[it would not be] for the Court to determine what shall be the final result ... It is for the Parties themselves to find an agreed solution"[90] – provided the negotiations are meaningful and "'pursue[d] as far as possible with a view to concluding agreements,' even if an obligation to negotiate did not imply an obligation to reach

expeditiously to an exchange of views regarding [their] settlement by negotiation or other peaceful means").

[82] *See* art. VI, Treaty on the Non-Proliferation of Nuclear Weapons, opened for signature July 1, 1968, 21 U.S.T. 483, 79 U.N.T.S. 161 ("Each of the Parties to the Treaty undertakes to pursue negotiations in good faith on effective measures relating to cessation of the nuclear arms race at an early date and to nuclear disarmament, and on a treaty on general and complete disarmament under strict and effective international control"), *available at* www.un.org/disarmament/WMD/Nuclear/NPTtext.shtml.

[83] *See* Cassese, *supra* note 69, at 566 (noting the Declaration includes "a host of *pacta de contrahendo* and also *pacta de negotiando*") [footnote omitted]. Ruth Lapidoth noted "many examples," as well. *See* Ruth Lapidoth, *Relation between the Camp David Frameworks and the Treaty of Peace – Another Dimension*, 15 Is. L.R. 193 (1980).

[84] *See* Owada, *supra* note 69, at 23–24.

[85] Cassese, *supra* note 69, at 566 n. 6 (summarizing Beyerlin's view).

[86] *See* Beyerlin, *Pactum de Contrahendo und Pactum de Negotiando im Völkerrecht?*, *supra* note 24, at 415–417.

[87] Cassese, *supra* note 69, at 566 n. 6.

[88] Kass, *supra* note 76, at 39

[89] *See* International Status of South-West Africa, Advisory Opinion, 1950 I.C. J. 128, 140 (July 11) (discussing whether the UN Charter articles 77 and 80 obligated Mandatory powers to negotiate placement of territory under the UN Trusteeship system).

[90] Gabčíkovo-Nagymaros Project (Hungary/Slovakia), 1997 I.C.J. 7, ¶141.

agreement."[91] Merely abiding by the formalities of a process of negotiation is not sufficient proof of good faith.[92]

The requirement of good faith in the performance of obligations is well established in international law and in domestic legal systems.[93] In civil law systems, a violation of good faith imputes fault, which is expressed in the doctrine of *culpa in contrahendo*.[94] Common law systems do not have an exact counterpart, but violations of good faith find similar expression in doctrines of negligence, [promissory] estoppel, and implied contract.[95] In international law, the law of state responsibility would provide the legal means for demanding the implementation of the obligation to conclude an agreement,[96] and although important scholars regard the obligation as an absolute obligation,[97] problems arise.

Articulating an operational standard that distinguishes good faith performance from bad faith performance presents challenges when applying the *pacta*.[98] Enforcing this elusive standard internationally, for instance through a judicial order to specifically perform an agreement or to resume negotiations in good faith, also challenges the integrity of an international court or tribunal. *Pacta de contrahendo* and *negotiando* are rudimentary expressions of agreement. At this base level, an agreement to agree at a later date amounts to an agreement to postpone an agreement – a distinction that may create the illusion of a good faith negotiation; it may serve as a cosmetic façade, masking nothing more than the intention *not* to reach an agreement.[99] Some doctrinal treatments view them

---

[91] North Sea Continental Shelf, Judgment, 1969 I.C.J. 87, 48; Railway Traffic between Lithuania and Poland (Railway Sector Landwarów-Kaisiadorys), 1931 P.C.I.J., Ser. A/B, No. 42, 108, 116; Case Concerning Claims Arising out of Decisions of the Mixed Graeco-German Arbitral Tribunal Set up under Article 304 in Part X of the Treaty of Versailles (Greece v. Federal Republic of Germany) 1972, 2 R.I.A.A. 27, 57 (Jan. 26), http://legal.un.org/riaa/cases/vol_XIX/27–64.pdf.

[92] *See* North Sea Continental Shelf Cases at 47.

[93] *See* art. 26, Vienna Convention on the Law of Treaties (*pacta sunt servanda*); Rogoff, *supra* note 24, at 144 and 146 (discussing good faith in conventional, customary, and municipal legal systems).

[94] Rogoff, *supra* note 24, at 146 n. 21 (citing, *inter alia*, the French *Code Civile*).

[95] *See generally* Friedrich Kessler & Edith Fine, *Culpa in Contrahendo, Bargaining in Good Faith, and Freedom of Contract: A Comparative Study*, 77 HARV. L. REV. 401 (1963–1964); Steven J. Burton, *Breach of Contract and the Common Law Duty to Perform in Good Faith*, 94 HARV. L. REV. 369–404 (1980); Willard L. Boyd III & Robert K. Huffman, *The Treatment of Implied-In-Law and Implied-In-Fact Contracts and Promissory Estoppel in the United States Claims Court*, 40 CATH. U. L. REV., 605 (1990).

[96] *See* Cassese, *supra* note 69, at 566.

[97] *See* David Simon, Article VI of the Non-Proliferation Treaty is a Pactum de Contrahendo and has Serious Legal Obligation by Implication 6, www.law.upenn.edu/journals/jil/jilp/articles/2-1_Simon_David.pdf 4 (citing McNair, Oppenheim, Lauterpacht, and Hahn).

[98] *See* Burton, *supra* note 95, at 396.

[99] Examples of categories of bad faith include the evasion of the spirit of the agreement, lack of diligence and slacking off, willfully rendering only "substantial performance," abuse of a

skeptically. Stephen Kass argued, "[e]ven when states are bound to reach agreement, international law requires no more than good faith efforts to fulfil that obligation."[100] Richard Baxter thought *pacta de contrahendo* "empty" and "rhetorical;" without appropriate machinery in place, "no court or other agency can determine whether a State has or has not negotiated in good faith and what the duty ... requires."[101] Myron Nordquist wrote that they are "largely declaratory of policy goals,"[102] and often couched in the language of guidelines – not legally enforceable as a legal duty.[103] Alternatively, US President Calvin Coolidge, acting as sole arbitrator in the *Tacna-Arica Arbitration* (1925), noted that a tribunal could nullify the original treaty based on one party's intentional frustration the good faith obligation to negotiate.[104] Of course, Coolidge was aware the original treaty traced to a peace treaty; and his rumination on a possible third-party remedy for nonperformance was kept squarely in the realm of *obiter dictum*. But bad faith could not be imputed from the failed implementation of a particular provision alone; "something more must appear" and "should not be lightly imputed."[105] Clear and convincing evidence was required to support the existence of bad faith, not disputable inferences.[106] Chile seemingly suggested this latter point, to no avail, during the preliminary stage, implying no meeting of the minds existed in support of a *pactum de contrahendo* and no measure of good faith in support of a *pactum de negotiando* could force a result amenable only to Bolivia.

UNILATERAL DECLARATIONS DISTINGUISHED FROM THE *PACTA*

By definition, *pacta de contrahendo* and *negotiando* are distinct from unilateral declarations, but they share many points of contact involving the intent to be bound. Deciphering the binding effect of unilateral declarations also involves

---

power to specify terms, abuse of a power to determine compliance, and interference with or failure to cooperate in the other party's performance. *See id.* at 350 n. 5 (summarizing Robert S. Summers, *"Good Faith" in General Contract Law and the Sales Provisions of the Uniform Commercial Code*, 54 VA. L. REV. 195 (1968)).

[100] Kass, *supra* note 76, at 40.

[101] R. R. Baxter, *International Law in Her Infinite Variety*, 29 INT'L & COMP. L.Q. 549, 552 (1980).

[102] Center for Oceans Policy, Univ. of Va., *U.N. Convention on the Law of the Sea 1982: A Commentary* 668 (Myron H. Nordquist et al.), *quoted in* Gaetan Verhoosel, *Beyond the Unsustainable Rhetoric of Sustainable Development: Transferring Environmentally Sound Technologies*, 11 GEO. INT'L ENVTL. L. REV. 49 (1988) (describing the technology transfer provision of art. 14 of the UN Convention on the Law of the Sea).

[103] Simon, *supra* note 97, at 6 (citing Colin M. Alberts, *Technology Transfer and Its Role in International Environmental Law; A Structural Dilemma*, 6 HARV. J.L. & TECH, 63, 71 (1992)).

[104] Tacna-Arica question (Chile, Peru), 1925, 2 R.I.A.A. 921, 929 (Mar. 4), http://legal.un.org/riaa/cases/vol_II/921–958.pdf.

[105] *Id.* at 930.

[106] Id.

consideration of their disputed consequences, factual circumstances, the clarity, consistency, and specificity of the declarations, the context in which they are made, and the authority on which they are based.[107] This tangled context, as President Coolidge noted in the failed *Tacna-Arica Arbitration*, required a thorough examination of the historical evidence and diplomatic record,[108] a difficult pathway that nevertheless invites the following review.

ORIGINS OF THE DISPUTE

The dispute before the ICJ traces to the nineteenth-century War of the Pacific (1879–1884), which pitted Bolivia and Peru against victorious Chile. In broader terms, the conflict originates with Spain's nineteenth-century retreat from empire in the New World and the fractious territorial disputes that followed the disintegration of Spain's three-hundred-year rule.

THE BROADER ISSUE: THE LEGACY OF SPANISH IMPERIAL RULE IN THE AMERICAS

The Spanish conquest of the Americas introduced an administrative system to govern its vast holdings. The system was known as vice kingdoms, or viceroyalties. Over time, the viceroyalties grew to include four administrative divisions, a system of royal courts (*Las Reales Audiencias*),[109] and the Captaincy-General of Chile.[110] The appointed vice-kings exercised tremendous regional authority and autonomy, none more absolutist than Peru's viceroy, José Abascal, marqués de la Concordia (1808–1816),[111] but they also represented the imperial ethos and prerogative power of the Spanish Crown.[112]

---

[107] *See* Armed Activities on the Territory of the Congo (New Application: 2002) (Dem. Rep. of the Congo v. Rwanda) Jurisdiction and Admissibility, 2006 I.C.J. 6, ¶¶ 45–53, 26–29.

[108] *See* Tacna-Arica question, *supra* note 104, at 930.

[109] *See generally* CHARLES HENRY CUNNINGHAM, THE AUDIENCIA IN THE SPANISH COLONIES AS ILLUSTRATED BY THE AUDIENCIA OF MANILA, 1583–1800 (1919). The Audiencias (and their capitals) included the Audiencias of Panama (Panama), Santa Fé (Bogotá), Quito (Quito), Lima (Lima), Charcas (La Paz), and Chile (Santiago). *See* HEIDE V. SCOTT, CONTESTED TERRITORY: MAPPING PERU IN THE SIXTEENTH AND SEVENTEENTH CENTURIES 12 (2009).

[110] *See* FARCAU, THE TEN CENTS WAR, *supra* note 2, at 31. Other Captaincies-General existed, for example, in Cuba, Guatemala, and Venezuela; while the latter two achieved practical autonomy, only the Captaincy-General of Chile was granted complete independence from its viceroy (of Peru) by order of the Spanish government, thus allowing it to exercise authority over the *audiencia* of Chile, with its seat in Santiago. *See* WILLIAM SPENCE ROBERTSON, RISE OF THE SPANISH-AMERICAN REPUBLICS AS OLD IN THE LIVES OF THEIR LIBERATORS 6 (1921).

[111] *See* Timothy E. Anna, *The Last Viceroys of Spain and Peru: An Appraisal*, 81(1) THE AM. HIST. REV. 38, 43 (1976).

[112] *See id.* at 41–42.

Land under Spanish control north of the Isthmus of Panama became known as the viceroyalty of New Spain (1535), which consisted of Central America, Mexico, and parts of what would become the western United States, the Spanish Caribbean, and the Philippines. The viceroyalty of Peru (1543) originally ruled throughout all of South America but it ceded territory to new viceroyalties as the Spanish presence penetrated the Southern Hemisphere.[113] It came to include Bolivia (known as Alto Peru) and Chile.[114] The viceroyalty of New Granada (1717) consisted of Venezuela, Colombia, and Ecuador, and the viceroyalty of Río de la Plata (1776) consisted of Argentina, Uruguay, and Paraguay. For a time, Bolivia/Alto Peru transferred to the jurisdiction of Río de la Plata to shore up defenses against the encroaching Portuguese,[115] but it reverted to Peru in 1810 in Spain's effort to consolidate dwindling power.

At the beginning of the nineteenth century, Spain nominally controlled the entire Pacific coast of South America. The Captaincy-General of Chile, one of the smallest and poorest colonies, contrasted starkly with the wealth of Peru and New Granada – "the two jewels in Spain's imperial crown."[116] Intense demand for New World minerals and metals spread throughout the empire.[117] Gold and silver not shipped back to Spain were distributed unevenly but effectively enough to facilitate Spain's lengthy rule.[118] But a sense of crisis enveloped the New World when word circulated in 1808 that the metropolitan power, already beset by popular uprisings, fell to Napoleon. Its two Bourbon kings, Charles IV, and his son, Ferdinand VII, abdicated, and Napoleon put his brother, Joseph, on the Spanish throne.[119]

THE END OF EMPIRE

A crisis of allegiance unfolded and the turmoil spurred pro-independence movements across South America, headed by *El Libertador*, Simón Bolivar

---

[113] ROBERTSON, *supra* note 110, at 2.

[114] *See* ST. JOHN, BOUNDARIES, TRADE, AND SEAPORTS, *supra* note 15, at 1.

[115] *See* OSCAR CORNBLIT, POWER AND VIOLENCE IN THE COLONIAL CITY: ORURO FROM THE MINING RENAISSANCE TO THE REBELLION OF TUPAC AMARU (1740–1782), 130 (1995).

[116] Christon I. Archer, *Review of Gabriel Paquette, Enlightenment, Governance, and Reform in Spain and Its Empire 1759–1808*, 82(1) J. MOD. HIST. 221, 222 (2010).

[117] *See generally*, HUGH THOMAS, RIVERS OF GOLD: THE RISE OF THE SPANISH EMPIRE (2003); *see also* LYLE N. MCALISTER, SPAIN AND PORTUGAL IN THE NEW WORLD, 1492–1700, 227–230 (1984) (estimating sixteenth-century gold and silver production).

[118] *See* Alejandra Irigoin & Regina Grafe, *Bargaining for Absolutism: A Spanish Path to Nation-State and Empire Building*, 88(2) HISP. AM. HIST. REV. 173, 191 (2008) (discussing the imperial distribution of revenue).

[119] *See id.* at 201 (summarizing historians' view that the Bourbon kings' forced abdication by Napoleon was the "turning point for the birth of modern republics in Spanish America").

(1783–1839), and José de San Martin (1778–1850). La Plata (Argentina) gained independence in 1810; Chile in 1818; New Granada (Ecuador, Colombia, Panama, and Venezuela) in 1819; Peru in 1821; and Bolivia in 1825.

The relatively rapid dissolution of the Spanish Empire in the New World affected borders that stretched across thousands of miles. But exact boundaries between viceroyalties or successor governments were inexactly defined because "colonial and post-colonial societies tended to cluster around a handful of urban centers," separated "by vast tracts of inhospitable, unproductive, and often impassable land, jungles, mountains, and deserts."[120]

THE APPLICATION OF *UTI POSSIDETIS*

Against the backdrops of decolonization and emerging statehood and to guard against contested boundary claims, emerging Latin American republics employed the principle of *uti possidetis*. As we have seen, the principle froze territorial title at the moment of independence, "no matter how arbitrary those boundaries may have been drawn."[121] As a convenient means of quieting title, the principle ensured that colonial boundaries instantly became international boundaries for Latin America's new republics.[122] It proved a costly means of securing nonviolent transitions to sovereignty,[123] and despite its indifferent regard for the human populations disrupted by the territorial divisions,[124] it retains legal significance.[125]

The principle's defense of the status quo[126] took two forms: *uti possidetis juris* pertained to border demarcations drawing from references to royal documents, or decrees (*cédulas*); *uti possidetis de facto* applied to territory actually possessed.[127] (Variances in the administrative practices of Spanish and Portuguese imperial holdings account for the distinction).[128] But "the borders between the various administrative units of the Spanish Empire were never meant to

---

[120] FARCAU, THE TEN CENTS WAR, *supra* note 2, at 32.

[121] Jan Klabbers & René Lefeber, *Africa: Lost between Self-Determination and Uti Possidetis, in* PEOPLES AND MINORITIES IN INTERNATIONAL LAW 37 (Catherine Brölmann et al., eds., 1993).

[122] *See* FARCAU, THE TEN CENTS WAR, *supra* note 2, at 31.

[123] *See generally* JOSHUA CASTELLINO & STEVE ALLEN, TITLE TO TERRITORY IN INTERNATIONAL LAW: A TEMPORAL ANALYSIS (2003).

[124] *See id.* at 10.

[125] Frontier Dispute (Burkina Faso/Mali), Judgment, 1986 I.C.J. 554, ¶ 26, 567 ("kept its place among the most important legal principles").

[126] Steven R. Ratner, *Drawing a Better Line: Uti Possidetis and the Borders of New States*, 90 AM J. INT'L L. 590, 601 (1996).

[127] *See* GIUSEPPE NESI, L'UTI POSSIDETIS IURIS NEL DIRITTO INTERNAZIONALE 7(1996) (discussing the dual purposes of the term).

[128] *See id.* at 7 ("in particolare dal Brasile").

be international boundaries;" they were vague, contradictory, and based on imprecise terms of travel and description "all done at a time when the accurate location of parallels of latitude was an inexact art and that of finding longitude was an unfathomable mystery."[129] This maw of undifferentiated boundary confusion transcended the Atacama Desert; Spanish colonial demarcations lacked precision in Patagonia, Tierra del Fuego, the Amazon, and in the sprawling basins of the Orinoco River.[130] The viceroyal administrative system of the Spanish Empire turned out to be an "entirely inadequate" precursor to the arrival of the state system in Latin America,[131] moreso in Africa.[132]

THE MORE IMMEDIATE CAUSE: THE WAR OF THE PACIFIC

Following South America's independence from Spain in the early nineteenth century, Bolivia's founding fathers, Simón Bolivar and General Antonio José Sucre, claimed for Bolivia the barren Atacama Desert, partly to provide a buffer between Peru and Chile, and partly to provide access to the Pacific Ocean through the tiny port at Antofagasta.[133] But Bolivia's southern border with Chile relied on Spanish colonial maps of the *Audiencia* of Charcas (a colonial subdivision of the viceroyalty of Peru), which variously placed the border along the Salado River or the Copiapó River; and the course of these rivers proved difficult to fix.[134] Chile also made overlapping historical claims,[135] and its constitutions of 1822, 1823, 1828, and 1833 claimed

[129] Farcau, The Ten Cents War, *supra* note 2, at 32.
[130] *See* Robert N. Burr, By Reason or Force: Chile and the Balancing of Power in South America, 1830–1905, at 5 (1965). The dispute between Chile and Argentina over Patagonia resulted in an award favoring Argentina in the Cordillera of the Andes Boundary Case (1902).
[131] *Id.* at 5 (claiming that Spanish colonial precedent as a means of demarcating with precision administrative units "was entirely inadequate as a legal basis for determining their boundaries").
[132] *See generally* Saadia Touval, The Boundary Politics of Independent Africa (1972).
[133] *See* Farcau, War of the Pacific (1879–1883), *supra* note 11, at 1624. The Bolivians referred to the coastline as the Departamento del Litoral. *See also* statement of Mr. Rodríguez Veltzé, Public sitting held on Wednesday 6 May 2015, at 10 a.m., at the Peace Palace, President Abraham presiding in the case concerning Obligation to Negotiate Access to the Pacific Ocean (Bolivia v. Chile), Preliminary Objection, Verbatim Record, CR 2015/19, ¶ 3, 10. But cf. Morales, *supra* note 41, at 78 (claiming Bolívar designated the port of Cobija as Bolivia's Pacific seaport in 1825). St. John noted that Bolivia quickly deemed the original port of Cobija inadequate, and far removed from the most logical trade route to the Peruvian port of Arica; an 1826 agreement between Peru and Bolivia secured Arica as a Bolivian port, but the Peruvian Congress refused to ratify the agreement. "[I]t proved to be the only time the Peruvian government ever agreed to give Arica to Bolivia." St. John, Boundaries, Trade, and Seaports, *supra* note 15, at 3–4.
[134] *See id.* at 3.
[135] *See* Luis Barros Borgoño, The Problem of the Pacific and the New Policies of Bolivia 45–55 (1924) (discussing, *inter alia*, references to Chile's historic title to and "possessory" occupation

all of the Pacific coast territory but made no mention of where its northern frontier ended.[136] Peru, on three occasions (1822, 1823, and 1825) recognized the need to demarcate its boundaries, but overriding territorial uncertainty forestalled efforts of its congressional boundary commission to come to any conclusion.[137] Bolivia and Peru disputed their frontiers between the Loa River in the north and Tocopilla in the south. At the time of independence in 1825, Bolivia "claimed a broad desert corridor between the Loa River and the Salado River with Peru and Chile making conflicting, overlapping claims to the north and south."[138] The only circumstance favoring these nascent republics and the enveloping border confusion was the inhospitable terrain, which negated conflicts over ownership.[139] There was nothing to fight over,[140] until reports surfaced in the 1840s of valuable fertilizer deposits. Instead, the republics focused on managing chaotic internal affairs, particularly Peru and Bolivia, which were wracked by political instability more than Chile.[141] But at this moment of resource discovery, the Grotian tendency appeared: a colonial boundary dispute gained impetus as a territorial temptation, which thereafter has "raised serious issues of economic development and regional hegemony."[142]

---

of the Atacama Desert, including references to the Liberator Bolívar; Law V, Title 15, Book 2 of the Laws of the Indies, November 1, 1681 organized by the Royal Audiencia of Lima, extended on January 2, 1791; a 1793 report commissioned by the viceroy of Peru, don Francisco Gil de Taboada y Lémus; twenty jurisdictional acts of Chilean authority over the desert region during the colonial period up to the beginning years of the nineteenth century, as recorded by historian MIGUEL LUIS AMUNÁTEGUI in THE BOUNDARY QUESTION BETWEEN CHILE AND BOLIVIA (1863); and the authority that emanates from "a true gem of national history," the Epítome Chileno (1648), published by Field marshal Santiago de Tesillo).

[136] *See* FARCAU, THE TEN CENTS WAR, *supra* note 2, at 33.

[137] *See* ST. JOHN, BOUNDARIES, TRADE, AND SEAPORTS, *supra* note 15, at 2.

[138] *Id.* at 3.

[139] SATER, CHILE AND THE WAR OF THE PACIFIC, *supra* note 4, at 6.

[140] *See* MORALES, *supra* note 41, at 79 (noting Chile did not seriously begin challenging Bolivian sovereignty in the Atacama until after the first reports of guano deposits in the 1840s). Cf. St. John at 7 (noting that Chilean indifference to the exact location of its northern border ended with the discovery of guano).

[141] *See* FARCAU, THE TEN CENTS WAR, *supra* note 2, at 26 (comparing Chile's small civil wars and less serious rebellions to "revolving door" political unease in Peru and Chile). Sater notes that whereas Chile elected four leaders over forty years beginning in the 1830s (not without strife), Peru adopted six different constitutions between 1823 and 1830 and Bolivia underwent eleven regime changes and more than 100 revolutions between 1839 and 1876. *See* WILLIAM F. SATER, ANDEAN TRAGEDY: FIGHTING THE WAR OF THE PACIFIC, 1879–1884, 15–16 (2007) [hereinafter SATER, ANDEAN TRAGEDY].

[142] *See* Ronald Bruce St. John, *Chile, Peru and the Treaty of 1929: The Final Settlement*, IBRU BOUNDARY AND SECURITY BULLETIN 98 (2000), www.dur.ac.uk/resources/ibru/publications/full/bsb8-1_john.pdf.

A CONTRIBUTING FACTOR: BOLIVIA'S LATE-STAGE DEVELOPMENT

By the mid-1800s, Bolivia was the weakest economy in the hemisphere. It was the last South American country to achieve independence (1825); it lacked democratic political tradition; it had no manufacturing base, a vast and variegated landscape (bigger than Texas and California), and a sparse population of perhaps two million.[143] Eighty percent of the inhabitants did not speak Spanish,[144] and seven-eighths of the population lived in five small cities in the western highlands.[145] It lacked the technology and finance capital to connect by railway its capital, La Paz, situated in the Andes twelve thousand feet above sea level, to the nearest port in Arica, Peru;[146] travel time using the most direct route between La Paz and the Pacific could take almost one month.[147] But in 1857, huge deposits of guano and nitrates also were discovered in the Mejillones region of the Atacama Desert,[148] an area remote from Bolivia's nascent commercial infrastructure located on the *Altiplano* (highland plateau). The land suddenly became valuable to Chile and Bolivia,[149] and potentially threatening to Peru's monopoly control over guano.[150]

THE CONDOMINIUM AGREEMENT OF 1866

Elsewhere, European intrigues in the Western Hemisphere put South American republics on high alert.[151] Spain became a direct concern again

---

[143] FARCAU, THE TEN CENTS WAR, *supra* note 2, at 20–22

[144] *Id.* at 21

[145] *See* SATER, ANDEAN TRAGEDY, *supra* note 141, at 12 (listing La Paz, Oruro, Cochabamba, Sucre, and Potosí).

[146] The port city is now the northernmost port of Chile. Chile is credited with the engineering feat of connecting Arica to the Bolivian border, hence La Paz, by rail, in fulfilment of one clause of the 1904 Peace Treaty.

[147] *See* SATER, ANDEAN TRAGEDY, *supra* note 141, at 9–10 and 11–12.

[148] *See* HERBERT S. KLEIN, A CONCISE HISTORY OF BOLIVIA 129 (2nd. edn., 2011); BURR, *supra* note 130, at 89 (citing "vast new guano deposits in the Mejillones region").

[149] *See* MORALES, *supra* note 41, at 80 (noting Chile's attempt to seize the guano-rich Mejillones region, bringing Chile and Bolivia to the brink of war). *See* SATER, CHILE AND THE WAR OF THE PACIFIC, *supra* note 4, at 6.

[150] The Chincha Islands off Peru's coast had provided the source of almost all of the world's supply of guano at this time, although, in addition to the Atacama Desert holdings, deposits later would be discovered in the Caribbean, on Pacific Atolls, and off Australia. *See generally*, Christopher R. Rossi, "A Unique International Problem": The Svalbard Treaty, Equal Enjoyment, and Terra Nullius: Lessons of Territorial Temptation from History, 15 WASH. U. GLOBAL STUD. L. REV. 93–136 (2016).

[151] With the United States consumed by civil war, politically unstable and weak Latin American republics looked with alarm at French, British, and Spanish interventions in Mexico to make good on Mexican foreign debt. *See* BURR, *supra* note 130, at 90 (noting European interventions and

when it retook the Dominican Republic (Santo Domingo) in 1861; suspicions heightened across South America when the Spanish fleet rounded the southern tip of South America, Cape Horn, and headed up the Pacific coast to Peru's chief port, Callao.[152] A local incident provoked the "revindication" of Spanish interests, and Spain seized Peru's guano-rich Chincha Islands in 1864.[153] Regional tensions, particularly between Chile and Bolivia over the Mejillones region,[154] were put aside and a quadruple alliance of the South American west coast states – Ecuador, Chile, Bolivia, and Peru – formed to oppose successfully Spain's irredentist meddling.[155] Following Spain's defeat – its last gasp at empire in South America – a brief period of amity facilitated an 1866 accord between the governments of La Paz and Santiago (the Mutual Benefits Treaty).[156] That agreement divided the contested Atacama territory at the 24th parallel South,[157] granted exploitation rights to each republic, and imposed a fiscal condominium arrangement over "guano deposits [and minerals] discovered in Mejillones, and in all such further deposits of this same fertilizer which may be discovered in the territory comprised between 23° and 25° South latitude."[158] Tax revenue generated from mining interests in the area were to be shared equally.[159] Bolivia agreed to construct a customs house and port facility at Mejillones and to use no other port for the export of guano or minerals from the shared territory.[160] An export duty exemption applied to all products produced between the 24° and 25° latitude, and was extended to cover natural products Chile exported through Mejillones.[161] Other export

particularly the French attempt to establish a monarchy in Mexico "deeply shocked the entire hemisphere").

[152] *See* BURR, *supra* note 130, at 90.

[153] *See id.*, at 90–92 (recounting the "Talambo" incident and the seizure of the Chincha Islands).

[154] In May 1863, the Bolivian National Assembly empowered the President to declare war on Chile regarding Bolivia's southern border and mineral dispute with Chile. *See* ST. JOHN, BOUNDARIES, TRADE, AND SEAPORTS, *supra* note 15, at 8.

[155] *See* BURR, *supra* note 130, at 99 (discussing formation of the quadruple alliance); WILLIAM E. SKUBAN, LINES IN THE SAND: NATIONALISM AND IDENTITY ON THE PERUVIAN-CHILEAN FRONTIER 8 (2007); ROBERT D. TALBOTT, A HISTORY OF THE CHILEAN BOUNDARIES at 35 (1974) (noting the subordination of regional differences in the combined Peru/Bolivia/Chile/Ecuador alliance against Spain). Spain would suffer a humiliating defeat against Chile's navy (the Chincha Island War), which would represent the last gasp of the Spanish Empire in South America, save for the remnant holdings of empire in Puerto Rico and Cuba.

[156] *See* The Treaty of 1866 Between Bolivia and Chile (Mutual Benefits Treaty), *reprinted in* VIII (3) WILLIAM JEFFERSON DENNIS, DOCUMENTARY HISTORY OF THE TACNA-ARICA DISPUTE 49–50 (1927).

[157] *Id.* art. 1 (establishing a "line of demarcation … between Bolivia and Chile" from the 24° South parallel subject to an exact survey to be undertaken).

[158] *Id.*, art. 2.

[159] *See id. See* SATER, CHILE AND THE WAR OF THE PACIFIC, *supra* note 4, at 6.

[160] *See id.*, art. 3.

[161] *See id.*, art. 4.

duty assessments required the mutual agreement of the parties.[162] The treaty also secured for the parties a *jus prohibendi* pledge: neither Chile nor Bolivia could transfer their right of joint possession to another state, association, or individual,[163] and remuneration for outstanding claims held in abeyance by previous political disruptions were to be indemnified equally by the two coparceners.[164]

It was a remarkable agreement – a historically important but now obscure attempt to share sovereignty. But it imploded under the weight of fatal non-starters: it was made practical through a cooperative spirit – albeit a negative spirit – directed against Spain rather than in support of mutual respect and regional accord. It fueled the personal greed of Bolivia's dictator, Mariano Melgarejo, who had secret personal connections to Chile's nitrate interests.[165] It ceded, from Bolivian perspectives, a disproportionate amount of Bolivian territory, including all claims south of the 25th parallel.[166] And it was predicated on a fictitious equality between the parties that appeared reasonable given the expansive, desolate environment. In fact, Chile was much more capitalized than Bolivia by this time. British financiers fortified its corporate strength with a network of heavy industries and rail lines,[167] contributing to arguments that the war "was more a British war against Peru using Chile as its instrument."[168] Chile benefited from a constellation of internal economic growth factors as well: relative demographic/linguistic homogeneity, a diversified agricultural economy,[169] and an amenable geographic station, which promoted, if not necessitated, seafaring transit and commerce. Indeed, Chile's use of the Pacific Ocean as a highway to circumvent the Atacama wasteland to its north facilitated migration and played an important role in

---

[162] *See id.*, art. 5.

[163] *See id.*, art. 6.

[164] *See id.*, art. 7.

[165] *See* MORALES, *supra* note 41, at 65.

[166] *See id.* at 80–81 (particularly after the discovery of silver near Caracoles, in territory south of the 25th parallel); Klein, *supra* note 148, at 133 ("justifiably condemned ... for selling the nation to the highest bidder").

[167] *See generally* JOHN MAYO, BRITISH MERCHANTS AND CHILEAN DEVELOPMENT 1851–1886 (1987). *See also* JOHN MAYO & SIMON COLLIER, MINING IN CHILE'S NORTE CHICO: JOURNALS OF CHARLES LAMBERT, 1825–1830 (1998) (noting the mining presence of more than forty British-organized companies as early as the 1820s); J. FRED RIPPY, BRITISH INVESTMENTS IN LATIN AMERICA, 1822–1949: A CASE STUDY IN OPERATIONS OF PRIVATE ENTERPRISE IN RETARDED REGIONS 133–141 (1966) (detailing British concessionaires in Chile's railway, telegraph, and nitrate industries).

[168] *See* Heraclio Bonilla, *The War of the Pacific and the national and colonial problem in Peru*, 81(1) PAST & PRESENT 92, 95 (1978) (summarizing a perspective from imperialist literature and quoting the 1882 view of the US Secretary of State).

[169] *See* FARCAU, THE TEN CENTS WAR, *supra* note 2, 24–26.

changing the region's history.[170] Ten thousand Chilean laborers accessed the Atacama through its desert ports,[171] ports essentially cut off from Bolivia's meager and distant population centers in the Andean highlands.[172] But 50 percent of Bolivia's revenue depended on taxes from Atacaman excavation ventures and the labor power provided by Chileans.[173] Stemming the influx of these migrants presented difficult economic repercussions for the cash-strapped Bolivian state. The situation replayed problems involving the settlement of Texas, or the northern frontier of New Spain in the 1820s: with encouragement of the Mexican government,[174] settlers from the United States began to populate *Teyshas/Tejas*,[175] and the rapid infusion of migrants threatened Mexican sovereignty;[176] within a generation a secession movement established Texas as a republic in 1836.[177]

Similarly, the northern migration of Chilean commerce, capital, and labor quickly dominated the economics of the Atacama.[178] This Chilean migration would encroach on the nitrate fields of Peru's Tarapacá province,[179] ultimately

[170] An important subchapter in the War of the Pacific involved the naval battles between Peru and Chile and the preceding arms race of the early 1870s between the republics to upgrade their respective fleets with British-built central battery ironclads. In a minor footnote to international legal history, the Chilean fleet included the wooden corvette *Abtao*, a combination sail-and-steam-engine vessel that was the sister ship of the Confederate raider, *Alabama*, outfitted also by the British, and the subject of one of the most famous cases in international law, the *Alabama* Arbitration. *See* SATER, ANDEAN TRAGEDY, *supra* note 141, at 96–116 (comparing the navies) and 99 (noting the *Abtao*).

[171] *See id.* at 13.

[172] *See* Barros, *supra* note 135, at 75 (noting specifically Antofagasta's remoteness for Bolivians and Chile's responsibility for its development).

[173] *See* SATER, ANDEAN TRAGEDY, *supra* note 141, at 13.

[174] Mark E. Nackman, *Anglo-American Migrants to the West: Men of Broken Fortunes? The Case of Texas, 1821–46*, 5(4) W. HIST. Q. 441, 445 (noting Mexico allowed expatriate American settlers in the country beginning in 1821).

[175] The "Texas" region under Mexican rule between 1821 and 1836 derives from the Caddo people. Its name was variously transcribed by the Spanish (tejas, tyshas, texias, thecas, techan, teysas, techas) before coming into English as Texas. *See Texas, Origin of Name*, Texas State Historical Association. https://tshaonline.org/handbook/online/articles/pft04.

[176] More than one hundred thousand Anglo-American settlers arrived in the "Texas" region between 1821 and 1846. *See* Nackman, *supra* note 174, at 441 (noting as well that expatriate Americans outnumbered Mexicans in the region by a factor of ten (30,000:3,000) by 1835).

[177] *See* ROBERT A. CALVERT, ARNOLDO DE LEÓN, & GREGG CANTRELL, THE HISTORY OF TEXAS 55–81 (5th edn., 2013), http://site.ebrary.com/lib/uiowa/reader.action?docID=10809696&ppg=5.

[178] *See* BURR, *supra* note 130, at 119 (noting the "efficient and aggressive business interests of Chile quickly began to exploit the [Atacama]"). Discovery of a silver lode at Caracoles provoked a dispute about the demarcations of the condominium zone. *See id.*, at 119.

[179] *See* BURR, *supra* note 130, at 131 (noting by 1875 that Tarapacá's nitrate fields attracted more than ten thousand Chilean workers, engineers, and administrators and 20 million Chilean pesos in investment).

against Peru's interests as well. Immediately preceding the outbreak of war, the estimated ratio of Chileans to Bolivians in the Atacama was 17:1.[180] Chilean labor discontent caused an uprising in Mejillones in 1861, which provoked a Bolivian threat to use force if its sovereignty was not respected.[181] In 1872, Bolivian forces put down an attempt by insurrectionists to seize Antofagasta; complaints of Chilean complicity in the matter (The *Paquete de los Vilos* Affair) stirred Bolivian passions about the security of its entire littoral area,[182] and prompted a secret mutual security pact with Peru.[183] In 1879, Chilean patriotic societies in the Atacama appealed to Santiago for relief from Bolivian misrule. The protection of Chilean nationals would factor into the initiation of war.[184]

CONDOMINIUM RESCINDED

In 1871, Bolivian General Melgarejo was overthrown by Colonel Agustín Morales,[185] and Bolivia rescinded the 1866 condominium agreement.[186] In practice, the condominium failed almost from the beginning.[187] Although a mixed commission did map and demarcate uncharted areas,[188] the treaty displeased both governments from the outset; without the common enemy of Spain to deflect animosity, sentiments of "resentment and distrust" quickly returned.[189] Bolivia began redirecting mineral exports above the 23rd parallel through Cobija to avoid revenue-sharing at the port of Mejillones; it withheld payment of half the customs receipts collected at Mejillones; and it refused to indemnify outstanding claims overtaken by the condominium agreement.[190] Chile objected to Bolivia's selective enforcement of the agreement,[191] resented the treatment of its nationals, and chafed at the Bolivian disregard of direct

---

[180] *See* SATER, ANDEAN TRAGEDY, *supra* note 141, at 11.

[181] *See id.* at 17.

[182] *See* BURR, *supra* note 130, at 122–123.

[183] *See id.* at 124 (discussing the 1873 secret treaty between Peru and Bolivia).

[184] *See* SATER, ANDEAN TRAGEDY, *supra* note 141, at 11.

[185] *See* MORALES, *supra* note 41, at 67–68 (later General Morales); *see* FARCAU, THE TEN CENTS WAR, *supra* note 2, at 36.

[186] *See* BURR, *supra* note 130, at 120.

[187] Talbott argues, "neither government found the treaty satisfactory at the time it was signed," and "each nation returned to its former position of resentment and distrust of the other." TALBOTT, *supra* note 155, at 36–37.

[188] *See id.* at 37.

[189] *Id.* at 36–37.

[190] *See id.* at 37.

[191] *See id.*

investment that was improving territory many Chileans regarded as historically and rightfully theirs.[192]

Following failed diplomatic efforts to reinstate the condominium arrangement,[193] which the Bolivian Congress again rejected (the 1873 Lindsay-Corral Treaty), Chile proposed a settlement – the 1874 Boundary Treaty – that affirmed the 24th latitude as the border with Bolivia,[194] and abandoned the joint sovereignty arrangement in exchange for Bolivia's pledge of a twenty-five-year moratorium on imposts levied against Chilean corporate interests or on excavated products in the Atacama region.[195] But Bolivia's abrogation of the 1874 Boundary Treaty convinced the *Moneda*, Chile's seat of executive power, to revindicate its rights,[196] propelling the region into war.

THE TEN CENTS TAX

A ten cents tax ignited the war. In 1873, Bolivia granted the Chilean-owned Antofagasta Railroad and Nitrate Company (*La Compañía de Salitres y Ferrocarril de Antofagasta*) a concession to mine nitrates in the Atacama. The Bolivian National Assembly failed to immediately approve the decree but the concessionaire continued doing business. In 1878, Bolivia approved the 1873 decree, but added a ten cents tax per hundredweight of nitrates exported.[197] The ten cents tax clearly violated the 1874 Boundary Treaty and the 1873 concession contract,[198] but Bolivia justified it on the grounds that the dictator Melgarejo illegally concluded the agreement in violation of domestic law.[199]

---

[192] *See* SATER, CHILE AND THE WAR OF THE PACIFIC, *supra* note 4, at 9–10 (discussing Chilean attitudes against Bolivia)

[193] *See* FARCAU, THE TEN CENTS WAR, *supra* note 2, at 36 (noting one unacceptable offer after another).

[194] The new boundary was established at the 24th parallel south from the Pacific Ocean to the Cordillera o the Andes. *See* TALBOTT, *supra* note 155, at 38.

[195] SATER, CHILE AND THE WAR OF THE PACIFIC, *supra* note 4, at 6; BURR, *supra* note 130, at 130–131.

[196] SATER, CHILE AND THE WAR OF THE PACIFIC, *supra* note 4, at 7.

[197] Historians have noted that the tax, in addition to generating revenue for Bolivia, brought prices for Bolivian guano and nitrates more in line with price hikes in Peru, which had nationalized its nitrate mines. Bolivia, with its secret security pact with Peru, depended on Peru's navy as a counterbalance to Chile's naval build up and could not afford to provoke Peru by granting Chile more congenial allowances for mining interests that would undercut Peru's price setting. *See* TALBOTT, *supra* note 155, at 41.

[198] *See* art. 4 of the 1874 Treaty and cl. 4 of the 1873 concession contract. *See* TALBOTT, *supra* note 155, at 43.

[199] *See* TALBOTT, *supra* note 155, at 37.

CHILE'S GEOSTRATEGIC CONCERN

Chile's attempts to accommodate Bolivia in the Atacama up to this time reflected geostrategic, not pan-Andean, concerns. A naval armament race with Peru and serious border disputes with Argentina made opening up a third foreign policy dispute with Bolivia unworkable.[200] But Chilean balance of power calculations changed with upgrades to its fleet, and although misconceived in terms of its naval preparedness at war's onset,[201] Chile quickly settled an outstanding border dispute with Argentina over Patagonia and the Straits of Magellan (the Fierro-Sarratea Treaty) in January 1879,[202] and turned full attention toward pressing Bolivia for an arbitral solution to the Atacama dispute, as required by the 1874 treaty.[203] Bolivia refused the request, effectively shut down concession operations, and issued an ultimatum, promising to expropriate the Antofagasta Railroad and Nitrate Company concession if the tax were not paid by February 14, 1879.[204] In a peremptory move, a Chilean militia of two hundred invaded the port of Antofagasta on that day, encountered no resistance from Bolivian gendarmes (who had retreated on orders of the prefect of the port), and immediately recruited a substantial number of disgruntled Chilean laborers as combatants from the overwhelming stock of Chilean nationals who had been put out of work by the *de facto* seizure of the concession.[205] Mediation efforts failed.[206] Bolivia declared war.[207] Aware of Peru's secret alliance with Bolivia, Chile demanded Peruvian neutrality

---

[200] Sater speculates that Bolivia's president, General Hilarión Daza, imposed the tax thinking the *Moneda* would be too preoccupied and "fearfully looking over its shoulder toward Argentina," thus affording Bolivia a propitious moment to levy the tax against Chile. SATER, ANDEAN TRAGEDY, *supra* note 141, at 55. *See also* FARCAU, THE TEN CENTS WAR, *supra* note 2, at 41 (discussing Daza's "serious miscalculation").

[201] *See* SATER, ANDEAN TRAGEDY, *supra* note 141, at 107 (describing Chile's navy at the outbreak of war as "in various states of disrepair").

[202] *See* BURR, *supra* note 130, at 135. The treaty ran into immediate problems regarding ratification in Buenos Aires. *See* George v. Rauch, CONFLICT IN THE SOUTHERN CONE: THE ARGENTINE MILITARY AND THE BOUNDARY DISPUTE WITH CHILE, 1870–1902, 167 (1999).

[203] *See* TALBOTT, *supra* note155, at 44.

[204] Before the decree was to take effect, Bolivia shut down operations of the company by preventing the loading of nitrates for export at the port, which caused massive unemployment among Chilean stevedores. Bolivia also ordered the arrest of the company's manager, who sought asylum aboard a Chilean warship menacingly anchored in Antofagasta's harbor, and ordered the seizure of 90,948 bolivianos and 13 centavos. *See id.* at 43–44. Chile dispatched two other warships in short order. *See* FARCAU, THE TEN CENTS WAR, *supra* note 2, at 42.

[205] *See* FARCAU, THE TEN CENTS WAR, *supra* note 2, at 42.

[206] *See* BURR, *supra* note 130, at 136.

[207] *See* SATER, CHILE AND THE WAR OF THE PACIFIC, *supra* note 4, at 9.

but Peru rejected the demand, and Chile declared war on both countries on April 5, 1879.[208]

A most interesting prelude to the War of the Pacific, an intrigue of such logical sense that Chile would propose it repeatedly during the war,[209] related to Chile's attempt to sever Bolivia from its long-standing relationship with Peru – to convert Bolivia into an ally – and to cement an irreparable division between Bolivia and Peru that would eliminate the threat of united opposition to Chile's north, cultivate Bolivia as an ally bordering Chile's nemesis to the east, Argentina, while at the same time substituting Bolivia not only as Peru's antagonistic neighbor to the south but as Chile's friendly buffer to the north.[210] To accomplish these objectives, Chile proposed exchanging Bolivian sovereignty in the Atacama between the 23rd and 24th parallels for Bolivian ownership over the coastal region of Arica above the Loa River – territory Chile did not own,[211] but would support Bolivia in securing.[212] This proposal sought to guarantee Bolivia its long sought after blue-water port, not at the remote and inaccessible Atacama sea outlets but at the much more proximate terminus at Arica. But Chile "could not cede what it [at that time] did not own," however appealing the thought of forcing "Peru to pay Chile's obligations."[213]

AFTERMATH AND THE FAILED PLEBISCITE

The War of the Pacific resulted in Chile's three-year occupation of Lima beginning in early 1881 and ultimately cost Peru its southernmost provinces, including the nitrate-rich provinces of Tarapacá and Arica.[214] The peace agreement reestablishing relations between Peru and Chile, the Treaty of Ancón, placed the provinces of Tacna and Arica under the control of Chile for ten years, after which the questions of dominium and sovereignty were to be put to a popular vote.[215] The plebiscite dashed Bolivian dreams of securing the port of Arica, "as Chile could not be expected to give Bolivia territory which would separate Tarapacá from the rest of Chile."[216] A "provision kept from the

---

[208] BURR, *supra* note 130, at 136; WILLIAM JEFFERSON DENNIS, TACNA AND ARICA: AN ACCOUNT OF THE CHILE-PERU BOUNDARY DISPUTE AND OF THE ARBITRATIONS BY THE UNITED STATES 80–81 (1931).

[209] *See* FARCAU, THE TEN CENTS WAR, *supra* note 2, at 36–37.

[210] *See* BURR, *supra* note 130, at 140–141.

[211] *See id.* at 141.

[212] *See* FARCAU, THE TEN CENTS WAR, *supra* note 2, at 37.

[213] SATER, CHILE AND THE WAR OF THE PACIFIC, *supra* note 4, at 224.

[214] Farcau estimates the Chilean conquest of the Atacama and Tarapacá regions garnered for Chile close to three billion pesos in nitrate exports within twenty years. *See* FARCAU, THE TEN CENTS WAR, *supra* note 2, at 194.

[215] *See* art. 3, Treaty of Ancón, *supra* note 7.

[216] ST. JOHN, BOUNDARIES, TRADE, AND SEAPORTS, *supra* note 15, at 15–16.

public at the time, prohibited the cession of any part of the territory in question to a third party [i.e., Bolivia] without the consent of the signatories ... a point of bitter frustration for Bolivia to this day."[217] This *jus prohibendi* provision negotiated bilaterally by Peru and Chile in the Treaty of Ancón worked against the interests of Bolivia in much the same way Chile and Bolivia used it to foreclose Peru's presence in the Atacama with the 1866 condominium agreement. And attempts to hold the plebiscite – a key feature of the peace agreement – met a fate similar to the quick demise of the condominium agreement, which was to be held ten years after the peace agreement had been concluded. Prior to the expiration of Chile's ten year control of Tacna and Arica, Chile fruitlessly attempted to purchase the territory in lump sum from Peru.[218] It then threatened the "Chileanization of the two provinces" through massive public works expenditures to entice twenty thousand Chilean citizens to the regions,[219] certainly with a mind toward determining the outcome of the required plebiscite. Such maneuvering stalled the plebiscite process. Attempts to hold the plebiscite involved three US administrations, a tortured series of negotiations, Coolidge's failed arbitration, and ultimately the repudiation of the promise to hold the plebiscite altogether.[220] The failure of this plebiscite – itself a failed *pactum de contrahendo* – complicated regional relations. It serves as a sly reminder of difficulties awaiting Bolivia in its quest to secure performance by Chile of an alleged *pactum* involving quite possibly the same disputed territory. Chile subsequently returned the province of Tacna in 1929, which now forms Peru's southernmost border with Chile and Bolivia, but it kept the port and province of Arica.[221] "[T]he only party

---

[217] Farcau, The Ten Cents War, *supra* note 2, at 198–199.

[218] Burr, *supra* note 130, at 180–181.

[219] *See id.* at 190; Alberto Díaz Araya, *Problemas y perspectivas sociohistóricas en el norte chileno: análisis sobre la "chilenización" de Tacna y Arica*, 5(4) Si Somos Americanos. Revista de Estudios Transfronterizos 49–81 (2014).

[220] A series of negotiations begun by the US Harding Administration led to failed arbitrations commencing in 1925 with US President Calvin Coolidge serving as arbitrator. This was followed by "Plebiscitary Commissioners" Generals John J. Pershing and William Lassiter in succession, which led to negotiations resulting in the treaty. *See* Dennis, *supra* note 208, at 225 and 282. Sater claims successive Chilean governments stalled and then refused to hold the plebiscite, fearful Peru would win. *See* Sater, Chile and the War of the Pacific, *supra* note 4, at 224. Ultimately, no plebiscite was held, and under the auspices of the US Hoover Administration, an agreement was reached: Tacna reverted to Peru; Arica, to Chile. *See* Farcau, The Ten Cents War, *supra* note 2, at 198.

[221] *See* art. 2, Treaty between Chile and Peru for the Settlement of the Dispute Regarding Tacna and Arica (the Treaty of Lima) and the Supplementary Protocol to the Treaty of Lima, both signed at Lima on 3 June 1929 (entry into force 28 July 1929) (Original in Spanish, French and English translations) 94 *League of Nations Treaty Series* 401, Annex 11,

that might have protested the Treaty" – Bolivia – "was allowed no role in the negotiations."[222]

The outcome for Bolivia was even more devastating. The war cost Bolivia 250 miles (400km) of its Pacific coastline – all of its coastline, in fact – including the province of Atacama, its largest port-city capital, Antofagasta, and its four other outlets to the ocean – Mejillones, Cobija, Huanillo, and Tocopilla; Bolivia lost one hundred and eight thousand square miles of mineral-rich land in the Atacama Desert (territory almost the size of Nevada), which Chile annexed. It altered collective memories as well as boundaries.[223] The defeat transformed Bolivians instantly into a nation of landlubbers. Its landlocked status weighs heavily on its national conscience and economy today,[224] and compels the Bolivian navy to maintain its fleet of ninety vessels, four thousand six hundred personnel, two thousand marines and naval aviation accompaniment in the brown water ports of Lake Titicaca and on other internal waterways[225] in wishful anticipation of a change in political fortune that will provide

---

www.icj-cij.org/docket/files/153/18616.pdf. Like the Treaty of Ancón, the supplementary protocol established a *jus prohibendi*, precluding Chile and Peru without previous agreement from ceding to any third power territories pertaining to the treaty (i.e., Tacna and Arica). *See id.*, art. 1, Supplementary Protocol. The maritime boundary implications of the Treaty of Lima later became an issue of dispute between the two countries, resulting in a partial delimitation by the I.C.J. in 2014. *See* Maritime Dispute (Peru v. Chile), Judgment, 2014 I.C.J. 3. The judgment retained the border for the first 80 miles offshore but partially redrew the demarcation thereafter, awarding to Peru more than half of the thirty-seven-thousand square miles it originally sought. *See* Adriana Leon and Chris Kraul, *Peru Wins Maritime Border Dispute with Chile over Key Fishing Grounds*, LA TIMES, Jan. 27, 2014, http://articles.latimes.com/2014/jan/27/world/la-fg-wn-peru-territorial-dispute-chile-20140127. The settlement of the maritime claim has been followed by yet another dispute over a 9-acre (37,610 sq. meter) "land triangle" in the La Yarada-Los Palos district of Tacna involving overlapping claims by Chile and Peru based on competing interpretations of the 1929 Treaty of Lima. *See Boundary Tensions between Peru and Chile Continue*, IBRU BOUNDARY NEWS, October 22, 2015, www.dur.ac.uk/ibru/news/boundary_news/?itemno=25974&rehref=%2Fibru%2Fnews%2F&resubj=Boundary+news+Headlines.

[222] Gordon, *supra* note 13, at 323.

[223] *See* SATER, ANDEAN TRAGEDY, *supra* note 141, at 1.

[224] *See* JONATHAN R. BARTON, A POLITICAL GEOGRAPHY OF LATIN AMERICA 65 (1997). Bolivia has indirect access to the Pacific and Atlantic Oceans via Chile, Peru, Paraguay, and Brazil; most exports and imports go through the Chilean ports of Antofagasta and Arica on the Pacific, as well as through the Peruvian ports of Ilo, Mollendo, Tachna, and Matarini (via Brazil's ports of Belem and Santos). *See* Daniel Arthur McCray, Eternal Ramifications of the War of the Pacific 4 (thesis, University of Florida, 2005), http://etd.fcla.edu/UF/UFE0009403/mccray_d.pdf.

[225] *See* ERIC WERTHEIM, THE NAVAL INSTITUTE GUIDE TO COMBAT FLEETS OF THE WORLD, 16TH EDITION, THEIR SHIPS, AIRCRAFT, AND SYSTEMS 52 (Naval Institute Press, Annapolis, 2013). Deprived of a coast to protect, the *Armada Boliviana* patrols ten thousand miles of internal waterways, principally three internal basins, including the Amazon basin, involving the Ichilo, Mamore Itenez, Yacuma, Orthon, Abuna, Beni, and Madre de Dios rivers, the central basin, comprising Lake

pelagic purpose to its admiralty. Ironically, Bolivia did not even have a navy to deploy during the War of the Pacific[226] (the *Armada Boliviana* was founded in 1963[227]); it offered instead Letters of Marque and Reprisal to hire privateers to cruise against the Chileans.[228] The plan failed, leaving its ally, Peru, to battle the Chilean ironclads alone,[229] which it did until Chile destroyed Peru's armada in early 1881.[230]

The annexation secured for Chile a monopoly over the world's supply of nitrates, a commodity as valuable then as oil is today. Nitrates were essential to the manufacture of gunpowder and made more lucrative because of a new use for it found by Alfred Nobel in 1867: dynamite.[231] Overall, the war increased the size of Chile by one-third,[232] and the Atacama would later reveal repositories of some of the world's richest copper deposits.[233]

Titicaca, and the Del Plata basin, including the Paraguay and Bermejo rivers. Advanced sea training is carried out in Argentina and Peru, which, pursuant to a 2010 agreement between the Presidents of Peru and Bolivia, granted Bolivia permission to construct and operate a small port near the Peruvian port of Ilo. *See* STEPHEN SAUNDERS, HIS JANE'S FIGHTING SHIPS 2014–2015 (116th rev. edn., 2014), 68–69.

[226] *See* Farcau, *War of the Pacific (1879–1883)*, *supra* note 11, at 1625.

[227] *See* SAUNDERS, *supra* note 225, at 68.

[228] Letters of Marque vexed international relations at sea for centuries, due to their loose supervision. The practice was outlawed only among signatories by the 1856 Paris Declaration, which Bolivia refused to sign. For the text of the Declaration, *see* *1856 Paris Declaration Respecting Maritime Law*, *in* THE LAW OF NAVAL WARFARE: A COLLECTION OF AGREEMENTS AND DOCUMENTS WITH COMMENTARIES 61 (Natalino Ronzitti ed., 1988); for a discussion of its abuse, *see* Todd Emerson Hutchins, *Structuring a Sustainable Letters of Marque Regime: How Commissioning Privateers Can Defeat the Somali Pirates*, 99 CAL. L. REV. 819, 855 (2011).

[229] For a comparison of Chilean and Peruvian navies during the War of the Pacific, *see* SATER, ANDEAN TRAGEDY, *supra* 141, at 96–116.

[230] For a description of the naval encounters during the War of the Pacific, encounters that demonstrated effective use of contact mines, torpedoes, and submarines, *see id.* at 117–169.

[231] *See* STEPHEN R. BROWN, A MOST DAMNABLE INVENTION: DYNAMITE, NITRATES, AND THE MAKING OF THE MODERN WORLD 4 (2005) (comparing nitrate's value to oil's twenty-first-century value); *id.* at 162 (noting Chile's virtual control over the entire global supply of industrial-scale commercial nitrates on the cusp of the world's greatest increase in demand); *id.* at 82 (discussing demand for dynamite immediately following its invention).

[232] *See* SATER, CHILE AND THE WAR OF THE PACIFIC, *supra* note 4, at 1–2.

[233] *See* SATER, ANDEAN TRAGEDY, *supra* note 141, at 1 (2007). Bolivia's Minister of Foreign Affairs estimated Chile earned more than 900 billion USD in copper exports from the Atacama since 1883. *Lo que gana Chile y pierde Bolivia por no tener acceso al mar*, CORREO DEL SUR (May 6, 2015), www.correodelsur.com/politica/20150506_lo-que-gana-chile-y-pierde-bolivia-por-no-tener-acceso-al-mar-.html (quoting David Choquehuanca). Chile produces almost a third of the world's copper; the vast majority of that copper comes from the Collahuasi, Chuquicamata and Radomiro Tomic, Escondida, and Los Pelambres mining operations in the Atacama. *See* Christopher Woody, *Chile and Bolivia are Still Arguing Over the Outcome of a War They Fought 131 Years Ago*, BUSINESS INSIDER (Oct. 4, 2015), www.businessinsider.com/chile-bolivia-sea-access-land-dispute-2015-10.

Bolivia signed an armistice – the Truce Pact – on April 4, 1884.[234] Pending a final settlement, Chile retained territories from the 23rd parallel South to the mouth of the Loa River (at the 21st parallel South).[235] Commercial relations and customs exemptions for natural products were reestablished, with Bolivia receiving free transit for goods introduced via the port of Antofagasta.[236] Bolivia received port access to Arica, but with conditions attached until outstanding obligations to Chile were satisfied, after which, Bolivia would be able to establish its own internal customs office, allowing foreign goods to transit freely through Arica.[237]

The 1904 Peace Treaty reestablished peaceful relations between Bolivia and Chile.[238] Bolivia recognized Chilean sovereignty over coastal territory that had been Bolivian.[239] Chile granted Bolivia in perpetuity a right of commercial free transit to the Pacific and at Chilean ports,[240] together with the right to establish Bolivian customs posts at Chilean ports.[241] Chile also agreed to build and pay for a railway from Arica (Chile's northernmost port) to the plateau of La Paz,[242] to guarantee obligations incurred by Bolivia to attract railway investment, to settle debts associated with coastal territory that had been Bolivian, and to make a substantial cash payment to Bolivia.[243]

But the 1904 Treaty cemented the loss of the Atacama Desert, psychologically scarring Bolivia's national identity.[244] It came on the heels of a rebellion that forced Bolivia to cede the southeast rubber-rich Acre region to Brazil (Treaty of Petropólis, 1903). Three decades later, Bolivia clashed with Paraguay over control of the oil-rich Gran Chaco region; the war lasted from 1932 to 1935, contained Bolivian elements of an unrealistic dream to access the Atlantic Ocean via the Paraguay River,[245] claimed one hundred thousand lives, wounded one hundred and fifty thousand, and became the bloodiest war in modern Latin American history and the bloodiest hemispheric war since the US Civil War.[246] It officially concluded with the Treaty of Buenos Aires (1938), which awarded

---

[234] *See supra* note 7.
[235] *See id.* art. 2.
[236] *See id.* art. 5.
[237] *See id.* art. 6.
[238] *See* 1904 Peace Treaty, *supra* note 6.
[239] *See id.* art. II.
[240] *See id.* art. VI.
[241] *See id.* art. VII.
[242] *See id.* art. III.
[243] *See id.* arts. III, V, and IV.
[244] Mesa Gisbert, *supra* note 40, at 242 (declaring: "El mar se convirtió en el gran cohesionador spiritual del país" and the loss of access to it "Un Tatuaje en el alma de Bolivia").
[245] *See* FARCAU, THE TEN CENTS WAR, *supra* note 2, at 194–195.
[246] *See* BRUCE W. FARCAU, THE CHACO WAR: BOLIVIA AND PARAGUAY, 1932–1935, ix (1996) (noting one hundred thousand men killed out of a total combined population of less than five million);

twenty thousand square miles of oil and gas fields to Paraguay.[247] Bolivia has disputed boundaries with all of its neighbors and it has lost most, if not all, of its disputes.[248] But the focal point of its foreign policy and national identity distills to the loss of the Atacama and the corridor it once provided to the sea.[249] It serves as a constant historical reminder of the poverty of the doctrine of *uti possidetis* despite its necessity, and the limited utility of competing historical narratives based on factual circumstances. These narratives tend to rely on evidence scattered along a historical arc of parochialism, confusion, and indeterminacy, voluminous in quantity but sparse in useful content.[250] Reliance on competing pre- and postcolonial narratives form part of Bolivia's case before the ICJ.[251] But the turbulent yet unavoidable history of *uti possidetis* suggests that the re-vindication of Bolivia's interests will follow a different legal route – a route alternatively informed by the application of *pacta de contrahendo* or *negotiando*, or a claim involving legal consequences associated with Chilean declarations.

BOLIVIA'S APPEAL TO ACCUMULATIVE EVIDENCE AND JUDGE GREENWOOD'S QUESTION

During oral proceedings, Judge Christopher Greenwood posed the following question to Bolivia's lawyers: "On what date does Bolivia maintain that an agreement

William R. Garner, The Chaco Dispute: A Study of Prestige Diplomacy 107 (1966) (citing fifty-five thousand Bolivian deaths and eighty-three thousand injured and forty-five thousand Paraguayan deaths and sixty-seven thousand injured); Paul H. Lewis, *Paraguay since 1930*, in 8 CAMBRIDGE HISTORY OF LATIN AMERICA 233, 234 (Leslie Bethell, ed., 1991) (declaring the Chaco War the "bloodiest war in Latin American history"); DAVID H. ZOOK, JR., THE CONDUCT OF THE CHACO WAR 23 (1960) (labeling it "the hemisphere's greatest struggle since the American Civil War).

[247] http://opinionator.blogs.nytimes.com/2012/04/03/how-bolivia-lost-its-hat/?_r=0.

[248] Bolivia unquestionably lost the War of the Pacific against Chile, the Acre War against Brazil, and the Chaco War against Paraguay; its defeat along with Peru in the War of the Confederation involved a coalition of opposing forces that included Chileans, Peruvians, and Argentines.

[249] *See* David Choquehuanca Céspedes, Minister of Foreign Affairs of Bolivia, EL LIBRO DEL MAR, *supra* note 49, at 19 ("Ninguna controversia internacional o conflagración bélica que afrontó Bolivia en su historia ocasionó una pérdida tan importante como la Guerra del Pacífico."); MESA GISBERT, *supra* note 40, at 242 ("Es que ni en el Acre ni en el Chaco habíamos perdido nuestra cualidad y acceso a las cuencas del Amazonas y del Plata, en cambio en la Guerra con Chile perdimos la cualidad marítima y el acceso a la Cuenca de Pacífico, cuya importancia es central en la economía mundial del siglo XXI").

[250] Award of the Arbitral Tribunal in the First Stage of Proceedings between Eritrea and Yemen (Territorial Sovereignty and Scope of the Dispute) (Eritrea v. Yemen), P.C.A. 1998, XXII R.I.A.A. ¶ 239, 268 (Oct. 9).

[251] Documents prepared and submitted to the I.C.J. postdate and predate Bolivia's independence from Spain, and date to ancient times and the connections of the Tiwanaku and Aymara peoples to contemporary Bolivia. Examples of Bolivia's historical account are contained in EL LIBRO DEL MAR, *supra* note 49, 23–33.

to negotiate sovereign access was concluded?"[252] Unlike the argument of Chile's counsel, who emphasized a need to show when the obligation crystallized,[253] Boliva's counsel pointed to an "accumulation of successive acts by Chile,"[254] arguing that no principal of international law requires a "magical moment when agreements or understandings appear out of nothingness, like the story of creation."[255]

Bolivia's appeal to the accumulative evidence implies a reliance on historical evidence dating to colonial rule, but centers on affirmations by Chilean officials, noting, the "particularly important" Treaty on the Transfer of Territories of May 18, 1895,[256] its protocol,[257] and a litany of subsequent official pronouncements.[258] With the 1895 Transfer of Territories document, Chile pledged to acquire dominion over Tacna and Arica and to "transfer them to" Bolivia by way of compensation of five million silver pesos.[259] Failing

---

[252] Public sitting held on Wednesday 6 May 2015, at 10 a.m., at the Peace Palace, President Abraham presiding, in the case concerning Obligation to Negotiate Access to the Pacific Ocean (Bolivia v. Chile), Preliminary Objection, Verbatim Record, CR 2015/19, ¶ 31, 60 (question of Judge Greenwood)

[253] Public sitting held on Thursday 7 May 2015, at 4.30 p.m., at the Peace Palace, President Abraham presiding, in the case concerning Obligation to Negotiate Access to the Pacific Ocean (Bolivia v. Chile), Preliminary Objection, Verbatim Record, CR 2015/20, ¶ 4, 32 (mentioning the need for a crystallization of the obligation: "Mais alors, de cet engagement,on ne sait toujours pas davantage à partir de quel moment ses différents éléments constitutifs sont réputés avoir atteint la phase de cristallisation nécessaire à la formation d'une obligation juridique, au-delà de simples pourparlers diplomatiques?") (M. Dupuy).

[254] Public sitting held on Friday 8 May 2015, at 3 p.m., at the Peace Palace, President Abraham presiding, in the case concerning Obligation to Negotiate Access to the Pacific Ocean (Bolivia v. Chile) Preliminary Objection, Verbatim Record, CR 2015/21, ¶ 9, 34 (Mr. Akhavan).

[255] *Id.* at ¶ 9, 33 (Mr. Akhavan). But *see* J. Klabbers & R. Lefeber, *supra* note 121 at 568 (1993) (discussing *uti possidetis*' immediate application, thus freezing territorial title at the critical date of independence); and Frontier Dispute, Judgment, I.C.J. ¶ 30, 568 (describing *uti possidetis* as "photographing" the territorial situation; "freez[ing]" territorial title"; and "stop[ping] the clock" but not putting back the hands). Bolivia's rejection of a "magical moment" signifying the crystallization of its claim distinguishes its argument from other examples involving the binding effect of unilateral declarations.

[256] Treaty on Transfer of Territory between Bolivia and Chile, signed at Santiago on 18 May 1895 (the 1895 Treaty) (Spanish transcription, English translation, original in Spanish). Original submitted by Bolivia as Annex 98 to its Memorial, Annex 3, 91 www.icj-cij.org/docket/files/153/18616.pdf.

[257] Protocol of 9 December 1895 on the scope of the obligations agreed upon in the treaties of 18 May between Bolivia and Chile, signed at Sucre on 9 December 1895 (the December 1895 Protocol) (Original in Spanish, English translation), Annex 4, 107 (binding Chile to "make use of all legal measures ... so as to acquire the port and territories of Arica and Tacna, with the unavoidable purpose of ceding them to Bolivia"), www.icj-cij.org/docket/files/153/18616.pdf.

[258] *See* EL LIBRO DEL MAR, *supra* note 49, 53–64 (cataloging Bolivian claims regarding Chilean presidents, foreign ministers, and ambassadors who undertook to negotiate a sovereign access to the sea with Bolivia).

[259] *See* Treaty on Transfer, *supra* note 256 (noting in the preamble agreement between Chile and Bolivia "that a higher need and the future development and commercial prosperity of Bolivia

that acquisition, Article 4 of the protocol recorded that "the said obligation undertaken by Chile will not be regarded as fulfilled, until it cedes a port and zone that fully satisfies the current and future needs of Bolivian trade and industry."[260] Although the agreements were signed, both states failed to approve the protocols. And in an 1896 exchange of notes, both countries agreed they were "wholly without effect."[261]

In 1910, Bolivian Foreign Minister Daniel Sánchez Bustamante restated the logic and justice of establishing an ocean passageway through Arica;[262] he noted Chile and Peru "should no longer be neighboring countries" and that Bolivia more properly should be the territorial sovereign of an intermediate buffer zone (containing "at least one convenient port") for the stability of Hispanic-American nations.[263] He later wrote Arica was "the natural port of Bolivia."[264] Bolivia claimed this memorandum reaffirmed expectations of a title transfer that had been created by Chile, which had survived the conclusion of the 1904 Peace Treaty.[265] A 1920 protocol signed by Bolivian and Chilean Foreign Ministers "agreed to ... exchange general ideas" and acknowledged "the aim of reaching an agreement pursuant to which Bolivia could satisfy its aspiration of obtaining its own access to the Pacific [independent of the 1904 Peace

---

require its free and natural access to the sea," and in art. 1 that if Chile acquired dominion over Tachna and Arica through a plebiscite, "it undertakes to transfer them to ... Bolivia" in return for compensation).

[260] Art. 4, Protocol of 9 December 1895 on the scope of the obligations agreed upon in the treaties of 18 May between Bolivia and Chile, signed at Sucre on 9 December 1895 (the December 1895 Protocol) (Original in Spanish, English translation), Annex 4, 105, 108 www.icj-cij.org/docket/files/153/18616.pdf (mentioning specifically the small port of Vitor or an analogous inlet).

[261] Note from Adolfo Guerrero, Minister of Foreign Affairs of Chile, to Heriberto Gutiérrez, Extraordinary Envoy and Minister Plenipotentiary of Bolivia in Chile, No 521, 29 April 1896 (Original in Spanish, English translation), Annex 6, 115; Note from Heriberto Gutiérrez, Extraordinary Envoy and Minister Plenipotentiary of Bolivia in Chile, to Adolfo Guerrero, Minister of Foreign Affairs of Chile, No 118, 30 April 1896 (Original in Spanish, English translation), Annex 7, 119, www.icj-cij.org/docket/files/153/18616.pdf.

[262] Memorandum from the Minister of Foreign Affairs of Bolivia, Daniel Sánchez Bustamante, 22 April 1910, Annex 8, at 42, International Court of Justice Application Instituting Proceedings filed in the Registry of the Court on 24 April 2013, Obligation to Negotiate Access to the Pacific Ocean (Bolivia v. Chile), www.icj-cij.org/docket/files/153/17338.pdf.

[263] Id.

[264] José E. Pradel B., *Daniel Sánchez Bustamante y el Memorándum de 1910*, EL DIARIO NUEVOS HORIZONTES (Nov. 4, 2014), www.eldiario.net/noticias/2014/2014_11/nt141104/nuevoshorizontes .php?n=5&-daniel-sanchez-bustamante-y-el-memorandum-de-1910 (noting the memorandum demostraba además la vinculación real del Puerto de Arica con Bolivia and that "Arica, siendo como es el puerto natural de Bolivia, y solo de Bolivia").

[265] International Court of Justice Application Instituting Proceedings filed in the Registry of the Court on 24 April 2013, Obligation to Negotiate Access to the Pacific Ocean (Bolivia v. Chile), ¶ 17, 14, www.icj-cij.org/docket/files/153/17338.pdf.

Treaty];" Article IV read: "Chile is willing to ensure that Bolivia acquires its own access to the sea, by ceding an important part of that area north of Arica and of the railway line that is located in the territories that are the object of the plebiscite provided for in the Treaty of Ancón."[266] Bolivia later claimed in a 1950 Exchange of Notes (reaffirmed in a memorandum in 1961[267]) that this 1920 *Acta Protocolizada* represented Chile's acceptance of the transfer to Bolivia of access to the Pacific Ocean, along with the "clear direction" of Chile's international policy.[268] The Chilean Foreign Ministry note indicated that Chile "has been willing to consider, in direct negotiations with Bolivia, the possibility of satisfying" Bolivia's aspirations and, in a spirit of fraternal friendship, "is willing to formally enter into a direct negotiation aimed at finding the formula which would make it possible to grant Bolivia its own and sovereign access to the Pacific and for Chile to obtain compensations that are not of a territorial nature."[269] This latter expression appears to be the sturdiest of the wet reeds on which leans Bolivia's *pactum de contrahendo* argument.

Bolivia has recounted numerous attempts over the last century to demonstrate Chile's intent to negotiate a sovereign access, but many of them seem to blur the distinction between a duty to negotiate and a duty to agree. In 1926, for instance, US Secretary of State Frank B. Kellogg fielded an inquiry from Chilean Ambassador to Washington, Miguel Cruchaga, about the prospect of ceding Tacna to Peru, Arica to Chile, and a four-kilometer wide corridor between Arica and Los Palos, Peru, to Bolivia.[270] Shortly after, Kellogg delivered to Chile and Peru a memorandum in 1926 offering the good offices of

[266] Protocol ("*Acta Protocolizada*") Subscribed between the Foreign Affairs Minister of Bolivia, Carlos Gutiérrez, and the Extraordinary Envoy and Plenipotentiary Minister of the Republic of Chile, Emilio Bello Codesido, 10 January 1920, Annex 9, at 44, International Court of Justice Application Instituting Proceedings filed in the Registry of the Court on 24 April 2013, Obligation to Negotiate Access to the Pacific Ocean (Bolivia v. Chile), www.icj-cij.org/docket/files/153/17338.pdf.

[267] See Memorandum from the Embassy of Chile in La Paz, 10 July 1961, Annex 12, at 50, International Court of Justice Application Instituting Proceedings filed in the Registry of the Court on 24 April 2013, Obligation to Negotiate Access to the Pacific Ocean (Bolivia v. Chile), www.icj-cij.org/docket/files/153/17338.pdf.

[268] See Note of 1 June 1950 from the Ambassador of Bolivia to the Minister of Foreign Affairs of Chile [Alberto Ostria Gutiérrez], Annex 10, at 46, International Court of Justice Application Instituting Proceedings filed in the Registry of the Court on 24 April 2013, Obligation to Negotiate Access to the Pacific Ocean (Bolivia v. Chile), www.icj-cij.org/docket/files/153/17338.pdf.

[269] Note of 20 June 1950 from the Minister of Foreign Affairs of Chile to the Ambassador of Bolivia [Horacio Walker Larraín], Annex 11, at 48, International Court of Justice Application Instituting Proceedings filed in the Registry of the Court on 24 April 2013, Obligation to Negotiate Access to the Pacific Ocean (Bolivia v. Chile), www.icj-cij.org/docket/files/153/17338.pdf.

[270] See EL LIBRO DEL MAR, *supra* note 49, at 38.

the United States to help find a solution to the stalled plebiscite disposition of Tacna and Arica. Of the three possible dispositions of the *res* contemplated – assign it to one or the other; divide it; or "effect some arrangement whereby neither contestant shall get any of the territory" – only the third option contained the essential element of compromise that made sense to him; he suggested the voluntary but compensated ceding of the provinces of Tacna and Arica to Bolivia.[271] Bolivia claims Chilean Foreign Minister Jorge Matte confirmed Chile's willingness to grant a strip of territory and a port to Bolivia once the definitive possession of Tacna and Arica was clarified.[272] In fact, Matte wrote, "the Chilean Government would honor its declarations in regard to the consideration of Bolivian aspirations," but he declared that Kellogg's suggestion "goes much farther than the concessions which the Chilean Government has generously been able to make."[273]

In 1975 Chilean leader Augusto Pinochet and Bolivian President Hugo Banzer met in the Bolivian border town of Charaña, where Pinochet offered Bolivia a small strip of demilitarized land between Arica and the Peruvian border (extending into the territorial sea) in exchange for equivalent territorial compensation taken from the Bolivian *Altiplano*.[274]

Bolivia reconsidered and ultimately balked at the idea of further relinquishing land to obtain territory improperly seized to begin with.[275] Additionally, the *jus prohibendi* provision in the 1929 Treaty of Lima required Peruvian consent, which was not given.[276] Peru President General Francisco Morales Bermúdez offered in 1976 a counterproposal: a zone of tripartite sovereigns between the city of Arica and the Peruvian border, "with Bolivia receiving a corridor feeding into this zone." Peru's plan masterfully reinserted its parochial interests into the buffer zone while offering "Bolivia at least as much as the Chileans

---

[271] Frank B. Kellogg, *Tacna-Arica*. Advocate of Peace through Justice 55, 56 and 57 (1927).

[272] El Libro del Mar, *supra* note 49, at 39.

[273] Memorandum issued by the Chancellor of Chile Jorge Matte to the Secretary of State Frank B. Kellogg of 4 December 1926, Annex 8, El Libro del Mar, *supra* note 49, at 120.

[274] See Note No. 686 of 19 December 1975 to the Ambassador of Bolivia from the Minister of Foreign Affairs of Chile [Patricio Carvajal Prado], Annex 14, at 54, International Court of Justice Application Instituting Proceedings filed in the Registry of the Court on 24 April 2013, Obligation to Negotiate Access to the Pacific Ocean (Bolivia v. Chile), www.icj-cij.org/docket/files/153/17338.pdf ("Chile would be prepared to negotiate with Bolivia the cession of a strip of land north of Arica up to the *Línea de la Concordia*"). The Chilean plan also demanded recognition of Chile's right to use the Rio Lauca. See Gordon, *supra* note 13, at 325. The I.C.J. recognized these negotiations in a separate case before the I.C.J. involving a maritime delimitation dispute between Chile and Peru. See Maritime Dispute (Peru v. Chile), ¶¶ 131–133.

[275] See St. John, *supra* note 142, at 94–95.

[276] See *id.* at 95.

had."[277] Chile regarded the trilateral economic development of the territory an undue complication and rejected the proposal.[278] Citing Chile's lack of sincerity, Bolivia broke diplomatic relations in March 1978,[279] and the diplomatic impasse remains to this date.

Attempts to resolve this dispute have historically oscillated between bilateral and trilateral negotiations, but Bolivia also has attempted periodically to internationalize the discussion. It sought a revision of the 1904 Peace Treaty through an appeal to the League of Nations in 1920,[280] which declared the complaint inadmissible because the League Assembly lacked capacity to modify any treaty.[281] It approached the Non-Aligned movement,[282] and the Organization of American States, first in 1962 by linking the Lauca River issue to access to the sea,[283] then on the occasion of the hundredth anniversary of the War of the Pacific in 1979,[284] and periodically thereafter. The OAS has approved resolutions encouraging the parties to find a "formula for giving Bolivia a sovereign outlet to the Pacific Ocean" while taking account of the rights and interests of all parties involved.[285] It also has appealed to the United Nations and to potential international mediators such as Jimmy Carter

---

[277] Gordon, *supra* note 13, at 325.

[278] *See* St. John, *supra* note 142, at 94–96.

[279] *See* Gordon, *supra* note 13, at 327.

[280] Letter from the Delegates of Bolivia to the League of Nations to James Eric Drummond, Secretary-General of the League of Nations, 1 November 1920 (Original in Spanish, English translation), Bolivia, Ministry of Foreign Affairs, Report of the Minister of Foreign Affairs to the Ordinary Congress (1921), 514–515, reprinted in 2 Obligation to Negotiate Access to the Pacific Ocean (Bolivia v. Chile) (Annexes 14–46), Annex 37, 577 www.icj-cij.org/docket/files/153/18618.pdf. *See* Figueroa, *supra* note 33, 43–58 (discussing Bolivia's efforts to secure a review by the League of Nations).

[281] League of Nations, Report of the Commission of Jurists on the Complaints of Peru and Bolivia, 21 September 1921 (extract) (Original in Spanish, English translation), Chile, Ministry of Foreign Affairs, Report of the Minister of Foreign Affairs to the National Congress (1924), 439–440, reprinted in 2 Obligation to Negotiate Access to the Pacific Ocean (Bolivia v. Chile) (Annexes 14–46), Annex 39, 589, www.icj-cij.org/docket/files/153/18618.pdf.

[282] *See* Figueroa, *supra* note 33, at 144.

[283] *See* Wehner, *supra* note 19, at 11 (discussing Bolivia's OAS claim linking the 1962 Lauca River dispute with Chile to the question of its access to the sea).

[284] AG/Res. 426, Access by Bolivia to the Pacific Ocean (Resolution adopted at the twelfth plenary session held on October 31, 1979), 1 OEA/Ser.P/IX.o.2, 2 July 1980, p. 55, www.oas.org/en/sla/docs/ago3793E01.pdf (calling for an equitable solution "for the purpose of providing Bolivia with a free and sovereign territorial connection with the Pacific Ocean" taking into account the rights and interest of the parties involved as well as the Bolivian proposal that no territorial compensation be included).

[285] 2, AG/RES. 686 (XIII-0/83), Report on the Maritime Problem of Bolivia (Resolution adopted at the seventh plenary session, held on November 18, 1983), 1 OEA/Ser.P/XIII.o.2, 14 December 1983, p. 100, www.oas.org/en/sla/docs/ago3797E01.pdf. *See also* AG/Res. 560 (XI-0/81), Report on the Maritime Problem of Bolivia (Resolution adopted at the eighth plenary session, held

and Kofi Annan.[286] The parties returned to numerous bilateral meetings in Uruguay (the Fresh Approach meetings, 1986–1987), at the XIII Ibero-American Summit in Bolivia (2003), at the Monterrey Summit of the Americas (2004), and on four occasions in 2005 (New York, Salamanca, Mar del Plata, and Montevideo).[287] During the Sixty-Seventh Session of the United Nations General Assembly in 2012, Bolivia affirmed that bilateral options remained open with Chile;[288] Chile responded by declaring Bolivia "lacks any legal basis for claiming a sovereign access to the Pacific Ocean by territories belonging to Chile,"[289] a claim repeated in 2012,[290] prompting Bolivia to bring the case before the ICJ.[291]

CONCLUSION

Should the case result in a judgment on the merits, the determination of the substantive law relating to the duty to negotiate presents many challenges for the ICJ and the parties. Outcomes appear less than satisfying: a finding that a *pactum de contrahendo* exists, based on the unilateral or repeated declarations of Chilean authorities, would compel the parties to return to diplomacy to

---

on December 10, 1981), 1 OE/Ser. P/XI.0.2, 24 June 1982, p. 95, www.oas.org/en/sla/docs/ago3795E01.pdf; and AG/Res. 481 (X-0/80), The Bolivian Maritime Problem (Resolution adopted at the sixth plenary session, held on November 27, 1980), p. 28, www.oas.org/en/sla/docs/ago3794E01.pdf.

[286] *See* Wehner, *supra* note 19, at 16.

[287] *See* EL LIBRO DEL MAR, *supra* note 49, 47–50.

[288] *See* Speech by the President of the Plurinational State of Bolivia, Mr. Evo Morales Ayma, on the occasion of the 13th plenary meeting of the Sixty-Sixth Session of the UN General Assembly, 21 September 2011, UN doc. A/66/PV.13, *available at* http://gadebate.un.org/66/bolivia-plurinational-state (claiming to "keep bilateral channels of negotiation open with Chile"). *See also* H.E. Mr. Evo Morales Ayma, President, speech of 26 September 2012 (67th Session), General Assembly of the United Nations, *available at* http://gadebate.un.org/node/396 (addressing Bolivia's right to Chile's return of its coastline).

[289] Declaración del Ministerio de Relaciones Exteriores de Chile sobre la entrega de una nota por parte de Bolivia a la Corte Internacional de Justicia, Sala de Prensa, Ministerio de Relaciones Exteriores de Chile, July 12, 2011, www.minrel.gob.cl/prontus_minrel/site/artic/20110712/pags/20110712144736.php ("Bolivia carece de todo fundamento jurídico para reclamar un acceso soberano al Océano Pacífico por territorios que pertenecen a Chile. Los límites entre Chile y Bolivia fueron establecidos con precisión hace más de 100 años, en el Tratado de Paz y Amistad de 1904, el cual es reconocido y respetado por ambos países y se encuentra plenamente vigente").

[290] *See* Speech by the Minister of Foreign Affairs of Chile, Mr. Alfredo Moreno Charme, during the 15th plenary meeting of the Sixty-Seventh Session of the UN General Assembly, 28 September 2012, UN doc. A/67/PV.15, 37 at 41, *available at* www.un.org/ga/search/view_doc.asp?symbol=A/67/PV.15 (categorically rejecting Bolivia's claim of an outstanding border issue).

[291] Obligation to Negotiate Access, Preliminary Objection, *supra* note 5, 47, 18.

find the specific modalities for a solution. Absent a timetable and conditioned only by the difficult-to-measure duty to negotiate in good faith, a Bolivian victory may result in a Pyrrhic victory. Similarly, a finding that a *pactum de negotiando* exists may only extend the rhetorical torpor that prompted Bolivia to seek third-party resolution – consigning all parties once again to the diplomatic *pergatorium* that has afflicted these Andean coastal countries since the War of the Pacific. A finding that Chile has been negotiating in bad faith institutionally presents the Court with the loathsome prospect of invalidating peace treaties, thereby opening up the prospect of another dispute involving redrawing boundary lines in the region. Were Bolivia to secure an outcome favorable to its Pacific coastline desires, it would be left to reconcile the economic equations of its geostrategic predicament and the attending costs of connecting, operationalizing, and developing additional infrastructure between the coast and its commercial centers on the *Altiplano*. A close look at Chile's less than clean hands also would probably prompt a judicial reconsideration of Bolivia's historical record, including its rescission of the 1866 condominium agreement and the double-dealing of the Melgarejo dictatorship, its imposition of the illegal ten cents tax, its refusal to arbitrate as required by the 1874 Boundary Treaty, and its nineteenth-century rejection of efforts to reinstate the condominium agreement. A finding that neither *pactum* exists would restate the status quo and underscore the realities of Chile's dominion over territory won in a war fought one hundred and thirty-five years ago. It would blunt the equitable momentum Bolivia has been able to muster within the OAS and elsewhere but also could radicalize regional relations demarcated already along radical/liberal and indigenous/postcolonial fault lines.[292] A judgment favoring Chile would underscore a primordial feature of territorial temptation: sentiments of comity and conscience do not motivate states to cede sovereignty. Chile negotiated a return of Tacna to Peru but in exchange secured Arica and its key port, and the fulfilment of its international legal obligation created by the *pactum de contrahendo* of the 1883 Treaty of Ancón. It also secured a *jus prohibendi* agreement with Peru regarding any future disposition of the territory. Most important, it secured for Chile a Peruvian sense of satisfaction. Peru long ago stopped refighting the War of the Pacific – and this dividend also remunerates Chile. That Chile historically has been willing to negotiate and accommodate a Bolivian access to the sea can signify Chile's

[292] *See generally* Steve Ellner, *Introduction: Latin America's Radical Left in Power: Complexities and Challenges in the Twenty-first Century*, 40(3) Latin American Perspectives 5–25 (2013); *South America's New Caudillos: Evo Morales of Bolivia and Democracy*, N.Y. Times (Oct. 16, 2014), www.nytimes.com/2014/10/17/opinion/evo-morales-of-bolivia-and-democracy .html?_r=0.

bona fides in attempting a regional accord as much as it can signify Chile's elaborate ruse to forestall good faith negotiations. But it is not clear Bolivian internal politics can accommodate this interpretation.

The more obvious path to an accord would require all parties to identify with the dissatisfaction of the existing situation and the poverty of seeking a resolution of this dispute inside the formal strictures of a third-party dispute settlement forum. That formal pathway to shaping a solution in many ways seems inferior to the social interactions constructed by other, informal or less formal, pathways to international law creation. In this constructivist sense, despite the perils it may invite, a ruling establishing a *pactum de negotiando* could support and enhance notable efforts crafted by the parties, efforts that may reflect a more meaningful pathway simply by not interfering with the parties' intersubjective determination of what exactly constitutes a sovereign access to the sea.

That phrase itself is oblique. As noted by Judge Owada, the phrase is "not a term of art in general international law," despite its usage by both sides in oral and written proceedings.[293] One should not presume that the language of international law is necessarily informing the outcome or the parameters of this case; rather, it would appear the social and diplomatic interactions of the parties could possibly affect the *legalect* of international law.

The legalect of this case, perhaps unself-consciously, has been informed by the parties, notwithstanding the "lengthy and convoluted nature of the Bolivia-Chile-Peru dispute."[294] A litany of creative, if forestalled, proposals creates modalities for an accord or future negotiations, including: an 1866 condominium-like arrangement based on a zone of tripartite occupation as suggested by Peru's President Morales in 1976; territorial concessions linked to resource exchanges, such as Bolivian liquefied natural gas production to supplement Chile's and Peru's energy needs in exchange for territorial concessions linked to maritime zones or riparian issues; territorial swaps as proposed by Chile during the Charaña discussions, then by Peru; special territorial corridors or shared sovereignty over ports as contemplated by Coolidge in the *Tacna-Arica Arbitration*; development of a Free City zone as contemplated by the 1866 condominium arrangement and US Secretary of State Kellogg;

[293] Public sitting held on Friday 8 May 2015, at 3 p.m., at the Peace Palace, President Abraham presiding, in the case concerning Obligation to Negotiate Access to the Pacific Ocean (Bolivia v. Chile), Preliminary Objection, Verbatim Record, CR 2015/21, at 38 (Judge Owada).
[294] APPROACHES TO SOLVING TERRITORIAL CONFLICTS: SOURCES, SITUATIONS, SCENARIOS, AND SUGGESTIONS 39 (The Carter Center, 2010), www.cartercenter.org/resources/pdfs/news/peace_publications/conflict_resolution/Solving_Territorial_Conflicts.pdf [hereinafter CARTER CENTER]

expansion of agreements to facilitate transportation networks modeled on Chile's construction of the Arica-La Paz railroad or infrastructure needs around the port of Ilo; or the "creation of a special transportation corridor of a nonterritorial nature,"[295] perhaps to accommodate Bolivia's and Chile's under-tapped worldwide comparative advantage in the production of lithium.[296]

These are the modalities the parties need to reconfigure, but within a trilateral rather than bilateral context. Clearly, a return to the thirteen-point agenda discussions would be of benefit, but with Peru's inclusion as well. Tri-national discussions are not only implied by the *jus prohibendi* provision agreed to by Chile and Peru, but would signify a fully integrated resolution strategy that could create intersubjective avenues for subregional economic, political, and legal development. The basis for the thirteen-point agenda already has been broached officially and unofficially by a group of diplomats, journalists, and scholars, who in 2001 launched the *Proyecto Trinacional* to remove conceptual and practical obstacles by advancing academic, cultural, and commercial ties.[297]

Trilateral discussions also would promote the possibility of this subregional growth triangle in ways only indirectly attempted. Subregional growth triangles have been well studied in a South-East Asian context,[298] as well as specifically within South American and West African comparative perspectives.[299] The unencumbered movement of labor, technology, and capital in these regions have been known to create significant political, social, and economic consequences.[300] Factors associated with successful examples seem possible within the Andean context: economic complementarity, geographical proximity, government commitment and policy coordination, infrastructure development, and private sector market forces.[301] South America's context, turbulence notwithstanding, presents relative macro-conditions not present elsewhere: since the War of the Pacific, it has not been the *situs* of major international war; it has been less impeded by ethnic or religious cleavages; although internally

[295] *See* CARTER CENTER, *supra* note 294, at 39.
[296] *See* Hodson, *supra* note 35.
[297] *See* Ronald Bruce St. John, *Same Space, Different Dreams: Bolivia's Quest for a Pacific Port*, 1(10) THE BOLIVIAN RESEARCH REVIEW (2001), www.bolivianstudies.org/revista/2001_07.htm. *See also* HACIA UN ENFOQUE, TRINACIONAL DE LAS RELACIONES ENTRE BOLIVIA, CHILE Y PERÚ (2001).
[298] *See* David Wadley & Hayu Parasati, *Inside South East Asia's Growth Triangles* 85(4) GEOGRAPHY (2000) 323–334.
[299] *See* ARIE M. KACOWICZ, ZONES OF PEACE IN THE THIRD WORLD: SOUTH AMERICA AND WEST AFRICA IN COMPARATIVE PERSPECTIVE (1998).
[300] *See* Brian Bridges, *Beyond Economics: Growth Triangles in Southeast Asia* 21(1) ASIAN PERSPECTIVE 55–77 (1997).
[301] Wadley & Parasati, *supra* note 298 at 324; Bridges, *supra* note 300, 55–77.

weak in terms of political structures, South American states escaped the *quasi*-status of less fully fledged nation-states; and peoples of the region have been better able to democratize while developing regional, cultural, normative, and transnational identities.[302] The establishment of a nascent pluralistic security community in the Southern Cone generates guarded optimism about transforming national identities and historical zones of conflict into "incipient zones of negative peace"[303] – which are conceived as "the absence of systemic, large-scale collective violence between political communities."[304] It may also have an effect on the regional construction of sovereignty. Taken for granted as an inflexible norm, "it is easy to overlook the extent to which sovereignty norms reflect an ongoing artifact of practice" – not a once-and-for-all creation of norms established by the War of the Pacific.[305] The most dynamic aspect of this problem is that the three parties could reconfigure sovereignty away from the limiting and seemingly intractable options presented by its Westphalian construction. Perhaps sovereignty in the Northern Atacama Desert is a *jus dispositivum* awaiting a sensible reconstruction by the parties most affected by the War of the Pacific.

A complicated history involving borders imposed by the fiat power of *uti possidetis* was meant to protect against postcolonial landgrabs throughout South America. But indeterminate territorial demarcations in the Atacama following the collapse of the Spanish Empire prompted competing claims of possession, occupation, and development,[306] but not immediately. Territorial temptations and the Grotian tendency exposed the weakness of *uti possidetis* for Bolivia, Chile, and Peru because of mid-nineteenth-century disputes over resources. Competing historical narratives, national interests, forestalled plebiscites, massive migration, secret and broken promises, and clean and dirty hands complicate the question of a sovereign access for Bolivia to the sea. The question involves, certainly for Bolivia and Chile, and, of late, Peru, national identity and honor. Chile and Peru litigated before the ICJ a maritime boundary dispute directly stemming from the 1929 Treaty of Lima, resulting in a 2014 ICJ judgment.[307] The settlement of that maritime claim, itself problematic because it leaves no maritime space for Bolivia to own should it achieve a

---

[302] *See* Kacowicz, *supra* note 299, at 178–180.
[303] *Id.* 177.
[304] *Id.* at 7.
[305] *See* Alexander Wendt, *Anarchy Is What States Make of It: The Social Construction of Power Politics*, 46(2) Int'l Org. 391, 413 (1992).
[306] *See* St. John, Boundaries, Trade, and Seaports, *supra* note 15, at 29.
[307] *See* Maritime Dispute (Peru v. Chile), *supra* note 221.

sovereign access to the sea, almost immediately has propelled Chile and Peru into a dispute over a nine acre (37,610 sq. meter) triangle (the La Yarada-Los Palos district of Tacna) landward of the point (*Punto Concordia*) used by the ICJ for its seaward delimitation.[308] The dispute has involved diplomatic exchanges and allegations of troop deployments,[309] the recall of both ambassadors,[310] and tensions fueled by other charges of espionage.[311]

The principle of *pacta tertiis*, itself a reflection of the sovereign equality of states, ensures that judicial settlements will not affect the interests of nonparties.[312] But as the recent maritime delimitation case between Peru and Chile suggests, it does not necessarily preclude the ICJ from ruling on a case before it as between Chile and Bolivia.

The question is whether the ICJ can impute more meaning to a sovereign access to the sea than would be suggested by finding, at best, that a *pactum de negotiandum* exits based on the historical record and factual *effectivités*. The essential indeterminacy of the historical record suggests that something more clear and convincing is needed other than the disputable inferences and references proffered by Bolivia. Given that indeterminacy, it is doubtful the ICJ will provide finality to this ongoing saga, and that does not appear to be its charge. Absent a *deus ex machina*, the opportunity costs to settlement increase for this subregional growth triangle, reinvigorating the prospect that the three principal parties, not the ICJ, already have constructed an array of intersubjective modalities that can lead to settlement, and indeed potential cooperation, informing along the way the rich and informal texture of international law creation.

---

[308] *See Boundary Tensions between Peru and Chile Continue, supra* note 221.

[309] *Chile and Peru in Border Spat over La Yarada-Los Palos area*, BBC NEWS (Nov. 8, 2015), www .bbc.com/news/world-latin-america-34759018.

[310] *See* Colin Post, *Border Rhetoric Heats up between Chile and Peru*, PERU REPORTS (Nov. 7, 2015), http://perureports.com/2015/11/07/border-rhetoric-heats-up-between-chile-and-peru/.

[311] *See Boundary Tensions between Peru and Chile Continue, supra* note 221.

[312] *See* MICHAIL VAGIAS, THE TERRITORIAL JURISDICTION OF THE INTERNATIONAL CRIMINAL COURT 187 (2014).

8

Conclusions on the Future of the Global Commons

Reflecting on three decades of empirical research, a group of scholars, including future Nobel Laureate Elinor Ostrom, once titled a study of commons management *The Drama of the Commons.*[1] The group recognized the main point of Garrett Hardin's tragedy of the commons: common ownership over valuable resources will result in the exhaustion of the resource. "If all users exercise restraint, then the resource can be sustained; if you exercise restraint but your neighbor does not, the resource still collapses and you have lost the short-term benefits of taking your share."[2]

Common-pool resource theorists drew inspiration from bio-economics, principally from the Gordon-Schaefer model of the late 1950s, which focused on fisheries management and maximum sustainable yield.[3] Ostrom's seminal work, *Governing the Commons: The Evolution of Institutions for Collective Action* (1990), displayed a deep regard for fisheries management systems as well. International relations specialists are historically familiar with Hardin's prototypical scenario, which common-pool resource theorists traced to fisheries, common use, and the law of the sea. It embraces key aspects of the Grotian Tradition.

These common-pool resource theorists focused on two challenges touched on in this study. One was the problem of free riders, who benefit from the resource but do not share in the costs of maintaining the resource. Russia and

---

[1] *See generally* ELINOR OSTROM ET AL., THE DRAMA OF THE COMMONS (2002).

[2] *See* Thomas Dietz, Nives Dolšak, Elinor Ostrom, & Paul C. Stern, *The Drama of the Commons* 3, *in* THE DRAMA OF THE COMMONS (E. Ostrom et al., eds., 2002) (citing the dilemma presented by Hardin) [hereinafter Dietz, Dolšak, Ostrom, & Stern].

[3] *See, e.g.*, H. Scott Gordon, *The Economic Theory of a Common-Property Resource: The Fishery*, 62 J. OF POL. ECON. 124–142 (1954); Milner B. Schaefer *Some Considerations of Population Dynamics and Economics in Relation to the Management of Marine Fishes*, 14 JOURNAL OF THE FISHERIES RESEARCH BOARD OF CANADA, 669–681 (1957); Dietz, Dolšak, Ostrom, & Stern, *supra* note 2, at 9 (citing the early formal analyses of Gordon and Schaefer).

other states quietly demonstrate this practice in view of Norway's administration of the FPZ around Svalbard's extended waters. The international community reflects this practice as well, with its muted response to Russia's widening administrative control over the Northern Sea Route, as if waiting to discern whether the Russians can make the passageway commercially viable. The other was the problem of subtractability or rivalness, where "what one person harvests from the resource subtracts from the ability of others to do the same."[4] Subtractibility and rivalness are primordial components of the Grotian tendency and its territorial temptations. They reflect the interplay between *dominium*, or ownership and *imperium*, or the power to rule and enforce rules.

Subtractibility and rivalness reduce to self-interest, which Aristotle addressed when he wrote: "Everyone thinks chiefly of his own, hardly at all of the common interest."[5] "[E]ven when they extend their concern beyond themselves," cautioned David Hume, "'tis not to any great distance[.]"[6] Attempts to achieve a better, more sustainable use by placing authority in the hands of a collective agency prove no easy fix. Free-market champion and Nobel Laureate Milton Friedman emphasized the illusion of collective schemes, which he reduced to the example of poor public housing in America,[7] a resource owned by all and maintained by none. Can management of the global commons be different?

Hardin understood the problem as a dilemma, warning of the consequence of overgrazing among herders individually compelled to pursue their own best interest. But common-pool resource theorists concluded Hardin's account was unduly inexorable, and that history indicated outcomes that were not always tragic, sometimes, even often, mutually beneficial. This conclusion makes room for a far more positive discussion of the commons,[8] even if the discussion invariably involves drama.[9] Ostrom's most important teaching derived from her finding that "humans have a more complex motivational structure and more capability to solve social dilemmas than posited in earlier rational-choice

---

[4]   Nives Dolšak & Elinor Ostrom, *The Challenges of the Commons, in* The Commons in the New Millennium: Challenges and Adaptation 7 (Nives Dolšak & Elinor Ostrom, eds., 2003).

[5]   Dietz, Dolšak, Ostrom, & Stern, *supra* note 2, at 8 (quoting Aristotle's Politics, Book II, Ch. 3).

[6]   1 David Hume, A Treatise of Human Nature: A Critical Edition 342 (David Fate Norton & Mary J. Norton, eds., 2007).

[7]   *See* Milton Friedman (With the assistance of Rose D. Friedman), Capitalism and Freedom 178–180 (1962); Milton & Rose D. Friedman, Free to Choose: A Personal Statement 109–112 (1980).

[8]   *See* Dietz, Dolsak, Ostrom, & Stern, *supra* note 2, at 3–4 (citing the work of B. J. McCay, J. M. Acheson, and C. Rose).

[9]   *See id.* at 4.

theory."[10] Common-pool resource associates claimed that multiple property rights arrangements exist; and that, for instance, condominium arrangements such as the common property meadows in the Swiss Alps, which have been managed by localized and self-organized groups since the Middle Ages, have avoided the problem of overexploitation and subtractibility.[11] Ostrom and others cited empirical examples of cooperation, discussing groundwater basins, lakes, forests, and irrigation systems.[12] The question is whether these successful localized examples – largely internal to states and closed to "outsiders" – present a template for global resource governance,[13] where group boundaries are controlled largely by statehood; where the connection between use of common goods and local needs and conditions are more diffuse, and involve at times more tenuously connected social relations; where those affected by the rules of state behavior unevenly participate in administering the rules; where decisions of rule-making authorities may not resonate with the interests of outside authorities;[14] where the glue of domestic social adhesion loses its binding character, resulting in rivalries for scarce or newly emergent resources. Global resource governance must bridge the gap between *dominium* and *imperium*.

Ostrom et al. have done much to develop the vocabulary and "untangle the various meanings" of the commons and associated terms.[15] Importantly, they claimed the concept of common property should not be confused with open access. Common property regimes arise "where the members of a clearly

---

[10] Elinor Ostrom, *Beyond Markets and States: Polycentric Governance of Complex Economic Systems*, Nobel Prize Lecture, December 8, 2009, reprinted in Work in Political Theory and Policy Analysis (Indiana University; and Center for the Study of Institutional Diversity, Arizona State University), 408, at 435, www.nobelprize.org/nobel_prizes/economic-sciences/laureates/2009/ostrom_lecture.pdf.

[11] *See, e.g.*, Ivo Baur & Claudia R. Binder, *Adapting to Socioeconomic Developments by Changing Rules in the Governance of Common Property Pastures in the Swiss Alps*, 18 ECOLOGY AND SOC'Y 60 (2013), http://dlc.dlib.indiana.edu/dlc/bitstream/handle/10535/9217/ES-2013-5689 .pdf?sequence=1&isAllowed=y.

[12] *See, e.g.*, ELINOR OSTROM ET AL., RULES, GAMES, AND COMMON-POOL RESOURCES (1994); Elinor Ostrom, *20 Years Into Our Common Future: The Challenge of Common-Pool Resources*, ENVIRONMENT (July/August 2008), www.environmentmagazine.org/Archives/Back%20Issues/July-August%202008/ostrom-full.html.

[13] *See, e.g.*, ELINOR OSTROM, GOVERNING THE COMMONS: THE EVOLUTION OF INSTITUTIONS FOR COLLECTIVE ACTION (1990); Ottmar Edenhofer, Christian Flachsland, & Berhnard Lorentz, *The Atmosphere as a Global Commons, in* THE WEALTH OF THE COMMONS: A WORLD BEYOND MARKET & STATE (David Bollier & Silke Helfrich, eds., 2014) (casting uncertainty on whether Ostrom's findings on a local level can be replicated at the global level).

[14] *See* OSTROM, *supra* note 13, ch. 3 (discussing her design principles: clearly defined boundaries; congruence between rules and local conditions; collective-choice arrangements; monitoring; graduated sanctions; conflict resolution mechanisms; respect for institutional authority not challenged by external governmental authorities).

[15] Dietz, Dolzack, Ostrom, Stern, *supra* note 2, at 3 and 17.

demarcated group have a legal right to exclude nonmembers of that group from using a resource. Open access regimes (*res nullius*) – including the classic cases of the open seas and the atmosphere – have long been considered in legal doctrine as involving no limits on who is authorized to use a resource."[16]

No limits? This powerful sentiment clearly subscribes to a classically constructed component of high seas freedom – an aspect lifted out of the Grotian Tradition and affirmed with a sense of invariance, adding to this *traditum's* handed-down, transhistorical significance as a received truth. But the concept of free use in an open access regime creates the misdirected impression of *laissez-faire* use, with few, if any, restrictions to serve the interests of other states and their exercise of free use.[17] The sentiment leads to confusion and does not capture the significance of the Grotian tendency, which pays attention to variance, and to the historical importance of *mare clausum*. And it underestimates challenges to repositioning the current and prospective fate of the global commons. It also forwards a selected or partial reading of Grotius, and draws support from his affirmation in *Mare Liberum* that the oceans were naturally ordained for common use.[18]

Constructing a bridge between open access and common property regimes – between the *international commons* and regimes that manage common-pool resources – attracts increasing scholarly attention. It reflects the project to establish a moral basis for future resource management in fairness to future generations;[19] where the commons comes to consist of "all the creations of nature and society that we inherit jointly and freely, and hold in trust for future generations."[20] It testifies to Ostrom's and common-pool resource theory's broadening appeal as an antidote to Hardin's tragedy of the commons and as a corrective for neoliberalism's implicit faith in the false rationality of market-oriented and state-centric systems.

Discussion of the commons now projects a model for ecological governance[21] operating in a quasi-sovereign manner similar to the "logic of Market

---

[16] OSTROM, *supra* note 13, at 335–336

[17] Prue Taylor, *The Common Heritage of Mankind: A Bold Doctrine Kept within Strict Boundaries*, in THE WEALTH OF THE COMMONS: A WORLD BEYOND MARKET AND STATE (Bollier & Helfrich, eds., 2014), http://wealthofthecommons.org/essay/common-heritage-mankind-bold-doctrine-kept-within-strict-boundaries.

[18] *See* BURNS H. WESTON & DAVID BOLLIER, GREEN GOVERNANCE: ECOLOGICAL SURVIVAL, HUMAN RIGHTS AND THE LAW OF THE COMMONS (2014).

[19] *See*, e.g., EDITH BROWN WEISS, IN FAIRNESS TO FUTURE GENERATIONS: INTERNATIONAL LAW, COMMON PATRIMONY, AND INTERGENERATIONAL EQUITY (1982).

[20] The State of the Commons: A Report to Owners from Tomales Bay Institute 3 (2003). http://bollier.org/sites/default/files/State%20of%20the%20Commons.pdf

[21] *See*, e.g., THE WEALTH OF THE COMMONS: A WORLD BEYOND MARKET AND STATE (David Bollier & Silke Helfrich, eds., 2014).

exchange."[22] In this preferred world, which draws from the rich legal tradition tracing to *Mare Liberum*,[23] a "vernacular law" governs. Vernacular law consists of "'unofficial norms', institutions, and procedures that a peer community devises to manage community resources on its own and typically democratically."[24] The vernacular commons is not only a geo-spatial regime challenging and replacing malleable and tired legal concepts such as *res nullius* and *terra nullius*, it is a social system with a democratic value-orientation, where commoners gain standing in open access areas designed for enclosure by states.

The advent of a new Arctic governance model in the form of the Arctic Circle Assembly reflects vernacular law and the commoners' democratic frustration with the clubbish Arctic Council, and commoners' desire for a more inclusive global Arctic concept. Vernacular law's ethos includes corporations, public associations, think tanks, and individuals to advance broad goals. But to what end? A global Arctic created for common use along lines of shared sovereignty and *res communis* is different than a global Arctic predicated on common access to support a command of the commons involving *jus navigandi*, freedom of fishing, and potential resource exploitation. Attempts to secure the former failed in the history of UNCLOS, and the Arctic Circle Assembly shrewdly avoids discussions signaling any redistributive designs for Arctic resource management. Its functional orientation makes it a worthy clearinghouse of information on circumpolar health, Arctic tourism, business cooperation, ecosystem management, indigenous peoples, and resource/transit/security issues. But its status as a soft law forum indicates, as commoners would acknowledge, that the Arctic Circle Assembly is but a first trestle constructing a bridge between open access and common property regimes in the international sphere. Do prospects for the ecological governance of the commons indicate arrival of a Grotian Moment?

Any declaration of an epochal Grotian Moment, where an alignment of global interests and common values secures resources for common use and benefit for humanity, must deal with the historical Grotian tendency – artfully nuanced by the master himself – of powerfully situated states, acting individually or in concert, to appropriate emerging resources to the exclusion of other states and to the detriment of a global common use doctrine. The arrival of vernacular law, even if more concrete than aspirational, must still come to terms with the *traditum* of the Grotian tendency.

[22] David Bollier & Burns Weston, *Greenkeeping Governance: Toward a Law of the Ecological Commons*, BOLLIER KOSMOS, www.kosmosjournal.org/article/greenkeeping-governance-toward- a-law-of-the-ecological-commons/.

[23] *Id.*

[24] *Id.*

The world is not witnessing a paradigm shift in High Arctic passageways, or in extended seaward reaches into Svalbard's continental shelf. It is witnessing historically based iterations to territorialize resources, if not by individual appropriations, then by nuanced course-of-dealing arrangements that preference parochial interests vis-à-vis the rest of the world. Iterations of this Grotian tendency, well-demonstrated within the so-called Grotian Tradition, arise also in the pelagic space of the Gulf of Fonseca, where manifold differences among the coparceners continue to daunt prospects for shared management except as against the interests of the rest of the world. Another iteration arises in the hyperarid corridor of the Atacama Desert leading to Bolivia's long-standing desire for access to a Pacific port. There, Chile's state-sponsored possessory interest in territorializing geo-spatial resources secured by conquest, together with economic, security, social, and cultural *effectivités* attending Chilean rule since the War of the Pacific, forestall a negotiated solution that could lead to inventive, regionally beneficial modalities for a shared sovereignty solution.

A variation of territorial temptation, with an inventive twist, now plays out in a different frontier, the 3.5 million square kilometer South China Sea. The South China Sea contains considerable energy and living resource reserves[25] and is a major thoroughfare for Indo-Pacific security. One-third of global trade passes through the Strait of Malacca,[26] to and from the South China Sea – through the same sea-lanes that carried so much European colonial history from the fifteenth through nineteenth centuries. Today this trade includes more than fifteen million barrels of oil per day; Asia-Pacific commerce involves eight of the world's ten busiest container ports, and approximately $1.2 trillion in shipborne trade bound annually for the United States alone.[27] An Award of the Permanent Court of Arbitration ruled in July 2016 that none of the disputed features of the South China Sea was capable of sustaining human habitation or economic life.[28] And in ways that does not bode well for the future of the commons, here is where the problem begins.

---

[25] A US Department of Defense 2015 report to Congress noted the South China Sea accounts for more than 10 percent of global fisheries production and contains approximately eleven billion barrels and 190 trillion cubic feet of proved and probable oil and natural gas reserves. US Department of Defense, Asia-Pacific Maritime Security Strategy 5, undated but released August 2015, www.defense.gov/Portals/1/Documents/pubs/NDAA%20A-P_Maritime_SecuritY_Strategy-08142015-1300-FINALFORMAT.PDF.

[26] *See* Gregory Poling, *US Interests in the South China Sea: International Law and Peaceful Dispute Resolution, in* POWER, LAW, AND MARITIME ORDER IN THE SOUTH CHINA SEA 64 (Tran Truong Thuy & Le Thuy Trang, eds., 2015).

[27] *See* Department of Defense, Asia-Pacific Maritime Security Strategy, *supra* note 25, at 1.

[28] *See* In the Matter of the South China Sea Arbitration before an Arbitral Tribunal Constituted under Annex VII to the 1982 United Nations Convention on the Law of the Sea between the

Seven states – China, Vietnam, Malaysia, Indonesia, Brunei, the Philippines, and Taiwan – enclose the South China Sea and the hundreds of skerries that dot its waters, break its surface at low-tide, and lay as submerged banks. Were some of these features habitable as islands for purposes of UNCLOS, they could generate an EEZ or a continental shelf. If classified merely as uninhabitable rocks within the meaning of Article 121(3) of UNCLOS, they would be capable of generating a territorial sea no greater than twelve nautical miles. If characterized as a low-tide elevation, or submerged bank, no legal assertion of title or attending claim of resource entitlement could result.

These coastal states have disputed territorial and maritime issues in the South China Sea since the 1930s,[29] with principal disputes arising between China and the Philippines (over Mischief Reef in 1995–1998),[30] and China and Vietnam (resulting in a negotiated maritime delimitation in the Gulf of Tonkin in 2000).[31] A 2002 Declaration of Conduct[32] stabilized relations until 2009, when Malaysia and Vietnam jointly, and Vietnam separately, presented to the CLCS extended continental shelf submissions, which projected parochial resource enclosure claims beyond the 200 nautical mile limit, in accordance with UNCLOS.[33]

But an ascendant China, ambitiously positioning itself as a maritime power,[34] complicates the regional calculus in a familiar way. China responded to the

Republic of the Philippines and the People's Republic of China, Award, P.C.A. Case No. 2013-19, 12 July 2016.

[29] *See* Jay Batongbacal, *Arbitration 101: Philippines v. China,* ASIA MARITIME TRANSPARENCY INITIA-TIVE, January 21, 2015, http://amti.csis.org/arbitration-101-philippines-v-china/ (noting the territorial and maritime issues in the South China Sea have technically been in existence since the 1930s).

[30] Mischief Reef is a rocky outcrop located in the Spratly archipelago; it is claimed by the Philippines as within its 200 mile EEZ and occupied and fortified with structures by China between 1995 and 1998, resulting in Philippine vessel interceptions by China and a series of diplomatic confrontations. *See generally* Ian James Story, *Creeping Assertiveness: China, the Philippines and the South China Sea Dispute,* 21 CONTEMPORARY SOUTHEAST ASIA 95–118 (1999).

[31] *See generally* Zou Keyuan, *The Sino-Vietnamese Agreement on Maritime Boundary Delimitation in the Gulf of Tonkin,* 36 OCEAN DEV. & INT'L L. 13–24 (2005).

[32] Declaration on the Conduct of Parties in the South China Sea, Association of Southeast Asian Nations, signed in Phnom Penh, November 4, 2002, www.asean.org/asean/external-relations/china/item/declaration-on-the-conduct-of-parties-in-the-south-china-sea (undertaking to resolve territorial and jurisdictional disputes by peaceful means through friendly consultations).

[33] Socialist Republic of Viet Nam, Submission to the Commission on the Limits of the Continental Shelf, Partial Submission in Respect of Vietnam's Extended Continental Shelf: North Area (April 2009) (Annex 222); Malaysia and the Socialist Republic of Viet Nam, Joint Submission to the Commission on the Limits of the Continental Shelf, in Respect of the Southern Part of the South China Sea (6 May 2009) (Annex 223), reprinted in The Republic of the Philippines and The People's Republic of China, Award on Jurisdiction and Admissibility, PCA Case No. 2013–19, October 29, 2015, at 5, www.pcacases.com/web/sendAttach/1506.

[34] *See* China's Military Strategy, The State Council Information Office of the People's Republic of China, May 2015, Beijing, http://eng.mod.gov.cn/Database/WhitePapers/.

Malaysian and Vietnamese submissions swiftly by presenting to the United Nations Secretary General for the first time in 2009 its claim of a U-Shaped Nine-Dash line.[35] This line encloses its neighbors' EEZs, rings approximately 90 percent of the South China Sea with China's claim of sovereign rights and jurisdiction, asserts but does not elaborate on a claim based on historic rights, and appears every bit as imperial as fifteenth-century Luso-Spanish designs to demarcate the geography of New World discoveries with the Treaty of Tordesillas, except that this twenty-first-century claim of sovereignty *ad absurdum* is certainly less likely to be ignored.

In the South China Sea Spratley Island chain, six countries – China, Taiwan, Malaysia, Brunei, Philippines, and Vietnam – claim sovereignty over all (China, Taiwan, and Vietnam) or some (the Philippines, Malaysia, and Brunei) of the scattered reefs. Owing to the territorial principle that the land dominates the sea, traditional international law established the principle that maritime claims had to derive from land features. UNCLOS contains no rule granting water rights to outcroppings incapable of supporting habitation. Where disputed or tenuous territorial imperatives once existed, China now assertively, if not inventively, creates a new one. With alarming speed, it has piled sea sediment onto low water reefs in the center of the Spratlys – 660 miles from the Chinese mainland – creating in a thirteen-month period an artificial island-complex, which it calls a reclamation project, complete with port facilities, airstrips, and structures with military capability. China's construction project generates serious conflict across Southeast Asia, principally with Vietnam, the Philippines, and the United States. It has polarized discussions within the Association of South East Asian Nations (ASEAN), as documented by the failure of the 45th ASEAN Ministerial Meeting in Phnom Penh in 2012, where members could not come to terms over a joint *communiqué* over the legal status of the South China Sea.[36] And it stokes regional tensions in a sea of overlapping claims. Sovereignty issues abound over extant land features in the South China Sea, including a dispute over the Paracel Islands (claimed by China and Vietnam and occupied by China), and a dispute over Scarborough Shoal (claimed by China, Taiwan, and the Philippines, and controlled since 2012 by

---

[35] *See* Figure 2: Map attached to China's Notes Verbales to the United Nations Secretary General, Nos. CML/17/2009 and CML/18/2009 (showing so-called "Nine-Dash Line") (Memorial, Figure 1.1), reprinted in The Republic of the Philippines and The People's Republic of China, Award on Jurisdiction and Admissibility, PCA Case No. 2013–19 (Oct. 29, 2015), at 5, www .pcacases.com/web/sendAttach/1506.

[36] *See* Kristine Kwok, *Beijing's South China Sea Island Building Has Polarized Asean Nations*, South China Morning Post (Aug. 9, 2015), www.scmp.com/news/china/diplomacy-defence/article/1847875/beijings-south-china-sea-island-building-has-polarised.

China). It extends into the East China Sea in disputes involving Senkaku or Diaoyu Islands (disputed by China, Taiwan, and Japan, and administered by Japan), and Dokdo or Takeshima islets (disputed by Japan and South Korea) in the Sea of Japan (East Sea). How China connects its Nine-Dash line may draw Indonesia into a dispute over the surrounding Natuna Islands and its natural gas fields.[37] Furthermore, while most signatories to UNCLOS recognize the right of military passage and peaceful activities within the EEZ but outside territorial waters, UNCLOS' actual silence on this issue stimulates China's position that coastal states may regulate foreign military activities in their EEZs in addition to economic activity.[38] Russia already has asserted coastal state authority in Arctic waters over foreign nonmilitary activities. In 2013, it denied the *Arctic Sunrise*, a Dutch Greenpeace vessel, a right to enter and freely navigate the Northern Sea Route; it then seized the vessel and detained its international crew (the "Arctic 30") as pirates for interrupting operations of Gazprom's Prirazlomnaya offshore oil platform.

Powerful Anglo-European maritime countries selectively incorporated package-deal provisions of UNCLOS favorable to their respective positions in the 1980s, discarding concessions negotiated to accommodate developing country interests in establishing an equitable distribution of resources in accordance with the Common Heritage of Mankind principle. China now follows suit. During UNCLOS negotiations, many of the smaller maritime powers in the South China Sea region ceded control over commercial straits in favor of the principle of freedom of navigation, with the expectation that they would secure in exchange control over the abundant fisheries within 200 nautical miles of shore.[39] China's Nine-Dash line upends this expectation and introduces China to strategic rivalries and shifting alliances similar to the seventeenth-century complications that undid the *Estado de Índia* and early-nineteenth-century Spanish imperial rule in the New World.

The dispute involved the Philippines' arbitration against China, which in 2015 survived jurisdiction and admissibility objections raised by China.[40]

---

[37] *See* Victor Robert Lee, *Is Indonesia Beijing's Next Target in the South China Sea?* THE DIPLOMAT, Oct. 2, 2014, http://thediplomat.com/2014/10/is-indonesia-beijings-next-target-in-the-south-china-sea/.

[38] *See* Ronald O'Rourke, *Maritime Territorial and Exclusive Economic Zone (EEZ) Disputes Involving China: Issues for Congress* 11 (Congressional Research Service Report, Dec. 22, 2015), www.fas.org/sgp/crs/row/R42784.pdf.

[39] *See* James Kraska, *The Nine Ironies of the South China Sea Mess*, THE DIPLOMAT, Sept.17, 2015, http://thediplomat.com/2015/09/the-nine-ironies-of-the-south-china-sea-mess/ (noting particularly Malaysia's and Indonesia's reluctance to cede free transit through the Strait of Malacca and Sunda Strait except in exchange for the EEX benefits of the package deal).

[40] *See* An Arbitral Tribunal Constituted Under Annex VII to the 1982 United Nations Convention on the law of the Sea between the Republic of the Philippines and the People's Republic of

Outside the purview of the Tribunal, China had sought discussions per the ASEAN Treaty of Amity and Cooperation and the 2002 Declaration of Conduct for Parties in the South China Sea. But the Permanent Court of Arbitration, *proprio motu*, affirmed that those soft law forms of dispute settlement did not bar application of UNCLOS Annex VII compulsory arbitration procedures.[41] China's nonappearance before the tribunal and refusal to participate mirrors a similar rejection of court authority by Russia in the *Arctic Sunrise* case,[42] and by the United States in the *Nicaragua* case. China also has been accused of resorting to a familiar form of foot-dragging: "over the course of the last [eight] ministerial meetings on the Declaration of Conduct and Code of Conduct, China has continued to assert its sovereignty over disputed waters ... Its participation in the talks has prevented any real progress, allowing Beijing to continue its activities in the contested Paracel and Spratly Islands without contest from any mutually agreed-upon framework (except the non-binding 2002 declaration)."[43] This two-track policy rhetorically supports negotiations in soft law policy-shaping *fora* while at the same time publicly laying down markers that solidify territorial *effectivités* leading to sovereign authority (*à titre de souverain*). It indicates China's creeping coastal state interest into a broader pelagic space. Using soft law *fora* as "smokescreens" for dispute resolution, while incrementally territorializing or buttressing control over resources, mimics the familiar complaint of Bolivia against Chile in the Atacama Desert dispute, and discontented voices within the Arctic Council and Arctic Assembly over resistance by powerful stakeholders to the concept of a globalizing Arctic. China's strategy adapts key features of *uti possidetis* and applies it analogously to spaces never contemplated by its nineteenth-century progenitors – testifying to Rosalyn Higgins' warning that *uti possidetis* may come to mean all things to all people. This terrestrial principle, modified from possessory presumptions created by Roman law *praetors*, solidified postcolonial borders to preempt belligerent assertions of *terra nullius*. Now it bears disconcerting application in pelagic space, over artificially "reclaimed" territory that never existed previously, as a means not of freezing entitlement, but of creating entitlement.

China, Award on Jurisdiction and Admissibility, PCA Case No. 2013–19 (Oct. 29, 2015), www .pcacases.com/web/sendAttach/1506.

[41]   *Id.* at 149.

[42]   *See*, In the Matter of the Arctic Sunrise Arbitration, The Kingdom of the Netherlands and the Russian Federation, PCA Case No. 2014-02, Award on the Merits (Aug. 14, 2015), www .pcacases.com/web/sendAttach/1438.

[43]   Ankit Panda, *For the ASEAN-China South China Sea Code of Conduct, Ninth Time Isn't the Charm*, THE DIPLOMAT, Aug. 1, 2015, http://thediplomat.com/2015/08/for-the-asean-china-south-china-sea-code-of-conduct-ninth-time-isnt-the-charm/.

Lost in much of the discussion about competitive landgrabs under the sea, or on top of the world, or the coming communal use questions involving Antarctica and outer space, is consideration of the nature of these races, extant or projected. Is there a "Race to the Pole" or a debate about the distributional consequences of resource accumulation through continental shelf extensions in areas originally deemed set-asides for humanity's common use, or have the capable participants sped ahead of the instrumentalities of international law, or perhaps created their own, to secure their own *faits accomplis* over pelagic space?

If pelagic space is subject to such appropriation, will international law's remaining three "traditional" global commons – the atmosphere (the ozone layer), Antarctica, and outer space – be different? Antarctica looms as an issue on the horizon. Seven states claim territory in Antarctica: Argentina, Australia, Chile, France, New Zealand, Norway and United Kingdom. Argentine, United Kingdom, and Chilean claims overlap. The 1959 Antarctic Treaty holds these sovereignty disputes in abeyance and precludes new claims while the treaty stays in effect.[44] A peaceful condominium arrangement presides, elevating scientific research aims above territorial claims. Supplementary environmental agreements safeguard flora and fauna, seals, marine living resources, mining, and environmental protection. A globalizing Antarctic attracts numerous new national research initiatives: China operates five research centers, India recently updated its Bharati base; Turkey, Belarus, Iran, and Colombia have announced plans to establish research colonies.[45] But despite its veneer, the Antarctic is geopolitically contested and its future provokes "fresh concerns over the ownership of the polar continent and its continental shelves."[46] China and South Korea intensify the hunt for krill off its waters; Russia forestalls efforts to create the largest ocean sanctuary in the Southern Ocean; pressures to commercialize its space grow with fishing, tourism, and biological prospects. Antarctica holds at least thirty-six billion barrels of oil and natural gas, diamonds, and other mineral resources; it holds 70 percent of the world's supply of fresh water, awaiting recovery by drilling deep into its aquifers or by harvesting its ice or icebergs.[47]

---

[44] Art. IV, Antarctic Treaty (No acts or activities taking place while the present Treaty is in force shall constitute a basis for asserting, supporting or denying a claim to territorial sovereignty in Antarctica or create any rights of sovereignty in Antarctica. No new claim or enlargement of an existing claim to territorial sovereignty in Antarctica shall be asserted while the present Treaty is in force.)

[45] *See* Simon Romero, *Countries Rush for Upper Hand in Antarctica*, N.Y. TIMES (Dec. 29, 2015), www.nytimes.com/interactive/2015/12/29/world/countries-rush-for-upper-hand-antarctica.html?_r=0.

[46] KLAUS DODDS, THE ANTARCTIC: A VERY SHORT INTRODUCTION 132 (2012).

[47] *See* Romero, *supra* note 44.

Reviewing the proliferation and fragmentation of international lawmaking in the atmospheric commons prompts concerns that competition "works systematically to the overall advantage and interests of the most powerful states, whose consent is essential for the functioning of the system."[48] Already conversations about possible new additives to the global commons – for instance, tropical rain forests, biodiversity, and bioprospecting – have been added to the post-2015 United Nations Development Agenda. But they have been added with the understanding that access to most resources within the global commons has been difficult historically and the resources they contain "have not been scarce."[49] Science, technology, and climate change combine to change access to these resources, and even to redefine these resources with the inclusion of an intangible resource, cyberspace. What has not changed has been territorial temptation. A true epochal shift in state behavior would record a shift away from the Grotian tendency, but any epochal shift in state behavior is moderated not by the penchant to share resources but to divide them. The geo-spatial races currently underway do not appear to be open races in the conventional sense, but, rather, invitational races, with place-markers extended to those proximate states most capable of exercising their territorial tendency to alienate and enclose. Though they pledge cooperation, they compete; though they compete, they unite to exclude all others; when they see no need to unite, they act unilaterally. In concert, they render indeterminate the future interests of the global commons, crowding out application of vernacular law before its arrival.

Indeterminacy works to the advantage of well situated states. Deep divisions swirl around the Svalbard Treaty's application beyond the territorial sea, yet Norway's long-range management claim has deftly introduced a 200-mile FPZ, with a future mind toward declaring an EEZ. Norway has not pressed the issue historically, and has relied on a degree of ambiguity to settle in on its long-range intentions, making for a delicate course of dealing with its pelagic neighbor, Russia, which itself exacts rewards from Svalbard's peculiar shared resource arrangement. Robert Lansing's early-twentieth-century separation of sovereignty from its post-Wesphalian identification with the territorial state facilitated an artificial understanding of *terra nullius* that assigned the benefits of commercial ownership over Svalbard's mineral resources without saddling states with the

---

[48] Peter H. Sand & Jonathan B. Wiener, *Towards a New International Law of the Atmosphere?* 7 Go. J. Int'l L. 1, 11 (2015).

[49] UN System Task Team on the Post-2015 UN Development Agenda: Global Governance and Governance of the Global Commons in the Global Partnership for Development Beyond 2015, 6 (2013), www.un.org/en/development/desa/policy/untaskteam_undf/thinkpieces/24_thinkpiece_global_governance.pdf.

political burdens of annexation. The significance of China's U-shaped line in the South China Sea, subsequently deemed irrelevant by the Tribunal as an indicator of China's sovereign and/or historic claims, has never been explained. China's continuing yet legally rejected claim of an *animus occupandi* established through uncontested and immemorial use is made more indeterminate by its presentation as a series of dotted lines, not an unbroken line. The world is left guessing as to when the lines will be connected, or how the gaps between them will be clearly delimited.[50] But this indeterminacy should come as no surprise if China is buying time to build up its historical case and maritime strength for a future redefinition of the South China Sea as one of its core national security interests. As probable, although rhetorically and currently denied by China's foreign policy establishment, China will land military aircraft on its "reclaimed" Spratly Islands airstrips as a 'revindication' of some future tort in a projection seaward of a Chinese Air Defense Identification Zone.

Legal historian Christina Duffy Burnett, in her study of the mid-nineteenth-century antecedents to the US Guano Islands Act, noted that constraints to territorial temptation sometimes invert the lurch toward more territory, plenary power, and extended sovereignty – "for purposes of reducing the number of contexts in which the government must take up the responsibilities that come with such power." States (principally the United States) sometimes drew lines around what counts properly as "national territory," that is, territory belonging to a nation but not fully part of it.[51] This practice purposely disclaimed sovereignty, and adopted indeterminate legal catch phrases – such as "appertaining to" – not to share resources but "to take control over territory while avoiding many of the responsibilities that sovereignty implies."[52] Perhaps China is taking a page from Robert Lansing's muddled playbook. The nomenclature is slightly different but the intent of eating one's sovereignty cake and disclaiming it, too, seems apparent. China's "indisputable sovereignty over the islands in the South China Sea" extends to "adjacent waters" and other "relevant waters as well as the seabed and subsoil thereof."[53]

China embarks on a reclamation project in the South China Seas; Chile rhetorically supports Bolivia's sovereign access to the sea. The lexicon of legal

[50] *See generally* Masahiro Miyoshi, *China's "U-Shaped Line" Claim in the South China Sea: Any Validity Under International Law?* 43 OCEAN DEV. & INT'L LAW 1–17 (2012).

[51] Christina Duffy Burnett, *The Edges of Empire and the Limits of Sovereignty: American Guano Islands*, 57 AM. Q. 779, 781 (disclaiming sovereignty/reducing the number of conflicts), 791 (appertaining to) and 798 (avoiding responsibilities) (2005).

[52] *Id.*

[53] *See Note Verbale* of the People's Republic of China to the United Nations to the Secretary-General of the United Nations, No. CML/17/2009 (7 May 2009), *available at* http://www .un.org/depts/los/clcs_new/submissions_files/mysvnm33_09/chn_2009re_mys_vnm_e.pdf;

indeterminacy grows. Similarly, Russia's ambiguous claim about the integral nature of the Northern Sea Route artfully blurs legal questions about those portions of it that may pass into the high seas. The artful shading of UNCLOS Article 234, the product of intense diplomatic negotiation by Canada and Russia, acknowledges the need for enhanced coastal state police powers in hazardous ice-covered areas, but its interplay with straits used for international navigation remains sublimely unclear. Martti Koskenniemi, *in The Gentle Civilizer of Nations: The Rise and Fall of International Law 1870–1960* (2001), devoted an entire chapter to European practices involving withholding or avoiding clarity on sovereignty declarations over their colonies in order to achieve ad hoc territorial advantages without moral or political costs.[54] What compels a different outcome for the twenty-first century?

The existing framework is complex; stewardship of the commons is fragmented. Current arrangements underestimate the impact of human activity; and newer arrangements lack specificity or hard regulatory standards.[55] Within this mix lurks the territorial temptation, which benefits from informal *non liquets* and a lack of hard regulatory standards. The Arctic Council retails as the leading intergovernmental forum promoting cooperation among Arctic states. Its eight members, six indigenous Permanent Participant organizations, six Working Groups, three Task Forces, one Expert Group, and thirty-two observers take on important functional issues, including, most recently, the problem of black carbon emissions and methane production, known to accelerate Arctic warming. The organization has ably contributed to the progressive development of resource management and international lawmaking, but its status, scrupulously maintained, as a soft law forum works in a way that also secures the more close-knit interests of the Arctic 5, the powers that rim the Arctic Circle. In closed meetings, these countries convene to manage the kinks and coming conflicts they alone share with regard to extended Arctic continental shelf claims. But continental shelves abound; and all coastal countries have a stake in the disposition of extended continental shelf claims. The mechanism created to manage these coming seaward projections of sovereignty, the CLCS, is also kept sufficiently soft.

and *Note Verbale* from the Permanent Mission of the People's Republic of China to the United Nations to the Secretary-General of the United Nations, No. CML/18/2009 (7 May 2009), *available at* http://www.un.org/Depts/los/clcs_new/submissions_files/vnm37_09/chn_2009re_vnm.pdf.

[54] *See generally* MARTTI KOSKENNIEMI, THE GENTLE CIVILIZER OF NATIONS: THE RISE AND FALL OF INTERNATIONAL LAW 1870–1960, ch. 2 (2001); Burnett, *supra* note 50, 798–799.

[55] UN System Task Team on the Post-2015 UN Development Agenda: Global Governance and Governance of the Global Commons in the Global Partnership for Development Beyond 2015, *supra* note 48, at 6. www.un.org/en/development/desa/policy/untaskteam_undf/thinkpieces/24_thinkpiece_global_governance.pdf.

Much scholarly attention currently focuses on the delimitation work of the overburdened CLCS, which must tediously review complicated scientific data provided by the same interested states that seek continental shelf extensions. The Commission itself is not an official United Nations agency, and doubt abounds as to its ability to render effective recommendations, making its work product a likely subject for future discussions of the problem of *non liquet* in international law,[56] rather than of international law's progressive development.

Grotius' idea of *mare liberum* remains a powerful expression of the Grotian Tradition in international law. The Grotian Tradition maintains its position of prominence in the historiography of international law, standing above or at least alongside new or revised versions of state relations. Its elevated position suggests a permanence to the *traditum* it represents, despite shifting contexts and historical upheavals. The Grotian Tradition remains a powerful reminder of the past, partly imagined, partly experienced, certainly constructed – as constructed as a Chinese reclamation project on previously submerged shoals. Perhaps portions of the tradition no longer fit where they once did, having been lifted out or reconstructed from an imagined past in pursuit of a wishfully preferred future.

Embedded in the *traditum* of the Grotian Tradition – that is, in its historical evolution – is Grotius' idea of common use. Successor generations have appropriated it in nostalgic recognition of his youthful brilliance, as a synergistic accompaniment to the onset of the Republican Tradition, and as an important stimulus for common-pool resource theory. It is now relied upon as a palliative and perhaps solution to globalizing concerns of resource management in an epoch of dramatic climate change. It shows promise in its enticing relation to the ideas of condominium and shared sovereignty. To some, it appears adequate to our time in the epochal arrival of vernacular law's *moment*. But will it be inadequate to the next generation? What if a portion of common use doctrine has been reconstructed or lifted out of the *traditum* of the Grotian Tradition by enthusiasts who inadvertently misrepresent this portion of the tradition as the sum total of a genuine want? The history of international

---

[56] The fact that the Commission provides recommendations as opposed to decisions invites consideration of justiciability. Julius Stone has noted that the doctrine of *non liquet* comes into play when the application of rules of appropriate content and precision are lacking, giving rise to questions regarding a decision-makers (in)ability to resolve disputes. *See* Julius Stone, *Non Liquet and the Function of Law in the International Community*, 35 Brit. Y.B. Int'l L. 125 (1959). Although chided for his piece on the Grotian Tradition, Lauterpacht's contributions to the discussion of *non liquet* are seminal. *See generally*, Hersch Lauterpacht, *Some Observations on the Prohibition of 'Non Liquet' and the Completeness of the Law, in* Symbolae Verzijl 196 (1958).

law teaches that states, through emergent technology and change, through innovation, geostrategic station, and good fortune, continue to validate the historical tendency – the Grotian tendency – to territorialize common space when means and interests allow, leaving international relations scholars to wonder in their wake whatever did Grotius mean by, and whatever remains of, his common use doctrine introduced in a small pamphlet on the Free Sea many years ago?

Selected Bibliography

Aalto, Pami, Helge Blakkisrud, and Hanna Smith. *The New Northern Dimension of the European Neighbourhood*. Brussels: Center for European Policy Studies, 2009.

A General Collection of Voyages and Discoveries made by the Portuguese and the Spaniards, during the Fifteenth and Sixteenth Centuries, Containing the Interesting and Entertaining Voyages of the Celebrated. Gonzalez and Vaz [and others]. London: W. Richardson, Royal Exchange; J. Bew, Paternoster Row; T. Hookham, New Bond-street; J. and T. Egerton, Whitehall; and C. Stalker, Stationers-Court, Ludgate-street, 1789.

Abate, Randall S. and Sarah Ellen Krejci. "*Climate Change Impacts on Ocean and Coastal Law: Scientific Realities and Legal Responses*." In *Climate Change Impacts on Ocean and Coastal Law: U.S. and International Perspectives*, 1–24. Edited by Randall S. Abate. Oxford: Oxford University Press, 2015.

Abbott, Kenneth W. and Duncan Snidal. "Hard and Soft Law in International Governance." 54(3) *International Organization* 421–456, 2000.

Abdy, John T. and Bryan Walker. *The Commentaries of Gaius*. Cambridge: University Press, 1870.

Abi-Saab, Georges. "*Cours Général de Droit International Public*." In *Recueil des Cours*. Vol. 207, 9–463. Edited by Academie de Droit International de la Haye. New York: Springer, 1987.

Agnarsdóttir, Anna. "*The Danish Empire: The Special Case of Iceland*." In *Europe and Its Empires*, 59–84. Edited by Mary N. II. Harris and Csaba Lévai. Pisa: Plus-Pisa University Press, 2008.

Aguirre III, Robert W. "The Panama Canal. International Straits of the World." In *International Straits of the World: The Panama Canal*, Vol. 15. Edited by Gerald J. Mangone. Leiden, Boston: Martinus Nijhoff Publishers, 2010.

Alberts, Colin M. "Technology Transfer and Its Role in International Environmental Law: A Structural Dilemma." 6(1) *Harvard Journal of Law & Technology* 63–84, 1992.

Albrethsen, S. E. and T. B. Arlov. "The Discovery of Svalbard–A Problem Reconsidered." 5 *Fennoscandia Archaeologica* 105–110, 1988.

Alexandrowicz, Charles Henry. "Freitas versus Grotius." 35 *British Yearbook of International Law* 1959, 162–182, 1960.

Allen, John L. "From Cabot to Cartier: The Early Exploration of Eastern North America, 1497–1543." 82(3) *Annals of the Association of American Geographers* 500–521, 1992.

Allot, Philip. "Power Sharing in the Law of the Sea." 77(1) *The American Journal of International Law* 1–30, 1983.

Anderson, Charles L. G. *Old Panama and Castilla del Oro*. Washington, DC: The Sudwarth Company, 1911.

Anderson, David H. "The Status under International Law of the Maritime Areas around Svalbard." 40(4) *Ocean Development and International Law* 373–384, 2009.

Andrews, Kenneth R. *Drake's Voyages: A Re-assessment of Their Place in Elizabethan Maritime Expansion*. New York: Charles Scribner's Sons, 1967.

Anghie, Antony. "International Law in a Time of Change: Should International Law Lead or Follow?" 26(5) *American International Law Review* 1315–1318, 2011.

Anna, Timothy E. "The Last Viceroys of New Spain and Peru: An Appraisal." 81(1) *The American Historical Review* 38–65, 1976.

Araya, Alberto Díaz. "Problemas y perspectivas sociohistóricas en el norte chileno: Análisis sobre la 'chilenización' de Tacna y Arica." 5(4) *Si Somos Americanos. Revista de Estudios Transfronterizos* 49–81, 2014.

Archer, Christon I. "Review of Gabriel Paquette, Enlightenment, Governance, and Reform in Spain and its Empire, 1759–1808." 82(1) *The Journal of Modern History* 221–223, 2010.

Arlov, Thor B. "The Discovery and Early Exploitation of Svalbard. Some Historiographical Notes." 22(1) *Acta Borealia* 3–19, 2005.

A Short History of Svalbard. Oslo: Norsk Polarinstitutt, 1989.

Armitage, David. *Foundations of Modern International Thought*. Cambridge: Cambridge University Press, 2013.

"Introduction." In *The Free Sea: Hugo Grotius*. Edited and with introduction by David Armitage. Translated by Richard Hakluyt with William Welwod's Critique and Grotius' Reply. Indianapolis: Liberty Fund, 2004.

Åtland, Kristian and Kristin Ven Bruusgaard. "When Security Speech Acts Misfire: Russia and the Elektron Incident." 40(3) *Security Dialogue* 333–354, 2009.

Aust, Anthony. *Handbook of International Law*. 2nd edn. Cambridge: Cambridge University Press, 2010.

Axworthy, Thomas S., Timo Koivurova, and Waliul Hasanat, eds. *The Arctic Council: Its Place in the Future of Arctic Governance*. Toronto: Munk-Gordon Arctic Security Program, 2012.

Baev, Pavel K. "Russia's Arctic Ambitions and Anxieties." 112(756) *Current History* 265–270, 2013.

"Sovereignty Is the Key to Russia's Arctic Policy." 37(4) *Strategic Analysis* 489–493, 2013.

Bailes, Alyson J. K. "Understanding the Arctic Council: A 'Sub-Regional' Perspective." 15(2) *Journal of Military and Strategic Studies* 31–49, 2013.

Spitsbergen in a Sea of Change in The Spitsbergen Treaty. In *The Spitsbergen Treaty: Multilateral Governance in the Arctic*, 34: 35–36. Edited by Diana Wallis and Stewart Arnold. Helsinki: Conexio Public Relations, 2011.

Baker, James S. and Michael Byers. "Crossed Lines: The Curious Case of the Beaufort Sea Maritime Boundary Dispute." 43(1) *Ocean Development and International Law* 70–95, 2012.

Balkin, Jack M. and Levinson, Sanford. "Legal Historicism and Legal Academics: The Roses of Law Professors in the Wake of Bush v. Gore." 90(1) *Georgetown Law Journal* 173–181, 2001.

Bantz, Vincent P. "International Legal Status of Condominia." 12 *Florida Journal of International Law* 77–152, 1998.

Bardonnet, Daniel. "Frontières terrestres et frontières maritimes." *Annuaire Français De Droit International* 35: 1–64, 1989.

Bartelson, Jens. *Sovereignty as Symbolic Form*, Vol. 6. London; New York: Routledge, 2014. *A Genealogy of Sovereignty*, Vol. 39. Cambridge, NY: Cambridge University Press, 1995.

Barton, Jonathan R. *A Political Geography of Latin America*. New York: Psychology Press, 1997.

Bartos, T. "Uti Possidetis. Quo Vadis." *Australian Year Book of International Law* 18, 37–96, 1997.

Baslar, Kemal. *The Concept of the Common Heritage of Mankind in International Law*. Leiden, Netherlands: Brill, 1998.

Bauer, K. Jack. *The Mexican War: 1846–1848*. Lincoln and London: University of Nebraska Press, 1974.
Surfboats and horse marines; U.S. naval operations in the Mexican War, 1846-48. Annapolis: U.S. Naval Institute, 1969.

Baur, Ivo and Claudia R. Binder. "Adapting to Socioeconomic Developments by Changing Rules in the Governance of Common Property Pastures in the Swiss Alps." 18(4) *Ecology and Society* 1–15, 2013.

Baxter, Richard R. "International Law in 'Her Infinite Variety'." 29(4) *International and Comparative Law Quarterly* 549–566, 1980.

Beaulac, Stéphane. "Emer de Vattel and the Externalization of Sovereignty." 5(2) *Journal of the History of International Law* 237–292, 2003.

Becker, Michael. "Russia and the Arctic: Opportunities for Engagement Within the Existing Legal Framework." 25(2) *American University International Law Review* 225–247, 2010.

Bederman, David J. *"Privateering."* In *Max Planck Encyclopedia of Public International Law*, Vol. 8, 475–477. Edited by Rüdinger Wolfrum. Oxford University Press, 2012.
"The Old Isolationism and the New Law of the Sea: Reflections on Advice and Consent for UNCLOS." 49(21) *Harvard International Law Journal* 21–27, 2008.

Bevans, Charles Irving. *Treaties and Other International Agreements of the United States of America, 1776–1949*. Vols. 1, 6, 10, and 12. Washington: US Government Print Office, 1968–1976.

Beyerlin, Ulrich. *"Pactum de Contrahendo, Pactum de Negotiando."* In *Encyclopedia of Public International Law* 854–858. Vol. 3. Edited by Rudolf Bernhardt. 1984.
"Pactum de Contrahendo und Pactum de Negotiando im Völkerrecht?" 36 *Zeitschrift für Ausländishes Offentliches Recht und Völkerrecht* 407–443, 1976.

Bicheno, Hugh. *Crescent and Cross: The Battle of Lepanto 1571*. London: Cassell, 2003.

Biersteker, Thomas J. and Cynthia Weber, eds. *State Sovereignty as Social Construct*. Vol. 46. Cambridge, NY: Cambridge University Press, 1996.
"The Social Construction of State Sovereignty." 46(1) *Cambridge Studies in International Relations* 1–21, 1996.

Bilder, Richard B. "*Beyond Compliance: Helping Nations Cooperate.*" In *Commitment and Compliance: The Role of Non-Binding Norms in the International Legal System*, 65–73. Edited by Dinah Shelton. Oxford: Oxford University Press, 2000.

Bleichert, Maura A. "The Effectiveness of Voluntary Jurisdiction in the ICJ: El Salvador v. Honduras, A Case in Point." 16(3) *Fordham International Law Journal* 799–847, 1992.

Blom, Hans. W., ed. *Property, Piracy and Punishment: Hugo Grotius on War and Booty in De Iure Praedae: Concepts and Contexts*. Leiden, Netherlands: Brill, 2009.

Bloom, Evan T. "Establishment of the Arctic Council." 93(3) *The American Journal of International Law* 712–722, 1999.

Blunden, Margaret. "Geopolitics and the Northern Sea Route." 88(1) *International Affairs* 115–129, 2012.

Blutman, László. "In the Trap of a Legal Metaphor: International Soft Law." 59(3) *International and Comparative Law Quarterly* 605–624, 2010.

Bockstoce, John R. and John J. Burns. "Commercial Whaling in the North Pacific Sector." 2(14) *The Bowhead Whale* 563–577, 1993.

Bodin, Jean. *Les Six Livres De La République*. Paris: Fayard, 1986.
  Six Books of the Commonwealth. Abridged and translated by M. J. Tooley. Oxford: Basil Blackwell, 1955.

Bonilla, Heraclio. "The War of the Pacific and the National and Colonial Problem in Peru." 81(1) *Past & Present* 92–118, 1978.

Booth, John A., Christine J. Wade, and Thomas W. Walker. *Understanding Central America: Global Forces, Rebellion, and Change*. 4th edn. Boulder, CO: Westview Press, 2006.

Borgerson, Scott G. "The Coming Arctic Boom: as Ice Melts, the Region Heats Up." *Foreign Affairs*. 92 (4): 76–89, 2013.
  "Arctic Meltdown: The Economic and Security Implications of Global Warming." 87(2) *Foreign Affairs* 63–77, 2008.

Borgoño, Luis Barros and John W. Davis. *The Problem of the Pacific and the New Policies of Bolivia*. Baltimore, MD: Sun Job Printing Office, 1924.
  Hugo Grotius, the Portuguese, and Free Trade in the East Indies. Singapore: National University of Singapore Press, 2011.

Borschberg, Peter. "*Grotius, Maritime Intra-Asian Trade and the Portuguese Estado Da Índia: Problems, Perspectives and Insights from De Iure Praedae.*" In *Property, Piracy and Punishment: Hugo Grotius on War and Booty in De Iure Praedae Concepts and Contexts*, 31–60. Edited by Blom, Hans W. Leiden: Brill, 2009.
  "Hugo Grotius' Theory of Trans-Oceanic Trade Regulation: Revisiting Mare Liberum (1609)." 29(3) *Itinerario* 31–53, 2005.

Boutrous-Ghali, Boutrous. "The Role of International Law in the Twenty-First Century: A Grotian Moment." 18(1) *Fordham International Law Journal* 1609–1613, 1995.

Bovenberg, Jasper A. "Mining the Common Heritage for Our DNA: Lessons Learned from Grotius and Pardo." 29(8) *Duke Law and Technology Review* 1–20, 2006.
  Property Rights in Blood, Genes and Data: Naturally Yours? The Hague. Boston: Martinus Nijhoff, 2006.

Bowett, Derek William. "Estoppel before International Tribunals and Its Relation to Acquiescence." 33(1) *British Year Book of International Law* 176–202, 1957.

Boxer, Charles Ralph. *Fidalgos in the Far East 1550–1770*. Hong Kong; London: Oxford University Press, 1968.

The Dutch Seaborne Empire, 1600–1800. New York: Knopf, 1965.

The Portuguese Seaborne Empire, 1415–1825. New York: A. A. Knopf, 1969.

Boyd III, Willard L. and Robert K. Huffman. "Treatment of Implied-in-Law and Implied-in-Fact Contracts and Promissory Estoppel in the United States Claims Court." 40(3) *Catholic University Law Review* 605–630, 1990.

Braudel, Fernand. *Civilization and Capitalism: 15th-18th Century. Vol. 2, The Wheels of Commerce*. Translated by Siân Reynolds. New York: Harper and Row, 1983.

Civilization and Capitalism: 15th-18th Century. Vol. 3, The Perspective of the World. Translated by Siân Reynolds. New York: Harper and Row, 1984.

Bridenbaugh, Carl and Roberta. *No Peace Beyond the Line: The English in the Caribbean, 1624–1690*. New York and London: Oxford University Press, 1972.

Bridges, Brian. "Beyond Economics: Growth Triangles in Southeast Asia." 21(1) *Asian Perspective* 55–77, 1997.

Brigham, Lawson W. "Arctic Marine Transportation." In *McGraw-Hill Yearbook of Science and Technology*, 8–11. Edited by Robert L. Weber. New York: McGraw-Hill, 2012.

"Russia Opens Its Maritime Arctic." 137(5) *United States Naval Institute Proceedings* 50–54, 2011.

"Edited Transcription of Q & A Session: Panels III & IV." In *Changes in the Artic Environment and the Law of the Sea*, 307–318. Edited by Myron H. Nordquist, John Norton Moore, and Tomas H. Heidar. Leiden: Martinus Nijhoff, 2010.

Brilmayer, Lea and Natalie Klein. "Land and Sea: Two Sovereignty Regimes in Search of a Common Denominator." 33(3) *New York University Journal of International Law and Politics* 703–768, 2001.

Bring, Ove. "The Westphalian Peace Tradition in International Law-From Jus ad Bellum to Jus Contra Bellum." In *International Law across the Spectrum of Conflict: Essays in Honour of Professor LC Green on the Occasion of His Eightieth Birthday*. Vol. 75, 57–80. Edited by Michael N. Schmitt and Green, Leslie C. Newport: Naval War College Press, 2000.

Brito Vieira, Monica. "Mare Liberum vs. Mare Clausum: Grotius, Freitas, and Selden's Debate on Dominion over the Seas." 64(3) *Journal of the History of Ideas* 361–377, 2003.

Brown, Stephen R. *Merchant Kings: When Companies Ruled the World, 1600–1900*. New York: Thomas Dunne Books, 2010.

A Most Damnable Invention: Dynamite, Nitrates, and the Making of the Modern World. New York: Thomas Dunne Books, 2005.

Brubaker, R. Douglas. *The Russian Arctic Straits*, edited by Gerard J. Mangone. Leiden; Boston: M. Nijhoff, 2005.

"Straits in the Russian Arctic." 32(3) *Ocean Development and International Law* 263–287, 2001.

Brubaker, R. Douglas and Willy Østreng. "The Northern Sea Route Regime: Exquisite Superpower Subterfuge?" 30(4) *Ocean Development and International Law* 299–331, 1999.

Brüel, Erik. *International Straits: A Treatise on International Law*. Vol. 1. London: Sweet & Maxwell, 1947.

Buck, Susan J. *The Global Commons: An Introduction*. Washington, DC: Island Press, 1998.

Bull, Hedley. *The Anarchical Society: A Study of Order in World Politics*. New York: Columbia University Press, 1977.

The Grotian Conception of International Society, in Diplomatic investigations: Essays in the Theory of International Politics. Butterfield, Herbert, Martin Wight, and Hedley Bull. London: Allen & Unwin, 1966.

Burch, Kurt. *"Property" and the Making of the International System*. Boulder: Lynne Rienner, 1998.

Burkhardt, Mike. "The German Hanse and Bergen – New Perspectives on an Old Subject." 58(1) *Scandinavian Economic History Review* 60–79, 2010.

Burnett, Christina Duffy. "The Edges of Empire and the Limits of Sovereignty: American Guano Islands." 57(3) *American Quarterly* 779–803, 2005.

Burns, John J., J. Jerome Montague, and Cleveland J. Cowles, eds. *The Bowhead Whale*. Lawrence, KA: Society for Marine Mammalogy, 1993.

Burr, Robert N. *By Reason or Force: Chile and the Balancing of Power in South America, 1830–1905*. Berkeley: University of California Press, 1965.

Burton, Steven J. "Breach of Contract and the Common Law Duty to Perform in Good Faith." 94(2) *Harvard Law Review* 369–404, 1980.

Bush, George W. "Address before a Joint Session of the Congress on the State of the Union." 38(5) *Weekly Compilation of Presidential Documents* 133–139, 2002.

Butler, William Elliott. *"Grotius and the Law of the Sea."* In *Hugo Grotius and International Relations*, 209–220. Edited by Hedley Bull and Benedict Kingsbury. Oxford: Oxford University Press, 1992.

Northeast Arctic Passage. Alphen aan den Rijn: Sijthoff and Noordhoff, 1978.

Buzan, Barry. "From International System to International Society: Structural Realism and Regime Theory Meet the English School." 47(3) *International Organization* 327–352, 1993.

Byers, Michael, with James Baker. *International Law and the Arctic*. New York; Cambridge: Cambridge University Press, 2013.

Byers, Michael. *Who Owns the Arctic?: Understanding Sovereignty Disputes in the North*. Vancouver, BC: Douglas and McIntyre, 2010.

Byers, Michael and Suzanne Lalonde. "Who Controls the Northwest Passage." 42(4) *Vanderbilt Journal of Transnational Law* 1133–1162, 2009.

Cable, Vincent. "The 'Football War' and the Central American Common Market." 45(4) *International Affairs* 658–671, 1969.

Caflisch, Lucius. *"Vattel and the Peaceful Settlement of International Disputes."* In *Vattel's International Law from a XXI St Century Perspective / Le Droit International de Vattel Vu Du XXI E Siècle*, 255–266. Edited by Vincent Chetail and Peter Haggenmacher. The Hague, Boston: Martinus Nijhoff, 2011.

Calvert, Robert A., Arnoldo De Leon, and Gregg Cantrell. *The History of Texas*. Hoboken, NJ: John Wiley & Sons, 2013.

Caminos, Hugo and Michael R. Molitor. "Progressive Development of International Law and the Package Deal." 79(4) *The American Journal of International Law* 871–890, 1985.

Carr, Edward Hallett. *What Is History?* New York: Alfred A. Knopf, 1962.

The Twenty Years' Crisis: 1919–1939; An Introduction to the Study of International Relations. London: Macmillan, 1946.

Cassese, Antonio. "The Martens Clause: Half a Loaf or Simply Pie in the Sky?" 11(1) *European Journal of International Law* 187–216, 2000.

"The Israel-PLO Agreement and Self-Determination." 4(4) *European Journal of International Law* 564–568, 1993.

Casson, Lionel. *"Seaborne Exploration in the Ancient World."* In *Maritime History as World History*, 35–46. Edited by Daniel Finamore. Salem, MA: Peabody Essex Museum, 2004.

Castellino, Joshua and Steve Allen; with special contribution on indigenous peoples from Jérémie Gilbert. *Title to Territory in International Law: A Temporal Analysis.* Aldershot; Hants; England; Dartmouth; Burlington, VT: Ashgate, 2003.

Cavallar, Georg. "Vitoria, Grotius, Pufendorf, Wolff and Vattel: Accomplices of European Colonialism and Exploitation or True Cosmopolitans." 10(2) *Journal of the History of International Law* 192–198, 2008.

The Rights of Strangers: Theories of International Hospitality, the Global Community, and Political Justice since Vitoria. London: Routledge, 2002.

Chan, Joseph. *Confucian Perfectionism: A Political Philosophy for Modern Times.* Princeton, NJ: Princeton University Press, 2013.

Chatterjee, Pratap. *Halliburton's Army: How a Well-Connected Texas Oil Company Revolutionized the Way America Makes War.* New York: Nation Books, 2009.

Chaturvedi, Sanjay. *"Geopolitical Transformations: 'Rising' Asia and the Future of the Arctic Council."* In *The Arctic Council: Its Place in the Future of Arctic Governance*, 225–260. Edited by Thomas S. Axworthy, Timo Koivurova, and Waliul Hasanat. Toronto: Munk-Gordon Arctic Security Program, 2012.

Cheng, Bin. *Studies in International Space Law.* Oxford: Clarendon Press; New York: Oxford University Press, 1997.

Chinkin, Christine M. "The Challenge of Soft Law: Development and Change in International Law." 38(4) *International and Comparative Law Quarterly* 850–866, 1989.

Christie, Eric William Hunter. *The Antarctic Problem: An Historical and Political Study.* London: Allen and Unwin, 1951.

Christol, Carl Q. "The Common Heritage of Mankind Provision in the 1979 Agreement Governing the Activities of States on the Moon and Other Celestial Bodies." 14(3) *International Lawyer* 429–483, 1980.

Christophe-Alexandre, Paillard. "Russia and Europe's Mutual Energy Dependence." 63(2) *Columbia Journal of International Affairs* 65–84, 2010.

Churchill, Robin and Geir Ulfstein. *"The Disputed Maritime Zones around Svalbard."* In *Changes in the Arctic Environmental and the Law of the Sea*, 551–593. Edited by Myron H. Nordquist, John Norton Moore, and Tomas H. Heidar. Leiden: Martinus Nijhoff, 2010.

Churchill, Robin Rolf and Alan Vaughan Lowe. *The Law of the Sea.* Manchester: Manchester University Press, 1999.

Churchill, Robin Rolf and Geir Ulfstein. *Marine Management in Disputed Areas: The Case of the Barents Sea.* London: Routledge, 1992.

Clegern, Wayne M. *Origins of Liberal Dictatorship in Central America: Guatemala, 1865–1873.* Niwot: University Press of Colorado, 1994.

Cochran, Patricia. "Indigenous Frameworks for Observing and Responding to Climate Change in Alaska." 120(3) *Climate Change* 557–567, 2013.

Cohen, Ariel. *"Russia in the Arctic: Challenges to US Energy and Geopolitics in the High North."* In *Russia in the Arctic*, 11–52. Edited by Stephen J. Blank. Carlisle, PA: Strategic Studies Institute, US Army War College, 2011.

Cohen, Morris Raphael. *The Meaning of Human History.* LaSalle, IL: Open Court, 1961.

Colletta, Paolo E., ed.; Jack Bauer, associate ed. *United States Navy and Marine Corps Bases, Overseas.* Westport, CN: Greenwood, 1985.

Collingwood, R. G.. *The Idea of History.* Oxford: Clarendon Press, 1946.

Combs, Jerald A. *The Jay Treaty, Political Battleground of the Founding Fathers.* Berkeley: University of California Press, 1970.

Conley, Heather A. *The New Foreign Policy Frontier: US Interests and Actors in the Arctic. A Report of the CSIS Europe Program.* Washington, DC: Center for Strategic and International Studies, 2013.

Connor, Michael. *The Invention of Terra Nullius: Historical and Legal Fictions on the Foundation of Australia.* Sydney: Macleay Press, 2005.

Conrad, Joseph. *Heart of Darkness.* Rockville, MD: Wildside Press, 2003.

Conway, Martin. *No Man's Land: A History of Spitsbergen from Its Discovery in 1596 to the Beginning of the Scientific Exploration of the Country.* Cambridge: Cambridge University Press, 2012.

Cookman, Scott. *Ice Blink: The Tragic Fate of Sir John Franklin's Lost Polar Expedition First Edition.* New York: Wiley, 2000.

Cornblit, Oscar. *Power and Violence in the Colonial City: Oruro from the Mining Renaissance to the Rebellion of Tupac Amaru, 1740–1782.* Cambridge: Cambridge University Press, 1995.

Croce, Benedetto. *History as the Story of Liberty.* Translated by Sylvia Sprigge. London: Allen and Unwin, 1941.

Crowe, Michael Bertram. "The 'Impious Hypothesis': A Paradox in Hugo Grotius?" 38 (3) *Tijdschrift Voor Filosofie* 379–410, 1976.

 "An Eccentric Seventeenth-Century Witness to the Natural Law: John Selden (1584–1654)." 12(1) *American Journal of Jurisprudence* 184–195, 1967.

Croxton, Derek. "The Peace of Westphalia of 1648 and the Origins of Sovereignty." 21(3) *The International History Review* 569–591, 1999.

Croxton, Derek and Anuschka Tischer. *The Peace of Westphalia: A Historical Dictionary.* Westport, CT: Greenwood Publishing Group, 2002.

Cryle, Peter Maxwell. *"Anachronistic Readings of Eighteenth-Century Libertinage in Nineteenth- and Twentieth-Century France."* In *Sex, Knowledge, and Receptions of the Past*, 65–85. Edited by Kate Fisher and Rebecca Langlands. Oxford: Oxford University Press, 2015.

Cunningham, Charles Henry. *The Audiencia in the Spanish Colonies, as Illustrated by the Audiencia of Manila, 1583–1800.* Berkeley: University of California, 1919.

Curci, Jonathan. *The Protection of Biodiversity and Traditional Knowledge in International Law of Intellectual Property.* Cambridge; New York: Cambridge University Press, 2010.

Curtin, Philip D. *Cross-Cultural Trade in World History.* Cambridge; New York: Cambridge University Press, 1984.

Cutler, A. Claire. "The 'Grotian Tradition' in International Relations." 17 *Review of International Studies* 41–65, 1991.

D'Amato, Anthony and John Lawrence Hargrove. *"Environment and the Law of the Sea: A Report of the Working Group on Ocean Environment of the American Society of International Law."* Studies in Transnational Legal Policy 1–60. Vol. 5. Washington, DC: American Society of International Law, 1974.

d'Aspremont, Jean. "Softness in International Law: A Self-Serving Quest for New Legal Materials." 19(5) *European Journal of International Law* 1075–1093, 2008.

Dando-Collins, Stephen. *Tycoon's War: How Cornelius Vanderbilt invaded a Country to Overthrow America's Most Famous Military Adventurer.* Cambridge, MA: Da Capo Press, 2008.

Davidson, George. *Francis Drake on the Northwest Coast of America in the Year 1579: The Golden Hinde Did Not Anchor in the Bay of San Francisco.* Vol. 5, Series II. Transactions and Proceedings of the Geographical Society of the Pacific, 1908.

The Discovery of San Francisco Bay: The Rediscovery of the Port of Monterey; the Establishment of the Presidio, and the Founding of the Mission of San Francisco. Vol. 4. Transactions and Proceedings of the Geographical Society of the Pacific. San Francisco: Geographic Society of the Pacific, 1907.

Davies, David W. *A Primer of Dutch Seventeenth Century Overseas Trade.* The Hague: Martinus Nijhoff, 1961.

Davis, Harold Eugene, John J. Finan, and F. Taylor Peck, eds. *Latin American Diplomatic History: An Introduction.* Baton Rouge and London: Louisiana State University Press, 1977.

Daube, David. "Turpitude in Digest 12.5.5". *Studies in Roman Law in Memory of A. Arthur Schiller.* Edited by Bagnall, Roger & Harris, William. 33–38, 1986.

de Freitas, Seraphim. *De Iusto Imperio Lusitanorum Asiatico.* Lisboa: Instituto Nacional de Investigação Científica, reimpr. 1983.

de La Fayette, Louise. "Access to Ports in International Law." 11(1) *The International Journal of Marine and Coastal Law* 1–22, 1996.

Dennis, William Jefferson. *Tacna and Arica; an Account of the Chile-Peru Boundary Dispute and of the Arbitrations by the United States.* Hamden, CT: Archon, 1967.

de Solis, Antonio. *The History of the Conquest of Mexico by the Spaniards.* Done into English from the Original Spanish by Thomas Townsend Esq. London: Printed for T. Woodward at the Half-Moon, and J. Hooke at the Flower-de-Luce, both against St. Dunstan's Church, in Fleet-Street; and J. Peele at Locke's-Head in Pater-Noster-Row, 1724.

De Sá, Hernane Tavares. *The Play within the Play: The Inside Story of the UN.* New York: Knopf, 1966.

De Vattel, Emer and Joseph Chitty. *The Law of Nations: Or, Principles of the Law of Nature, Applied to the Conduct and Affairs of Nations and Sovereigns.* Philadelphia: P. H. Nicklin and T. Johnson, 1835.

De Visscher, Charles. *Les effectivités du droit international public.* Paris: Editions A. Pedone, 1967.

de Vries, Jan. *Economy of Europe in an Age of Crisis, 1600–1750.* Cambridge: Cambridge University Press, 1976.

Dilthey, Wilhelm. "*The Understanding of Other Persons and Their Life-Expressions.*" In *Theories of History*, 213–215. Edited by Patrick L. Gardiner. London: Allen and Unwin, 1959.

Dodds, Klaus. "The Ilulissat Declaration (2008): The Arctic States, 'Law of the Sea', and Arctic Ocean." 33(2) *SAIS Review of International Affairs* 45–55, 2013.

"*Anticipating the Arctic and the Arctic Council: Pre-emption, Precaution and Preparedness.*" In *The Arctic Council: Its Place in the Future of Arctic Governance*, 1–28. Edited by Thomas S. Axworthy, Timo Koivurova, and Waliul Hasanat. Toronto: Munk-Gordon Arctic Security Program, 2012.

The Antarctic: A Very Short Introduction. Oxford; Oxford University Press, 2012.

Dolšak, Nives, and Elinor Ostrom. "The Challenges of the Commons," *The Commons in the New Millennium.* 3–34, 2003.

Donnelly, Mark P. and Daniel Diehl. *Pirates of Virginia: Plunder and High Adventure on the Old Dominion Coastline.* Mechanicsburg, PA: Stackpole Books, 2012.

Dotson, John E. "Foundations of Venetian Naval Strategy from Pietro II Orseolo to the Battle of Zonchio 1000–1500." 32(32) *Viator: Medieval and Renaissance Studies* 113–123, 2001.

Dufresne, Robert. *Controversial Canadian Claims over Arctic Waters and Maritime Zones.* Ottawa: Parliamentary Information and Research Service, 2008.

Dumbauld, Edward. *Life and Legal Writings of Hugo Grotius.* Norman, OK: University of Oklahoma Press, 1969.

Dunai, Tibor J., Gabriel A. González López, and Joaquim Juez-Larré. "Oligocene–Miocene Age of Aridity in the Atacama Desert Revealed by Exposure Dating of Erosion-Sensitive Landforms." 33(4) *Geology* 321–324, 2005.

Dunlap, William V. *Transit Passage in the Russian Arctic Straits.* Durham: International Boundaries Research Unit, University of Durham, 1996.

Dyke, Jon Van and Christopher, Yuen. "'Common Heritage' v. 'Freedom of the Seas': Which Governs the Seabed?" 19(3) *San Diego Law Review* 493–551, 1982.

Earle, Peter. *The Pirate Wars.* New York: Thomas Dunne Books; St. Martin's Press, 2003.

Ebinger, Charles K. and Evie Zambetakis. "The Geopolitics of Arctic Melt." 85(6) *International Affairs* 1215–1232, 2009.

Edenhofer, Ottmar, Christian Flachsland, and Berhnard Lorentz. "*The Atmosphere as a Global Commons.*" In *The Wealth of the Commons: A World Beyond Market & State* Part 5. Edited by David Bollier and Silke Helfrich. Amherst: Levellers Press, 2014.

Edmundson, William. *A History of the British Presence in Chile: From Bloody Mary to Charles Darwin and the Decline of British Influence.* New York, NY: Palgrave Macmillan, 2009.

Elferink, Alex G. Oude. "*Arctic Maritime Delimitations: The Preponderance of Similarities with Other Regions.*" In *The Law of the Sea and Polar Maritime Delimitation and Jurisdiction*, 179–183. Edited by Alex G. Oude Elferink and Donald R. Rothwell. The Hague: Martinus Nijhoff, 2001.

El Libro Del Mar (The Book of the Sea). 2. ed. La Paz: *Ministerio de relaciones exteriores de Bolivia, Dirección estratégica de reivindicación marítima,* 2014.

Elliot-Meisel, Elizabeth B. "Still Unresolved after Fifty Years: The Northwest Passage in Canadian-American Relations, 1946–1998." 29(3) *American Review of Canadian Studies* 407–430, 1999.

Elliott, John Huxtable. *Empires of the Atlantic World: Britain and Spain in America, 1492–1830.* New Haven: Yale University Press, 2006.

Ellner, Steve. "Latin America's Radical Left in Power Complexities and Challenges in the Twenty-first Century." 40(3) *Latin American Perspectives* 5–25, 2013.

Elshtain, Jean Bethke. *Sovereignty: God, State, and Self.* New York: Basic Books, 2008.

Emmerson, Charles. *The Future History of the Arctic.* New York: Public Affairs, 2010.

Engel, Kristen H. and Saleska, Scott R. "Subglobal Regulation of the Global Commons: The Case of Climate Change." 32(2) *Ecology Law Quarterly* 183–233, 2005.

Esquemeling, John. *Bucaniers of America: Or, A True Account of the most Remarkable Assaults Committed of Late Years Upon the Coasts of the West Indies, by the Bucaniers of Jamaica and Tortuga, Both English and French.* 2 Vols., 2nd edn., Corrected and Enlarged with Two Additional Relations, viz. the One of Captain Cook, and the Other of Captain Sharp. London: Printed for William Crooke at the Green Dragon without Temple-bar, 1684.

Estes, Donald H. *Asama Gunkan: The Reappraisal of a War Scare.* San Diego Historical Society, 1978.

Evensen, Jens. "The Anglo-Norwegian Fisheries Case and Its Legal Consequences." *The American Journal of International Law.* 46 (4): 609–630, 1952.

Falk, Richard. "Some Thoughts on the Decline of International Law and Future Prospects." 9(2) *Hofstra Law Review* 399–410, 1980.

Falk, Richard, Friedrich Kratochwil, and Saul H. Mendlovitz, *International Law: A Contemporary Perspective.* Boulder: Westview Press, 1985.

Farcau, Bruce W. "Pacific, War of the (1879–1883)." In *The Encyclopedia of War III,* 1628–1633. Edited by Gordon Martel. Hoboken: Wiley-Blackwell, 2012.

The Ten Cents War: Chile, Peru, and Bolivia in the War of the Pacific, 1879–1884. Westport, CT: Greenwood Publishing Group, 2000.

The Chaco War: Bolivia and Paraguay, 1932–1935. Westport, CT: Greenwood Publishing Group, 1996.

Fawcett, J. E. S. "How Free Are the Seas?" 49(1) *International Affairs* 14–15, 1973.

Fernández-Armesto, Felipe. "Maritime History and World History." In *Maritime History as World History,* 7–34. Edited by Daniel Finamore. Salem, MA: Peabody Essex Museum, 2004.

Vasco Da Gama and the Linking of Europe and Asia. Edited by Anthony R. Disney and Emily Booth. New Delhi; New York: Oxford University Press, 2000.

Columbus. Oxford: Oxford University Press, 1991.

Figueroa Pla, Uldaricio. *La demanda marítima boliviana en los foros internacionales.* Santiago: RIL editores, 2007.

Finamore, Daniel. ed. *Maritime History as World History.* Salem, MA: Peabody Essex Museum; Gainesville: University Press of Florida, 2004.

Finch, George A. "The Treaty with Nicaragua Granting Canal and Other Rights to the United States." 10(2) *The American Journal of International Law* 344–351, 1916.

Findling, John E. *Close Neighbors, Distant Friends: United States-Central American Relations.* Westport, CT: Greenwood Press, 1987.

Finnemore, Martha and Stephen J. Toope. "Alternatives to 'Legalization': Richer Views of Law and Politics." 55(3) *International Organization* 743–758, 2001.

Fischer, David Hackett. *Champlain's Dream: The European Founding of North America*. New York; London; Toronto; Sydney: Simon & Schuster, 2008.

Fisher, F. C. "The Arbitration of the Guatemalan-Honduran Boundary Dispute." 27(3) *American Journal of International Law* 403–427, 1933.

Fitzmaurice, Andrew. "The Genealogy of Terra Nullius." 38(129) *Australian Historical Studies* 1–15, 2007.

Fitzmaurice, Gerald. "Judicial Innovation–Its Uses and Its Perils–As Exemplified in Some of the Works of the International Court of Justice During Lord McNair's Period of Office." In *Cambridge Essays in International Law: Essays in Honour of Lord McNair*. London: Stevens,1965.

Flake, Lincoln E. "Russia's Policy on the Northern Sea Route in an Era of Climate Change." 158(3) *Rusi Journal* 44–52, 2013.

Fleischer, Carl A. *"The New International Law of the Sea and Svalbard."* Norwegian Academy of Science and Letters 150th Anniversary Symposium, Jan. 25, 2007, 1–15.

Frakes, Jennifer. "The Common Heritage of Mankind Principle and the Deep Seabed, Outer Space, and Antarctica: Will Developed and Developing Nations Reach a Compromise?" 21(2) *Wisconsin International Law Journal* 409–434, 2003.

Francioni, Francesco. "Resource Sharing in Antarctica: For Whose Benefit?" 1(1) *European Journal of International Law* 258–268, 1990.

Francioni, Francesco and Tullio Scovazzi, eds. *International Law for Antarctica*. 2nd edn. The Hague; Boston: Kluwer Law International, 1996.

Franckx, Erik. "Pacta Tertiis and the Agreement for the Implementation of the Straddling and Highly Migratory Fish Stocks Provisions of the United Nations Convention on the Law of the Sea." 8(1) *Tulane Journal of International and Comparative Law* 49–81, 2000.

   "New Developments in the Northeast Passage." 6(1) *International Journal of Estuarine and Coastal Law* 33–40, 1991.

   "Non-Soviet shipping in the Northeast Passage, and the legal status of Proliv Vil'kitskogo". *Polar Record*. 24 (151): 269–276, 1988.

Friedman, Milton. *Capitalism and Freedom*. Chicago and London: The University of Chicago Press, 1962.

Friedman, Milton and Rose Friedman. *Free to Choose: A Personal Statement*. New York and London: Houghton Mifflin Harcourt, 1990.

Friedmann, Wolfgang. "Selden Redivivus – Towards a Partition of the Seas?" 65(4) *The American Journal of International Law* 757–763, 1971.

   "The North Sea Continental Shelf Cases – A Critique." 64(2) *The American Journal of International Law* 229–232, 1970.

Friel, Ian. "Guns, Gales and God: Elizabeth I's 'Merchant Navy'." 60(1) *History Today* 45–51, 2010.

Fruin, Robert. "An Unpublished Work of Hugo Grotius's." 5(1) *Bibliotheca Visseriana* 13–26, 1925.

Fukuyama, Francis. *The End of History and the Last Man*. New York: Avon Books, 1992.

Fulton, Thomas Wemyss. *The Sovereignty of the Sea, an Historical Account of the Claims of England to the Dominion of the British Seas, and of the Evolution of the Territorial Waters*. Edinburgh: W. Blackwood, 1911.

Gadamer, Hans-Georg. *Truth and Method*. Translation revised by Joel Weinsheimer and Donald G. Marshall. London: Sheed and Ward, 1975.

Garner, William R. *The Chaco Dispute: A Study of Prestige Diplomacy*. Washington: Public Affairs Press, 1966.

Gassama, Ibrahim J. "International Law at a Grotian Moment: The Invasion of Iraq in Context." 18(1) *Emory International Law Review* 1–52, 2004.

Gau, Michael Sheng-ti. "The Commission on the Limits of the Continental Shelf as a Mechanism to Prevent Encroachment upon the Area." 10(1) *Chinese Journal of International Law* 3–33, 2011.

Gellinek, Christian. *Hugo Grotius*. Boston: Twayne Publishers, 1983.

George, William P. "Grotius, Theology, and International Law: Overcoming Textbook Bias." 14(2) *Journal of Law and Religion* 605–631, 1999.

Glamann, Kristof. *Dutch-Asiatic Trade, 1620–1740*. Copenhagen: Danish Science, 1958.

Gobat, Michel. *Confronting the American Dream: Nicaragua Under U.S. Imperial Rule*. Durham, NC: Duke University Press, 2005.

Goldstein, Judith, Miles Kahler, Robert Keohane, and Anne-Marie Slaughter. "Introduction: Legalization and World Politics." 54(3) *International Organization* 385–399, 2000.

Golitsyn, Vladimir. "*Climate Change, Marine Science and Delineation of the Continental Shelf*." In *Arctic Science, International Law and Climate Change*, 245–260. Vol. 235 Beiträge zum ausländischen öffentlichen Recht und Völkerrecht. Edited by Susanne Wasum-Rainer, Ingo Winkelmann, and Katrin Tiroch. Berlin Heidelberg: Springer, 2012.

Golts, Aleksandr. "*The Arctic: A Clash of Interests or Clash of Ambitions?*" In *Russia in the Arctic*, 43–62. Edited by Stephen J. Blank. Carlisle, PA: Strategic Studies Institute, US Army War College, 2011.

Gordon, Dennis R. "The Question of the Pacific: Current Perspectives on a Long-standing Dispute." 14(4) *World Affairs* 321–335, 1979.

Gordon, Edward. "Grotius and the Freedom of the Seas in the Seventeenth Century." 16(2) *Willamette Journal of International Law and Dispute Resolution* 252–254, 2008.

Gordon, H. Scott. *The Economic Theory of a Common-Property Resource: The Fishery*. London: Palgrave Macmillan UK, 1954.

Gosse, Philip. *The Pirates' Who's Who*. Boston: Lauriat, 1924.

The History of Piracy. New York: Tudor Publishing Company, 1946.

Graczyk, Piotr. "*The Arctic Council Inclusive of non-Arctic Perspectives: Seeking a New Balance*." In *The Arctic Council: Its Place in the Future of Arctic Governance*, 261–305. Edited by Thomas S. Axworthy, Timo Koivurova, and Waliul Hasanat. Toronto: Munk-Gordon Arctic Security Program, 2012.

Gregory XVI. *Index librorum prohibitorum sanctissimi domini nostri Gregorii XVI pontificis maximi jussu editus. In qua libri omnes ab apostolica sede usque ad annum MDCCCLII, EDITIO NOVISSIMA*. Romae: Ex Typographia Reverendae Camerae Apostolicae, 1835.

Griffiths, Franklyn. "New Illusions of a Northwest Passage." *International Energy Policy, the Arctic and the Law of the Sea*. 303–319, 2005.

Griffiths, Martin. *Rethinking International Relations Theory*. Basingstoke: Palgrave Macmillan, 2011.

Grotius, Hugo. *Mare Liberum 1609–2009*. Translated and edited by Robert Feenstra. Introduction by Jeroen Vervliet. Leiden: Brill, 2009 [1609].

    The Free Sea. Edited and with introduction by David, Armitage. Translated by Richard Hakluyt with William Welwod's Critique and Grotius' Reply. Indianapolis: Liberty Fund, 2004.

    De Iure Praedae Commentarius. Translated by Gwladys L Williams and Walter H Zeydel. Edited by James Brown Scott. Oxford: Clarendon, 1950.

    De Jure Belli Ac Pacis Libri Tres. Vol. 2. Translated by Francis W. Kelsey with the collaboration of Arthur E. R. Boak, Henry A. Sanders, Jesse S. Reeves, and Herbert F. Wright, and an introduction by James Brown Scott. Oxford: Clarendon, 1925 [1625].

Grotius, Hugo., ed. *Martianus Capella, Martiani Capellae de nuptii Philologiae et Mercurii*. Leiden, 1599.

Grunewald, Donald. "The Anglo-Guatemalan Dispute over British Honduras." 5(2) *Caribbean Studies* 17–44, 1965.

Grydehøj, Adam, Anne Grydehøj, and Maria Ackrén. "The Globalization of the Arctic: Negotiating Sovereignty and Building Communities in Svalbard, Norway." 7(1) *Island Studies Journal* 99–118, 2012.

Hacia un enfoque trincional de las relaciones entre Bolivia, Chile y Perú. Centro de Estudios Estratégicos para la Integración Latinoamericana. Caracas, La Paz, Lima, Santiago, 2001.

Haakonssen, Knud. *Grotius, Pufendorf, and Modern Natural Law*. Aldershot, England; Dartmouth; Brookfield, VT: Ashgate, 1999.

    "Hugo Grotius and the History of Political Thought." 13(2) *Political Theory* 239–265, 1985.

Haanappel, Peter P. C. *The Law and Policy of Air Space and Outer Space: A Comparative Approach*. The Hague, New York: Kluwer Law International; Frederick, MD: Distributed in North, Central and South America by Aspen Publishers, 2003.

Haas, Peter. "Knowledge, Power and International Policy Coordination." 46(1) *Special Issue of International Organization* 1–390, 1992.

    "Do Regimes Matter? Epistemic Communities and Mediterranean Pollution Control." 43(3) *International Organization* 377–403, 1989.

Hackworth, G. H. *Digest of International Law*. Vol. 1. Washington: Government Printing Office, 1940–1944.

Hacquebord, Louwrens, Frits Steenhuisen, and Huib Waterbolk. "English and Dutch Whaling Trade and Whaling Stations in Spitsbergen (Svalbard) before 1660." 15(2) *International Journal of Maritime History* 117–134, 2003.

Haggard, Stephan and Beth A. Simmons. "Theories of International Regimes." 41(3) *International Organization* 491–517, 1987.

Haggenmacher, Peter. *Grotius et la doctrine de la guerre juste*. Paris: Presses universitaires de France, 1983.

Hakluyt, Richard. *The Principall Navigations, Voiages and Discoveries of the English Nation, Made by Sea or over Land, to the Most Remote and Farthest Distant Quarters of the Earth at Any Time within the Compasse of These 1500. Yeers: Devided into Three Severall Parts, According to the Positions of the Regions Whereunto They were Directed*. London: George Gishop and Ralph Newberie, Deputies to Christopher Barker, Printer to the Queens most excellent Majestie, 1589.

Hale, John Rigby. *Renaissance Exploration*. New York: W. W. Norton and Company, 1972.

Hardin, Garrett James. *The Tragedy of the Commons*. Washington, DC: American Association for the Advancement of Science, 1968.

Harrington, Matthew Craig. *"The Worke Wee May Doe in the World": The Western Design and the Anglo-Spanish Struggle for the Caribbean*. M.A. thesis, Florida State University, 2004.

Hart, Herbert Lionel Adolphus. *The Concept of Law*. Oxford: Clarendon Press, 1961.

Hasani, E. "Uti Possidetis Juris: From Rome to Kosovo". *The Fletcher Forum of World Affairs*. 27: 85–98, 2003.

Haskell, John D. "Hugo Grotius in the Contemporary Memory of International Law: Secularism, Liberalism, and the Politics of Restatement and Denial." 25(1) *Emory International Law Review* 269–270, 2012.

Haslam, Jonathan. *No Virtue Like Necessity: Realist Thought in International Relations Since Machiavelli*. New Haven: Yale University Press, 2002.

Hattendorf, John B. *"The Sea as an Arena for Conflict."* In *Maritime History*, 130–139. Edited by Hattendorf, John B. Malabar, FL: Krieger Publishing Company, 1996.

    ed. *Maritime History. Vol. 1. The Age of Discovery*. Malabar, FL: Krieger Publishing Company, 1996.

Havercroft, Jonathan. *Captives of Sovereignty*. Cambridge, NY: Cambridge University Press, 2011.

Hemming, John. *The Conquest of the Incas*. New York: Harcourt, Brace, Jovanovich, 1970.

Henrat, Philippe. "French Naval Operations in Spitsbergen During Louis XIV's Reign." 37(4) *Arctic* 544–551, 1984.

Herwig, Holger. *The First World War: Germany and Austria-Hungary 1914–1918*. New York: St. Martin's Press, 1997.

Hillgenberg, Hartmut. "A Fresh Look at Soft Law." 10(3) *European Journal of International Law* 499–515, 1999.

Hinsley, Francis Harry. *Sovereignty*. Cambridge: Cambridge University Press, 1986.

Hitchman, James H. "The Platt Amendment Revisited: A Bibliographical Survey." 23(4) *The Americas* 343–369, 1967.

Hobbes, Thomas. *Leviathan, or The Matter, Forme, & Power of a Common-Wealth Ecclesiasticall and Civill*. London: Printed for Andrew Crooke, at the Green Dragon in St. Paul Church-yard, 1651.

Hobsbawm, Eric J. "Introduction: Inventing Traditions." In *The Invention of Tradition*, 1–14. Edited by Ranger, Terence O. and Eric J. Hobsbawm. Cambridge, NY: Cambridge University Press, 1983.

Hoffman, Paul E. "Diplomacy and the Papal Donation 1493–1585." 30(2) *The Americas* 151–183, 1973.

Hoffman, Philip T. *Why Did Europe Conquer the World?* Princeton, NJ: Princeton University Press, 2015.

Holland, Ben. "Sovereignty as Dominium? Reconstructing the Constructivist Roman Law Thesis." 54(2) *International Studies Quarterly* 449–480, 2010.

Honneland, Geir. *"Fisheries in the Svalbard Zone: Legality, Legitimacy and Compliance."* In *The Law of the Sea and Polar Maritime Delimitation and Jurisdiction*, 317–336.

Edited by Alex G. Oude Elferink and Donald R. Rothwell. The Hague: Martinus Nijhoff, 2001.

Horensma, Pier. *The Soviet Arctic*. London: Routledge, 2003.

Hossain, Kamrul. "*Governance of Arctic Ocean Marine Resources*." In *Climate Change Impacts on Ocean and Coastal Law: U.S. and International Perspectives*. Edited by Randall S. Abate and Robin Kundis Craig. Oxford: Oxford University Press, 2015.

Hough, Peter. *International Politics of the Arctic: Coming in from the Cold*. New York: Routledge, 2013.

Howse, Derek and Norman J. W. Thrower, eds. *A Buccaneer's Atlas: Basil Ringrose's South Sea Waggoner: A Sea Atlas and Sailing Directions of the Pacific Coast of the Americas, 1682*. Berkeley; Los Angeles; Oxford: University of California Press, 1992.

Hoyt, Edwin C. "Law and Politics in the Revision of Treaties Affecting the Panama Canal." 6(2) *Virginia Journal of International Law* 289–310, 1965.

Hudson, Manley O. "The Central American Court of Justice." 26(4) *The American Journal of International Law* 759–786, 1932.

Huebert, Rob. *Climate Change and Canadian Sovereignty in the Northwest Passage*. Edited by P. Whitney Lackenbauer. Calgary: University of Calgary Press, 2011.

Hume, David. *A Treatise of Human Nature: A Critical Edition*. Edited by David Fate Norton and Mary J. Norton. Oxford: Clarendon Press, 2007.

Humpert, Malte & Raspotnik, Andreas. "The Future of Arctic Shipping Along the Transpolar Sea Route." *Arctic Yearbook*. 281–307, 2012.

Hurst, Cecil. "The Continental Shelf." 34 *Transactions of the Grotius Society* 153–169, 1949.

Hutchins, Todd Emerson. "Structuring a Sustainable Letters of Marque Regime: How Commissioning Privateers Can Defeat the Somali Pirates." 99(3) *California Law Review* 819–884, 2011.

Ibrahim, Ahsraf Ray. "The doctrine of laches in international law." *Virginia Law Review*. 83 (3): 647–692, 1997.

Irigoin, Alejandra and Regina Grafe. "Bargaining for Absolutism: A Spanish Path to Nation-State and Empire Building." 88(2) *The Hispanic American Historical Review* 173–209, 2008.

Irwin, Douglas A. "Mercantilism as Strategic Trade Policy: The Anglo-Dutch Rivalry for the East India Trade." *Journal of Political Economy*. 99 (6): 1296–1314. 1991.

Isaac, Larry W. and Daniel M. Harrison. "*Corporate Warriors: The State and Changing Forms of Private Armed Force in America*." In *Globalization between the Cold War and Neo-Imperialism*, Vol. 24, 153–188. Edited by Jennifer M. Lehmann and Harry F. Dahms. Bradford: Emerald Group Publishing, 2006.

Israel, Jonathan Irvine. "Conflicts of Empires: Spain, the Low Countries and the Struggle for World Supremacy, 1585–1713." 21(3) *The International History Review* 731–733, 1999.

   Dutch Primacy in World Trade: 1585–1740. Oxford: Clarendon Press; New York: Oxford University Press, 1989.

Ivanov, Yuri and Alexander Ushakov. "The Northern Sea Route – Now open." 12(1) *International Challenges* 15–19, 1992.

Jackson, C. Lan. *The Arctic Whaling Journals of William Scoresby the Younger, Vol. I The Voyages of 1811, 1812 and 1813.* London: Hakluyt Society, 2004.

Jackson, Gordon. *The British Whaling Trade.* London: Shoe String Press, 1978.

Jackson, Robert H. *Quasi-States: Sovereignty, International Relations and the Third World*, Vol. 12. Cambridge: Cambridge University Press, 1993.

Jacobs, Els M. *In Pursuit of Pepper and Tea: The Story of the Dutch East India Company.* Amsterdam: Netherlands Maritime Museum; Zutphen: Walburg Press, 1991.

Jakobsson, Thor Edward. *"Climate Change and the Northern Sea Route: An Icelandic Perspective."* In *International Energy Policy, the Arctic and the Law of the Sea*, 285–301. Edited by John Norton Moore and Alexander S. Skaridov. Leiden: Martinus Nijhoff, 2005.

James, Alan. *Sovereign Statehood: The Basis of International Society.* London: Taylor and Francis, 1988.

Janis, Mark Weston. *America and the Law of Nations 1776–1939.* Oxford; New York: Oxford University Press, 2010.

Janzen, Olaf U. *"A World-Embracing Sea: The Oceans as Highways, 1604–1815."* In *Maritime History as World History*, 102–114. Edited by Daniel, Finamore. Salem, MA: Peabody Essex Museum, 2004.

Jares, Vladimir. "The Continental Shelf Beyond 200 Nautical Miles: The Work of the Commission on the Limits of the Continental Shelf and the Arctic." 42(4) *Vanderbilt Journal of Transnational Law* 1265–1305, 2009.

Jasinski, Marek E. "Russian Hunters on Svalbard and the Polar Winter." 44(2) *Arctic* 156–162, 1991.

Jeffery, Renée. "Hersch Lauterpacht, the Realist Challenge and the 'Grotian Tradition' in 20th-Century International Relations." 12(2) *European Journal of International Relations* 223–250, 2006.

Hugo Grotius in International Thought. New York: Palgrave Macmillan, 2006.

Jennings, Robert Y. "A Changing International Law of the Sea." 31(1) *The Cambridge Law Journal* 32–34, 1972.

"The Caroline and McLeod Cases." 32(1) *The American Journal of International Law* 82–99, 1938.

Jensen, Øystein and Svein Vigeland Rottem. "The Politics of Security and International Law in Norway's Arctic Waters." 46(1) *Polar Record* 75–83, 2010.

Joyner, Christopher C. "Legal Implications of the Concept of the Common Heritage of Mankind." 35(1) *International and Comparative Law Quarterly* 190–199, 1986.

"Ice-covered regions in international law." *Natural Resources Journal.* 31 (1): 213–242, 1991.

Kacowicz, Arie Marcelo. *Zones of Peace in the Third World: South America and West Africa in Comparative Perspective.* Albany, NY: State University of New York Press, 1998.

Kankaapää, Paula. *"Knowledge Structures of the Arctic Council for Sustainable Development."* In *The Arctic Council: Its Place in the Future of Arctic Governance*, 84–112. Edited by Thomas S. Axworthy, Timo Koivurova, and Waliul Hasanat. Toronto: Munk-Gordon Arctic Security Program, 2012.

Kankaapää, Paula and Oran R. Young. "The Effectiveness of the Arctic Council." 31(1) *Polar Research* 1–14, 2012.

Kao, Shih-Ming, Nathaniel S. Pearre, and Jeremy Firestone. "Adoption of the Arctic Search and Rescue Agreement: A Shift of the Arctic Regime toward a Hard Law Basis?" 36(2) *Marine Policy* 832–838, 2012.

Kaplan, Edward S. *U.S. Imperialism in Latin America: Bryan's Challenges and Contributions, 1900–1920.* Westport, CT; London: Greenwood Press, 1998.

Kass, Stephen L. "Obligatory Negotiations in International Organizations." 3 *Canadian Year Book of International Law* 36–38, 1965.

Keene, Edward. *Beyond the Anarchical Society: Grotius, Colonialism and Order in World Politics.* Cambridge, NY: Cambridge University Press, 2002.

Kefferpütz, Roderick. "On Thin Ice? (Mis)Interpreting Russian Policy in the High North." 205(15) *Centre for European Policy Studies Policy Brief* 10–19, 2010.

Kellogg, Frank B. "TACNA-ARICA." 89(1) *Advocate of Peace through Justice* 55–57, 1927.

Kelsen, Hans. "Absolutism and Relativism in Philosophy." 42(5) *American Political Science Review* 906–914, 1948.

"The International Legal Status of Germany to be Established Immediately upon Termination of the War." 38(4) *The American Journal of International Law* 689–694, 1944.

"The Legal Status of Germany According to the Declaration of Berlin." 39(3) *The American Journal of International Law* 518–526 (1945).

Kelsey, Harry. *Sir Francis Drake: the Queen's pirate.* New Haven: Yale University Press, 1998.

Kempe, Michael. "*Beyond The Law. The Image of Piracy in The Legal Writings of Hugo Grotius.*" In *Property, Piracy and Punishment: Hugo Grotius on War and Booty in De Iure Praedae Concepts and Contexts,* 379–395. Edited by Hans W. Blom. Leiden: Brill, 2009.

Kempen, Barbara. *Der völkerrechtliche Status der Inselgruppe Spitzbergen.* Berlin: Duncker and Humblot, 1995.

Kennedy, Paul. *The Rise and Fall of the Great Powers: Economic Change and Military Conflict from 1500–2000.* New York: Vintage Books, 1987.

Kent, Heinz Sigfrid Koplowitz. "Historical Origins of the Three-Mile Limit." 48(4) *The American Journal of International Law* 537–553, 1954.

Keskitalo, Eva Carina Helena. *Negotiating the Arctic: The Construction of an International Region.* New York: Routledge, 2004.

Kessler, Friedrich and Edith Fine. "Culpa in Contrahendo, Bargaining in Good Faith, and the Freedom of Contract: A Comparative Study." 77(3) *Harvard Law Review* 401–449, 1964.

Keyuan, Zou. "The Sino-Vietnamese Agreement on Maritime Boundary Delimitation in the Gulf of Tonkin." 36(1) *Ocean Development and International Law* 13–24, 2005.

Kingsbury, Benedict. "A Grotian Tradition of Theory and Practice: Grotius, Law, and Moral Skepticism in the Thought of Hedley Bull." 17(3) *Quinnipiac Law Review* 3–33, 1997.

Kinney, Arthur F. and David W. Swain, eds. *The Routledge Encyclopedia of Tudor England.* New York: Routledge, 2001.

Klabbers, Jan. "The Redundancy of Soft Law." 65(2) *Nordic Journal of International Law* 167–182, 1996.

Klabbers, Jan and René Lefeber. "Africa: Lost Between Self-Determination and Uti Possidetis." In *Peoples and minorities in International law,* 37–63. Edited by Catherine Brölmann, René Lefeber, and Marjoleine Zieck. Dordrecht: Martinus Nijhoff, 1993.

Klein, Herbert S. *A Concise History of Bolivia.* 2nd edn. Cambridge: Cambridge University Press, 2011.

Knecht, Sebastian. "Arctic Regionalism in Theory and Practice: From Cooperation to Integration?" In *Arctic Yearbook 2013,* 164–183. Edited by Lassi Heininen, Heather Exner-Pirot, and Joël Plouffe. Akureyri: Northern Research Forum, 2013.

Knight, Franklin W., ed. *Bartolomé de las Casas, An Account, Much Abbreviated, of the Destruction of the Indes, with Related Texts.* Translated by Andrew Hurley. Indianapolis, IN: Hackett Publishing, 2003.

Knutsen, Jan Normann. "Norway in the First World War." 5 *Folia Scandinavica Poznań* 43–58, 1999.

Kohen, Marcelo Gustavo. "L'"Uti possidetis iuris" et les espaces maritimes". *Procès International : Liber Amicorum Jean-Pierre Cot,* 154: 159–167, 2009.

Koivurova, Timo. "Limits and Possibilities of the Arctic Council in a Rapidly Changing Scene of Arctic Governance." 46(2) *The Polar Record* 146–156, 2010.

Koivurova, Timo and David L. Vanderzwaag. "The Arctic Council at 10 Years: Retrospect and Prospects." 40(1) *University of British Columbia Law Review* 121–194, 2007.

Kolodkin, Anatoliy L. and M. E. Volosov. "The Legal Regime of the Soviet Arctic: Major Issues." 14(2) *Marine Policy* 158–168, 1990.

Koselleck, Reinhart. *Futures Past: On the Semantics of Historical Time.* Translated and with an Introduction by Keith Tribe. New York: Columbia University Press, 2004.

Critique and Crisis: Enlightenment and the Pathogenesis of Modern Society. Cambridge, MA: MIT Press, 2000.

Koskenniemi, Martti. "Empire and International Law: The Real Spanish Contribution." 61(1) *University of Toronto Law Journal* 1–36, 2011.

The Gentle Civilizer of Nations: The Rise and Fall of International Law, 1870–1960. Cambridge, NY: Cambridge University Press, 2002.

"Lauterpacht: The Victorian Tradition in International Law." 8(2) *European Journal of International Law* 215–263, 1997.

Kovalev, Aleksandr Antonovich and William Elliott Butler. *Contemporary Issues of the Law of the Sea: Modern Russian Approaches.* Vol. 1. Utrecht: Eleven International Publishing, 2004.

Kraska, James. *Deep Currents and Rising Tides: The Indian Ocean and International Security.* Edited by John Garofano and Andrea J. Dew. Washington, DC: Georgetown University Press, 2013.

Maritime power and the law of the sea: expeditionary operations in world politics. Oxford: Oxford University Press, 2011.

"International Security and International Law in the Northwest Passage." 42(4) *Vanderbilt Journal of Transnational Law* 1109–1132, 2009.

"The Law of the Sea Convention and the Northwest Passage." *The International Journal of Marine and Coastal Law.* 22 (2): 257–282, 2007.

Krasner, Stephen D. *Sovereignty: Organized Hypocrisy*. Princeton, NJ: Princeton University Press, 1999.

"Westphalia and All That." In *Ideas and Foreign Policy: Beliefs, Institutions, and Political Change*, 235–264. Edited by Judith Goldstein and Robert O. Keohane. Ithaca, NY: Cornell University Press, 1993.

"Compromising Westphalia." 20(3) *International Security* 115–151, 1995.

"*Structural Causes and Regime Consequences: Regimes as Intervening Variables.*" In *International Regimes*, 1–21. Edited by Stephen D. Krasner. Ithaca, NY: Cornell University Press, 1983.

"Structural Causes and Regime Consequences: Regimes as Intervening Variables." 36(2) *International Organization* 185–205, 1982.

Kratochwil, Friedrich. "*Sovereignty as Dominium: Is There a Right of Humanitarian Intervention?*" In *Beyond Westphalia* 21–42. Edited by Gene M. Lyons and Michael Mastanduno. Baltimore, MD: Johns Hopkins University Press, 1995.

Kratochwil, Friedrich and John Gerard Ruggie. "International Organization: A State of the Art on an Art of the State." 40(4) *International Organization* 753–775, 1986.

Kronfol, Zouhair A. "The Exclusive Economic Zone: A Critique of Contemporary Law of the Sea." 9 *Journal of Maritime Law and Commerce* 461–463, 1977.

Ku, Charlotte. "The Concept of Res Communis in International Law." 12(4) *History of European Ideas* 459–477, 1990.

Kuhn, Thomas S. *The Structure of Scientific Revolutions*. 4th ed. Chicago: University of Chicago Press, 2012.

The Structure of Scientific Revolutions. Chicago: University of Chicago Press, 1962.

Kuran, Timur. *Private Truths, Public Lies: The Social Consequences of Preference Falsification*. Cambridge, MA: Harvard University Press, 1997.

Kütting, Gabriela. *Environment, Society and International Relations: Towards More Effective International Environmental Agreements*. New York: Routledge, 2000.

Lafleur, Gérard and Lucien Abénon. "*The Protestants and the Colonialization of the French West Indes.*" In *Memory and Identity: The Huguenots in France and the Atlantic Diaspora*, 267–284. Edited by Bertrand Van Ruymbeke and Randy J. Sparks. Columbia, SC: The University of South Carolina Press, 2003.

Lakhtine, W. "Rights over the Arctic." 24(4) *The American Journal of International Law* 703–717, 1930.

Lalonde, Suzanne. *Determining Boundaries in a Conflicted World: The Role of Uti Possidetis*. Montreal; McGill-Queen's University Press, 2002.

Lalonde, Suzanne and Frédéric Lasserre. "The Position of the United States on the Northwest Passage: Is the Fear of Creating a Precedent Warranted?." 44(1) *Ocean Development and International Law* 28–72, 2013.

Lalonde, Suzzane and Ronald St J. Macdonald. "Donat Pharand: The Arctic Scholar." 44(3) *Canadian Yearbook of International Law* 3–93, 2006.

Lane, Kris E. *Pillaging the Empire: Piracy in the Americas 1500–1750*. Armonk, NY: M. E. Sharpe, 1998.

Langley, Lester D. and Thomas Schoonover. *The Banana Men: American Mercenaries and Entrepreneurs in Central America, 1880–1930*. University Press of Kentucky, 1995.

Lansing, Robert. "A Unique International Problem." 11(4) *The American Journal of International Law* 763–771, 1917.

"Notes on Sovereignty in a State." 1(1) *The American Journal of International Law* 105–128, 1907.

Lapidoth, Ruth. "Relation between the Camp David Frameworks and the Treaty of Peace –Another Dimension." 15(2) *Israel Law Review* 191–196, 1980.

"The reopened Suez canal in international law." *Syracuse Journal of International Law and Commerce.* 4: 1–49, 1976.

Larschan, Bradley and Bonnie C. Brennan. "The Common Heritage of Mankind Principle in International Law." 21(2) *Columbia Journal of Transnational Law* 305–336, 1983.

Lasserre, Frédéric and Sébastien Pelletier. "Polar Super Seaways? Maritime Transport in the Arctic: An Analysis of Shipowners' Intentions." 19(6) *Journal of Transport Geography* 1465–1466, 2011. Web.

Lauterpacht, Elihu, ed. *International Law: Being the Collected Papers of Hersch Lauterpacht.* Vol. 2. Cambridge: Cambridge University Press, 1975.

Lauterpacht, Hersch. *The Function of Law in the International Community.* Oxford: Oxford University Press, 2011.

International Law: Being the Collected Papers of Hersch Lauterpacht. Edited by Elihu Lauterpacht. Vol.1. Cambridge England: University Press, 1970.

"Some Observations on the Prohibition of 'Non Liquet' and the Completeness of the Law." In *Symbolae Verzijl*, 196–221. Edited by Jan Hendrik Willem Verzijl. La Haye: Nijhoff, 1958.

"Sovereignty over Submarine Areas." 27 *British Yearbook of International Law* 376–394, 1950.

"The Grotian Tradition in International Law." 23(1) *British Yearbook of International Law* 1–3, 1946.

Laver, Roberto C. *The Falklands/Malvinas Case: Breaking the Deadlock in the Anglo-Argentine Sovereignty Dispute.* The Hague: Martinus Nijhoff, 2001.

Lawson, Philip. *The East India Company: A History.* London: Longman, 1993.

Lee, Daniel. "Popular Liberty, Princely Government, and the Roman Law in Hugo Grotius's De Jure Belli ac Pacis." 72(3) *Journal of the History of Ideas* 371–392, 2011.

Lee, Dwight E. and Robert N. Beck. "The Meaning of 'Historicism'." 59(3) *The American Historical Review* 568–577, 1954.

Lenz, Lawrence. *Power and Policy: America's First Steps to Superpower, 1889–1922.* New York: Algora Publishing, 2008.

Leonard, Thomas M. *"'Keeping the Europeans Out': The United States and Central America since 1823."* In *Central America: Historical Perspectives on the Contemporary Crises*, 5–20. Edited by Ralph Lee Woodward, Jr. New York; Westport, CT; London: Greenwood Press, 1988.

Lesaffer, Randall. *"A Schoolmaster Abolishing Home-Work? Vattel on Peacemaking and Peace Treaties."* In *Vattel's International Law from a XXI St Century Perspective / Le Droit International de Vattel Vu Du XXI E Siècle*, 352–359. Edited by Vincent Chetail and Peter Haggenmacher. The Hague, Boston: Martinus Nijhoff, 2011.

"The Grotian Tradition Revisited: Change and Continuity in the History of International Law." 73(1) *British Yearbook of International Law* 103–140, 2003.

Lewis, Paul H. *"Paraguay since 1930."* In *The Cambridge History of Latin America*, 233–234. Vol. 8. Edited by Leslie Bethell. Cambridge: Cambridge University Press, 1991.

Lieberman, Victor B. *Strange Parallels: Southeast Asia in Global Context, C 800–1830.* Vol. 1, *Integration on the Mainland.* Cambridge, NY: Cambridge University Press, 2003.

Strange Parallels: Southeast Asia in Global Context, C 800–1830. Vol. 2, *Mainland Mirrors: Europe, Japan, China, South Asia, and the Islands.* Cambridge, NY: Cambridge University Press, 2009.

Lincoln, Margarette, H. V. Bowen, and Nigel Rigby, eds. *The Worlds of the East India Company.* Rochester, NY: D. S. Brewer, 2002.

Lipson, Charles. "Why Are Some International Agreements Informal?" 45(4) *International Organization* 495–538, 1991.

Liu, Miaojia, and Jacob Kronbak. "The potential economic viability of using the Northern Sea Route (NSR) as an alternative route between Asia and Europe". *Journal of Transport Geography.* 18 (3): 434–444, 2010.

Llamzon, Aloysius P. "Jurisdiction and Compliance in Recent Decisions of the International Court of Justice." 18(5) *European Journal of International Law* 815–852, 2007.

Locke, John. *The Second Treatise on Civil Government.* New York: Prometheus Books, 1986.

López Martin, Ana G. *International Straits: Concept, Classification and Rules of Passage.* Heidelberg: Springer Science and Business Media, 2010.

Lyons, Gene M. and Michael Mastanduno, eds. *Beyond Westphalia?: State Sovereignty and International Intervention.* Baltimore, MD: Johns Hopkins University Press, 1995.

Mackenzie, Thomas and L. H. A. Stubbs. *Studies in Roman Law, with Comparative Views of the Laws of France, England, and Scotland.* Edited by John Kirkpatrick. Edinburgh; London: W. Blackwood and Sons, 1880.

Mackie, Sedley J., ed. *An Account of the Conquest of Guatemala in 1524 by Pedro de Alvarado, with a Facsimile of the Spanish Original, 1525.* New York: The Cortes Society, 1924.

MacMillan, Ken. *Sovereignty and Possession in the English New World: The Legal Foundations of Empire, 1576–1640.* Cambridge, NY: Cambridge University Press, 2006.

Macnab, Ron. "Submarine Elevations and Ridges: Wild Cards in the Poker Game of UNCLOS Article 76". *Ocean Development and International Law: The Journal of Marine Affairs.* 39 (2): 223–234, 2008.

"The Case for Transparency in the Delimitation of the Outer Continental Shelf in Accordance with UNCLOS Article 76." 35(1) *Ocean Development and International Law* 1–10, 2004.

MacQuarrie, Kim. *The Last Days of the Incas.* New York: Simon and Schuster, 2007.

Mancke, Elizabeth. "Early Modern Expansion and the Politicization of Oceanic Space." 89(2) *The Geographical Review* 225–229, 1999.

"Oceanic Space and the Creation of a Global International System, 1450–1800." In *Maritime History as World History*, 149–66. Edited by Daniel Finamore. Salem, MA: Peabody Essex Museum; Gainesville, FL: University of Florida Press, 2004.

Maritain, Jacques. "The Concept of Sovereignty." 44(2) *American Political Science Review* 343–357, 1950.

Markham, Clements R. *The War between Peru and Chile, 1879–1882.* London: Sampson Low. Marston, Searle and Rivington, 1882.

Mattingly, Garrett. "No Peace beyond What Line?" 13 *Transactions of the Royal Historical Society* 145–162, 1963.

Matzat, Heinz L. and Friedrich Meinecke. *Die Entstehung des Historismus.* München, Deutschland: R. Oldenbourg Verlag, 1959.

Matz-Lück, Nele. "Planting the Flag in Arctic Waters: Russia's Claim to the North Pole." 1(2) *Göttingen Journal of International Law* 235–255, 2009.

Maurer, Noel and Carlos Yu. *The Big Ditch: How America Took, Built, Ran, and Ultimately Gave Away the Panama Canal.* Princeton and Oxford: Princeton University Press, 2011.

Mayo, John and Simon Collier. *Mining in Chile's Norte Chico: Journal of Charles Lambert, 1825–1830.* Boulder: Westview, 1998.

British Merchants and Chilean Development, 1851–1886. Boulder: Westview, 1987.

McAlister, Lyle N. *Spain and Portugal in the New World, 1492–1700.* Minneapolis: University of Minnesota Press, 1984.

McColl, R. W., ed. *Encyclopedia of World Geography.* Vol. 1. New York: Facts on File, 2005.

McCullough, David. *The Path Between the Seas: The Creation of the Panama Canal, 1870–1914.* New York; London; Toronto; Sydney; Singapore: Simon & Schuster, 1977.

McKitterick, T. E. M. "The Validity of Territorial and Other Claims in Polar Regions". *Journal of Comparative Legislation and International Law.* 21 (1): 89–97, 1939.

McNair, Baron Arnold Duncan. *The Law of Treaties.* Oxford: Clarendon Press, 1961.

McNeily, Jack. "A Condominium Approach to Abyei." 13(1) *Chicago Journal of International Law* 265–290, 2012.

McWhinney, Edward and Mariko Kawano, eds. *Judge Shigeru Oda and the Path to Judicial Wisdom: Opinions (Declarations, Separate Opinions, Dissenting Opinions) on the International Court of Justice, 1993–2003.* Leiden, Boston: Martinus Nijhoff Publishers, 2006.

Means, Philip Ainsworth. *The Spanish Main: Focus of Envy, 1492–1700.* New York: C. Scribner's Sons, 1935.

Melville, Herman. *Moby-Dick; or, The Whale. 1851.* Evanston, Chicago: Northwestern University Press, 1988.

Mesa Gisbert, Carlos D. *Presidencia sitiada: Memorias de mi Gobierno.* La Paz: Fundación Comunidad, 2008.

Miller, Jon. "Hugo Grotius." In *The Stanford Encyclopedia of Philosophy.* Edited by Edward N. Zalta. Stanford, CA: Center for the Study of Language and Information, Stanford University, 2014.

Milun, Kathryn. *The Political Uncommons: The Cross-Cultural Logic of the Global. Commons* London: Ashgate Publishing, 2011.

Miyoshi, Masahiro. "China's 'U-Shaped Line' Claim in the South China Sea: Any Validity under International Law?" 43(1) *Ocean Development and International Law* 1–17, 2012.

Moe, Arild. "Russian and Norwegian Petroleum Strategies in the Barents Sea." 1(2) *Arctic Review on Law and Politics* 225–248, 2010.

Molenaar, Erik J. "Current and Prospective Roles of the Arctic Council System within the Context of the Law of the Sea." 27(3) *The International Journal of Marine and Coastal Law* 553–595, 2012.

Montes Gomez, Esteban. *Archaeology of the Colonial Period Gulf of Fonseca, Eastern El Salvador*. Dissertation, Graduate Division of the University of California, Berkeley, 2010.

Moore, John Bassett. *Costa Rica-Panama Arbitration: Memorandum on Uti Possidetis*. Rosslyn: Commonwealth, 1913.

Moore, John Norton. "The Regime of Straits and the Third United Nations Conference on the Law of the Sea." 74(1) *The American Journal of International Law* 77–100, 1980.

Morales, Waltraud Q. *A brief history of Bolivia*. Second edition. New York: Facts On File, 2010.

Mousourakis, George. *The Historical and Institutional Context of Roman law*. Burlington, VT: Ashgate, 2003.

Munro, Dana G. "Dollar Diplomacy in Nicaragua, 1909–1913." 38(2) *The Hispanic American Historical Review* 209–234, 1958.

Nabulsi, Karma. "An Ideology of War, Not Peace: Jus in Bello and the Grotian Tradition of War." 4(1) *Journal of Political Ideologies* 13–37, 1999.

Nackman, Mark E. "Anglo-American Migrants to the West: Men of Broken Fortunes? The Case of Texas, 1821–46." 5(4) *The Western Historical Quarterly* 441–455, 1974.

Naldi, Gino J. "The Case Concerning the Frontier Dispute (Burkina Faso/Republic of Mali): Uti Possidetis in an African Perspective." *International & Comparative Law Quarterly*. 36 (04): 893–903, 1987.

Documents of the Organization of African Unity. London: Mansell, 1992.

Nanda, Ved P. "Maritime Piracy: How Can International Law and Policy Address This Growing Global Menace?" 39(2) *Denver Journal of International Law and Policy* 177–207, 2011.

Nansen, Fridtjof. *In Northern Mists. Arctic Exploration in Early Times*. Translated by Arthur G. Chater. London: W. Heinemann, 1911.

Naylor, Robert A. "The British Role in Central America Prior to the Clayton-Bulwer Treaty of 1850." 40(3) *The Hispanic American Historical Review* 361–382, 1960.

Nellen, Henk J. M. *Hugo De Groot: Een Leven in Strijd Om De Vrede, 1583–1645*. Amsterdam: Balans, 2007.

"The History of Grotius and His Printers, Explained on the Basis of Five Portraits." 39(2) *International Journal of Legal Information* 210–212, 2011.

Hugo Grotius's Political and Scholarly Activities in the Light of his Correspondence. In *Property, Piracy and Punishment: Hugo Grotius On War and Booty in de Iure Praedae*. Edited by H. W. Blom. Leiden: Brill, 2009.

Nelson, L. D. M. "The Patrimonial Sea." 22(4) *International and Comparative Law Quarterly* 668–669, 1973.

Nesi, Giuseppe. *L'Uti Possidetis Iuris Nel Diritto Internazionale*. Padova: Cedam, 1996.

"Uti possidetis iuris e delimitazioni marittime." 74(3) *Rivista di diritto internazionale* 534–570, 1991.

Neumann, Thilo. *Die norwegische Arktis im Völkerrecht. Landgebiete – Seegebiete – Grenzgebiete*. Hamburg: Verlag Dr. Kovac, 2013.

Neves, Juan Carlos. *United Nations Peace-Keeping Operations in the Gulf of Fonseca by Argentine Navy Units.* An Occasional Paper of the Center for Naval Warfare Studies. Strategic Research Department Research Report 1–93: US Navy War College, 1993.

Newey, Glen. *Routledge Philosophy Guidebook to Hobbes and Leviathan.* London and New York: Routledge, 2008.

Newson, Linda A. *Indian Survival in Colonial Nicaragua.* Norman, OK: University of Oklahoma Press, 1978.

The Cost of Conquest: Indian Decline in Honduras under Spanish Rule. Boulder: Westview Press, 1986.

Nicholson, Graham. "The Common Heritage of Mankind and Mining: An Analysis of the Law as to the High Seas, Outer Space, the Antarctic and World Heritage." 6 *New Zealand Journal of Environmental Law* 177–197, 2002.

Nielsen, Fred K. "The Solution of the Spitsbergen Question." 14(1–2) *The American Journal of International Law* 232–235, 1920.

Nilsson, Annika E. *"Knowing the Arctic: The Arctic Council as a Cognitive Forerunner."* In *The Arctic Council: Its Place in the Future of Arctic Governance,* 190–224. Edited by Thomas S. Axworthy, Timo Koivurova, and Waliul Hasanat. Toronto: Munk-Gordon Arctic Security Program, 2012.

Nordquist, Myron H. and Choon-ho Park, eds. "Resolutions of the Third United Nations Conference on the Law of the Sea." 4(1) *Ocean Yearbook Online* 483–491, 1983.

Nordquist, Myron H., John Norton Moore, and Alexander S. Skaridov, eds. *International Energy Policy, the Arctic and the Law of the Sea.* Leiden/Boston: Martinus Nijhoff Publishers, 2005.

Nordquist, Myron H., John Norton Moore, and Ronán Long, eds. *Challenges of the Changing Arctic: Continental Shelf, Navigation, and Fisheries.* Brill: Nijhoff, 2016.

Nossova, Irina. *Russia's International Legal Claims in its Adjacent Seas: The Realm of Sea as Extension of Sovereignty.* Tartu: University of Tartu Press, 2013.

Noyes, John E. "The Common Heritage of Mankind: Past, Present, and Future." 40(1–3) *Denver Journal of International Law and Policy* 447–471, 2011.

"Judicial and Arbitral Proceedings and the Outer Limits of the Continental Shelf." 42(4) *Vanderbilt Journal of Transnational Law* 1211–1264, 2009.

Numminen, Lotta. "A History and Functioning of the Spitsbergen Treaty." In *The Spitsbergen Treaty: Multilateral Governance in the Arctic,* 7–13. Edited by Diana Wallis and Stewart Arnold. Helsinki: Conexio Public Relations, 2011.

Nye, Joseph S. *Soft Power: The Means to Success in World Politics.* New York: Public Affairs, 2004.

O. Henry. *The Gift of the Magi.* Illustrations by Steve Edwards. The Printery: Kirkwood, 2005.

Obama, Barack. *National Security Strategy of the United States.* Collingdale, PA: Diane Publishing, 2010.

O'Connell, Daniel P. *The International Law of the Sea.* Vol. 1. Edited by I. A. Shearer. Oxford: Clarendon, 1982.

Oda, Shigeru. "The Concept of the Contiguous Zone." 11(1) *International and Comparative Law Quarterly* 131–153, 1962.

Ogilby, John, *America: being the latest, and most accurate description of the New World: containing the original of the inhabitants, and the remarkable voyages thither: the conquest of the vast empires of Mexico and Peru, and other large provinces and territories, with the several European plantations in those parts: also their cities, fortresses, towns, temples, mountains, and rivers: their habits, customs manners, and religions: their plants, beasts, birds, and serpents: with an appendix containing, besides several other considerable additions, a brief survey of what hath been discover'd of the unknown south-land and the Arctick region.* London: Printed by the Author, and are to be had at his House in White Fryers, 1671.

Okhuizen, Edwin. "Dutch Pre-Barentsz Maps and the Pomor Thesis about the Discovery of Spitsbergen." 22(1) *Acta Borealia* 21–41, 2005.

Olenicoff, Serge M. *Territorial Waters in the Arctic: The Soviet Position.* Report prepared for Advanced Research Projects Agency, Santa Monica: Rand Corp., 1972.

Olivecrona, Karl. "Appropriation in the State of Nature: Locke on the Origin of Property." 35(2) *Journal of the History of Ideas* 211–230, 1974.

Onuf, Nicholas Greenwood. *The Republican Legacy in International Thought.* Cambridge: Cambridge University Press, 1998.

"Civitas Maxima: Wolff, Vattel and the Fate of Republicanism." 88(2) *The American Journal of International Law* 280–303, 1994.

"Sovereignty: Outline of a Conceptual History." 16(4) *Alternatives: Global, Local, Political* 425–446, 1991.

Onuf, Nicholas Greenwood and Peter S. Onuf. *Nations, Markets, and War: Modern History and the American Civil War.* Fairfax, VA: University of Virginia Press, 2006.

Onuma, Yasuaki. *A Normative Approach to War: Peace, War, and Justice in Hugo Grotius.* Oxford: Clarendon, 1993.

Oppenheim, Lassa. *International Law: A Treatise (Peace).* Vol. 1. New York and Bombay: Longmans, Green, and Co., 1905.

Oppenheim, Lassa and Hersch Lauterpacht. *International Law: A Treatise.* Vol. 2. 8th edn. London: Longmans, 1955.

Opsahl, Torkel. "Norwegian Dependencies, Particularly Spitsbergen and the European Communities." In *Legal Problems of an Enlarged European Community,* 179–321. Edited by M. E. Bathurst, K. R. Simmonds, N. March Hunnings, and Jane Welch. London: Stevens, 1972.

O'Rourke, Ronald. *Coast Guard Polar Icebreaker Modernization: Background and Issues for Congress.* Washington, DC: Congressional Research Service, 2015.

Maritime Territorial and Exclusive Economic Zone (EEZ) Disputes Involving China: Issues for Congress. Washington, DC: Congressional Research Service, 2015.

Changes in the Arctic: Background and Issues for Congress Congressional Research Service, 2014.

Changes in the Arctic: Background and Issues for Congress. Washington, DC: Congressional Research Service, 2011.

Ostrom, Elinor. "Beyond Markets and States: Polycentric Governance of Complex Economic Systems." 2(2) *Transnational Corporations Review* 1–12, 2010.

Governing the Commons: The Evolution of Institutions for Collective Action. Cambridge, NY: Cambridge University Press, 1990.

Ostrom, Elinor and Charlotte Hess. *"Private and Common Property Rights."* In *Property Law and Economics*, 53–56. Edited by Boudewijn Bouckaert. Massachusetts: Edward Elgar Publisher, 2010.

Ostrom, Elinor, Thomas Dietz, Nives Dolšak, Paul C. Stern, Susan Stonich, and Elke U. Weber, eds. *The Drama of the Commons*. Washington: National Academy Press, 2002.

Ostrom, Elinor, Roy Gardner, and James Walker. *Rules, Games, and Common-Pool Resources*. Michigan: University of Michigan Press, 1994.

Owada, Hisashi. *"Pactum de Contrahendo, Pactum de Negotiando."* In *Max Planck Encyclopedia of Public International Law*, 18–19. Edited by Kunig, Philip. Oxford: Oxford University Press, 2008.

"Study on treaty reservations and declarations." International law, UN and Japan. Tokyo, Festschrift Takano, 1988.

Oxman, Bernard H. "The Territorial Temptation: A Siren Song at Sea." 100(4) *The American Journal of International Law* 830–851, 2006.

"The Third United Nations Conference on the Law of the Sea: The Tenth Session (1981)." 76(1) *The American Journal of International Law* 1261–1285, 1982.

Ørebech, Peter Thomas. "Terra Nullius, Inuit Habitation and Norse Occupation – With Special Emphasis on the 1933 Eastern Greenland Case." 7 *Arctic Review on Law and Politics* 20–41, 2016.

"The 'Long-Arm' Reach of the Svalbard Treaty?" 1–69. Revised draft article on file with author.

Østreng, Willy. "The Northern Sea Route: A New Era in Soviet Policy?" 22(3) *Ocean Development and International Law* 259–287, 1993.

Politics in High Latitudes: The Svalbard Archipelago. Translated by R. I. Christophersen. Montreal: McGill-Queen's University Press, 1978.

Pannikar, Kavalam M. *Asia and Western Dominance: A Survey of the Vasco Da Gama Epoch of Asian History*. London: Allen and Unwin, 1959.

Pardo, Arvid. *The Common Heritage: Selected Papers on Oceans and World Order 1967–1974*. Msida: Malta University Press, 1975.

Parish, Helen Rand and Harold E. Weidman. "The Correct Birthdate of Bartolome de las Casas." 56(3) *The Hispanic American Historical Review* 385–403, 1976.

Parker, Geoffrey. *Global Crisis: War, Climate Change and Catastrophe in the Seventeenth Century*. New Haven: Yale University Press, 2013.

Parry, John T. "What is the Grotian Tradition in International Law?" 35(2) *University of Pennsylvania Journal of International Law* 2013–2023, 2014.

Pattberg, Philipp. "Conquest, Domination and Control: Europe's Mastery of Nature in Historic Perspective." 14(1) *Journal of Political Ecology* 1–9, 2007.

Pearce, Charles E. M. and Frances M. Pearce. *"Transoceanic Trade and Migration (1): Following Currents from the West Pacific Warm Pool into the Indian Ocean: The Cinnamon Route and the Colonization of Madagascar."* In *Oceanic Migration: Paths, Sequence, Timing and Range of Prehistoric Migration in the Pacific and Indian Oceans*, 67–86. Edited by Charles E. M. Pearce and Frances M. Pearce. Netherlands: Springer, 2010.

Pedersen, Torbjørn. "Debates over the Role of the Arctic Council." 43(2) *Ocean Development and International Law* 146–156, 2012.

"International Law and Politics in US Policymaking: The United States and the Svalbard Dispute." 42(1–2) *Ocean Development and International Law* 120–135, 2011.

"Denmark's Policies toward the Svalbard Area." 40(4) *Ocean Development and International Law* 319–332, 2009.

"The Dynamics of Svalbard Diplomacy." 19(2) *Diplomacy and Statecraft* 236–262, 2008.

"The Constrained Politics of the Svalbard Offshore Area." 32(6) *Marine Policy* 913–919, 2008.

"The Svalbard Continental Shelf Controversy: Legal Disputes and Political Rivalries." 37(3–4) *Ocean Development and International Law* 339–358, 2006.

Pedersen, Torbjørn and Tore Henriksen. *Conflict and Order in Svalbard Waters.* Tromsø: University of Tromsø, 2009.

Pellet, A. The Opinions of the Badinter Arbitration Committee Second Breath for the Self-Determination of Peoples. *European Journal of International Law* 3(1), 178–185, 1992.

Perera, Victor. *Unfinished Conquest: The Guatemalan Tragedy.* Berkeley: University of California Press, 1993.

Petersmann, Ernst-Ulrich. *"The Doha Development Round Negotiations on Improvements and Clarifications of the WTO Dispute Settlement Understanding 2001–2003: An Overview."* In *The WTO Dispute Settlement System 1995–2003,* 3–17. Edited by Federico Ortino and Ernst-Ulrich Petersmann. The Hague: Kluwer Law International. 2004.

Pharand, Donat. Soviet Union Warns United States Against Use of Northeast Passage. *The American Journal of International Law,* 62(4), 927–935. 1968.

"Innocent passage in the Arctic." *The Canadian Yearbook of International Law.* (6): 3–60, 1968.

"Canada's Sovereignty over the Northwest Passage." 10(2) *Michigan Journal of International Law* 653–676, 1989.

"The Arctic Waters and the Northwest Passage: A Final Revisit." 38(1–2) *Ocean Development and International Law* 3–69, 2007.

Phillips, Mark Salber. *On Historical Distance.* New Haven: Yale University Press, 2013.

"What Is Tradition When It Is Not Invented? A Historiographical Introduction." In *Questions of Tradition,* 3–29. Edited by Gordon Schochet. Ontario: University of Toronto Press, 2004.

Philpott, Daniel. *"Ideas and the Evolution of Sovereignty."* In *State Sovereignty: Change and Persistence in International Relations,* 15–47. Edited by Sohail H. Hashmi. University Park, PA: Pennsylvania State University Press, 2010.

Pinto, M. C. W. "The International Community and Antarctica." 33(2) *University of Miami Law Review* 475–487 (1978–1979).

Pois, Robert A. "Two Poles within Historicism: Croce and Meinecke." 31(2) *Journal of the History of Ideas* 253–272, 1970.

Poling, Gregory. *"US Interests in the South China Sea: International Law and Peaceful Dispute Resolution."* In *Power, Law, and Maritime Order in the South China Sea,* 61–75. Edited by Tran Truong Thuy and Le Thuy Trang. Lanham; Boulder; New York; London: Lexington Books, 2015.

Popper, Karl Raimund. *The Poverty of Historicism.* New York, Hagerstown; San Francisco; London: Harper Torchbooks, 1964.

The Open Society and Its Enemies, Vol. 1: The Spell of Plato. Princeton, NJ: Princeton University Press, 1966.

The Open Society and Its Enemies, Vol. 2: The High Tide of Prophecy: Hegel, Marx and the Aftermath. Princeton, NJ: Princeton University Press, 1966.

Prescott, Victor and Clive H. Schofield. *The Maritime Political Boundaries of the World*. 2nd edn. The Hague, Boston: Martinus Nijhoff, 2005.

Prickett, Stephen. *Modernity and the Reinvention of Tradition: Backing in to the Future*. Cambridge, NY: Cambridge University Press, 2009.

Pryor, John H. *Geography, Technology, and War: Studies in the Maritime History of the Mediterranean, 649–1571*. Cambridge: Cambridge University Press, 1988.

Purchas, Samuel. *Purchas His Pilgrimes. In Five Bookes*. Vols. III & IV. London: William Stansby for Henrie Fetherstone, 1625.

Purver, Ronald. "Arctic Security: The Murmansk Initiative and its Impact." 11(4) *Current Research on Peace and Violence* 147–158, 1988.

Ragner, Claes Lykke. "The Northern Sea Route." In *The Barents: A Nordic Borderland*, 114–127. Edited by Tomas Hallberg. Stockholm: Arena Norden, 2008.

Rajabov, M. Melting Ice and Heated Conflicts: Multilateral Treaty as Preferable Settlement for the Arctic Territorial Dispute. *Southwestern Journal of International Law* 15(2), 419–448, 2009.

Ralston, Jackson H. and W. T. Sherman Doyle. *Venezuelan Arbitrations of 1903*. Washington: Government Printing Office, 1904.

Ranger, Terence O. and Eric J. Hobsbawm, eds. *The Invention of Tradition*. Cambridge, UK: Cambridge University Press, 1983.

Ratner, Steven R. "Drawing a Better Line: Uti Possidetis and the Borders of New States." 90(4) *The American Journal of International Law* 590–624, 1996.

Rauch, George V. *Conflict in the Southern Cone: The Argentine Military and the Boundary Dispute with Chile, 1870–1902*. Westport, CT: Greenwood Publishing Group, 1999.

Raustiala, Kal. "Form and Substance in International Agreements." 99(3) *The American Journal of International Law* 581–614, 2005.

Rediker, Marcus. *Between the Devil and the Deep Blue Sea: Merchant Seamen, Pirates and the Anglo-American World, 1700–1750*. Cambridge and New York: Cambridge University Press, 1987.

Reeves. Jesse S. "Clearing the Way for the Nicaragua Canal." 17(2) *The American Journal of International Law* 309–313, 1923.

Reisman, W. Michael. "Judge Shigeru Oda: A Tribute to an International Treasure." 16 *Leiden Journal of International Law* 57–65, 2003.

"Protecting indigenous rights in international adjudication". *American Journal of International Law*. 89 (2): 350–362, 1995.

Reisman, W. Michael and Mahnoush H. Arsanjani. "The Question of Unilateral Governmental Statements as Applicable Law in Investment Disputes." 19(2) *ICSID Review* 328–343, 2008.

Reppy, Alison. "The Grotian Doctrine of the Freedom of the Seas Reappraised." 19(3) *Fordham Law Review* 243–285, 1950.

Reynolds, Clark G. *History and the Sea: Essays on Maritime Strategies*. Columbia, SC: University of South Carolina Press, 1989.

Riddell-Dixon, Elizabeth. "Canada and Arctic Politics: The Continental Shelf Extension." 39(4) *Ocean Development and International Law* 343–359, 2008.

Riley, Patrick. "The Legal Philosophy of Hugo Grotius." In *A Treatise of Legal Philosophy and General Jurisprudence*, 365–377. Edited by Damiano Canale, Enrico Pattaro, and Hasso Hofmann. Netherlands: Springer, 2009.

The Philosophers' Philosophy of Law from the Seventeenth Century to Our Days. Dordrecht, NY: Springer, 2009.

Rippy, James Fred. *British Investments in Latin America, 1822–1949: A Case Study in the Operations of Private Enterprise in Retarded Regions.* Minneapolis: University of Minnesota, 1959.

Risse, Mathias. Who Should Shoulder the Burden? Global Climate Change and Common Ownership of the Earth. Harvard Kennedy School Working Paper, RWP08-075, December 2008.

"Common Ownership of the Earth as a Non-Parochial Standpoint: A Contingent Derivation of Human Rights." 17(2) *European Journal of Philosophy* 277–304, 2008.

Riste, Olav. *The Neutral Ally: Norway's Relations with Belligerent Powers in the First World War.* Oslo: Universitetsforlaget, 1965.

Roach, J. Ashley and Robert W. Smith. "Straight Baselines: The Need for a Universally Applied Norm." 31(1–2) *Ocean Development and International Law* 47–80, 2000.

United States Responses to Excessive Maritime Claims. 2nd edn. Leiden: Martinus Nijhoff, 1996.

Robertson, William Spence. *Rise of the Spanish-American Republics as Told in the Lives of Their Liberators.* New York: D. Appleton, 1918.

Rodriguez Gonzalez, Salvador. "The Neutrality of Honduras and the Question of the Gulf of Fonseca." 10(3) *The American Journal of International Law* 509–542, 1916.

Roelofsen, C. G. "Grotius and the 'Grotian Heritage' in International Law and International Relations; the Quartercentenary and Its Aftermath (circa 1980–1990)." 11(1) *Grotiana* 6–28, 1990.

Rogoff, Martin A. "Obligation to Negotiate in International Law: Rules and Realities." 16(1) *Michigan Journal of International Law* 141–185, 1994.

Ronzitti, Natalino, ed. *The Law of Naval Warfare: A Collection of Agreements and Documents with Commentaries.* Dordrecht: Martinus Nijhoff Publishers, 1988.

Rossi, Christopher R. "A Unique International Problem: The Svalbard Treaty, Equal Enjoyment, and Terra Nullius: Lessons of Territorial Temptation from History." *Washington University Global Studies Law Review.* 15 (1): 93–136, 2016.

"A Particular Kind of Dominium: The Grotian Tendency and the Global Commons in a Time of High Arctic Change." 11(1) *Journal of International Law and International Relations* 1–60, 2015.

"Jura Novit Curia? Condominium in the Gulf of Fonseca and the 'Local Illusion' of a Pluri-State Bay." 37(3) *Houston Journal of International Law* 793–801, 2015.

"The Club within the Club: The Challenge of a Soft Law Framework in a Global Arctic Context." 5(1) *The Polar Journal* 8–34, 2015.

"A Nicaraguan Feast: Having the Jurisdictional Cake and Eating It Too." In *Historic U.S. Court Cases: An Encyclopedia*, 228–232. Vol. 1. Edited by John W. Johnson, 2001.

Broken Chain of Being: James Brown Scott and the Origins of Modern International Law. The Hague, Boston: Kluwer Law International, 1998.

Equity and International Law: A Legal Realist Approach to International Decisionmaking. Irvington, NY: Transnational Publishers, 1993.

"Jus ad Bellum in the Shadow of the 20th Century." 15 *New York Law School Journal of International and Comparative Law* 49–82, 1994.

Roth, Brad R. "Enduring Significance of State Sovereignty." 56 *Florida Law Review* 1017–1050, 2004.

Rothwell, Donald R. "*The Arctic in International Law: Time for a New Regime?*" 15(1) *Brown Journal of World Affairs* 241–243, 2008.

The Polar Regions and the Development of International Law. Vol. 3. Cambridge: Cambridge University Press, 1996.

"The Canadian-U.S. Northwest Passage Dispute: A Reassessment." 26(2) *Cornell International Law Journal* 331–345, 1993.

Rothwell, Donald R. and Stuart Kaye. "Law of the Sea and the Polar Regions: Reconsidering the Traditional Norms." 18(1) *Marine Policy* 41–58, 1994.

Rottem, Gideon. "Land, Island and Maritime Frontier Dispute." 87(4) *The American Journal of International Law* 618–626, 1993.

Rouvière, Laetitia and Perrier Bruslé, Latetitia. "Bolivia-Chile-Peru: Sea Access." In *Border Disputes: A Global Encyclopedia*, Volume 1, 53–68. Edited by Brunet-Jailly, Emmanuel, Santa Barbara, CA: ABC-CLIO., 2015.

Rowen, Herbert H. "'L'État c'est à moi': Louis XIV and the State." 2(1) *French Historical Studies* 83–98, 1961.

Ruddy, F. S. "Res Nullius and Occupation in Roman and International Law." 36(2) *University of Missouri-Kansas City Law Review* 274–287, 1968.

Rudmose Brown, Robert Neal. "Spitsbergen in 1914." 46(1) *Geographical Journal* 10–21, 1915.

Ruggie, John Gerard. "Territoriality and Beyond: Problematizing Modernity in International Relations." 47(1) *International organization* 139–174, 1993.

Runciman, Steven. *The Fall of Constantinople, 1453*. Cambridge: Cambridge University Press, 1990.

Ryan, A. N. "*The New World and Asia 1492–1606*." In *Maritime History: The Age of Discovery*, 257–277. Edited by John B. Hattendorf. Malabar: Krieger Publishing Company, 2004.

Samuels, Joel H. "Condominium Arrangements in International Practice: Reviving an Abandoned Concept of Boundary Dispute Resolution." 29(4) *Michigan Journal of International Law* 727–730, 2008.

Samuelson, Paul A. *Economics*. 9th edn. New York: McGraw-Hill, 1973.

Sand, Peter H. and Jonathan B. Wiener, "Towards a New International Law of the Atmosphere." 7(2) *Göttingen Journal of International Law* 1–25, 2015.

Saperia, Jordie. "Jerusalem: Legal Status, Condominium and Middle East Peace." 3 *Journal of East Asia and International Law* 175–198, 2010.

Sater, William F. *Andean Tragedy: Fighting the War of the Pacific, 1879–1884*. Lincoln: University of Nebraska Press, 2007.

Chile and the War of the Pacific. Lincoln: University of Nebraska Press, 1986.

Saunders, Stephen. *IHS Jane's Fighting Ships 2014–2015*. 116th rev. edn. London: Jane's Information Group, 2014.

Sánchez Ramos, Belén. "*Strengthening the Capacity of the Arctic Council: Is the Permanent Secretariat a First Step?*" In *The Arctic Yearbook 2013*, 264–278. Edited by Lassi Heininen, Heather Exner-Pirot, and Joël Plouffe. Akureyri: Northern Research Forum, 2013.

Scelle, Georges. *Plateau continental et droit international*. Paris: A. Pedone, 1955.

Schachter, Oscar. "The Twilight Existence of Nonbinding International Agreements." 71(2) *The American Journal of International Law* 296–304, 1977.

Schaefer, Milner B. "Some Considerations of Population Dynamics and Economics in Relation to the Management of the Commercial Marine Fisheries." 14(5) *Journal of the Fisheries Board of Canada* 669–681, 1957.

Schafer, Joseph. "The British Attitude toward the Oregon Question, 1815–1846." 16(2) *The American Historical Review* 273–299, 1911.

Scharf, Michael P. *Customary International Law in Times of Fundamental Change: Recognizing Grotian Moments*. Cambridge: Cambridge University Press, 2013.

"Seizing the 'Grotian Moment': Accelerated Formation of Customary International Law in Times of Fundamental Change." 43(3) *Cornell International Law Journal* 439–441, 2010.

Schermaier, Martin J. "Res Communes Omnium: The History of an Idea from Greek Philosophy to Grotian Jurisprudence." 30(1) *Grotiana* 20–48, 2009.

Schmitt, Carl. *The Leviathan in the State Theory of Thomas Hobbes: Meaning and Failure of a Political Symbol*. Westport, CT: Greenwood Press, 1996.

The Nomos of the Earth in the International Law of the Jus Publicum Europaeum. New York: Telos, 2003.

Schmitt, Michael N. "Humanitarian Law and Direct Participation in Hostilities by Private Contractors or Civilian Employees." 5(2) *Chicago Journal of International Law* 511–535, 2004–2005.

Schneider, Peter. "Condominium." In *Encyclopedia of Public International Law I*, 58–60. Vol. 10. Amsterdam; New York; Oxford; Tokyo: North-Holland, 1987.

Schoolmeester T. and Baker E., eds. *Continental Shelf: The Last Maritime Zone*. Norway: UNEP/GRID-Arendal, 2009.

Schoonover, Thomas David. *The French in Central America: Culture and Commerce, 1820–1930*. Wilmington, DE: Scholarly Resources, 2000.

Germany in Central America: Competitive Imperialism, 1821–1929. Tuscaloosa: University of Alabama Press, 1998.

"Metropole Rivalry in Central America, 1820s to 1929: An Overview." In *Central America: Historical Perspectives on the Contemporary Crisis*, 21–46. Edited by Ralph Lee Woodward, Jr. Westport, CT. Greenwood Publishing Group, 1988.

Schrijver, Nico. "The changing nature of state sovereignty." *British Year Book of International Law*. 70: 65–98, 2000.

Schwarzenberger, Georg. *Power Politics: An Introduction to the Study of International Relations and Post-war Planning*. London: J. Cape, 1941.

Title to Territory: Response to Challenge. *American Journal of International Law* 51(2), 308–324, 1957.

Scobbie, Iain. "The ICJ and the Gulf of Fonseca: When Two Implies Three but Entails One." 18(3) *Marine Policy* 249–262, 1994.

Scoresby, William. *An Account of the Arctic Regions: With a History and Description of the Northern Whale-fishery*. Vol. I. Newton Abbot: David & Charles, 1969.

An Account of the Arctic Regions: With a History and Description of the Northern Whale-fishery. Vol. II. Newton Abbot: David & Charles, 1968.

Scotcher, Nkeiru. "The Sovereignty Dilemma." In *The Spitsbergen Treaty: Multilateral Governance in the Arctic,* 21–33. Edited by Diana Wallis and Stewart Arnold. Helsinki: Conexio Public Relations, 2011.

Scott, Heidi V. *Contested Territory: Mapping Peru in the Sixteenth and Seventeenth Centuries.* Notre Dame, IN: University of Notre Dame Press, 2009.

Scott, James Brown. "Arctic Exploration and International Law." 3(4) *The American Journal of International Law* 928–941, 1909.

"The Central American Peace Conference of 1907." 2(1) *The American Journal of International Law* 121–143, 1908.

Scroggs, William O. *Filibusters and Financiers; the Story of William Walker and his Associates.* New York: The Macmillan Company, 1916.

Selden, John. *Ioannis Seldeni mare clausum, seu, De dominio maris libri duo I. Mare, ex iure naturae seu gentium, omnium hominum non esse commune, sed dominii privati seu proprietatis capax. pariter ac tellurem. esse demonstratur(1636).* Latin edn. Lugduni Batavorum: Apud Joannem and Theodorum Maire, 1636.

Of the Dominion: Or, Ownership of the Sea. The Evolution of Capitalism. New York: Arno, 1972.

Selden, John, James Howell, and Marchamont Nedham. *Mare Clausum: The Right and Dominion of the Sea in Two Books. In the First, the Sea Is Proved by the Law of Nature and Nations, not to Be Common to All Men, but to Be Susceptible of Private Dominion and Propriety as Well as the Land. In the Second, It Is Asserted That the Most Serene King of Great Britain Is the Lord and Proprietor of the Circumfluent and Surrounding Sea, as an Inseparable and Perpetual Appendix of the British Empire.* Written at First in Latin by That Late Famous and Learned Antiquary John Selden, Esquire. Formerly Translated into English, and Now Perfected and Restored by J. H. Gent. London: Printed for Andrew Kembe and Edward Thomas, and Are to Be Sold at Their Shops on St. Margarets-hill in Southwark, and at the Adam and Eve in Little-Britain, 1663.

Shackelford, Scott J. "Was Selden Right?: The Expansion of Closed Seas and Its Consequences." 47(1) *Stanford Journal of International Law* 1–50, 2011.

"The Tragedy of the Common Heritage of Mankind." 28(1) *Stanford Environmental Law Journal* 109–149, 2009.

Shaffer, Gregory C. and Mark A. Pollack. "Hard vs. Soft Law: Alternatives, Complements, and Antagonists in International Governance." 94(3) *Minnesota Law Review* 706–799, 2009–2010.

Shaw, Malcolm. "Case Concerning the Land, Island and Maritime Frontier Dispute (El Salvador/Honduras: Nicaragua Intervening), Judgement of 11 September 1992." 42(4) *The International and Comparative Law Quarterly* 929–937, 1993.

"The heritage of States: the principle of "uti possidetis juris" today." *British Year Book of International Law.* 67: 75–154, 1996.

"Peoples, territorialism and boundaries". *European Journal of International Law.* 8(3): 478–507, 1997.

"The International Court of Justice and the Law of Territory." In *The Development of International Law by the International Court of Justice,* ed. by Christian J. Tams, and James Sloan, 2013.

Shils, Edward. *Tradition*. Chicago: University of Chicago Press, 1981.

Shusterich, Kurt M. "International Jurisdictional Issues in the Arctic Ocean." 14(3) *Ocean Development and International Law* 235–272, 1984.

Simmonds, Kenneth R. "*Grotius and the Law of the Sea: A Reassessment.*" In *Grotius et L'ordre juridique International*, 43–45. Edited by Alfred Dufour, Peter Haggenmacher, Jíf Toman. Lausanne: Payot, 1985.

Simsarian, James. "The Acquisition of Legal Title to Terra Nullius." 53(1) *Political Science Quarterly* 111–128, 1938.

Singer, Peter W. "Outsourcing War." 84(2) *Foreign Affairs* 119–133, 2005.

Singh, Elen C. *The Spitsbergen (Svalbard) Question: United States Foreign Policy, 1907–1935*. Oslo: Universitetsforlet, 1980.

Singh, Elen C. and Artemy A. Saguirian. "The Svalbard Archipelago: The Role of Surrogate Negotiators." In *Polar Politics: Creating International Environmental Regimes*, 56–95. Edited by Gail Osherenko and Oran R. Young. Ithaca: Cornell University Press, 1993.

Singh, Nagendra. *The Role and Record of the International Court of Justice*. Dordrecht; Boston; London: Martinus Nijhoff Publishers, 1989.

Siorat, Lucien. *Le problème des lacunes en droit international: contribution à l'étude des sources du droit et de la function judiciaire*. Paris: *Librairie générale de droit et de jurisprudence*, 1958.

Skagestad, Odd Gunnar. *The 'High North': An Elastic Concept in Norwegian Arctic Policy*. FNI Report 10/2010. Lysaker, Norway: Fridtjof Nansen Institute, 2010.

Skaridov, Alexander S. "Northern Sea Route: Legal Issues and Current Transportation Practice." In *Changes in the Arctic Environment and the Law of the Sea*, 283–306. Edited by Myron H. Nordquist, Tomas H. Heidar, and John Norton Moore. The Hague: Martinus Nijhoff, 2010.

Skinner, Quentin. "*The Sovereign State: A Genealogy.*" In *Sovereignty in Fragments: The Past, Present and Future of a Contested concept*, 26–28. Edited by Hent Kalmo and Quentin Skinner. Cambridge University Press, 2010.

"Meaning and Understanding in the History of Ideas." 8(1) *History and Theory* 3–53, 1969.

Skuban, William E. *Lines in the Sand: Nationalism and Identity on the Peruvian-Chilean Frontier*. Albuquerque: University of New Mexico Press, 2007.

Smith, Alan K. *Creating a World Economy: Merchant Capital, Colonialism, and World Trade, 1400–1825*. Boulder: Westview, 1991.

Smith, Daniel Malloy. *Robert Lansing and American Neutrality, 1914–1917*. Vol. 59. California: University of California Press, 1958.

Smith, Jeffrey J. "'Notre mer?' An Independent Québec's Maritime Claims in the Gulf of St. Lawrence and Beyond." 35 *Canadian Yearbook of International Law/ Annuaire canadien de droit international* 113–177, 1997.

Smith, Laurence C. "Agents of Change in the New North." *Eurasian Geography and Economics*. 52 (1): 30–55, 2011.

Smith, Robert Freeman. "A Note on the Bryan-Chamorro Treaty and German Interest in a Nicaraguan Canal, 1914." 9(1) *Caribbean Studies* 63–66 1969.

Smith, S. "Piracy in Early British America." *History Today* 46: 29–37, 1996.

Somos, Mark. "Secularization in De Iure Praedae: From Bible Criticism to International Law." In *Property, Piracy and Punishment: Hugo Grotius on War and*

Booty in De Iure Praedae: Concepts and Contexts, 147–191. Edited by Hans W. Blom. Leiden: Brill, 2009.

Soroos, Marvin S. *The Endangered Atmosphere: Preserving a Global Commons.* Columbia: University of South Carolina Press, 1997.

"The Commons in the Sky: The Radio Spectrum and Geosynchronous Orbit as Issues in Global Policy." 36(3) *International Organizations* 665–677, 1982.

Squire, E. G. *The States of Central America: Their Geography, Topography, Climate, Population, Resources, Productions, Commerce, Political Organization, Aborigines, etc., etc., Comprising Chapters on Honduras, San Salvador, Nicaragua, Costa Rica, Guatemala, Belize, the Bay Islands, the Mosquito Shore, and the Honduras Interoceanic Railway.* New York: Harper & Brothers, 1858.

Nicaragua, Its People, Scenery, Monuments, and the Proposed Interoceanic Canal. Vol. II. New York: D. Appleton, 1852.

Stahl, William Harris, Richard Johnson, and E. L. Burge. *Martianus Capella and the Seven Liberal Arts.* Vol. I. New York and London: Columbia University Press, 1971.

Stansifer, Charles L. *"United States-Central American Relations, 1824–1950."* In *United States-Latin American Relation, 1800–1850,* 25–45. Edited by T. Ray Shurbutt. Tuscaloosa and London: The University of Alabama Press, 1991.

"E. George Squier and the Honduras Interoceanic Railroad Project." 46(1) *The Hispanic American Historical Review* 1–27, 1966.

Starkov, V. F. "Russian Arctic Seafaring and the Problem of the Discovery of Spitsbergen." 3 *Fennoscandia Archaeologica* 67–72, 1986.

Staten, Clifford L. *The History of Nicaragua.* Santa Barbara; Denver; Oxford: Greenwood, 2010.

Steinberg, Philip E. and Jeremy Tasch, eds. *Contesting the Arctic: Politics and Imaginaries in the Circumpolar North.* London: IB Tauris, 2015.

Steinmetz, Sara. *Democratic Transition and Human Rights: Perspectives on U.S. Foreign Policy.* New York: State University of New York Press, 1994.

Sterio, Milena. "A Grotian Moment: Changes in the Legal Theory of Statehood." 39(2) *Denver Journal of International Law and Policy* 209–695.

Stevens, Kenneth R. *Border Diplomacy: The Caroline and McLeod Affairs in Anglo-American-Canadian Relations, 1837–1942.* University of Alabama Press, 1989.

St. John, Ronald Bruce. *The Bolivia-Chile-Peru Dispute in the Atacama Desert.* Durham University: IBRU, 1994.

"Same Space, Different Dreams: Bolivia's Quest for a Pacific Port." 1(1) *The Bolivian Research Review* 1–21, 2001.

"Chile, Peru and the Treaty of 1929: The Final Settlement." 8(1) *Boundary and Security Bulletin* 91–100, 2000.

Boundaries, trade, and seaports: power politics in the Atacama Desert. Latin American Studies Program, University of Massachusetts at Amherst, 1992.

St. Leger, James. *The "etiamsi Daremus" of Hugo Grotius: A Study in the Origins of International Law.* Romae, 1962.

Stokke, Olav Schram. "Regime Interplay in Arctic Shipping Governance: Explaining Regional Niche Selection." 13(1) *International Environmental Agreements, Politics, Law and Economics* 65–85, 2013.

"A Legal Regime for the Arctic?: Interplay with the Law of the Sea Convention." 31(4) *Marine Policy* 402–408, 2007.

Stokke, Olav Schram and Geir Hønneland. *International Cooperation and Arctic Governance: Regime Effectiveness and Northern Region Building.* New York: Routledge, 2007.

Stone, Julius. "Non Liquet and the Function of Law in the International Community." 35 *British Year Book of International Law* 124–161, 1959.

Story, Ian James. "Creeping Assertiveness: China, the Philippines and the South China Sea Dispute." 21(1) *Contemporary Southeast Asia* 95–118, 1999.

Strati, Anastasia. *The Protection of the Underwater Cultural Heritage: An Emerging Objective of the Contemporary Law of the Sea.* The Hague, Boston: Martinus Nijhoff Publishers, 1995.

Straumann, Benjamin. "Is Modern Liberty Ancient? Roman Remedies and Natural Rights in Hugo Grotius's Early Works on Natural Law." 27(1) *Law and History Review* 55–85, 2009.

Stuart, Graham H. and James L. Tigner. *Latin America and the United States.* 6th edn. Englewood Cliffs, NJ: Prentice-Hall, 1975.

Summers, Robert S. "'Good Faith' in General Contract Law and the Sales Provisions of the Uniform Commercial Code." 54(2) *Virginia Law Review* 195–267, 1968.

Syrjämäki, Sami. *Sins of a Historian: Perspectives to the Problem of Anachronism.* Tampere, Finland: Tampere University Press, 2011.

Talbott, Robert Dean. *A History of the Chilean Boundaries.* Ames: Iowa State University Press, 1974.

Tanaka, Y. Case Concerning the Territorial and Maritime Dispute between Nicaragua and Honduras in the Caribbean Sea (8 October 2007). *International Journal of Marine and Coastal Law* 23(2), 327–346.

Taylor, Prue. *"The Common Heritage of Mankind: A Bold Doctrine Kept within Strict Boundaries."* In *The Encyclopedia of Sustainability, Vol. 3: The Law and Politics of Sustainability,* 64–69. Edited by Klaus Bosselmann, Daniel Fogel, and J. B. Ruhl. Great Barrington: Berkshire Publishing, 2011.

Teschke, Benno. *The Myth of 1648: Class, Geopolitics, and the Making of Modern International Relations.* London: Verso, 2003.

Theriault, Sophie. "Northern Frontier, Northern Homeland: Inuit People's Food Security in the Age of Climate Change and Arctic Melting." 15(2) *Southwestern Journal of International Law* 224–249, 2008–2009.

Theutenberg, Bo Johnson. "Mare Clausum et Mare Liberum." 37(4) *Arctic* 481–490, 1984.

Thiel, Johannes Hendrik. *Studies on the History of Roman Sea-Power in Republican Times.* Amsterdam: North-Holland Publishing, 1946.

Thierry, Hubert. "The Thought of Georges Scelle." 1(1) *European Journal of International Law* 193–209, 1990.

Thomas, Hugh. *Rivers of Gold: The Rise of the Spanish Empire.* London: Weidenfeld & Nicolson, 2003.

Thompson, William R. *Great Power Rivalries.* Columbia, SC: University of South Carolina Press, 1999.

Thuy, Tran Truong and Le Thuy Trang. *Power, Law, and Maritime Order in the South China Sea.* Lanham; Boulder; New York; London: Lexington Books, 2015.

Thürer, Daniel. *"Soft Law."* In *IV Encyclopedia of Public International Law,* 452–460. Edited by Rudolf Bernhardt. Amsterdam: Elsevier, 2000.

Tiller, Rachel and Elizabeth Nyman. "Having the Cake and Eating It Too: To Manage or Own the Svalbard Fisheries Protection Zone." 60 *Marine Policy* 141–148, 2015.

Timchenko, Leonid. *"The Northern Sea Route: Russian Management and Jurisdiction over Navigation in Arctic Seas."* In *The Law of the Sea and Polar Maritime Delimitation and Jurisdiction*, 269–292. Edited by Alex G. Oude Elferink and Donald R. Rothwell. The Hague: Martinus Nijhoff, 2001.

"The Russian Arctic Sectoral Concept: Past and Present." 50(1) *Arctic* 29–35, 1997.

Quo Vadis Arcticum?: The International Law Regime of the Arctic and Trends in Its Development. Osnova: State University Press, 1996.

Titley, David W. and Courtney C. St John. "Arctic Security Considerations and the US Navy's Roadmap for the Arctic." 63(2) *Naval War College Review* 35–48, 2010.

Tomasek, Robert D. "The Chilean-Bolivian Lauca River Dispute and the O.A.S." 9(3) *Journal of Inter-American Studies* 351–366, 1967.

Toulmin, Stephen. *Cosmopolis: The Hidden Agenda of Modernity.* New York: The Free Press, 1990.

Touval, Saadia. *The Boundary Politics of Independent Africa.* Cambridge, MA: Harvard University Press, 1972.

Tønnessen, Johan Nicolay and Arne Odd Johnsen. *The History of Modern Whaling.* Translated by R. I. Christophersen. Berkeley: University of California, 1982.

Tschudi, Felix H. "Time Equals Money: Developing a Profitable Shipping System Using the Northern Sea Route." 70(2) *Proceedings* 17–18, 2013.

Tuchman, Barbara. *The Guns of August: The Outbreak of World War I.* New York: Macmillan, 1962.

Tuck, Richard. *Philosophy and Government, 1572–1651.* Cambridge: Cambridge University Press, 1993.

Ulfstein, Geir. *The Svalbard Treaty: From Terra Nullius to Norwegian Sovereignty.* Oslo: Scandinavian University Press, 1995.

Unger, Richard W. *"Politics, Religion and the Economy of Renaissance Europe."* In *Maritime History as World History*, 3–19. Edited by Daniel Finamore. Salem, MA: Peabody Essex Museum, 2004.

"Power and Domination: Europe and the Sea in the Middle Ages and the Renaissance." In *Maritime History as World History*, 143–144. Edited by Daniel Finamore. Salem, MA: Peabody Essex Museum, 2004.

"Theoretical and Practical Origins of Methods of Navigation." In *Maritime History as World History*, 21–33. Edited by Daniel Finamore. Salem, MA: Peabody Essex Museum, 2004.

Upton, Francis H. *The Law of Nations Affecting Commerce during War: With a Review of the Jurisdiction, Practice and Proceedings of Prize Courts.* New York: J. S. Voorhies, 1863.

Vagias, Michail. *The Territorial Jurisdiction of the International Criminal Court.* Cambridge: Cambridge University Press, 2014.

Vaihinger, Hans. *The Philosophy of 'As If': A System of the Theoretical, Practical and Religious Fictions of Mankind.* Translated by C. K. Ogden. New York: Harcourt, Brace and Company, 1924.

Van Alstyne, Richard W. "British Diplomacy and the Clayton-Bulwer Treaty, 1850–60." 11(2) *Journal of Modern History* 149–183, 1939.

Van Bynkershoek, Cornelis. *De Dominio Maris Dissertatio*. Translated by Ralph Van Deman Magoffin [of 1744 edn.]. Oxford University Press, 1923.

Van Holk, L. E., Ben Vermeulen, and C. G. Roelofsen, eds. *Grotius Reader: A Reader for Students of International Law and Legal History*. The Hague: T. M. C. Asser Instituut, 1983.

Van Ittersum, Julia Martine. "Hugo Grotius in Context: Van Heemskerck's Capture of the Santa Catarina and its Justification in De Jure Praedae (1604–1606)". *Asian Journal of Social Science*. 31 (3): 511–548. 2003.

Profit and Principle: Hugo Grotius, Natural Rights Theories and the Rise of Dutch Power in the East Indies, 1595–1615. Leiden: Brill, 2006.

Preparing *Mare liberum* for the Press: Hugo Grotius' Rewriting of Chapter 12 of *De iure praedae* in November-December 1608. *Grotiana* 26 (1): 246–280, 2007.

Knowledge Production in the Dutch Republic: The Household Academy of Hugo Grotius. *Journal of the History of Ideas* 72 (4): 523–548, 2011.

Van Vollenhoven, Cornelius. "Grotius and the Study of Law." 19(1) *The American Journal of International Law* 1–11, 1925.

The Three Stages in the Evolution of the Law of Nations. Gravenhage: Martinus Nijhoff, 1919.

De drie treden van het volkenrecht. Gravenhage: Martinus Nijhoff, 1918.

Van Warmelo, P. "Aspects of Joint Ownership in Roman Law." 25(2) *Tijdschrivt voor Rechtsgeschiedenis* 125–195, 1957.

Vander Linden, H. "Alexander VI and the Demarcation of the Maritime and Colonial Domains of Spain and Portugal." 22(1) *The American Historical Review* 1493–1494, 1916.

Varmer, Ole. "The Third World's Search for Equitable Access to the Geostationary Satellite Orbit." 11 *International Law Students Association: Journal of International Law* 175–198, 1987.

Verhoosel, Gaetan. "Beyond the Unsustainable Rhetoric of Sustainable Development: Transferring Environmentally Sound Technologies." 11(1) *Georgetown International Environmental Law Review* 49–76, 1998.

Verlinden, Charles. "*The Big Leap under Dom João II: From the Atlantic to the Indian Ocean*." In *Maritime History as World History*, 79–80. Edited by Finamore, Daniel. Salem, MA: Peabody Essex Museum, 2004.

Vervliet, Jeroen. "*General Introduction*." In *Mare Liberum 1609–2009*, xv. Edited by Robert Feenstra. Leiden: Brill, 2009.

Verzijl, Jan Hendrik Willem. *International Law in Historical Perspective*. Vol. 6. Leyden: A. W. Sijthoff, 1973.

Von Humboldt, Alexander. *Personal Narrative of Travels to the Equinoctial Regions of the New Continent during the Years 1799–1804*. Translated by Helen Maria Williams. Amsterdam: Theatrum Orbis Terrarum, 1972.

Vylegzhanin, Aleksandr Nikolaevich, Vjačeslav K. Zilanov, and William Elliott Butler. *Spitsbergen: Legal Regime of Adjacent Marine Areas*. Utrecht: Eleven International Publisher, 2007.

Wadley, David and Hayu Parasati. "Inside South East Asia's Growth Triangles." 85(4) *Geography* 323–334, 2000.

Waldock, C. Disputed Sovereignty in the Falkland Islands Dependencies. *British Year Book of International Law* 25, 311–353, 1948.

Walker, Thomas W. and Christine J. Wade. *Nicaragua: Living in the Shadow of the Eagle*. 5th edn. Boulder, CO: Westview Press, 2011.

Wallerstein, Immanuel Maurice. *The Modern World-System: Capitalist Agriculture and the Origins of the European World-Economy in the Sixteenth Century*. New York: Academic Press, 1974.

Wallis, Diana, Introduction. In *The Spitsbergen Treaty: Multilateral Governance in the Arctic*. Edited by Diana Wallis and Stewart Arnold. Helsinki: Conexio Public Relations, 2011.

Waugh, Teresa and Maria Bellonci. *The Travels of Marco Polo*. New York: Facts on File, 1984.

Weber, Mel. "Defining the Outer Limits of the Continental Shelf across the Arctic Basin: The Russian Submission, States' Rights, Boundary Delimitation and Arctic Regional Cooperation." 24(4) *The International Journal of Marine and Coastal Law* 653–681, 2009.

Weeks, Edythe E. *Outer Space Development a Method for Elucidating Seeds*. Newcastle upon Tyne: Cambridge Scholars Publishing, 2012.

Weeramantry, Christopher. "The Grotius Lecture Series: Opening Tribute to Hugo Grotius." 14(6) *American University International Law Review* 1516–1518, 1999.

Wegge, Njord. "The Political Order in the Arctic: Power Structures, Regimes and Influence." 47 (2) *Polar Record* 165–176, 2011.

Weil, Prosper. "Towards Relative Normativity in International Law." 77(3) *The American Journal of International Law* 413–442, 1983.

Weiss, Edith Brown. *In Fairness to Future Generations: International Law, Common Patrimony, and Intergenerational Equity*. Tokyo: The United Nations University; Dobbs Ferry, NY: Transnational Publishers, 1989.

"Planetary Trust: Conservation and Intergenerational Equity." 11(4) *Ecology Law Quarterly* 495–551, 1984.

Weitzel, George T. *American Policy in Nicaragua. Memorandum on the Convention between the United States and Nicaragua Relative to an Interoceanic Canal and a Naval Station in the Gulf of Fonseca, Signed at Managua, Nicaragua, on February 8, 1913*. US Senate Document No. 334. Washington: Government Printing Office, 1916.

Welwod [Wellwood], William. *An abridgement of all sea-laws: gathered forth of all writings and monuments which are to be found among any people or nation upon the coasts of the great ocean and Mediterranean Sea: and specially ordered and disposed for the use and benefit of all benevolent sea-farers within His Maiesties dominions of Great Britanne, Ireland, and the adiacent isles thereof*. Digital edition compiled and edited by Colin Mackenzie, 2001 [London: Thomas Man, London: Printed by Humfrey Lownes, 1613].

Welwood, William. "*Of the Community and Propriety of the Seas*." In *The Free Sea*, 54–59. Edited by David Armitage. Indianapolis: Liberty Fund, 2004.

Wendt, Alexander. "Anarchy is What States Make of It: The Social Construction of Power Politics." 46(2) *International Organization* 391–425, 1992.

Wertheim, Eric. *The Naval Institute Guide to Combat Fleets of the World, 16th Edition: Their Ships, Aircraft, and Systems*. Annapolis: Naval Institute Press, 2013.

Weston, Burns H. and David Bollier. *Green Governance: Ecological Survival, Human Rights, and the Law of the Commons*. Cambridge: Cambridge University Press, 2013.

White, Christopher M. *The History of El Salvador*. Westport, CT: Greenwood Press, 2009.

Wight, Martin. *International Theory: The Three Traditions*. Edited by Gabriele Wight and Brian Porter, with an introductory essay by Hedley Bull. New York: Holmes and Meier for the Royal Institute of International Affairs, 1992.

"Western Values in International Relations." In *Diplomatic Investigations: Essays in the Theory of International Politics*, 89–131. Edited by Martin Wight and Herbert Butterfield. Cambridge, MA: Harvard University Press, 1968.

Wijkman, Per Magnus. "Managing the Global Commons." 36(3) *International Organization* 511–536, 1982.

Wilkes, Charles. *Narrative of the United States Exploring Expedition during the Years 1838, 1839, 1840, 1841, 1842*. Philadelphia: Lea and Blanchard, 1845.

Williams, Glyn. *Voyages of Delusion: The Northwest Passage in the Age of Reason*. New York: Harper Collins, 2002.

Arctic Labyrinth: The Quest for the Northwest Passage. Oakland: University of California Press, 2011.

Williams, Mary Wilhelmine. "The New Central America." 214 *The North American Review* 297–305, 1921.

Wilson, Eric. "The VOC, Corporate Sovereignty and the Republican Sub-Text of De iure praedae." 26(1) *Grotiana* 310–313, 2007.

"Erasing the Corporate Sovereign, Inter-Textuality and an Alternative Explanation for the Publication of Hugo Grotius' Mare Liberum (1609)." 30(2) *Itinerario* 78–103, 2006.

Wines, Richard A. *Fertilizer in America: From Waste Recycling to Resource Exploitation*. Philadelphia: Temple University Press, 1985.

Winkel, Laurens. "Problems of Legal Systematization from De Iure Praedae to De Iure Belli Ac Pacis. De Iure Praedae Chapter II and the Prolegomena of De Iure Belli Ac Pacis Compared." 26(1) *Grotiana* 61–78, 2007.

Wood, James C. "Intergenerational Equity and Climate Change." 8(2) *Georgetown International Environmental Law Review* 293–325, 1995–1996.

Xue, Guifang. "Deep Danger: Intensified Competition in the South China Sea and Implications for China." 17(2) *Ocean and Coastal Law Journal* 307–313, 2012.

Young, Oran R. "Building an International Regime Complex for the Arctic: Current Status and Next Steps." 2(2) *Polar Journal* 391–407, 2012.

"Whither the Arctic? Conflict or Cooperation in the Circumpolar North." 45(1) *Polar Record* 73–82, 2009.

Creating Regimes: Arctic Accords and International Governance. Ithaca: Cornell University Press, 1998.

"Institutional linkages in international society: polar perspectives." *Global Governance*. 2 (1): 1–23, 1996.

"Regime dynamics: the rise and fall of international regimes." *International Organization.* 36 (02), 1982.

Zemanek, Karl. "Was Hugo Grotius Really in Favour of the Freedom of the Seas?" 1(1) *Journal of the History of International Law* 46–59, 1999.

Zook, David H. *The Conduct of the Chaco War.* New York: Bookman Associates, 1961.

Zysk, Katarzyna. "Russia's Arctic Strategy: Ambitions and Constraints." 57(2) *Joint Force Quarterly* 103–110, 2010.

Author Index

Subject Index

Table of Cases Index

Lightning Source UK Ltd.
Milton Keynes UK
UKHW03f0131130918
328808UK00017B/419/P